CADOGAN GUIDES

"Intelligently organized and obviously well researched, these books strike a balance between background and sightseeing information and the practicalities that travelers need to make a trip enjoyable. As a travel bookseller, I am happy to see guides focusing on destinations that people would like to visit but have been unable to gather enough information until now."

—Harriett Greenberg, *The Complete Traveller Bookstore, New York City*

"Rochelle Jaffe, owner and manager of Travel Books Unlimited in Bethesda, Maryland, attributes (Cadogan Guides) popularity to both their good, clean-looking format and the fact that they include 'information about everything for everyone'. . . . These guides are one of the most exciting series available on European travel."

—*American Bookseller* magazine

Other titles in the Cadogan Guide series:

IRELAND
TURKEY
THE SOUTH OF FRANCE
ITALIAN ISLANDS
THE CARIBBEAN
SPAIN
INDIA
SCOTLAND
ITALY
AUSTRALIA

Forthcoming:
TUSCANY &
UMBRIA
THAILAND &
BURMA
BALI
PORTUGAL
MOROCCO

ABOUT THE AUTHOR

DANA FACAROS is a professional travel writer. Over the past ten years she has lived in several countries concentrating mainly on the Mediterranean area. In collaboration with her husband, Michael Pauls, she has written many travel books including guides to the Spanish Islands, the Italian Islands and Turkey. Her roots, however, are in the Greek Islands as her father comes from Ikaria. Her first guide to the Greek Islands was published in 1979, and she returned there recently to produce the present edition.

CADOGAN GUIDES

GREEK ISLANDS

DANA FACAROS
updated with the help of Michael Davidson & Brian Walsh

Illustrations by Pauline Pears

A Voyager Book

The
Globe
Pequot
Press

Chester, Connecticut 06412

First published as *Greek Island Hopping*

Library of Congress Cataloging-in-Publication Data

Facaros, Dana.
  Greek islands.

  (Cadogan guides)
  Rev. ed. of: Greek island hopping. 1979.
  Bibliography: p.
  Includes index.
  1. Aegean Islands (Greece and Turkey)—Description and
travel—1981–   —Guide-books. 2. Ionian Islands
(Greece)—Descriptions and travel—1981–   —Guide-
books. I. Facaros, Dana. Greek island hopping.
II. Title. III. Series.
DF895.F3 1987   914.99′0476   86–1165
ISBN 0–87106–827–3 (pbk.)

Manufactured in the United Kingdom

ACKNOWLEDGEMENTS

I would like to thank the many members of the National Tourist Organisation of Greece for their kind assistance in writing this guide, and the following people without whose moral, physical and financial assistance it would not have been possible: my parents and my grandmother, Mrs Despina Facaros; Joseph Coniaris, Sotiros S. Kouvaras of Ithaki, Filia and Kosta Pattakos, Carolyn Steinee, and Julie Wegner.

The updaters would like to thank all the girls at the NTOG; Wendy and Fanis Meletis, Pat and George Shepherd and family, Sofia Sampsaki, Cindy and Alexis Kimissis, Romy Most and Jack Stauf.

To the memory of my great-uncle,
Theologos Facaros,
former mayor of Ikaria

CONTENTS

Introduction

Part I

General Information *Page 1*

LIST OF MAPS

INTRODUCTION

Since 1972 (when I made my first trip) the Greek islands have undergone a remarkable transformation. Signs of prosperity – new houses and villas, airports, improved harbours and breakwaters, asphalted roads (and new cars and buses to use them), bright consumer durables, supermarkets, and trendy shops – are nearly everywhere. Part of this new wealth comes from islanders living abroad, who send money home, then return themselves to retire in style. Much of the rest has been provided by tourism.

After shipping, tourism is the most important source of revenue in Greece. It is unavoidable (unless you go in the winter) and indeed has been adapted into the cycle of seasons: first you have Lent, then the tourists, the grapes, and in December, the olives. From June until September the ferryboats from Piraeus are packed with holiday makers, both foreigners and Greeks. Popular sites and beaches are crowded by day and often by night as well with those unable to find a room, anywhere – they've been booked solid for months in advance.

The growth of international tourism in traditional insular cultures has (not surprisingly) had some undesirable effects. A number of resort areas have been built up willy nilly in search of the fast buck, and other islands have sacrificed many charming old customs and even sanity itself in their desire to please all-comers. And then there are other islands and villages, more self reliant, that cling stubbornly to their traditions and do all they can to keep outside interests from exploiting their coasts. Others, including some of the most visited islands, are enjoying a reassuring renaissance of traditional arts and customs, often led by the young people who see their heritage eroding into Common Market Euro-blandness.

Every island has its own personality, and I hope with the aid of this book that you'll find what you seek – a holiday with all the comforts of home, modern recreational facilities, and dancing until dawn, or a tour of the ancient and Byzantine sites, or an escape to a secluded shore, where there's the luxury of feeling obliged to do nothing at all. Or perhaps you want a bit of each. For, in spite of all the rush to join the 20th century, the Greek islands have retained the enchantment that inspired Homer and Byron – the wine dark sea, the transcendentally brilliant light, the scent of lemon blossom and jasmine at twilight, the nights alive with shooting stars. The ancient Greeks made the islands sacred to the gods, and they have yet to surrender them entirely to us mortals.

Every effort has been made to ensure the accuracy of
the information in this book at the time of going to
press. However, practical details such as opening
hours, travel information, standards in hotels and
restaurants and, in particular, prices are liable to
change.

Greece suffers from a high rate of inflation (up to
30%), but the drachma is often devalued against other
Western currencies, so the actual costs of your holiday
remain the same. We have tried to take inflation into
account when quoting hotel prices in this edition, but
please bear in mind that prices should only be used as
a guideline.

We intend to keep this book as up-to-date as possible
in the coming years. Please write to us if there is
anything you feel should be included in future
editions.

Part I

GENERAL INFORMATION

Fisherman on Mykonos

Getting To and Around Greece and the Islands

By air

Charter flights to Athens and occasionally to the islands are frequent in the summer from European and North American capitals. Check the travel sections in newspapers, or get advice from travel agencies. In London peruse the so-called "bucket shops", which have made spare charter tickets their speciality, although beware: these may only be issued a day or two ahead of time, and if you miss your flight there are no refunds. Americans and Canadians with more time than money may well find their cheapest way of getting to Greece is to take a trans-Atlantic economy flight to London and from there to buy a bucket shop ticket to Greece. This may be difficult in July or August, however. Trans-Atlantic bargains can still be found, but bear in mind that the peak season runs from late May to mid September. CIEE are a reliable US charter company (tel. 800 223 7402). To be sure of your seat, book APEX (Advanced Purchase Excursion Fare) which grants you confirmed reservations and is more flexible than charters. Many charters go direct to the islands—Rhodes, Crete, Corfu, Kos, Skiathos, Zakynthos, Lesbos, Samos, Mykonos, Kefallonia and Santorini—as well as to Athens

1

and Thessaloniki, whereas scheduled flights rarely go from London to the islands.

There are several rules about charters to Greece. One is that a charter ticket is valid for no more than four weeks. Visitors to Greece using a charter flight may visit Turkey or any other neighbouring country for the day, but must not stay overnight. To be on the safe side, make sure you don't get a Turkish stamp on your passport. The Turkish officials will happily stamp a removable piece of paper. Even if you intend to stay longer than four weeks or travel to other countries using just half a charter ticket may still come out less than a scheduled flight, so shop around.

Scheduled flights direct to Athens are daily from London and New York and less frequently from Toronto and Montreal. There are also direct flights from London to Thessaloniki and Corfu. While the basic carriers from the United States are Olympic Airways and TWA, from London there's a vast and ever-changing number of airlines, so again it's advisable to shop around and see which offers the best deal. Card-carrying students under 24 are eligible for discounts; Worldwide Student Travel, 37 Store St, London WC1 can get you the best current deal. Returning from Greece, it is advisable to confirm your return flight a few days prior to departure.

Flights from Athens to the islands are available on Olympic Airways. To be assured of a seat, especially in the summer, you should book your ticket as far in advance as possible. Groups of 15 or more receive a 5% discount, infants up to 2 years old a 90% discount, and children of 2 to 12 years a 50% discount. Americans who do not have an Olympic Airways office in their town can call a toll-free no. 800–223–1226 for information.

In the past few years Olympic Airways have been offering island to island flights in season, a pleasant innovation that precludes the need to go to Athens. Although these have a habit of changing from year to year, routes between Crete and Rhodes, Crete and Santorini, Crete and Mykonos, Rhodes and Kos, Rhodes and Santorini, and Rhodes and Mykonos seem fairly well established.

At the time of writing the following prices in drachmas are:

Athens to	Frequency	dr.
Alexandroupolis (for Samothraki)	daily	6250
Chania (Crete)	daily	5580*
Chios	daily	4570
Corfu	daily	7680*
Herakleon (Crete)	daily	6630
Kavala (for Thassos)	daily	6470
Kefallonia	daily	5290
Kos	daily	6400
Kythera	daily	4500
Leros	daily	8620
Limnos	daily	4770

Milos	daily	4200
Mykonos	daily	5020
Mytilini (Lesbos)	daily	5290
Paros	daily	5610
Rhodes	daily	8400*
Samos	daily	5290
Santorini	daily	5960
Skiathos	daily	5020
Skyros	daily	6400
Thessaloniki (for N. Aegean Is.)	daily	6400*
Zakynthos	daily	5290

* denotes prices of peak time flights.

Addresses and telephone numbers of airlines in Athens (area code 01) are as follows:

Aeroflot: 14 Xenofondos; tel. 3220986
Air Canada: 10 Othonos; tel. 3235143
Air France: 4 Karageorgi Servias; tel. 3230501. Airport tel. 9699707
Air Zimbabwe: 39 El. Venizelou; tel. 3239101
Alitalia: 10 Nikis; tel. 3244315. Airport tel. 9613512
Austrian Airlines: 8 Othonos; tel. 3230844. Airport tel. 9610335
British Airways: 10 Othonos; tel. 3222521. Airport tel. 9610402
Canadian Pacific: 4 Karageorgi Servias; tel. 3230344. Airport tel. 9702001
Cyprus Airways: 10 Filellinon; tel. 3246965. Airport tel. 9610325
Iberia: 8 Xenofondos; tel. 3245514. Airport tel. 9699813
Japan Airlines: 4 Amalias; tel. 3248211. Airport tel. 9613615
JAT: 4 Voukourestiou; tel. 3223675. Airport tel. 9613629
KLM: 22 Voulis; tel. 3242991. Airport tel. 9613639
Lufthansa: 4 Karageorgi Servias; tel. 3294235. Airport tel. 9699244
Olympic: 6 Othonos; tel. 9292555 (Int.), 9292444. (Dom.). Also 96 Leoforos Syngrou; tel. 9292333. East Airport tel. 9699317. West Airport tel. 9892111
Pan Am: 4 Othonos; tel. 3235242. Airport tel. 9699669
Qantas: Filellinon & Nikis; tel. 3232792. Airport tel. 9699323
Sabena: 8 Othonos; tel. 3236821. Airport tel. 9613903
SAS: 6 Sina & Vissarionos; tel. 3634444. Airport tel. 9614201
South African Airways: 4 Karageorgi Servias; tel. 3229007. Airport tel. 9612724
Swissair: 4 Othonos; tel. 3231871. Airport tel. 9610203
TWA: 8 Xenofondos; tel. 3236831. Airport tel. 9610012

Getting to and from Ellinikon Airport, Athens: Ellinikon Airport is divided into two: East (international airlines) and West (Olympic Airlines, both international and domestic flights). A bus leaves for the West Airport from the Olympic Agency at 96 Syngrou Avenue every half-hour, and public bus no. 133 (Ag. Kosmos) from Syntagma Square, or no. 122 from Vass. Olgas Avenue. East

3

Airport may be reached by bus no. 121 from Vass. Olgas Avenue or bus no. 18, express yellow bus, from Vass. Amalias Avenue, near Syntagma Square. From Piraeus, bus nos. 107 and 109 from Klissovis St go to the West Terminal. Bus no. 101 from Klissovis St and bus no. 19 from Akti Tselepi go to the East Terminal. Note that the bus stops are along the road in front of the terminals, not on the airport grounds themselves. A taxi between Athens and the airport will cost you about 700 dr. (more at night).

By train

From London to Athens there are three daily trains, the Athenai Express, the Akropolis Express and the Hellas Express, all of which take about three days. And a hot, crowded, stuffy, three days they are too, especially in Yugoslavia. A more pleasant, though slightly costlier route, is to go through Italy to Brindisi and take the night ferry over to Corfu and Patras. Anyone under 26 can get a 25% reduction in fare with Transalpino, 214 Shaftesbury Avenue, London WC2; many travel agents also sell Transalpino tickets. British people under age 26 can also travel by Interail passes, good for a month's rail travel in Europe—which gets you there and back, at a reasonable price; and Americans and Canadians can buy two-month Eurail and Youth Eurail passes before leaving home. However, the Eurail Pass is a bad bargain if you're only going to Greece, which has a limited rail service. For men over 65 and women over 60, the Rail Europ senior card saves up to 50% on rail fares in Greece and several other European countries, 30% in Germany and Yugoslavia, 30% on most sea crossings. It costs £5 and can be purchased at any British Rail Travel Centre.

Hardy souls who deny themselves even one night in a couchette are advised to bring with them three days' provisions, including water, and some toilet paper. Those who intend to sleep in a prone position, beneath seats and feet, should also bring something to lie on. Wear the oldest and most comfortable clothes you own (and save yourself the trouble of washing them before you go).

Domestic train routes of possible interest to island hoppers are as follows:

	Frequency
Athens—Thessaloniki (for NE. Aegean Is)	7 a day
Athens—Alexandroupolis (for Samothraki)	4 a day
Thessaloniki—Alexandroupolis	4 a day
Athens—Chalki (Evia)	17 a day
Athens—Patras (for Ionian Is)	7 a day
Athens—Kalamata (for Kythera)	9 a day
Athens—Volos (for Sporades)	7 a day

Students with valid identification can obtain a 50% reduction on domestic train fares, and groups of more than ten people a 30% discount.

In Athens, the railway station for northern Greece is Larissa Station, Delighianni St, tel. 8213882. The station for the Peloponnese is across the tracks, tel. 5131601. In Piraeus, the station for the Peloponnese is near the Piraeus–Athens metro on Akti Kalimassioti. The station for northern Greece lies further down the road on Akti Kondili. For further information telephone the OSE (Hellenic Railways Organization): 5222491 or 3624402/6.

By bus

Taking a bus from London to Athens is always a possible alternative for those who decide that a train trip is too expensive or too easy a route to travel. With three and a half days (or more) on the road, adventures are practically included in the ticket price but it probably isn't worth while unless you intend to spend some time in Greece; otherwise you'll be spending most of your holiday with a serious bus hangover. Also, make sure you go with a reputable company, like the Magic Bus. In Greece, you'll find agencies selling Magic Bus tickets on the most obscure islands, as well as in Athens; Filellion St near Syntagma Square is Athens' budget travellers' boulevard, so check there for other possibilities.

The domestic bus service in Greece is efficient and regular, if not always a bargain. Each bus is decorated at the whim of its driver, with pin-ups, saints, wallpaper, tinsel, tassels, and plastic hands which wave violently when the bus falls into a pothole. Bus services from Athens relevant to this book are as follows:

Athens to	No. per day	Terminal	Tel. no.	Duration
Chalki (Evia)	30	Liossion	8317153	1.30 hrs
Edipsos (Evia)	3–5	Liossion	8317153	3.30 hrs
Gythion	4	Kifissou	5124913	6.30 hrs
Igoumenitsa (for Corfu)	3	Kifissou	5125954	8.30 hrs
Kavala (for N.E. Aegean Is.)	2	Kifissou	5129407	11.00 hrs
Kephallonia	4	Kifissou	5129498	800 hrs
Kerkyra (Corfu)	3	Kifissou	5129443	11.00 hrs
Lefkas	4	Kifissou	5133583	7.00 hrs
Patras (for Ionian Is.)	19	Kifissou	5124914	3.30 hrs
Rafina (for Cyclades and Evia)	frequent	Mavromateon	8210872	1.00 hrs
Thessaloniki (for N.E. Aegean Is.)	frequent	Larissa Rlway Sta. and Kifissou	5222491	8.00 hrs
Volos (for Sporades)	9	Liossion	8317186	5.00 hrs
Zakynthos	4	Kifissou	5129432	7.00 hrs

To get to the terminal at 100 Kifissou St, take bus no. 51 from Omonia Square (Villara and Menadrou Sts). For the terminal at 260 Liossion St take bus no. 24 from Leoforos Amalias, by the National Garden. Take a bus or tram north, towards Areos Park on 28th Octovriou St for the Mavromateon terminal.

During the summer it is advisable to reserve seats in advance on the long-distance buses. Tickets for these journeys must normally be bought before one boards the bus, although on short trips one pays in transit. (Handing the conductor a 1000-dr. note for a 30-dr. ride does not improve foreign relations.)

There are never enough buses on the islands in the summer nor is it customary to queue. However, you will not be left behind if it is humanly possible for you to

5

squeeze on. If you can wake up in time, you will find that buses are rarely crowded early in the morning.

By ship

The most popular sea route to Greece is from Italy, with daily ferry services from Ancona, Bari, Brindisi, Otranto, and Venice. The most popular of these is the daily service from Brindisi, which leaves at 10 pm (connecting with the train from Rome) and arrives in Corfu the next morning. Passengers are allowed a free infinite stopover in Corfu if that island is not their ultimate destination, before continuing to Igoumenitsa or Patras, though make sure it is noted on your ticket. If you plan to sail in the summer, it's advisable to make reservations in advance, especially if you bring a car (most travel agents can do this for you). Students and young people get a 30% discount.

Steamer and ferry services of varying regularity also connect Piraeus to the ports listed on the next 3 pages.

Sealink has a luxury shipping service from Venice to Istanbul calling at Piraeus on the outward journey and Patmos on the return journey. Check with their UK offices for details and times of sailing.

A new service in the summer connects Rijeka and/or Dubrovnik in Yugoslavia with Corfu. Like most of the services listed, it runs only once or twice a week. Tourist offices or travel agents can quote you on fares, these change frequently because of fluctuating exchange rates and local inflation. The George Papazoglou travel agency, in the arcade at 41 Stadiou St (open 8 am–1 pm and 4 pm–7.30 pm; Sundays 10 am–12 noon; tel. 3213075) can give you further information on these or any other ship or plane service; along with tickets. The daily newspaper *I Nay Temporiki* lists all the activities of the port at Piraeus and publishes weekly ship schedules. The National Tourist Office also publishes a weekly list of ship departures, both abroad and to the islands.

Boats to the Islands

A little travelling through the islands will soon show you that each boat is an individual. The many new ones are clean and comfortable and often air-conditioned. The older boats may lack some modern refinements but nevertheless they can be pleasant if you remain out on deck. The drinking water is never very good on the boats, but all sell beer, Coca Cola and lemon or orange soda. Biscuits and cigarettes complete the fare on the smaller boats, while the larger ones offer sandwiches, cheese pies or even full meals.

All the boats are privately owned and although the Greek government controls the prices some will charge more for the same journey, depending on the facilities offered, speed, etc. If caiques relay you from shore to ship, you will pay more. In most cases children under the age of 4 travel free, and between 4 and 10 for half-fare. Over 10 they are charged the full fare. In the summer it is wise to buy tickets in advance, to guarantee a place and also because they are often 20% more

Ferries

Ports	Frequency	Company
Brindisi–Corfu–Igoumenitsa–Patras	Every day March–Oct.	Fragline, 5A Rethimnou St Athens, tel. 821 4171
Brindisi–Corfu–Igoumenitsa–Patras	Every day, all year round	Hellenic Mediterranean Lines Electric Train Station Piraeus, tel. 411 5611
Brindisi–Corfu–Igoumenitsa–Patras	3/4 times a week Oct.–June; Every day, June–Sept.	Adriatica Car Ferry 97 Akti Miaouli Piraeus, tel. 418 1901
Brindisi–Corfu–Igoumenitsa–Kephalonia–Patras	4 times a week late June–mid Sept.	Adriatic Ferries 15–17 Hatzikyriakou Piraeus, tel. 418 0584
Brindisi–Corfu–Paxos–Ithaka–Kephalonia–Patras	3/4 times a week June–mid Sept.	Ionis, 12 Akti Possidonos Piraeus, tel. 411 0948
Brindisi–Patras	Every day, May–Oct. Almost every day March and April	Anco Ferries 33 Akti Miaouli Piraeus, tel. 452 0135
Brindisi–Patras	Every day in high season. Every other day in low season	Cross Med. Maritime Co. 89 Kolokotroni Piraeus, tel. 417 1304
Bari–Corfu–Igoumenitsa–Patras	Every day, July–Sept. Infrequently in low season	Ventouris Ferries 7 Efplias St Piraeus, tel. 418 1001
Ancona–Corfu–Igoumenitsa–Patras	4 times a week June–Sept. Twice a week April, May, Oct.	Strinzis Lines 48 Amalias Ave. Athens, tel. 322 6400
Ancona–Igoumenitsa–Patras	4 times a week in high season, twice a week in low season	Minoan Lines 21 Leof. Vass. Konstantinos Athens, tel. 751 2356
Ancona–Patras	4 times a week June–Oct. Twice a week otherwise. None in Feb./March	Karageorgis Lines 26–28 Akti Kondyli Piraeus, tel. 417 3001
Ancona–Igoumenitsa–Patras	Twice a week April–Jan.	Marlines 38 Akti Possidonos Piraeus, tel. 411 0777
Ancona–Igoumenitsa–Patras Herakleon–Smyrni (Turkey)	Once a week June–Sept.	Marlines (address & tel. as above)
Ancona–Corfu–Patras–Piraeus–Herakleon–Rhodes–Limassol–Haifa	Every 10 days June–Oct.	Stability Lines Viamare Travel Ltd. 33 Mapesbury Rd London, tel. 452 8231
Trieste–Patras	3 times a week in summer	Hellenic Cypriot Mediterranean Lines S.A. 2 Iassonos Piraeus, tel. 413 3879
Venice–Piraeus–Herakleon–Alexandria	Every 10 days March–Dec.	Adriatica, 97 Akti Miaouli Piraeus, tel. 418 1901
Haifa–Limassol–Rhodes–Piraeus	Once a week, year round	Avroessa Lines S.A. 1 Charilaou Tricoupi Piraeus, tel. 418 3777
Odessa–Istanbul–Piraeus	Twice a month May–Oct.	Black Sea Shipping Co 25 Akti Miaouli Piraeus, tel. 411 8705

7

Piraeus to	2nd Class (dr.)	Tourist Cl. (dr.)	3rd Class (dr.)	Dura-tion
Ag. Nikolaos, Crete	4035	3037	2285	14.00 hrs
Amorgos	1781	1369	1311	11.15 hrs
Anafi	3206	2454	1889	18.40 hrs
Astypalaia	2706	2021	1582	13.00 hrs
Chania, Crete	2937	2181	1590	12.00 hrs
Chios	2558	1845	1369	9.00 hrs
Donoussa	3045	2307	1778	10.30 hrs
Elafonnissos	2223	1778	1450	10.00 hrs
Folegandros	2550	1944	1509	12.00 hrs
Halki	4510	3321	2470	18.00 hrs
Herakleon, Crete	3153	2318	1719	12.00 hrs
Heraklia	3045	2307	1778	15.30 hrs
Ikaria	2195	1589	1228	12.00 hrs
Ios	2307	1824	1509	10.00 hrs
Kalymnos	2706	2021	1562	13.00 hrs
Karlovassi, Samos	2677	2021	1541	12.00 hrs
Karpathos	4539	3352	2520	18.00 hrs
Kassos	4338	3206	2404	18.00 hrs
Kimolos	1875	1477	1224	8.00 hrs
Kos	3367	2520	1916	15.00 hrs
Koufonissia–Shinoussa	3045	2307	1778	14.30 hrs
Kythera	2490	1964	1582	10.00 hrs
Kythnos	1369	1013	795	4.00 hrs
Leros	2706	2021	1582	11.30 hrs
Lesbos (Mytilini)	2918	2141	1719	15.00 hrs
Limnos	3037	2376	1916	18.00 hrs
Milos	1875	1477	1224	8.00 hrs
Mykonos	1845	1427	1178	6.00 hrs
Naxos	1875	1457	1224	8.00 hrs
Nissyros	3367	2520	1916	22.00 hrs
Paros	1633	1268	1065	6.00 hrs
Patmos	2706	2021	1582	8.00 hrs
Rhodes	3683	2793	2153	20.00 hrs
Samos	2918	2141	1645	12.00 hrs
Santorini	2307	1824	1509	12.00 hrs
Serifos	1547	1158	897	5.00 hrs
Sifnos	1692	1310	1112	6.30 hrs
Sikinos	3045	2307	1778	10.30 hrs
Sitia, Crete	4510	3381	2648	14.00 hrs
Symi	3367	2520	1916	24.00 hrs
Syros	1547	1224	1060	4.30 hrs
Tilos	3367	2520	1916	24.00 hrs
Tinos	1731	1369	1178	5.00 hrs

Not included in the above prices are embarkation taxes and contributions to the seamen's union; these, however, are minimal.

Argosaronic Line (tel. 4115801, 4511311)

Piraeus to	1st Class (dr.)	3rd Class (dr.)	Duration
Aegina	486	342	1.30 hrs
Hydra	790	578	4.10 hrs
Poros	720	523	3.40 hrs
Porto Heli	1005	764	4.00 hrs
Spetses	1005	764	5.25 hrs

Sporades Line (tel. 4178084 4172415)

Ag. Konstantinos to			
Alonissos	2160	1439	6.00 hrs
Glossa	1691	1216	4.25 hrs
Limnos	2192	1569	10.30 hrs
Skiathos	1510	1068	3.15 hrs
Skopelos	1932	1268	5.25 hrs
Kymi, Evia to			
Ag. Efstratios	1890	895	6.00 hrs
Alonissos	1800	1386	3.00 hrs
Glossa	2100	1571	5.00 hrs
Skiathos	2310	1703	5.30 hrs
Skopelos	2100	1513	3.30 hrs
Skyros	1050	714	1.45 hrs
Volos to			
Alonissos	1470	1150	5.00 hrs
Glossa	1260	942	3.30 hrs
Skiathos	1150	802	3.00 hrs
Skopelos	1365	1007	4.30 hrs

Evia and Cyclades Line (tel. (0294) 23300)

Rafina to	Passenger fares (dr.)	Duration
Andros	675	1.30 hrs
Karystos, Evia	543–607	2.00 hrs
Marmari, Evia	361	5.00 hrs
Mykonos	1200	5.00 hrs
Naxos	1224	6.30 hrs
Paros	1051	5.00 hrs
Syros	976	3.30 hrs
Tinos	1034–1546	4.00 hrs

Kea–Kythnos Line (tel. (0292) 25249)

Lavrion to	Tourist Class (dr.)	Duration
Kea	503	2.30 hrs
Kythnos	751	4.00 hrs

when bought on board. Refunds are rarely given unless the boat itself never arrives, stuck in Piraeus for tax delinquencies. Boats will arrive late or divert their course for innumerable reasons so if you have to catch a flight home allow for the eccentricities of the system and leave a day early to be safe.

When purchasing a ticket, either in Piraeus or on the islands, it's always best to do so from your ship's central agency. Other agencies may tell you that the boat is full, when in truth they've merely sold all the tickets allotted them by the central agency. On many islands, agents moonlight as bartenders or grocers and may only have a handwritten sign next to the door advertising their ship's departures.

Because Piraeus is so busy there's a new trend to use smaller mainland ports, especially Rafina and Lavrion. Neither of these is far from Athens, and bus connections are frequent. They are a bit of a bother for most tourists, though, which means that islands mainly served by these outlying ports are often quieter, if you take the trouble to go.

Most inter-island ferries have three or four classes: the first class, with an air-conditioned lounge and cabins (and often as expensive as flying); the second class, often with its own lounge as well, but smaller cabins; tourist class, for which you can reserve a cabin, segregated by sex, and deck class, which usually gives you access to the typically large, stuffy rooms full of 'airline seats' and the snack bar area. As a rule the Greeks go inside and the tourists stay out—on summer nights in particular perhaps the most pleasant alternative if you have a sleeping bag.

You'd do well to always keep your ticket with you on a Greek ship, at least until the crew enacts its "ticket control", a comedy routine necessitated by the fact that Greeks never check tickets when passengers board. Instead, after one or two pleas on the ship's loudspeaker system for passengers without tickets to purchase them forthwith, you suddenly find all the doors on the boat locked or guarded by a sailor with the bored but obdurate expression of a eunuch guarding a harem, while bands of officers rove about the boat checking tickets. Invariably mix-ups occur: children are separated from their parents, others have gone to the wc, someone has left a ticket with someone on the other side of the immovable sailor, crowds pile up at the doors, and stowaways are marched to the purser's office. In the worst cases, this goes on for an hour; on smaller ships it's usually over in fifteen minutes.

Prices, though no longer cheap, are still fairly reasonable for passengers, rather dear for cars. However, there's one unbeatable bargain (subject to annual renewal by the Greek Tourist office): free tickets in the months of April and May and September and October to 25 of the less visited islands. These class C tickets are available as follows:

Dodecanese: between Rhodes and Kastellorizo, Halki, Kassos or Tilos; Kos and Nyssiros; Patmos and Lipsi; Patmos and Agathonisi; Kalymnos and Pserimos; and Kalymnos and Astypalaia.

Cyclades: between Sifnos and Kythnos, Kimolos, Milos or Serifos; between Naxos and Shinoussa, Amorgos, Heraklia, Donoussa and Koufounissia; from Ios to Sikinos, Folegandros or Serifos; from Santorini to Anafi.

10

Northern Aegean Islands: between Chios and Psara.

Since the free ticket programme is up for renewal each year, contact the National Tourist Organisation of Greece for the latest details. The following is a list of some of the more popular scheduled mainland and inter-island connections. Duration of each boat trip and approximate prices are given in drachmas but are subject to change without notice.

Hydrofoils

There are currently five fleets of hydrofoils thumping over the Greek seas. The Flying Dolphins leave Piraeus Zea Marina for all four of the Saronic islands, and links them with neighbouring mainland ports at Porto Heli and Nauplion; one goes as far as Kythera. Two services ply the Dodecanese, from Rhodes all the way north to Samos, calling at Kalymnos, Kos, Leros and Patmos in between. Another connects Kilini to Zakynthos. The fifth services the Sporades. All the hydrofoils run throughout the year but are less frequent in winter.

Hydrofoils as a rule travel twice as fast as ships and are twice as expensive (in some cases as much as a plane). In the peak season they are often fully booked, so buy tickets as early as you can. Another advantage of hydrofoils is that they don't usually make you seasick, though a choppy sea may leave you saddle-sore.

Tourist Excursion Boats

These are generally slick and clean, and have become quite numerous in recent years. They are more expensive than the regular ferries or steamers, but often have schedules that allow visitors to make day excursions to nearby islands (though you can also take them one way), and are very convenient, having largely taken the place of the little caique operators, many of whom now specialise in excursions to remote beaches instead of island hopping on request. They may well be the only transport available to the most remote islands, but do inquire about scheduled ferries. Friendly yachtsmen may give you a lift—it never hurts to ask.

Boats to Turkey

Whatever axes are currently being ground between Greece and Turkey, a kind of *pax tourista* has fallen over the mutually profitable exchange of visitors from the Greek islands to the Turkish mainland. Connections run daily year-round between Rhodes and Marmaris ($3\frac{1}{2}$ hrs); between Kos and Bodrum daily in summer, less frequently in winter ($1\frac{1}{2}$ hrs); from Chios to Cseme several times a week from spring to autumn (1 hr); from Samos to Kuşadasi (near Ephesus) at least twice a day, April–October ($1\frac{1}{2}$ hrs); and from Lesbos to Ayvalik daily in summer (2 hrs). While there isn't much difference in crossing times, prices can vary enormously according to when you go and whose boat you take (both Greek and Turkish boats make the crossings). I have paid $20 in May from Chios to Cseme, $5 in June from Marmaris to Rhodes, $25 from Kuşadasi to Samos in July, and nothing in September once, just because I was in the right place at the right time. There is a mysterious array of taxes, everywhere different (sometimes less if you only make a day excursion); generally speaking, though, the fare is 5000–6000 dr. Generally the Turkish shops around the ports will take drachma, but the Greeks will not take Turkish lira—and the exchange rate between the two is pretty dreadful. Also, beware the charter restriction: things as they are, a sidetrip to Turkey can bring the Greek airport authorities to invoke the law and refuse you passage home on your flight.

For the most recent information on Greek sea connections, get a copy of the National Tourist Organisation's *Greek Travel Pages* or *Key Travel Guide*, which is updated every week. Travel agents in Great Britain often have a copy, and it is easy to find in Greece itself.

By yacht

Yachting is by far the best way of seeing the Greek islands, and more and more people do it every year. A vast effort has been made by the National Tourist Organisation to construct marinas and yacht supply stations, and one is never very far from a safe anchorage. There are 27 official ports of entry and exit in Greece: Ag. Nikolaos (Crete), Alexandroupolis, Argostoli (Kephallonia), Chania (Crete), Chios, Corfu, Glyfada (Attica), Herakleon (Crete), Hermoupolis (Syros), Itea, Kalamata, Katakolo, Kavala, Kos, Lavrio (Attica), Myrina (Limnos), Mytilini (Lesbos), Nauplion, Patras, Preveza, Pylos, Rhodes, Samos, Thessaloniki, Volos, Vouliagmeni (Attica), Zakynthos and Zea Marina (Piraeus).

Yachts entering Greek waters must fly the code flag 'Q' until cleared by entry port authorities. Afterwards it is customary to fly a Greek courtesy flag. Upon arrival the **port authority** (*Limenarkion*) issues all yachts with a transit log, which entitles the yacht and crew to unlimited travel in Greek waters. It also allows crew members to buy fuel, alcohol and cigarettes duty free. The log should be renewed yearly, or after leaving and re-entering Greek waters. Yachtsmen who intend to spend a night ashore should first get their passports stamped.

Any boat smaller than a yacht is defined as a pleasure craft, whether it is a sailing, motor or rowing boat. These are noted down in the owner's passport upon entry to Greece and are allowed to circulate for four months, a period which is renewable at customs.

Anyone taking a yacht by road is strongly advised to obtain boat registration documentation from the Royal Yachting Association, Queen St, Gillingham, Dorset (tel. 07476 4437).

The greatest **navigational hazard** in the Aegean Sea is the meltemi, the strong north wind. It generally peaks in August, and is also often encountered in July and September. The suffocating sirocco from Africa blows occasionally in western Greek waters.

The Greek meteorological service issues warnings of any likely hazards on the radio telephone service (three minutes after every hour and half-hour in English). The Greek radio network transmits weather bulletins in English every day at 6.50 am–7.00 am in winter (6.30 am–6.50 am in summer), 1.10 pm–1.25 pm and 9.45 pm–10.00 pm.

More details on radio services and other information are given in the National Tourist Organisation's handbook *Greece for the Yachtsman*, which can be found at any of the organisation's offices abroad. Also helpful, if somewhat outdated, are H. M. Denham's books, *The Aegean—A Sea Guide to its Coasts and Islands* and *The Ionian Islands to Rhodes*.

Chartering yachts is very popular these days, and as the promotional literature says, can be cheaper than staying in a hotel (if you have enough friends or family to share expenses). Between the various firms (the National Tourist Organisation has a list) there are over a thousand vessels currently available in all sizes, with or without a crew (though without a crew both the charterer and another member of the party must show proof of seamanship: a sailing certificate or letter of recommendation from a recognised yacht or sailing club). For more information, write to the Association of Boat and Yacht Rental Agents, P.O. Box 341, Piraeus.

A number of English based flotilla companies offer one or two week sailing holidays, the air fare being included in the total cost of around £600 per person in high season.

By car

Driving from London to Athens at a normal pace takes around $3\frac{1}{2}$ days, which is why one sees so few British cars in Greece. Unless you are planning to spend a few weeks on one or two islands, a car is not really worth the expense and trouble of bringing it to Greece. If you do decide to bring one, the smaller the better, both for squeezing it onto the ferry, and for negotiating the sometimes very narrow village roads.

One of the best bets for **North Americans and Australians** who want to drive in Greece is to buy a car for the duration of your trip, with an agreement to sell it back to the company when you leave. Several companies in Paris can arrange this, though it is not possible in Greece itself. Alternatively, there are many rent-a-car companies on the mainland and the islands.

An **International Driving Licence** is not required by British, Austrian, Belgian or German citizens. Other nationals can obtain an international licence at home, or at one of the Automobile Club offices in Greece (ELPA), by presenting a national driving licence, passport and photograph. The minimum age is 18 years.

The Motor Insurance Bureau at 10 Xenofontos St, Athens, tel. (01) 3236733, can tell you which Greek insurance company represents your own, or provide you with additional cover for Greece.

There are five **frontier posts** for Greece, all open day and night:
Yugoslavia: Evzoni and Niki
Bulgaria: Promahon

13

Turkey: Kastania and Kipi

Customs formalities are very easy and usually take very little time. One is allowed a year of free use of the car in Greece, and after that can apply for a four-month extension. North Americans and Australians are allowed two years. If you leave Greece without your car, you must have it withdrawn from circulation by a customs authority. ELPA has a list of lawyers who can offer free legal advice on motorcars. They also have a 24-hour recording of information useful to foreign motorist, tel. 174.

Parking in the centre of Athens, or the Green Zone, is forbidden outside designated parking areas. The following streets form the borders of the Green Zone: Sekeri, Botassi, Stournara, Marni, Menandrou, Pireos, Likourgou, Athias, Mitropoleos, Philellinon, Amalias and Vassilissis Sophias.

While driving in the centre of Athens may be a hair-raising experience, the rest of Greece is easy and pleasant. There are few cars on most roads, even in summer and all signs have their Latin equivalents. Traffic regulations and signalling comply with standard practice on the European Continent (i.e. driving on the right). Crossroads and low visibility in the mountains are probably the greatest hazards. Where there are no right of way signs at a crossroads, give priority to traffic coming from the right, and always bleep your horn on blind corners. Take special care when approaching an unguarded railway level crossing. It is also advisable to take a spare container of petrol along with you, as petrol stations are inconsistent in their frequency. There is a speed limit of 50 kmh (30 mph) in inhabited areas: other speed limits are indicated by signposts in km. Horn blowing is prohibited in Athens and other big cities. The Greek Automobile Club (ELPA) operates a breakdown service within 60 km (40 miles) of Athens, Salonika, Larissa, Patras and Herakleon: dial 104.

Greek Automobile Club (ELPA) addresses
Athens: 2–4 Messogion St, Tower of Athens. Tel. (01) 7791615. Telex: 215763
Chania (Crete): 1 Apokoronou & Skoula. Tel. (0821) 26059
Corfu: Pat. Athinagora. Tel. (0661) 39504
Herakleon (Crete): Knossos Ave. & G. Papandreou. Tel. (081) 289440
Kavala: 109 7th Merachias. Tel. (051) 229778
Larissa: At the 3rd km or the national road Athens/Larissa. Tel. (041) 239660
Patras: Astingos & 127 Korinthou. Tel. (061) 425411
Rhodes: 38 Akti Miasuli. Tel. (0241) 25066
Thessaloniki: 228 Vass. Olgas & 34 Egeou. Tel. (031) 426319
Tripolis: 3 Vass. Pavlou. Tel. (071) 224101
Volos: 2 Eolidos. Tel. (0421) 25001

By motorbike, scooter or moped

Scooters, and even more popular, mopeds are ideal for the islands in the summer. It almost never rains and what could be more pleasant than a gentle thyme-scented breeze freshening your journey over the mountains? Scooters are both more economical and more practical than cars. They can fit into almost any boat and travel paths where cars fear to tread. Many islands have scooter rentals which are not expensive, and include third party coverage in most cases. For larger motorbikes you may be asked to show a driver's licence. However, be warned that not a few hospital beds in Greece are occupied every summer by tourists who have been careless about moped safety rules.

By bicycle

Cycling has not caught on in Greece, either as a sport or as a means of transport, though you can usually hire an old bike in most major resorts. Trains and planes carry bicycles for a small fee, and Greek boats generally take them along, for nothing. Crete and Evia are the best islands for cycling enthusiasts, Crete being the more rugged by far. On both islands you will find fresh water, places to camp, and a warm and surprised welcome in the villages.

Hitch-hiking

With the rarest of exceptions, hitch-hiking, or autostop as it is known in Greece, is perfectly safe. However, the lack of cars makes it a not particularly speedy mode of transport. The Greek double standard produces the following percentages for hopeful hitch-hikers:
> Single woman: 99% of the cars will stop. You hardly have to stick out your thumb.
> Two women: 75% of the cars will find room for you.
> Woman and man: 50%; more if the woman is pretty.
> Single man: 25% if you are well dressed with little luggage; less otherwise.
> Two men: start walking.
> The best time for soliciting a ride is when you disembark from a ship. Ask around your fellow passengers, or better still write your destination on a piece of paper (in Greek if possible) and pin it to your shirt with a naive and friendly smile. What you lose in dignity you will generally gain in a lift.

Customs and immigration

The formalities for foreign tourists entering Greece are very simple. Citizens of all English-speaking countries (except South Africa) can stay for up to three months in Greece simply on presentation of a valid passport. South Africans are permitted two months.

If you want to extend your stay in Greece, you must report to the police ten days before your visa runs out. (If you are staying in Athens, register at the Athens Alien Dept, 9 Chalkokondyli St, tel. 362 8301). Take your passport, four photographs, and if possible, the name of a reference in Greece. You will receive a slip of paper authorising you to stay for a period of up to six months. This has to be stamped at the end of every three succeeding months that you remain in Greece.

What you can bring into Greece duty free

Private cars and pleasure craft for four months without further documents. Trailers and caravans need additional documentation: contact the National Tourist Organisation or your automobile club for more information.
Books
Camera (still and/or movie) and film
Sporting equipment
Typewriter
Record player and up to 20 records
2 packs playing cards
Dogs and cats with a veterinary certificate
Bicycle
Binoculars
2 guns and 20 cartridges (must be declared)
Tape recorder
Portable radio
Portable musical instrument
75 grams perfume
$\frac{1}{4}$ litre eau de Cologne
1 bottle spirits
150 grams tobacco
300 cigarettes (200 if non EEC)
10 kg sweets
1500 drachma
Any amount of money in other currencies which is more than US$500-worth should be declared.

What you can take out of Greece duty free

1 container olive oil up to 18 kg
Art objects made after 1830. (Anything of earlier date, either bought or found, must first be licensed by the Greek Archaeology Service, Section of Antiquity Sales, 13 Polygnotou St. Antique shop owners will give you further details, and an exportation tax must be paid. Those caught with even the most innocent un-licensed potsherd in their baggage will be severely prosecuted.) Make sure that any drachmas you have when leaving are not in denominations of more than 500 dr.—many foreign banks will refuse to change them (or give you a very low exchange rate).

Where to Stay, Drinking, Dining and Dancing

Hotels

All hotels in Greece are divided into six categories: Luxury A, B, C, D and E. Prices are set and strictly controlled by the Tourist Police. Off season you can generally get a discount, sometimes as much as 40%. In the summer season prices can be increased by up to 15%. Other charges include an 8% government tax, a 45% community bed tax, a 12% stamp tax, an optional 10% surcharge for stays of only one or two days, an air-conditioning surcharge, as well as a 20% surcharge for an extra cot. All of these prices are listed on the door of every room and authorised and checked at regular intervals. If your hotelier fails to abide by the posted prices, or if you have any other reason to believe all is not on the level, take your complaint to the Tourist Police.

1988 rate guideline in drachma
Prices for E hotels are not quoted officially, but should be about 20% less than D rates.

During the summer, hotels with restaurants may require guests to take their meals in the hotel, either full pension or demi pension, and there is no refund for an uneaten dinner. Twelve noon is the official check-out time, although on the islands it is usually geared to the arrival of the next boat. Most Luxury and class A, if not B, hotels situated far from the town or port supply buses or cars to pick up guests.

Musicians from the Tomb of the Leopards 480–470 BC Fresco

17

	L	A	B	C	D
Single room with bath	8000–27000	4200–9000	3500–7000	2500–4500	1200–2000
Double room with bath	15000–33000	7000–14000	6000–10000	3000–6500	1600–3000
Breakfast	600–1200	400–700	300–600	300–500	
Lunch or dinner	1500–3000	1000–2500	800–2000		

Hotels down to class B all have private bathrooms. In C some do and some don't. In D you will be lucky to find a hot shower, and in E forget it. In these hotels neither towel nor soap is supplied, although the bedding is clean.

The importance of reserving a room in advance, especially during July and August, cannot be overemphasised. Reservations can be made through the individual hotel or

The Hellenic Chamber of Hotels, 24 Stadiou St, Athens.

Tel. Athens 3236962 (from Athens: between 8 am and 8 pm)

Telex 214269 XEPE GR. Cable EXENEPEL

Rooms in private homes

These are for the most part cheaper than hotels and are sometimes more pleasant. On the whole, Greek houses aren't much in comparison to other European homes mainly because the Greeks spend so little time inside them; but they are clean, and the owner will often go out of his or her way to assure maximum comfort for the guest. In most houses you can also get an idea of Greek taste, which is sometimes simple and good, but at other times incredibly corny, from plastic cat pictures that squeak to lamps in the shape of ships made out of macaroni. Increasingly, however, rooms to rent to tourists are built in a separate annexe and tend to be rather characterless.

While room prices are generally fixed in the summer, out of season they are always negotiable with a little finesse, even in June. Speaking some Greek is the biggest asset in bargaining, although not strictly necessary. Claiming to be a poor student is generally effective. Always remember, however, that you are staying in someone's home, and do not waste more water or electricity than you need. The owner will generally give you a bowl to wash your clothes in, and there is always a clothes line.

The Tourist Police on each island have all the information on rooms and will be able to find you one, if you do not meet a chorus of Greeks when you leave the boat, chanting "Rooms? Rooms?". Many houses also have signs.

Youth Hostels

Some of these are official and require a membership card from the Association of Youth Hostels, or alternatively an International Guest Card from the Greek Association of Youth Hostels, 4 Dragatsaniou St, Athens, tel. 323–4107; other hostels are informal, have no irksome regulations, and admit anyone. There are official youth hostels on the islands of Corfu, Santorini and Crete, which has several. Most charge extra for a shower, sometimes for sheets.

Camping out

The climate of summertime Greece is perfect for sleeping out of doors. Unauthorised camping is illegal in Greece, although each village on each island enforces the ban as it sees fit. Some couldn't care less if you put up a tent at the edge of their beach; in others the police may pull up your tent pegs and fine you. All you can do is ask around to see what other tourists or friendly locals advise. In July and August you only need a sleeping bag to spend a pleasant night on a remote beach, cooled by the sea breezes that also keep hopeful mosquitoes at bay. Naturally, the more remote the beach, the less likely you are to be disturbed. If a policeman does come by and asks you to move, though, you had best do so; be diplomatic. Many islands have privately-operated camping grounds—each seems to have at least one. These are reasonably priced, though some have only minimal facilities. The National Tourist Office controls other, 'official', campsites which are rather plush and costly.

There are two main reasons behind the camping law: one is that the beaches have no sanitation facilities for crowds of campers, and secondly, Greece in the summer has a major problem with forest fires. Every summer they rage through the dry timberlands on the islands and mainland. If the police are in some places lackadaisical about enforcing the camping regulations, they come down hard on anyone lighting any kind of fire in a forest, and may very well put you in jail for two months.

Renting a house or villa

On most islands it is possible to rent houses or villas, generally for a month or more at a time. Villas can often be reserved from abroad: contact a travel agent or the National Tourist Organisation for names and addresses of rental agents. In the off season houses may be found on the spot with a little inquiry; with luck you can find a house sleeping six, eight or ten people, and depending on the facilities it can work out quite reasonably per person. Islands with sophisticated villa rentals (i.e. with a large number of purpose-built properties with all the amenities, handled by agents in Athens, Great Britain and North America) are Rhodes, Skiathos, Corfu, Mykonos, Crete, Paros and Symi. The NTOG has a list of agents offering villas and apartments. In Athens an agent which handles a number of island properties is Starlite Tours and Travel, 12 Amalias Avenue. Facilities normally include a refrigerator, hot water, plates and utensils, etc. Generally, the longer you stay the more economical it becomes. Things to check for are leaking roofs, water supply (the house may have a well) and a supply of lamps if there is no electricity.

Traditional Settlements in Greece

This is a programme sponsored by the National Tourist Organisation of Greece to preserve old villages and certain buildings while converting their interiors into

19

tourist accommodation with modern amenities. Often these are furnished with handmade furniture and weaving typical of the locale. The aim is to offer visitors a taste of rural life while improving the economy in these areas. So far guest-houses are available on Santorini, Chios, Psara and Kephallonia, and in several villages on the mainland; others are planned for the future. Prices are quite reasonable (especially when compared with the going rate for villas) and reservations and information may be had by writing to the Greek National Tourist Organisation/EOT dieftynsi Ekmetalefseos, 2 Amerikis St, Athens 10564.

Art centres of the School of Fine Arts

Four of the five annexes of the Athenian School of Fine Arts are located on the islands, namely, Hydra, Mykonos, Rhodes and Lesbos (Mythimna). These provide inexpensive accommodation for foreign artists (for up to 20 days in the summer and 30 in the winter) as well as studios, etc. One requirement is a recommendation from the Greek embassy in the artist's home country. Contact its Press and Information Office for further information.

A note on the Greek toilet

Greek plumbing has improved remarkably in the past eight years, especially in the hotels. However, public toilets and those in the cheaper hotel and pensions often have their quirks. Tavernas, *kafeneíons*, and sweetshops almost always have facilities (it's good manners to buy something before you excuse yourself). Popular beaches usually have public toilets nearby as well, though you may have to pay a small fee.

Often the plumbing makes up in inventiveness for what it lacks in efficiency. Do not tempt fate by disobeying the little notices "the papers they please to throw in the basket"—or it's bound to lead to trouble. Also, a second flush in immediate succession will gurgle and burp instead of swallow. Many places in Greece have only a ceramic hole. Women who confront this for the first time should take care not to wet their feet: squat about halfway and lean back as far as you can. Always have paper of some sort handy.

If you stay in a private room or pension you may have to have the water heater turned on for about 20 minutes before you take a shower, so if you were promised hot water but it fails to appear, ask the proprietor about it. In larger hotel often there is hot water in the mornings and evenings, but not in the afternoons. Actually "cold" showers in the summer aren't all that bad, because the tap water itself is generally lukewarm, especially after noon. A good many showers are of the hand-held variety, but if a black cat has recently crossed your path you may get the Special Greek Squirt, where a quarter of the water trickles on your head and the rest ricochets off the ceiling and onto your towel. If the water stops, try jiggling the sink or toilet. Sinks in Greece rarely have rubber stoppers.

Greek tap water is perfectly safe to drink, though big plastic bottles of spring water are widely available, even on most ships. On dry islands, remember to ask what time the water is turned off.

Dining

Eating establishments in Greece are categorised into Luxury, A, B, and C classes. Prices are controlled by the Tourist Police, who also enforce sanitary and health regulations.

The menu in Luxury restaurants is often international; in others you will rarely find more than the basic Greek cuisine. This is steeped in rich golden olive oil and the ingredients are fresh and often produced locally. You may go back into the kitchens to examine the offerings before making a choice. There is usually a menu posted on the door with an English translation, listing the prices. The availability and variety of fish depends on the catch. Sadly, seafood has become one of the most expensive meals you can order. A combination of increased demand, marketing to Athens, and greedy, unsound fishing practices (such as illegal dynamiting) has decreased the fish population in the Mediterranean, so that what was once common and cheap is now costly and in some places quite rare. Each type of fish has its own price, and your choice is usually weighed for you before it's cooked. Remember, the redder the gills the fresher the fish.

Pork has taken the place of lamb as the most common meat in Greek tavernas since the country joined the Common Market. Almost all souvlaki (the ubiquitous chunks of meat grilled on a stick) you get these days is pork, though lamb, roasted or stewed, is still widely available. Beef and chicken are often stewed in a sauce of tomatoes and olive oil, or roasted, accompanied by potatoes, spaghetti or rice. Village feasts, or *paneyéri* often feature wild goat meat with rice or potatoes. A Greek salad can be just tomatoes or just cucumbers, or village style with tomatoes, cucumbers, black olives, peppers, onions and feta cheese—a small one for one person and a big one for two or three. You eat this during the meal, dipping your bread in the olive oil. In the summer dinner is generally followed by melon or watermelon.

Restaurants (*estiatórion*) serve baked dishes and often grills as well. Those serving just a grill and roasts are called *psistariá*. A taverna may serve baked dishes or a grill or both, and is less formal than a restaurant. A sweet shop, or *zacharoplasteíon*, sells honey pastries, cakes, puddings and drinks and sometimes home-made ice cream. Many also serve breakfast, along with the less common dairy shops, or *galaktopoleíon* which sell milk, coffee, bread, yoghurt, rice pudding and custard pies. Cheese pies and "tost" can appear almost anywhere.

Prices on Greek menus are written first without, then with, service and tax charges. If you are served by a young boy (*mikró*), give him something or leave it on the table—tips are generally all he earns. If you've been given special service, you may leave a tip for your waiter on the plate.

Bavarian-type beer is now common in most restaurants and tavernas, and many have several wines to choose from. Even if you've tried the national

21

favourite, retsina (resinated white wine), once and couldn't bear it, some local brands are quite delicate—and nothing cuts down the oil in Greek cooking better. There is also an infinite variety of red and white labels, mostly from Patras, Attica, Samos, Rhodes and Crete.

More and more rare are the tavernas with huge wooden barrels lining the walls; in many, however, you can buy wine by the jug or glass. You can also come with your own container and have it filled with local wine—the cheapest way to buy it. Cafés or *kafeneíons* serve Turkish coffee—now known more often as Greek coffee (*café hellinikó*). There are 40 different ways to make this, although *glykó* (sweet), *métrio* (medium) and *skéto* (no sugar) are the basic orders. It is always served with a glass of water. Nescafé with milk has by popular tourist demand become available everywhere, though Greeks prefer it iced, with or without sugar and milk, which they call *frappé*. Soft drinks and ouzo round out the average café fare. Ouzo—like its Cretan cousin raki—is a clear anise-flavoured aperitif which many dilute (and cloud) with water. It can be served with a little plate of snacks called *mezédes* which can range from grilled octopus through nuts to cheese and tomatoes, though often these days you must request mezédes specially. Brandy, or Metaxas (the Greeks know it by the most popular brand name), is usually a late night treat. The more stars on the label (from three to seven) the smoother the drink. In the tourist haunts, milk shakes, fruit juices, cocktails and even capuccinos are readily available; in the backwaters you can usually get ice cream and good Greek yoghurt.

Greek *kafeneíons* in small towns are frequented mostly by men, who discuss the latest news, and play cards or backgammon.

In the last few years the influx of tourists has resulted in the birth of a new type of bar on the Greek scene—the British style pub, usually playing the latest hit records and serving fancy cocktails as well as standard drinks. These establishments usually come to life later in the evening, when everyone has spent the day on the beach and the earlier part of the evening in a taverna. They close at 3 or 4 am. In general they're not cheap, and it can be disconcerting to realise that you have paid the same for your Harvey Wallbanger as you paid for the entire meal of chicken and chips, salad and a bottle of wine, half an hour before in the taverna next door. Cocktails have now risen to beyond the 700 dr. mark in many bars, but before you complain remember that the measures are triples by British standards. If in doubt stick to beer, ouzo, wine and Metaxa (Metaxa and coke is generally about half the price of the better known Bacardi and coke). You may have difficulty in finding beer, as the profit margin is so small that many bars stop serving it in the peak season, thus obliging you to plump for the higher priced drinks. One unfortunate practice on the islands is the doctoring of bottles, whereby some bar owners buy cheaper versions of spirits and refill brand name bottles with them (Tequilla made in Piraeus?). The only way to be sure is to see the new bottle being opened in front of you.

A list of items which appear frequently on Greek menus is included in the language section at the end of the guide (pp. 403—413).

Music and dancing

Greek music is either city music or village music. The music of the city includes the popular tunes and most bazouki music, whereas village music is played on the bag pipes (*tsamboúna*), the clarinet (*klaríno*), the violin and sometimes the dulcimer (*sandoúri*). Cretan music specialises in the lyre and is in a class by itself.

On the islands you can hear both city and village music, the former at the *baóukia*, or Greek night clubs, which usually feature certain singers. Many play records or washed-out musak until midnight as the customers slowly arrive. One generally buys a bottle of white wine and fruit and dances until 4 in the morning, though expect to pay a pretty drachma for the privilege. To hear the village, or folk music, you must go into the villages, to the festivals or weddings. In many places Sunday evening is an occasion for song and dance. Village music is generally modest, with city music not only do the professional singers perform, but any local with a good voice will often get up to sing a few songs. After an hour of drinking, a particular favourite or a good dancer is liable to make the enthusiasts forget the law against *spásimo*, or plate breaking, and supporters may end up paying for missing place settings.

On a particularly energetic evening someone is bound to get up and dance holding a fully set table between his teeth, while others dance with wine glasses or bottles on their heads. When matrons begin to belly dance on the table, you know it's time to go.

In the tavernas one may hear either city or village music. Some put on permanent shows, and others have music only occasionally. Athens is awash with tourist shows and discotheques during the summer but starts pulsating to all kinds of Greek music in November, when Plaka is returned to the Athenians. Most musicians on the islands go to Athens in the winter.

The lyrics to most Greek songs deal with the ups and downs of love. Serious composers (Mikis Theodorakis is the best known) often put poetry to music, providing splendid renderings of the lyrics of George Seferis and Yannis Ritsos. The guerrillas (*partizanis*) and the Communists have a monopoly of the best political songs, many by Theodorakis. Cretan songs are often very patriotic (for Crete) and many are drawn from the 17th-century epic poem, the *Erotókritos*, written in the Cretan dialect by Vincento Kornaro.

Every island in Greece has its special dance, although today it is often only the young people's folk dance societies that keep them alive, along with the island's traditional costumes. The best time to find them dancing is on each island's Day of Liberation from the Turks or any other anniversary of local significance. Here are details of two excellent folk dance companies:

Athens:
Dora Stratou Greek Folk Dances, Dora Stratou Theatre, Philopapou Hill.
Tel. 3224861 mornings, 914650 afternoons.
From beginning of May to end of September.

The Dolphin Fresco at Knossos

Shows begin at 10 pm every day, with an additional show at 8 pm on Wednesdays and Sundays
Tickets: 400 or 550 dr.; 150–200 dr. for students.

Rhodes:
Nelly Dimoglou Greek Dances, The Old City Theatre.
Tel. (0241) 29085.
From June to October.
Performances at 9 pm daily except Saturdays.
Tickets 500 dr.; 300 dr. for students.

Although these shows are beautiful and interesting, there's nothing like getting up to dance yourself—a splendid way to work off the big dinner just consumed at a paneyeri. The one dance everyone knows is the basic one two three kick kickie, or Stae Tria, done in a circle with hands on shoulders. The circle is never complete, however: even in this simple dance someone leads, setting the pace and variation of the dance (for all know each dance a little differently) and generally supplying the special effects with leaps, foot slaps, kicks, little skips or whatever he or she likes. Cretans are the best leaders—some are almost contortionists.

Stae Tria often begins at a slow pace and picks up towards the end. The Sýrto, on the other hand, retains its slow graceful pace throughout. It has only six easy steps which are repeated until the end, but watch the leader for variations. This is considered the oldest Greek dance of all, dating back at least to Hellenistic times. The Kalamatíano, a 12-steo dance, is a little more difficult. If a Greek invites you to dance the Bállo, a couple's dance, follow your partner's lead. While there are certain set steps to the Tsíphte Téli, or belly dance, it has become a free-spirited dance for the loose limbed.

24

The Zeybetiko is normally performed by men, although upon occasion women also dance it. This is the serious deliberate solo dance that inspires the most spásimo, for everyone loves to watch a good Zeybetiko dancer with his friend before him on one knee-clapping out the rhythm. The Hasápiko, better known as the Zorba dance in the West, and traditionally performed by two men, will require some practice but is well worth learning. This is even more true of the Cretan dances with their small furious steps and hops, which have a habit of lasting until your adrenalin has pumped its last. The remedy for this is a glass of raki, and before you know it you'll be dancing another Pentozale or Pedekto.

Almost all Greeks love to dance and are never surprised when visitors want to join in the fun. People interested in learning Greek dancing can often find local people to teach them, or they can follow the steps in a book published by Lycabettus Press: *Greek Dances* by Ted Petrides.

Wild Animals and Other Concerns

Animals

The only ferocious animal most visitors will encounter is the mosquito,which can easily be outsmarted with a lotion, spray or insect coil, all of which are widely available. Electric mosquito killers, which you plug into a wall socket, are also inexpensive and effective, and don't stink like the coils—but make sure you get one with the proper electrical fitting. Some islands have very few mosquitoes, while others have swarms of them. Some mules can be bad-tempered, but may be foiled by avoiding their rear legs. Pincushiony sea urchins live by rocky beaches, and if you step on one with bare feet, you'll know it. The spines may break and embed themselves even deeper if you try to force them out, olive oil and a lot of patience is recommended, to get the spine to slip out. Pale brown jellyfish (*médusas*) may drift in anywhere depending on winds and currents. Unless they find a tender spot, a jellyfish sting is not very painful, although they can sometimes leave scars.

The truly dangerous creatures are much more difficult to find. Poisonous snakes and scorpions live only in rural areas. Scorpions hide in small, dark places and though their sting is extremely painful, it is not fatal. One kind of snake is poisonous—a small, grey-brown snake that lives in the nooks and crannies of stone walls, where it is well camouflaged, it only comes out occasionally to sun itself. Although it is rare, and seldom seen, the Greeks are terrified of it, the mere word "fithi" (snake) makes their blood pressure rise. If you have the misfortune to be bitten, you should apply a pressure immobilization bandage, full details of the application, and what this bandage is, are to be found in a First Aid book. Most importantly, stay calm. Get to a doctor as soon as possible, but never run. Mountain sheepdogs are a more immediate danger in outer rural areas, by stooping as if to pick up a stone to throw at it, you might keep a dog at bay. If bitten, go immediately to a doctor.

Sharks are seldom found near the coastal regions of Greece. Blood attracts them, so if you are wounded, swim for shore without delay. Underwater fishermen should ask their Greek confrères about other dangerous fish in the area, such as the Dracula, an unlikely delicacy, whose razor-sharp fins can kill.

Again, these dangers are very rare, and most people never hear of them, much less see them. However, if you do plan to camp in an out-of-the-way area, it never hurts to have a tetanus shot before travelling.

The hunting season (mainly for hare and fowl) is from 25 August to 15 March. For further information contact the Greek Federation of Hunting Societies, 2 Korai St, Athens; tel. 3231271.

Banks and money

The word for bank in Greek is *trápeza*, derived from the word *trapezi*, or table, and thus from the days of the money changers. On all the islands with more than goats and a few shepherds there is some sort of banking establishment. If you plan to spend time on one of the more remote islands, however, such as Antikythera or Kastellorizo, it is safest to bring enough drachma with you. On the other hand, the small but popular islands often have only one bank, where exchanging money can take a long time. Waiting can be avoided if you go at 8 in the morning, when the banks open (normal banking hours are 8 am to 1 pm). Most island banks are closed on Saturdays and Sundays.

Traveller's cheques are always good to bring, not only in case of theft, but also because they command a better exchange rate than currency. The major brands of traveller's cheques and international banking cards are accepted in all banks (travel agents and hotels can also give you drachma for most of these when the banks are closed). Athens and Piraeus, with offices of many British and American banks, are the easiest places to have money sent if you run out, though even if you're a customer it may take a few days—it's easiest if you have someone at home who can send it to you.

The **Greek drachma** is circulated in coins of 50, 20, 10, 5, 2 and 1 drachma and in notes of 50, 100, 500, 1000 and 5000 drachma. You are allowed to bring 3000 drachma in to Greece with you, which is a good idea if you intend to arrive on a Saturday or Sunday.

If you run out of money in Greece, it usually isn't too difficult to find a **temporary job** on the islands, ranging from polishing cucumbers to laying cement. The kafeneions are good places to inquire. Work on yachts can sometimes be found by asking around at the Athenian marinas. The theatre agents, for work as extras in films, are off Academias Ave. by Kanigos Square. Teachers may apply to the American Community Schools of Athens Inc., 129 Ag. Paraskevis, Ano Neo Chalandri, Athens. The *Athens News*, the country's English daily, often has classified advertisements for domestic, tutorial, and secretarial jobs.

Children

If you have children, they won't be alone if you bring them to the islands—more and more come to Greece all the time. However, if they're babies, don't count on island pharmacies stocking your baby's brand of milk powder or baby foods—they may have some, but it's safest to bring your own supply. Disposable nappies, or diapers are widely available except in the smaller villages. Pushchairs or prams are convenient on the larger islands with big towns and pavements, but are less useful in hilly villages, where there tend to be more steps than smooth stretches. A back carrier, however, can come in handy.

Greeks adore children and, with the aid of a long afternoon nap, keep theirs up till all hours. They will probably give yours all kinds of sticky sweets and chocolate on the hottest of days, and offer you an endless supply of advice on their upbringing.

Children, depending on their age, go free or receive discounts on domestic flights, ships and buses. On the last two, the policy towards children varies—sometimes we paid full fare for our six-year-old, sometimes half, and sometimes he went free. You can also save money on hotels by bringing sleeping bags for the children.

Climate and Conversion tables

AVERAGE DAILY TEMPERATURES

	ATHENS		CRETE (HERAKLION)		CYCLADES (MYKONOS)		DODECANESE (RHODES)		IONIAN (CORFU)		N.E. AEGEAN (MYTILINI)		SARONIC (HYDRA)		SPORADES (SKYROS)	
	F°	C°	F°	C°	F°	C°	F°	C°	F°	C°	F°	C°	F°	C°	F°	C°
JAN	48	11	54	12	54	12	54	12	50	10	50	10	53	12	51	10
FEB	49	11	54	12	54	12	54	13	50	10	48	10	53	12	51	10
MAR	54	12	58	14	56	13	58	14	52	12	52	12	56	13	52	11
APR	60	16	62	17	62	17	60	17	60	15	60	16	61	16	58	15
MAY	68	20	68	20	68	20	66	20	66	19	68	20	68	20	66	19
JUNE	76	25	74	24	74	23	73	21	71	21	74	24	76	25	74	23
JUL	82	28	78	26	76	25	78	27	78	27	80	27	82	28	77	25
AUG	82	28	78	26	76	25	79	27	78	26	80	27	81	28	78	25
SEP	76	25	76	24	74	23	78	25	74	23	74	23	76	25	71	22
OCT	66	19	70	21	68	20	72	21	66	19	66	19	71	21	65	19
NOV	58	15	64	18	62	17	66	17	58	15	58	15	62	17	58	15
DEC	52	12	58	14	58	14	58	14	54	12	52	12	58	15	51	12

Two Greek measurements you may come across are the *sremma*, a Greek land measurement (1 sremma = ¼ acre), and the *oka*, an old-fashioned weight standard, divided into 400 *drams* (1 *oka* = 3 lb; 35 *drams* = ¼ lb, 140 *drams* = 1 lb).

The **electric current** in Greece is mainly 220 volts, 50 Hz. In more out-of-the-way places you may find 110 volts. US 60-cycle appliances equipped for dual voltage will function on 50 Hz but will work more slowly than normal.

Greek time is Eastern European, or two hours ahead of Greenwich time.

Embassies and consulates in Greece

Australia:	15 Messogion St, Athens. Tel. 775 7651/4
Austria:	26 Leof. Alexandras, Athens. Tel. 821 1036
Canada:	4 Ioannou Genadiou St, Athens. Tel. 723 9511
France:	7 Vass. Sofias, Athens. Tel. 361 1663
Germany (Fed. Rep.):	3 Karaoli & Dimitrou St, Athens. Tel. 36941
Ireland:	7 Vass. Konstantinou, Athens. Tel. 723 2771
Japan:	2–4 Messogion St, Athens (Athens Tower). Tel. 775 8101
New Zealand:	15–17 Tsoha St, Athens. Tel. 641 0311
South Africa:	124 Kifissias & Iatriou St, Athens. Tel. 692 2125
United Kingdom:	1 Ploutarchou St, Athens. Tel. 723 6211
USA:	91 Vass. Sofias, Athens. Tel. 721 2951
United Nations Office:	36 Amalias, Athens. Tel. 322 9624

Health

In theory there is at least one doctor (*iatrós*) on every island, whose office is open from 9 am to 1 pm and from 5 pm to 7 pm. On many islands too there are hospitals which are open all day, and usually have an outpatient clinic, open in the mornings. British travellers qualify for treatment here, and need to have Form EIII, available at all DHSS offices. Otherwise you'll have to pay, although it's usually reasonable. Private doctors and hospital stays can be very expensive, and you should seriously consider taking out a traveller's insurance policy, these being fairly reasonably priced.

Most doctors pride themselves on their English, as do their friends the pharmacists, whose advice on minor ailments is also good, although their medicine is not particularly cheap.

Coca Cola or retsina cuts down the oil in Greek foods. Lemon juice can also help stomach upsets. The sea quickly cures cuts and abrasions. If anything else goes wrong, the Greek villagers will advise you to pee on it.

Holidays

Note that most businesses and shops also close down for the afternoon before and the morning after a religious holiday. If a national holiday falls on a Sunday, the following Monday is observed. The Orthodox Easter is generally a week or so after the Roman Easter.

1 January	New Year's Day	*Protochroniza*
6 January	Epiphany	*Ton Theofanzıon*
25 March	Greek Independence Day	*Ikosi pémpti martíou*
	Shrove Tuesday	*Kathari Théftera* (follows a three-week carnival)
	Good Friday	*Megáli Paraskeví*
	Easter	*Páscha*
	Easter Monday	*Théftera tou Páscha*
1 May	May Day (International Labour Day)	*Protomayíou*
15 August	Assumption of the Virgin	*Koímisis tis Theotókou*
28 October	*"Ochi"* Day (in celebration of Metaxas' "no" to Mussolini)	*Ekosi októo oktovríou*
25 December	Christmas	*Kristoúyena*
26 December	St Stephen's Day	*Théfteri i méra ton Kristoúyena*

Museums

All significant archaeological sites and museums have regular admission hours. Nearly all are closed on Tuesdays, and open other weekdays from 8 or 9 am to around 2 pm, though outdoor sites tend to stay open later, until 5 or 6 pm. As a rule, plan to visit cultural sites in the mornings to avoid disappointment, or unless the local tourist office can provide you with current opening times. Hours tend to be shorter in the winter. Students with a valid identification card get a discount on admission fees; on Sundays everyone gets in free.

If you're currently studying archaeology, the history of art or the Classics and intend to visit many museums and sites in Greece, it may be worth your while to obtain a free pass by writing several weeks in advance of your trip to the Museum Section, Ministry of Science and Culture, Aristidou 14, Athens, enclosing verification of your studies from your college or university.

Greek National Tourist Organisation

In Greece the initials come out: EOT. If they can't answer your questions about Greece, at least they can refer you to someone who can.

In Athens:
Head Office: 2 Amerikis St, Athens 10564.
Tel. (01) 322 3111; telex 5832.
EOT Information desk: National Bank of Greece, Syntagma Square, 2 Karageorgi Servias St.
Tel. (01) 322 2545, 323–4130.
EOT, East Airport: Tel. (01) 979 9500, 970 2396.
EOT, West Airport: Tel. (01) 979 9264.

In Australia:
Greek National Tourist Organisation, 51–57 Pitt St, Sidney, NSW 2000.
Tel. 2411 663/4; telex 25209.
In Canada:
Office National Hellénique du Tourisme, 2 Place Ville Marie, Esso Plaza,
  Montréal H3B 2C9, Quebec.
Tel. 871 1535; telex 60021.
In Great Britain:
National Tourist Organisation of Greece,
195 Regent St, London W1R 8DR.
Tel. 01 734 5997, telex 21 122.
In USA:
Head Office: Olympic Tower, 645 Fifth Ave, 5th Floor, New York, NY
  10022.
Tel. (212) 421 5777; telex 664 89.
168 N. Michigan Ave, Chicago, Ill. 60601.
Tel. (312) 782 1084; telex 283468.
National Bank of Greece Building, 31 State St, Boston, Mass. 02109.
Tel. (617) 227 7366; telex 940493.
611 West Sixth St, Suite 1998, Los Angeles, Calif. 90017.
Tel. (213) 626 6696; telex 686441.

Islands without a branch of the EOT often have some form of local tourist office; if not, most have **Tourist Police** (often located in an office in the town's police station). They offer information about the island, and can often help you find a room. In Athens there are three Tourist Police stations, and a magic telephone number—171. The voice on 171 not only speaks good English, but can tell you everything from ship departures to where to spend the night. Tourist Police stations in Athens are at:
7 Syngrou St (the home of 171).
Larissa Train Station, tel. 821 3574.
East Airport, tel. 981 9730 and 981 4093.
At Piraeus the Tourist Police are on the Akti Miaouli, tel. 452 3670.
You can always tell a Tourist Policeman from other policemen by the little flags he wears on his pocket, showing which language he speaks.

Photography

Greece lends herself freely to beautiful photography, but a fee is charged at museums. For an 8- to 16-mm still camera, without tripod, one buys a ticket for the camera; with a tripod one pays per photograph.

A large variety of film, both instamatic and 35mm, can be found in many island shops, though it tends to be expensive. Large islands even have 24-hour developing services, though again this tends to cost more than at home.

The light in the summer is often stronger than it seems and is the most common cause of ruined photographs. Greeks invariably love to have their pictures taken, and although it's more polite to ask first, you should just go ahead and take the photo if you don't want them to rush off to beautify themselves and strike a pose. You should avoid taking pictures of the communications systems on the mountain tops.

If you bring an expensive camera to Greece, it never hurts to insure it. Above all, never leave it alone "for just a few minutes". Although Greeks themselves very rarely steal anything, other tourists are not so honest.

Post Offices

Signs for post offices (*tachidromío*) as well as post boxes are bright yellow and easy to find. Many post office employees speak English. Stamps can also be bought at the kiosks, although they charge a small tax. A stamp is a *grammatósima*.

If you do not have an address in Greece, mail can be sent to you Poste Restante to any post office in Greece, and can be picked up with proof of identity. After three months all unretrieved letters are returned to sender. If someone has sent you a parcel, you will receive a notice of its arrival, and you must go to the post office to collect it. You will often have to pay some handling fee, if not customs charges and duties if the parcel contains dutiable articles. Fragile stickers attract little attention. In small villages, particularly on the islands, mail is not delivered to the house but to the village centre, either a café or bakery. Its arrival coincides with that of a ship from Athens.

If you want to mail a package, any shop selling paper items will wrap it sturdily for you for a small fee.

Sports

Water Sports
Naturally they predominate in the islands. All popular beaches these days hire out pedal boats and wind surf boards. Two islands, Corfu and Syros, have **sailing schools**; islands with **water skiing centres** are:

Chios:	The Chios Naval Club
Corfu:	The Kassidokosta School Komeno Bay
Crete:	The Chania Naval Club
	Water Ski School Elounda Beach
	The Kasidokosta School also at Elounda Beach
Kythera:	The Kythera Island Naval Club
Lesbos:	The Naval Club
Poros:	The Zannou School
Rhodes:	The Rhodes Naval Club
Skiathos:	The P. Kassidokosta School

Nudism by law is forbidden in Greece, except in designated areas (Mykonos has one), and every year the media carry stories of offended villagers, crackdowns and arrests of naked tourists. In practice, however, many people shed all in isolated coves, ideally on beaches accessible only by private boat. On the other hand, topless sunbathing has become the norm (though I've yet to see a Greek woman go topless) on a majority of popular beaches. Elsewhere, do exercise discretion, it isn't worth wounding local sensibilities, no matter how prudish other people's attitudes may seem to you.

Underwater activities with any kind of breathing apparatus are strictly forbidden to keep divers from snatching any antiquities. However, three islands have diving schools—Rhodes, Evia (Halkida) and Corfu (Paleokastritsa)— where, even if you already know how to dive, you have to go out with their boats.

AVERAGE SEA TEMPERATURES

Jan	Feb	Mar	Apr	May	June	July	Aug	Sep	Oct	Nov	Dec
59°F	59°F	59°F	61°F	64°F	72°F	75°F	77°F	75°F	72°F	64°F	63°F
15°C	15°C	15°C	16°C	18°C	22°C	24°C	25°C	24°C	22°C	18°C	17°C

Land Sports

Tennis is slowly catching on among the Greek elite. Island with courts and their addresses are:

Corfu: 4 Romanou St. Tel. 37021.
Crete: in Herakleon, 17 Beaufort Ave. Tel. (081) 28 30 15.
    in Chania, Dimokratias Ave., in the stadium. Tel. (0821) 21 293.
Rhodes: Rhodes Tennis Club. Tel. (0241) 2230
Evia: Halkida Tennis Club. Tel. (0221) 25 230.

There are **golf** courses on Corfu and Rhodes, and both admit non-members.
The Corfu Golf Club, Ropa Valley, P.O. Box 71, tel. 94220/1. The course has 18 holes, par 72, practice range, equipment shop, changing rooms, and restaurant.
The Afandou Golf Club, 19 km (12 miles) from Rhodes town, tel. 51451, 18 holes, par 70. The club has an equipment shop, lounges, changing rooms, and a restaurant.
Organised **horse riding** is offered only on Corfu at the Corfu Riding Club, Korkira Beach, Gouvia, tel. 30770. Open April–October, 7–10 am and 5–9 pm.
Mountain climbing and skiing. Crete is the island queen of Greek mountain sport, with three mountain refuges. A fourth is on the island of Evia.
Lefka Ori (White Mountain), Crete:
Kallergi, alt. 1680 m (5510 ft); 40 beds. Tel. Chania (0821) 24 647.
Volikas, alt. 1480 m (4860 ft); 30 beds. Tel. as above.
Psiloritis (Mt Ida), Crete:
Prinias, alt. 1100 m (3610 ft); 16 beds. Tel. Herakleon (081) 28 71 10.
Mount Dirfys, Evia:

Liri, alt. 1100 m (3610 ft); 36 beds. Tel. Chalki (0221) 25 230.

There is skiing from December to March at both Kallergi and Liri.

Three important addresses in Athens for mountaineers and skiers are:
The Hellenic Alpine Club, 7 Karageorgi Servias. Tel. 32 34 555.
The Hellenic Touring Club, 12 Polytechniou St. Tel. 52 48 600/1.
The Hellenic Federation of Excursion Societies, 4 Dragatsaniou. Tel. 32 34 107.

Telephones

The Organismos Telephikinonion Ellathos, better known as OTE, has offices in the larger towns and at least one on every island that has a telephone service. One can call both direct and collect (reverse charges), although the latter usually takes at least half an hour to put through. On the larger islands one may dial abroad direct (for Great Britain dial 0044 and for the USA 001 before the area code). You should also use OTE for calling other places in Greece. Telegrams can be sent from either OTE or the post office.

Payphones take 5, 10 and 20 dr. coins dated 1976 or later. In addition calls can be made from kiosks, kafeneíons, and shops (always ask first).

It is often impossible to call Athens from the islands in mid-morning, the chances are far better in the evening. To defeat the beeps, whirrs, and buzzes you often get instead of a connection, try dialling as fast as you can. This somehow seems to work the best.

What to bring to Greece

Even in the height of summer, evenings can be chilly in Greece, especially when the meltemi wind is blowing. Always bring at least one warm sweater, if not a pair of long trousers. Those who venture off the beaten track into the thorns and rocks should bring sturdy and comfortable shoes—tennis shoes are very good. They should cover the ankles if you really like wilderness, where scorpions and harmful snakes can be a problem. Plastic swim shoes are recommended for rocky beaches, where there are often sea urchins.

Summer travellers following whim rather than a pre-determined programme should certainly bring a sleeping bag, as lodgings of any sort are often full to capacity. Serious sleeping baggers should also bring an air-mattress to cushion them from the gravelly Greek ground. Torches are very handy for moonless nights, caves and rural villages.

On the pharmaceutical side, seasickness pills, insect bite remedies, tablets for stomach upsets and aspirin will deal with most difficulties encountered. Soap, washing powder, a clothes line and especially a towel are necessary for those staying in class C hotels or less. Bring a sink plug if you like sinks full of water. A knife is a good idea for paneyeria, where you are often given a slab of goat meat with only a spoon or fork to eat it with. A photo of the family and home is always appreciated by new Greek friends.

Zeus or Poseidon. Detail of Bronze Statue, National Archaeological Museum, Athens

On all the Greek islands except for the most remote of the remote you can buy whatever you forgot to bring. Toilet paper and mosquito coils are the two most popular purchases on arrival. However, special needs such as artificial sweeteners, contact lens products and so on can generally be found only in Athens and the more popular islands.

Let common sense and the maxim "bring as little as possible and never more than you can carry" dictate your packing.

Women

Greece is a perfect destination for women travelling on their own. Not only is it safe, but because they fundamentally respect them, Greeks refrain from annoying women as other Mediterranean men are known to do. Yet they remain friendly and easy to meet. While some have a difficult time believing that women are their equals, imagining that for a woman a night without company is unbearable mortification of the flesh, they are ever courteous and will rarely allow even the most liberated female (or male) guest to pay for anything. Any Greek who tries to take advantage of a woman or chases tourists earns himself a bad reputation.

On the other hand, young Greek women rarely travel alone, and although many in the larger towns now have jobs, old marriage customs still exert a strong influence, even in Athens, and weddings are sometimes less a union of love than the closing of a lengthily negotiated business deal. In the evenings, especially at weekends, you'll see many girls of marriageable age join the family for a seaside promenade, or *volta* in Greek, sometimes called "the bride market". A young man generally in his late 20s or early 30s, will find a likely girl there or through certain inquiries. He will then approach the father, to discover the girl's dowry—

34

low wages and high housing costs demand that it contains some sort of living quarters from the woman's father, often added on top of the family house. The suitor must have a steady job. If both parties are satisfied, the young man is officially introduced to the daughter, who can be as young as 13 or 14 in the villages. If they get along well together, the marriage date is set. The woman who never marries and has no children is sincerely pitied in Greece. The inordinate number of Greek widows (and not all wear the traditional black) is due to the 10- to 20-year age difference which often occurs between husband and wife.

Because foreign men don't observe the Greek customs, their interest in a Greek woman will often be regarded with suspicion by her family. Although the brother probably won't knife a man for glancing at his sister, he is likely to tell him to look elsewhere.

The Greeks of Today

History

Unless you're one of those travellers who unplug themselves from their earphones and novels only to take photographs of donkeys, then you'll want to meet the Greeks. Although the massive influx of foreign visitors in recent years has had an inevitable numbing effect on the traditional hospitality offered to strangers, you will find that almost everyone you meet is friendly and gracious, and the older islanders—especially in the small villages—full of wonderful stories.

And rare indeed is the Greek who avoids talking about politics. It was Aristotle, after all, who declared man to be a political animal and if Greeks today have any link with their Classical past it is in their enthusiasm for all things political. (This enthusiasm is no more evident than during an election, when all means of transport to the Greek islands are swamped with Athenians returning to their native villages to vote.) Some knowledge of modern history is essential in understanding current Greek views and attitudes, and for that reason the following outline is included. It is only an outline, and those with further interests can refer to the small collection of books in English on the subject or to the Greek people themselves. Ancient and Byzantine history, which touches Greece less closely today, is dealt with under Athens and the individual islands.

From ancient times to the end of the Byzantine Empire, Greek people lived not only within the boundaries of modern-day Greece but throughout Asia Minor, in particular that part of Asia Minor which is now Turkey. Constantinople was their capital, and it was Greek. Not even during the 400-year Turkish occupation did these people and their brethren in Europe stop considering themselves Greeks— and the Turks, for the most part, were content to let them be Greek as long as they paid their taxes.

The revolutionary spirit that swept through Europe at the end of the 18th and beginning of the 19th centuries did not fail to catch hold in Greece, by now more than weary of the lethargic inactivity and sporadic cruelties of the Ottomans. The Greek War of Independence was begun in the Peloponnese in 1821, and it continued for more than six years in a series of bloody atrocities and political intrigues and divisions. In the end the Great Powers, namely Britain, Russia and France, came to assist the Greek cause, especially in the decisive battle of Navarino (20 October 1827) which in effect gave the newly formed Greek government the Peloponnese. Count John Capodistria of Corfu, ex-secretary to the Tsar of Russia, became the first President of Greece, which included the Peloponnese and the peninsula up to a line between the cities of Arta and Volos. While a king was sought for the new state, Capodistria followed an independent policy which succeeded in offending the pro-British and pro-French factions in Greece—and also the powerful Mavromikhalis family who assassinated him in 1831. Before the subsequent anarchy spread too far, the Great Powers appointed Otho, son of King Ludwig I of Bavaria, as King of the Greeks.

Under Otho began the Great Idea, as it was called, of uniting all the lands of the Greek peoples with the motherland, although it made little advance at the time. Otho was peaceably ousted in 1862 and the Greeks elected William George, son of the King of Denmark, as "King of the Hellenes". By this they meant all the Greek people, and not merely those within the borders of Greece. The National Assembly drew up a constitution in 1864 which made the nation officially a democracy under a king, a system that began to work practically under Prime Minister Kharilaos Trikoupis in 1875. With the long reign of George I, Greece began to develop with an economy based on sea trade. The Great Idea had to wait for an opportune moment to ripen into reality.

In 1910 the great statesman from Crete, Eleftherios Venizelos, became Prime Minister of Greece for the first time. Under his direction the opportune moment came in the form of the two Balkan Wars of 1912–13, as a result of which Crete, Samos, Macedonia and southern Epirus were annexed to the Greek nation. In the meantime King George was assassinated by a madman, and Constantine I ascended to the throne of Greece. Constantine married the sister of Kaiser Wilhelm and had a close relationship with Germany. When the First World War broke out, so did a dispute as to whose side Greece was on. Venizelos supported the Allies and Constantine the Central Powers, although he officially remained neutral until the Allies forced him to mobilise the Greek army. Meanwhile, in the north of Greece, Venizelos had set up his own government with volunteers in support of the Allied cause. After the war the Great Idea still smouldered, and Greek forces were sent to occupy Smyrna (present-day Izmir) and advance on Ankara, the new Turkish capital. It was a disaster. The Turks, under Mustapha Kemal (later Ataturk) had grown far more powerful after their defeat in the Balkan War than the Greeks had imagined. In August 1922 the Greek army was completely routed from Smyrna, and many Greek residents who could not escape were slaughtered. Constantine immediately abdicated in favour of his son George II, and died soon afterwards. The government fell and Colonel Plastiras with his officers took over, ignobly executing the ministers of the previous government. Massive population exchanges were made between Greece and Turkey to destroy the main reason behind Greek expansionist claims, and the Greeks were confronted with the difficulties of a million Anatolian refugees.

In 1929 a republic was proclaimed which lasted for ten shaky years, during which the Greek communist party, or KKE, was formed and gained strength. After the brief Panglos dictatorship, the Greeks elected Venizelos back as President. He set the present borders of Greece (except for the Dodecanese Islands, which belonged to Italy until 1945). During his term of office there was also an unsuccessful uprising by the Greek Cypriots, four-fifths of the population of what was then a British Crown Colony, who desired union with Greece.

The republic, beset with economic difficulties, collapsed in 1935, and King George II returned to Greece, with General Metaxas as his Prime Minister. Metaxas had dictatorial control of the country under the regime of the 4 August, which crushed the trade unions and all leftist activities, exiling the leaders. Having prepared the Greek army long in advance for the coming war, Metaxas died in 1941 after his historic "No!" to Mussolini. Indeed, in 1940, with Italian troops on the Albanian border, Greece was the first Allied country to join Britain voluntarily against the Axis. The Greek army stopped the Italians and then pushed them back into Albania.

But by May 1941 all of Greece was in the hands of the Nazis, and George II was in exile in Egypt. Bad as the Occupation was in Greece, political strife compounded it, fired by the uncertain constitutionality of a monarch who had been acting for so many years without parliamentary support. The Communist-organised EAM, the National Liberation Front, attacked all the competing resistance groups so rigorously that they came to support the monarchy as a lesser evil than the Communists. These Monarchists, as they were called, were supported in turn by the British. Nothing could be done, however, to prevent Civil War from breaking out three months after the liberation of Greece. The army of the EAM almost took Athens when the King finally agreed not to return to Greece without a plebiscite.

After the World War and the Civil War the country was in a shambles, economically and politically. Americans began to supersede the British in Greek affairs; Britain had her own difficulties. The elections of March 1946 were observed by the Americans and ran peaceably. A few months later the King was welcomed back to Greece, although he died a year later to be succeeded by his brother Paul.

Recovery, especially in the sphere of economics, was very slow, despite American assistance. Stalin was also very interested in the strategic location of Greece. In a roundabout way this caused the second Civil War in 1947 between the Communists and the government. The USA became deeply involved trying to defend the recent Truman Doctrine and government forces finally won in October 1949, allowing the country to return to the problems of reconstruction.

With the Korean War in 1951 Greece and Turkey became full members of NATO, although the Cyprus issue again divided the two countries. The Greek

Cypriots, led by Archbishop Makarios in 1954, clamoured and rioted for union with Greece. Either for military reasons (so believe the Greeks) or to prevent a new conflict between Greece and Turkey, the Americans and British were hardly sympathetic to Cyprus' claims. Meanwhile Prime Minister Papagos died, and Konstantinos Karamanlis replaced him, staying in office for eight years. The stability and prosperity begun under Papagos increased, agriculture and tourism becoming the major industries. The opposition to Karamanlis at this time criticised him for his pro-Western policy, basically because of the Cyprus situation, which grew worse all the time. Because of the island's one-fifth Turkish population and its locality, the Turks would not agree on union for Cyprus—the independence or partitioning of the island was as far as they would go. Finally in 1960, after much discussion on all sides, Cyprus became an independent republic and elected Makarios its first President. The British and Americans were considered to be good friends again.

Then once more the economy began to plague the government. The royal family became unpopular, there were strikes, and in 1963 came the assassination of Deputy Lambrakis in Thessaloniki, for which police officers were tried and convicted. Anti-Greek government feelings rose in London, just when the King and Queen were about to visit. Karamanlis advised them not to go, and their insistence sparked off his resignation. George Papandreau of the opposition was eventually elected Prime Minister. King Paul died and Constantine II became King of Greece.

In 1964 violence broke out in Cyprus again, owing to the disproportional representation in government of the Turkish minority, problems temporarily solved at the time. A quarrel with the King caused Papandreau's resignation, and there was much bitterness, leaving political allegiances between Monarchists and Republicans. The party system deteriorated and on 21 April 1967 the colonels established their military dictatorship. George Papandreau and his son Andreas were imprisoned, the latter charged with treason. George Papadopoulos became dictator, imprisoning thousands without trial. In 1967 another grave incident occurred in Cyprus, almost leading to war. Shortly afterwards, Constantine II fled to Rome.

The proclaimed aim of the colonels' junta was a moral cleansing of "Christian Greece". Human rights were suppressed, and the secret police were guilty of the most cruel tortures. Yet the British and American governments tolerated the regime, the latter very actively, for its NATO interests. The internal situation went from bad to worse, and in 1973 students of the Polytechnic school in Athens struck. Tanks were brought in and many were killed. After this incident popular feeling rose so high that Papadopoulos was arrested, only to be replaced by his arrester, the head of the military police and an even worse dictator, Ioannides. The nation was in turmoil. Attempting to save his position by resorting to the appeal of the Great Idea, Ioannides tried to launch a coup in Cyprus by assassinating Makarios, intending to replace him with a president who would declare the long-desired union of Cyprus with Greece. It was a fiasco. Makarios fled, and the Turkish army invaded Cyprus. The dictatorship resigned and Karamanlis returned to Athens from Paris where he had been living in self-exile. He immediately formed a new government, released the political prisoners and legalised the Communist party. He then turned his attention to Cyprus, where Turkish forces had occupied 40% of the island. But the Greek army was not strong enough to take on the Turks, nor did the position taken by the British and the American governments help in the least.

On 17 November 1974 an election was held, which Karamanlis easily won. The monarchy did less well and Greece became the republic it is today. In 1977 Archbishop Makarios died leaving the Cyprus issue even more up in the air than before in the minds of the Greeks, although the Turks seem to consider it well nigh settled. This is still one of the major debating points in Greek politics, along with continued membership in the Common Market and NATO (the Greeks are understandably slow to forgive the Americans for their support of the junta). Social reform is also a very important issue with the left, and proved, along with an independent foreign policy, to be the ticket to Andreas Papandreau's Socialist victories in the 1980s.

Religion

With the exception of some Roman Catholics, in the Cyclades nearly all Greeks belong to the Orthodox church; indeed being Orthodox and speaking Greek were traditionally the two most important criteria in defining a Greek, no matter where he was born. The church has so much to do with being "Greek" that even the greatest doubters can hardly think of marrying outside the church, or neglecting to have their children baptised. Much emphasis is put on ceremony and decorum, which has changed very little since the foundation of the church in the 4th century by Constantine the Great, Emperor of Constantinople. As Constantinople took the place of Rome as the political and Christian capital of the world, the Greeks believe their church to be the only true successor to the original church of Rome. Therefore, a true Greek is called a *Romiós* or Roman, and the Greek language of today is called *Romaíka*.

The Orthodox church is considered perfect and eternal; if it is not, its adherents cannot be saved. This explains the violence of the controversy over the icons in the 8th century, when iconoclasts, influenced by the mid-Eastern religions, declared images of divine beings sacrilegious. This debate served to sever the Roman Catholic church from the Orthodox, compounded by the crowning of Charlemagne as the Emperor of Rome, which had previously been subject to the Emperor of Constantinople. Further divisions arose over the celibacy of the clergy (Orthodox priests can marry before they are ordained) and the use of the phrase "and the son" in the Holy Creed, the issue which caused the final schism in 1054 when the Pope's representative Cardinal Humbert excommunicated the Patriarch of Constantinople.

After the fall of the Byzantine Empire, the Turks not only allowed the church was thus able to preserve many Greek traditions through the dark age of Ottoman rule, including education, on the other hand it often abused this power against its own flock, especially on a local scale. According to an old saying, priests, headmen and Turks were the three curses of Greece and the poor priests (who in truth are usually quite amiable fellows) have not yet exonerated themselves from the list, which now includes the king and the cuckold.

The vast quantity of churches one sees on some islands has little to do with the priests, however, for they were built by families or individuals, especially by sailors, seeking the protection of a patron saint. Some were built to keep a promise, others in simple thanksgiving. Architecturally there is an endless variety of styles depending on the region, period and terrain, as well as the wealth and whim of the builder. All but the tiniest of chapels have an *iconostasis*, either of wood or stone, which separates the *heiron* or sanctuary, where only the ordained are allowed, from the rest of the church. Unfortunately, most of the churches are now locked up all the time, since light-fingered tourists have decided that icons make lovely souvenirs; to get inside you must locate the caretaker. Once you have gained access, it's good form to dress discreetly (no shorts!) and to leave a few drachmas for upkeep.

Almost all these churches have only one service a year, on the name day of the patron saint (name days are celebrated in Greece far more widely than birthdays: "Many years!" *(Chrónia pollá!)* is how to greet people on their nameday). This annual celebration is called a *yiortí* or more frequently *paneyéri*, and is the cause for feasts and dancing before or after the church service. If feasible *paneyeria* take place in the churchyard, otherwise you'll find them in neighbouring wooded areas or in tavernas. The food can be superb but is more often basic and plentiful; for a set price you receive more than your share and a doggy bag full, generally of goat. These parties are also the best places to hear the traditional island music and learn the accompanying dances, and it's sad that they're only a fond memory in most major tourist centres (although alive and well in less frequented areas). *Fifteen August*, the Assumption of the Virgin *(tis* paneyeri) is the largest paneyeri in Greece apart from Easter, the biggest holiday. The faithful sail to Tinos, the Lourdes of Greece, and other centres connected with Mary, and for that reason mid-August is a difficult time to travel among the islands, especially the Cyclades. Not only are the boats filled to more than capacity, but the meltemi wind also blows with vigour, and Greek matrons, the most ardent pilgrims of all, are some of the worst possible sailors.

Greek weddings are another very interesting and lovely spectacle. The bride and groom stand solemnly before the chanting priest, while the surrounding family and friends often do everything but watch the proceedings. White crowns, bound together by a white ribbon, are placed on the heads of bride and groom, and the *koumbáros*, or best man, exchanges them back and forth. The newly-weds are then led around the altar three times, which spurs the guests into action as they bombard the happy couple with fertility-bringing rice and flower petals. After congratulating the bride and groom one is given a small gift of sweetened

40

After congratulating the bride and groom one is given a small gift of sweetened almonds, a *boboniéra*. This is followed by the marriage feast and dancing, which lasted up to five days in the past. If you are in the vicinity of a wedding you will be offered a sweet cake, and if you are interested you may be invited to come along as a special guest.

Baptisms are cause for similar celebration. The priest immerses the baby completely in the Holy Water three times (no vulnerable spots on modern Greeks!) and almost always gives the little one the name of a grandparent. For extra protection from the forces of evil, village babies often wear a *filaktó*, or amulet, the omnipresent blue glass eye bead. If you visit a baby at home you may well be sprinkled first with Holy Water, and it's wise to keep your compliments to the little one's parents to a minimum; old gods do get jealous.

Funerals in Greece, for reasons of climate, are carried out as soon as possible after death, and are announced by the village churchbells. The dead are placed in the earth for three to five years (longer if the family can pay) after which time the bones are dug up and placed in the family box to make room for the next resident. It is curious that the *aforismós*, or Orthodox excommunication, is believed to prevent the body decaying after death. Ceremonies are performed in memory of the departed, three, nine and forty days after death, and on the first anniversary. They are sometimes repeated annually. Sweet buns and sugared wheat *koúliva* are given out after the ceremony.

Part II
ATHENS AND PIRAEUS

The Caryatid Porch of the Erechtheion

As most travellers to the Greek islands eventually find themselves in Athens and Piraeus, they are included in this book; those making their first journey to Greece will particularly want to spend two or three days in the capital. It's rarely love at first sight, though, as Athens can give a very poor initial impression, with its ramshackle architecture and grubby, dusty exterior. Look closely, however, and you'll find a fascinating city: a collection of villages each maintaining its own individuality; small hidden oases of green parks amidst the hustle and bustle; tiny family run tavernas tucked away in the most unexpected places; and friendly people who belie the reputation of most inhabitants of capital cities.

Orientation
Athens

Syntagma (or **Constitution**) **Square** is to all intents and purposes the centre of the action, and it's here that the **Parliament Building** is to be found, backing on to the **National Gardens** and **Zappeion Park**. The square itself is the perfect place to sit and let the afternoon or evening slip by. From here it's a short walk down to the **Plaka,** the old part of Athens, with its interesting network of lanes and traditionally styled houses, and **Monastiraki,** home of the flea market, although this is not quite an accurate description. However, it does have a colourful assortment of shops, with bargains to be had for the dedicated souvenir hunter.

A ten-minute walk from Syntagma will take you to **Kolonaki Square**, Athens' Knightsbridge in miniature. It has a lot of chi-chi shops and restaurants (all of course expensive) with plenty of well-heeled Athenians to patronise them; it's a hive of activity in shopping hours. Up from the square (it's a long hike on foot, but there's a funicular to take you) is the hill of **Lycavitos**, looking as if it sprang out of a fairy tale, at least at night. On the top sits the chapel of **St George**, a cannon that is used on national holidays, and a restaurant/bar. It's the best place to go for panoramic views of the whole city, including, *nefos* permitting (the black cloud of pollution that often plagues Athens), a sweeping vista down to the sea at Piraeus.

At the other end of Vass. Sophias from Syntagma Square, the Hilton Hotel serves as another useful landmark. Behind it are the areas of **Ilissia** and **Pangrati**; here is the real essence of Athens—shops, tavernas, bars and cinemas for the city's inhabitants, unlike the touristy haunts of the centre.

Omonia Square, lying at the end of the Panepistimiou or Stadiou St from Syntagma, is where the centre of the city really runs out, and, if it's not quite as pristine as Syntagma at the moment, this is soon changing; the municipality is giving it a face-lift, closing many streets to make pedestrian shopping walkways. Omonia is not as sleazy as it once was and is alive with shops, street traders, snack bars, and restaurants, some serving delicious suckling pig.

From Zappeon Park buses run frequently down to the coast and suburbs of **Glyfada, Voula** and **Vouliagmenis**. Glyfada, close to the airport which also accommodates the controversial US Airforce base, is a green and pleasant suburb, and the town itself has grown into a busy resort, and even more recently, a rival Kolonaki. Many smart city dwellers shop at the ritzy boutiques, and there are even a couple of well-designed (but small, fortunately) indoor shopping centres. Here and further down the coast at Voula are beaches run by NTOG, and there's an entrance fee. The water is generally clean, but nothing quite like some of the islands. There's also good swimming beyond Voula at Vouliagmenis, which has a succession of rocky coves. The road continues along the coast from here to **Sounion** and the **Temple of Apollo**, as famous for its beautiful position and sunsets as the graffiti of **Lord Byron**, who scrawled his name on one of the columns.

Athens does her best by tourists, offering the memorials of a glorious past and almost unlimited wine, song and dance festivals for entertainment, making a short stay, before you take off for your island, a very enjoyable experience.

Historical outline of Athens

Traces found by archaeologists prove that Athens was inhabited from the Neolithic Age, c. 3500 BC. In the second millennium Ionians from Asia Minor invaded these pre-Hellenic people and established small city states throughout Attica, the main one being Kekropia (from the serpent god Kekrops, who later became connected with the real or mythical King Erechtheus, considered to be half snake and the original founder of Athens). The owl was sacred to Kekropia—as it was to the goddess Athena, and her worship and name gradually came to preside in the city.

In the 14th century BC Athens, as part of the Mycenaean empire of the Acheans, invaded Crete, fought Thebes, and conquered Troy, but escaped the subsequent Dorian invasion which brought chaos into the Mycenaean world. Two hundred years later Attica was conquered, and the Greek dark ages began which lasted until the 8th century BC. The Ionians and the Aeolians went back to the lands in Asia Minor and settled many of the Aegean islands.

Sometime during the 8th century all the towns of Attica were peaceably united, an accomplishment attributed to the mythical King Theseus. Athens was then ruled by a king (the chief priest), the polemarch (or general), and the archon (or civil authority), positions that by the 6th century became annually elective. The continued conflict between the landed aristocracy and lower and rising commercial classes gradually brought about the solution of democratic government, especially under the reforms of Solon and Kleisthenes. In between these two rulers the tyrant Pisistratos, head of the popular party, began to make Athenian naval might a force to be feared by the other independent city states of Greece.

Kleisthenes' reforms broke down the old unsatisfactory political classifications by dividing the population into ten tribes. Each selected by lot 50 members of the people's assembly, from which a further lot was drawn to select an archon, creating ten archons in all, one from each tribe. The head archon gave his name to the Athenian year. Meanwhile, as Persian strength grew in the east, Ionian intellectuals and artists settled in Athens, bringing with them the roots of Attic tragedy.

After the fall of Ionia to the Persians (Athens had briefly assisted the Ionian case), Darius, the King of Kings, turned to subdue Greece, and in particular Athens, which posed the only threat to his fleet. In 490 BC his vast army landed at Marathon only to be defeated by a much smaller Athenian army, led by Miltiades. Powerful Sparta and the other states then recognised the eastern threat, but the defence of Greece was left primarily in the hands of the Athenians and their fleet, which grew in strength under Themistokles. In 480 BC Xerxes, the new Persian king, invaded Greece with a massive fleet and army. The Athenians fled and their city was destroyed, yet the Persian navy floundered against the Greeks at Salamis, and the whole issue of the invasion was finally settled by the Athenians and Spartans at the battle of Plataea.

Having proved her naval might, Athens set about creating a maritime empire for the stability of her internal politics. She ruled the confederacy at Delos, demanding contributions (later tributes) from the islands in return for protection from the Persians. Sea trade also became necessary to support the city's population, whose agriculture was based on the olive and the vine, and colonisation ensured a continual food supply to Athens. The democracy became truly imperialistic under Perikles, who had the Delian treasury brought to Athens for safe keeping and also in order to beautify the city. This was the golden age of Athens, during which she led the world in art, architecture, theatre and philosophy.

Phidias, Herodotos, Sophocles, Aristophanes and Socrates are just a few names from that period.

The Peloponnesian War (431–404 BC) was caused in part by Athenian expansion in the west. Sparta, Athens' great foe had superiority on land, Athens on the seas. Back and forth the struggle went, exhausting each side with little benefit to either, until Lysander captured Athens, razed the walls, and set up the brief rule of the Thirty Tyrants.

Democracy was restored but Athens' imperialist ideas were not, and she built up a second maritime hegemony. The Peloponnesian War, however, had struck a blow from which Athens could not totally recover, the population grew dissatisfied with public life, and refused to tolerate innovators and critics such as Socrates, whom they put to death. Economically Athens also had trouble keeping a balance of trade, which she so desperately needed. Yet her intellectual tradition held true in the 4th century, bringing forth such men as Demosthenes, Praxiteles, Menander, Plato and, later, Aristotle.

Philip II of Macedon took advantage of this turmoil to bring the city states together under Macedon for an expedition against Persia, whose ruler, Artaxerxes Ochus, was threatening the Greek states. A last torch of patriotic independence was held up against the Macedonians by Demosthenes, the Athenian orator, but with little success. Philip subdued Athens and had begun to plan his campaign against Persia when he was assassinated, leaving his son Alexander to conquer the East. When Alexander died, Athens had to defend herself against his striving generals. In 294 BC Dimitrios Poliorketes (the Besieger) took the city, followed by Antigonas Gonatas. Alexandria and Pergamon became Athens' intellectual rivals, although Athens continued to be honoured by them.

In 168 BC the Romans took Athens and gave her Delos. Eighty years later Athens betrayed Roman favour by siding with Rome's enemy, Mithridates of Pontos, for which Sulla destroyed Piraeus and the walls of the city. But Rome always remembered her cultural debt to Athens, and many leading Romans attended Athens' schools and gave the city great gifts. Conversely many Greek treasures ended up in Rome. St Paul preached to the Athenians in AD 44, and they were gradually converted to Christianity. In the 3rd century AD Goths and barbarians sacked Athens, but were eventually driven away leaving the city to join the growing Byzantine Empire.

The Byzantine Emperors closed the philosophy schools and changed the temples to churches, including the Parthenon which became a cathedral. By now Athens had lost almost all of her former importance. She became the plaything of the Franks after they pillaged Constantinople at the beginning of the 13th century. St Louis appointed Guy de la Roche as Duke of Athens, a dukedom which passed through many outstretched hands, including the Catalans', the Neapolitans' and the Venetians'. In 1456 the Turks took Athens, turning the Parthenon into a mosque and the once sacred Erechtheion into a harem. The Venetians under Morosini attacked the Turks in 1687 and accidently blew up part of the Parthenon, where the Turks had stored their gunpowder. A year later the Venetians left, unsuccessful, and the citizens who had fled returned to Athens. In 1800 Lord Elgin began the large-scale removal of monuments from Athens to European museums.

During the War of Independence, the Greeks under Gouras took the Akropolis, and were besieged by the Turks, who succeeded in retaking the heights, although their blockade was broken by the French. But finally, by 1833 all of Athens was free again, and in 1834 she was declared the capital of the new Greek state.

The few hundred war-scarred houses deteriorating under the Akropolis hardly fitted the bill as a capital city, however. When Otho of Bavaria, the first King of the Greeks, arrived, he brought his own architects with him. The new city was laid out on the lines of Stadiou and El. Venezelou Sts which boast most of Otho's neo-Classical public buildings. The rest of the city's architecture was abandoned to unimaginative white and grey concrete structures, spared monotony only by the hilly Attic terrain.

Modern Athens, with over three million inhabitants (a third of the Greek population), has a busy life of its own during the day. The depopulation of the villages for the suburbs has produced the woes common to many a great city, and Athens spreads out further and further. Transportation is a big problem. But at night, especially in the winter, things begin to cook, and not only in the egg–lemon soup pots of Plaka. Athenians rarely eat before 10 or 11 at night, and they want to be entertained afterwards. If a day of sightseeing hasn't numbed the tourist to further delights, he or she should make every effort to come along and join in.

Museums and sites in Athens

Agora Museum (the Theseum and Ancient Agora)
Open daily 9 am–2.45 pm; Sundays and holidays 9 am–1.45 pm. Closed Tuesdays.

The **stoa of Attalos,** in which the museum is housed, was reconstructed by John D. Rockefeller from the original 2nd century BC stoa or gallery built by King Attalos II of Pergamon. The items inside are finds from the Agora.

The **Theseum,** actually dedicated to Hephaistos, the god of metals and smiths, was built in the middle of the 5th century BC and is the best-preserved Greek temple in existence. Architecturally it belongs to the Doric order, and was perhaps designed by the architect of the temple at Sounion. It is constructed almost entirely of Pentelic marble. Metopes with scenes from the lives of Heracles and Theseus (for whom the temple was named) decorate the temple. It became a church in the 5th century and English protestants were buried there during the last century. In 1834 the government declared it a national monument.

The **Agora,** excavated by the American School of Archaeology, was the centre of Athenian civic and social life. Here the citizens spent much of their day; here

Socrates questioned their basic conceptions of life and law. In 480 BC the Persians destroyed all the buildings of the Agora, which were then rebuilt in a newer and grander style. Most suffered greatly from the Roman and barbarian destructions. Only the foundations are left of the **Bouleuterion** or council house, and the neighbouring Temple of the Mother of the Gods or **Metroon,** built by the Athenians in reparation for their slaying of a priest from the cult. The round **Tholos** or administration centre is where the administrators or *prytanes* worked, and as some had to be on call all hours of the day, kitchens and sleeping quarters were included. Its final reconstruction took place after Sulla's rampage in 88 BC. Only a wall remains of the **Sanctuary of the Eponymous Heroes of Athens,** the ten who gave their names to Kleisthenes' ten tribes. The **altar of Zeus Agoraios** received the oaths of the new archons, a practice initiated by Solon.

The 4th century **Temple of Apollo** was dedicated to the mythical father of the Ionians, who believed themselves descended from Ion, son of Apollo. In the museum is the huge statue which once stood inside the temple, representing the god. Almost nothing remains of the **Stoa Basileios,** or of Zeus Eleutherios, which played a major role in Athenian history as the court of the annual archon, where trials concerning the security of the state took place. By the Stoa of Zeus stood the **Altar of the Twelve Gods,** from which all distances in Attica were measured. Beside it ran the **Panathenaic Way,** of which some Roman signs remain by the Church of the Holy Apostles. It went to the Akropolis, crossing the Agora from which the population would watch the ceremonial procession that celebrated the union of Attica. South of the Altar of Twelve Gods was a **Temple to Ares,** built in the Doric style in the 5th century BC, perhaps by the Theseum architect. The **Three Giants** stood before a 5th century AD gymnasium that had been built in the same place as the **Odeon of Agrippa,** of which parts of the orchestra remain further on. This had been built in 15 BC and collapsed 200 years later. The later gymnasium was a part of the University of Athens which Justinian closed in the 6th century AD. By the **Middle Stoa** (2nd century BC) one finds the ruins of a **Roman temple** and the ancient shops and booths. On the other side of the Middle Stoa is the popular court, or **Heliaia,** organised by Solon and built in the 6th century BC. The Heliaia was the largest court of Athens which heard questions dealing with politics well into Roman times.

Between the **South and East Stoas** (2nd century BC) is the **Holy Apostles Church** (Ag. Apostoli) originating from the 11th century. When St Paul visited Athens, he spoke in the Agora, and the church commemorates the event. In 1956 the American School of Classical Studies restored it and the many fine Byzantine paintings within. Across the Panathenaic Way are some remains of **Valerian's Wall** thrown up in AD 257 against the barbarian threat and created out of the ruins of the Agora which remained outside its protection. The ruins between Valerian's Wall and the Stoa of Attalos belong to the **Library of Pantainos,** built by Flavius Pantainos in AD 100 and destroyed 167 years later.

Akropolis
Open daily 7.30 am–7.30 pm; Sundays and holidays 8 am–6.30 pm. Tel. 32 10 185.

Two nights before and two nights after a full moon the Akropolis is open from 9 pm to 11.45 pm. On nights without a full moon there is a **sound and light show,** 1 April–31 October presented daily in English 9 pm–9.45 pm. Tickets are 150 dr., or 80 dr. for students. They can be obtained at the Athens Festival Box Office, 4 Stadiou St (in the arcade), tel. 32 21 459 or 32 23 111 extension 240; or at the entrance gate at Ag. Dimitriou, Loumbardis Hill before the performance, tel. 92 26 210.

The **Akropolis,** supplied by the spring Klepsydra, was inhabited from the end of the Neolithic Age, and people being attracted by its natural fortified position. The Mycenaeans added a Cyclopean wall and built the palace of their king by the present Erechtheion. This palace was replaced by a temple to the god of the spring, Poseidon, and to Athena. In mythology, these two gods took part in a contest to decide who would be the patron of the new city. With his trident Poseidon struck a spring out of the rock of the Akropolis, while Athena invented the olive tree, which the Athenians judged the best.

Under the tyrant Pisistratos a great gate was constructed in the wall, but the Athenians later dismantled it and Delphi cursed it. When the Persians arrived in 480 BC the cult statue of Athena was hurried to the protection of Salamis and in good time, for the Persians burnt the Akropolis. Themistokles built a new rampart out of the old Parthenon, and under Perikles the present plan of the Akropolis buildings was laid out.

The path to the Akropolis follows the Panathenaic way, built at the consecration of the Panathenaic Festival in 566 BC. Following it one comes first to the **Beulé Gate** (named after its discoverer Ernest Beulé) which includes monumental stairways built by the Romans and two Venetian lions. Up the reconstructed Panathenaic ramp one enters the **Propylaia,** the massive gateway built in the same place as Pisistratos' gate by the architect Mnesikles under Perikles. This was considered the architectural equal of the Parthenon by the ancient Greeks, but was damaged when a Turkish powder magazine inside blew up in the 17th century. Now the Propylaia has been carefully restored.

On either side of the actual entrance are the north and the south wings. The north wing held a picture gallery (Pinakotheke); the smaller south wing consisted of only one room of an unusual shape, because the priests of the neighbouring Nike temple didn't want the wing in their territory. The actual entrance had five doors, the middle one opening on the Panathenaic Way. Of the Doric and Ionic orders, it was never finished because of the Peloponnesian War.

The **Temple of Athena Nike,** or Wingless Victory, was built by the architect Kallikrates in 478 BC of Pentelic marble. Inside was kept a statue of Athena, a copy of a much older wooden statue. Its lack of wings, unlike later victory statues, gave it its second name. In 1687 the Turks destroyed the temple to build a tower. It was rebuilt in 1835 and again in 1936, as the bastion beneath it was crumbling.

It is of the Ionic order, and decorated with friezes, although the north and western ones were taken to England by Lord Elgin and are now replaced by cement casts. From the temple of Athena Nike one can see the whole Saronic Gulf, as Aegeus could when watching for the return of his son Theseus from his Cretan adventure with the Minotaur. Theseus was to have signalled his victory with a white sail but forgot. Seeing the black sail, the king threw himself off the precipice in despair.

The **Parthenon,** the glory of the Akropolis and probably the most famous building in the world, if not the most imitated, was constructed between 447 and 432 BC under the direction of Perikles' artist Phidias, the 5th century's greatest sculptor. The name Parthenon, which means the Chamber of Virgins, was first used a hundred years after its construction; before that it was called the Great Temple. It is constructed entirely of Pentelic marble, of the Doric order. Inside it once stood the famous statue of Athena Parthenos by Phidias, more than 36 feet high and made of ivory and gold. In the National Museum one can see a small copy of it.

The genius of the Parthenon may be observed in its foundation, which is curved slightly to prevent an illusion of drooping caused by straight horizontals. To make the columns appear straight the architect bent them a few centimetres inward. Corner columns were made wider to complete the illusion of perfect form.

The outer colonnade consists of 46 columns and above them are the remains of the Doric frieze: on the east was portrayed the battle of giants and gods, on the south the Lapiths and Centaurs (much of this is in the British Museum today), on the west the Greeks and the Amazons, and on the north the battle of Troy. Little remains of the pediment sculptures which represented the gods. The Ionic frieze above the interior colonnade depicts the Panathenaic Procession and was designed by Phidias. This representation of the quadrennial procession bringing Athena a golden crown and sacred garment, or *peplos*, is considered one of the masterpieces of Greek art.

As previously mentioned, the Parthenon was severely damaged in 1687 when a Venetian bomb hit the Turks' powder stores inside; the destruction was continued in 1894 by an earthquake, after which reconstruction began. Today air pollution threatens to give the kiss of death to this graceful prototype of bulky bank buildings. Entrance within the Parthenon itself is forbidden, to save on wear and tear. What is intriguing—and sometimes you can see the work in progress on the Akropolis—is that after all these years the Greek government has decided to pick up all the pieces of the columns and stones, lying scattered since Morosini's day, and reconstruct as much of the temple as possible.

The last great monument on the Akropolis is the **Erechtheion,** a peculiar building of the Ionic order, owing its idiosyncrasies to the various cult items and older sanctuary it had to encompass. Beneath it stood the Mycenaean House of Erechtheus, mentioned in Homer, and the primitive cult sanctuary of Athena; on one side of this was the Sacred Olive Tree which Athena created, and under the north porch the mark formed by Poseidon's trident when he brought forth his sea spring in their contest. The tomb of Kekrops, the legendary founder of Athens, is in the Porch of the Maidens or Caryatids, there Erechtheus died at the hand of either Zeus or Poseidon. Within the temple stood the cult statue of Athena Polias, who received the sacred *peplos* and crown of the Panathenaic Procession. It was she whom the Athenians hid during the Persian offensive.

The sanctuary was quickly restored after the Persian fire, but the marble temple which had been planned by Perikles, was not started until 421 BC. It became a church in the 7th century and a harem under the Turks, the sacred place of the trident marks being used as a toilet. Lord Elgin took parts of the temple, including one of the maidens. In 1909 reconstruction work on the Erechtheion was finished.

Basically the Erechtheion is a rectangular building with three porches. Inside were two cellas or chambers, the largest East Cella dedicated to Athena Polias, the smaller cella to Poseidon–Erechtheus. The north porch consists of six tall Ionic columns; and an opening was made in the roof and floor to reveal the trident marks, for it was considered sacrilegious to hide something so sacred from the view of the gods. The six famous maidens gracefully supporting the roof on their heads are also an Ionian motif. To escape pollution, the originals are now in the Akropolis Museum and have been replaced by casts.

The **Akropolis Museum** houses a collection of sculptures and reliefs from the temples, in particular of maidens, or Kores.

Beside the Akropolis is the **Areopagos,** or hill of Ares, the god of war. There sat the High Council, who figured so predominantly in Aeschylos' play *The Eumenides* where mercy defeated vengeance for the first time in history during the trial of the matricide Orestes. Although Perikles removed much of the original power of the High Council, under the control of the ex-archons it continued to advise on the Athenian constitution into the Roman period.

On the south side of the Akropolis are two theatres. The older, the **Theatre of Dionysos,** was used from the 6th century BC when Thespis created the first true drama, and was often modified up to the time of Nero. In this theatre the annual Greater Dionysia was held, in honour of the god of wine and patron divinity of the theatre, Dionysos. The dramatic competitions included in the festival led to the staging of some of the world's greatest tragedies, which were premiered here. Beside the theatre stood two temples to Dionysos Eleutherios, and the stage that remains is from the 4th century BC. The area before the stage, the **proskenion,** is decorated with scenes from the life of Dionysos, made in the 1st century AD.

Above the theatre is an **Asklepieion,** a sanctuary to the god of healing. The stoa which remains is from the second sanctuary. The first and oldest to the west originally belonged to the water goddess, but very little of it remains. Both Asklepieions were connected with the parent cult at Epidauros.

The **Theatre of Herodes Atticus** was built by a private citizen, Atticus, in AD 161 and was partially covered. Now it hosts the annual **Festival of Athens,** which combines the modern European with the ancient Greek in presenting theatre, ballet, and concerts of classical music by companies and orchestras from all over the world. Performances are given from mid-May until September. Prices vary greatly and there are always student tickets. Children under 10 are not admitted. Advance booking begins 10 to 15 days before the start of each programme and further information and tickets may be obtained from:

The Athens Festival Box Office, 4 Stadiou St (in the arcade).
Tel. 32 21 459 or 32 23 111 extension 240.
Open daily 8.30 am–1.30 pm and 6 pm–8.30 pm; Sundays 9 am–12 noon.
The Herod Atticus Theatre. Tel. 32 32 771 or 32 23 111 extension 137.
Open 6.30 pm–9 pm before each performance (performances begin at 9 pm).

Tickets for the **National Theatre** can be bought at the National Theatre Box Office, at the corner of Ag. Konstantinou and Menandrou Sts, tel. 52 23 242 and tickets for the **State Opera** at Olympia Box Office, 57 Akedemiou St, tel. 36 21 2461.

Benaki Museum: On the corner of Vassilis Sophias and Koumbari St. Tel. 36 11 617. Open daily 8.30 am–2 pm; Sundays and holidays 8.30 am–2 pm. Closed Tuesdays. This museum holds the collection of Antonios Benaki, who spent 35 years of his life amassing objects from Europe and Asia, Byzantine and Islamic. It holds the finest Greek folk costume collection and other objects of interest ranging from letters of Venizelos, through a wooden Macedonian library and paintings attributed to El Greco, to George Seferis' Nobel Prize.

National Archaeology Museum: Patission and Tossitsa Sts. Tel. 82 17 717. Open daily 8 am–7 pm. Closed Mondays; free Thursdays and Sundays. The National Museum contains some of the most spectacular finds in Greece including the frescoes from Santorini, gold from Mycenae, statues, reliefs, tomb stelai, and a superb pottery collection from all periods. The ancient art of Cyprus is also on display, until it is deemed safe to send it back home.

National Gallery: Across from the Athens Hilton. Tel. 72 11 010. Open 9 am–3 pm; Sundays 10 am–2 pm. Closed Mondays. Also called the Alexander Soustou Museum the National Gallery contains works by modern Greek artists and other contemporary exhibits.

Historical and Ethnological Museum: At the Palea Vouli (Old Parliament), Stadiou St. Tel. 32 37 617. Open 9 am–2 pm. Closed Mondays. Contains memorabilia from the War of Independence including, Lord Byron's sword and portraits of the heroes.

Popular Art Museum: 17 Kydathinaion St. Tel. 32 13 018. Open 10 am–2 pm. Closed Mondays. The museum has a collection of Greek folk art, both religious and secular, along with paintings by primitive artists.

The Pnyx: On the hill west of the Akropolis. Nowadays the setting for the Akropolis Sound and Light Show, the Pnyx once hosted the General Assembly of Athens and the great speeches of Perikles and Demosthenes. On assembly days citizens were literally rounded up to fill the minimum attendance quota of 5000, but they were paid for their services to the state. Later the assembly was transferred to the theatre of Dionysos. On the summit of the nearby Hill of the

Cape Artemision, Jockey, National Museum, Athens

Muses is the **Philopappos Monument,** the tomb of Caius Julius Antiochos Philopappos, a Syrian Prince and citizen of Athens. The monument was built for him by the Athenians in AD 114 in gratitude for his beneficence to the city.

Roman Agora: Located between the Agora and the Akropolis. Open daily 10 am–4.30 pm. Dating from the end of the Hellenistic age, the Roman Agora contains the **Tower of the Winds,** or Clock of Andronikos, built in the 1st century BC. Run by a hydraulic mechanism, it stayed open day and night so that the citizens could know the time. The name Tower of the Winds derives from the frieze of the eight winds that decorates its eight sides. The Roman Agora also contains the **Gate of Athena Archegetis,** dating from the 1st century BC and built with funds from Julius and Augustus Caesar; there is also a court and the ruins of stoas. Beside the Agora is the Fehiye Camii, the Victory or Corn Market Mosque.

Byzantine Museum: 22 Vassilis Sophias Ave. Tel. 72 11 027. Open 9 am–3 pm; Sundays 9.30 am–2.30 pm. Closed Mondays. Entrance 300 dr., 100 dr. with student card; free Thursdays and Sundays. The museum includes some examples of Early Christian art and a fine collection of Byzantine sculpture, icons gospels and other objects from the Byzantine Empire.

Keramikos and Museum: 148 Hermou St. Tel. 34 63 552. Open daily 9 am–3 pm. Museum closed Tuesdays. The Keramikos Museum contains the most interesting finds from the ancient cemetery, the Keramikos. The site was used for burials from the 12th century BC and continued to be used into Roman times. Roads to the academy, the Agora and the Sacred Way passed through the Keramikos which was just outside the city walls and thus to the Sacred Gate and the Dipylon Gate.

Following the Streets of the Tombs the visitor can see the rich private tombs built by the Athenians in the 4th century BC. Those with large stone vases are for the unmarried dead, others are in the form of miniature temples and stelai the best of which are now in the National Museum.

Temple of Olympian Zeus: Open daily 9 am–3 pm; Sundays 9.30 am–2.30 pm. Admission fee 200 dr. Fifteen columns remain of one of the hugest temples of the ancient world, begun under the tyrant Pisistratos but stopped when the tyrants fell from power. Work was continued in 175 BC under a Roman architect, Cossutius, in Pentelic marble, but again halted when the temple was half finished by the death of Cossutius' patron, Antiochos IV, Epiphanes of Syria. Hadrian had the temple finished in AD 131. Nearby are the ruins of ancient houses and a bath and at the far end stands **Hadrian's Arch,** which divided the city of Theseus from the city of Hadrian. It was built in the 2nd century AD. It is in the area of the Temple of Zeus that the Athenians celebrate the Easter Resurrection.

War Museum: Located at Vasilis Sophias and Rizari Sts. Tel. 72 90 543. Open daily 9 am–2 pm. Closed Mondays. Inside are weapons from various periods, uniforms, models, etc.

Wine Festival at Dafni: 10 km (6 miles) outside Athens. Take bus 282 from Eleftherias Square. 9 July–11 September, every day 7 pm–1 am. Admission at the gate. A variety of Greek wines and foods, music, singing and dancing make up a Greek wine festival and Greeks attend as much as foreigners. Wine is free once the admission price is paid.

Museum of the City of Athens: Plateia Klafthmonos. Open Mondays, Wednesdays, Fridays 9 am–1.30 pm; free Wednesdays. Located in the re-sited neo-Classical palace of King Otho, this new museum contains photos, memorabilia and model of Athens soon after it became the capital of modern Greece.

Byzantine churches and monasteries in Athens

Agii Apostoli: see under Agora (page 47).

Agii Theodori: 11th century church at Klafthmonos Square at the end of Dragatsaniou St. It has a beautiful door; the bell tower and some of the decorations inside are more recent additions.

Kapnikarea Church: A few blocks from Agii Theodori, on Ermou St. It is from the late 11th century and built in the shape of a cross, its cupola sustained by four large columns. Kapnikarea is the church of the University of Athens.

Panayia Gorgoepikoos (or Ag. Eleftherios, on Mitropoleos Square): also known as the little Metropolitan Church to distinguish it from the nearby cathedral, this is considered the loveliest church in Athens. Built in the 12th century and restored in the 19th, it still contains the marbles placed inside at its construction, including an ancient calendar.

Dafni Monastery: Take bus 282 from Eleftherias Sq. for the 10-km (6-mile) trip both to the wine festival and to the monastery, one of the finest Byzantine monuments in Greece. The name Dafni derives from the temple of Apollo Dafneios, upon which the monastery was founded in the 6th century, near the

Sacred Way. The monastery church dates back to the 11th century, and contains some of the most wonderful mosaics in Greece especially of Christ Pantokrator, considered a masterpiece of the mosaic art.

WHERE TO STAY IN ATHENS

Athens is a big noisy city, especially so at night when you want to sleep (unless you do as the Greeks do and take a long afternoon siesta). I myself prefer Piraeus, which dies down at around 7 pm, and is so much more convenient when sailing to the islands (though many people, especially women on their own, find it a bit spooky). Be that as it may, you won't be surprised to learn that every type of accommodation fills up quickly in the summer and if you don't have a reservation, or if the boat schedules played havoc with one you did make, it's best to head straight for the NTOG office on Syntagma Square (in the National Bank building) and use their hotel finding service.

New luxury chain hotels are mushrooming up seemingly everywhere just outside the city centre—there's the **Ledra Marriott** at 113–115 Syngrou (tel. 93 47 711), featuring, of all things, a Polynesian–Japanese restaurant, and a hydro-therapy pool you can soak in with a view of the Parthenon. A single room in season costs 21 000 dr. a double 28 000. Another new addition to the scene (and one on a human scale) is the 76 room **Astir Palace Athens Hotel** on Syntagma Square (tel. 36 43 112), owned by the National Bank of Greece. While it was under construction, ancient foundations and waterpipes were uncovered and these are incorporated into the decor of the hotel's restaurant, the **Apokalypsis,** located below the street level (Greek and international cuisine). Despite its location, specially insulated glass windows keep out the hubbub below. There's a sauna, and each room features a mini bar and colour TV (with an in-house movie channel). Singles cost 18 000 dr. doubles from 22 000 dr.

Directly across the square from the Astir is the **Grande Bretagne** (tel. 32 30 251), originally built in 1862 to house members of the Greek royal family who couldn't squeeze into the main palace (the current Parliament building) up the square. The Grande Bretagne is the only "grand" hotel in Greece worthy of the description, with a vast marble lobby, elegant rooms (now air conditioned and appointed with such modern conveniences as direct dial phones and colour TV), a formal dining room, perfect service, and a grandeur and style that the newer hotels, with all their plushness, may never achieve. Even if you can't afford to stay there (singles average 20 000 dr. and doubles rocket to over 30 000 dr.) you may want to poke your head in to see where the crowned heads of Europe lodge in Athens—and where the Nazis set up their headquarters during the Second World War. Winston Churchill spent Christmas 1944 at the Grande Bretagne and was lucky to escape an assassination attempt—a bomb had been planted in the hotel's complex sewer system.

On a less exalted level, but with a far more fetching view is the **Royal Olympic Hotel** at 28 Diakou (tel. 92 26 411), facing the Temple of Olympian Zeus and Mt Lykavitos. Rooms here are American in spirit, with a number of family sized suites, and if you have the misfortune to get a room without a view, there's the wonderful panorama from the rooftop bar. Rates are 13 000 dr. for a single, 18 000 dr. for a double. In the same category the **Electra Palace** at 18 Nikodimou St (tel. 32 41 401) has views of the Acropolis and a wonderful rooftop swimming pool in a garden setting—something you don't find every day in Athens. Rooms are air conditioned and there's a garage adjacent to the hotel. Half-board is obligatory—unfortunately, because the hotel is quite close to the good tavernas of Plaka. Prices are 8000 dr. for a single, 12 000 dr. for a double.

The best value in the C category (and a big favourite with Americans) has long been the **Hotel Alkistis** at 18 Plateia Theatrou (tel. 32 19 811), all rooms with private baths and phones, all very modern and perfectly clean. Rates are 2800 dr. for a single, 4500 dr. for a double. If the Alkistis is full, a good second bet is the **Hotel Museum** at 16 Bouboulinas St (tel. 36 05 611), right at the back of the Archaeology Museum. The rooms are about the same, but the prices are a bit higher—about 3200 dr. for a single, 5000 dr. for a double.

If you're going on the cheap, there are currently three official places to stay. The **YWCA** (XEN) is the best of the lot—central, clean, and accommodating both women and married couples. It's at 11 Amerikis St (tel. 36 26 180) a single room costs 1200 dr., a double 1600 dr. The **YMCA** (XAN) is nearby at 28 Omirou St (tel. 36 26 970) and should now be reopened after its renovations. Less savoury is the city's **IYHF Youth Hostel** inconveniently located far from the centre at 57 Kypselis St (tel. 82 25 860). Rates there are 500 dr. a night, sheets extra.

Most of the other inexpensive hotels are around Plaka. For better or worse, the government has shut down many of the old dormitory houses. Survivors of the purge have upgraded themselves but are still a bargain—and many still let you sleep on the roof for a few hundred drachmas (not an unpleasant option in the thick heat of August). Best bets in the cheaper category include:

Hotel Phaedra, 16 Herefondos St (tel. 32 38 461), just off Filellinon St. Free hot showers. A double here will set you back at least 3000 dr., but expect to pay a lot more when the big squeeze is on.

John's Place, 5 Patroou St (tel. 32 29 719). Singles 1500 dr., doubles 2800 dr.

Hotel Cleo, 3 Patroou St (tel. 32 29 053). Small and near Plaka; doubles are 2800 dr.

Joseph's House, 13 Markou Botsari (tel. 92 31 204), in a quieter area on the south side of the Acropolis. Prices about 1300 dr. a head; washing facilities available (take advantage of it—if you're travelling in the islands for any length of time, washing clothes is the biggest bore).

Hotel Tempi, 29 Eolou St (tel. 32 13 175). Near Monastraki, also with washing facilities. Singles 1500 dr., doubles 2500 dr.

The nearest campsite to Athens is at Dafni Monastery (see above).

EATING OUT IN ATHENS

When the Athenians themselves go out to dinner, they often head out to the suburbs or to the sea shore. **Glyfada,** near the airport, is a popular destination and on a summer evening the cool sea breeze can be a life saver after the oppressive heat of Athens. The obvious meal to choose is something from the sea, and most of the tavernas specialise in fish, lobster, squid and shrimp, although, as everywhere in Greece, it's the most expensive food you can order. Try the red mullet (*barbounia*). Remember that prices marked for fish usually indicate how much per kilo, not per portion.

Leading off the main square in Glyfada is a street almost entirely devoted to excellent restaurants and friendly, inexpensive bars. At reasonably priced **George's,** the steak will be served according to your specifications and the meatballs (*keftedes*) are a speciality. A large number of Americans and British live in the area and so fast food joints abound, with fried chicken take-aways, hamburger houses and ice cream parlours galore. Lately, expensive Arab restaurants (complete with imported Middle Eastern singers and belly dancers) have made an appearance on the scene. **La Bussola,** on Vass. Georgiou and Grigori Lambraki, serves authentic Italian food and marvellous pizzas from its outside oven. A full dinner runs to about 1800 dr. (less if you only have pizza).

If rugby is your game, head for **Flanagan's Pub** (just up from the main square), which the local rugby lads finally bought as an investment when they realised how much money they were spending there. It's unusually packed with a chatty crowd, and as the name suggests, it serves Irish coffee.

Back in central Athens, **Gerofinikas** at 10 Pindarou St off Kolonaki Square, is the most popular restaurant with tourists and Greek businessmen alike. Whatever the origin of the specialities here (the management and staff hail from Istanbul) many Greeks will tell you this is what true Greek cuisine should be, and indeed the standard of the food and service is high. One superb speciality is lamb with artichokes and aubergine (eggplant) purée. By Greek standards the place is expensive—a typical meal will cost about 2000 dr. upwards. Fewer tourists know about **Costayiannis,** near the National Archaeology Museum, with a mouth watering display of food in the glass cabinets near the entrance preparing you for a memorable culinary evening. Apart from the excellent seafood, the 'ready food' is unbeatable—try the quail with roast potatoes, the roast pork in wine and herb sauce and the rabbit *stifado*. If you've developed a taste for it, order barreled retsina to accompany your meal. Prices here are very reasonable—1000–1500 dr. for a full meal.

Just off Mikalakopoulou St, and not far from the Hilton Hotel is **John's Village (To Chorio tou Yianni),** a cut above the ordinary taverna and warmly decorated with hand woven rugs and island pottery. The accompanying music, played by a strolling minstrel, makes this a favourite spot to spend an evening without breaking the bank. There's a good variety of well prepared Greek dishes and a meal will cost about 1500 dr. For a really Athenian evening don't miss **To Katoi,** a couple of hundred metres up from the Holiday Inn on Mikalakopoulou, also with live music in the wintertime. The food is great, especially the meat—chops, steaks and sausages and there is a large selection of starters (something you'll appreciate in Greece after a while). Order a selection before you choose your main course. If you point your forefingers at each other about four inches apart and revolve them in the same direction, you should be served some superb hot cheese and ham rolls. Either that of they'll show you where the bathroom is!

The Plaka is, of course, the perennial favourite with both Greeks and tourists; the atmosphere at night is exciting with its crowded tavernas perched precariously on uneven steps, Greek dancers whirling and leaping on stages the size of postage stamps, light bulbs flashing and *bouzouki* music filling the air. A typical charming Plaka taverna is the rooftop **Thespes,** 100 metres along from the Plaka Square, where a selection of starters, such as *tzatziki*, *taramasalata*, fried aubergine (eggplant) followed by lamb chops and several flagons of wine won't cost you much more than 800 dr. In some of the other tavernas you may not be as lucky and will have to pay well over the odds, particularly if there's live music, for food that rarely rises above the mediocre. One other outstanding exception is the **Platanos,** the oldest taverna in the Plaka, near the Tower of the Four Winds. The same people have been eating there for donkey's years, and if George is still around accept with good grace the carafe of wine he'll probably send over, but none of his other suggestions. The food here is good and wholesome, but forget about perusing the menu—it's definitely an 'in the kitchen and point' joint, and inexpensive at 800 dr. for a meal.

Athens is well supplied with ethnic eating places—Italian, Spanish, Chinese, Japanese, Indian and restaurants of other nationalities are scattered around the capital. Of particular note for lovers of German food is the **Rittenburg** at 11 Formionos in Pangrati, where the boiled and grilled sausages, and pork with sauerkraut are the tops. There are a number of Chinese restaurants and they're all relatively expensive. One of the better deals can be had down on the coast at Voula, where **Loon Fung Tien** does Dim Sum (buffet) lunchtimes on Sunday for 1500 dr. A collection of top class, expensive French restaurants cluster around the Hilton Hotel, the most notable being **Le Calvados,** with specialities from Normandy and **L'Orangerie,** whose lonely atmosphere complements the specialities of filet with green pepper, risotto mediterranée and a wide range of seafood dishes. For both these places take a full wallet, if not your credit card. In Kolonaki **Je Riviens** serves a selection of good French dishes and has outdoor seating. Dinner here costs at least 2000 dr.

The **Hilton** itself, on Vass. Sophias, is justifiably proud of its **Taverna Ta Nissia.** Although the name is a bit phoney (I never saw an island taverna that had a redwood ceiling) the emphasis is on the best of the national cuisine, with plenty of delicious mezedes (hors d'oeuvres) which for Greeks is the litmus test of a good restaurant. A dinner here costs about 3000 dr. Behind the Hilton (again, on Mikalakopoulou) is the Cypriot restaurant **Othello's,** with very tasty dishes at around 1600 dr. for a meal.

Watering holes abound in Athens, many of them serving bar food, and most of the English speaking community do the rounds of the **Red Lion,** the **Underground** and the **Ploughman's,** all within a stone's throw of the Hilton.

Piraeus

The port of Athens, Piraeus—pronounced "Pirefs"—was the greatest port of the ancient world and today is one of the busiest in the Mediterranean. In a way it's the true capital of Greece, which derives most of its livelihood from the sea in one way or another, Athens being merely the sprawling suburb where the bureaucrats live. Still, it takes a special tourist to find much charm in the tall grey buildings and hurly-burly in the streets, though Marina Zea and Mikrolimani with their yachts and brightly-lit tavernas and bars make pretty (and most prosperous) tableaus, as do the neon kinetics of the advertisements when one sails from Piraeus in the evening. The tall, half-finished building on the waterfront was built and abandoned by the junta when they found that the foundations were mixed with sea water. Somehow its useless silhouette makes a fitting monument to that ignorant and often cruel government.

Historical outline of Piraeus

Piraeus was inhabited from pre-Hellenic times by an Artemis-worshipping people who left only the Serangeion (also called the cave of Paraskevas or Zeno) to their memory. The Serangeion can be found at Kastelli, by Mikrolimani, and was used as baths into Roman times. When Phaliron, the old port of Athens, could no longer cater for the growing needs of the city, Themistokles founded the port of Piraeus (in the 5th century BC) and his work was finished by Kimon and Perikles. The Miletian geometrician Hippodamos planned the city in the straight right-angled weave of streets which still exists today. At this time the famous Long Walls were built, connecting Athens to Piraeus, of which a few vestiges remain at Marina Zea.

The Piraeus of antiquity was a progressive cosmopolitan centre, its heart at the huge agora in the middle of the city. In its stoas were held the world's first commercial fairs and trade expositions, some on an international scale. All religions were tolerated, and women were allowed for the first time to work outside the home.

As Piraeus was so crucial to Athens' power, the conquering Spartan Lysander destroyed the Long Walls in 404, at the end of the Peloponnesian War. Piraeus made a brief comeback under Konon and Lykurgos, who rebuilt the port's arsenals. After the 100-year Macedonian occupation and a period of peace, General Sulla decimated the city to prevent any anti-Roman resistance, and for 1900 years Piraeus remained an insignificant village with a population as low as 20. A huge lion at the entrance of the port, placed there in 1040 by the Viking Harold Haardrada, gave Piraeus the Venetian names Porto Leone or Porto

Draco. Since the selection of Athens as the capital of free Greece after the War of Independence, Piraeus has regained its former glory as the reigning port of a sea-going nation.

Piraeus today

In recent years the port of Piraeus has been simplified and should pose no problems to those who want to leave it as quickly as possible.

Ships are grouped according to their destination and almost anyone you ask will be able to tell you the precise location of any particular vessel. There is no lack of ticket agents in the port area. They are all very competitive, but prices to the islands are fixed, so the only reason to shop around is to see if there is an earlier or quicker ship to the island of your choice. For complete information on boat schedules, it is best to visit the **Tourist Police** on Akti Miaouli by Skouze St. Ticket agents often don't know or won't tell you information on lines other than their own.

There are three main **railway stations**. The electric train service serves Athens, as far north as Kifissia the most beautiful suburb of the city. The terminal is right across the street from the quay and frequent trains run from 6 am to 1.30 am. The railway stations for northern Greece and for the Peloponnese are a bit further down the road.

Buses to Athens run day and night, the main "Green" line taking you directly to Syntagma Square. The 107/109 bus service to West Airport leaves from Klissovis St.

The quickest route to a **youth hostel** from Piraeus is to take the train or bus to Ommonia, and walk down Stadiou St to Pragastaniou Rd. Here you will find Youth Hostel 4. In Piraeus itself there are many **hotels,** but unless you move away from the business district they are generally noisy. Some people sleep out in the squares, particularly in Karaiskaki, but they have to put up with lights, noise, and the neighbouring discotheques.

If you find yourself in Piraeus with time on your hands, you could visit the new **Archaeology Museum,** at 38 Filellion St, with a surprisingly interesting collection. Open daily 9 am–1 pm and 4 pm–6 pm; Sundays 10 am–2 pm. Closed Tuesdays. Free Thursdays and Sundays. The **Marine Museum** on Akti Themistocles by Freatidos St is also very interesting open daily 9 am–12.30 pm; Sundays and holidays 10 am–1 pm and 6 pm–9 pm. Entrance free. It has plans from the great Greek naval battles, ship models and mementoes from the War of Independence. You could also visit the **Hellenistic Theatre** at Zea, which occasionally has performances in the summer.

Beaches are not far away, although on most you must pay. Kastella is the closest followed by New Phaliron which is free. Buses leave for Ag. Kosmos by the airport, where you can play tennis or volleyball; at Glyfada, further down the road, you can swim and play golf.

Zea, Glyfada and Vouliagmeni are the three **marinas** organised by the

National Tourist Organisation. Prices are comparable to other European marinas. Piraeus is also the place to charter yachts or sail boats, from 12-foot dinghies to deluxe twin-screw yachts. You must have a diploma from a sailing club to rent a boat without a crew (see Chartering a yacht, p. 13).

WHERE TO STAY

Hotel accommodation in Piraeus is chiefly geared towards businessmen; most of the other people who stay in Piraeus do so because they arrived on a late night ship or plan to depart on an early morning one. The port definitely quietens down at night—except for the sailors of all nationalities who hang around hoping for something to happen. If you're with the kids, try the quiet and very clean **Hotel Anemoni,** at Karaoli Demetriou and Evripidou 65–67 (tel. 41 36 881); since it's not directly on the port you miss the sailors; doubles go for around 4500 dr., singles 2800 dr. If you want to be within walking distance of the docks, the **Hotel Triton** (tel. 41 43 457) is one of the best of the many in the area; its B class doubles start at 5500 dr., but go shooting up in high summer. All rooms have private bath and breakfast is available. On the lower end of the scale there are many D & E class hotels, some of which are not as clean as they might be, but their rates range from 2000 dr. to around 3000 dr.

EATING OUT

Around the port the fare is generally fast food and the tavernas are so greasy it's a wonder they don't slide off the street. For real food hike over the hill to Zea Marina, the large pleasure boat harbour and a vast necklace of neon. The locals' favourite spot here seems to be the inexpensive **American Pizza,** but there are places with Greek pizza and other fare as well, both on the harbour and on the streets giving into it. On a hot summer afternoon or evening sit out at **Ziller's** on Akti Koundouriotou 1, which overlooks the sea and Votsalaki Beach. It's tastefully decorated and popular, with a floor to ceiling wall of liqueurs and a complete and reasonably priced menu, including Chateaubriand for 2. Dinner costs about 1500 dr. For seafood **Mikrolimano** (previously known as **Turkolimano**) is the traditional place to go, but is overpriced and touristy, serving food that is neither interesting or fresh. A far better idea is to eat somewhere else, for example the excellent **Kaliva** in Vass. Pavlou, Kastella, with a splendid view down over the harbour (excellent meat dinners for 900 dr.) followed by a stroll through Mikrolimano for a coffee and Metaxa on the harbour front. If you do eat by the water and are prepared to pay the hefty prices (a full dinner will cost you about 4000 dr.) the best known restaurants here are the **Semiramis** and the **Black Goat** but there's really not all that much to distinguish one from another; just stroll around until you find a fish that winks at you.

TOURIST POLICE
Akti Miaouli, tel. 45 23 670
Irron Politechniou, tel. 41 20 325

Kavala
Komotini
Alexandroupolis
Thessaloniki
Igoumenitsa
Volos
6
4
3
Evia
Chalki
Patras
Piraeus Athens
Nauplion
Lavrion
Porto Cheli
5
Kalamata
1
Gythion
Monemvassia
3
2

1 The Cyclades
2 The Dodecanese
3 The Ionian Islands
4 The North-Eastern Aegean Islands
5 The Saronic Islands
6 The Sporades

Crete

GREECE AND THE ISLANDS

THE ISLANDS

For all practical purposes the islands of Greece have been divided into seven major groupings: the Cyclades, the Aegean islands surrounding Delos; the Dodecanese, the 13 main islands lying off the south-west coast of Asia Minor; the north-eastern Aegean islands, stretching from Thassos to Ikaria; the Ionian islands between Greece and Italy; the Saronic islands, in the Saronic Gulf; the Sporades, spread off the coast of Thessaly and Evia; and Crete, the largest island in Greece.

This wealth of islands (over 3000 all told, although a mere hundred or so are inhabited) has created a great variety of cultural nuances, and a thriving business for Greek ships. Islands by their very nature are the individualists of the geographic world, and the Greek islands are not only different from the mainland and from one another, but every islander has a sneaking suspicion, if not a burning belief, that his or her island is the best in Greece, debates between two islanders as to whose homeland is preferable are always highly inconclusive. One island may have more resources, but on the poorer island the people are better because they must work harder. On an island with tourists the people make money, but islands without tourists have peace and quiet. And so on. Thus the visitor must also choose, according to his own taste, where to spend a holiday, a few months, or perhaps a lifetime. Each island has its own special charm, and the only general rule that can be made in "doing the islands" is to do them leisurely so as not to miss it.

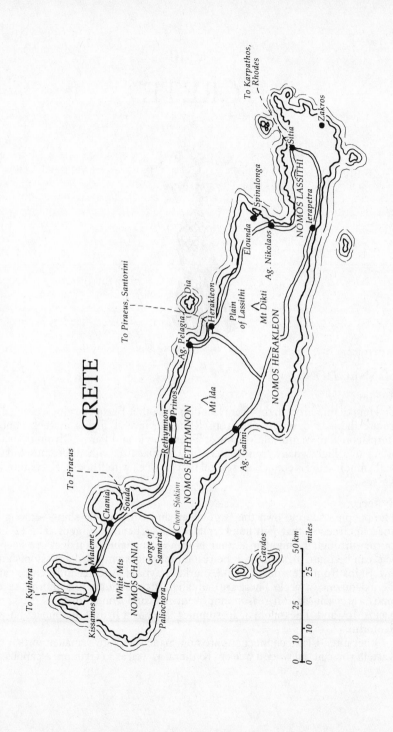

CRETE

To Piraeus

To Kythera

Kissamos

White Mts
It
NOMOS CHANIA

Gorge of
Samaria

Paliochora

Maleme

Chania

Souda

Chora Sfakion

Rethymnon
Prinos

NOMOS RETHYMNON

Mt Ida

Ag. Galini

Ag. Pelagia

Dia

To Piraeus, Santorini

Herakleon

NOMOS HERAKLEON

Plain
of Lassithi

Mt Dikti

Elounda
Spinalonga

Ag. Nikolaos

NOMOS LASSITHI

Ierapetra

Sitia

To Karpathos,
Rhodes

Zakros

Gavdos

50 km   miles

0   10   25   25
0   10   25

Part III

CRETE

The Faience Snake Goddess

CONNECTIONS

By air:
To Herakleon, direct flights from London and other European cities; seven daily from Athens and one a day from Rhodes. Several flights a week connect Herakleon with Santorini, Mykonos, Thessaloniki and Paros. Olympic Airways offers five flights daily from Athens to Chania, two with direct bus links to Rethymnon. Sitia is connected several times a week with Rhodes, Karpathos and Kassos.

By ferry:
The people of Crete own the large clean and comfortable ships—among the finest in Greece—that daily link Herakleon and Chania to Piraeus. The 12-hour journey through the night, in a cabin, or on a warm night out on deck in a sleeping bag, can be quite pleasant and the restaurant prices on board are astonishingly low. Ships from Alexandria, Haifa, Turkey, Cyprus, Ancona and Venice call at Herakleon once a week. There are daily ships in the summer to Santorini, several times a week in the off season, and frequent connections to Paros, Mykonos, Naxos, Ios and Thessaloniki. In summer there is a hydrofoil connection with Santorini.

Other inter-island connections are now made via Crete's smaller ports. From Kastelli you can sail twice a week to Kythera, as well as to Gythion, Neapolis and

Monemvassia in the Peloponnese. Ag. Nikolaos has a twice weekly connection with Anafi, Santorini, Folegandros, Milos, Piraeus, Kassos, Karpathos, Halki and Rhodes; once a week with Symi, Tilos, Nissyros, Kos, Kalymnos, Astypalaia, Amorgos and Paros. From Sitia there are boats three times a week to Piraeus, twice a week to Santorini, Karpathos, Kassos and Rhodes, once a week to Milos, Folegandros, Paros, most of the other Cyclades and Dodecanese.

By bus

There is now a bus which you can board in Crete which combines with the ferries to Piraeus/Athens and takes you all the way to Thessaloniki.

Greece's largest island, Crete, is at once very old and very new. Here lie the ruins of Europe's first civilisation, the Minoan, so wonderfully sophisticated and peaceful (the only weapons archaeologists have found in the palace date from the later Mycenaean period) that one can't help wondering if the first was not also the best. From Crete, too, come some of the most ancient Greek myths, and in its remote mountain villages old customs have survived that were long abandoned in the rest of Greece. And yet, in the past few years, no island has undergone such a striking metamorphosis. Guides used to warn foreign men not to cast an admiring eye on a Cretan woman, for fear that her father and brothers would be tempted to use their famous daggers; now the main danger in many places is suffocation under wave after wave of package tours. There are even rumours that Crete's main attraction, Knossos, may eventually be closed owing to the wear and tear inflicted on the soft gypsum by half a million visitors a year. Hotels, like giant concrete weeds have sprung up along the beaches, and the north-east coast is rapidly becoming one unplanned, ecologically disastrous, unaesthetic mess. There is a definite extremist streak in the Cretan character, and the island's headlong rush to realise its tourist potential is only its most recent manifestation.

But for most people Crete's many natural charms and the monuments of its grand, often turbulent, history more than compensate for an occasional lack of elbow room in the summer months. No less than four mountain ranges stretch across its 260-km (160-mile) length, lending Crete a dramatic grandeur which is disproportionate to its size. Threading its way through the White Mountains in the west is Europe's longest gorge, Samaria; innumerable sandy beaches soften the coastline; 1500 species of wild flowers, some unique to Crete, brighten the landscape at every turn, with a Technicolor intensity in the springtime that a moviemaker might envy. Vineyards, olive and citrus groves and plastic-covered greenhouses filled with vegetables cover the plains and terraces. Two of the island's main cities, Chania and Rethymnon, rival one another in the charm of their Venetian buildings, while some of the small mountain villages are excellent examples of folk architecture, their churches often adorned with Byzantine frescoes and icons so seldom seen on the other islands. Then of course there are the Minoan sites and the archaeology museum in Herakleon, which along with the National Museum in Athens rates as the finest in Greece.

Crete also has its own distinct culture, dialect, music and dances, and it is an encouraging sign that many young Cretans are taking an active role in preserving the island's traditional arts. You can see even the younger men donning the baggy trousers, high boots and black headbands, and taking up the *lyra*, the three-stringed instrument held upright on the lap, principal conveyor of Crete's Eastern-influenced melodies accompanied by the *lauto*, similar to a large mandolin and often a violin and clarinet. On some occasions you can still hear men singing *Mantinadhes*, the improvised couplets, or *rizitika*, "songs from the roots" which deal primarily with themes of Cretan patriotism. Then there is the *Erotokritos*, a 10 000-line romance, written in the Cretan dialect, composed in the 17th century by Vincenzo Kornaros; it is one of the masterpieces of popular Greek poetry and is still memorised and recited today. Other Cretans have earned world-wide acclaim, like El Greco, Nikos Kazanzakis, the composer Mikis Theodorakis, and Greece's most famous statesman, Eleftherios Venizelos.

If you have any choice in the matter, go to Crete towards the end of April. That way not only will you avoid the worst crowds, but the Libyan Sea is usually warm enough for bathing, the flowers are glorious and the higher mountains are still capped with snow. Note, however, if you intend to walk through the gorge of Samaria, that it doesn't officially open until 1 May, when its torrent recedes sufficiently for safe passage.

History

Midget hippopotamus *Pentlandi* bones discovered on Crete have given rise to the view that in not so distant times, geologically speaking, Crete was part of the mainland. Separation stranded the beasts, which, faced with diminished food supplies, slowly diminished themselves until, sadly, they finally disappeared altogether. The first human inhabitants arrived around 6000 BC, a people probably from Asia Minor, who built their small houses in Knossos and other future Minoan capitals. In 3000 BC, at the end of the Neolithic period, a new population arrived, inspiring new forms in pottery and a move from stone tools to copper. This period is called the Early Minoan. The Middle Minoan (1900 BC) saw the advent of palaces towns and a system of writing in pictographs, but in 1700 BC an earthquake (probably) devasted the buildings, forcing the people to start afresh.

From 1700 to 1450 BC was the height of the Minoan civilisation. The palaces were rebuilt and decorated with frescoes, and equipped with water and drainage systems. Colonies were settled on the islands, and the Minoans, ruling the seas made contact with cities in Africa, Asia Minor and on the Greek mainland, inspiring the myths of the great King Minos, which was probably the dynastic name of the Knossos kings. Linear A, the as yet undeciphered system of writing was developed. But disaster struck Crete again in 1450 BC, thought to have been caused by a volcanic eruption, tidal waves and earthquakes from nearby Santorini. The magnificent Minoan kingdom was left in ruins.

Many believe that at this time Mycenaeans from the mainland invaded Crete, taking advantage of its now fallen state. In this late Minoan period (1550-1050 BC) only Knossos was built up again, and Linear B writing, which in translation proved to be a very ancient form of Greek, predominated (similar Linear B tablets were also found at Mycenae and Thebes). Other towns began to be repopulated and Chania prospered in particular, although Crete no longer exerted external influence. By 1100 BC and the beginning of the Iron Age the civilisation had slowed down into a dark age, and the people took to the hills.

The Dorians invaded Crete, and by the Geometric period (8th century BC) Crete thrived. It is thought that the invaders co-existed peacefully with the native Minoans; inscriptions in Greek letters have been found that spell non-Greek words. As on the mainland, by the 5th century BC, small city states were gradually formed which fought among themselves, built walls, and minted their own coins, ruled by a powerful aristocracy. Romans under Q. Metellus Creticus conquered Crete in 67 BC, and Gortyna, inhabited since Minoan times, became the capital of the province of Crete and Cyrenaica in West Africa.

Rich churches were constructed in Crete in the early Byzantine period, but in AD 823 Saracen Arabs conquered the island and stayed until its liberation in 961 by the Emperor Nikephoros Phokas. In the 13th century the Genoese ruled Crete, but later sold it to the Venetians, who occupied the island from 1210 to 1669. On the whole Crete prospered under the Venetians, in particular after the fall of Constantinople, when the island became a refuge for scholars and painters fleeing the capital. The so-called Cretan school of art flourished in the 15th and 16th centuries, working both at home and in the rest of Greece, and nurtured El Greco, who at that time still called himself Domeniko Theotokopoulos. The epic romance *Erotokritos* was written by Kornaros. Great fortifications and public buildings were built by the Venetians.

However, benevolent though the Venetians were, Cretans—being Cretans— yearned to control their own destiny. On several occasions they attempted to revolt, and many actually welcomed the advent of the Turks. Yet when the Ottomans finally took Herakleon from Venice (after a 21-year siege), in 1669, Crete fell into a new dark age, spiritually and economically. The Cretans rose up against the Turks more than 400 times, notably in 1821, but were inevitably the losers to the superior Muslim forces. In 1898 the Great Powers appointed Prince George High Commissioner of an independent Crete, and with the work of Venizelos the island became part of Greece in 1913. During the Second World War, Nazi paratroopers launched the world's first successful invasion by air on Crete, routing the Allied troops who had fled there from the mainland. Once again the Cretan guerrillas took to the mountains and along with British agents waged a heroic resistance, despite brutal reprisals by the Germans.

Mythology

As Cronus, the ruler of the world, had been warned that a child of his would usurp his place, he swallowed every baby his wife Rhea, daughter of the Earth, presented to him. After this had happened five times, Rhea determined a different fate for her sixth child, Zeus. When he was born she smuggled him to Crete and gave Cronus a stone instead, which the god duly swallowed. Mother Earth hid the baby in the Diktean cave and set the Kouretes to guard him, to shout and beat their shields should the baby cry and arouse Cronus' suspicions.

After Zeus grew up and had indeed taken his father's place by the simple expedient of castrating him, a girl named Europa caught his fancy. To avoid making his wife Hera jealous, Zeus abducted the maiden in the form of a beautiful bull and took her to Crete, where she bore him three sons: Minos, Rhadamanthys and Sarpedon. Minos became the King of Crete at Knossos. When he was requested to prove that his claim to the throne was sanctioned by the gods, he remembered the form his father had taken and asked Poseidon to give him a bull from the sea to sacrifice. However, the bull of Poseidon was so magnificent that instead of killing it, Minos sent it to service his herds.

The kingdom of Minos prospered, ruling the seas and exacting tribute from all over the Mediterranean. But Poseidon never forgot Minos' lack of piety in not sacrificing the bull. In revenge he made Minos' wife Pasiphae (daughter of the sun and the nymph Crete, who gave the island its name) fall in love with it. Poor Pasiphae confided this problem to the great inventor Daedalus, who had been banished from Athens for murder and was now living at Minos' court. Daedalus responded by making her a hollow wooden cow, which she entered and with which the bull mated. This resulted in the birth of a monster with the head of a bull and the body of a man, the Minotaur.

Naturally revolted by this new member of his household, Minos asked Daedalus to hide it. Obediently Daedalus built the Labyrinth, an impossible maze of corridors, and there he put the Minotaur. As this strange beast also showed a great liking for human meat, Minos took advantage of an Athenian insult and ordered that city to pay in reparation a tribute every nine years of seven maidens and seven youths, whom he would feed to the Minotaur.

Two tributes had been paid when Theseus, the son of Aegeus, King of Athens, appeared and demanded to be one of the victims. With great reluctance his father agreed, and Theseus went to Crete as part of the tribute. But Ariadne, daughter of Minos, fell in love with him at first sight and turned to Daedalus for help in saving his life. Daedalus gave her a ball of thread. Theseus slew the Minotaur with his bare hands, retraced his way out of the Labyrinth with Ariadne's ball of thread and escaped, taking the Cretan princess and the other Athenians along with him. Although he left Ariadne on Naxos, he later married her younger sister Phaedra.

Minos was furious when he discovered the part Daedalus had played in the business and threw the inventor and his young son Ikaros into the Labyrinth. Although they managed to find their way out, escape from Crete itself was impossible, as Minos controlled the seas and was on the lookout for them. But Daedalus was never at a loss, and decided that what they couldn't accomplish by sea they would do by air. He made wings of wax for himself and Ikaros, and on the

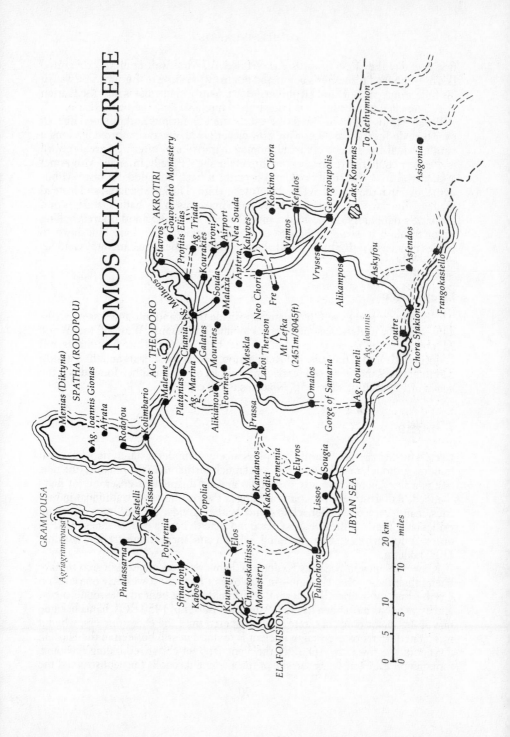

NOMOS CHANIA, CRETE

GRAMVOUSA

SPATHA (RODOPOU)

AG. THEODORO

AKROTIRI

Menias (Diktyna)

Ag. Ioannis Gionas

Afrata

Rodofou

Agriagrambousa

Kolimbario

Maleme

Mathios

Stavros

Gouverneto Monastery

Profitis Elias

Ag. Triada

Kourakies

Aroni

Airport

Souda

Aptera, Nea Souda

Malaxa

Kalyves

Nea Souda

Kokkino Chora

Kefalos

Vamos

Georgioupolis

Lake Kournas

To Rethymnon

Asigonia

Kastelli

Kissamos

Platanias

Ag. Marina

Galatas

Mournies

Fournes

Chania

Alikianou

Meskla

Lakoi Therison

Neo Chori

Fre

Vryses

Askyfou

Asfendos

Prassa

Mt Lefka
(2451m/8045ft)

Alikampos

Loutre

Frangokastello

Polyrenia

Topolia

Kandanos

Temenia

Kakodiki

Omalos

Gorge of Samaria

Ag. Roumeli

Ag. Ioannis

Chora Sfakion

Phalassarna

Sfinarion

Kabos

Kounenii

Elos

Chrysoskalitissa
Monastery

Elyros

Lissos

Sougia

Paliochora

LIBYAN SEA

ELAFONISION

20 km

miles

20

10

10

5

5

0

0

10

first fine day they flew towards Asia Minor. All went well until an exhilarated Ikaros disobeyed his father's command not to fly too close to the sun. The wax in his little wings melted, and he plunged down to drown in what is now the Ikarian Sea. The island on which Daedalus buried him also took the name Ikaria.

When Minos heard of Daedalus' escape he was furious and pursued him all over the Mediterranean. Knowing how clever Daedalus was he brought along a nautilus shell and a piece of thread, hoping to trap him by offering a great reward to whoever could figure out a way to thread the shell. Finally, in Sicily, Minos met a king who took the shell away and brought it back threaded. At once Minos demanded that the king turn Daedalus over to him. The king hedged, and instead invited Minos to stay at his palace. When Minos was in his bath, Daedalus and the king's daughters introduced a pipe through the ceiling and poured boiling water through it, scalding him to death. Thereupon Zeus took him down to Hades to act as a judge of the dead along with his brother Rhadamanthys and his enemy Aeacus.

Crete today

The mountain ranges of Crete naturally divide the island into four major areas, and these have also become Crete's political divisions. West of the White Mountains is the *nomos* (county) of Chania; between the White Mountains and Psiloritis (Mt Ida) is the *nomos* of Rethymnon; between Psiloritis and the Lassithi Mountains lies the *nomos* of Herakleon; and east of the Lassithi Mountains is the *nomos* of Lassithi; of which Ag. Nikolaos is the capital.

Chania

Crete's former capital, **Chania,** is a pleasant city of modern, stately neo-Classical buildings, though most visitors never get much further than the old port (the new one is a few kilometres away in Souda) and its dilapidated ensemble of half-bombed, half-restored Venetian buildings. Two of the city's traditional industries, hand-carved wooden chairs and leather goods, are still very much in evidence; Chania is the cheapest place in Crete to have a pair of shoes made to order. If nothing else, it's a charming, relaxed (and increasingly trendy) antidote to Herakleon.

Known in ancient times as Kydonia, Chania was recently discovered to have been inhabited by the Minoans—it was one of their most westerly outposts on Crete—but unfortunately almost all their buildings lie beneath the modern city, and excavations have been limited. After the disaster of 1450 BC Chania became one of the major cities of Crete, and prospered until the Byzantine era, when it was ruined. Parts of the wall of ancient Kydonia can still be seen in the Kastelli district of the town. In AD 1252 the Venetians set about rebuilding Kydonia, renaming it La Canea. On the site of the ancient akropolis they constructed the fortress Kastelli, within which were built the lovely homes of the Venetian noblemen. This fortress was surrounded by a wall. In the late 15th century, alarmed by the threat of the pirate admiral Barbarossa, who had struck in neighbouring Rethymnon, the Venetians created a wall around the entire town and surrounded it with a moat more than 45 metres (150 ft) wide and 9 metres (30 ft) deep. A long jetty divided the harbour in two.

All these precautions were, however, to no avail, and in 1645 less than 60 years after the completion of the walls, the Turks besieged and took Chania, installing pashas and beys at Kastelli and raising further fortifications. In 1850 they transferred the capital of Crete from Herakleon to Chania, where it remained until the island's annexation to Greece.

On 20 May 1941, while General Student's parachutists invaded Crete, the Nazis bombed Chania, demolishing a large section of the old walls and houses. While the Battle of Crete was a victory for the Nazis, their specially trained parachutists were almost all killed. Chania commemorates the anniversary of the battle during the **Chania Festival,** which runs from the middle to the end of May, and includes folk dancing on the waterfront.

The centre of daily life in Chania is the **market,** which resembles a train depot and is also the stop for buses from Souda, Chania's port. It's a short walk from here to the old **Venetian Quarter.** The whole neighbourhood is a National Historical Landmark, and while the façades of the buildings may not be altered, the interiors are rapidly being restored to house pensions, restaurants and jazz clubs. On one side of the harbour, is the **Mosque of the Janissaries** (1645), with its funny little domes, where the crack troops of the Ottoman Empire once worshipped; information is now dispensed by a very helpful **National Tourist Office,** open all year 8.30 am-3 pm.

On the other side of the harbour, where one can still see sections of the Inner Venetian wall (quarried from the stones of ancient Kydonia), is the **Naval Museum of Crete,** located within the walls. (open every day 10 am-2 pm, also Tuesday, Thursday and Saturday 5 pm-7 pm). Wandering through the nearby maze of tiny streets, look for the ruined synagogue and the church of San Salvatore, used by the Turks as a mosque. On nearby Theofanous St a gate bears the Venieri coat-of-arms, dated 1608.

Chania has two interesting museums. On Khaldon St, in the Venetian church of San Francesco, is the **Archaeology Museum,** containing not only Chania's Minoan finds, but also pottery from Cyprus, with which ancient Kydonia traded, and other Classical finds (open weekdays 8 am-5 pm, closed Tuesday). The **Historical Museum and Archives,** on Sfakianaki St, has Greece's second largest collection of historical material, dating back from the Venetian occupation to the liberation of Crete (open weekdays 9 am-1 pm, closed weekends).

The **Outer Venetian Walls** are intact to the west (dated 1590 on the Koum Kapissi Gate on Minos St) and to the east. It is to the east that you will find the large church of **Ag. Nikolaos,** built by the Venetians and used by the Turks to shelter a magical healing sword when they converted it to a mosque and claimed by the Orthodox church in 1918. In the same vicinity is San Rocco (1630) and **Ag. Anargyrii,** built in the 16th century and the only church to hold Orthodox services throughout the Venetian and Turkish occupations. It contains several very old icons. By the harbour here note the seven arches that remain from the original **Venetian Arsenali,** or shipbuilding yard.

In the **Chalepa** quarter of town, amid its many 19th-century mansions and public gardens, stands the house and statue of Eleftherios Venizelos, as well as the residence of the High Commissioner, Prince George. Across from Venizelos' house is a historical oddity: a Russian Orthodox church donated by Prince George's mother.

The harbour now has a yacht marina; Chania is an official port of entry and supplies general provisioning. The nearest beach, **Neo Chora,** is a 15-minute walk from the harbour. It's sandy, shallow, and safe for children, and has several tavernas. The beaches tend to improve the further west you go, towards Platanais and Galatas. A kilometre or so west of Chania stands the monument of the diving eagle, a German memorial to the 2nd Parachute Regiment, oddly adopted by the Cretans as their own monument to the bitter Battle of Crete.

PANEYERIA
On 15 August Chania hosts the Pan Cretan Festival. The Chania festival runs from the middle to the end of May. In the neighbouring village of Chryssopigi there is a festival on Good Friday at Zoodochos Pigi.

WHERE TO STAY
Although there are several modern (and rather sterile) hotels in the newer quarters of Chania, most people prefer to stay near the harbour. A charming new addition to the roster there is actually quite old, located in a refurbished Venetian house the **Contessa Hotel** on Theofanous Street (tel. 0821 23 966). It has the intimate air of an old fashioned guest house, with only six rooms, furnished in traditional Cretan style, each with a private bath. The Contessa's owners speak little English, but make up for it by being extremely helpful in any way they can. Because it's so small, reserve well in advance. Doubles start at 5000 dr. On the waterfront at Akti Enosseos is the B class **Porto Veneziano,** a modern but comfortable hotel with 63 rooms, doubles for 7000 dr. (tel. 0821 29 311).

Chania is also blessed with a large number of pleasant pensions, most with rates below the Cretan norm. One of the nicer ones, the **Kydonia Pension,** is just off the harbour, on a narrow lane leading to the cathedral: 15 Isodian St (tel. 0821 57 179). The rooms are simple, the shower (shared) is hot, there's a small bar and the rates are low—1000 dr. a head. For the same price the **Hotel Piraeus** has clean rooms, marvellously situated overlooking the bustling harbour front and the friendly Greek-American owner encourages a relaxed family atmosphere. There are cooking and washing facilities (tel. 0821 54 154). A little more done up is the **Pension Kastelli,** 39 Kanevarou St, on the quieter east end of the harbour. Rates are in the same price range.

There's also a **Youth hostel,** which is very decent and very quiet because it's almost out of the city limits, at 33 Drakonianou (tel. 0821 53 565). To get there, take the Ag. Ioannes bus from in front of the market. You don't need a card to stay, and rates—including showers—are only 390 dr. a person.

There are two campsites near Chania, though again you'll need a bus to reach them: **Camping Ag. Marina** (tel. 0821 68 555), is 5 miles west of the town and open throughout the season; and **Camping Chania,** three miles west of town, tel. 51 090. The former is the nicer of the two. Buses leave every hour from the station.

EATING OUT

It's hard not to find a restaurant in Chania—the harbour is one great crescent of tavernas, almost all specialising in fish. It's worth your while to check over their prices: some have succumbed to tourism mark-ups, others are still at true Greek prices. If you are visiting Chania in the off season, the **Aposperida** on Kordilaki Street will provide something different. Located in a Venetian soapworks, the tables are set out on different levels in the great multi-storey space. The food is Cretan and a dinner there (open only in the evenings) will set you back about 1500 dr.

Another good, local place is directly across from the Kydonia Penison on Isodion Street, called **Taverna Apovrado.** For around 800 dr. you can try a number of Chaniote specialties, including the local wine and sausage, of which the natives are quite proud. Just off the harbour in Halidon St, the **Lukulos Restaurant** offers a fairly wide selection, from pizzas to pepper steak, at reasonable prices. For a taste of France, **Les Vagabonds,** in the back streets of the old town, makes a valiant effort, with smoked trout, salade Niçoise and Beef Bourgignon on the menu. A full meal with wine will run to 2000 dr. The market is an excellent source of cheap food and snacks, and at lunchtime possibly the liveliest place in Chania.

In the many bars on the harbour you can get practically anything you want, including such un-Greek concoctions as fruit and ice cream drinks. For genuine local entertainment, and the cheapest raki in all Crete, go to the little hole-in-the-wall called **Lyraki,** just beyond the NTOG office. The owner, like all good bar keepers, has a particular grouchy charm and serves some wonderful mezedes to go with his raki. The music is all impromptu—men stop in to play with their friends—and if you stay long enough, you're bound to see some equally impromptu Cretan dancing. Less spontaneous, but also featuring good Cretan music is **Zamania's** on Apokoronou Street. You can eat here as well (about 800-1000 dr. for dinner); the lyraki and laouto do their magic every evening except Monday and Tuesday.

TOURIST INFORMATION
NTOG Turkish Mosque (0821) 43 300.
Tourist Police: 44 Karaiskaki St. tel. (0821) 24 477.

Nomos of Chania

The city of Chania is the best point of departure for the rest of the nomos, the land of the White Mountains. This west side of Crete is slowly rising out of the sea, while eastern Crete is subject to a gradual sinking, noticeable through the centuries. Nomos Chania is the home of the gorge of Samaria, the last place in the world where the Cretan wild goat, the kri kri, lives in its natural habitat. The Chaniotes are known in Crete as the best musicians and warriors, especially those from Chora Sfakion. Excellent oranges, honey and olive oil are produced, and west Chania is Crete's big chestnut producer. Kastelli and Kissamos wines are well known throughout Greece.

Buses for the nomos leave from 7 Kydonia St, near the Samaria Hotel.

Akrotiri, one of the three "heads" of Crete, is directly east of Chania. Eleftherios Venizelos and his son are buried there, by Profitis Elias church where Cretans raised the Greek flag in 1897 in the midst of a bombardment by international navies. The story runs that the admirals were so impressed by the courage of the Cretans, who at the risk of their lives held up the flag that had fallen from its pole during the battle, that they stopped fighting and applauded them. A Russian shell destroyed the church, but it is said that Prophet Elijah avenged the action by blowing up part of the Russian ship the next day, killing many sailors.

Not only does Akrotiri have Chania's airport, but here too are many new villas of its wealthier citizens. There are two monasteries on the headland. **Ag. Triada,** near Kabani, was founded by the Venetian Tzangarol at the beginning of the 17th century and has a lovely Renaissance church. On 8 October many pilgrims come to celebrate a large paneyeri held at the monastery of **Ag. Ioannes Gouvernetou,** near the stalactite cave Kimisios or Katholikon, where St John the Hermit lived and died. Although cave enthusiasts may not mind, it's a good hour's walk to Gouvernetou, nor will there be monks at the end of the trek to ply you with refreshments; they abandoned the monastery long ago. At Spiliani another cave, **Anemospilia** (Cave of the Wind), has a pond and stalactites, and **Arkoudia** (Bear) cave has a rock bear inside and also an ancient church. A pretty beach can be found at the small village of **Stavros.**

Souda, at the head of the bay of Akrotiri, is Chania's port and wins no prizes for charm, but it has restaurants, snack bars and hotels. Frequent buses connect it with the capital. A major NATO base is located at Souda and its air force exercises can be rather obnoxious. But NATO is not the first to appreciate the superb harbour of Souda Bay, one of the best in the Mediterranean Sea. The Venetians fortified the bay's islet **Nea Souda,** and it was the last place on Crete to hold out against the Turks, despite their repeated attempts to capture it. At one time they tried to disarm the defenders psychologically by piling 5000 Christian heads around the walls. The fort, however, remained in the hands of the Venetians and Greek rebels, who took shelter there, until 1715 when Venice surrendered it to Turkey. The Turks built another fort, **Idzeddin,** at the south

74

end of the bay by the ancient city Aptera, whose ruins supplied the stone for its construction. Together with Nea Souda, Idzeddin guarded the bay of Souda. As for **Aptera,** an important centre into the Christian era, little remains except the story of its name, for here the Muses were said to have defeated the seductive Sirens in a musical contest, whereupon the Sirens, in a fit of pique, tore out their feathers and plunged into the sea, hence "aptera" or "featherless". Among the ruins you can pick out the Cyclopean walls, two temples and a Roman theatre. South-west of Idzeddin is the village **Malaxa,** an ancient mining centre. Ruins of two Byzantine churches, Ag. Saranta and Ag. Eleousa remain, but most spectacular is the ravine to the south, said to be 400 metres (1300 ft) deep, riddled with caves. The neighbouring village of **Mournies** was the birthplace of Venizelos.

Heading towards the middle "head" of Crete, called Rodopou but also known locally by its cape, **Spatha,** one comes to **Ag. Marina** with its old Venetian and Turkish houses. The islet facing Ag. Marina is **Ag. Theodoro,** and it, too, attracted the Venetian fortification architects. Its cave with its wide open mouth originally belonged to a hungry sea monster, with an appetite as big as Crete; Zeus, however, couldn't bear to see his home island devoured, and petrified the monster with a thunderbolt. Ag. Theodoro today is a refuge for the wild Cretan goat, the kri kri.

Close to Ag. Marina is **Platanias** with sandy beach and bamboo forest. Another beach is near **Maleme,** further west, where the Battle of Crete began. German dead are buried in a large cemetery nearby. The village of **Kolimbario** at the foot of Spatha, is the point of departure for excursions on the "head". Its church Ag. Georgios celebrates paneyeri on 23 April but its monastery **Gonias,** also known as Hodegetria, is much better known. Founded in the early 17th century, it is a rich monastery with many lovely icons, some dating from its foundation. Its festival is on 15 August; on 29 August pilgrims make the long two-hour trek to the **Church of St John the Hermit Gionas,** north of Rodofou. **Afrata,** the last village on the head accessible by car, has a huge cave, Hellenospilios, with corridors 90 metres (300 ft) long containing stalactites and stalagmites and other geographic wonders. From Afrata it is a few hours on foot (or $1^{1}/_{2}$ hours by caique from Kolimbario) to **Menias,** the port of ancient **Diktyna,** the most famous shrine to Artemis in Greece. Menias has a rocky beach and shady caves, and there are some ruins of the ancient port. Diktean Artemis had a popular following up to the end of the Roman Empire. The Diktean mountains in Lassithi were named for her, and Agamemnon stopped by to offer a sacrifice at her shrine in Polyrenia on his return home from Troy.

Polyrenia itself is south of Kastelli and more of it remains than of Diktyna. Founded by the Acheans and Dorians, Polyrenia ("many flocks") supported a large population, supplied by a still visible aqueduct. Parts of the ancient walls remain, added to by the Romans and perhaps the Turks. The church of the 99 Holy Fathers was built on the site from temple material, and the cemetery lies in a temple's foundations. There are also ruins of roads and houses. The road leading

Storage Jars at Knossos, Crete

to Polyrenia from Kastelli is also a ruin; buses attempt it twice a day from Kastelli (but it's a charming 5 mile walk).

Kastelli (ancient Kissamos) is situated on a plain surrounded by knobbly hills which produce olives and grapes. To distinguish it from the various other Kastellis of Crete, the town's proper name is Kastelli Kissamou, a most proper name as Kastelli's castle was Kissamos' temple and theatre refashioned by the Venetians in 1550. This castle has a long and at times most melodramatic history. When the Cretan Kantanoleo captured it from the Venetians, they, as if recognising Kantanoleo's authority, offered a highborn Venetian girl as his son's bride. At the wedding feast the Cretans were given drugged wine and the Venetians murdered them, taking the fort once more.

In the Kastelli post office is a small museum with a few discoveries from ancient Kissamos. Wine is the major product of the town, and there are paneyeria on 30 May, 27 June (Ag. Pandeliemenon) and 29 August (Ag. Ioannes). There is a rocky beach with a taverna.

Up at the ancient city of **Phalassarna** the beach is large and sandy, one of the finest in Crete. Unfortunately it is also an hour's walk from the nearest bus in Platanos. As well as a couple of tavernas, there's a stone "throne" and a marker to show where Phalassarna once stood, some walls also remain by Koutri. Phalassarna was once a port and the fact that its remains are set back so far from the sea is evidence of western Crete's gradual uptilt. Further north, on an islet off the Gramvousa head, lies the famous Venetian fort, taken during the War of Independence by Greek refugees, in particular those from the two small islands of Psara and Kassos, which had been devastated by the Turks. Forced to make a living in troubled times, these refugees took to pirating so successfully that Capodistria had to intervene personally to stop them, and Gramvousa fort became Turkish once more. Caiques in Phalassarna may be hired to make the trip to the fortress. More isolated sandy beaches lie further south, at Sfinarion and Kabos.

WHERE TO STAY
On Maleme Beach the Crete **Chandris Hotel** provides the luxury. Its A class doubles are around the 11 000 dr. mark. Once a week the hotel has a Cretan dance evening (tel. 0821 62 221). In Ag. Marina there are a number of C class hotels in the 3000–5000 dr. range, and one B class, the **Santa Marina,** on the beach, with doubles going for 6500 dr. (tel. 0821 68 570). In Kastelli, in fact right in the centre of town is the **Kastelli Hotel** (Plateia Kastelliou, tel. 0822 22 140), a decent fairly modern place, with a double going for around 3800 dr. with private bath. There are also a number of pensions and rooms, both in town and on the beach. In Phalassarna you can rent rooms in a taverna for 1200 dr. or simply camp out—that's about it.

EATING OUT
In Kastelli there are several seaside fish restaurants; try **Makedonas** near Teloniou Square, where prices are fairly moderate (about 1200 dr. for a full dinner). Others may be found by the pretty caique harbour (where you can also swim before eating) just west of town. On the road to Chania there are small tavernas here and there, only open in the summer; to the east there's precious little. At Phalassarna there are a couple of tavernas on the beach (expect to pay a bit more because of transport costs). There's also a restaurant up at Polyrenia—the village is small and you can't miss it. The food is average, but the view is quite wonderful.

Further south, on the Libyan Sea, via slow and often rough roads, is the **Monastery Chrysoskalitissa,** "Our Lady of the Golden Stair" (though only the faithful, or according to some, non-liars can see the steps of gold). Remote though it is, many people come to its paneyeri on 14–15 August. Wonderfully isolated, amid many fine beaches, is the islet **Elafonision,** popular with Chaniotes who want to escape from the cares of the world, or at least from those of Crete.

Once a day a bus leaves Kastelli for **Topolia,** with its pretty stalactite cave of Ag. Sophia, used since Neolithic times and still the shelter for a little church. At the nearby church of Ag. Kyryianni (960) are the remains of a Bishop Psaromilingos, who was martyred in the cave. We are now in Chania's chestnut region, an area of dramatic, mountainous beauty reminiscent of Corsica. The main village, **Elos,** hosts a chestnut harvest festival (Yiorti tou Kastanas) on the second Sunday of October. Eight other villages in the area claim the chestnut as their major product; in July they also have some of the best weddings in Crete.

Kouneni is the next large village, with three Byzantine chapels, in particular Ag. Georgios, constructed in 1284, and Michail Archangelos (14th century), both with frescoes. East of Kouneni lies the village of **Kandanos,** inhabited from ancient times and known for its freedom-loving inhabitants. The Nazis destroyed it after much resistance, and the present village is all new. Ruins of the ancient walls remain on the hill, and there are many Byzantine churches in the area with frescoes, **Kakodiki** to the south-west has a hundred springs with soft mineral waters known for curing kidney stones. Kali Keratai is the most famous. Michail Archangelos church (1387) contains frescoes. The springs at Temenia, Dzanoudianon and Limbinari are also known for their curative properties. Muscat-producing **Temenia** was built on the site of ancient Yrtakina, near the far grander Elyros, one of the largest Doric settlements on Crete. According to legend two sons of Apollo, Philakides and Philandros, founded the town, which worshipped them. Arrows, bows and bronze were exports of the pugnacious town of **Elyros,** which prospered until the Saracens destroyed it in the 9th century. Walls from the town and akropolis still exist.

In 1279 the Venetian conquerors built **Castel Selino,** on a narrow peninsula, more with the aim of subduing the rebellious Greeks than of protecting their new territory. The castle did not last, however; the terror of the islands, Khair Eddin Barbarossa, arrived in 1539 and destroyed it on his pillaging path. Below the ruins of its walls is a lovely sandy beach. The small town of Selino, now known as **Paliochora** (bus from Chania) was once known as the Bride of the Libyan Sea, a sobriquet that must have been due to its location rather than to any architectural splendour, though the church, Panayias, has a lovely campanile.

From Paliochora it is an hour's caique trip to the ancient city of **Lissos,** another victim of the Saracen conquest and perhaps once the port of both Elyros and Yrtakina. A theatre, baths, houses and temples can still be seen of this once prosperous Doric–Roman–Byzantine town. Very close to Lissos was ancient Syia, modern **Sougia,** also a harbour of Elyros. Many signs of ancient times remain, including walls, an aqueduct and a bath. On the floor of the 6th-century church are lovely mosaics, both geometrical and scenic. Ag. Antonios (1382) is painted with frescoes. A cave near Sougia, Spyliara, is one of a multitude believed to have housed the Cyclops Polythemos. On 8 September Sougia has a paneyeri.

The next village going eastwards along the coast of the Libyan Sea is Ag. Roumeli, which also boasts a frescoed church, Panayia, built on a temple of Artemis by the Venetians. The town itself was constructed on the site of ancient Tarra with its sanctuary of Tarranean Apollo. Tarra was known for its fine glass made in the Roman period.

Gorge of Samaria

Of course, the most scenic way to reach Crete's southern coast is by walking through the **gorge of Samaria,** among the most spectacular 11 miles in Crete. Once considered a rather adventurous excursion, the hike has become a "must" for nearly everyone, and unless you can manage to go very early or very late in the year you may as well forget any private communion with Mother Nature (especially at weekends). The gorge is open officially from 1 May to 31 October, when the water is low enough to ensure safe fording of the streams, and when the gorge is patrolled by the staff of the National Forest Service. Usually, however, you can pass through from mid-April to mid-November without too much danger—ask at the tourist office in Chania. To walk all the way through (it takes most people between five and six hours going down, and about twice that going up towards **Omalos,** the small village at the head of the gorge) you must be in the gorge by 3 pm, although almost everyone starts much earlier, to avoid the midday heat, and to make the excursion a single day's outing. The first bus (or buses, depending on demand) departs from Chania for Omalos at around 5 in the morning, the tour buses leave almost as early, some even setting out from Herakleon and Rethymnon. In the high season, consider paying the extra drachmas for a tour bus, for once you reach the end of the gorge at Ag. Roumeli there is often a mad rush to catch a caique either to Chora Sfakion, Sougia or Paliochora, and another dash once you're at one of these villages to buy a bus ticket home. Everyone seems to want to catch the last bus of the afternoon, to allow time beforehand for lunch and a swim on the coast. The tour buses do allow for this, and also assure you of a seat going back. However you go, wear good walking shoes and bring something to eat (it is safe to drink water from any of the streams in Samaria).

If you haven't the time or energy to make the whole trek, you can at least sample Samaria (the bus trip from Chania, twisting around the steep slopes of the White Mountains, is itself an experience) by descending only a mile or so into the gorge down the **Xyloskalo,** the great wooden stair from Omalos, or alternatively, if you're based in the south, by going a mile up from Ag. Roumeli to the famous Sideropontes ("the iron gates"), the oft-photographed section of the gorge where the sheer rock walls rise almost 300 metres (1000 ft) on either side of a passage only 3 metres (10 ft) wide. The Forest Service will admit visitors until nearly dusk for either of these short excursions.

The name Samaria derives from a chapel (1379) and ruined village in the centre of the gorge, Ossa Maria, which over the years was corrupted to Samaria. There are several other abandoned chapels along the way, about 20 fords in the stream, and if you're very, very lucky, you'll catch a glimpse of the wild kri kri, the long-horned native Cretan goat that for many years was near extinction. The White Mountains National Park, of which Samaria is a part is the only place on mainland Crete where they may be found, others have been to offshore islets where they are also carefully protected. In the springtime there are also many wild flowers.

Ag. Roumeli, at the southern mouth of the gorge, was built on the site of ancient Tarra with its sanctuary of Tarranean Apollo. In Roman times Tarra was famed for its fine glassware. The Venetians built a frescoed church, tis Panayias, on the foundation of a temple to Artemis. Since it has no roads, Ag. Roumeli was all but abandoned until the 1960s, when people began to come in through the gorge. Now it has numerous places to stay and eat, it also has a pebbly beach.

From Ag. Roumeli the caiques take 1¹/₂ hours either to Paliochora or to Chora Sfakion less to Sougia which is less tourist-oriented but also less frequently served by bus. Between Ag. Roumeli and Sfakion, **Loutre** has many quiet beaches. South of Ag. Roumeli is the triangular islet **Gavdos** (ancient Clauda), which along with the tiny Italian island of Lampedusa vies for the title of the southernmost point in Europe. It also vies (with many more islands) to have been the home of the fair Calypso. Boats leave twice a week from Paliochora for this place of charming beaches and shepherds but little tourist accommodation. The castle, Gozzo, is Venetian.

Ag. Ioannis is a three-hour mule ride east of Ag. Roumeli. An autonomous ancient city, Aradin, once inhabited the site of which a few vestiges remain. The old church of Archistratigos Michail was built from the stones of ancient Aradin. The region surrounding it is full of caves. Drakolakki cave is noteworthy—an underground labyrinth with a bottomless lake that requires both torch and string to explore.

Legendary in Crete for the ferocity and courage of its inhabitants, **Chora Sfakion** today is hardly distinguishable from the island's other coastal villages, with its seaside tavernas, hotels, souvenir shops and pebble beach. At one time, however, it was the capital of its own province, one that Crete's various occupiers never quite subdued. Situated by the sea, it supplied the innumerable Cretan revolutions, and often turned to smuggling and piracy. At one time Chora Sfakion was said to have a hundred churches, enabling people to gather at seemingly harmless paneyeria to plot the next moves of a revolt. Villages in the province of Sfakia are often fortified on small hills, as the independent Sfakians also fought great feuds among themselves. The Venetians constructed a castle on the hill after the revolt of 1570, while 14 km (9 miles) down the coast stood their fortress Ag. Nikitas, known today as **Frangokastello,** built in 1317, and used mainly to keep the Cretans under control. During the War of Independence a great massacre took place there. An Epirot insurgent, Khatzimichalis Dalianis, held Frangokastello with 650 Cretans until 8000 Turkish troops arrived to force them out. The Turks took the fort, and all of the Greeks inside were slain, including Dalianis although groups of Cretans who had remained outside the fort quickly recaptured it. Meanwhile other Cretan chieftains captured the mountain passes and caused havoc when the remainder of the Turkish army turned to the north, seizing guns and much needed supplies.

This event, the Massacre of Frangokastello, has given rise to the most authenticated of the million or so Greek ghost stories that exist. On 17 May, the anniversary of the massacre, the phantoms of the Cretan dead rise up at dawn, fully armed, and march silently towards the fortress to disappear into the sea. These are the famous Drosoulites, the "dew shades", still ready to fight the enemy Turk. They have been seen so often that scientific explanations have been attempted, although as yet none has proved satisfactory. A less spooky paneyeri of the Virgin takes place at Frangokastello on 15 August.

WHERE TO STAY

There are quite a few places to stay in the main centres here, especially in Ag. Roumeli, Chora, Sfakion and Paliochora. Unfortunately, in the first two places the word "rip-off" is all too often heard, especially since the gorge has become so popular. In Ag. Roumeli there are several restaurant-pension combos, like **Tara** (tel. 0825 29 391) which charges about 3500 dr. for a double. You may do better in Chora Sfakion, where there's more choice; some average Class C hotels, and the long established **Xenia,** a class B pension (tel. 0825 91 202) located on the dour quay, with doubles about 4000 dr. More friendly, less expensive, and run by an English speaking lady is the **Pension Sofia,** next to the supermarket near the waterfront. In Paliochora there are a large number of rooms built especially for tourists, and the pleasant class D **Livykon Hotel** at the top of Venizelou Street (tel. 0823 41 250). Doubles are around 2500 dr. If the above towns are crowded—and they do get crowded—consider hopping in one of the many little ferry boats that ply the southern coast to Loutro (connections from Chora Sfakion and Ag. Roumeli) where there's a little clump of inexpensive pensions, or to Sougia (boat from Paliochora), where the rooms are even cheaper and quieter. There's also a taverna that rents rooms at Frangokastello.

EATING OUT

There honestly isn't anything very special along the coast; after a trek through the gorge you may just be happy for anything Ag. Roumeli can produce at whatever price. In Chora Sfakion ask around for the current favourite; in Paliochora try the **Dionysios Taverna,** where you can eat well for about 700 dr.—including wine.

North of Frangokastello one finds the village of **Asfendos** among the trees, with a brook of roaring water; **Askyfou,**the village with the ravine that spelt doom to enemy armies trapped inside; and pretty little **Asigonia,** with a large paneyeri on 23 August at the church of Ag. Georgios, a site surrounded by plane trees and springs. Mountain villages such as these are rarely visited by foreign tourists, and are ideal for those who want to experience Cretan rural life. Closer to civilisation is **Alikampos,** whose frescoed Church of the Virgin (1315) celebrates on 15 August.

Georgioupolis east of Chania was named in honour of Prince George and has a long sandy beach, part of the stretch which extends intermittently all the way to Rethymnon and is a favourite area for hotel builders, although you can still find cheap rooms to rent around the village. Many people who stay there return year after year, which speaks well for the place. Hundreds of eucalyptus trees provide welcome shade, and a fresh stream flows into the sea in the centre of the village. In the nearby village of **Mathe** is the church of Ag. Antonios with a carob tree for its roof.

Crete's only lake, **Lake Kournas,** is near here, deep and eerie and full of eels. Inland, **Vryses,** though on the main road, has retained much of its shady charm, interspersed with busts of heroic, grandly moustachioed Cretans. Locals come

81

here to picnic and swim in its creek. In the Evangelistria church of **Fre** an icon works wonders, and a large paneyeri is held on 25 March. **Neo Chorio** with its vast citrus orchards has a paneyeri on the Sunday following Easter Sunday, and there are a few remains of ancient habitations. Most, however, will find a detour to **Kokkino Chora,** on Cape Drapanon, more rewarding for its scenery and beaches, and the village that was selected as the location for the film *Zorba the Greek* although it seems too bright in summer; for the brooding, overcast atmosphere portrayed on celluloid you must come to Kokkino Chora in the winter.

West of Kokkino Chora is **Kalyves** with a long beach, near the fortress Apokorona, built by the Genoese before they turned Crete over to the Venetians.

In the heart of the nomos of Chania some of the best oranges in Crete are grown—and Cretan oranges have a reputation for being the best in the world. **Fournes** claims to have more than 120 000 orange trees; it also boasts the Cave of the Pig, and has a large paneyeri to Ag. Panteleimon on 27 July. At **Alikianou** the wedding massacre of Kantanoleo's Cretans took place, at the Venetian tower of Da Molin. Besides more bright green orange groves, Alikianou has a church of Ag. Georgiou (1243) with exceptional frescoes. Another orange-growing village, **Meskla,** is a lovely little place. One church has mosaics from a temple of Aphrodite, left by the ancient city of Rizinia; another, the Transfiguration of the Saviour, has lovely frescoes dating back to 1303. Byzantine frescoes can also be seen in the church of Christ the Saviour. **Lakoi** is yet another picturesque village, situated on a mountainside near the Plain of Omalos.

Beside these villages runs the majestic Therisson ravine, traversed by a road. It is known in Cretan history for the 1905 Revolution of Therisso, when the Cretans rose for union with Greece. Prassa to the west has a smaller ravine beside it and unusual rock formations and caves.

Rethymnon

Rethymnon, Crete's third city, and according to many, its most charming, has long bemoaned its lack of a proper harbour. The Venetians dug one, but even now it keeps silting up. But in several ways this has proved a blessing, for much of what passes for progress has passed Rethymnon by. Like Chania it is a National Historical Landmark, noted for its Venetian architecture, but one that suffered far less Nazi bombing. Two minarets lend the skyline an exotic touch; wooden balconies, remnants of the Turkish occupation, project overhead, darkening the already narrow streets. This medieval atmosphere and the long stretch of sandy beach in front of the town are Rethymnon's major attractions.

The modern city was built over ancient Rithymna, a Classical city, though the discovery of Late Minoan tombs indicate even earlier inhabitants. A fortress was built where the ancient akropolis stood, and the Venetians reinforced it with a further wall upon their arrival. Below, by the sea, the town began to grow unprotected. However, its relative isolation attracted many of the scholars who

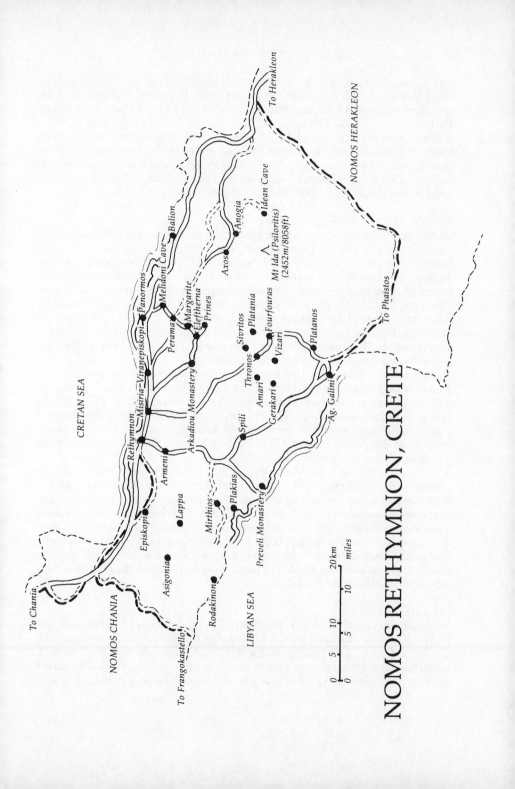

NOMOS RETHYMNON, CRETE

CRETAN SEA

To Chania

NOMOS CHANIA

To Frangokastello

LIBYAN SEA

Episkopi

Asigonia

Rodakinon

Lappa

Mirthios

Plakias

Preveli Monastery

Armeni

Rethymnon

Misiria—Viranepiskopi

Perama

Panormos

Melidoni Cave

Balion

Margarite

Eleftherna

Prines

Arkadiou Monastery

Spili

Gerakari

Amari

Thronos

Sivritos

Platania

Vizari

Fourfouras

Axos

Anogia

Idean Cave

Mt Ida (Psiloritis)
(2452m/8058ft)

Platanos

Ag. Galini

To Phaistos

NOMOS HERAKLEON

To Herakleon

20 km
miles

0   5   10   20 km
0   5   10   miles

fled Constantinople, giving Rethymnon a reputation for intellectual activity which it retains to this day. It was three times raided by pirates, beginning with the wily Barbarossa in 1538, and followed by Uluch Ali in 1562 and 1571, when Rethymnon was burnt. The Venetians finally decided something should be done, and walled in the city. They also built the Fortezza, one of the best-preserved Venetian castles in Greece, although it was captured by the Turks in 1645. For a vivid account of Rethymnon as it existed under the Turks at Independence and during the exchange of populations read *The Tale of a Town* by Pandelis Prevelakis, a native son. (The English translation can be found in the city.)

WHAT TO SEE IN RETHYMNON
All that remains of the city wall is the **Goora,** the grand gate that leads into the old city off the Plateia of the Four Martyrs, honouring four young men who were beheaded by the Turks. Note the 17th-century **Rimondi Fountain,** a quaint architectural hodgepodge at the junction of several main streets, nearby on the corner of Arkadio and Petihaki Sts, the **Archaeology Museum** is located in the Venetian Loggia, or military club, built around 1600. Inside are Neolithic items from Amari cave, Late Minoan pottery, etc. Ornate Turkish headstones lie scattered about the yard. For a good view over Rethymnon, climb the minaret of the **Neradzes Mosque,** on Manouli Vernadou St. Built in the 18th century, the mosque is now used for musical programmes.

Rethymnon's waterfront has inevitably been given over to the tourist trade. Restaurants line the beach and the old Venetian harbour, where they specialise in fish. From here you may consider a trip to the **Fortezza,** built in 1574, with its fine view of the town and sea. The best preserved building within the powerful walls is the mosque; otherwise there is a wonderfully deserted air about the place, inducive to just poking around. (Built by forced labour, then surrendered by the Venetians, it has never really been loved.)

In the new part of town, the city park has been made over the old Turkish cemetery. A bit dishevelled, it contains a small zoo, where one unhappy kri kri, forced to share quarters with the peacocks, hides in his little den; however, it will probably be the only one you'll see. The Cretan Wine Festival and Handicrafts Exhibition takes place here for two weeks in mid-July. Also in the new part of Town, on Leoforos Koundouri is the little glass **National Tourist Office,** still run single-handed by the indefatigable Kostas Palierakis, who loves his town dearly, and who is on the whole five times more helpful than the people in most other tourist offices in Greece.

WHERE TO STAY
Within the city itself the **Hotel Brascos,** at Ch. Daskalaki and Th. Moatsou (tel. 0831 23 721), is slick and clean and charges its full class B rates—around 7500 dr. for a double. On a more reasonable level, there are two good class E establishments; for cleanliness and an excellent bathroom, the **Hotel Paradisos** at 35 Ig. Gavril (tel. 0831 22 419) is a good deal at 1400 dr. a single, 2200 dr. a

double, showers extra. For former elegance and a view of the harbour from the balcony, the **Hotel Achillion,** at 151 Arkadiou (tel. 0831 22 581) offers more in the way of atmosphere (and noise at night). For peace and quiet, **Zorba's** is reasonably priced and located at the east end of the beach; expect to pay about 2000 dr. a person for the private shower and WC (tel. 0831 28 540). Before trekking out there, give them a ring to see if there's a vacancy. The **Youth hostel** is exceptionally nice and convenient, only a few blocks from the tourist office at 7 Pavlou Vlastou (tel. 0831 22 848). You don't need a card to stay there; breakfast and cooking facilities are available. Rates are 390 dr. a person, showers extra.

Just outside Rethymnon in Adele (6.5 km/4 miles) is the very popular (especially with American families) class A **Rethymnon Beach Hotel** and **Bungalows** on a lovely beach (tel. 0831 29 491). It fills up early in the spring and stays that way, so book early. Rates are 15 000 dr. upwards a night in season for a double, and the bungalows reach the giddy heights of 20 000 dr. a day.

A couple of miles east of Rethymnon there are two neighbouring campsites, **Elizabeth** (tel. 0831 28 694) and **Arkadia Campings** (tel. 0831 22 361).

EATING OUT
The trendy place to eat, with its tiny fish restaurants is the Venetian harbour, but expect to pay at least 2000 dr. for the privilege (though the quality and variety is excellent). Cheaper food can be had along the beachfront, including pizza (the **Parthenon** is good in this respect). On the west side of the Fortezza, all by itself, is the **Sunset Taverna,** with good solid Greek food (about 600 dr. a person for kalamari, salad, chips and retsina) and a view of you know what, as well as of the numerous cranes that frequent the shore. For something different, try **Famagusta** on Nikalou Plastira, a moderately priced eatery specialising in Cypriot dishes. To hear traditional music, seek out the little place on Koronaiou Street near the church of the Mikri Panayias; if it has a name, no one remembers it.

TOURIST INFORMATION
NTOG, L. Venizelou, tel. (0831) 29 148.
Tourist police, Rethymnon, 52 Vass. Georgiou, tel. (0831) 28 156.

Nomos of Rethymnon

The **nomos of Rethymnon** is rugged, dominated in the east by Mt Ida, or Psiloritis (2456 metres/8058 ft); several paths lead to its summit and to its sacred cave, one of two on Crete sacred to Zeus. Also here are Crete's two famous fortress-monasteries, Preveli and Arkadiou. In the south are several undeveloped beaches, as well as everyone's favourite fishing village, Ag. Galini.

A small road south of Episkopi leads to the ancient city of **Lappa,** also called Phoenix in the past, and Lambe during the Byzantine period. Ruins remain dating from the still standing Classical wall. To the tiny southern village of

Rodakinon ("the village of the peach") the only public transport is from Frangokastello in nomos Chania. Rodakinon has a lovely beach and caves where you can shelter from the hot sun.

Further east along the coast of the Libyan Sea is the village of **Plakias,** near another lovely beach. Plakias is a little more ready for tourists than Rodakinon, with more accommodation of every type added each year. From Plakias it's a four-hour walk to **Preveli Monastery;** alternatively, back-track along the road.

Beautifully situated between the coast and Kouraliotiko ravine, this 17th-century monastery was a great resistance centre during the Turkish and German occupations. In gratitude for its assistance to the Allies in 1941, the British gave Preveli two silver candlesticks and a marble plaque in gratitude to the monastery and to surrounding villages for sheltering Allied soldiers from the Nazis until they could be picked up by submarine and taken to Egypt. Preveli's paneyeri takes place on 8 May.

Another route south of Rethymnon leads to **Armeni,** where a Late Minoan cemetery has been discovered. Almost the entire Armeni population between the ages of 20 and 40 works in Germany now. **Spili** is a large mountain village on the way south. It is known for its greenery and has a long fountain of 17 lion heads, built by the Venetians. The town's churches celebrate paneyeria on 29 June and 27 May. South of Spili the road leads to **Ag. Galini,** its jumble of houses spilling down the hill, a picturesque fishing village that now does most of its fishing for the tourists. The beach isn't all that good, but some of the best cooks in Crete work in the numerous restaurants here.

On the west slopes of Mt Ida in the heart of the nomos is a group of small villages famed for their resistance. Beautiful **Gerakari,** east of Spili, stood unconquered under Venetian, Turkish and German occupations, and has many houses from the Middle Ages, along with a tower. At **Amari,** the capital of the province, the church Asomatos has the oldest dated frescoes in Crete, from 1225. The nearby monastery also has frescoes, and an agricultural college. Two ancient towns are near the village of **Thronos: Vene,** founded by Ptolemy and **Sivritos,** destroyed by the Saracens in the 9th century. A remarkable amount of their walls remains and Sivritos even retains a gateway, **Vizari** to the south was built beside a later Roman settlement and among the ruins are a mosaic floor and part of an Early Christian basilica. From **Fourfouras** village a shale path leads up to one of the peaks of Mt Ida, a five-hour trip in good walking shoes. There is a little chapel and well on top, as well as an unforgettable view of Crete. Another ascent can be made from **Platania** to the Cave of Pan (two hours).

North of these villages, on a good road from Rethymnon, lies the **Arkadiou Monastery,** founded in the 11th century, although the present building dates from the 17th century. The decorative façade (pictured on the 100-drachma note), however, is from 1587. Even so, Arkadiou resembles a small fort rather than a religious building, which is perhaps why the rebel Koroneos used it to hide his powder magazine, and why surrounding villagers took refuge there. On 7 November 1866, the Turks under Mustafa Kyrtil Pasha attacked Arkadiou. After a two-day siege they had begun to enter the monastery when the Abbot Gaberiel had it blown up rather than surrender, killing 829 people, both Cretan and Turkish. The event caused a furore in Europe, and many influential writers, Swinburne and Hugo among them, took up the cause of Cretan independence. At the monastery one can visit the Gunpowder Room, where Giambudakis fired the shot that exploded the powder, and three rooms of relics, which include the skulls of the martyrs in an old windmill. The heroic event is celebrated every year on 8 and 9 November at the monastery. There is also a tourist pavilion at Arkadiou and a small hotel.

Viranepiskopi is on the north coast and possesses two churches of interest: a 10th century basilica near a sanctuary of Artemis, and a 16th century Italian church. The area is popular for camping. **Panormos** to the east is by the mouth of the Milopotamos river and the fortress Castelli of Milopotamos, built by the Genoese in 1206, but taken by the Venetians only six years later. Also in Panormos are the ruins of a 5th century basilica. Further east, **Balion** is a quiet fishing village that has just built its first hotel, the Bali Beach. Just south of Perama, **Melidoni cave** is another of Crete's famous grottoes, this one quite large, so large that mythographers have made it the residence of Talos, a bronze giant with a bull's head, given by Zeus to Minos to guard the coasts of Crete. Talos ran around the island three times each day, flinging boulders at foreign ships. It was also his duty to visit all the towns of Crete with tablets bearing Minos' laws, until Medea slew him by removing a pin from his heel, draining away all his blood. In the same cave, 270 women and children took refuge in 1824 during the War of Independence. When the Turk Houssein discovered their refuge, he smoked them to death.

From Perama another road leads to **Margarite** with its thriving pottery industry and Maranthospilios cave and ancient **Eleftherna,** dating from the Classical period and inhabited into the Byzantine age. Ruins of the walls, the akropolis, a bridge, a Byzantine tower, and huge Roman cisterns remain, the latter handy in times of siege. Eleftherna is built on a plateau and supplied by water from the Milopotamos river. Higher and more precipitous is ancient **Axos,** of which the akropolis walls, dating from the 8th century BC, remain.

Near Axos is **Anogia,** a major resistance centre, which was burned by both the Turks and the Germans, the latter in reprisal for the famous kidnapping of General Kriepe, who was hidden for a while in the village by the Resistance. Today it produces some of Crete's finest woven cloth, with 700 traditional patterns in all, and also Crete's best raki, ouzo's stronger cousin, also known as *tsikoutha*. Recently Anogia has taken advantage of its weaving traditions to become a "typical" village for package tour excursions. From Anogia a path leads to the **Idean cave,** where Zeus lived as a young man before dethroning his father Cronus, although some say he was born there. At any rate the Idean cave was very sacred in antiquity, a cult centre that preserved remnants of Minoan religion into Classical times. Pythagoras was initiated into its mysteries; Robert Graves, for one, believed it was the source of his mystical theories on numbers.

An ascent to the summit of **Mount Ida** can be made from Anogia, taking more than 12 hours. Other approaches begin from nomos **Herakleon,** in the east.

WHERE TO STAY
Ag. Galini is packed with all sorts of accommodation and if you arrive in the summer without a reservation, you'll very likely find them packed with people, especially package tourists. In town the best value is the **Pantheon,** with private baths, located at Kountouriotou (tel. 0842 91 293), doubles cost about 2000 dr. There are a number of pensions on the roads leading into Ag. Galini and the **Hotel Minos,** class D (tel. 0842 91 218), where a double with a good view costs 2500 dr. In Plakias there are rooms to rent and a youth hostel (tel. 0832 31 202): ditto at Mythios. Beds in the hostels are about 400 dr. a night, and neither demands a card. In Spili, that verdant oasis in the centre of the province, there's the wonderful **Green Hotel** (tel. 0832 22 225) run by some friendly relatives of Kostas Palierakis in Rethymnon's NTOG office. The hotel—a class C—is bedecked with flowers and plants and costs about 3500 dr. a night for a double.

EATING OUT
In Ag. Galini the restaurants cluster around Vassili Ioannis St, where you can test the local chefs' reputations—before sitting down, be sure to check prices. Elsewhere the food is typical.

Herakleon

Herakleon (also Iraklion among other spelling variations), Crete's capital and Greece's fifth largest city, with a population nearing 120 000, holds little charm for most visitors. It's all very urban and much is new—which in Greece translates as lots of concrete—and the centre especially is full of the noisy hustle and bustle that most foreigners come to the Greek islands to get away from at home. However, nearly everyone visiting Crete ends up here at least once, for not only is Herakleon the central point for transport in Crete, with its busy international port and airport, but it also has the world's greatest collection of Minoan artefacts in its museum, and the grand palace of Knossos in its suburbs. The Venetians too have left their mark, with some of Crete's finest public buildings and churches.

History

Herakleon was used as one of Knossos' two ports into the Roman era. The invading Saracens built a new town over it and called it "Kandak" for the moat they dug around its walls. As their base of piracy, Kandak also became a leading slave trade centre for the world. When Nikephoros Phokas liberated Crete in 961, the Byzantines called Kandak "Kandax". This turned into Candia or Candy when the Venetians made the town their Cretan capital in 1210, and the whole

88

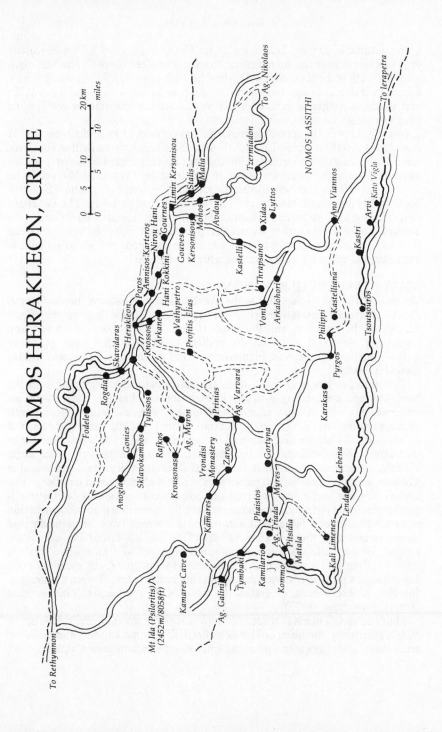

NOMOS HERAKLEON, CRETE

To Rethymnon

Mt Ida (Psiloritis)/\
(2452m/8058ft)

Kamares Cave

Ag. Galini

Fodele

Rogdia

Skavidaras

Herakleon

Knossos

Anogia

Gonies

Sklavokambos

Tylissos

Rafkos

Krousonas

Ag. Myron

Vrondisi Monastery

Zaros

Kamares

Prinias

Ag. Varvara

Arkane

Hani Kokkini

Vathypetro

Profitis Elias

Paros

Amnisos Karteros

Nirou Hani

Gournes

Limin Kersonisou

Stalis

Malia

Gouves

Kersonisou

Mohos

Avdou

Tzermiadon

Xidas

Lyttos

To Ag. Nikolaos

Kastelli

Thrapsano

Voni

Arkalohori

Kastelliana

Philippi

Pyrgos

Karakas

Gortyna

Phaistos

Ag. Triada

Myres

Pitsidia

Kamilario

Kommo

Matala

Tymbaki

Lebena

Lenda

Kali Limenes

Ano Viannos

Kastri

Arvi

Kato Vigla

Tsoutsouros

To Ierapetra

NOMOS LASSITHI

20 km

miles

0   5   10
0   10

island became known as Candia or Candy. The Greeks called it Megalo Kastro, or just Kastro, after the huge fortifications constructed there by the Venetians from the 15th to 17th centuries. During the 16th century Michele Sammicheli, the greatest defence expert of his era, worked on Candia's walls and the city, the seat of the Venetian-appointed Duke of Crete, became one of the leading Mediterranean sea ports.

In a tribute to Sammicheli's genius, the Turkish siege of Candia lasted for 21 years, from 1648 to 1669. Louis XIV sent the French to assist the Venetians towards the end of the struggle although the venture ended in disaster for his forces. By the time Francesco Morosini (uncle of the Francesco Morosini who blew the top off the Parthenon) surrendered the city to the Turks on 5 September, 30 000 Christian defenders and 117 000 Turks had perished. The Venetians were allowed to leave in safety. Candia remained the capital of Crete under the Turks until 1850 when they transferred it to Chania. After independence the Greeks rechristened the city Herakleon, and it was made the island's administrative capital when Crete was united with Greece.

WHAT TO SEE IN HERAKLEON

On the top of everyone's list is the **Archaeology Museum,** in the central Plateia Eleftheria. By law every important archaeological find on the island belongs to the museum, and the result is that the collection is both vast and fascinating. As usual, to avoid the endless flood of guided tours get, here early—the doors open at 8 am in the summer and at 9 am from November to May (closed Mondays).

The museum has been laid out in chronological order beginning with the Neolithic Age and ending with the Roman period, although it's the Minoan collection in between that is most fascinating, with its delicate beauty and intricate craftsmanship, the famous Kamares ware vases, the snake goddess, and the mysterious Phaistos disc, believed by some to be the world's first example of moveable type, although no one has been able to translate the script's language. There are examples of Linear A and Linear B scripts, the game board found at Knossos, models of towns and palaces, exquisite seal stones and jewellery. The famous frescoes and painted sarcophagus are upstairs; almost as fascinating as the paintings themselves is the amount of work that went into their reconstruction by two Swiss artists, father and son, called Gillieron. Note in particular the border surrounding the well-known fresco of the Bull leapers, or Toreadors: it is a ritual Minoan calendar, its vari-coloured markings and moon-like symbols corresponding very accurately to the lunar and solar cycles. An excellent book that details its meaning, as well as deciphering much of the Minoan culture and thought, is *The Thread of Ariadne* by Charles F. Herberger (Philosophical Library, New York, 1972).

The **National Tourist Office** is directly across the street from the museum in Plateia Eleftheria, the heart of Herakleon, where evening strollers mingle in the many cafés, sweetshops and pizzerias amid monuments to great Cretans.

Daedalou St leads from the Plateia Eleftheria to Herakleon's other main square, Venizelou. In the centre water trickles (usually) from the lions of the **Morosini Fountain,** commissioned in 1626 by the then Venetian governor. Here also stands San Marco, the first church built by the Venetians in Herakleon, now used as a concert hall and permanent exhibition hall housing reproductions of Crete's best Byzantine frescoes (so if you can't get into any of the churches, you can at least get an idea of what you're missing). Also here, at the top of 25 Augostou St, is the reconstruction of the lovely **Venetian Loggia,** originally built in the 1620s. On one side of the Loggia you can see what remains of the Sagredo Fountain, with its figure of a woman representing Crete, on the other side, the old Venetian Armeria now bristles with local politicians instead of weapons in its role as Herakleon's city hall.

Next to it, set back in its own square, is the **Church of St Titus,** founded in the Byzantine era and reconstructed after various earthquakes, used by the Turks as a mosque and by the Cretans to house the head of their patron saint, Titus. He is credited with converting the island to Christianity, and received one of the Epistles from St Paul. When the Venetians gave up Crete, they took Titus' skull, the island's most precious relic, and only returned it in 1966. As well as an atmospheric interior, St Titus' from the outside has a marvellous simplicity and grace in its fine old stone.

The street named 25 Augostou leads straight down to Herakleon's port, and is lined with ticket agencies, car rental shops, banks, etc. Along the waterfront here stand the great arches of the restored **Venetian Arsenali.** In the nearby square one of Crete's most revered heroes met a cruel end. Called Daskaloyiannis, or "John the teacher", he led the major revolt against the Turks in 1770, believing that the Russians intended to assist his cause. The Russians never appeared, and in order to save the rest of his men, Daskaloyiannis surrendered to the Turks and was publicly flayed to death. The event inspired one of the island's best known popular poems, "The Song of Daskaloyiannis".

Out on the harbour mole is the Venetian fortress **Rocco al Mare** (16th century), recently restored to its original condition and guarded by the Lion of St Mark. For a small fee you can explore the interior (open daily 8 am–3 pm).

From here you can stroll west along the coast past the Xenia Hotel to the **Historical Museum of Crete,** in a mansion once belonging to the Kalakairinou family. Inside is a variety of items from Roman times to the present, notably the fine Venetian and traditional arts, and the reconstructed library of modern Herakleon's most famous son, Nikos Kazanzakis.

Also in central Herakleon, south of Plateia Venizelou, 1866 St is the home of the city's busy outdoor market, and the narrow alleys are crowded with in-expensive restaurants. At one end of the market, in Kornarou Sq, are two old fountains, Venetian and Turkish. Take Karterou St from here to Herakleon's elephantine 19th-century cathedral dedicated to the city's patron saint, **Ag. Minas.** Just below the cathedral is an older, smaller church with a more in-teresting interior. Even better is **Ag. Katerina** (1555), in the same square. Used

A Minoan Bull's Head found at Knossos

today to display an impressive collection of Cretan–Byzantine art, Ag. Katerina once housed a famous school, and some believe El Greco studied there before leaving for Venice. The museum's pride and joy are six icons by Mikalis Damaskinos, the 16th-century contemporary of El Greco who also went to Venice but returned to Crete to adorn his motherland with his Renaissance–Byzantine icons.

Massive and unavoidable are the great **Venetian walls** which Sammicheli built around the old city. Restored to a wonderful degree, they are nearly as vexing to attain today as they were for the besieging Turks—4000 metres (14 000 ft) in their total length, in places 14 metres (45 ft) thick, with 12 fort-like bastions. Tunnels have been dug through the old gates, though the **Chania Gate** at the end of Leoforos Kalokairnou preserves much of its original character. The only place where you can successfully gain access to the walls is by the Bastion St Antonio, from where you can walk south to the Martinengo Bastion and the tomb of Nikos Kazanzakis. This great Cretan writer, who died in 1957, had inscribed on his tombstone: "I believe in nothing, I hope for nothing, I am free." Perhaps some of his ancestors shared his sentiments, for from his tomb you can make out Mt Iouktas in the distance—the burial place of Zeus. See if you can make out the god's profile in the shape of the mountain.

Knossos

Knossos may be reached by city bus from Herakleon (no. 2, every 15 minutes, begins at the harbour and passes through Plateia Venizelou). The site is open daily except for important holidays, from 8 am to 7 pm (8 am to 5 pm in winter). Again, to avoid the crowds, come early, there are rooms to rent near the site, as well as restaurants and cafés.

"Knossos, a mighty city", wrote Homer in the *Odyssey*, "where Minos was king for nine years, a familiar of mighty Zeus." The chronology of the spot is quickly told: remains indicate that the first inhabitants of Knossos came during the 7th millennium BC. Circa 1950 BC they built a palace, which fell down in the earthquake of 1700. Construction of a new palace followed, and it is the remains of this that one sees today. In 1400 BC it was destroyed by a great fire. The inhabitants at the time were probably Mycenaean, as shown by the finds of Linear B tablets. The lack of later construction on the immediate palace site and the discovery of coins depicting the Minotaur are thought to prove the subsequent sanctity of the spot as the ancient Labyrinth.

After the destruction of the palace, a Geometric community flourished which was to become one of the leading cities of Crete in the 3rd century BC, although following a war with Lyttos it lost its supremacy to Gortyna. The Romans built a large city in the area, and habitation here continued until the early Byzantine period. The bishop of Knossos is mentioned in the annals of the church. Afterwards Knossos lay abandoned, but not forgotten. It seems that its location was never a mystery, although the discovery and excavation of its Minoan past had to wait until Heinrich Schliemann electrified the world with his excavations of Troy and Mycenae. In 1878 a merchant from Herakleon named Minos Kalokairinos dug the first trenches, at once striking part of the palace and uncovering the first known Linear B tablet, which he showed to Sir Arthur Evans in 1894. Evans, excited by what he saw, negotiated for the property (something Schliemann himself attempted to do unsuccessfully) and began excavations in March 1900.

Evans thought at first that he was excavating a Mycenaean site, then to his astonishment realised he had found something far older—a whole civilisation right out of the myths of the ancient Cretans. It was one of history's great archaeological discoveries, and Evans took it upon himself to try to reconstruct what he could of Minos' palace. In recent years scholars have bitterly disagreed on the accuracy of these reconstructions and on the various names Evans chose for the different chambers and courts of Knossos, but to the casual visitor they are quite extraordinary, and give one a sense of a Middle Minoan palace circa 700 BC that none of the other, unreconstructed sites can hope to achieve.

Space doesn't permit a detailed description of Knossos, although there are several guides for sale at the excavations (try to find that of J. D. S. Pendlebury). The excavations at Knossos are entered by the west court of the palace. If one continues directly to the left, one finds the oldest road in Europe, the Royal Road, which leads to the so-called Little Palace. At the head of it stands the "theatre"— perhaps used to view religious processions (it looks more like a large stairway). To the right of the west court is a porch leading to the Corridor of the Procession and the Propylaeum, south entrance, of the palace with frescos on the wall. A staircase from the Propylaeum leads to an upper floor, some of the rooms of which are used for storage a descending staircase brings one to the Throne Room and Lustral Basin believed to have held water used in rituals. Unfortunately wear and tear by so many visitors has made it necessary to rope off the stone throne so that you can no longer sit where Minos sat in 1400 BC (though if you're elected judge of the Court of International Justice in The Hague you may sit on its reproduction). Evans found evidence in the Throne Room of a last-ditch effort, perhaps by the King himself, to placate the gods as disaster swept through Knossos. From the large central court back up the stairs one can enter a series of rooms which include huge storage pithois and rooms with their frescoes recopied on the walls. On the north side of the palace one sees the brightly painted charging bull. As is the case throughout Knossos, the columns are peculiar to Minoan architecture, thickening at the top. These are thought to be in imitation of a certain cyprus tree native to the gorge of Samaria.

On the east side of the palace one can see the huge pithoi from the first palace, and the excellent water system that supplied Knossos, also visible under the floor in the Queen's Megaron and its bathroom, complete with a flush toilet. Also in this area are the upper and main Halls of the Double Axes, the Grand stairway, the Corridor of the Draught-board, the separate House of the Chancel Screen and others, most labelled in English. A path to the south leads to the House of the High Priest and the Royal Temple tomb, although these can only be visited with special authorisation. The same is true of the Little Palace across the road, though not of the Caravanserai, where travelling caravans could spend the night. This lies up the main road, across the ravine.

It is intriguing to speculate on exactly how the Minoans lived at Knossos, and how the myths of Minos, Ariadne, the Minotaur and the Labyrinth grew up. Many believe they describe Minoan religious rituals: that Ariadne was the Great Goddess, the Moon Goddess of the snakes, and that Minos (a title like that of Pharaoh) was her consort, a sacred sun king, who ruled a prescribed number of years before his sacrifice. The word "labyrinth" comes from the ancient word *labrys*, or "Double Axe", and means "House of the Double Axe". The double axe, a symbol seen throughout Knossos, would kill both the victim and slayer; among other things, the Labyrinth was the descent into the underworld, from which only an exceptional hero (like Theseus) could emerge alive, "reborn". The maze story may also have been suggested by the complicated spiral dance, described by Homer in the *Iliad*, "a dancing floor like that which Daedalus once fashioned in spacious Knossos for Ariadne of the lovely hair", a fertility dance that culminated in the acrobatic bull leaping. The Minotaur, or "Bull of Minos", is thought to have been the form the king would take in his ritual matings with the Moon Goddess, since Pasiphaë, means "the shining one", or moon, and was herself disguised as a cow.

Amnisos (take bus no. 1 from Plateia Eleftheria) was the harbour of Minoan Knossos, and ruins remain from that period as well as from the Archaic (the sanctuary of Zeus Thenatas). Fom here Idomeneus and his 90 ships set sail for Troy. In a more recent vein, here Greek archaeologist Spyridon Marinatos discovered pumice flung from Santorini's volcano, evidence that led him to formulate his well known theory on Knossos' untimely demise (see **Santorini**).

Within walking distance, up the Episkopi road, is the *Cave of Eileithia*, the protectress of childbirth. Sacred even among the early Minoans, this cave held many Minoan ritual objects; for the modern visitor it holds a fair crop of stalactites. Amnisos is the closest beach to Herakleon, if not the cleanest. Tidier strands may be found at **Hani Kokkini**. Large hotels dot sandy beaches along the coast east to Malia.

PANEYERIA
Herakleon Flower Festival 2–6 June; grape Festival 11–19 September; and a huge paneyeri for the patron saint Ag. Minas on 11 November.

WHERE TO STAY
Convenient for the archaeological museum and other sights in the central city, yet located on the quiet (well, traffic-less) pedestrians-only Daedaluo Street, is the **Hotel Daedalos** (tel. 081 22 43 91), a spacious class C establishment with 115 beds, and paintings by local artists in the lobby. Otherwise it's plain and modern; doubles with bath cost 4500 dr. and breakfast is available. Also near the museum is the imposing **Atlantis Hotel,** an A class with imposing prices to match. Reckon 12 000 dr. for a double (tel. 081 22 91 03). The quiet **Hotel Rea** near the sea at Kalimeraki St (tel. 081 22 36 38), is much lower on the price scale at 2200 dr. for a double. There's also a large number of pensions scattered all over the city and a **Youth hostel** of so-so quality at 24 Chandakos (tel. 081 22 29 47). You don't need a card but there's a curfew and you can't be in the building between 10 am and 1.30 pm. There's also a rather notoriously bizarre option if you're in the mood; the class E **Hotel Chania,** run by a certain George who has covered the walls with murals and planted mannequins in the recesses. Prices are low—around 700–1000 dr. a head; the address is 19 Kydonias St (tel. 081 28 42 82), but be prepared to deal with Mr Thiakakis' whims. Five km west of town is an A class campsite with all modern facilities (tel. 081 25 09 86).

EATING OUT
The **Glasshouse** on the quay near the Xenia hotel has long been a fashionable place to eat among the locals and prices are accordingly expensive, as are the restaurants near the fountain, one of which is Italian and quite good, but pricey. Increasingly popular are the ten or so tavernas along Fotiou ("Dirty") Lane between Odos 1866 and Evans Street, all jammed together in the narrow confines, and all offering your basic Greek cuisine and grilled meats at moderate prices (700–1000 dr. for a dinner). If you've a hankering for fish, **Ta Psaria** at the foot of 25 Augustou Street has it at reasonable prices (for fish, anyway) and there's seating outside, if you don't mind the constant hum of traffic. Herakleon is awash with pizzarias, especially around Plateia Eleftherias and Daedaluo Street. In the latter the **Victoria Pizza Café** certainly has the widest variety of pies—22 kinds, no less, averaging out at 600 dr. Less expensive, and a real oasis if you can no longer stand the sight of mousaka is the **Curry House** near Daedaluo

Street off Perdikari Street, featuring several curry specialities daily at around 500 dr. a dish. There's also a respectable Chinese restaurant in the same area.

TOURIST INFORMATION
NTOG, 1 Xanthoudidou St, across from the archaeology museum tel. (081) 22 24 87

TOURIST POLICE
Dikeosinis St, tel. (081) 28 31 90.

Nomos of Herakleon

There are four **bus stations** in Herakleon. From the harbour station just below the city walls buses depart for destinations along the north coast as far as Vai, and to Ierapetra and the Lassithi Plateau; from outside the Chania Gate the buses cover all other destinations in the nomos; from the Evans Gate buses head to Ano Vianos, Myrtos and Thrapsano; from the west side of the harbour near the Xenia Hotel, buses go to Rethymnon and Chania. The nomos of Herakleon has not only most of Crete's Minoan sites, but also its ancient Roman capital Gortyna and once notorious Matala Beach, on the south coast.

West of Herakleon, along the road to Rethymnon, is the village of **Rogdia**, with a Venetian fort, Kastro of Rogdia, located by the shore **Fodele**, further north, is considered the birthplace of El Greco, although there isn't much to see beyond a monument sent in his honour by the University of Valladolid. To the south of it lies the **Minoan Tylissos** by a pretty village of the same name. There are three large villas from the Late Minoan period, destroyed in 1400 BC. These can be seen throughout the day for a small fee. There is another Minoan country house at **Sklavokambos** along the road towards Gonies **Ag. Myron** is a large village south of Tylissos with paneyeri on 8 August. Ancient **Rafkos** with scanty ruins is to the north; **Krousonas**, a small village in the afternoon shadow of Mt Ida, celebrates Ag. Charalambos' Day with a big fete on 10 February.

Prinias further south has the ruins of ancient Ryzenia on its akropolis with two Archaic temples and a later Hellenistic fort. In **Ag. Varvara** a large rock to one side of the village is said to mark the centre of Crete, its "omphalos", or navel, and a road leads to **Kamares,** from whence one can climb to the Kamares cave on Mt Ida. The cave is famous for the discovery of fine Minoan pottery there, called Kamares ware. By mule the trip takes four hours and one can travel all the way to the top of Mt Ida from Kamares in ten hours. (For information on the Hellenic Alpine Club shelter, see **Sports,** page 32/33.)

Vrondisi Monastery lies on the same road, just before Kamares. Its church, Ag. Antonios, has good 14th-century frescoes while the nearby Ag. Fanourios, the church of Valsamonero, has 15th-century frescoes considered to be some of the finest in Crete.

South of Ag. Varvara lies Crete's largest plain, Mesara, richly cultivated, and the ancient city of **Gortyna,** partially excavated by the Italians in 1880 and 1961. Although inhabited from Neolithic times, its fame began after the fall of Knossos when it became one of the ruling cities of Crete, with ports at Matala and Lebena. In 189 BC Hannibal passed through Gortyna, and later the Romans made it the capital of their provinces of Crete and Cyrenaica. Although in the *Iliad* Homer describes Gortyna as walled, the walls that remain were begun by Ptolemy Philopator but left unfinished. St Paul sent St Titus to convert Gortyna and Titus was its first bishop. In 828 the Saracens destroyed the city.

The most remarkable of the vast remains at Gortyna is the Law Code of Gortyna, which was inscribed at the beginning of the 5th century BC, and discovered in a mill stream in the 19th century AD; it may now be seen in the Roman Odeon. Written in boustrophedon, "as the ox plows" from left, to right then right to left, the laws are mainly of a civil nature, covering marriage, sex offences and property law. Other remains include a theatre, a temple on the akropolis, the residence of the Roman governor (Praetorium), and temples of Pythian Apollo and of Isis and Serapis. The ruins of the great basilica at the entrance date from the 6th and 10th centuries. Dedicated to Ag. Titos, it was the oldest one on Crete.

The Minoan city of **Phaistos,** was also excavated by the Italian School of Archaeology, starting in 1900. It was one of the earliest inhabited places in Crete, dating from the same time as Malia and Knossos and mentioned by Homer. It was destroyed in Hellenistic–Roman times by the more powerful Gortyna. Its first palace was constructed in the Middle Minoan period, 2100 BC, and destroyed in 1700 BC; the second palace was built on top of the first and destroyed in 1400 BC. Below the palace, 50 000 people lived and worked for the king, and one can see the ruins of the villages surrounded by the rich and lovely Mesara Plain. The palace was three storeys high, and the grand stairway leading to it has traces of the sacred snakes carved in it. Below it in the West Court lies the theatre. In the palace one can see the rooms of the king and queen, with bathrooms, the cisterns for storing rain water, and one of the oldest metal forges in the world. Near the excavations is a tourist pavilion with a café and food.

Neighbouring **Ag. Triada** (connected to Phaistos by a dirt road) supplied much of the gypsum and alabaster for the building of Phaistos. It was a Late Minoan settlement in its own right, where many people lived after the great destruction of 1400. The name Ag. Triada is derived from a small Venetian church near the site, the other church at the excavations is Ag. Georgios Galatas (1302), which contains some frescoes. A small palace or villa remains at Ag. Triada that contained some of the Minoans' finest art work. No one knows why it was built so close to Phaistos (the walk takes less than an hour); maybe a wealthy Minoan simply fell in love with the splendid site.

A road west of Myres leads to **Matala,** the lovely and very popular beach which is enclosed by sandstone cliffs riddled with ancient tombs. Over the years Cretans have enlarged these into cosy little rooms, which in the 1960s and '70s attracted a sizeable colony of young troglodytes. Now the local authorities prefer people to sleep on the beach if they must sleep out. The night life is pretty lively, and the inexpensive bars and tavernas do a brisk trade. The beach here is safe for children, and too at nearby **Limenes**. During Easter it's nearly impossible to find a room in the area, many Greeks come here regularly for their first swim of the year. On the road between Matala and Pitsidia a track leads to **Kommo,** where archaeologists in the last few years have uncovered sizeable Minoan remains of Phaistos' port. Eastwards along the Coast (road from Myres) is **Kali Limenes** the "fair havens" where St Paul is thought to have stopped, and east of that lies the port of **Gortyna,** near the quiet fishing village of **Lebena,** known for its healing waters. In late Classical times an Asklepieion, a temple to Asklepios, the god of healing, was built here. Both it and the Hellenistic floor of the treasury have mosaics and there are also two large bath tubs.

Pyrgos is the largest village east of Gortyna, and east of that, at **Philippi,** is a Byzantine fortress renovated by the Genoese, called Castel Belvedere for its remarkable view. This region of small villages and the monastery Foundadon is called the Kastelliana. East of this is **Ano Viannos,** or ancient Vienna, the inhabitants of which might have founded Vienne in France. On the old akropolis are the ruins of a Venetian castle and Turkish tower. Ag. Pelagia (1360) has frescoes. There is a castle near **Kastri** (of Mt Kairatos), and a Venetian fortification at **Vigla** which is very well preserved, called Vigla of Kairatokambos. It was here that the Saracens entered Crete in 823. Down the coast is the **Monastery Arvi, and a pretty beach**.

North from Ano Viannos is **Arkalohori** with a large paneyeri on 21 May. Minoan tombs and a sacred cave have been found there. In the small village of **Voni,** on the way to Kastelli, a folk festival takes place from 17 to 20 July. **Kastelli** is the chief village of the Pethiada, and is topped by the ruins of a Venetian castle; the 15th-century church Eisodia Theotokon has very interesting frescoes. To the east is the ancient city of **Lyttos,** or Lyktos, the enemy of Knossos in Doric times. High up on the foothills of Mt Dikti, Lyttos was wealthy and minted its own coins in Classical times, but in 220 BC Knossos destroyed it to put an end to the rivalry. Hellenistic walls remain, as does a Christian basilica with mosaics. Another ancient city, **Kersonisou,** to the north of Kastelli, was the port of Lyttos, but independent. It had a famous temple to Artemis. There is a later fort on the islet across from it (the larger, more distant islet, **Dia** is now a sanctuary for Crete's wild goat, the kri kri). Limin Kersonisou is a strip of big hotels and two campsites. **Gournes** is the home of an American Air Force Base; **Nirou Hani** has a Minoan villa.

Further east lies **Malia,** also well supplied with all possible tourist amenities and a comfortable youth hostel. The Minoan palace and city (closed Sundays) has been excavated by the French School of Archaeology since the 1920s. The history of the palace of Malia follows the same pattern as that of the other sites: built in 1900 BC it was devastated by the earthquake 200 years later, and the second palace, built over the first, was ruined in the mysterious catastrophe of the

15th century BC. From the west court is the entrance to a long rectangular central court with a pit in the middle. In the Pillar Crypt to the left one can discern symbols carved in the pillars. Another little room further north is set at an oblique angle to the others, and might have been used for moon study or worship. On the same side are the Megaron, Lustral Basin and archives. Outside the palace a paved Minoan road still exists, the sunken Hypostyle Crypt and, most famously, the great court full of gargantuan pithoi. By the sea is the cemetery, and to the west are the remains of a 6th-century basilica.

Last of all, in the centre of the nomos is **Arkane,** where most of the island's table grapes are produced. There are actually two villages, Kato Arkanes and the larger, Epano Arkanes. In the Asomatos church (1315) are good frescoes of the same period as those in Ag. Triada. There are many Minoan remains in this region, including the walls in the village, a well, tombs and other buildings. However, two of the sites—the large nekropolis at Phouri and the temple at Anemopilia—are closed (though the Herakleon tourist office may be able to refer you to the caretaker who can let you in). The cemetery contained many wealthy burials in a wide variety of tomb styles, the earliest dating back to 2500 BC. Above Arkane's town dump, on a windswept promontory called Anemopilia, a Minoan temple was discovered in 1979, containing four skeletons, apparently of people caught in the temple as the great earthquake struck and toppled it over them. The archaeologists who excavated the site, Sakellarakis, husband and wife, concluded that one of the skeletons, a young man, was in the act of being sacrificed to appease the furious god. Their findings have only poured oil on the flaming controversy among scholars as to whether or not the Minoans practised human sacrifice.

In nearby **Vathypetro** a Minoan villa has been found. Kanli Castelli, or the Bloody Fortress, is also in the Arkane region, and is believed to have been built by Nikephoros Phokas when he liberated Crete from the Saracens in 961. It later sheltered a harried Duke of Crete, much tried by the Duke of Naxos, Marcos Sanudo, who captured towns in Crete in defiance of Venice.

WHERE TO STAY

Outside the capital most people opt for hotels down in Matala or along the crowded coast to the east around Malia. Matala is expensive and police are tough cookies if you disobey the notices about no sleeping in the caves or on the beach. The **Bamboo Sands Hotel** near the main square is rated class C but is cheaper than most in the village—at 3200 dr. for a double (tel. 0892 42 370). If you've a sleeping bag, though, head straight for **Matala Camping** near the beach, a good cool place to stay with ridiculously low prices. There are also cheap beds in the neighbouring villages of Kalamaki and Pitsidia.

In Malia, the centre of the over-developed coast, you can ensconce yourself in the **Ikaros Village,** class A (tel. 0897 31 267), intriguingly designed as a traditional Cretan village (most of the big hotels lack any design whatsoever). Rates are approximately 8000 dr. (single) and 13 000 dr. (double). Don't despair if your budget won't stretch to this—there are a large number of smaller hotels but probably one of the cheapest you'll find is the E class **Ermioni** at about 2000 dr. for a double (tel. 0897 31 093). A pleasant economy alternative is the charming **Youth hostel** just east of town (tel. 0897 31 338), where beds are 400 dr. a night. In Hersonisou there are untold pensions and hotels covering every price range, the most luxurious being the **Creta Maris Hotel** and **Bungalow** complex where a double in season will set you back a hefty 14 000 dr. (tel. 0897 22 115). A double at any of the C class hotels will run from 3000 dr. to 5000 dr. There's a camping site nearby (tel. 0897 22025).

EATING OUT
Both coasts can be hard on the wallet, and the food tends to be Greek-international-bland to please all tastes. In Matala people tend to drink more than eat; in Malia, among the many on the packed road to the beach, is **Oroscopio** with reasonable prices and good Greek food (500–700 dr.). One pleasant surprise is the **Bombay Curry House** in Hersonisou, where authentic Indian meals need not be too hard on the pocket if you choose carefully.

Ag. Nikolaos

Ag. Nikolaos, the capital of the nomos of Lassithi, was the ancient port of Lato, with the name of Lato Pros Kamara. Mandraki, a later name, lasted into Venetian times. The Genoese built the fortress of Mirabello above the bay of the same, name but the Turks demolished it and now the administration building of Lassithi occupies its place. When Ag. Nikolaos (named for a 9th-century church) became capital of the nomos only 95 people lived there, although today its summertime population reaches 10 000. Of all the Cretan capitals, Ag. Nikolaos caters most obviously to the cosmopolitan crowd, which provides the major income for the town. For that reason it tends to be rather expensive, its oft-extolled smallness, charm and quaintness is its business. However, because of ever increasing displays of drunkenness and rowdiness, and surly service in most cafés and restaurants, it's not the place to find the real Crete.

A small lake, more than 60 metres (200 ft) deep, occupies the centre of town. In 1907 it was connected to the sea, and the channel is crossed by a small bridge. An odd bird or two is pent up in the cages at its far end. Restaurants and cafés line every available space on the waterfront. The Akti Koundourou follows the sea shore, past rocky places where you can swim. There is a beach at the very end and a church. Ag. Nikolaos, patron of sailors, with 9th- and 14th-century frescoes (ask at the police station for the key). In town, off Plateia Venizelou, the 12th-century church **Panayia** is by the cathedral. The **Archaeology Museum** may be found up the hill on Kon. Palaiologo (closed Tuesdays), and shows Minoan and later artefacts discovered in Eastern Crete. The local police, who double as the Tourist Police, may be found halfway up the hill.

Ag. Nikolaos bus station is near a rocky beach at the end of Sof. Veñizelou St, beaches within bus range are Elounda, Kalo Chorio (on the road to Sitia), Ammoudi and Almyros, a couple of kilometres to the east, the local nudist beach, lined with bamboo. There are also daily boat excursions from the port to other beaches, as well as to Spinalonga and to the so-called sunken city, Olous.

PANEYERIA
6 December, Ag. Nikolaos: 29 May, Ag. Triada. Nautical week 27 June–3 July, with fireworks on the last day.

WHERE TO STAY
Sometimes it seems as if all of Europe has descended on Ag. Nikolaos, and if you come unprepared, sleeping on the beach is a wretched alternative. There are a number of very luxurious hotels in the area, of which the most famous is the **Astir Palace** in Elounda, 10 km (6 miles) outside the town (tel. 0841 41580), with 200 rooms and 96 bungalows. Of the many luxury hotels in Greece, this is one of the best; it sits in its own bay and because of its privacy was chosen as the meeting place for Gaddafi and Mitterrand in 1985 for their peace talks over Chad. Its plush double rooms go for 18 500 dr. (half pension obligatory in midsummer) and bungalows for 22 000 dr. Equally sumptuous is the bungalow-hotel **Minos Beach** at Akti Elia Sotirchou (tel. 0841 22 345)—all spanking new and modern, with twin bungalows reaching the 22 000 dr. mark in high season. On a more modest level, the **Hotel New York** at 21a Kontogiani St (tel. 0841 28 577) is known for having rooms when the other hotels are all booked up with package tours. It's very near the bus station and a double in season is around 3500 dr. Less costly are the charming **Green House** pension at 15 Modatsou (tel. 0841 22 025) and the pension **Argyro** at 1 Solonos St (tel. 0841 28 707); the rates for both are 1800–2000 dr. for a double. If you plan to stay for several days, immediately next to the Youth hostel on Strat. Koraka is a small family run pension (it has no name) with cooking facilities and immaculately clean modern rooms at a very reasonable 2000 dr. Otherwise, your best bet may well be taking potluck at the bus station, where anyone with an available room to let will offer it as you arrive.

EATING OUT
One of the few tavernas in town that has kept its prices in line with the rest of Greece is **Agtalon,** next to the bridge; one that hasn't is the **Cretan Restaurant,** although if you have the money the food and service are excellent. What makes the Cretan special is its delightfully kitschy decor, crammed full of seashells, fountains, stuffed fish and so on. British and American visitors make up nearly all the clientele at the **Limni Restaurant** on Paleologou Katechaki; apparently some television actors from the BBC used to eat there, and the food is good and prices moderate (1200 dr. for a meal). The speciality is fish or shrimp cooked in earthenware pots. Another place that hasn't succumbed to tourist mark-up prices is the taverna **Itanos** near Plateia Venizelou, where a full meal with Cretan

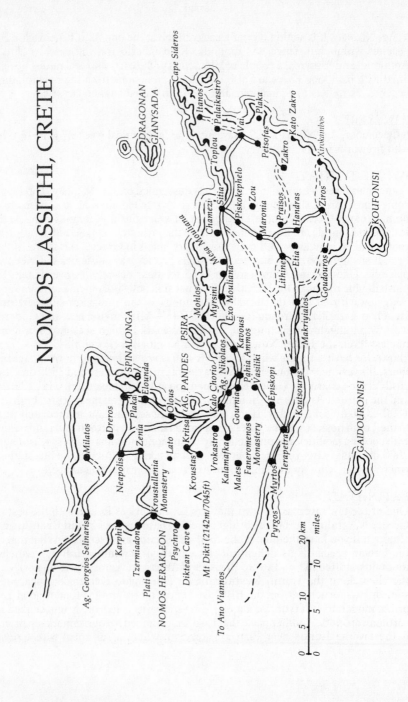

NOMOS LASSITHI, CRETE

barreled wine can come to as little as 600 dr. The locals, like most Greeks, prefer to dine in the country, where the prices are lower, there are fewer tourists, and the food is more to their tastes. Currently the **Blue Sea Taverna** near the Minos Beach hotel is the most popular.

TOURIST INFORMATION
Tourist office, by the lake, tel. (0841) 22 357.
Tourist police, up the hill, tel. (0841) 22 321.

Nomos Lassithi

Nomos Lassithi (the name comes from a corruption of the Venetian La Sitia) is the most varied in Crete: its famous mountain plain, where there are many windmills, is too cold for olives, but produces apples, wheat and potatoes, while at the eastern end there is Vai, a luxuriant palm-lined tropical beach. Lassithians claim to be the best lovers in Crete, although this is not by any means unanimously agreed by other Cretans; they do, however, give credit to the nomos for its potatoes and pigs. The *Erotokritos* poet Kornaros was from Lassithi, as well as a pope and Zeus himself, and a church near Ag. Nikolaos, Panayia Kera, has the best fresco paintings in Crete.

Directly off the coast of the city of Ag. Nikolaos is the islet **Ag. Pandes,** a refuge for the kri kri and site of a church of the same name, drawing pilgrims on 20 June. Otherwise one needs special permission to visit the goats. Other islets in Mirambelou Bay are **Psira** and **Mohlos,** both with Minoan ruins, dug by the American School of Archaeology. One can hire caiques from Ag. Nikolaos or the village of Mohlos to visit them. North of Ag. Nikolaos is **Elounda,** on the site of the unexcavated port of Dreros, **Olous.** Inscriptions from the 2nd century BC prove a treaty between Rhodes and Olous, and the walls of the port can still be observed in the sea. Artemis Britomartis was worshipped at the city, which was reported to have a wooden statue of the goddess made by Daedalus. Salt works of the Venetians exist in the area as well as a windmill, and a basilica with mosaics. Elounda itself is a pleasant little resort town that sprang up overnight and is an attractive alternative to Ag. Nikolaos.

Spinalonga, a half-hour caique trip from Elounda (the journey can also be made from Ag. Nikolaos) is a small islet created by Venetian engineers when they dug a canal separating it from the Kolokytha (squash) peninsula. In 1579 they built a huge fortress on Spinalonga, on the ruins of the ancient fort of Olous. During the Turkish occupation Spinalonga held out like the other small island forts of Nea Souda and Grambousa, until a Venetian treaty handed it over to the Ottomans in 1715. The Turks settled it with soldiers and civilians. When they evacuated in 1904, it became a leper colony until 1952. The walls, houses and cisterns make very impressive remains, **Plaka,** opposite the islet, was the supply centre for the lepers and is popular today with those seeking rest and relaxation.

West of Elounda a road leads to ancient **Dreros,** on a saddle between two hills and discovered at the beginning of this century. Its remains include walls, a cistern an Archaic agora and a Geometric temple to Apollo Delphinios built in the 7th century BC, which produced the oldest hammered bronze statues to be found in Greece. **Milatos** to the north of Dreros was considered an enemy. Tradition has it that Sarpedon, one of Minos' brothers, won the affections of a certain boy the brothers quarrelled over and left Crete for Asia Minor. He took with him not only the boy but people from Milatos, and they founded the great city of Miletus. In the 3rd century BC the Lyttians destroyed Milatos. The **Cave of Milatos** served as a refuge during the War of Independence for 2700 people. Upon their discovery the Turks besieged them, and after two battles the refugees surrendered, as the Turks had previously promised them safe conduct. However, the Turks massacred all the old men and children, and enslaved the women.

West of Milatos, on the highway from Herakleon many, Greek buses and cars stop at the shrine of **Ag. Georgios Selinaris** with its miraculous icon. **Neapolis** is the largest village en route to Ag. Nikolaos; the old village on which it was built, Kares, witnessed the birth of Petros Filagros in 1340. Raised by Catholics, he became a professor of theology and was elected Pope Alexander V in 1409, during the schism. A year later, however, he died. Kares was destroyed in 1347 in a rebellion against the Venetians and renamed "new town", or Neapolis. There is a small museum with items from Elounda and Dreros, and on 14–15 August a large paneyeri celebrates the Assumption.

A small village on the road to Tzermiadon, **Zenia,** has the following tale, during the Turkish occupation there lived a lovely young girl in the village who had hair down to her knees. Her beauty caught the eye of the Turkish captain, who threatened to destroy all of Zenia if she would not marry him. On those terms, she reluctantly agreed. During the wedding feast she poured him more wine than he could hold, and during the night she decapitated him. Running to the church, she cut off her hair and took the clothes of a soldier and the name of Captain Manolis. She performed many heroic deeds before she was killed. Her hair and the decapitating knife are still on display in the Zenia church.

The spectacular high **Plain of Lassithi** is connected by regular public bus with both Herakleon and Ag. Nikolaos; many tour buses full of day trippers make the ascent too, and you may want to spend a night or two in one of the 18 villages on the plain—Tzermiadon, the largest, Psychro and Ag. Georgios all have rooms—to get an idea of what the place is really like. For it is unique: a green carpet of a plateau hemmed in by the Lassithi Mountains, irrigated by white-sailed windmills, 10 000 in all. This scenic way of supplying water was designed by Venetian engineers in 1464, after a crop shortage and after the fruit trees had been destroyed to punish rebellious locals. Although fewer than 6000 of the wind water pumps are in use today, they still make a splendid sight against the mountains and green plain.

Of all the villages on Lassithi Plain, **Tzermiadon** has the most tourist facilities and a paneyeri on 6 November. The **Trapeza cave** here was inhabited in

Neolithic times, but today one can only see the entrance, as the cave has been boarded up to prevent accidents. From Tzermiadon one can walk (with a guide if possible) to the ancient city of **Karphi** ("the nail"), excavated by the British School of Archaeology under John Pendlebury from 1937 to 1939. Karphi served as a city of Minoan refuge from the Doric invaders in the Sub-Minoan period, but its difficult situation caused it to be abandoned later. One can see the temple, the house of the chieftain, the tower and barracks, and there is an especially lovely view of Lassithi. The trip up takes about 1¹/₂hours.

Kroustallenia Monastery, in Tzermiadon, was built in 1541, and housed the local revolutionary council during the war. **Psychro,** on the other side of the plain, is the base for visiting the **Diktean cave,** the birthplace of Zeus. Ascent can be made easily by foot or on donkeys which are available at the site, as are local guides. Descent into the cave is rather more difficult, and it is advisable to wear old trousers and rubber-soled shoes and to bring a torch, although candles are available at the site. The cave only rediscovered in the 1880s, and excavated by D. G. Hogarth of the British School of Archaeology, contained relics from Middle Minoan up to Archaic times. According to the ancient Hymn of the Kouretes, Zeus was hidden in this cave by his mother Rhea (see **Mythology,** page 67). A crevice in the cave wall is known as his cradle while a row of large stalactites is called "Zeus' mantle". Other stories claim that Europa conceived Minos in the cave, and that when he became king he went there every nine years for paternal advice from Zeus. While the cult objects found prove a continuity of worship at Dikti before and after the Doric invasion, in a later period the worship of Zeus was transferred to the Idean cave.

In Psychro a tourist pavilion caters to cave visitors, and there are other restaurants and small hotels and rooms. On 29–31 August there is a three-day paneyeri in the village, nearby **Ag. Georgios,** site of a new folklore museum, celebrates the saint of the same name on 23 April, and **Magoula** has a paneyeri for Ag. Spyridon on 12 December. A village on the nomos border, **Plati,** contains the remains of a Minoan settlement, inhabited before and after the Doric invasion.

Lovely **Kritsa** village a few miles above Ag. Nikolaos is the "authentic" Cretan village visited by tourists from Ag. Nikolaos. It is indeed worthy of a visit for its architecture (although destroyed by the Saracens, it was reconstructed after the liberation of Crete by Nikephoros Phokas), for the view of the bay below, and for excursions to ancient Lato, and particularly to the church **Kera Panayia.** Built in the early part of the Venetian period, this church is open from 9 am to 12 noon and from 2 pm to 5 pm. Almost the entire wall surface is covered with magnificent frescoes, depicting the life of Mary's mother, St Anne, of Mary herself, and other scenes from the New Testament. On 15 August a paneyeri is held at the church, and around this time traditional Cretan weddings take place with food and dancing in which one can participate for a fee. Ancient **Lato,** also known as Goulas, is an hour's walk from Kritsa, or a rough drive. It was excavated by the French School of Archaeology and is splendidly situated in a depression between two hills which formed its akropolises. It is an Archaic town, built in the 7th century BC and influences from Minoan palaces have been noted in the agora and stairway. The streets are paved with flagstones, and the walls have a double gateway. There are remains of temples, houses, a cistern and a Hellenic prytaneion, or meeting place of the town elders. Goulas is the fortified part of the town.

From Kritsa one can also visit **Kroustas,** a village untouched by the tourism further down the road. Kroustas has some very old frescoed churches and a huge festival on 25 June, the feast of St John, with bonfires and dances. The bus to Kritsa goes to Kroustas occasionally. More frequent buses from Ag. Nikolaos go south to the popular beach at **Kalo Chorio;** from Kalo Chorio's model farm one can visit **Vrokastro,** inhabited from 1000 BC and used as a refuge settlement during the Doric invasion. A Geometric fort stands on the hill. Nearby, to the east, is **Gournia,** a site excavated by Harriet Boyd Hawes between 1901 and 1904, the first woman to lead a major archaeological dig. It is the best preserved Minoan town on Crete, reaching its peak in 1600 BC, and many workshops, storerooms, houses and a small palace remain, as well as signs of a mine near the shore.

From Gournia one can take a path to **Pahia Ammos,** a growing resort with a good beach. To the south (the road turns near Gournia) is the late Byzantine monastery **Faneromenos,** high on the hill and the site of many resistance activities during the Turkish occupation. South of Pahia Ammos lies **Vasiliki,** where an Early Minoan settlement was discovered at the beginning of this century by two Americans, Boyd and Seager. Mottled pottery produced from the site has been given the name Vasiliki ware. Red-plastered rooms, corridors and a courtyard of the palace remain among other ruins. If you're heading east to Sitia from Pahia Ammos, the new road is perhaps the island's most scenic, a long winding serpent slithering along a jagged and often precipitous coast.

If you're heading south, the road bisects the narrowest part of Crete (12 km/7½ miles) to **Ierapetra,** the largest town on the Libyan Sea, and the furthest south in Greece, only 370 km (230 miles) from Egypt. In mythology Ierapetra was founded by the Telchines from Rhodes, who had the heads of dogs and the flippers of seals. The name they gave Ierapetra was Kamiros, like that of another city they had founded on Rhodes, but when their presence on Crete, continued to foul up the weather, Zeus sent them elsewhere. The Doric name of the town was Ierapytna. It prospered in the Hellenistic period as the most powerful city in eastern Crete, and although destroyed by the Romans the last city in Crete to resist their invasion, it was rebuilt by them in even grander style. In the Byzantine period it was the seat of a bishop, but it was ruined by the Saracens and later by an earthquake in 1508. In the 13th century the Genoese or Venetians built Kastelli on the coast, a fort which is well preserved today. Nearby is the house where tradition claims that Napoleon spent the night of 26 June 1798 before his campaign in Egypt. Beside it is an interesting mosque and minaret. There are also a few Roman remains to be seen to the west of the town, including a theatre. The most beautiful item in this rather dull town is in its one-room museum, in the

CRETE

Town Library: a lovely sarcophagus found in the village of Episkopi to the north. While in summer it can be very hot, Ierapetra is very pleasant in the winter. There is a youth hostel and some hotels, but the best beaches are towards Makriyialos. On 3 October every year a big festival celebrates the 1821 revolution.

Along the coast west of Ierapetra is **Myrtos,** where in 1968 the British School of Archaeology excavated an early Minoan town which had been a weaving centre, dating from 2500 to 2100 BC. Some of the finds are in the Myrtos schoolhouse, while the more important ones are in the Ag. Nikolaos museum. In nearby **Pyrgos** a villa has been found with large rooms and a stairway. One popular way of going to Myrtos, other than by the new road, is to walk through the river bed from Males, which has a frescoed Byzantine church, Panayia Messochoritissa (1431). There is another church, Ag. Georgios, further south in a ruined village.

Along the coast east of Ierapetra, old houses at **Koutsouras** have been restored and are rented out to visitors; in **Markiyialos,** which has an excellent sandy beach, there are pensions and a campsite. To the north the village **Etia** was one of the major towns in the Byzantine and Venetian periods, noted for its lovely setting. The region was ruled by the De Mezzo family, who built a palace fortress in the 15th century, considered one of the greatest Venetian constructions in Crete. It was three storeys high, with vaulted ceilings and sculptured decorations. The Turks were besieged in the palace, however, and a later fire and earthquake finished the destruction, although today it has been partially restored. Of the many outlying buildings, the wall and gate and fountain house bear inscriptions.

The **Ag. Sofia monastery** is close by, towards the village of Handras. During the Turkish occupation it served as a fortress and secret school, and was often besieged and destroyed. **Praisos,** the ancient city north of Handras, has three akropolises. Habitation dates from Late Minoan to Hellenistic times, and the walls and houses remain. The capital of the Eteocretans—the "true Cretans" or descendants of the Minoans—Praisos was destroyed by the city of Ierapetra in 155 BC. East of Praisos is **Zakro** with a restaurant called The Maestro's, where the Maestro serenades diners with his violin. A huge gorge leads down from Zakro—a good five-mile walk—to the palace of **Kato Zakro** . The Minoan tombs found within have given it the name "the Gorge of Death". One can also go by the road along the top of the ravine.

The town of Zakro was excavated by the English archaeologist Hogarth in 1901, but the palace itself was found in 1961 by N. Platon, and because this side of Crete is sinking, part of it now lies under water. Built in the Late Minoan period, the palace was destroyed by a sudden collapse, followed by fire. Among its remains are a central court, a west wing with inscriptions, magazines, a Lustral Basin, archives, and a once-decorated banquet hall. After the great destruction the surrounding town of narrow cobblestoned streets was rebuilt, but the palace lay untouched. The evidence of such a large settlement in Zakro, which could hardly have supported it, demonstrates how extensively the Minoans traded by sea. There are rooms to let in Kato Zakro and a pebble beach. In Zakro itself a

107

Minoan villa has been uncovered with wall paintings and wine presses, and on a summit is a round, Hellenistic beacon tower.

The road north of Zakro leads to **Petsofas,** where a peak sanctuary was dedicated to the fertility goddess, and where many votive offerings have been found. Further north is **Palaikastro,** the last bus stop for **Vai,** a beach with palm trees said to have been brought by the Saracens. Unfortunately, it has become a stop on the package tour itinerary, so on any given day expect to share this little tropical paradise with hundreds of other people. There is a late Minoan settlement with streets and houses by the sea, at a place called Roussolakos. Another site is Kastri on a hill by the shore, where remains dating from Geometric to Hellenistic times have been uncovered. A Classical temple to Diktean Zeus existed there, and a hymn to Zeus from the 4th century was found engraved on a stone. Palaikastro has a fine beach lined with restaurants and tavernas.

To the north, near Cape Sideros, lies ancient **Itanos,** which can be reached by the road from Palaikastro or Toplou. Also known as Erimoupolis, this was inhabited from Early Minoan times, although the ruins existing today are Geometric to Hellenistic. Ptolemy used it as a naval station, and the city thrived on the trade of dyes and glass. Early Christian ruins are below, but this settlement and the small 15th-century village, were deserted because of the Saracen and pirate raids.

The famous **monastery of Toplou** lies south west of Itanos. Its real name is Panayia Akroteriani, but the name *toplou* (meaning "cannon" in Turkish from the huge cannon once possessed by the monastery) is more popular. Believed to have been founded by the Kornaros family, Toplou was built in the late 15th century and was repaired after earthquake destruction in 1612. It is three storeys high and a veritable fortress with a tall Italianate bell tower dated 1558. Above the monastery gate is a hole, Fonias, through which the besieged monks used to pour hot oil onto their attackers. It has a long history as a place of refuge and resistance. At the beginning of the War of Independence in 1821, the Turks captured it and hung the bodies of 12 monks on the gate. At the end of the war, however, the Turks found themselves in turn attacked by Cretans. They surrendered the monastery when the Cretans offered to spare the lives of other Turkish prisoners and to give them transport. Cretan occupation ended when the Great Powers decided the island should remain Turkish. There is a very beautiful icon in the monastery painted by Ioannis Kornaros in 1770 entitled "Great is the Lord", one of the masterpieces of Cretan art. There are other icons, manuscripts and a Hellenistic inscription describing the arbitration of Magnesia in an argument between Itanos and Ierapytna. One of the aisles is believed to have been part of a chapel to Ag. Isidoros, built when Nikephoros Phokas liberated Crete, which also gave its name to Cape Sideros.

West of Toplou is the sleepy town of **Sitia** (Sithia in the softer Cretan pronunciation). The site was once occupied by ancient Eteia, which produced Myson, one of the Seven Sages of Greece. Sitia later produced Vincenzo Kornaross author of the *Erotokritos*, the 17th-century Cretan national epic of a love formed, lost, and found again between Erotokritos and Aretousa, daughter of the King of Athens. Once surrounded by Byzantine, Genoese and Venetian walls, as well as a Venetian fortress, little now remains of these defences, thanks to earthquakes and the bombardment of Barbarossa. The **Archaeology Museum** on the road out of town to the south coast has interesting exhibits from the Neolithic to the late Roman period, most locally excavated. There's also a small **folklore museum** on G. Arkadion St with some colourful examples of local arts and crafts. Today Sitia exports raisins and is known for its wine. In the middle of August, a three-day wine festival is held here. There is a lovely youth hostel run by a slightly mad Englishman, and there are many tavernas and restaurants along the shady waterfront.

South of Sitia is **Piskokephelo**, another peak sanctuary, near which a farmhouse has been excavated. On 24 June a large festival is held in the village, **Zou** to the south has a Minoan village and a cave in **Maronia** contained Early Minoan finds. **Lithine** even further south is a charming village with the remains of a once important Venetian tower. In **Chamezi** west of Sitia an oval, prehistoric house or sanctuary was discovered. Two beehive tombs in **Mesa Mouliana** date from the end of the Bronze Age; and in **Exo Mouliana**, famous for its wine, is a frescoed church, Ag. Georgios (1426). **Myrsini** is a Venetian village with important Minoan tombs in the vicinity; and **Kavousi** had a small Sub-Minoan settlement and a peak sanctuary, although little now remains of them.

WHERE TO STAY

There are several places to stay on the plain of Lassithi, the best hotel being in Tzermiado, the capital. This is the **Kourites** (tel. 0844 22 194) where the doubles can be as low as 2500 dr. up to 3500 dr. a night. Things are cheaper in Ag. Georgios, where the **Dias Hotel** (tel. 0844 31 207) has doubles at 2000 dr. In Psychro, where most people stay, there are quite a few rooms to supplement the class D **Zeus** (tel. 0844 31 284), where doubles are 2500 dr. and the class E **Dikteon Andron** (tel. 0844 31 504), where rooms are 2100 dr. for a double, 1500 dr. for a single.

In Sitia there are many places to choose from. **Hotel Itanos** on Plateia Venizelou (tel. 0843 22 146) is a classy class C near the park; doubles here begin at 3000 dr. In the lower priced category, the **Hotel Stars**, at 37 M. Kolyvaki (tel. 0843 22 917) offers some peace and quiet, convenience for ferry boats and doubles at 2400 dr. The **Youth hostel** at 4 Therissou St (tel. 0843 22 693) is just east of town and again, quite pleasant and friendly, with kitchen facilities and a garden.

In Ierapetra there are also many hotels and pensions; the **Hotel Atlantis** at Ag. Andreas (tel. 0842 28 555) is east of town (there is really nothing to hold you in the city limits) and is about the best of the class C hotels, with doubles going for 4500 dr.

In town the nicest cheap hotel is the **Ierapytna** on Plateia Ag. Ioannou Kale (tel. 0842 28 530) with doubles at 2500 dr. But far better to go west of Ierapetra to

Myrtos and the **Myrtos Hotel** (tel. 0842 51 215) where you can get one of its C class doubles with bath for 4500 dr. There are campsites at Pahia Ammos (tel. 0842 93 243) and Ierapetra (tel. 0842 61 351).

EATING OUT

There are plenty of little tavernas on the Lassithi, some catering to the local trade, some to the tourists. **Kronias Restaurant** in Tzermiado is somewhere in between; the food is good and the price is surprisingly low. In Elounda the culinary hot spot is **Marilena's**, a Cypriot restaurant specialising in delicious hors d'oeuvres, including humus and toasted cheese from Cyprus. It's definitely worth the higher bill. The **Venus** restaurant is another local favourite, serving international cuisine. Again, the prices are high. In Sitia, **Yuras** on 4 Dimokritou St is very reasonably priced; you can eat well for 600 dr.; as usual the long line of seaside tavernas specialising in fish tend to be dear, but the food is fresh and delicious. **Zorba's** has a wide range of other specialities, and you are invited to go and inspect them in the kitchen. Apart from the usual Greek dishes, the restaurants on the front in Ierapetra offer such rare delicacies as beans on toast and bacon and eggs, and you get a discount if you have a copy of yesterday's *Daily Mirror*. If you're not tempted by all this, wander into the back streets where the locals eat. Out at Vai there's a mediocre taverna overlooking the crowded beach—and if you wonder why people are hopping about in the water, it's because the fish there actually bite!

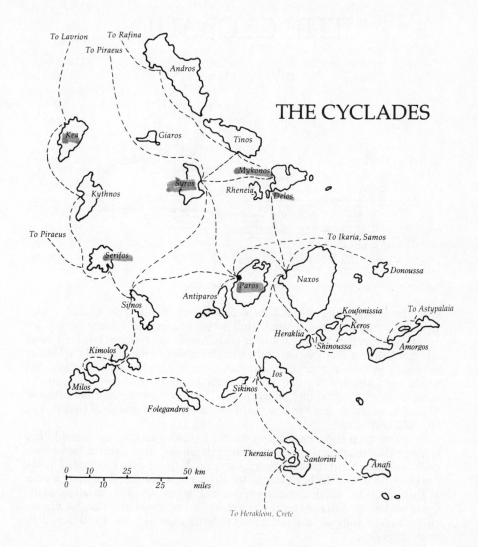

To Lavrion

To Rafina

To Piraeus

Andros

Kea

Giaros

Tinos

THE CYCLADES

Mykonos

Syros

Rheneia

Delos

Kythnos

To Piraeus

Serifos

To Ikaria, Samos

Donoussa

Paros

Naxos

Sifnos

Antiparos

Koufonissia

To Astypalaia

Keros

Heraklia

Amorgos

Shinoussa

Kimolos

Ios

Milos

Sikinos

Folegandros

Therasia

Santorini

Anafi

0   10   25   50 km

0   10   25   miles

To Herakleon, Crete

Part IV

THE CYCLADES

The Street of Lions, Delos

When imagining a Greek island, many people picture one of the Cyclades, with archetypal rocky terrain, asymmetrical white houses and streets fit only for dwarfs, with a church squeezed in at every corner. As they are relatively close together, one can visit a variety of the islands without losing much of the holiday in transit; in the summer there are daily communications between them. Yet within the Cyclades (the "circling" islands around Delos, the tiny centre of ancient Greek spiritual life), one can find, besides such constant favourites as Mykonos, Santorini and Paros, some of the most unspoilt islands in Greece, like Heraklia and Anafi.

Archaeological evidence suggests that the Cyclades have been inhabited since at least 6000 BC, the first settlers traditionally coming from Karia in Asia Minor and speaking a non-Greek language. Later the Karians were supplanted by the Phoenicians, who at the beginning of the Bronze Age developed a culture known as Early Cycladic, which lasted from 3000 to 2000 BC, or until the advent of the Cretan–Minoan thalassocracy. The most familiar products of the Early Cycladic civilisation are the marble figurines of the fertility goddess, so beautiful in their utter simplicity.

Mythology mentions Minos of Crete conquering the Aegean Islands in order to rid himself of his overly just brother Rhadamanthys, whom he sent to administer the new Cretan colonies. This period of Minoan influence on the islands occurred during the Middle Cycladic period; the Late Cycladic period coincides

112

with the fall of Crete and the rise of the Mycenaeans. When the Mycenaeans in turn fell to their Dorian conquerors, a dark age fell on the islands which lasted for hundreds of years. Many islands, however, were under the Ionian influence, and spoke the Ionian dialect.

Towards the end of the 8th century BC, a new culture, the Archaic, flourished in Ionia and on the islands. The rise of the Persians, however, caused the Ionians to flee westwards to Attica, and the islands were left at the mercy of the Persians, whom some of them actively supported at Marathon and Salamis. The Athenians punished those who had sided with their enemy and obliged the islands to enter into the new maritime league they had formed at Delos in 478 BC. This replaced an older Ionian council, or Amphictyony. But what began as a council of allies gradually turned into a tribute to the Athenians, as their fleet was the only one capable of protecting the islands from the Persian menace. As the islands were proud of their independence, they naturally resented Athenian encroachment in their affairs, and the Athenians were compelled to put down many a rebellion and to extort the yearly contribution of money and ships.

During the Peloponnesian War the islands generally sided with the city which was winning at any given time, although many jumped at the chance to support Sparta against their Athenian oppressors. But when Athens recovered from the war in 378 BC, she formed a second Delian league, again subjugating the Cyclades. Most of the islands turned to Philip of Macedon as his star rose into ascendancy, and they were later to become the subject of many battles between the generals of Alexander the Great.

In the beginning of the 2nd century BC the Romans captured the islands, bringing a certain amount of peace with their conquest. Some of the islands were later given to Rhodes, a less kind ruler. The fall of Rome, however, spelt centuries of hardship for the islands. Although they were officially part of the Byzantine Empire, Constantinople could not protect them from the numerous marauders prowling the high seas, and the islanders were left to fend for themselves, building villages in the most inaccessible places possible.

When Constantinople fell in 1204, the Frankish conquerors allotted the Aegean to the Venetians, and the islands became a free for all between young noblemen and the pirates (sometimes one and the same). The Cyclades became the special territory of Marco Sanudo, nephew of the leader of the Fourth Crusade, Doge Enrico Dandolo. Marco Sanudo as Duke of Naxos ruled that island and Paros himself, and gave the smaller islands to his barons, who still owed allegiance to Naxos. The Crispi dynasty followed the Sanudos in 1383, but as pirates and the growing Ottoman Empire caused increasing difficulties Venice herself stepped in to bring about a certain amount of control at the end of the 15th century. A few decades later, however, the islands were systematically decimated by the pirate admiral Khair-ed-din-Barbarossa, and by the mid-16th century they were under Turkish domination.

The Venetians had managed to convert many of the Greeks on the Cyclades to the Catholic faith, in particular on Syros, and during the Ottoman occupation

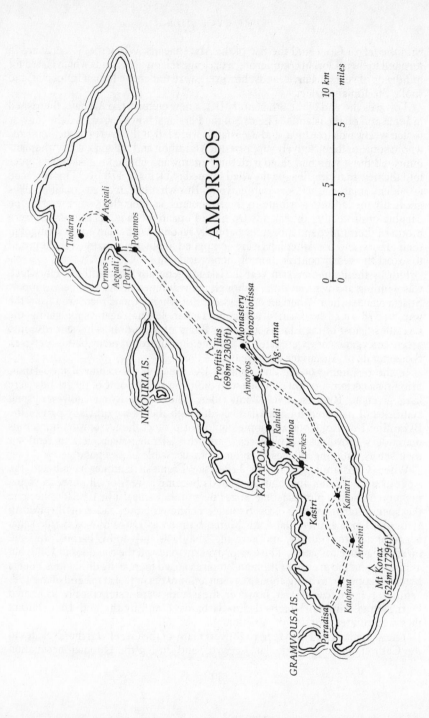

AMORGOS

both Orthodox and Catholic monasteries thrived. Nominally the islands continued to be ruled by the Duke of Naxos, but he was now a mere puppet of the Sultan. Turkish rule was only harsh in economic terms and most of the islands were spared the cruelties inflicted on Crete. The Turkish occupation was broken for three years (1771–74) in one of the more outlandish episodes in Greek history. At the time Russia and Turkey were at each other's throats over Poland, and rumours reached Catherine the Great of Greek discontent under the Turkish yoke. She sent her fleet into the Aegean to lead an insurrection against the Sultan and occupied some of the Cyclades. The adventure failed and the Russians went home, unpopular with all parties.

When the Greek War of Independence broke out, Cycladic participation consisted mainly of naval support and of harbouring refugees, since under French protection (for the Catholic population) many islands retained a neutral stance in the conflict. However, in the early years of the Greek nation the Cyclades were added to its territory. Syros led the ports of Greece at the time, but lost the position to Piraeus with the advent of the steamship. Today that island's capital, Ermoupoulis, is still the largest town and administrative centre of the Cyclades.

Before the advent of tourism, the Cyclades had suffered a serious drop in population; it was just too hard to make a living from the dry, rocky soil. Even now, on the most popular islands, the winter months can be lonely, as many people spend the winter in Athens. The climate, more than anywhere else in Greece, is much influenced by the winds. The winter months are plagued by the voreas, the north winds that turn ship schedules into a fictional romance. After March the main wind, the sirocco, blows gently from the south, warming the islands, which are still green from the winter rains. By July many of the Cyclades look brown and parched, except where there are sources of underground water. From July to September the notorious meltemi wind blowing off the Russian steppes periodically huffs and puffs like the big bad wolf, and terrorises those who venture out on excursion boats (you may get so sick you wish the boat would sink—but it doesn't usually); the big ships usually aren't too bad, and if you're really a landlubber you can fly: Paros, Mykonos, Milos, Santorini and Naxos have airports.

Water continues to be a problem on some islands, and it may be turned off for part of the day. However, since these islands are so popular with visitors (and thus important to the national economy) efforts have been made to ensure that they and their new hotels have ample water supplies, even in August.

AMORGOS

CONNECTIONS
Daily with Naxos, Heraklia, Koufonissia and Shinoussa; also several times a week with Piraeus and Syros; twice a week connections with Astypalaia and the other Dodecanese.

Easternmost of the Cyclades, Amorgos is rugged, in many places dramatically so. On the south coast the cliffs plunge down into the sea; crossing the island from north to south the road is so rough that most people prefer to get about by caique. For many years Amorgos was a destination for the adventurous, then all of a sudden crowds of travellers came seeking the quiet Cycladic life they had dreamed about. They swooped down on Amorgos until there were people literally sleeping in the streets. Things, however, now seem to have quietened down a bit. There still aren't enough available rooms to accommodate everyone who would like to stay, so if you come in the summer without a reservation be prepared to sleep under the stars.

HISTORY

Both Amorgos and its neighbouring islet Keros have produced artefacts from the pre-Mycenaean period, some tombs on Amorgos dating back to 3300 BC. In 1885 the German archaeologist Dummler found 11 ancient cemeteries, with many fine ceramics now to be seen in Oxford and Copenhagen. Much work in marble has also been found, along with signs of trade with Milos and Egypt. There were three ancient, independent cities on Amorgos in Cycladic times, each minting its own coins and worshipping Dionysos and Athena. Kastri (modern Arkesini) was settled by Naxians, Minoa by Samians, and Aegiali by Milians.

In the 5th century BC Amorgos joined the Delian alliance; later the Alexandrian gods, Serapis and Isis, were worshipped widely, for Ptolemy of Egypt was the Hellenistic ruler of the island. The Romans sent exiles to Amorgos and this downhill trend continued when the island was ravaged by Goths, Vandals and Slavs during the Byzantine period. One bright moment in this dark history was during the War of the Iconoclasts, when a miraculous icon sailed to Amorgos, set adrift, according to tradition, by an icon-loving lady from Constantinople. As the icon showed a preference for staying by the cliffs on Amorgos' south coast, Emperor Alexis Comnenus founded the Chozoviotissa monastery there in 1088 to house it. In 1209 the Duke of Naxos, Marco Sanudo, seized the island with an army of Naxians, and Gizi later built the town castle. The 17th century saw an increase of wealth on the island, in spite of the Turkish occupation, much of it derived from the export of the exquisite embroideries made by the women of Amorgos; some of these are on display at the Victoria and Albert Museum in London. Between the 17th and 19th centuries so many of these extraordinary pieces were sold, that a hero of the revolution, General Makriyiannis, threatened to declare war on Amorgos should the island send any more abroad: but Amorgos heeded not. However, rather than battling with Makriyiannis, the island simply ran out of embroideries, and no one now remembers how to make them. The highlight of the island's later history occurred when Brigitte Bardot paid it a visit in 1973.

116

WHAT TO SEE

Because of the condition of the road linking the two halves of Amorgos, many ships call at both of the island's ports, Katapola in the south and Aegiali in the north. **Katapola** isn't much: a yacht supply station, a place to swim and a few pensions, and there is a bus to the capital. From Katapola you can walk up the hill to the ancient city of **Minoa** of which walls, part of the akropolis, a gymnasium and a few remains of a temple to Apollo can still be seen. The inhabitants believe the name Minoa comes from Minos, the King of the Mountain, or Minos, the King of Crete, although the great city states of Amorgos were a product of the Ionian culture; the island is closer to Asia Minor than the other Cyclades. Also near Katapola is **Rahidi** with the church Ag. Georgios on the site of an oracle used in antiquity.

The town of **Amorgos,** also known as Chora, is a typical white Cycladic town, which sits more than 300 metres (1000 ft) above sea level. A neat column of windmills (each family had its own) once laboured with the winds that rose up the dizzying precipices from the sea. In the middle of town, on a rocky mount, is the castle built by Geremia Gizi in 1290. The locals call it Apano Kastro, and steps lead up to it; it is well preserved and affords a panoramic view of the island.

A road has been built to the island's main sight, the grand **Monastery of Chozoviotissa** ("life saving") and cars have replaced mules as the easiest form of transport. Most people, however, prefer to walk down from the bus stop—a dramatic 20-minute walk down a serpentine path. At the foot of the steep 180-metre (600-ft) orange cliff lies the monastery—a huge, white fortress, resembling one great wall built into the living rocks. (Be sure to dress modestly; the monastery is open mornings and after 5 pm.)

Inside, the monastery has some 50 rooms, 2 churches and 3 monks. The miraculous icon of the Madonna from Constantinople is still there, along with 98 hand-written manuscripts in its library. For many years a mysterious spear, thrown by unknown hands, was seemingly impossibly stuck in the rock of the cliff over the monastery, and although it finally fell down, worn away by time, there are still many stories about it. In 1976 a less mysterious rock fell on the monastery and went through three floors, but repairs have been carried out by the government.

The other ancient city in the southern half of Amorgos is **Arkesini,** which has extensive tombs, walls and houses, near the modern hamlet of **Kastri.** A well-preserved Hellenistic tower may be seen near here at **Ag. Trias.** There are several quiet beaches (like **Kalofana**) in the south. Most people who stay in Chora go to white **Ag. Anna** beach, the closest to town and the monastery.

Although it's easiest to reach the north side of Amorgos by boat, there is a track that crosses the rough terrain, guarded on either side by an occasional tower (the walk takes about five hours). **Aegiali,** small and charming, is Amorgos' northern port and main resort, with the island's one real sandy beach. In some shops here, and in Chora, you can find embroidered scarves made locally, but they are nothing like the original embroideries of Amorgos. Near Aegiali are the scant remains of ancient **Aegiali;** at **Tholaria** you can see Greek vaulted tholos tombs which date from the Roman period. A pleasant walk from Aegiali takes you along the mule paths to **Potamos,** which has a tiny café on a terrace with a commanding view of the port below, with its amphitheatre of hills, and the sunset.

PANEYERIA
The good people of Amorgos have yet to become bored by tourism, and they go out of their way to invite guests to their celebrations: 26 July, Ag. Paraskevi at Arkesini; 15 August at Langada and 21 November at the Chozoviotissa Monastery.

WHERE TO STAY
In the port Katapola, there are several pensions, most prominently the **Pension Amorgos** (tel. 0285 71 214) where doubles cost around 1300 dr., showers included. Most people prefer to stay elsewhere—in one of the numerous rooms in Chora (there are no official pensions or hotels here) or Aegiali, where you can choose between the ageing **Mike Hotel** (tel. 0285 71 252, open only in the summer) where rooms are 3000 dr. or the **Pension Lakki,** where singles are around 1400 dr., doubles an economical 2000 dr. Both are on the beach, where those who can't get rooms (or don't care to) can sleep out without too many hassles. Ag. Anna beach serves the same function on the south half of the island.

EATING OUT
Amorgos has good, inexpensive, and very Greek tavernas in its main centres. Try asking around which is the best and you'll most likely receive the gentle response that they're all the best, so as not to hurt anyone's feelings.

Between Amorgos and Naxos lie a bevy of tiny islands, three of which—Heraklia (or Iraklia), Shinoussa and Koufonissia—are served by the daily boat between Naxos and Amorgos, and the occasional steamer from Piraeus. These three all have rooms to rent; they are certainly quiet places, and not prepared to take many visitors. If you plan to stay any length of time, you should bring some food along, and be prepared to be sparing with the water.

Heraklia, the most westernly and the largest, has rooms in its port, Ag. Georgios; from here it's a 20-minute walk to the large sandy beach at **Livadi.** The one excursion, other than to the beach, is to walk along the mule path from Ag. Georgios to the tiny hamlet of **Iraklia,** and from there to the large cave overlooking Vourkaria Bay, then back along the west coast to Ag. Georgios. **Shinoussa,** a short hop from Heraklia, has a hotel in its "capital" of the same name, and two beaches, one at the charming, miniature port, and the other across the island at **Psili Ammos.** Shinoussa is blessed with fresh springs, and supports a species of mastic bush on its relatively flat surface.

Koufonissia is two islands; lower, or Kato, Koufonisi, is just barely inhabited, while **Koufonisi** itself has two restaurants and two beaches, at **Harakopou** and **Pori.** From here you may be able to take a caique to **Keros,** which has the ruins of a Neolithic settlement at **Daskalio** on the west coast, and those of an abandoned medieval settlement in the north. To reach **Donoussa**, east of Naxos, you have to take the steamer from Piraeus or the small boat from Naxos. A Geometric settlement was excavated on the island, but most of its visitors come for its fine sandy beaches on the south coast near the villages of Donoussa, the port, and **Mersini**

ANAFI

CONNECTIONS
Twice a week with Piraeus, Santorini, Ag. Nikolaos and Sitia, in Crete, Kassos, Karpathos and Rhodes. Once a week with Milos and Folegandros.

Anafi, most southerly of the Cyclades, is a primitive island, difficult of access, its one village lacking many amenities, its coasts unblessed with beaches. Food is not easy to find, and visitors should bring along provisions to supplement the little fish and macaroni available locally. But if the crowds and noise seem too thick elsewhere, Anafi may be the antidote of peace and quiet you seek; here the inhabitants continue to go about their lives as they always have. Little contact with the outside world has meant that several old customs have been preserved, and some have found in the Anafiotes' songs and paneyeria traces of their origins from the ancient worship of Apollo.

HISTORY
Apollo had a particularly strong following on Anafi. According to mythology, Anafi rose at the command of Apollo to shelter Jason and the Argonauts, besieged by a tempest, and has ever since kept its 28-sq,. km (11-sq. mile) head out of the water. In the 15th century BC, however, a great deal of volcanic rock, 5 metres (16 ft) thick in some places, was added to Anafi from the explosion of Santorini, brought to the island by wind and tidal wave. Both Apollo and Artemis were worshipped on the island from early times, and the ruins of their temple remain on the site of the ancient town. The twelfth Duke of Naxos, Giacamo Crispi, gave Anafi to his brother who built a castle, which did very little when the terror of the Aegean, Barbarossa, turned up, enslaving the entire population. For a long time Anafi remained deserted, people trickling back only when it was safer.

WHAT TO SEE
The island's one village **Chora,** with some 300 people, is a short walk up from the landing. A path leads east of the village to **Katelimatsa,** with a few ruins of ancient houses, and to the island's main attraction, the **Monastery of Panayia Kalmiotissa,** built near the remains of the ancient temple to Apollo, dedicated by Jason in gratitude to the god. The **Kastro** built by Guglielmo Crispi is to the north of the village and half ruined; a path leads up to its rocky height.

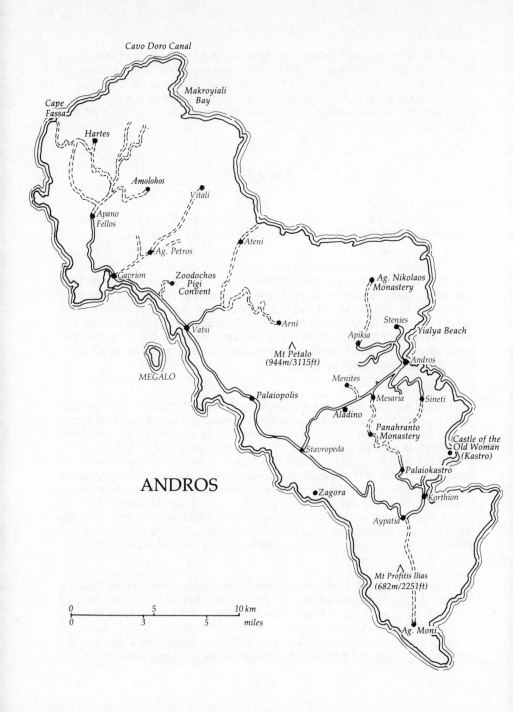

Cavo Doro Canal

Makroyiali
Bay

Cape
Fassa

Hartes

Amolohos

Vitali

Apano
Fellos

Ateni

Ag. Petros

Gavrion

Zoodochos
Pigi
Convent

Ag. Nikolaos
Monastery

Stenies

Yialya Beach

Vatsi

Arni

Apikia

MEGALO

Mt Petalo
(944m/3115ft)

Andros

Menites

Palaiopolis

Mesaria

Sineti

Aladino

Panahranto
Monastery

Castle of the
Old Woman
(Kastro)

ANDROS

Stavropeda

Palaiokastro

Zagora

Korthion

Aypatia

Mt Profitis Ilias
(682m/2251ft)

0   5   10 km
0   3   5   miles

Ag. Moni

PANEYERIA
15 August, Panayia at the monastery, known for its special folk dances.

WHERE TO STAY
There are a few primitive rooms to rent in Chora; ask around if you're not offered one of them when you get off the ship.

EATING OUT
Food, as mentioned above, is another problem, but such is the price of solitude these days.

ANDROS

CONNECTIONS
Daily with Rafina, Tinos and Mykonos, less often with Syros.

One of the largest and most populated of the Cyclades, Andros, like Kea, is an island much more visited by Greeks with summer villas than by foreigners. In the south only the narrowest of straits separates Andros from Tinos, while in the north the blustery Doro Channel, long dreaded by sailors, lies between the island and Evia. However, the same irksome wind also makes Andros, and especially its capital, one of the coolest spots in the Aegean in July and August. Vegetation, even forest, covers the land between the rocks, and fresh water is abundant, especially mineral water which is commercially exploited. Like Tinos, Andros was embellished by the Venetians with lovely white dovecots. It is a prosperous island, famed for its captains and ship-owners, and the people are known for their friendly nature.

HISTORY
The name Andros is thought to be derived from the Phoenician Arados, or perhaps from Andrea, the general sent by Rhadamanthys of Crete to govern the island. In 1000 BC Ionians colonised Andros, leading to its early cultural bloom in the Archaic period. Dionysos was the most popular god worshipped at the pantheon on Palaiopolis, the leading city at the time, and a certain temple of his had the remarkable talent of turning water into wine during the Dionysia.

After the Athenian victory at Salamis, Themistokles tried to fine Andros for supporting Xerxes. As the Andrians refused to pay, he besieged the island, but was unsuccessful and had to return home empty handed. Although the islanders later assisted the Greeks at Plataea, Athenians held a grudge against Andros, and in 448 BC Perikles divided the island between Athenian colonists, who taxed the inhabitants heavily. In response the Andrians supported Athens' enemies whenever they could: when the Peloponnesian War broke out, they withdrew from the Delian alliance and sided with Sparta, supporting that city throughout the war, in spite of siege by Alcibiades and Konon. Spartan oppression, however, proved just as awful as Athenian oppression, and things were no better during the succession of Hellenistic rulers, although a magnificent statue of Hermes, the Conductor of the Dead, dating from the 1st or 2nd century BC and found at Palaiopolis, suggests that at least art survived the constant change of kings.

For putting up resistance to their conquest, the Romans banished the entire population of Andros to Boetia, and gave the island to Attalos I, King of Pergamon. When permitted to return, the inhabitants found their homes pillaged and faced many a rough year. Byzantium proved a blessing compared with the past, despite Saracen raiding. In the Venetian free for all, another nephew of Doge Enrico Dandolo, Marino Dandolo, took Andros, and allied himself with his cousin Marco Sanudo, the Duke of Naxos. Most of the surviving fortifications were constructed under the Dandoli.

In 1566 the Turks took the island. Apart from collecting taxes, they left the island more or less to its own devices, and many Albanians from nearby Karystos (Evia) settled on Andros. In 1821 Andros' famous son, the philosopher Theophilos Kairis, declared the revolution at the cathedral of Andros. The island contributed money and weapons to the struggle. In 1943 the Germans bombed the island for two days when the Italians stationed there refused to surrender.

WHAT TO SEE
The capital, alternatively known as Chora or **Andros,** is built on a long, narrow tongue of land, and adorned with the grand neo-Classical mansions of the island's ship-owners, its main thoroughfare (pedestrians only) paved with marble slabs. At the edge of the town a bridge leads to the Venetian castle, **Kato Kastro,** built by Marino Dandolo and damaged in the 1943 bombardment, now watched over by a statue of the Unknown Soldier. **Plateia Riva,** the square before the arch, has a small **museum** dedicated to Andros' seafaring history, but you may have to ask around for the key. Below here at a spot called **Kamara** the locals dive into the sea—there are sandy beaches on either side of town, but they're often windswept.

Up the main street (often scented with cheese and custard pies made at the local bakery), some of the island's public offices are located in the old mansions: the post office, banks and telephone office are in the centre of town, and the bus station is just a few steps away.

The town's inadequate port, **Emborios,** is no longer used for large boats (the ferry calls at Gavrion) and it is now a popular beach; a small church, **Ag. Thalassini,** guards one end of the harbour from a throne of rock. The town's cathedral, **Ag. Georgios,** is built on the ruins of a 17th-century church.

The following legend is told about a third church, **Theoskepasti,** built in 1555. When the wood for the church's roof arrived in Andros from Piraeus, the priest found that he couldn't afford the price demanded for it by the captain of the ship. Angrily, the captain set sail again only to run into a fierce, boiling tempest. The sailors prayed to the Virgin, promising to bring the wood back to Andros should she save their lives. Instantly the sea grew calm again, and Theoskepasti, or Roof of God, was completed without further difficulty. It was dedicated to the Virgin Mary, who also has a miracle-working icon inside the church.

From Chora frequent buses leave for the **island's villages,** Many go to Gavrion when a ship is coming in (check the timetable at the bus station). At nearby **Stenies** is a lovely beach, Yialya. **Apikia** bottles the mineral water Sariza and owns the 16th-century monastery Ag. Nikolaos to the north. The main road to the west coast passes through the fertile Mesaria Valley with its numerous villages, winding stone walls and dovecots. **Menites,** a mountain village, is gifted with waters and might have been the location of Dionysos' miraculous temple, at the church Panayias tis Koumulous. By Menites is **Mesaria,** with a church of the Taxiarchos built in 1158 by the Emperor Manuel Comnenos. Mesaria was the home of a legendary nun named Rose. She lived during the 18th century, curing people and making an icon of Ag. Nikolaos from her hair, which she gave to the church of that saint, built in 1732.

From Mesaria a path and an hour's walk takes you to the most important monastery on Andros, **Panahranto,** founded shortly after Nikephoros Phokas' liberation of Crete in 961, and supposedly visited by the emperor himself. South of Mesaria, at **Aladino,** a cave with the picturesque name of Chaos may be visited—it has several chambers with stalactites (bring a light—the villagers know its location as Lasthinou).

Buses go to the Bay of Korthion in the south-east, with its beach, hotel and rooms. The fishing here has an excellent reputation, but if they're not biting you can always eat in one of the fish tavernas along the waterfront. To the north of the bay is the ruined **castle of the Old Woman,** so named for a certain lady who abhorred the Venetians. She tricked them into letting her inside the fort, and later opened the door to the Turks who slaughtered many of the Venetians. Very upset by this, the old woman leapt from the castle and landed on a rock now known as "Tis Grias to Pidema" or Old Lady's Leap. **Palaiokastro,** another fortification built by Dandolo, is a bit north of Korthion, and in ruins.

Palaiopolis on the west coast was the ancient capital of Andros, inhabited until around AD 1000 when the people moved to Mesaria. An earthquake in the 4th century AD destroyed part of it, and pirates finished the job. Walls and part of the akropolis are preserved, along with the ruins of buildings and temples, although the site has yet to be thoroughly explored. **Vatsi.** to the north, is Andros' most popular tourist resort. Occasionally the steamer calls here, as well as at Gavrion. From Vatsi you can visit the convent **Zoodochos Pigi,** built in the 14th century and containing icons from that century onwards. The nuns of the convent run a weaving factory. **Arnas,** on the northern slopes of Andros' highest peak, Mt Petalo, is the garden of the island, with its greenery, trees and water.

The main port, **Gavrion,** is further up the coast, with many facilities and a beach, though in itself it has little charm. From here it's a 40-minute or so walk up to **Ag. Petros,** the best-preserved ancient monument on Andros. Dating from

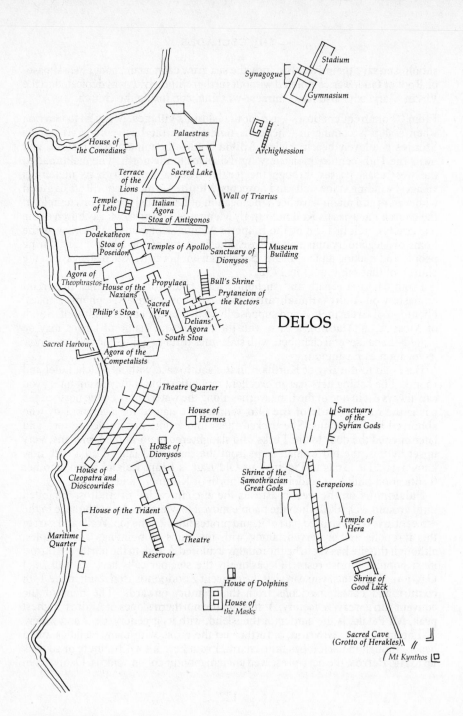

Stadium

Synagogue

Gymnasium

House of
the Comedians

Palaestras

Archighession

Terrace
of the
Lions

Sacred Lake

Temple
of Leto

Italian
Agora
Stoa of Antigonos

Wall of Triarius

Dodekatheon

Stoa of
Poseidon

Temples of Apollo

Sanctuary of
Dionysos

Museum
Building

Agora of
Theophrastos

House of the
Naxians

Propylaea

Bull's Shrine

Prytaneion of
the Rectors

Philip's Stoa

Sacred
Way

Delians'
Agora

South Stoa

DELOS

Sacred Harbour

Agora of the
Competalists

Theatre Quarter

House of
Hermes

Sanctuary
of the
Syrian Gods

House of
Dionysos

House of
Cleopatra and
Dioscourides

Shrine of the
Samothracian
Great Gods

Serapeions

House of the Trident

Temple of
Hera

Maritime
Quarter

Theatre

Reservoir

Shrine of
Good Luck

House of Dolphins

House of
the Masks

Sacred Cave
(Grotto of Herakles)

Mt Kynthos

the Hellenistic era, the tower stands some 20 metres (65 ft) high—the upper storeys were reached by ladder—and its inner hall is still topped by a corbelled dome. The landscape around here squirms with stone walls that resemble caterpillars with humps.

Amolohos, an isolated mountain village in the north, is well known for its beauty. Another ancient tower is located further north at Zorkos Bay.

PANEYERIA
15 August, at Korthinon; Theoskepasti, 15 days before Easter, and 19 June, Analapsis, both at Andros; 23 August, at Menites.

WHERE TO STAY
Like Kea, Andros is an island whose tourism infrastructure is geared to long term stays. The Athenians who don't own villas fill up the hotels and it may well be difficult, especially in the capital, to find a hotel or pension that will let you stay for only a few nights. The most elegant place in the capital nevertheless is the **Paradissos Hotel** (tel. 0282 22 187/9) in a graceful, neo-Classical confection near the centre of town. A double here is in the 6000 dr. range. The **Xenia** has rooms at about the same price (tel. 0282 22 270).

Most visitors end up staying in Gavrion or Vatsi, both of which have small hotels and numerous rooms to rent. The latter is much the nicer and of its pensions the **Lykion** (tel. 0282 41 214) is the most pleasant, its immaculate doubles costing 3500 dr.

Apikia, just north of the capital, also has rooms and bungalows. **Helena.** (tel. 028 22 2281) is quiet and small, but again likely to be completely booked unless you call before the season. Rates here are 3000–4000 dr.

EATING OUT
Waves of foreign tourists always hike up prices, but this hasn't happened yet in Andros. The best restaurants are in Andros town, and near the beach.

TOURIST POLICE
See regular police, Gavrion, tel. (0282) 71 220.

DELOS

CONNECTIONS
Tourist boat from Mykonos daily at 9 am, returning at 12.30 pm, or at 10.15 am, returning at 1.30 pm, with a guide (cost 2000 dr.), or hire a private boat at the main harbour, or Platis Gialos. Admission fee to land on the island, which is a 3.50-km^2 (1.35 sq. mile) outdoor archaeology museum.

Today Delos, holy island of the ancient Greeks, centre of the great maritime alliance of the Greek golden age, a major free port in Hellenistic and Roman times that controlled much of the east–west trade in the Mediterranean, is deserted except for the government-appointed guardian of the ruins, a small hotel, and scores of lizards sporting among the broken marble. Even though the ancients allowed no burials on Delos, the island feels haunted, not so much in the morning when the crowds descend on it from Mykonos, but in the evening and at night.

MYTHOLOGY
The ancient name of Delos was Ortygia, derived from one of Zeus' love affairs, this time with a maiden named Asteria. Asteria fled the lusty king of the gods in the form of a quail, and Zeus turned himself into an eagle the better to pursue her. The pursuit proved so hot that Asteria turned into a rock and fell into the sea. This rock was known as Ortygia, or Adelos, the invisible one, as it floated all over Greece just below the surface of the sea. Some time later Zeus fell in love with Asteria's sister Leto, whom he approached in the form of a swan to avoid the difficulties he had with her sister. But Zeus' wife, Hera, soon discovered the affair and in a fit of jealousy begged Mother Earth not to allow Leto to give birth anywhere under the sun. All over the world wandered poor, suffering Leto, unable to find a rock to stand on, as all feared the wrath of Hera. Finally in pity Zeus turned to his brother Poseidon and asked him to help his miserable mistress. Poseidon thereupon ordered Ortygia to halt, and anchored the islet with four columns of solid diamond. Thus Adelos the Invisible, not under the sun but under the sea, became Delos, the Visible. Delos, however, was reluctant to have Leto, fearing her son would give her a resounding kick back into the sea. But Leto promised the islet that no such thing would happen; indeed her son would make Delos the richest sanctuary in Greece. The island conceded, and Leto gave birth first to Artemis, goddess of the hunt and virginity, and then nine days later to Apollo, the god of truth and light.

HISTORY
In the 3rd millennium BC Delos was settled by the Karians, and by 1000 BC the Ionians had made it their religious capital, introducing the cult of Apollo whom they believed to be the father of the founder of their race, Ion. This cult is first mentioned in a Homeric hymn of the 7th century BC. Games and pilgrimages took place, and Delos was probably the centre of the Amphictyonic league of the Ionians (a maritime confederation). In 550 BC Polycrates, the Tyrant of Samos, conquered the Cyclades but respected Delos, giving the island the islet Rheneia, and symbolically binding it to Delos with a chain.

With the rise of Athens, notably under Pisistratos, Delos' greatest glory and greatest difficulties begin. What was once entirely sacred started to take on a political significance, and the Athenians invented stories to connect themselves to Delos—did not Erechtheus, the King of Athens, lead the first delegation to Delos? After slaying the Minotaur on Crete did not Theseus stop at Delos and

126

dance around the altar of Apollo? In 543 BC the Athenians even managed to find an oracle at Delphi ordering the purification of the island, which meant removing the old tombs, a manoeuvre designed to alienate the Delians from their past and thus diminishing the island's importance in comparison to Athens'.

In 490 BC the population of Delos fled to Tinos before the Persians under Darius, who, according to Herodotos, respected the sacred site and sacrificed 300 talents' worth of incense to Apollo. The Delians, furthermore, were told they could return home in safety. The Persians lost the war, and after the Battle of Salamis the Athenians, to prevent further invasions, organised a new Amphictyonic league, or Delian alliance, for its centre was to be at Delos. Only the Athenian fleet could guarantee protection to the island allies, who were required to contribute a yearly sum and ships to support the navy. Athenian archons administered the funds.

The Delian alliance was effective, despite the resentment among the islanders who disliked being lorded over by the Athenians, for the contributions became more like tributes. In 454 BC Perikles, in order better to "protect" or rather spend the league's treasury, placed it on Athens' akropolis; some of the money went to repair damage incurred during the previous Persian invasion, and some to beautify Athens generally. To make matters worse, a terrible plague hit Athens, and as it was determined to have been caused by the wrath of Apollo, a second purification of Delos was called for. This time not only did the Athenians remove all the old tombs, but they forbade both births and death on Delos, forcing the pregnant and the dying to go to Rheneia. Thus the alienation of the Delians was complete. When the people turned to Sparta for aid during the Peloponnesian War, the Spartans remained unmoved: since the inhabitants couldn't be born or die on the island, it wasn't really their homeland, and why should they help a group of foreigners? In 422 BC Athens punished Delos for going to Sparta by exiling the entire population (for being "unpure") to Asia Minor, where all the leaders were slain by cunning. Athenians moved in to take the Delians' place, but Athens herself was punished by the gods for her greed and suffered many drawbacks in the Peloponnesian War. After a year, hoping to regain divine favour, Athens allowed the Delians to return home. From 403 to 394 BC Delos had a breath of freedom when the Spartans defeated Athens, and 50 years later the islanders applied to the Amphictyonic league to oust the Athenians from the shrine altogether. The head of the league at the time, Philip II of Macedon, refused the request, wishing to stay on good terms with the city that hated him most.

In the confusion following the death of Philip's son, Alexander the Great, Delos became free and prosperous, supported by the pious Macedonian kings. Many new buildings and shrines were constructed and by 250 BC Delos was a cosmopolitan, commercial port, flourishing through the business of merchants from all over the Mediterranean. When the Romans defeated the Macedonians in 166 BC they returned the island to Athens, which exiled the Delians to Achaia. But by 146 BC and the fall of Corinth, Delos was the centre of all east–west trade, and declared a free port by the Romans in order to undermine business at Rhodes. People from all over the world settled on the island and set up their own cults in complete tolerance. Roman trade guilds, each with its own *lares*, centred on the Italian Agora. New quays and piers were constructed to deal with the heavy flow of vessels. Markets thrived.

In the battle of the Romans with Mithradates of Pontus in 88 BC, Delos was robbed of many of her treasures; 20 000 people were killed, and the women and children carried off as slaves. This was the beginning of the end of Delos. General Sulla regained the ruined island, but 19 years later Delos was again destroyed by pirates allied to Mithradates, and the population was again dragged off to the slave markets. General Triarius retook the island and fortified it with walls, and Hadrian attempted to revive the waning cult of Apollo with new festivities, but failed. Delos went into such a decline that when Athens tried to sell the wretched place, no one offered to buy it. In AD 363 the Emperor Julian the Apostate tried to renew paganism on Delos, but the oracles solemnly warned: "Delos shall become Adelos", and he gave up the idea. Later Theodosius the Great banned all heathen ceremonies. A small Christian community survived on Delos until the 6th century, when it was given over to the rule of pirates. House builders on Tinos and Mykonos used Delos for a marble quarry, and it became a pasture land.

After the independence of Greece, Delos and Rheneia were placed in the municipality of Mykonos. Major archaeological excavations were begun in 1872 by the French School of Archaeology in Athens under Dr Lebeque, and the work continues.

WHAT TO SEE

A trip to **Delos** begins as one clambers out of the caique and pays the entrance fee. After this the rest is easy. All the major sites are labelled, and at a normal walking pace everything of interest to the average dilettante can be seen in three hours. Basically Delos is laid out as follows.

To one's left from the boat landing stage is the **Agora of the Competalists**. Compita were Roman citizens or freed slaves who worshipped the Lares Competales, or crossroad gods. These established the Roman trade guilds, along with the others under the protection of Hermes, Apollo or Zeus. Many of the remains in the Agora are votive offerings to these gods; there are also ruins of the shops. A road, once lined with statues, leads to the sanctuary of Apollo. To the left of the road is the long **Philip's Stoa,** built by Philip V of Macedon in 210 BC. Only the foundations remain of this once tall and splendid building of the Doric order. General Sulla once placed a votary statue inside it for his victory over Mithradates. The kings of Pergamon built the **Southern Stoa** in the 3rd century BC, and one can also see the remains of the **Delians' Agora,** the local marketplace in the area.

The **Sanctuary of Apollo** is announced by the **Propylaea,** a gateway built in the 2nd century BC of white marble. Little remains of the sanctuary itself, once crowded with temples, votive offerings and statues. Next door to it is the **House of the Naxians,** built in the 6th century BC. Once a huge kouros, or statue, of Apollo as a young man stood there, of which only the pedestal remains. According to Plutarch the statue was destroyed by a huge bronze palm tree placed near it by the Athenians, which toppled in the wind and brought the Naxian Apollo down with it.

Next one comes upon the **three temples of Apollo.** The first and largest was begun by the Delians in 476 BC. The second was an Athenian construction of Pentelic marble, built during the Second Purification, and the third, of porous stone, was made by the 6th-century Athenian tyrant Pisistratos. Dimitrios the Besieger contributed the **Bull's Shrine** which held a trireme in honour of the sacred delegation ship of Athens—the very one Theseus sailed in on his return to Athens after slaying the Minotaur, the ship whose departure put off executions, most famously that of Socrates, until its return to Athens. Other buildings in the area had an official purpose—the **Prytaneion of the Rectors** and the **Councillor's house.** Towards the museum is the **sanctuary of Dionysos** of the 4th century BC, flanked by its marble phalli. The **Stoa of Antigonos** was built by a Macedonian king of that name in the 3rd century BC. Outside the stoa is the **Tomb of the Hyperborean Virgins,** who came to help Leto give birth to Apollo and Artemis, thus making the tomb sacred and irremovable during the purifications.

On the other side of the Stoa stood the **Abaton,** the holy of holies, where only the priests could enter. The **Minoan fountain** nearby is from the 6th century BC. Through the **Italian Agora** one comes to the **Temple of Leto** (6th century) and the **Dodekatheon,** dedicated to the 12 gods of Olympos in the 3rd century BC. Beyond, where the **Sacred Lake** has dried up, is the famous **Terrace of the Lions,** ex-votos made by the Naxians in the 7th century BC. The lake, sacred for having witnessed the birth of Apollo, was surrounded by a small wall which still exists. When Delos' torrent Inopos stopped flowing, the water evaporated. Along the shore are two **Palaestras** (buildings for exercises and lessons) along with the foundation of the **Archighession,** or temple to the first mythical settler on Delos, worshipped only on that island. Besides the **Gymnasium** and **Stadium** there are the remains of a few houses and a **synagogue** built by the Phoenician Jews in the 2nd century BC.

A dirt path leads from the tourist pavilion to Mt Kynthos (110 metres/360 ft). Along the way one comes to the **Sanctuary of the Syrian Gods** of 100 BC with a small religious theatre within. The first of **three Serapeions** follows, dedicated to the Egyptian god Serapis. All three shrines were built in the 2nd century BC. Between the first and second Serapeions is the **shrine to the Samothracian Great Gods,** the Cabiri or underworld deities. Next is the third Serapeion, perhaps the main sanctuary, with temples to both Serapis and Isis, half a statue remaining. In the region are houses with mosaics, and a **temple to Hera** from 500 BC. **The Sacred Cave** is on the way to the top of Mt Kynthos, where Apollo ran an oracle. Later it was dedicated to Herakles. On the mountain itself is the

Shrine of Good Luck, built by Arsinoe Philadelphos, wife of her brother, the King of Egypt. On the summit of Kynthos signs of a settlement dating back to 3000 BC have been discovered, but better yet is the view, encompassing nearly all the Cyclades.

The **Theatre Quarter** consists of the private houses surrounding the **Theatre of Delos** from the 2nd century BC, which seated 5500; beside it is a lovely eight-arched **reservoir.** The houses of the quarter date from the Hellenistic and Roman ages and many have mosaics, some beautifully preserved, such as in the **House of the Dolphins** and the **House of the Masks.** All houses have a cistern beneath the floor, spaces for oil lamps and sewage systems. Some are built in the peristyle "style of Rhodes" with a high-ceilinged guest room. Columns bordered the central courts, open to the sun. Other special houses include the **House of the Trident** and the **House of Dionysos,** both with mosaics, and the **House of Cleopatra and Dioscourides,** where the statues stand a headless guard over the once great town.

Surrounding Delos are the islets **Ag. Georgios** (named for the monastery there), **Karavonissi, Mikro** and **Megalo Rematiaris,** the last was consecrated to Hecate, the Queen of the Night. **Rheneia,** also known as Greater Delos, lies just west of Delos and is also uninhabited. Here came the pregnant or dying Delians—a large number of little rooms were excavated which probably received them as well as tombs and sepulchral altars. A nekropolis, discovered near the shore, was the repository of the coffins which the Athenians exhumed in the 2nd purification. On the other side of Rheneia are the ruins of a lazaretto, used more recently by Syros-bound ships which were in quarantine.

WHERE TO STAY
There's one small hotel, the **Xenia,** with four rooms and seven beds, so naturally you have to book well in advance. Prices range from 4000 dr. to 6000 dr., depending on the time of the year (tel. 0289 22 259).

FOLEGANDROS

CONNECTIONS
Daily with Ios and Sikinos; several times a week with Piraeus, Santorini, Milos, Paros, Naxos, Crete, Karpathos and Rhodes; once a week with Sifnos, Serifos and Kythnos.

The name Folegandros comes from the Phoenician "Phlegundum" meaning "the rocky island", a name which fits it well. The ancient city of the island is located on a high plateau above the modern capital, Chora, which itself dates back to the Middle Ages, set high above the sea away from would-be pirates. In the 13th century Marco Sanudo built a fortress by the ancient town; the houses themselves, two storeys high, formed a wall around Chora.

Folegandros is a small dry island of 650 inhabitants, one of the smallest in Greece with a permanent population. It has become a popular place for escapists, though there is an occasional day trip from Ios. Boats land at **Karavostassis,** the tiny harbour, which has restaurants and rooms to rent, and is within walking distance of shady **Livadi** beach, from where a rough path wil take you inland to visit the remote **Evangelistra monastery** on top of the rocky southern shores of the island. An easier path leads back to **Chora** from here. If you are going on any long walks in high-summer, wear a hat and take a bottle of water with you. A bus runs from the port to **Chora,** the capital, perched on the cliffs some 300 metres (1000 ft) above the sea. It is a pretty village with shady, sleepy squares. The ancient city with its sparse remains was on the hill above; Marco Sanudo's **medieval kastro** is delineated by the solid square of houses, whose backs once formed the outside wall.

The church **Panayia** stands high up on a commanding headland; beyond it there is a large cave, **Chrisispilio** (the Golden Cave), with stalactites and stalagmites, but access is difficult; ask in Chora for someone to guide you.

Ano Mera, 5 km (3 miles) west, is the only other village on Folegandros, and has two tavernas and a limited number of rooms to rent; from here; on a clear day, you can see Crete. Tracks from here lead down to seldom-visited beaches at Vigla, Livadaki and Vathi. From the road between Ano Mera and Chora a path descends to Agali beach, which has two simple tavernas and 13 rooms for rent, but no electricity. Next door is the quiet Ag. Nikolaos beach with a basic canteen. Both of these beaches can be reached by the boat which leaves Karavostassis at 11.15 am, returning at 5 pm.

PANEYERIA
15 August at Panayia; and Easter, when an icon is paraded and trips are made in boats around the island.

WHERE TO STAY
There are rooms to let in private homes in Chora, at 1700 dr. on average in the summer, as well as the island's one real hotels: the small **Odysseus** (tel. 0286 41 239), where the doubles in season are 2300 dr. with shower, singles 1800 dr. The larger and more comfortable B class **Fani-Vevie** (tel. 0286 41 237) has doubles at 2700 dr. with shower; the **Danassis** is a class E hotel with simple double rooms for 2200 dr. (tel. 0286 41 230). Down in Karavostassis the pleasant **Aeolos** (tel. 0286 41 205) on the beach has doubles fro 3100 dr. The beach at Livadi has a **campsite** (350 dr. a night per person, tents 500 dr.) with taverna, bar and laundry facilities. However, there are always more visitors than available space in the summer, so be prepared to sleep out, and, if it comes to that, be sure to find shelter from the strong, nagging winds.

EATING OUT
In Chora the taverna **O Kritikos** (the owner is Cretan) has delicious chicken on the spit, and with wine a meal will run to an exorbitant 500 dr., more if you opt for

Monastery on Ios

the freshly caught lobster sizzling on the grill. Also in Chora **Nicos taverna** serves standard chops and salads for 600 dr. a person in an unpretentious garden setting. Possibly the owner fears that a lick of paint and a tidying up of the courtyard could take away from its rustic charms. On Livadi beach **To Kati Allo** ("the something else") has a small army of ladies in the kitchen producing an excellent selection of ready cooked dishes, which you can enjoy while gazing out across the serene bay.

IOS

CONNECTIONS
In summer there are daily connections with Santorini, Paros, Naxos, Syros and Piraeus, and excursion boats to Sikinos and Folegandros; several times a week to Mykonos, Anafi, Milos, Serifos, Sifnos and Herakleon.

Ios has become the Fort Lauderdale of Europe, the resort for throngs of young people who spend their days lounging on the best beach in the Cyclades, their evenings sauntering from one watering hole to another, and their nights sleeping out on the beach. If that's the hard life you're seeking, Ios is the place. Otherwise, despite the loveliness of Ios and its beach, you may well feel disenchanted by the crowds and the rock'n'roll. I know people who go back to Ios every summer, and I know people you couldn't pay to ever return there again.

Tradition has it that the mother of Homer came from Ios, and it is to this island that the great poet returned at the end of his life. Some say it was a riddle told by the fishermen of Ios that killed Homer in a fit of perplexity: to wit, "What we

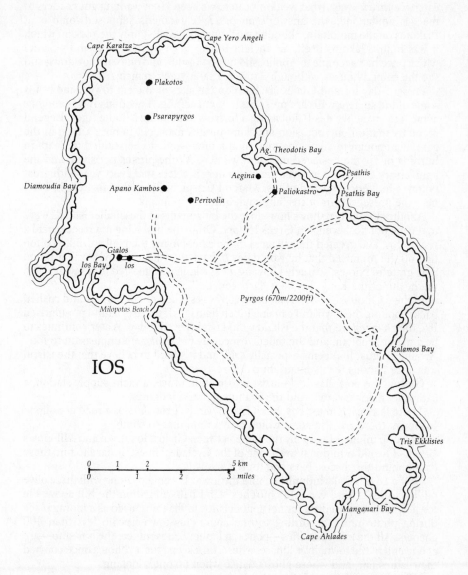

Cape Karatza   Cape Yero Angeli

● Plakotos

● Psarapyrgos

Ag. Theodotis Bay

Aegina ●   ● Psathis

Diamoudia Bay   Apano Kambos ●   Paliokastro   Psathis Bay

● Perivolia

Gialos ●
Ios Bay   ● Ios

Milopotas Beach

Pyrgos (670m/2200ft)

IOS

Kalamos Bay

| 0 | 1 | 2 | 5 km |
| 0 | 1 | 2 | 3 miles |

Tris Ekklisies

Manganari Bay

Cape Ahlades

catch we throw away; what we don't catch, we keep" (not wanting any readers to meet a similar fate, the answer's on p. 135!). Homer's supposed tomb is at Plakotos on the mountain, although earthquakes have left only the rock on which it was built. Plakotos itself, an ancient Ionian town (hence the island's name) which once had a temple to Apollo, slid down the cliff, and one can look down and see the ruined houses, although a tower, Psarapyrgos, remains.

Present-day Ios and Gialos are built on the sites of ancient towns, and at Ios some of the ancient walls are preserved. Aegina on Ag. Theodotis Bay is another ancient town; above it is Paliokastro, a fortress built in the Middle Ages. Legend recounts that on one occasion attacking pirates managed to bore a hole in the gate, big enough to allow one man in at a time—only to be scalded to death in burning oil by the besieged men and women. All the pirates perished, and the anniversary of the victory over the marauders is celebrated every year with great pomp. The Venetian Lord of Ios, Marco I Crispi, built another fortress in 1400 near the present town of Ios, although little of it remains.

Another local story shows how close the inhabitants of the smaller islands were to the big political events in Greek history: Otho, the first King of Greece, paid a visit to Ios, and greeted the villagers in the café, buying them all a drink. To top that off, he promised that he would pay to have the village cleaned up for them. The grateful Niotes, scarcely knowing what a king was, toasted him saying: "To the health of the King, Ios' new garbageman!"

In the earthquake of 1951, all the water was sucked out of Ios Bay and rushed back, flooding the town and causing much damage. If tourists hadn't popularised Ios, the chances are that the island would be deserted today. Water continues to be a major problem, and the toilets, especially in Gialos, are unpleasant to foul. Around August Ios seems especially arid, and it's hard to believe that the island was once famous for its luxuriant oak forests.

Gialos, the port, has Ios' tourist information office, a yacht supply station, a campsite, many tavernas and the island's quietest lodgings.

There is a beach in the bay, but it is very windy. From Gialos a road goes up to Ios town: there are also steps which take 15 minutes to climb.

Every 30 minutes buses ply the route between Gialos, **Ios town** and Milopotas Beach. The old traditional town, one of the Cyclades' finest, is hard to find these days behind the discos, bars and tourist shops.

Of the 18 original windmills behind the town, 12 remain, along with three olive oil "factories". Two very old churches stand half-ruined on the hill above the town, where supposedly a tunnel connects Ios to Plakotos, used as a hiding place during pirate raids; according to one count, Ios town has no less than 400 chapels. All the main facilities—police, telephone, post office, the bus stop—are at one end of the town, by a square, where, on a swing there, Niotes once courted their ladies fair, and where ghosts dance when no one's looking.

Milopotas with its superb sandy beach has several tavernas and two campsites, though most people just sleep where they can find room. Don't rely on that sleep, though, as Ios' all night beach parties have become infamous, even unfortunately ending in the deaths of several young people, due to overdoses of drugs and alcohol. Excursion boats leave Gialos every day for **Manganari Bay** (700 dr.), where there is a smart German-built bungalow resort, and **Psathis Bay,** where a certain church of the Virgin fell into the sea; at another church, **Ag. Ioannis Kalamos,** a huge paneyeri takes place on 29 August.

More remote (either hire a private boat or walk across Ios, a three-hour trek), is the fine beach at **Ag. Theodotis Bay** with the ruined Paliokastro. At the nearby monastery, Ag. Theodotis, one can even see the door the pirates broke through on the way to their doom. On 8 September a big celebration there commemorates the event with food and dance. **Perivolia,** a small settlement in the middle of the island, has water and trees; a church in the valley, **Ag. Barbara,** has a paneyeri on 26 July. **Apano Kambos.** once inhabited by a hundred families but today reduced to three or four, is another pretty place. Nearby, at a place called Hellinika, are huge monoliths of mysterious origin.

The island's speciality, megithra—a hard white cheese similar to Parmesan, mixed with perfume and fermented in a goatskin—is hard to find these days (all the better, some might add). But megithra cheese is not the answer to Homer's riddle: what the fishermen caught was lice.

WHERE TO STAY
Ios, the paradise of the footloose and fancy free, is surprisingly reasonable. You would get more peace and quiet staying in the port, but it's not much fun, and there are hundreds of rooms to let and several small hotels up in Chora. The **Afroditi Hotel** (tel. 0286 91 546), a bit outside of the tumultuous town centre is one of the best values you'll find, a double going for 3100 dr. **Homer's Inn,** in the town, has doubles for 3500 dr., but in high season you must book ahead (tel. 0286 91 365). On Milopotas Beach, the **Hotel Delfini** (tel. 0286 91 341) tends to fill up fast, but if you can get a room, it's one of the most genteel and civilised places to stay on Ios. Rates are 3500 dr. for a double, with showers. For something a little grander the **Ios Hotel** has bungalows near the beach for 8000 dr. in season, but these rates drop by as much as 50% in the off season (tel. 0286 91 224).

Down at Manganari Bay, the **Manganari Bungalow complex** offers luxury suites for 15 000 dr. (tel. 0286 91 215). Accessible only by boat from Gialos. For peace and quiet head for **Koumbara Beach** where there are a few rooms to let and one taverna; lovely after sunset. If you want to sleep out—but the police are cracking down—stay at **Soulis Campground** on the beach, the best of Ios' three grounds with showers and a place to wash clothes (tel. 0286 91 554).

EATING OUT
The **Ios Club,** on the footpath up from the harbour, has long been renowned for its views of sunset, its good drinks and Classical music (programme posted daily). At night it turns into a discotheque; it now has a restaurant as well with good food, some Greek and some more exotic dishes (800–1000 dr. a meal). In town, **The Nest** continues to be good and popular, especially for its prices—you can eat well

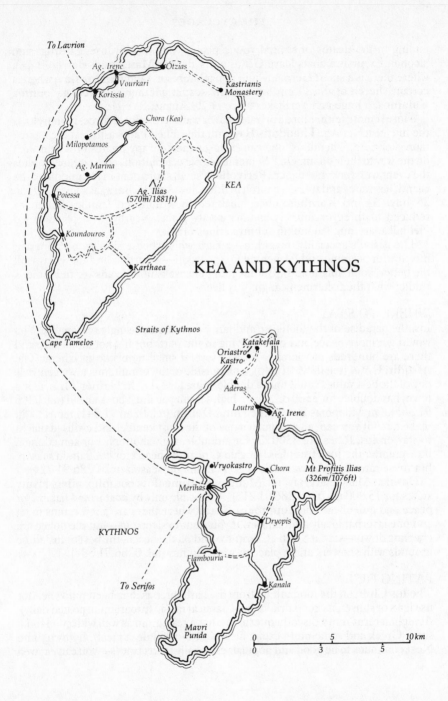

To Lavrion

Ag. Irene
Vourkari
Korissia

Otzias

Kastrianis
Monastery

Chora (Kea)

Milopotamos

Ag. Marina

Poiessa

Ag. Ilias
(570m/1881ft)

KEA

Koundouros

Karthaea

KEA AND KYTHNOS

Cape Tamelos

Straits of Kythnos

Katakefala

Oriastro
Kastro

Aderas

Loutra

Ag. Irene

Vryokastro

Chora

Mt Profitis Ilias
(326m/1076ft)

Merihas

KYTHNOS

Dryopis

Flambouria

To Serifos

Kanala

Mavri
Punda

0   5   10 km
0   3   5

for 500 dr. For psuedo-ethnic dishes try the **Why Not pub** which advertises chicken curry, chilli con carne, Alfredo's spaghetti and goulash. The more discerning head for **Calypso,** where the good music and civilised atmosphere is matched by the food. 1500 dr. per person. Down in Gialos the **Afroditi** is worth a look-in; choose well and some fine Greek food can be sampled for 1000 dr. per person. Fish 'n' chips, hamburgers and hot dogs can be found everywhere.

TOURIST INFORMATION
Information office in the port of Gialos (tel. 0286 91 207). Also see regular police in Chora (tel. 0286 91 228).

KEA (TSIA)

CONNECTIONS
Daily with Lavrion, weekly with Kythnos and Piraeus.

Closest of all the Cyclades to Athens, Kea has for many years been a favourite place to build a summer villa—timed correctly, the island can be reached from the metropolis in less than four hours. It also has a different feel to it: it is well watered, famed since antiquity for its fertility, renowned for its red wine, lemons, honey and almonds. Its traditional architecture, while interesting, lacks the pristine white cubism of its sister isles. Its beaches are lovely, but hardly empty in the summer, and more and more hotels materialise each year to cater for the needs of the increasing numbers of tourists.

HISTORY
Traces of a Neolithic fishing settlement were discovered at Kefala on Kea's north coast, dating back to 3000 BC. These aborigines must have been men of some mettle, for when the Minoan thalassocrats came to found a colony at modern-day Ag. Irene, they had to build defences to protect themselves from landward attacks. The discovery (1960) of the settlement, by John L. Caskey of the University of Cincinnati, was one of the more intriguing in recent years. Founded on a small peninsula around 1650 BC, the colony coincides nicely with the myth that Minos himself visited Kea and begot the Kean race by a native lady named Dexithea; it also revealed a fascinating chronicle of interaction between the Minoans and their Cycladic predecessors, and later, after the fall of Crete, with the Mycenaeans.

In the Classical era, Kea was dominated by four towns: Ioulis, near modern Chora, Karthea, Poiessa and Korissia. The 5th-century BC Lyric poets, Simonides and Bacchylides, the philosopher Ariston and the physician Erasistratos were all sons of Kea. During the Middle Ages, the Venetian Domenico Michelli used Ioulis' temple of Apollo to build a castle; in the 1860s the Greek government dismantled the Classical pieces to put in a museum.

WHAT TO SEE

Kea's port **Korissia** has recently expanded beyond its purely functional role, anxious to become a resort like Kea's other coastal villages. Korissia, of course, recalls the ancient town that once stood on the site; most locals, however, still call it Livadi, as they continue to call their island Tsia instead of the official Kea. Just north on attractive Ag. Nikolaou Bay, **Vourkari** is a pretty fishing village and resort, and north of that, on the peninsula of Ag. Irene (named after the small church there) is a **Bronze Age – Minoan – Mycenaean settlement.** Although you have to be an archaeology student to appreciate it to the full, it's not hard to make out the temple, originally constructed in the Bronze Age, a late Minoan palace-type hall, walls and a road. Among the artefacts found at Ag. Irene are inscriptions in the Minoan script Linear A.

From here the coastal road continues to the delightful but very popular beach resort at **Otzias,** the bay a mass of almond blossom in the spring, and to **Kastrianis,** with its 18th-century monastery dedicated to the Virgin, famous for its views.

Buses connect Korissia, the port, with **Chora,** the capital, which is hidden inland, high above the sea, as are so many Cycladic towns. The Kastro quarter of town is located on the site of ancient Ioulis' akropolis and medieval walls; all that can now be seen are the stone blocks from the original temple of Apollo. A small museum in town contains other pieces of it, and artefacts from the sites of the four ancient cities. A few old Venetian mansions may be seen around Kastro; several churches date back to the Byzantine era. One, **Panayia Kastrianni,** has an icon that worked many a miracle during the Turkish occupation, a ten-minute walk east of Chora leads to its most curious attraction—the **petrified Lion,** an ancient guardian some 3 metres high and 6 metres long (9 ft by 20 ft), chiselled out of the rock, mighty in form, gazing out with a bemused glare.

Equally majestic is the beautiful Hellenistic tower at the ruined monastery of **Ag. Marina,** south-west of Chora. The square tower, considered one of the finest in all Greece, has been restored, and its excellent masonry has stood up to time better than the monastery built around it. From Ag. Marina the road cuts across to the west coast beaches and resort communities at **Pisses** and **Koundouros.** The ancient city of **Poiessa** is near here, though more can be seen of **ancient Karthaea** on the south-east shore at Poles Bay; here Simonides is believed to have had his school. Inside the walls you can see the remains of a Doric temple dedicated to Apollo, and several other buildings.

PANEYERIA

1 July, Ag. Marna; 10 February, Ag. Charalambos, patron of Kea, at Chora; 15 August, Panayia, at Chora; 7 September, Ag. Soustas, at Otzias.

WHERE TO STAY

Nearly all the places to stay are along the coast, though you may find some rooms to let in Chora. In Korissia you can stay at something you don't find every day on a

Greek island—a motel, the **I Tzia Mas** (tel. 0288 31 305), a clean and friendly place where a double is 4000 dr. Book well in advance for the summer. The same warning holds for the **Kea Beach** (tel. 0288 22 144), a hotel and bungalow complex at Koundoros. Bungalows, which can accommodate two to four persons, are 9000 dr., a double 8000 dr. There are also several pensions and rooms at Pisses.

EATING OUT
Although foreign visitors have begun trickling in, Kea is still very Greek and the tavernas serve up typical Greek fare at reasonable prices.

TOURIST POLICE
On the quay, tel. (0288) 31 300.

KIMOLOS

CONNECTIONS
Three times a week with Piraeus, Kythnos, Serifos, Sifnos; caique twice a day from Apollonia, Milos.

Once known as Echinousa, or sea urchin, the island's modern name is thought to be derived from its first inhabitant. But Kimolia means chalk in Greek, and whether the name comes from the producer (chalk was once a main export of Kimolos) or the other way around, no one is quite sure. Another ancient export is fuller's earth, used in the manufacture of cloth. At one time Kimolos was attached to Milos (today they are separated by a channel only a kilometre wide). An ancient town was built where the sea now flows, but its nekropolis, dating back to 2500 BC, survives on Kimolos at a site called Elliniko.

Kimolos is a quiet island, a perfect place to relax and do nothing. Most of it is rocky and barren (the Venetians chopped down the once plentiful olive groves and nothing has grown there since), and the largest building on the island is a retirement home built by a local philanthropist, where Kimolos' elderly live free of charge. Apart from the one town, there are several shady beaches, but the only chalk you'll find these days is in the local grammar school.

At the little port, **Psathi,** caiques relay passengers to shore, and from here it's a 15-minute walk up to the typically white **Chora,** passing on the way the retirement home, which has a small museum in the basement to which the locals bring whatever potsherds and ancient bric-à-brac they happen to find. Chora has a few small cafés, a taverna and the main church, **Evangelistra,** built in 1614. From here you can walk up to the ruined Venetian castle of Marco Sanudo at **Paliokastro,** at Kimolos' highest point (355 metres/1164 ft). Within its forbidding walls is the island's oldest church, Christos. Another excursion, taking in the Elliniko cemetery (which has graves dating from the Mycenaean period to the

139

early centuries AD), may be made by mule path to the west coast, near **Ag. Andreas.** There's a beach near here at **Kambana.**

A small hamlet near Psathi has the odd nickname of **Oupa;** Oupa is the most abundant fish in the Aegean these days, and here, supposedly, people scooped it out by the basketful. There's a beach here, and another at **Prassa,** 6 km (4 miles) to the north, which also has an undeveloped radioactive spring. Goats are the only inhabitants of **Poliegos,** the large islet facing Psathi.

PANEYERIA
27 August, Ag. Fanouris; 27 July, Ag. Panteleimonos; 21 November, Panayias; 20 July, Profitis Elias; 4 August, Ag. Theothoso.

WHERE TO STAY
Not many people stay overnight on Kimolos, and if you want to you'll have to ask around in the bars and tavernas to see who currently has a room. Camping is usually "no problem" as the Greeks say—try Klima and Aliki beaches.

EATING OUT
There's one little place in Chora and another in the port that have souvlaki, scrambled eggs and other simple fare, but that's about it.

KYTHNOS

CONNECTIONS
Six times a week with Piraeus, Serifos, Sifnos and Milos; frequent links with Lavrion, Kea, Kimolos, Syros and Rafina.

Like its neighbours, Kea and Serifos, Kythnos receives relatively few foreigners—it is far more accustomed to receiving the afflicted at its thermal spa than holidaymakers. But it does its best by them; since the previous source of Kythnos' prosperity, the iron ore mines, closed in 1940, many of the people who didn't emigrate have had to get by as well as they can by fishing, farming and basket weaving. Perhaps because of their rigorous lives they tend to celebrate paneyeria and special days with great gusto, donning their traditional costumes; carnival is a big event here. Best of all, it's the kind of island where the old men still offer to take you fishing.

HISTORY
In Classical times the tale was told that Kythnos was long uninhabited because of its wild beasts and snakes, Ofiouso ("snake") being one of the island's ancient names. Recently, however, archaeologists have uncovered a Mesolithic settlement (7500–6000 BC) just north of the port of Loutra that not only spits in the eye of tradition, but currently holds the honour of being the oldest habitation yet discovered in the Cyclades.

Much later the Minoans held the island, followed by the Driopes, a semi-

140

mythical tribe, who were chased out of their home on the slopes of Mt Parnassos by Heracles and around the 12th century BC were scattered to Evia, Cyprus and Kythnos; their king Kythnos gave his name to the kingdom, whose capital was at a town still known today as Dryopis. During the Hellenistic period Kythnos was dominated by Rhodes. Two great painters came from the island, Timatheus (416–376 BC), who was known in antiquity for a certain portrayal of Iphegenia, and Kydian. In 198 BC all of Kythnos was pillaged, except for Vyrokastro, which proved impregnable. Marco Sanudo later took the island, and for 200 years it was under the rule of the Cozzadini family who still live in Bologna today. In order to maintain their authority the Cozzadini paid taxes both to the Venetians and to the Turks.

WHAT TO SEE

Kythnos has two ports; most ships these days put in at **Merihas** on the west coast, though when the winds are strong they'll put in at Loutra in the north-east. Merihas is a typical Greek fishing harbour, with a small beach. Just to the north are the meagre ruins of the once impregnable Hellenistic **Vyrokastro,** and another beach.

Buses make the 10-km (6-mile) trip from Merihas to **Chora,** the capital, also known as Messaria. Although as Cycladic towns go it's on the dull side, it does have a pretty church, **Ag. Saba,** founded in 1613 by its medieval masters, the Cozzadini, who left it their coat-of-arms. Other churches in the town claim to have icons by the Cretan–Venetian master Skordilis. There's also a restaurant and post office in the town.

Buses from Chora continue up to **Loutra,** the most important thermal spa in the archipelago. The iron once mined on Kythnos is in the water here, leaving a characteristic reddish deposit. Since ancient times Loutra's two springs have been used for bathing and as a cure for gout, rheumatism, eczema and other complaints. There is a beach here too and the Tourist Police. The Mesolithic settlement was found on the promontory just to the north; on the northernmost tip of Kythnos, Cape Kefalos, stood the **medieval citadel** (known variously as Paliokastro or Kastro tou katakefalou). About an hour's walk from Loutra, it is interesting to explore its derelict churches (one, **Our Lady of Compassion,** still has some of its frescoes), towers and houses, all abandoned around the middle of the 17th century.

A paved road leads from Merihas up to **Dryopis,** the only other inland village, visited mainly because it is the departure point for **Katafiki cave,** the most accessible of several on the island, where the people of Dryopis hid during pirate raids. From Dryopis you can walk down to the beach at **Ag. Stefanos,** or go by four-wheeled transport to the one at **Kanala,** Overlooking the bay, the monastery **Panayia tin Kanala** houses the island's most venerated icon, painted by St Luke.

Other beaches on the island, reached by foot or boat, include Fikiado, Lefkas and Episkopi.

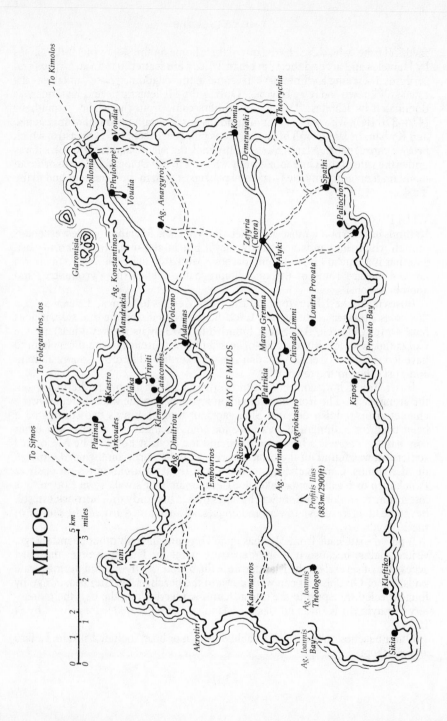

MILOS

5 km

3 miles

To Kimolos

To Folegandros, Ios

To Sifnos

Glaronisia

Pollonia
Phylokope!
Voudia
Voudia
Ag. Konstantinos
Mandrakia
Kastro
Plaka
Tripiti
Catacombs
Klema
Platina
Arkoudes
Volcano
Adamas
Ag. Dimitriou
Vani
Embourios
Rivari
Patrikia
Akrotiri
Kalamavros
Ag. Ioannis Bay
Ag. Ioannis Theologos
Ag. Marina
Agriokastro
Profitis Ilias
(883m/2900ft)
Mavra Gremna
Chivado Limni
Kipos
Provato Bay
Loutra Provata
Alyki
Zefyria
(Chora)
Ag. Anargyroi
Komia
Demenayaki
Theorychia
Spathi
Paliochori
BAY OF MILOS
Sikia
Kleftiko

PANEYERIA
15 August and 8 September, at Kanala; 2 November, Ag. Akindinos, at Merihas.
On Sundays you can often hear the island's music at Dryopis.

WHERE TO STAY
Merihas is the most convenient place to stay on Kythnos and there are quite a few
rooms to rent as well as the large, modern class C **Possidonion Hotel** (tel. 0281
31 244), where doubles are 3800 dr. In Loutra the **Xenia Anagenissis** overlooks
the beach and has doubles at 4000–6000 dr. (tel. 0281 31 217). There are also
rooms to rent in Loutra, and pensions catering primarily to those coming to take
the waters. You can also find rooms in Chora.

EATING OUT
There's an average restaurant in Chora and several tavernas in Merihas and
Loutra that have good fish. When you eat out, ask for the locally made cheese,
which is excellent.

TOURIST POLICE
Chora, tel. (0281) 31 201.

MILOS

CONNECTIONS
Daily by air from Athens; daily ferry from Piraeus. Frequent connections to
Sifnos, Serifos and Kythnos. In summer there are boats to Ios, Santorini,
Folegandros, Anafi, Kos, Rhodes, Karpathos and Crete. Ship to Kimolos daily;
caique from Pollonia to Kimolos.

Like Santorini, Milos is a volcanic island, but where the former is a glamorous
beauty associated with misty tales of Atlantis, Milos is a sturdy fellow who has
made his fiery origins work for a living. Although it lacks drama, it certainly has a
catalogue of geological eccentricities: hot springs bubble up here and there amid
its low rolling hills, the rocks startle with their colours, and the land is gashed with
the quarrying that has been going on here since the Mesolithic era and which
continues to this day (producing obsidian, sulphur, kaolin, barium, alum, benso-
nite and perlite). Milos also has one of the finest natural harbours in the whole of
the Mediterranean. It seems an odd trick of Mother Nature to so endow such a
small, out-of-the-way island. In spite of all its strange and wonderful rocks, Milos
still mourns for the one which it lost—the renowned Venus, now in the Louvre.

HISTORY
Milos has enjoyed (and suffered) a history as dramatic as its geology. At the dawn
of the Neolithic era people braved the sea to mine its precious obsidian, that hard

black, volcanic glass, prized for the manufacture of tools. Until the recent discovery of the Mesolithic settlement in Kythnos, Milos could claim to have the oldest habitation in the Cyclades, at Phylokope, settled by either Phoenicians or Cypriots. Obsidian tools from Milos have been found in the earliest Minoan and even pre-Minoan settlements on Crete, dating from before 3000 BC. Under the Cretans and later the Mycenaeans the island became rich from the obsidian which was traded all over the Mediterranean. As the inhabitants of Milos in later years were Dorian, they sided with the Dorian Spartans in the Peloponnesian War. When the Athenians made war in the east, the Milians again refused to fight with them. Athens sent envoys to Milos to change their minds. Their discussion, "The Milian dialogue", included in the fifth chapter of Thucydides' history, is one of the strangest and most moving passages of Classical literature. When Milos still refused to bend, the Athenians besieged the island, and when its defenders unconditionally surrendered, they massacred all men of fighting age, enslaved all the women and children, and resettled the island with colonists from Athens. After the fall of Athens, however, the island prospered until the inhabitants asked the Romans to come to protect them from the pirates. General Pompey put an end to the pirates, but the Romans moved in for good at Klema, the Dorian town which the Athenians had previously destroyed, and asserted their authority. Christianity came to Milos in the 1st century and the faithful built a great series of catacombs. Marco and his brother Angelo Sanudo captured Milos, and the island was later placed under the Crispi dynasty. In 1580 Turkish rule began, even though Milos was infested with pirates. One of them, John Kapsis, declared himself King of Milos, a claim which Venice recognised for three years, until the Turks tricked Kapsis into coming to Istanbul, where they slew him. In 1680 a party of colonists from Milos emigrated to London, where James, Duke of York, granted them land to build a Greek church—the origin of Greek Street in Soho.

In 1820, farmer George Kentrotis or Betonis found a cave while planting his corn. Inside there was a beautiful statue, in several pieces, of the goddess Aphrodite. What happened next is uncertain; either the Turkish authorities seized it, or George's friends warned him that they would do so, and advised him to sell it to (or give it into the safe keeping of) the French consul in Istanbul. Whatever happened, the Venus lost her arms and pedestal in transit. It was presented to Louis XVIII, and he added the piece to the Louvre museum.

In 1836 Cretan war refugees from Sfakia fled to Milos and founded the village Adamas, the present port. During the Crimean War the French navy docked at the great harbour of Milos and left many monuments, as they did during the First World War, and at Korfos you can see the bases of the anti-aircraft batteries installed during the German occupation in World War Two.

WHAT TO SEE
Even before you reach Milos' port, Adamas, you can see a sample of its bizarre rocks, the **Arkoudes,** or bears, the guardians of the great Bay of Milos (on the left

as you sail into the harbour). **Adamas** was founded by the Cretans, who brought along their holy icons, now in the churches of **Ag. Triada** and **Ag. Charalmbos:** in the latter, one picture, dating from 1576, portrays a boat attacked by a raging fish; the captain prayed to the Virgin, who resolved the struggle by snipping off the fish's nose. West of town a monument commemorates the French who died here during the Crimean War.

Adamas has most of the hotels and rooms available on the island; the tourist office has information on these. Bicycles can be hired here, and it's the main departure point for the island's buses. Above the village a site known locally as "the Volcano" is actually a steaming fissure in the ground.

A bus leaves frequently for **Plaka,** the pleasant but modern capital. Next to the bus stop the **Archaeology Museum** is marked by a queue of broken statues, and contains some of the finds on Milos dating back to Neolithic times; in a back room is a plaster cast of the Venus which Milos lost, a consolation prize from the French. Many signs direct one to the **Folklore and Laographic Museum,** which is worthy of a visit, especially if you can find someone to tell you the stories behind the exhibits, which include almost everything from a kitchen to a wine press. The Frankish castle on top of **Plaka Kastro** affords good views of the island. Within its ruined walls the most interesting building is the church **Thalassitras** (13th century); its name evokes Milos' great seafaring past.

Archaeologists believe that Plaka is built over the akropolis of ancient **Melos,** the town destroyed by the Athenians and resettled by the Romans. In the 1890s the British school excavated the site at **Klema,** a short walk below Plaka (if you take the bus, ask to be let off at Tripiti). Here you can see the **Catacombs,** dating from the 1st century and one of the best-preserved Early Christian monuments in Greece. The church area and long corridors lined with arched tombs remain, each with a little light before it that you can move about in order to examine an area more closely. When first discovered, the Catacombs were still full of bones, but the fresh air turned them to dust. Some tombs held five or six bodies; others are buried in the floor. On some of the tombs inscriptions in red still remain (all writing in black is later graffiti). Strangely enough, the modern cemetery of Milos near Plaka is constructed like a row of catacombs above ground.

A path from the Catacombs leads to the place where the Venus of Milos was discovered (there is a marker by the fig tree) and past the tall walls to the well-preserved **Roman Theatre,** where spectators looked out over the sea. Part of the stage remains, but the fact that there are still three tiers of seats left unexcavated is claimed to be a manifestation of the Milians' lack of interest in tourism. However, a theatre company from Athens sometimes performs in the theatre in August. There are also the remains of a **temple** on the path back to the main road.

Most of the population of Milos is concentrated here in the north, in the villages around Plaka. On the coast here, and around the Bay of Milos, there are many beaches, some adorned with wonderfully-coloured rocks, many accessible only on foot. Two popular beaches near Adamas are at **Platina,** near the

Arkoudes, where people go to watch the exquisite sunsets, and **Mandrakia,** on the opposite side of the peninsula, where you can also try the **waters of Tsillorneri** to "clear the system".

It is from Adamas and Plaka that buses leave for Pollonia, with its many trees, tavernas, rooms and places to camp, as well as the caiques to Kimolos. Pollonia is within walking distance of **Phylokope** (or Filokopi) one of the great centres of Cycladic civilisation, also excavated by the British in the 1890s. The dig yielded three successive levels of cities: the early Cycladic (3500 BC), the Middle Cycladic (to around 1600 BC) and Late Cycladic, which was considerably influenced by the Mycenaean culture.

Even in Early Cycladic days Milos traded its precious obsidian far and wide—pottery found in the lowest levels at Phylokope shows an Early Minoan influence. Great advances were made in the Middle Cycladic period: a wall was built around the more spacious and elegant houses, some with frescoes—one depicts the well-known flying fish. A palace, rather on the Minoan style, was built; fine vases were imported from Knossos and Minoan ware from the mainland; obsidian from the island reached the coasts of Asia Minor. Late in this period it is likely that Phylokope, like the rest of the Cyclades, came under the total domination of the Minoans: a script similar to Linear A was found in the excavations. The third, Late Cycladic level revealed a Mycenaean wall around the palace, a shrine, and Mycenaean pottery and figurines. This city saw the decline of Milos' importance in the Mediterranean, as the use of metals began to replace the need for obsidian. Unfortunately there's not very much to see at the site, and what can be seen—walls, mostly—are quite overgrown and inexplicable to the layman.

From Adamas you can take an excursion boat to the beach across the bay at **Embourios,** which also has rooms to rent and a taverna, or to see the curious **Glaronisia,** four islets north of Milos with caves, the largest of which is shaped like a massive basalt pipe organ. Near **Ag. Konstantinos**, off the road to Pollonia, steps lead down to **Papafragas** cave, a pool of brilliant blue water enclosed by a circular rock formation, once used by trading boats as a hiding place from pirates. More remote, on the south-west coast of Milos, is **Kleftiko** with its fantastic rock formations, accessible only from the sea. You can also sail near **Andimilos** to the north-west, home only of a rare variety of chamois goat.

No buses—and therefore few tourists—visit the rest of the island, but there are many rewards for anyone willing to walk. South of Pollonia, at **Komia,** are the ruins of Byzantine churches and nearby at **Demenayaki** are some of Milos' obsidian mines. **Zefyria** further inland is also known as Chora, for it was the capital of Milos in the Middle Ages, up to the 18th century. Panayia Portani was the main church of the village. A story recounts that a priest of this church was guilty of fornication. When accused by the villagers he denied it, but the villagers refused to believe him. With that the priest angrily cursed the people, a plague fell on the town, and everyone moved to Plaka. Today Zefyria is a very quiet village of old crumbling houses surrounded by olive trees. Alyki on the bay is a good beach near the **Mavra Gremna,** the black cliffs, strange formations in the rock. At several places out in the bay the sea bubbles from the hot springs released below.

At **Loutra Provata** you can see remains of Roman mosaics, and then take a sauna. The waters there are known for curing rheumatism; indeed since the time of Hippocrates, the waters of Milos have been praised for their healing properties. Local legend has it that the big **Alikis** spring, near the airport, has solved many an infertile woman's problem. **Kipos,** towards the south coast, has two churches. One, the Panayia tou Kipou, is the oldest in Milos, dating back to the 5th century. The old monastery Chalaka is at **Ag. Marina,** along with a well. From here one can climb to the top of **Profitis Ilias,** from where all of Milos and other islands are visible. Beaches can be found both at **Patrikia** and at **Ag. Dimitriou** further north, although it is often windy.

Ag. Ioannis Theologos, in the south-west corner of Milos, has the biggest paneyeri on the island, on 7 May. Ag. Ioannes is also known here as the Iron Saint, for during one paneyeri the partygoers were attacked by pirates. The people begged the saint to save them, and he complied by turning the door of the church to iron (one can still see a scrap of a dress caught in the door as the last woman entered). The pirates could not break in, and when one of them tried to kill someone left outside, Ag. Ioannes made his arm fall off!

PANEYERIA
17 July, Ag. Marina; 19 July, Profitis Elias on the mountain; 20 June and 31 October, Ag. Anargyroi (Byzantine church); 7 May and 25 September, Ag. Ioannes Theologos at Chalaka; 14 August at Zefyria; 28 August, Ag. Ioannes Prodromou; 5 August, Sotiris at Paraskopou; 26 July, Ag. Panteleimonos at Zefyria; and 25 July, Ag. Paraskevi at Pollonia.

WHERE TO STAY
Except for a few scattered rooms to let in Plaka and near the more popular beaches, the only accommodation is at Adamas. New here is **Venus Village,** a large hotel and bungalow complex on the beach (tel. 0287 22 020/22 132) that dwarfs the local competition. Rates are 6800 dr. for a double.

Prettiest among the less expensive hotels is the D class **Semiramis** (tel. 0287 22 118), each room with private bath. A single here is 2600 dr., a double 2800 dr.

In Kilma the **Panorama** has singles for 1800 dr. and doubles for 3000 dr. (tel. 0287 21 623). Rooms in private houses on the island go for around 1800 dr. If you want to sleep out, do so with caution—the local police can be sticky and do levy big fines.

EATING OUT
Again, nearly everything is in Adamas, and the best food there is at **Ta Haria tis Afroditis,** right on the waterfront where a delicious seafood dinner costs about 1500 dr. Also on the waterfront is the friendly, if somewhat disorganised, **Flisvos** taverna, where you can eat well for 600 dr.

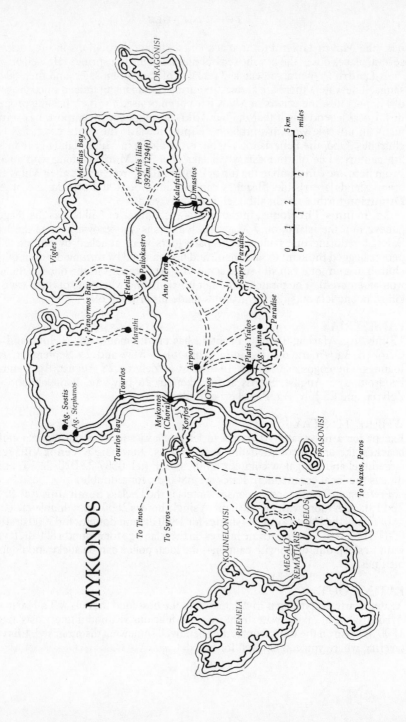

MYKONOS

DRAGONISI

Merdias Bay

Profitis Ilias
(392m/1294ft)

Vigles

Panormos Bay

Ftelia

Paliokastro

Ano Mera

Kalafati

Dimastos

Super Paradise

Marathi

Ag. Sostis

Ag. Stephanos

Tourlos

Tourlos Bay

Mykonos
(Chora)

Korfos

Ornos

Airport

Platis Yialos

Ag. Anna

Paradise

PRASONISI

To Tinos

To Syros

KOUNELONISI

MEGALO
REMATIARIS

DELOS

RHENEIA

To Naxos, Paros

0   1   2
0   1   2   3   5 km
                    miles

TOURIST INFORMATION
Tourist information booth, on the quay (tel. 0287 22 290).
Tourist police, see regular police, Plaka (tel. 0287 21 204).

MYKONOS

CONNECTIONS
By air: frequently with Athens, several times a week with Santorini, Rhodes and
Herakleon, Crete. Less frequently with Chios, Mytilini and Samos. By ship daily with
Athens, Tinos, Syros; several times a week with Naxos, Paros, Ios, Santorini, Sifnos,
Seriphos, Rafina, Amorgos; infrequent links to the Dodecanese and Crete. Daily to
Delos at 9 am, 10.15 am with a guide (2000 dr.), returning at 1.30 pm. Hydrofoil
service every Wednesday to Paros, Naxos, Ios, Santorini and Heraklion, Crete.

Mykonos, dry, barren and frequently plagued by high winds, has earned its reputation
as the most popular island in the Cyclades for three main reasons: its proximity to
Delos, the charm of its port, and its exquisite, fine, sandy beaches. If the surge in
tourism in recent years caught the other islands unawares, Mykonos, at least, didn't
bat an eyelid, having made the transformation long ago—relatively speaking—from a
traditional economy to one dedicated to the whims of the international set. Most
lovers of the simple and the unadorned—those seeking something distinctly Greek—
abhor Mykonos, looking upon it as the Sodom and Gomorrah of the Aegean. It has
the distinction of being one of the most expensive islands in Greece, and it was the
first officially to sanction nudism on some of its beaches.

HISTORY
In mythology Mykonos is the rock tomb of the last giant slain by the hero
Herakles; it also has the grave of Ajax of Oileus, one of the Achean heroes of the
Trojan War. (This Ajax is called little Ajax to differentiate between another hero
of the same name, who committed suicide when the arms of the dead Achilles
were not given to him but to Odysseus.) After the capture of Troy, little Ajax
raped Priam's daughter Cassandra who sought protection in a sanctuary of
Athena. Athena avenged this blasphemy by wrecking Ajax's ship off the coast of
Mykonos as he was returning home. Poseidon saved him in the storm but rather
than being grateful, Ajax declared that he would have been perfectly able to save
himself without the god's assistance. Poseidon's trident finished Ajax then and
there, and his Mycenaean tomb can still be seen at Linos.

The Ionians, who settled on the island, built three cities, one on the isthmus
south of Chora, the second at Dimastos, dating back to 2000 BC, and the third at
Panormos near Paliokastro. During the war between the Romans and Mithridates of Pontos, all of these ancient cities were destroyed. Chora was rebuilt
during the Byzantine period, and the Venetians surrounded it with a wall that no
longer exists; however, at Paliokastro a fort built by the Guizzi rulers still remains.

WHAT TO SEE

Prosperity has kept the homes of Chora, the island's picture postcard capital and port, well maintained, gleaming and whitewashed, with brightly painted wooden trims. In the main square a bust of Manto Mavroyenous (the heroine from Mykonos who fought in the War of Independence) once served as the island's guardian of left luggage; now dire little notices keep the backpacks away. The square is also the main taxi stand, and there are several inexpensive snack bars here. Further up the waterfront is the departure quay for the boats to ancient Delos, Mykonos' main excursion. The pelican mascot of Mykonos, the successor of the original Petros, may often be found preening himself in the shadow of the small church here. This side of the harbour also has the Tourist Police office, and on the hill overlooking the harbour are several windmills. Until recently one of them still ground wheat; another has been converted into a cottage. They are a favourite subject for the many local artists, as is "the little Venice of Mykonos", the houses of Alefkandra, tall and picturesque and built directly beside the sea, just below the windmills.

Mykonos claims to have 400 churches, and the most famous of these is the unusual **Panayia Paraportiani,** an asymmetrical masterpiece of folk architecture. Next to it is the island's **Ethnographic Museum,** with an interesting collection of bric-à-brac salvaged from Mykonos' past. Upstairs there is a re-created bedroom and kitchen, and a gallery of 19th-century prints of sensuous Greek odalisques gazing dreamily into space; downstairs is an exhibition, "Mykonos and the Sea". Open every day 5.30 pm–8.30 pm (no admission charge).

The **Archaeology Museum** is on the far side of the harbour near the Leto Hotel, and features artefacts from the islet of Rheneia, excavated by the Greek archaeologist Stavropoulos. Rheneia served as the nekropolis of Delos after the Athenian purifications. Other finds include a pithois carved with scenes from the Trojan War, discovered on Mykonos itself (9.30 am–3.30 pm except Tuesday, admission 100 dr.).

In ancient times Mykonos had the dubious distinction of being well known for the baldness of its men; curiously enough, the old fishermen of the island never take off their distinctive caps. Despite all the changes they've seen on their island, they have remained friendly and jovial, and if you speak a little Greek they'll regale you with stories of the good old days—before all the tourist girls began chasing them around! The only other town on Mykonos is **Ano Mera,** where the **Tourliani Monastery** with its 15th-century carved steeple is the main attraction (open mornings only). Sandy **Panormos Bay** to the north was the site of one of Mykonos' three ancient cities. The second ancient city, **Dimastos,** is believed to have been on top of Mt Ayios, Mykonos' highest point. At Linos are the remains of a Hellenistic tower and walls; at **Portes** is the tomb of Ajax, the troublemaker. The greenest spot on the island is the **Garden of Rapaki,** east of Chora (a good half-hour walk).

Dragonisi, the islet off the east coast of Mykonos, has lost its dragon but has numerous caves, and if you're lucky you may see a seal in one of them. Private

150

boats for the excursion may be hired at **Platis Yialos,** where you may also hire a boat of your own to Delos to avoid the crowds. **Paradise** and gay **Super Paradise** are the main nudist beaches on the island; there are so many others scattered along the island's coasts that you could spend an entire holiday visiting them all. Particularly popular are **Psarrou,** just before Platis Yialos, and **Ornos.** Both have a selection of tavernas serving fresh fish.

WHERE TO STAY
There's certainly no lack of places to stay on Mykonos, although not too surprisingly prices tend to be higher than almost anywhere else in Greece. Sleek new hotels, many incorporating elements of the local architecture, occupy every feasible spot on the coast, especially along the road to Platis Yialos; the **Anargyros Hotel** (tel. 0289 22 116) at Ornos is a prime example. It's a class C, but in season the rates soar up to 4500 dr. a double. If you want to hobnob with celebrities and Riviera types, stay in the **Leto** in Mykonos town (tel. 0289 22 207) with its wonderful view over the harbour and town. It has for many years been the classiest place to stay on the island, and again the price reflects this—a double in season costs 8000 dr. If you go in the off season, prices drop by around 20% or more. The **Apollon** (pictured below) is a comfortable, friendly hotel, perfectly situated in the middle of the windy seafront with doubles at 2800 dr., dropping to 1800 dr. in low season (tel. 0289 22 223).

Yet even if you arrive in the middle of summer without a reservation, you may well be greeted by a convoy of hotel vans and people with rooms to let in town or along Ag. Stefanos beach (unless, that is, you arrive on a late boat), where the C class **Artemis** (tel. 0289 22 345) has doubles for 3800 dr., or the smaller **Mina** hotel charges 2900 dr. for its D class doubles with bath (tel. 0289 23 024). Rooms in private houses are at least 900 dr. a person; for a little more you can make

The Harbourside at Mykonos

151

NAXOS

Ormos Abram

Apollon

Pachia Ammos • Chilia Vrisi

Mirisis

Ormos Amyti

Komiaki • Mesi

Lionas

Akrotiria Amilis

Chalandra • Skado
• Mytria Castle

Galini • Egares Koronos

Keramoti • Mine Railroad

Grotta

Palatia Kinidaros

Naxos • Agidia Kourounochori

(Chora) • Ag. Thaleleos

Ag. Georgios • Melanes • Mili Moni

Stelida Mutsuna

Apano Kastro Apiranthos

Glinado • Galanado Kaloxilos

Ag. Prokopios Potamia Chalki

Ag. Anna Filoti • Danakos

Tripodes Damarionas

Plaka Sangri Mt Zas

(1004m/3295ft)

Parthenos Psili Ammos

Mikri Vigla

Kastraki

T'apaliru Castle Chimarou

Kyripia • Pirgaki Marathos

Aliko

Agiasou

Panormos

Kalandou

0 1 2   5 km

0   1   2   3 miles

reservations at the delightful **Hotel Philippi,** located in the heart of Mykonos town at 32 Kalogera St (tel. 0289 22 295). The rooms are pleasant spotless and scented by the hotel's lovely garden (doubles here are 3000 dr.). All campers are referred to the large campground at Paradise Beach (continuous boat service from Platis Yialos, tel. 0289 22 129).

EATING OUT
Again, no lack of opportunities here, especially if you have deep pockets. Within a few blocks you can sample a genuine American doughnut, top that off with a seafood pizza, and wash it down with a pint from the Irish Bar. There are numerous snack bars and two bakeries with cheese pies, etc. if you're counting pennies. You can eat swordfish kebabs and squid and not pay an arm and a leg for it at the large restaurant connected to the motel on Platis Yialos Beach (dinner for 1000 dr.); **Philippi's** restaurant (connected to the Hotel Philippi) has the best reputation in town for international and Greek cuisine, served in the lovely garden—2000 dr. per person. Close by and in the same price range is the **Edem,** also offering a varied international menu in a garden setting. Centrally placed **Katrin's,** again fairly expensive, has many French specialities, and the recently opened **La Taverna Italiana** is proving very popular, with enough pasta dishes to keep the most fastidious Italian happy. If, in the wave of international food and music, you feel the need for a dose of the Greek, then head for **Niko's** taverna, in the centre of town or **Maky's,** just around the corner. You'll feel you're back in Greece, especially with dinner at 750 dr. a head. Eat at least once at **Spiro's,** below the windmills, with a lovely view of waves rolling up to the foot of the houses of "little Venice"; seafood specialities in the medium price bracket.

To a certain extent the international jet set left Mykonos long ago, and in the main the gay crowd followed suit, leaving in their wake a definite 'after the party' feeling. The chic little bars and clubs, so used to the big spenders, are now half full, their clients nursing an ouzo or a beer for the evening. A visit to the famous **Pierro's** will restore your faith, however, and remind you of former days, with hordes of young people dancing to the loud, lively music and spilling out all over the square, and in the **Mykonos Dancing Bar** the crowds jam in to join the others in the frantic dancing, led by the friendly waiters.

TOURIST POLICE
On the quay, tel. (0289) 22 482.

NAXOS

CONNECTIONS
Every day by ferry to Paros and Piraeus; daily boat to Amorgos via Koufonissia, Heraklia and Shinousa; daily excursion to Mykonos in summer. Other frequent

links are to Rafina, Syros, Tinos, Ios, Santorini, Sifnos and Serifos; less frequently to Anafi and the Dodecanese and Crete. A new airport should be completed by 1988/89, capable of handling large planes.

Naxos, 448 km² (173 sq. miles) in area, is the largest of the Cyclades and the most mountainous, its highest point, Mt Zas (or Zeus), crowning the archipelago at 1004 metres (3295 ft). It can also claim to be the most fertile, its cultivated valleys a refreshing green even in the height of the dry, sun-browned Cycladic summer. Lemons, and kitro, a liqueur distilled from them, are Naxian specialities, as is emery, found nowhere else in Greece. Souvenirs of the island's ancient, Byzantine and Venetian past abound, and the entire west coast is almost one uninterrupted beach. It's not surprising, then, that this once little known island attracts more visitors each year. The new airport will accelerate the island's tourist industry; until now it has served mostly as a retreat for people overwhelmed by the summer hordes on Mykonos and Paros.

HISTORY
Naxos was one of the major centres of Cycladic culture, the first signs of which appeared around 3000 BC. Then, as now, the main settlements appear to have been near Chora, on the hill of the Kastro, and at Grotta, where the sea-eroded remains of the Cycladic town can still be seen just off shore. Tradition has it that the island was later colonised by a party of Karians led by a son of Apollo named Naxos.

Mythology recounts that Theseus and the Cretan princess Ariadne stopped at Naxos on their way to Athens after the slaying of Ariadne's half-brother, the Minotaur. Yet the next morning, while Ariadne slept, Theseus set sail and abandoned her. This, even in the eyes of the Athenians, was seen as dishonourable, especially since Theseus had promised to marry the princess in return for the vital assistance she had rendered him in negotiating the Labyrinth, and various explanations for Theseus' behaviour have sprung up over the centuries. Did he simply forget about her, did he find a new mistress, or did the god Dionysos, who later found her and married her, desire her from the moment she set foot on Naxos, and warn Theseus away? Historically, some believe the myth demonstrates the rise of a late Cycladic civilisation after the fall of Crete, or that Ariadne, as a priestess of Crete, would have forfeited her rights and authority if she had gone to Athens. Many say it was her curse on Theseus that made him forget to change his black sails to white, inadvertently causing his father's death. In all events, Ariadne lived happily ever after with Dionysos, who taught the Naxians how to make their excellent wine and set Ariadne's crown, the Corona Borealis, in the firmament. The incident also inspired many later artists and poets, including Richard Strauss, who composed the well-known opera *Ariadne auf Naxos*.

Later Naxians were originally Ionians, and their most troublesome enemy was Miletus in Asia Minor, where some Naxian refugees, eager to take back the island for themselves, helped stir up trouble. According to Plutarch, many battles

154

were fought between the two rivals at the fort called Delion, of which a few vestiges remain near Naxos town. It was here that the Naxian heroine Polykrite fled when her island was besieged by these enemies, only to find the gate of the fortress already closed. One of the Miletian leaders found her there and fell so much in love with her that he agreed to help her people, informing her of all the movements of his armies. Thus the Naxians were able to make a sudden and vicious attack on the Miletians. However, in the confusion of the battle, Polykrite's lover, turned traitor for her sake, also perished, and the girl died in sorrow the next day, despite being acclaimed a great heroine.

Naxos was one of the first islands to work in marble, later producing in the Archaic period the lions of Delos and huge koures statues. Indeed, for a period, "huge" was the vogue on Naxos; in 523 the tyrant Lugdamis declared he would make the buildings on the island the highest and most glorious in all Greece. All that remains today of Lugdamis' ambition is the massive lintel from the gate of the Temple of Apollo located next to the town on the islet of Palatia. An ancient mole connects Palatia to the mainland, attesting to the former glory of Naxos when the island was the leader of the Ionic Amphictyonic league. As with most of the islands, Naxos declined in importance in the Classical age. In Hellenistic times it was governed by Ptolemy of Egypt who fortified Apano Kastro and Chimaru. The Byzantines continued to build defences on this rich and strategic island: and at their Castle T'apaliru, Marco Sanudo besieged them for two months in 1207.

With the taking of T'apaliru, Marco Sanudo became the Duke of Naxos and held sway over all the Venetians who had seized the Aegean Islands in the free for all after the conquest of Constantinople in 1204. When Venice refused to grant Sanudo the independent status he desired, he broke away in 1210 and went over to the side of the Latin Emperor, becoming the Duke of the Archipelago. The word archipelago, "the chief sea", was the Byzantine name for the Aegean; under Sanudo and his successors, it came to have its modern meaning, "a group of islands", in this case the Cyclades, which the Venetians ruled as a fief for 300 years. They built a palace and a Catholic cathedral on the top of Chora, and a second residence at Apano Kastro, used in defence against both outsiders and rebellious islanders. Even after the Turkish conquest in 1564 the Dukes of Naxos remained in nominal control of Naxos and the Cyclades, although always answerable to the Sultan.

A latter-day Naxian, Petros Protopapadakis, planned the Corinth canal and gave many public works to the island. He was the Minister of Economics in 1922 during the misadventure in Asia Minor, and was executed with other members of that sad government by the subsequent regime. His statue now stands by the port.

WHAT TO SEE
Naxos, or Chora, the island's port and capital, is a fine Cycladic town, though there are those who find its twisting streets so narrow as to be almost claustrophobic, and certainly bewildering, which is just as the natives intended them to

be, to confuse invading marauders. The old town, up on the hill, is divided into two neighbourhoods: **Bourgos** where the Greeks lived, and **Kastro** above, residence of the Venetian–Catholic nobility. In the former, the Orthodox cathedral, the **Metropolis of Zoodochos Pigi,** was built in the 18th century out of an old temple and older churches, and has an iconostasis painted by Dimitrios Valvis of the Cretan school. Archaeologists have made some interesting discoveries near the Metropolis and would knock it down if the bishop would let them.

Although the city walls have all but disappeared, the inner walls of the Kastro remain. Inside, some 19 Venetian houses still wear their coats-of-arms. Most of the residents claim descent from the Venetians, and many of their grandparents' tombstones in the **Catholic Cathedral** boast grand titles. The cathedral was founded in the 13th century by Marco Sanudo, whose own palace, or what remains of it, can be seen directly across the square. Only one of the seven original towers of Kastro survives, locally known as **Pirgos,** guarding one of the three entrances to the enceinte. During the Turkish occupation Naxos had a reputation for its educational facilities. In the Kastro there was the **School of Commerce,** and a school run by Catholic friars, attended for two years by the young Nikos Kazanzakis. One of the school's buildings, not far from the cathedral, is now an **Archaeology Museum,** This has been closed for several years, but there are plans to reopen it in 1986, with improved lighting to display its collection of Cycladic figurines, Mycenaean pottery, a Roman mosaic of Europa, pieces of Archaic kouroi and a statuette of a pig about to be sick in a sack.

A causeway north of the port leads to the islet of Palatia and the unfinished **Temple of Apollo,** begun in 522 BC. The massive lintel on the platform is all that stands, a lone gateway to nowhere, a popular frame for sunset photos. A small sandy beach curves around the causeway, protected by the ancient **harbour mole,** rebuilt by Marco Sanudo. **Grotta,** so named for its numerous caves, occupies the north shore of Chora, and it is here that you can see remains of the Cycladic buildings under the water. In one place a few steps are discernible; the locals claim that in ancient times a tunnel went from Grotta to Palatia. It is near the site of the ancient **Fort Delion.**

The busy waterfront has filled up with tourist establishments; in mid-August the main square, near the ferry port and bus station, is the site of the Dionysia, a festival of folk music and dance, wine and souvlaki. To the south, above the Agrarian Bank, is the **Church of Panayia Pantansassa,** once the church of a Byzantine monastery, dating back to the 11th century, and famous for its very early icon of the Virgin. Further south numerous hotels and a whole new suburb of Chora, Nea Chora, has sprung up around popular **Ag. Georgios beach.**

The busiest beach on the sandstrewn west coast of Naxos is **Ag. Anna,** frequented by public bus and caique from Chora; a 15-minute walk to the north will take you to the quieter Ag. Prokopios, and to the south is **Plaka,** (the best beach), which has a campsite. Further south there are rooms to rent along the beach at **Kastraki;** its name derives from the ruined Mycenaean fortress, built over the remains of a Cycladic akropolis. From here you can walk up to **T'apa-**

Iiru, the Byzantine castle high on its rock that defied Marco Sanudo and his mercenaries for two months. There's a more remote beach beyond Kastraki at **Pirgaki.**

The main asphalted road south of Chora leads up to the fertile **Livadi Valley.** A couple of kilometres up the road it splits, the left branch leading towards **Melanes** and the ancient marble quarries in the heart of Naxos; at the one called Flerio, 3 km (2 miles) east, lie two 7th-century BC kouroi, each 5 metres (15 ft) high. Kouros, in Greek, means "young man", and in the Archaic period such statues—highly stylised, stiff figures, their arms hugging their sides, one foot stepping forward—were probably inspired by Egyptian art; the young men they portray are believed to have been Zeus' ancient guardians, in Crete called the Curetes. At **Kourounochori** near Melanes is the site of a Venetian castle; **Ag. Thaleleos** in the same area has a monastery with a fine 13th-century church.

Back on the main road the right branch leads to **Galanado,** with its ruined Venetian tower **Belonia,** and the interesting twin church of St John, built in the Venetian period, with a Catholic chapel on one side and an Orthodox church on the other. The recently restored **Ag. Mamas,** dating from the 8th century and Naxos' original cathedral, is a short walk from the road on the way to **Sangri.** Sangri's name is the Hellenised version of Sainte Croix, in turn the French name for the Monastery Timious Stavrou (16th century). Sangri actually consists of three small villages spread out over the plateau, with many Byzantine and medieval towers and churches in the area; one of these, **Ag. Ioannes Gyroulas** in Ano Sangri, is built over a temple of Demeter.

From Sangri the road descends into the beautiful **valley of Tragea,** flanked on either side by Naxos' highest mountains. Olives are the main product of the numerous small villages in the valley, the most interesting of which is **Chalki.** Both the Byzantines and Venetians built towers here: **Francopoulo,** in the centre of the village, and up a steep path the **Apano Kastro,** last repaired by the Venetians and used, it is believed, as Marco Sanudo's summer home. He was not, however, the first to enjoy the splendid panorama of forests, olive groves and mountains from the summit: the fortress is built on Cyclopean foundations, and Mycenaean tombs have been discovered in the immediate area. In Chalki itself there are two fine churches with frescoes: **Panayia Protothronis** (12th century) and **Ag. Diasoritis** (9th century).

From Chalki a paved road leads up to **Moni,** home of the most unusual church on Naxos, the **Panayia Drossiani,** a mixture of ancient domes built of field stones. The main road through the valley, however, continues to **Filoti,** on the slopes of Mt Zas, the largest village in the region. There are many good paths in the region, and one leads up Mt Zas. Some say the mountain was dedicated to the goddess Za, others to Zeus, the father of the gods. A cave near the summit was probably used as a religious sanctuary. Another path (a three-hour walk) from Filoti follows the west flanks of the mountain to the excellently preserved **Tower of Chimarou,** built by Ptolemy in the Hellenistic age, its isolation no doubt a reason for its survival over the centuries. In Filoti itself there's the Venetian stronghold of the De Lasti family, and the church **Koimisis tis Theotokou** with a fine carved marble iconostasis, and **Panayia Filotissa** with a marble steeple.

From Filoti the road skirts the slopes of Mt Zas on its way to **Apiranthos,** where the Venetian families Crispi and Sommaripa built towers, and where many families today claim Cretan origin, having migrated here during the Turkish occupation to work in the emery mines. Apiranthos is one of the island's more traditional villages, where some women still weave on looms; it's also the site of a small **museum,** devoted to mostly Neolithic finds. A road from here descends to the port of **Mutsuna,** where the emery would be brought down from the mountains near Koronos by a rope funicular and loaded onto ships. Mutsuna has a fine beach; from here a dirt road follows the east coast south to the remote beach of **Psili Ammos.** Another beach, **Lionas,** is linked by paved road to **Koronos.**

Beyond Koronos the road turns into a winding, hairpin serpent leading to pretty **Komiaki,** highest of the island's villages, and **Apollon,** a popular summertime destination with its beach and pensions. On the slopes of the mountain here are ancient marble quarries, and in one steps lead up to a colossal **kouros,** abandoned in the 7th century BC before it was finished. Because the village was sacred to the god Apollo, the statue is said to represent him. Apollon is as far as the bus goes; by car you can chance the unpaved road along the north coast back to Naxos town, passing the isolated beaches of Ormos Abram and Pachia Ammos, near the 1606 **monastery of Faneromerni,** There is another beach at **Ormos Amyti; Galini,** where the road once more is paved, has the Byzantine fortified monastery **Ipsiloteras,** From here it's 6 km (4 miles) back to Chora.

PANEYERIA
Like the Cretans, the Naxians sometimes improvise verses at their paneyeria, a custom dating back to ancient times. Some of the many celebrations are: 20 May, Ag. Thaleleos; 17 July, at Koronos; 15 August, Panayia at Filoti; 1 July, Ag. Anargyroi at Sangri; 23 August, at Tripodes; 14 July, Ag. Nikodimos at Naxos; 29 August, Ag. Ioannes at Apollon and Apiranthos; 23 April, Ag. Georgios at Kinidaros.

WHERE TO STAY
Naxos is still one of the less expensive of the popular islands in this group, and even in August there still seem to be plenty of private rooms available, especially in the Nea Chora part of town. If you take one, however, make sure you can find it again. This new addition to the capital is as bewildering as the old with its anonymous streets and countless skeletons of future buildings. Rooms here are cheap—between 800 and 1200 dr. a person. If you want to lodge in a more historical setting, there are also several places that rent rooms in the Kastro, and three small hotels in Bourgos, just outside the walls; the **Panorama** on Amphitris Street is the loveliest, with a marvellous sea view (tel. 0285 22 330). Rates here are about 1800 dr. a single, 3000 dr. a double. Another charmer, the **Pension**

Ariadne on Ariadnis Street (tel. 0285 22 452), is right on the sea and has about the same prices. Cheapest of all is the dormitory at the **Dionysos,** up near the Kastro (tel. 0285 22 331), where beds go for 700 dr. a night. A new campground has been organised at Stelida near the town.

Outside the capital in **Ag. Anna** is a C class hotel of the same name with doubles going for 3000 dr. In Ag. Georgios there's a fairly wide selection of moderately priced hotels in the 2500–5000 dr. range, including the **St. George Pension** on the beach (tel. 0285 23 162). You can find rooms in most of the seaside villages, but as yet the pickings are a bit slim. There are bungalows at Pirgaki, accommodating three people for 2000–3000 dr. per person, and rooms at Chalki, Filoti and Apollon.

EATING OUT

There's a restaurant or taverna to suit all tastes and wallets in Naxos, and you don't have to depend on the numerous fast food joints if you're on a budget. There's **Thomas' Grill,** near the Hotel Coronis, with a fine version of everyone's favourite, *souvlaki,* for 500 dr. Another inexpensive place is **Meltemi,** an old favourite on Ag. Georgios beach, where a good Greek meal will set you back 600–800 dr. On the main square in the old town there's another good taverna with outdoor seating; prices are moderate, but get there early as it fills up fast.

TOURIST POLICE

See regular police, Naxos town, tel. (0285) 22 100

PAROS

CONNECTIONS

Three flights daily (six in the summer) from Athens; in the summer daily flights from Rhodes and three times a week from Herakleon, Crete. Summer hydrofoil connections with Naxos, Mykonos, Tinos and Syros. There are daily ferry connections to Piraeus and Naxos, Ios, Santorini, Amorgos and Rafina, in season you can also get to Ikaria, Samos, Sifnos, Mykonos, Donoussa, Koufonissa, Astipalaia, Kalymnos, Kos, Nissyros, Tilos, Symi and Rhodes. Frequent boats to Antiparos from Paroikia and Pounta.

Paros is one of the larger and more fertile Cyclades, with vineyards, wheat and barley fields, citrus and olive groves, and—an unusual sight in the archipelago—pastures of grazing cattle and sheep. But underneath the gentle slopes of Paros' one mountain, Profitis Elias (771 metres/2530 ft) lies some of the finest, most translucent marble in the world, prized by Classical sculptors and architects. It is also the main building material of Paros' charming villages. Although the island has several other attractions, including a famous Byzantine cathedral and a valley

PAROS

Platis Ammos
Filitzi
Langeri
Ag. Ioannis
Prodromos
Naousa
Kolimbithres
Fikia
Tris Ekklisies
Delion
Kalami
Krios
Argo
Parokia
Asklepieion
Longovardes Monastery
Marathi
Ag. Minas
Thapsana
Petaloudes
Kamari
Pounta
Kanali
Vathia Psaria
Voutakos
Panayia
Antiparos
Sifnaikos
Yialos
Kambos
Kastro (Antip.)
ANTIPAROS
Cave
Ag. Georgios
DESPOTIKO
Kavouras
SALIGOS
Dipla
STROGILONISI
Strogilonisi
Ambelas
Glyfada
Marmara
Piso Livadi
Tsou Kalia
Marpissa
Prodromos
Lefkas
Kostos
Mt Profitis Ilias
(771m/2530ft)
Ag. Theodoron Monastery
Lagadas
Spilion
Kalampaki
Molos
Dryos
Aspro Chorio
Glifa
Chrysi Akti
Agkairia
Akrotiri
Tripiti
Alyki
PRASONISI
KRISPI
DRIONISI
SANDRO
Faneromeni

0 1 2 5 km
0 1 2 3 miles

filled in the summer with butterflies, most people come for its soft, sandy beaches.

HISTORY

With the trade of the famous Parian marble, the island of Paros prospered very early in history. An Early Cycladic town thrived, and was connected with Knossos and the Mycenaeans in the Late Cycladic period (1100 BC). In the 8th century BC Ionians settled the island and brought it a second prosperity. The poet Archilochos (7th century BC), inventor of Iambic verse, and the sculptor Ariston were famous sons of ancient Paros. During the Persian Wars the Parians supported the Persians at both Marathon and Salamis. When Athens' General Miltiades came to punish them after Marathon, they withstood his month-long siege, leaving Miltiades to go home with a broken leg and die of gangrene. During the destructive Peloponnesian Wars Paros remained neutral until forced to join the second Delian league in 378 BC. Paros produced the great sculptor Skopas in the Hellenistic period, and the island did well until Roman times, trading its marble, which was used in the Temple of Solomon, for the Venus of Milo, and many of the structures on Delos and, later, Napoleon's tomb. When the Romans took over Paros, they also took over the marble business. After various other invaders the island was then left practically uninhabited. In 1207 Marco Sanudo ruled Paros from Naxos. The pirate Barbarossa, that red-bearded terror, took the island in 1536, and from then on the Turks ruled via the Duke of Naxos. At this time the interior village of Lefkas became the capital of Paros, owing to the innumerable pirate raids. The Catholics set up Capuchin schools and missions but had little success in converting the locals. In 1770 the Russians began to fortify Paros against the Turks, but they left long before the work was finished. Paros joined the War of Independence, and the heroine Manto Mavroyenous, whose parents were from Paros and Mykonos, came to Paros after the revolution and died there. She had led guerrilla attacks against the Turks throughout Greece.

WHAT TO SEE

Paroikia is the island's chief town and main port. It rolls out the welcome mat for visitors: opposite the landing pier, in a windmill, you can find the Tourist Police, and a list of all the island's hotels. Here too are the bus stop for the rest of Paros, up-to-date charts listing all sea connections and the usual seaside watering places. Yet in spite of the welcome, the first impression of Paroikia is one of neglect: its municipal gardens are untended, its sidewalks crumbling—a direct contrast to the immaculate streets and houses within the town. The architecture is pure Cycladic, and, what is more, one can explore it without climbing hundreds of stairs. The main street winds through the centre of town, lined by shops, both tourist and non-tourist. Near the heart of the town a narrow 13th-century wall, part of the old Venetian castle, is amalgamated into neighbouring houses, built out of the temples of Apollo and Demeter. Some objects in the museums are from this strange conglomerate.

161

On the west side of town, by a shady park of pine trees, is "the church of a hundred doors", the **Ekatontapyliani**. According to tradition, it was founded by St Helen, mother of Constantine the Great, whose ship put into port at Paros during a storm. However, the first known structure was built by Justinian in the 6th century. Designed by Ignatius, an apprentice of the master architect of Ag. Sofia in Constantinople, the original church was so lovely that when his master came to visit it, he was consumed by jealousy and pushed Ignatius off the roof of the church—but not before Ignatius had seized his foot and dragged him down to his death as well. In the north corner of the walled courtyard a frieze portrays the two unhappy architects. Another story accounts for its name: so far people have only found 99 doors (personally I could find only about 10), but when the 100th is discovered, it is a sign that Constantinople will return to the Greeks. The cathedral has suffered several restorations since the 6th century, and in the 1960s an attempt was made—though not entirely successfully—to restore the façade to its early Byzantine appearance. But inside the church, built in the form of a Greek cross with a dome, the atmosphere is shadowy yet jewel-like, in a sort of Byzantine–pre-Raphaelite way. Throughout the interior you can see evidence that its stones have been recycled from earlier Byzantine and pagan structures. Pagan tombs and a well are beneath the church floor.

On the carved wooden iconostasis is an icon of the Virgin, worshipped for its healing virtues; the church also contains the mortal remains of the Parian Ag. Theoktisti. Captured by pirates, she managed to flee into the trees of Paros. For 30 years she lived a pious life alone in the wilderness. A hunter finally found her, and when he brought her the communion bread she asked for, she died. For a good omen he cut off her hand (now on display in a box) and made to sail away, but he was unable to depart until he had returned it to the saint's body. Beneath a wooden pallet is Theoktisti's footprint: the Greeks take off their shoes and fit their feet into her's for good luck. Behind the iconostasis are frescoes and a carved marble Holy Table. The Baptistry next to the church has a sunken font.

Near the church is the **Archaeology Museum** in a new building (closed Tuesdays). Inside it has a fragment of the renowned "Parian Chronicles"—a history of Greece from Kerkops (approximately 1500 BC) to Diognetos (264 BC). Of great importance to scholars, the marble chronicle was discovered in the 17th century and the vast majority of it may now be seen in the Ashmolean Museum in Oxford. The Paros museum also contains finds from the local temple of Apollo, a 5th-century Winged Victory, and a short biography and frieze of the poet Antilochos, who took part in the colonisation of Thassos before he turned to lyric verse. The small church of **Ag. Nikolaos** is also nearby, built at the same time as the Ekatontapyliani. Just outside Paroikia, by a spring, are the Classical ruins of an **Asklepieion** (temple to the god of healing). Nearby was a temple to Pythian Apollo, which no longer exists.

Also in Paroikia is the **Aegean School of Fine Arts,** founded by Brett Taylor in 1966 and accredited by many American universities.

Frequent buses connect Paroikia with the island's second port, the lovely Naousa, Here, as well as a **Byzantine Museum** and icons in the church of Ag. Nikolaos Mostratos, there are a number of interesting churches. Near the harbour stand the half-submerged ruins of the Venetian castle. Naousa is a busy fishing port and thus a good place to find fresh fish; there are beaches within walking distance, and excursions to others, notably **Kolimbithres,** with its bizarre, wind-sculpted rocks. There are other beaches at Langeri, Santa Maria, and at the fishing village of **Ambelas,** which also has a taverna and a quiet hotel.

Between Naousa and Paroikia, men only may visit the **Monastery of Longo-vardes,** founded in 1683 by Christophoros Paleiologos. The walls are covered with 17th-century frescoes, and there are many old icons and an icon painting school. The **Tris Ekklisies,** a 7th-century basilica nearby, was built over the site of a 4th-century BC heroon of poet Archilochos. Northeast of Paroikia the marble foundation and altar of the **temple of Delian Apollo** still remain. Curiously, together with temples to Apollo on Delos and Naxos, it forms part of a perfect equilateral triangle.

In the centre of the island is Paros' medieval capital and one of its prettier towns, **Lefkas,** Farming, textiles and ceramics are its major industries. Paros' ancient marble quarries may be visited at **Marathi,** between Paroikia and Lefkas, not far from Ag. Minas, a fortified but abandoned monastery. The quarries too are abandoned, for economic reasons (they were last used to grace the mortal remains of Napoleon), but it's still fun to poke around. Bring a light to explore—the longest tunnel stretches 90 metres (300 ft) underground. The marble mined here was called "Lychnites" by the ancients, or "candlelit marble", for its wonderful ability to absorb light. An ancient inscription may be seen at one of the quarries.

East of Lefkas **Prodromos** is an old farming village; **Marmara,** another village, lives up to its name ("marble")—even some of the streets are paved with it. Prettiest of the three, though, is **Marpissa,** Above its windmills are the ruins of a 15th-century Venetian fortress and the 16th-century monastery Ag. Antonios, constructed out of Classical materials and containing lovely marbles and paint-ings (note the 17th-century fresco of the Second Coming of Christ). The ancient city of Paros is believed to have been in this area.

Piso Livadi historically served as the port for these villages and the marble quarries; now it's the centre of Paros' main beach colonies: **Molos, Dryos,** and the island's best, **Chrysi Akti,** the golden beach. Luxurious villas line the bay at Dryos where the Turkish fleet used to put in on its tribute-gathering tour of the Aegean.

South-west of Paroikia **Petaloudes** or Psychopiani literally swarms with butterflies in July and August; they fly up in clouds as you walk by. Here also are the ruins of a 17th-century Venetian tower, and just outside the village is the convent of Paros' patron saint, **Ag. Arsenios,** the schoolteacher, abbot and prophet who was canonised in 1967. The saint is buried inside the convent, but men are not allowed to enter. At **Pounta** there is a beach, and from here the small boat crosses to Antiparos. There's another beach at **Alyki** which has some facilities—and Paros' airport.

PANEYERIA
15 August, Ekatontapyliani at Paroikia; 23 April, Ag. Georgios at Agkairia; 21 May, Ag. Konstantinos at Paroikia; 40 days after Orthodox Easter, Analypsis at Piso Livadi; in July, Fish and Wine Festival, Paroikia; 29 August, Ag. Ioannis at Lefkas; 18 August, Petaloudes.

WHERE TO STAY
Paros is packed in the summer, and it's very hard to find a place if you just drop in. Nearly everyone stays in Paroikia, Naousa and Piso Livadi, but an alternative is the stone walled **Xenia Hotel** up in Lefkas, a ten minute bus ride from the Piso Livadi. The **Xenia** (class B) has a lovely view out over the village in its green amphitheatre, and there's a bar and restaurant. Prices here are 6000 dr. for a double (tel. 0284 71 248). If you want to book a place in town, the **Dina** (tel. 0284 21 325) with its garden is the most charming, and its prices, though high, are typical of Paros—3000 dr. for a double. In Naousa prices tend to be about the same, the nicest place here being the **Pension Naousa,** right on the sea (tel. 0284 51 207) which will set you back 2000 dr. for a single, 2800 dr. for a double. In Piso Livadi the class B pension **Marpissa** (tel. 0284 41 288) has the same prices and an attractive view. There are three campsites on the island—**Camping Koula** (tel. 0284 22 082) and **Paros** (tel. 0284 21 670) near Paroikia, and **Capt. Kafkis Camping** near Piso Livadi (tel. 0284 41 392).

EATING OUT
The best food in Paroikia, or on all of Paros for that matter, is at **To Tamarisko,** where you can dine delectably in a garden for around 1400–2000 dr. Near the Aegean school, tucked away and a bit hard to find, is **May Tey,** with a Vietnamese menu; if you're fond of oriental cooking, it's intriguing to see how differently it's prepared in other countries. The menu's limited, though, and prices are high—expect to pay 1500 dr. for dinner. In Naousa there's a string of good sea-food restaurants on the harbour, some with prices still in this stratosphere: check them out. Inexpensive souvlaki, hamburgers, etc, abound; you can even have the Parian version of the McDonald's favourite, in this case, a Big Nick.

TOURIST POLICE
24 Marrogenou, tel. (0284) 21673. There is also an information centre in Windmill.

ANTIPAROS

CONNECTIONS
At least two boats a day from Paroika, Paros; caique from Pounta, Paros.

Antiparos ("before" Paros) was the site of the ancient Oliaros, and was once connected to its larger neighbour Paros by a causeway. In the time of Alexander the Great a large, deep cave full of stalactites was discovered on Antiparos, which has been attracting tourists for 2000 years. Unprotected, the island was uninhabited in Byzantine times. The Venetians, under Leonardo Lorentani, built a tower there and what is left of it can still be seen in the harbour of Antiparos' one town, **Kastro.**

Many tourists who find Paros too tourist-ridden end up on a quiet Antiparian beach (there are good beaches at Kastro, at Sifnaikos Yialos in the north, and Ag. Georgios in the south). Fish is plentiful, even in the restaurants, and there are many rooms to rent besides the three hotels. Of the islands off the coast, **Strogilonisi** and **Despotiko** are known for their rabbit hunting. On the islet **Saliagos,** a fishing village from the 5th millennium has been excavated by John Evans and Colin Renfrew, the first Neolithic site found in the Cyclades.

The **cave,** is still the major attraction on the islet, despite the centuries of tourists taking free souvenirs. In the summer boats run not only from Kastro, but also from Paroikia and Pounta. From the boat landing stage one must ascend, half an hour by foot and less by donkey, and then descend into the 70-metre (230-ft) deep chamber. The cave is about twice as deep, but the rest is closed. Steps have been built to prevent visitors from killing themselves. Inside, the cave is fantastic and spooky. To make up for the many stalactites that have been broken off, famous visitors of the past have smoked and carved their names on the walls, including Lord Byron and King Otho, the King of Greece (1840). One stalagmite attests in Latin to a Christmas mass celebrated in the cavern by Count Nouantelle in 1673, attended by 500 (paid) locals. Unfortunately, an older inscription is now lost; its several authors declared that they were hiding from Alexander the Great, who accused them of attempted assassination. The church by the entrance of the cave, **Ag. Ioannis,** was built in 1774. To see the cave in the winter, it is necessary to go to the village for the key.

In Antiparos there are two 17th-century churches, the cathedral **Ag. Nikolaos,** and **Evangelismos.**

PANEYERIA
23 April, Ag. Georgios; 21 May, Ag. Konstantinos at Kambos; and 8 May, Ag. Ioannis Theologos, by the cave.

WHERE TO STAY
Many people who can't find a place to stay in Paros come to Antiparos, though prices are only a tiny bit lower here. The little **Chryssi Akti** on the beach is an elegant class C hotel (tel. 0284 61 206) with rates to match: up to 4500 dr. for a double in season. Less expensive is the **Mantalena Hotel** in town (tel. 0284 61 220) where you can get a single for 2300 dr. and a double for 3500 dr. There are also quite a few pensions and rooms to let, and although there's an organised campsite (tel. 0284 61 221), freelancers are winked at if they distance themselves from town.

SANTORINI
(THIRA)

Oia Finikia

Ormos

THERASIA

Imerovigli Vourvoulos

Potamos
Therasia
Agrilia

Skola Fira Fira
Cable car Karterathos

Monolithos

NEA KAMENI
Messaria Airport
Athinios Vothon

PALIA KAMENI Pirgos
Episkopi
ASPRONISI Mesa Gonia
Exo Gonia
Kamari
Megalochori

Profitis Ilias (566m)
Ancient Thira
Akrotiri Perissa
Ancient Akrotiri
Emborion

0   1   2   5 km
0   1   2   3 miles

Eleusis
Exomitis

EATING OUT
Unfortunately demand has also jacked up the price of food here, and it's not any cheaper than Paros. **Yorgos Taverna** in town has good solid fare at reasonable prices.

TOURIST POLICE
See regular police in town, tel. (0284) 61 202.

SANTORINI (THIRA)

CONNECTIONS
Daily flights from Athens; frequent air connections with Mykonos, Herakleon (Crete) and Rhodes. A hydrofoil goes to Santorini from Herakleon, and a small ferry makes the trip approximately four times a week in the summer. Daily ferry from Piraeus. Summer connections with Milos, Serifos, Sifnos, Kimilos and Ag. Nikolaos (Crete); year-round connections with Ios, Paros, Naxos and Anafi. Depending on the weather, most ships call at Athinios and Fira, the capital, and sometimes at Oia.

Considered by many to be the fairest of the Cyclades (indeed, the island's oldest name was Kalliste, or "the most beautiful") volcanically fertile Santorini has (literally) had its ups and downs: throughout history parts of the island and its circular archipelago have appeared then disappeared beneath the waves. Human endeavours on the island have fared similarly: one can visit no less than three former "capitals"—the Minoan centre of Akrotiri (many people's favourite candidate for Metropolis, the capital of the legendary Atlantis), the Classical capital Thira at Mesa Vouna, and the medieval Skaros, as well as the picturesque modern town of Fira, perched on the edge of Santorini's awesome, looming, multicoloured cliffs. But this, too, was flattened by an earthquake in 1956 (though lovingly rebuilt). Though nowadays trendy and chic and a must on the itinerary of most cruise ships, older inhabitants can remember when their island hosted more political prisoners than tourists, and nights were filled with the rumour of vampires rather than the chatter of café society sipping Bloody Marys, watching the sun go down in one of the world's most enchanting settings.

HISTORY
The history of Santorini, or Thira, is tied up with its geology. In the long distant past the island was created from volcanic debris. It was circular in shape, with a volcano called Strogyle in the centre. From prehistoric times, regular volcanic eruptions have created a rich, volcanic soil, which attracted inhabitants very early. First came the Karians, who were chased out by the Cretans. Their colony at Akrotiri dates back to the height of the Minoan civilisation. Then, in approximately 1450 BC, the volcano erupted again, destroying not only Akrotiri, but

Church and Cliffs on Thira, Cyclades

probably causing irreparable damage to the mighty Minoan civilisation in Crete as well.

This relatively recent theory was proposed by the Greek archaeologist Spirydon Marinatos. In 1939 he decided that the destruction of Amnisos, the port of Knossos on Crete, could only have been caused by a massive natural disaster, such as a tidal wave from the north. What, he wondered, could have caused such a catastrophic force? There were the following clues: south-east of Santorini oceanographers discovered volcanic ash from Strogyle on the sea bed, covering an area of 900×300 km^2 (350×115 sq. miles); on nearby Anafi and Eastern Crete itself is a layer of volcanic tephra 3mm ($\frac{1}{8}$ inch) thick. This, thin as it was, would be sufficient to destroy existing plant growth and cause a famine. A Classical clue came from the Athenian reformer and writer Solon, who in 600 BC wrote of his journey to Egypt, where the scribes told him of the disappearance of Kreftia (Crete?) 9000 years before, which Solon might have mistaken for a more correct 900. The Egyptians, who had steadily traded with Crete and Santorini, described a lost land of Atlantis, which had red, white and black volcanic rock (like Santorini today); they spoke of the ancient city vanishing in 24 hours under a tremendous wave. In his *Critias*, Plato described Atlantis as being composed of one round island and one long island, connected by one culture and rule (Santorini and Crete, under Minos?). He describes Atlantis as a sweet land of art, flowers and fruit (which are portrayed on the frescoes discovered at Akrotiri). In the 19th century French archaeologists discovered Minoan pots at Akrotiri, and it was there that Marinatos began to dig in 1967, bringing to light from under its deep tephra tomb a well-preserved Minoan town.

Whether or not Santorini was the glorified Atlantis of the ancients, the theory of the ruin of Minoan life by its volcanic explosion and subsequent tidal waves and earthquakes has historical support in a similar explosion in 1883. This was when the volcano Krakatoa exploded creating a caldera (a crater left by an explosion) of 8.3 km² (3¼ sq. miles). This caused a tidal wave of more than 200 metres (660 ft) high, which spread great damage over 150 km (100 miles). The caldera left by Strogyle, ie. the present bay of Santorini, is 22 km² (8½ sq. miles). After the volcano had sunk into it, it was filled by a rushing sea, which caused a truly enormous wave. As no bodies have been found at Akrotiri it is supposed that earthquakes and other omens warned the inhabitants in time for them to flee. The present islets of Therasia and Aspronisi mark the edges of the caldera.

In the 8th century BC the Dorians settled at Santorini, building their capital at Mesa Vouna on Mt Profitis Elias, which survived until the early decades after Christ. Thira was the island's Doric name, and legends have it that the Thirians founded the city of Cyrene in Libya. In Hellenistic times, Ptolemy of Egypt fortified the island and dedicated temples to Dionysos and to his own family.

Like the Ptolemies, the Byzantines also considered the island to be of strategic importance and fortified it, but most of these fortifications have since been destroyed by earthquakes. Skaros near Imerovigli became the Frankish capital when Marco Sanudo captured the island, and it was eventually taken over by the Crispi family. At this time the island was called after its patron saint Saint Irene, which has been elided into Santorini. In 1534 the pirate admiral Barbarossa stopped by and gave the island to the Turks. Throughout its history Santorini has enjoyed a considerable reputation for its wine, which is quite strong.

WHAT TO SEE

Traditionalists will disembark beneath the towering cliffs at Fira, taking a motor launch to the tiny port of Skala Fira, and from there hire a donkey to travel the winding path to the town 270 metres (900 ft) above. Those in more of a hurry can now ride the Austrian-built (1982) cable car which will take you up in two minutes. Donated to the island by ship-owner Evangelos Nomikos, profits from the fares go to Santorini's communities—and to the donkey drivers, who receive a percentage of each ticket. It operates every 15 minutes from 6.45 am to 8.15 pm.

Those who remember **Fira,** the capital, before 1956 say that the present town bears no comparison architecturally to its present version, though it's pleasant enough—Cycladically white, built on several terraces, adorned with pretty churches. The cliff side has numerous cafés and restaurants, all boasting magnificent views.

The **museum** is near the cable car on the north side of town. It houses finds from Akrotiri and Mesa Vouna and Early Cycladic figurines found in the pumice mines. The famous Santorini frescoes are still in the National Museum in Athens, although there are rumours that a new museum will one day be built in Fira to house them on the island. As well as the museum one can also visit the handicraft workshop founded by Queen Frederika, where women weave large carpets on looms. Some places serve local wines by the glass. The most famous labels are Atlantis, Santina, Nikteri, Kaldera, Vulcan and Vissanto.

Buses to other destinations on the island all depart from the central bus station. Several times a day the buses run to **Akrotiri** (9 am–1.30 pm and 4 pm–6 pm), the Minoan outpost discovered in 1967 by Professor Marinatos. Archaeological work is still very much in progress. Excavation proved very difficult due to the thick layer of tephra, or volcanic glass rock, which covered Akrotiri: one can see how deep the archaeologists had to dig.

The tephra is now quarried to make cement for tombstones. The ancient city revealed beneath it is wonderful and strange, made even more unreal by the huge roof which protects it from the elements. A carpet of volcanic dust silences all footsteps as one walks amid houses up to three storeys high, many still containing their huge pithoi, or storage pots. In one of the houses is the rather controversial grave of Marinatos, who died recently after a fall on the site. The huge filing cabinets hold pottery sherds yet to be pieced together. Good reference reading is the locally available *Art and Religion in Thera: Reconstructing a Bronze Age Society*, by Dr Nanno Marinatos, son of the archaeologist. Below the excavation site is a black rock beach and taverna; there are also some coffee shops and rooms in the vineyard-surrounded villages above.

East of Akrotiri is **Exomitis** where one of the best-preserved Byzantine fortresses of the Cyclades can be seen; submerged near here are the ruins of ancient Eleusis. The island's best beach, **Perissa,** is north of here. Like the other beaches of Santorini, the sand here is volcanic and black. Perissa has a campsite and good restaurants and tavernas. A modern church stands on the site of the Byzantine Saint Irene, for whom the island is named.

Up on the rocky headland of Mesa Vouna (a track leads up from Perissa) is **Ancient Thira,** its extensive ruins built on great terraces. Excavated by the German archaeologist Hiller von Gortringen in the late 19th century, the site produced the fine "Santorini vases" in the museum. Most of the present remains date from the Ptolemies, who used the city as a base for their enterprises further north. There are temples to the Egyptian gods, Dionysos, Apollo, the Ptolemies and founding father Thira; impressive remains of the Agora and theatre, with a dizzying view down to the sea; several cemeteries; and a gymnasium. Numerous houses still have mosaics; graffiti dating from 800 BC may be seen on the Terrace of Celebrations, recording the names of competitors and dancers of the gymnopedies. Note the unusual Cyclopean walls near here.

North of Ancient Thira stretches another black beach, **Kamari,** with tavernas, etc; inland, up the slope from Mesa Vouna, is the 1712 **Monastery Profitis Ilias** on Santorini's highest point (566 metres/1857 ft). On a clear day you can see Crete from here, and on an exceptionally clear day, it is said, even Rhodes is visible on the horizon. The locals, remembering the earthquake of 1956, say it is the only place on Santorini which will remain above sea level when the rest of the island sinks into the sea to join its other half. Profitis Ilias has a museum of valuable church objects, diamond gospels, the mitre of Gregory V, a crusader's cross and local folk items. For the time being, however, the monastery is closed to visitors. At the foot of Profitis Ilias, by the village of Mesa Gonia, is **Panayia**

Episkopi or Kimisis Theotokou, built in the 11th century. The Venetians converted the church to the Catholic faith when they conquered Santorini, but under the Turks the Orthodox recovered their own. Inside are Byzantine icons, and on 15 August the biggest paneyeri on the island takes place there.

Emborion and **Pirgos** are two of the oldest surviving villages on the island, with interesting old houses, Byzantine walls, and the latter with a Venetian fort. At the port, **Athinios**, are a couple of cafés and a taverna with food, including breakfast, and a small stretch of sand to sleep on if you arrive in the middle of the night.

Skaros, on the way to Oia was the medieval capital of Santorini, but it has been much damaged by earthquakes. Ag. Stephanos there is the oldest church on the island, and there are also the crumbling ruins of a Catholic convent of Santa Katerina, built after a young girl's vision in 1596. The nuns lived a life of hardship there until they changed residence in 1818 for Fira, and now the desolate convent is about to tumble down. In **Imerovigli** is another convent, still inhabited, dedicated to Ag. Nikolaos and built in 1674.

Oia, or Ia, is the third port of Santorini, and at least one ship still calls here regularly. Half-ruined by the earthquake, its white houses are piled on top of one another up the steep slope. Although it's a long hard walk up from the beach, you can come back with pumice-stone souvenirs for friends at home.

Santorini's caldera is 10 km (6 miles) wide and 380 metres (1248 ft) deep. Curving about the north-western edge is the islet **Therasia**, part of Santorini until they were separated by an eruption in 236 BC. Pumice is mined here; part of it went into the building of the Suez Canal. In one of the quarries a Middle Cycladic settlement was discovered, pre-dating Akrotiri, though there are no traces of it now. There are three villages on Therasia. The largest, **Manolas,** has tavernas and rooms to rent. There are also excursion boats to the "burnt isles", **Palia and Nea Kameni,** both still volcanically active, especially the Metaxa crater on Nea Kameni. However, although one local brochure refers to it as "the strange volcano which cause you greatness", be forewarned that half the people who visit it come away disappointed.

PANEYERIA
19 and 20 July, at Profitis Ilias; 20 October, Ag. Artemiou in Fira; 26 October, Ag. Dimitriou in Karterthos; 15 August, at Mesa Gonia and Fira.

WHERE TO STAY
There's nothing like staying in Fira with a view over the great caldera, but if you want to stay in town, do book in advance. Still at the top of the list for luxury and the view is the **Hotel Atlantis** (tel. 0286 22 232), a class A establishment near the heart of town, where a double in season costs 14 500 dr. There is a **Youth hostel** (tel. 0286 22 722) open from April till October, card not required and rates are 390 dr. a bed, including shower. It, too, is north of Fira ($\frac{1}{2}$ km); in town, however, there's the **Kamares Hostel,** where beds go for the same price. You'll find it near the cable car.

If Fira is full, you can almost always find a room elsewhere on the island, and as bus connections are good it's not all that hard getting about. Kamari has many modest sized hotels and pensions, although the prices tend to be rather bold—the C class **Artemis Beach** has doubles starting at 6000 dr. (tel. 0286 31 198). The island's campsite is also here (tel. 0286 31 451). If you land in Athinios, the owners of rooms (mostly in Messaria, Emborion and Karterados) will meet you in their vans and whisk you away.

In Oia there are a number of inexpensive rooms and pensions. Better yet, the NTOG has restored 30 traditional homes to let out to visitors at reasonable prices, furnished with native embroideries and handcarved furniture. Each house accommodates between two and seven people; for reservations and current prices, contact the NTOG or Paradosiakos at Ikismos Oias, Oia (tel. 0286 71 234).

EATING OUT

For international cuisine and reputedly the best food on Santorini, **Castro,** near the cable car will set you back a good 2500 dr. or more for one of its lavish spreads. At the opposite end of the scale is **Nikolaos Taverna,** with good Greek food at the lowest prices in town. Located in the heart of Fira, it's easy to find by the line of people waiting at the door (so get there early). For the view alone, it would be worth the price to eat at **Leschi's,** but the food is good, too, and the atmosphere charming; dinner here costs around 1400 dr., with good Santorini wine. In Oia there are two excellent choices—**George's,** where the typical Greek menu is served with much more love and care than usual, and **Kyblos,** built into the caves and romantically atmospheric; it's a bit more expensive than George's, with main courses starting at 500 dr.

TOURIST POLICE

See regular police, 25 tou Martiou St, tel. (0286) 22 649.

SERIFOS

CONNECTIONS

Daily with Piraeus, Sifnos and Milos. Almost every day to Kythnos. Twice a week with Ios and Santorini. Once a week to Syros.

Where its neighbour Sifnos greets the visitor with green terraces and dovecots, Seriphos tends to intimidate travellers with its barren rockiness. Its capital seems impossibly inaccessible, its port hemmed in by rocky masses, and a lack of vegetation (at first sight) makes it seem terribly hot in the summer. More than the other Cyclades, Serifos' water shortage problem is acute. The visitors who disembark here, though, are rewarded with some of the most pleasant and quiet beaches in the Cyclades.

HISTORY   *Very interesting*

Serifos, "the barren", owed much of its limited prosperity in antiquity to its iron and copper deposits, among the richest in Greece, and mined from the earliest days. However, when other sources were discovered in Africa which could be exploited more economically, the mines on Serifos were abandoned, and the island's population decreased drastically. Historically, the fate of Seriphos follows that of the other Cyclades; Chora, high above the sea, was once fortified with a Byzantine–Venetian castle and walls, and here and there on the island are odd remains left by other conquerors.

What Serifos may lack in historical interest is more than compensated for by its **mythology,** for it was the destination of Princess Danaë, who was set adrift in a box with her infant son Perseus. This cruel deed was done by her own father, the King, for it had been prophesied that a son of Danaë would slay him. In order to foil the oracle the King locked his daughter in a tower, but even there her beauty did not fail to attract the amorous attentions of Zeus, who came to Danaë in a shower of golden rain and fathered Perseus.

Enraged but unable to put his daughter or grandson to death, the King decided to leave the issue to fate and set them adrift in the box. Zeus guided them to the shores of Serifos, where a fisherman discovered them and brought them to Polydectes, the King of the island. Struck by her beauty, Polydectes wanted to marry Danaë but she refused him, and as Perseus grew older he supported his mother. Although Polydectes pretended then to lose interest in Danaë, he desired her more than ever and plotted to remove Perseus by asking a favour of him. Perseus, glad that the King had stopped chasing his mother, could not refuse. Then Polydectes explained what he wanted: nothing less than the head of the gorgon Medusa, the only mortal of the three horrible sisters, whose hair was of living snakes, whose eyes bulged and whose teeth were fangs. The sisters were so ugly that a mere glance at one of them turned a human to stone.

Despite Danaë's horror at this treachery of Polydectes, Perseus accepted the task and went about accomplishing it, assisted by the goddess Athena, and a mirrorlike shield, winged shoes and cloak of invisibility. With Medusa's awful head in his pouch Perseus returned to Serifos (saving Andromeda from a sea monster on the way), to find his mother hiding in the hut of the fisherman who had saved them so long ago, for Polydectes had tried to force her to marry him. Angrily Perseus went up to the palace, where he found a very surprised Polydectes at a great banquet. Perseus told him that he had succeeded in his quest and held up the prize as proof, instantly turning everyone in the room into stone.

The kind fisherman was declared King of Serifos by Perseus, who with his mother went home to the mainland. Still fearing the old prophesy, Danaë's father fled before them. But fate caught up with the old King when he later met Perseus

173

in another town. They did not recognise one another, and Perseus accidently killed his grandfather

WHAT TO SEE

Most people who visit Serifos stay in **Livadi,** the port, where there's a beach and many rooms to rent. A sweetshop on the waterfront is renowned for its loukoumades, hot doughnut seeped in cinnamon and honey, with a fragrance that fills the night air, an advertisement many find irresistible. There are two other beaches within easy walking distance from Livadi, towards the south; the second has become the unofficial campsite on the island.

Serifos, or Chora, the main town, is a 20-minute walk from the port. There is also an hourly bus service. (This is as far as the bus goes—you'll have to see the rest fo the island under your own steam). It is a pretty town, still retaining some medieval characteristics. Some of the houses are made from pieces of the old fortress and others date back many centuries. One can see the old windmills, and a certain rare carnation which is only grown on Serifos. The **bank, post office** and **OTE,** are all located here, but rooms are hard to find. From Chora a 20-minute walk leads to **Psili Ammos,** an excellent beach on the west coast.

The road continues from Chora past the **Aspropirgos** (White Castle), from the 6th century AD, to **Megalo Chorio,** believed to be the site of ancient Serifos; below, **Megalo Livadi** with a beach served as the loading dock for the iron and copper mined near Megalo Chorio. From here you can walk around **Mesa Akrotiri** where there are two caves: the cave of the Cyclops Polythemus with stalactites, and the other, at **Koutala,** where signs of prehistoric settlement were found. Unfortunately they are now closed as they are considered unsafe. Koutala also has a beach, and a mule path from here follows the south coast back to Livadi.

Sikamia Bay in the north, with its beach and one store, is a good place to get away from it all, for there are also trees and fresh water. **Galani,** another beach with a taverna, is half an hour on foot from Sikamia, and from here one can visit the **Taxiarchos Monastery,** built in 1500. Inside is a lovely old table, 18th-century frescoes by Skordilis, and Byzantine manuscripts in the library. The oldest church on Serifos is at **Panayia** village, built in the 10th century. **Kalitsos,** not far from Galani, is another pleasantly green place, with two restaurants.

Other beaches on Serifos are Karavi, Lia, Ag. Sostis, Platys Yialos, Halara and Ganima. Most of these are remote and accessible only on foot. Karavi is a popular nudist beach.

PANEYERIA

Fava beans are the big speciality at these celebrations: 5 May, Ag. Irene at Koutala; 27 July, Ag. Panteleimonos at Livadi; 7 September, Ag. Sosoudos at Livadi; 6 August, Sotiros at Kalobelli; 15–17 August, Panayia near the Monastery (at a different village each day)

WHERE TO STAY

Serifos is well known enough for its hotels and rooms to fill up in the summer. These are all near the sea, most of them in Livadi. There's the new **Serifos Beach Hotel,** the island's biggest with doubles at 3500 dr. (tel. 0281 51 209). More expensive is the **Maistrali,** also on the beach, with high season rates of 4500 dr. for its C class doubles (tel. 0281 51 381). Smaller and older, the **Pension Perseus** is also on the beach (tel. 0281 51 273) with doubles going for 2500 dr. Slightly more expensive is the **Areti Pension** in Livadi, with doubles at 2800 dr. (tel. 0281 51 117).

EATING OUT

The sea is clean and the fish is especially good in Serifos' seaside tavernas. Popular with locals and tourists alike is **Teli's,** on the waterfront in Livadi, where the food is excellent and the service friendly; inexpensive. Further round the harbour you can find fish restaurants, ouzeries and pizzeria. In Chora look out for **Stamatis'** restaurant and the **Orea Cleo ouzeri,** well known for its good fresh *mezedes.*

TOURIST INFORMATION

N.T.O.G., Livadi, tel. (0281) 51 300.
Tourist police, see regular police, Chora.

SIFNOS

CONNECTIONS

Daily with Piraeus, Serifos, Milos; twice-weekly with Ios and Santorini; frequently with Kythnos and Kimolos; less frequently with Syros.

The Chapel on Sifnos

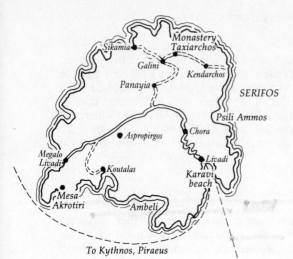

Sikamia

Monastery
Taxiarchos

Galini

Kendarchos

Panayia

SERIFOS

Psili Ammos

Aspropirgos

Chora

Megalo
Livadi

Livadi

Koutalas

Karavi
beach

Mesa
Akrotiri

Ambeli

To Kythnos, Piraeus

SERIFOS AND SIFNOS

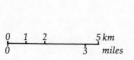

0   1   2   5 km
0   3   miles

O. Ag. Georgiou

Ag. Marina

SIFNOS

Kamares

Artemon

Kastro

Kato Petali

Apollonia

Ormos
Seralia

Pofitis Ilias
(678m/2237ft)

Exambela

Katavati Faros

Ag.
Andreas

Chrissopig
Monastery

Vathi

Platis Yialos

To Milos

KITRIANI

To Naxos

Sifnos in recent years has become the most popular island in the western Cyclades, with good reason—it's the prettiest, with its peaceful green hills and terraces, charming villages, friendly people and one long sandy beach. Here and there the landscape is dotted with Venetian dovecots, windmills, some 40 ruined Classical towers and over 300 miniature chapels. It is an exceptionally pleasant island for walks. In Greece Sifnos has a reputation for its pottery and its cooks, both of which have been in such demand elsewhere in Greece that few remain on Sifnos. Its olives are said to produce the best oil in the Cyclades, but sadly agriculture on the island is in decline (as is often the case, in direct correlation with the rise in tourism), and once-fertile Sifnos now has to import almost all of its foodstuffs

HISTORY
The Phoenicians, one of the first groups of people to settle on Sifnos, named the island Meropia (mentioned by Pliny) and began to mine gold. They were followed by the Cretans, who founded Minoa near Apollonia, and were in turn replaced by the Ionians who lived near Ag. Andreas and elsewhere. Meropia, meanwhile, had become famous for its gold mines; at one time, it is said, there was so much of the precious metal that the inhabitants simply divided it among themselves each year and in the 6th century could afford to pave their main square with Parian marble. In the 6th century Apollo demanded that the Sifniotes send a tithe of gold in the form of an egg to his sanctuary at Delphi, and in 530 BC they constructed a magnificent treasury for the gold and adorned it with a fine frieze and pediment which can still be seen at Delphi. For many years the Sifnian Treasury was the richest of all. But one year the Sifniotes, who had a reputation for greed and cunning, decided they needed the gold more than Apollo, and sent the god a gilded rock. Apollo accepted this fraud, but soon discovered he had been duped and cursed the island. This gave Polycrates, the Tyrant of Samos, a good excuse to extract a huge fine from Sifnos; 40 triremes plundered and ransomed most of the island's gold, and the curse supposedly caused the mines to sink and give out. Thus the island became empty, or "sifnos", which is what the name means. Nowadays most of the ancient mines are under water, at Ag. Mina, Kapsalos and Ag. Suzon.

After these events the island went into decline and the inhabitants moved to Kastro, where a Roman cemetery has been discovered. In 1307 the Da Koronia family ruled the island in place of Venice. In 1456 Kozadinos, the Lord of Kythnos, married into the family and the Kozadini ruled Sifnos until the Turks took the island in 1617. Towards the end of the 17th century the Ottomans made an attempt to re-open the mines, or at least got as far as sending out experts to examine them. Supposedly, when they got wind of these plans, the islanders hired a band of French pirates to sink the Sultan's ship bringing the experts. The experts, in turn, heard of the plot, and simply went home. Later the French exploited the local deposits of iron ore and lead; mining ended in 1914.

Sifnos has also made an important contribution to Greek letters. At the end of the 17th century the "School of the Holy Tomb" was founded on the island to keep alive the ancient Greek classics during the Turkish occupation, attracting students from all over Greece. Nikolaos Chrysogelos, its most famous head-master, led a contingent of Sifniotes in the War of Independence, and went on to become modern Greece's first Minister of Education. Another islander, the 19th-century poet-satirist Cleanthis Triandafilos, who wrote under the name Rabagas, was a thorn in the side of the monarchy until he committed suicide, imprisoned for his poisoned pen. Ioannis Gyparis (died 1942) was another Sifniote who, like Cadafy, was one of the first poets to espouse the use of the demotic language (as opposed to katharevousa) in literature.

WHAT TO SEE
The island's port, shady **Kamares,** has become in recent years a typical water-side jumble of tourist facilities. Situated between two steep, barren rocks that belie the fertility inland, it has some good places to camp, tavernas, etc. Only two of the many pottery workshops that once lined the north side of the harbour still survive. Sifnos' single bus route begins from Kamares: a dramatic climb up to the capital **Apollonia,** then on to Artemon, Chrissopigi and the resort Platys Yialos.

Apollonia is a Cycladic idyll, spread out across the hills, a circle of white from the distance. Its name derives from a temple of Apollo, built in the 7th century BC but superseded by the 18th-century church **Panayia Ouranoforia** in the highest quarter of town. Fragments of the temple can still be seen, though most interesting is the marble relief of St George over the door. Another church worth visiting, **Ag. Athanasios** (next to the pretty square dedicated to Cleanthis Triandafilos), has frescoes and a carved wooden iconostasis. In the bus stop square the **Museum of Popular Arts and Folklore** houses a fine ethnographic collection, including a selection of locally made pottery, embroideries and cos-tumes (open every day except Monday, 6–10 pm, entrance 20 dr.). There are numerous dovecots in the region with triangular designs which are repeated in the architecture of some of the houses. In Apollonia there are the island's banks, post office, Tourist Police and many rooms to rent. Local music, played on the violin and laouto, can frequently be heard in the cafés on Sundays.

Artemis is Apollo's twin sister; similarly **Artemon** is Apollonia's twin village and the second largest on Sifnos. Beneath its windmills are the island's most ambitious residences and churches. The church of **Kochi,** with its cluster of domes, is built over the ancient temple of Artemis, though not a sign of this remains. Two churches of note in Artemon are little **Ag. Georgios tou Afendi,** built in the 1600s and containing several fine icons from the period, and **Panayia ta Gournia,** near the bridge, with a beautiful interior (keys next door). Between Apollonia and Platis Yialos the monastery of **Ag. Andreas,** sitting on a hill, has some ruins of the double walls that once encircled the ancient citadel, and a little further north, but not accessible by road, is the monastery of **Profitis Ilias,** with a small network of catacombs and cells. Check that these are open before setting out.

Kastro, overlooking the east coast, is a 3-km (2-mile) walk from Artemon. This was the Classical and medieval capital of the island. It is a charming village, situated on a hill by the sea, surrounded by Byzantine-style walls made from the backs of the houses. On some of the old houses one can still discern Venetian coats-of-arms. Ruins of the Classical akropolis and walls remain, and there are many interesting churches, among them the two of the Panayia, Eleoussa (1653) and Koimmissi (1593), and Ag. Aekaterini (1665). All of these churches have noteworthy floors. The old Catholic church, St Antonio, may soon be converted into a museum of local antiquities. The site of the School of the Holy Tomb, closed in 1834, now serves as Kastro's cemetery. From Kastro paths lead down to **Seralia** and **Poulati** and their beaches.

Just south of Artemon the bus passes through **Exambela,** a quiet village in the middle of one of Sifnos' most fertile areas. The village's name derives from the Turkish "aksam bela" ("Trouble in the Evening"): during the occupation the inhabitants were notorious for their rowdy mischief-making. Further south, by the seaside village and beach at **Faros** is the island's most famous church, **Panayia Chrissopigi,** built in 1650 on a holy rock. Long ago two women fled to the monastery from a band of approaching pirates. Desperately they prayed to Mary for help and she answered their pleas by splitting the cape right in the pirates' path, creating a gap 18 metres (60 ft) wide, which today is spanned by a bridge. The icon of the Virgin in the church was discovered in the sea by fishermen attracted by the light it radiated. To see the church ask the bus driver to let you off at Chrissopigi and walk down the mule path. There is also a paved road for cars.

Platys Yialos with its broad sandy beach is the island's busiest resort, though you can escape its worldly concerns by lodging in the serene convent of **Panayia tou Vounou** up on the cliff, with a gorgeous view over the bay below. The last nuns left nearly a century ago, but the church with its ancient Doric columns is still used for island paneyeria. Two other seaside hamlets, **Vathi** and **Herronissos** are accessible only by boat from Kamares. **Vathi,** surrounded by high hills, has several tavernas on the beach and rooms (without electricity)—some available in the old monastery of Taxiarchis, dating from the 16th century. Another monastery on Sifnos near the village of Exambela, called **Vrissi** was built in 1612 and contains many old manuscripts and objects of religious art

PANEYERIA
1 September, Ag. Simeon near Kamares, 20 July, Profitis Ilias near Kamares; 29 August, Ag. Ioannes in Vathi; 25 March and 21 November, Panayia tou Vounou; 15 August, Panayia ta Gournia; 14 September, Stavros, at Faros; Ascension (Analypsis) at Chrissopigi

WHERE TO STAY
Most of the island's accommodation is in Kamares and Apollonia, and in high season you can pay 2000 dr. for a simple room. In Kamares the **Stavros Hotel**

179

has rooms with baths for 3200 dr. a double (tel. 0284 31 641). For the same price you can stay at the B class **Kamari** (tel. 0284 31 710). Up in Apollonia there's the charming class B **Pension Apollonia** (tel. 0284 31 490) with nine rooms, doubles going for 2000 dr. in high season. In Platis Yialos, the **Platis Yialos Hotel** (it used to be the Xenia) charges a cheeky 6500 dr. in season (tel. 0284 31 224). In Chrissopigi the small, family run **Flora** pension has double rooms with bath for 2800 dr. (tel. 0284 31 778). There are also rooms in Kastro, Artemon and Faros, and freelance camping is tolerated, so much so that there are even showers for campers on Kamares beach and elsewhere. If you come in summer without a room reservation, you'll be grateful for them after a night out under the stars.

EATING OUT
The local speciality is rivithia—oven baked chick peas—and on Sunday they are served in many Sifniot homes and at the taverna **Mangana** in Artemon. In general, the restaurant fare on Sifnos is better than on the other islands (undoubtably the influence of its famous chefs); a good place to enjoy it and a view besides is **Zorba's** up in Kastro. Both of the above are reasonably priced (600–800 dr. for a meal). For seafood **Captain Andreas** on the waterfront in Kamares has a good selection of fresh temptations and, as seems to be the trend these days, an Italian restaurant, **Lorenzo's,** has opened to entice the jaded palate. For lively evenings the **Smaragti bouzouki** restaurant in Platis Yialos is very popular, but pricey—2500 dr. a head.

TOURIST INFORMATION
N.T.O.G., Kamares, tel. (0284) 31 977.
Tourist police, see regular police, Apollonia, tel. (0284) 31 210.

SIKINOS

CONNECTIONS
Daily connections with Folegandros and Ios; less frequently with Santorini, Piraeus, Paros, Naxos, Sifnos and Syros.

If you find the other Cyclades too cosmopolitan, or you want to try out your Greek, you can always visit Sikinos, which is small and charming, untouched by history, unaffected (as yet) by organised tours (although its proximity to Ios may soon change all that). The one town on Sikinos is very pretty if sleepy, there is a pleasant beach, and a few other things to see if you should begin to tire of the simple pleasures of old-fashioned island life. The main ways of getting around are on foot and by mule. Vines still cover much of the fertile areas. In ancient times it was one of several islands called Oenoe, or "wine island".

The island's port, **Alopronia,** affords little shelter from the winds or for weary

SYROS

Kambos
Kastri
Ferekides' Cave
Chalandriani
Megas Lakkos
Ag. Loukas
Koraki
Aetov
VARVAROUSA
Mytakas
Ag. Dimitrios
Delfini Bay
Platos
Pyrgos
(411m/1350ft)
Ano Syros
Kini
Ag. Barbara
Ermoupolis
Piskopio
FANARI
Danakos
STROGULO
Galissas
Manna
Pagos
Messaria
Ag. Stefanos
Ano Mano
Azolimnos
Faneromeni
Vissas
Finikas
Adiata
Hroussa
Vari
Posidonia
Ormos
Ambela
Agathopes
Varis Bay
Komito
Megas Gialos

0   1   2   5 km
0   1   2   3 miles

visitors—most facilities are up at the capital, known as **Sikinos,** Chora or Kastro, the island's only real town, and an hour's walk up from the jetty, if the bus hasn't shown up. Looming over the village is the ruined **monastery of Zoodochos Pigi,** fortified against the frequent pirate incursions which the island endured in the past. The 300 inhabitants are most proud, however, of their "cathedral" with its icons by the 18th-century master Skordilis.

There are two walks to make on Sikinos, each taking about $1\frac{1}{2}$ hours. The path to the north-east leads to the rather scant remains of a Classical fortress at **Paliokastro;** the second, to the south-west, heads for **Episkopi,** where a Roman heroon of the 3rd century was converted into the Byzantine church Koimisis Theotokou; the church itself was remodelled in the 17th century after an earthquake.

Sikinos' beaches may be found along the south-eastern coast, from the port Alopronia to Ag. Georgiou Bay; the most popular being **Spilia,** so named because of the island's many caves.

WHERE TO STAY
Only a handful of rooms are available in private houses up in Chora, where you'll also find two small tavernas. In Alopronia there are also a few rooms, and three simple tavernas. If the rooms fill up people sleep out on Spilia Beach.

SYROS

CONNECTIONS
In summer daily with Mykonos, Tinos, Piraeus, Paros and Naxos. Three times a week to Amorgos, Santorini, Ios, Sikinos and Folegandros. Twice a week to Andros. Once a week to Milos, Sifnos, Serifos, Kythnos and Kea. Almost everyday to Rafina. Once a week to Patmos, Leros, Kalymnos, Kos, Rhodes, Samos and Ikaria.

Inhabitants of Syros have affectionately nicknamed their island home "our rock", as dry and barren a piece of real estate as you can find in Greece. But at the beginning of the 19th century and the beginning of the Greek War of Independence in 1821 it was blessed with three important qualities: a large, natural harbour, the protection of the King of France, and a hardworking population. The result was Syros' capital, Ermoupolis, once the major port in Greece, and today the largest city and capital of the Cyclades. It is also the best-preserved 19th-century neo-Classical town in the whole of Greece.

Syros is an island that doesn't need tourism, and looks upon its visitors as guests rather than customers—except when it comes to loukoumia, better known as Turkish Delight. These sweet, gummy squares, smothered in icing sugar, are an island speciality, and vendors stream aboard any ship that calls at Syros to peddle it to passengers, who are often just as eager to buy it

HISTORY

According to Homer, Syros was a rich, fertile isle, whose inhabitants never suffered any illness nor died of disease, and died only when they were struck by the gentle arrows of Apollo or Artemis after living long, happy lives. The first inhabitants, believed to be Phoenicians, settled at Dellagracia and at Finikas. Poseidon was worshipped on the island, and in connection with his cult one of the first observatories in the world, a heliotrope, was built here. It was constructed by the philosopher Ferekides, who also designed sundials and was a teacher of Pythagoras. In Roman times the population emigrated to the site of present-day Ermoupolis, at that time known as "the Happy" with its splendid natural harbour and two prominent hills. By the dark ages, however, Syros was uninhabited until the Venetians founded a town up on one of the hills, Ano Syros, in the 13th century.

Because Ano Syros was Catholic, it enjoyed the protection of the French king, and it remained neutral at the outbreak of the War of Independence in 1821. However, it welcomed war refugees from Chios, Psara and Smyrna, who brought their Orthodox faith with them and founded settlements on the other hill, Vrontatho, and down at the harbour. This port town boomed—it became the premier port and "warehouse" of the new Greek state, where cotton from Egypt and spices from the East would be stored and later shipped to the west; it was also the central coaling station for the whole eastern Mediterranean. When the time came to name the new town, Ermoupolis—"the city of Hermes" (the god of commerce)—was the natural choice.

For 50 years Syros ran much of the country's economy, and great fortunes were made and spent not only on elegant mansions, but also on schools, public buildings and streets, and on financing the war effort; the first theatre in modern Greece was built here, and the first high school, which was financed by a joint effort of the people; when they died, some of the most extravagant monuments to be seen in any Greek cemetery were erected in their memory. By the 1870s, however, oil replaced coal and Piraeus replaced Ermoupolis as Greece's major port; Syros declined, but always remained the largest city in the archipelago, supporting itself with its remaining shipyards and various industries, prospering just enough to keep its grand old buildings occupied, but not enough to tear them down to build new concrete blocks. Today the city is a National Historical Landmark.

WHAT TO SEE

You can either visit the monuments of neo-Classical **Ermoupolis** on your own, or take an excellent guided tour offered by the Teamwork travel office in the port. The city, as you arrive at the **commercial port,** presents an imposing sight, much commented on by early travellers. On either side are hills; catholic Ano Syros is on the right (or north), and Vrontatho on the left. The rest of the city is built on a 20° angle in a grand amphitheatre. On the other side of the harbour are the revitalised shipyards which declare this to be a working island.

The **Plateia Miaoulis** is the centre of the city, with its grand **town hall** and numerous cafés and pizzerias. Inside are full-length portraits of King George I and Queen Olga painted by Prossalendis. The **Archaeology Museum** is up the steps to the left. It contains proto-Cycladic and Roman finds from Syros and other islands. In front of the town hall is a statue of the revolution's hero—Admiral Miaoulis—and a bandstand with seven Muses. Sadly, the local Philharmonic Society, owing to lack of money, not interest, no longer performs there, but the municipality is endeavouring to raise funds for its revival. To the right, behind the square, stands the **Apollon Theatre,** the first in Greece since ancient times, a copy of La Scala in Milan; until 1914 it supported a regular Italian opera season. Currently you can get in only if you happen to be there when people are working on it—it needs extensive repairs. Up the street a little way from here you can wander through the central **Union Hall,** formerly a private mansion, and one of the few places you can get into to see the elaborate ceiling and wall paintings characteristic of old Ermoupolis.

In the next square up, **Ag. Nikolaos** is one of the city's best churches, boasting a carved marble iconostasis by the 19th-century sculptor Vitalis. In front of the church, a monument topped by a stone lion, also by Vitalis, is the world's first **monument to an Unknown Warrior.** The Cyclades capitol building is near here.

On the other side of the square, on St. Prioiou St the church **Koimesis** has an elegant neo-Classical interior and bell tower, one of the landmarks of Syros, and inside is an icon painted by **Dominicos Theotokopoulos**, better known as **El Greco.** Another fine church in Ermoupolis is the **Metamorphosis,** the Orthodox cathedral.

On top of **Vrontatho Hill** (take the main street from behind the Plateia Miaoulis) is the church Anastasis with a few old icons and superb views of the surrounding area, including Tinos and Mykonos. It is more intriguing, though, to make the hours' climb up Omirou St to the medieval Catholic quarter of **Ano Syros,** On the way up don't miss the **Orthodox cemetery of Ag. Georgios,** with its elaborate marble mausoleums of Syros' wealthy shipowners and merchants. Many of the families who have lived in Ano Syros since the Crusades have been Catholic, and some contemporary members of these families still live in picturesque old mansions. The hill is crowned by the **Catholic cathedral of St George.** A large **Capuchin convent of St Jean** was founded there in 1535 by the French King Louis XIII, and it is very beautiful, with archives dating from the 15th century. Another church, **St Nicolaos,** was founded in the 15th century as a house for the poor. Every year the **Apano Syria** takes place there in May or October (outside the high tourist season) celebrating the glorious history of Syros.

A 45-minute walk from Ermoupolis brings one to the pretty seaside church of **Ag. Dimitriou,** founded after the discovery of an icon there in 1936. Another excursion close to the city is a 15-minute walk to the **Temple of Isis** at Dili, built in 200 BC. At **Lazaretta** across the harbour there was once a temple of Poseidon dating from the 5th century BC, although all that remains are a few objects in the museum. In ancient times this was probably the Poseidonia mentioned in the *Odyssey*. A **cemetery,** from Roman times is at Pefkakia, also near Ermoupolis, although nothing remains of the actual tombs.

Other ancient sites are in the north of the island. At **Grammaton Bay** (reached only by boat), a blessing to protect ships from sinking is carved in the rock, dating back to Hellenistic times. **Kastri,** just north of Chalandriani, was settled in the Bronze Age, and walls, the foundations of houses and an overgrown nekropolis remain; all of these add greatly to the understanding of this period in the Cyclades. Signs suggest it was later inhabited for a brief period around 8000 BC. The **cave** where the philosopher Ferekides supposedly lived in the summer is just north of Kastri; his winter cave is at Alythini. Another path in the north leads to the quiet beach at **Megas Lakkos.**

Buses from Ermoupolis travel to the other seaside resorts of Syros. One is **Kini,** a small fishing village with a beach and tavernas, locally popular for its sunsets, another **Galissas,** which has the best beach on the island. Further south is another beach at **Finikas** (Phoenix), originally settled by the Phoenicians and also mentioned by Homer. **Vari** has become a major resort, while **Dellagracia,** better known as **Posidonia,** and **Megas Gialos** have fewer tourists. **Azolimnos** is particularly popular with the Syriani for its ouzeries and cafés, but there are no hotels or rooms. **Piskopio,** in the middle of the island has the oldest Byzantine church on Syros, Profitis Ilias, situated in the pine-covered hills. **Ag. Barbara,** a pleasant Orthodox monastery, has an orphanage for girls and produces items of popular art. Around the walls inside the church are frescoes depicting the saint's martyrdom. **Hroussa,** an inland, pine-shaded village has become a favourite place to build a villa. Nearby **Faneromeni** (meaning "can be seen from every-where") has panoramic views of the island. **Agathopes** is a fairly quiet, sandy beach with a couple of snack bars.

PANEYERIA

6 December, Ag. Nikolaos in Ermoupolis; the last Sunday in May, the finding of the icon at Ag. Dimitriou; 26 October, also at Ag. Dimitriou; 24 September, an Orthodox and Catholic celebration at Faneromeni.

Every two years, in either the last week of July or the first week of August, the **Apanosyria Festival** is organised by the municipality of Apanosyros, with exhibitions of local handicrafts and performances of folkloric plays. Another folklore festival is held, usually in June, at **Azolimnos** with three days of dancing, wine and song.

WHERE TO STAY

Syros is one island where you may well be able to book a flat at a moment's notice; the Teamwork Agency by the port has an extensive listing of sea-side properties; its owner, Panayiotis Boudouris, also manages the municipally owned **Hotel Europe,** in a building that originally served as Syros's first hospital (early 19th

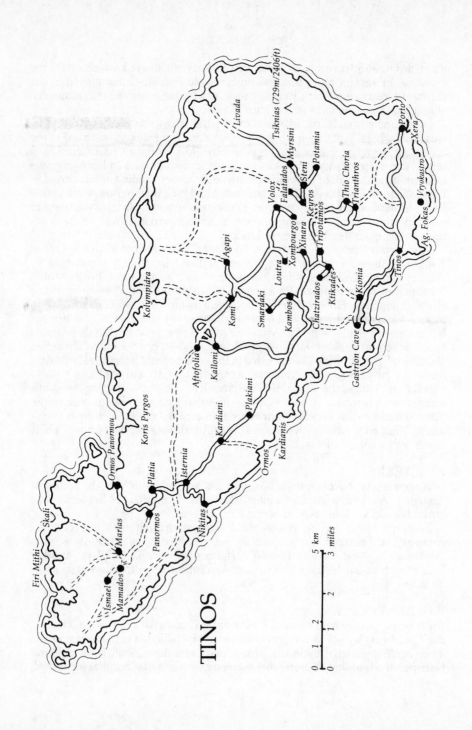

TINOS

Firi Mithi
Skali
Ismael
Mamados
Marlas
Ormos Panormou
Panormos
Platia
Koris Pyrgos
Isternia
Nikitas
Kardiani
Plakiani
Kolympidra
Aftofolia
Kalloni
Komi
Smardaki
Kambos
Agapi
Loutra
Xombourgo
Chatzirados
Ktikades
Kionia
Gastrion Cave
Kardianis
Ormos
Livada
Tsiknias (729m/2406ft)
Myrsini
Steni
Potamia
Volox
Falatados
Xinara
Keyros
Tripotamos
Thio Choria
Trianthros
Tinos
Ag. Fokas
Vryokastro
Xera
Porto

0   1   2   3   4   5 km
0   1   2   3 miles

century). Designed like a cloister, with a serene pebble mosaic courtyard, it has much larger rooms than the average hotel, each with a private bath (tel. 0281 28 771/2). Rates are 4500 dr. for a double, 3300 dr. for a single. The ageing but pleasant **Hermes,** right next to the ferry boat docks (tel. 0281 28 011) is a low priced class B with doubles at 3500 dr; try to get a room on the top floor facing the square. It has access in the back to a windy and rocky little strand where the locals swim. In the lower price range, there are several old houses in Ermoupolis that have rooms to let—two colourful and inexpensive choices are the **Kastro** and the **Apollon** (tel. 0281 22 158). There are also quite a few hotels and pensions on Syros' beaches, at Vari, Posidonia and Finikas, all catering for longer stays and you may be able to get a room without a reservation as is not always the case with beach hotels on the other Cyclades. There is a **campsite** at **Galissa** (tel. 0281 42 418).

EATING OUT
International dishes including crêpes, filet mignon, shrimp hors d'oeuvres and various soups can be found at the **Eleanna** restaurant on the main square, but of course a meal will be in the 1500–2000 dr. range. Behind that is the cheaper **Esperides** taverna-cum-snack bar with simple food at low prices. For tasty seafood *mezedes*, go to the small **Delfini ouzeri** where all the locals eat, despite the grumpy owner; to be found at the other end of the harbour from where the ferries dock. **Mama Anna,** opposite the bus station, serves good priced pizzas. In Azolimnos locals flock to the **Balopitas taverna** right on the waterfront and in Kini one of the favourite spots is the **Bouzouki** restaurant run by the Dakrotsi brothers, well known Syriani musicians. In the off season you can work up an appetite hiking up to one of the tavernas on the hills, both for good food and the view over the town and port. Most beaches have low-cost tavernas.

TOURIST INFORMATION
N.T.O.G. on quay, Ermoupolis.
Information at Town Hall, tel. (0281) 22 375.
Tourist police, see regular police, tel. (0281) 22 610.

TINOS

CONNECTIONS
Daily ferry from Piraeus, Mykonos, Syros, Andros and Rafina. Frequently with Paros and Naxos.

If Delos was the sacred island of the ancient Greeks, Tinos occupies the same place in the hearts of modern Greeks. One can't help but imagine that in ancient times Delos had much the same atmosphere—numerous lodgings and eating places, shaded stoas (in Tinos, awnings over the street) where merchants sell votives and other holy objects, and busy harbours. Delos, however, evolved into a booming free trade port, an unlikely fate for Tinos—although it is the only island in the archipelago to have a roller-skating rink! Besides its miraculous icon, Tinos is best known for its beautiful dovecots which were built by the Venetians; according to some, 1848 of these are scattered over the island's great sloping terraces. Many of the best have been kept in good repair, little houses of whitewashed stone embroidery, masterpieces of folk art. Tinos may be the centre of Orthodox pilgrimage, but of all the Cyclades it has the largest percentage of Catholics, and most of the island's pretty white villages are adorned with a campanile, which is unusual in Greece.

HISTORY

Inhabited by the Ionians in Archaic times, Tinos was occupied by the Persians in 490 BC, but set free after the Battle of Marathon. In the 4th century a sanctuary of the sea god Poseidon was founded on the island (after he cleared it of snakes) and it became a sacred place, where pilgrims would come to be cured by the god and to participate in the Poseidonia, December festivals. There were two ancient cities on the island, both named Tinos, one where the present town is and the other at Xombourgo. When the war between the Romans and Mithridates of Pontos broke out in 88 BC, the latter destroyed Tinos. In the 13th century the Venetians built a fortress at Xombourgo, out of the ancient akropolis and city there, and called it Santa Elena. It was one of the strongest fortresses of the Cyclades, and stood impregnable to 11 assaults by the Turks. Even the terrible Barbarossa was defeated by Santa Elena and its Venetian and Greek defenders. The frustrated Turks often pillaged and destroyed the rest of Tinos, venting their anger at Santa Elena's defiance.

In 1715, long after the rest of Greece had submitted to Ottoman rule, the Turkish admiral arrived in Tinos with a massive fleet and army. After sustaining a terrible attack, the Venetians decided that this time Santa Elena would not hold out, and, to the surprise of the Greeks, surrendered. The Turks allowed the Venetians to leave in safety, but in Venice the officers were put on trial for treason. It was decided that they had been bribed to surrender, and all were executed. Meanwhile the Turks blew up a good deal of Santa Elena in case the Venetians should change their minds and come back. Tinos was thus the last territorial gain of the Ottoman Empire.

In 1822, during the Greek War of Independence, a nun of the convent Kehrovouni, Sister Pelagia (now a saint), had a vision of the Virgin directing her to a certain rock. Here she discovered a miraculous icon of Mary and the Archangel at the Annunciation. The icon was found to have incredible healing powers for the faithful, and a church was soon built for it in Tinos town, called Panayia Evangelistra or Christopiliopsia. This has become the most important place of pilgrimage in Greece, called the Lourdes of the Aegean, a shrine of Greek nationalism; the discovery of the icon at just that moment in history helped to give the fight the aura of a holy war, and boosted morale. On 15 August 1940,

188

during the huge annual celebration at the church, an Italian submarine entered the harbour of Tinos and sank the Greek cruise boat *Elli*—one of the major incidents directly before the war with Mussolini. In the Colonels' regime the entire island was declared a holy place (part of that government's so-called "moral cleansing") and the women of Tinos were required to behave at all times as if they were in church, by wearing skirts, etc. This rule, however, was abolished along with the junta.

WHAT TO SEE

As your ship pulls into **Tinos,** the port and capital, you can see the famous yellow outline of the **Panayia Evangelistra** crowning the town, a short walk up Evangelistra St. Closed to traffic, this street becomes a solid mass of pilgrims on the two principal feast days of the Virgin, 15 August and 25 March, some ascending on their knees. As well as plastic bottles for holy water, candles and incense, you can buy almost anything under the great awnings from coffee cups bearing the IKE logo to Monopoly games.

A red carpet covers the grand marble stair leading up to the church itself, open daily 8.30 am–8.30 pm, as are the museums inside the church complex. The church, neo-Classical in style, is hung with hundreds of gold and silver ex-votos and lamps donated by the faithful; note especially the silver ship with a silver fish plugging up the hole in its side—one of the icon's many miracles. The many lamps strung overhead create a magical effect. There are men who spend the whole day removing these from the stands so that new arrivals will in turn have somewhere to put their own candles. Some of these candles are so huge one wonders how the pilgrims carried them up the hill. The icon itself, which people queue to kiss, can hardly be seen under the gold and diamond and pearls. Near the church four houses have been built for those waiting to be healed by the icon, but there is not enough room and many people camp out patiently in the courtyard.

You can visit the crypt of the church where Ag. Pelagia discovered the icon, now the **Chapel of Evreseos.** Silver lines the spot in the rocks where the icon lay; the spring here, believed to be holy, is said to have curative properties. Many people from all over Greece bring their children here in August to be baptised in the font. Next to the chapel the victims of the *Elli*, are interred in a mausoleum, which also contains a piece of the fatal torpedo.

Among the museums that surround the church's courtyard there's a **painting gallery,** with works from the Ionian school, a Rubens or two, a Rembrandt (or a copy?) partially hidden by the radiator, and many 19th-century works. Another museum contains the works of the Tiniote sculptor **Antonios Soxos,** above it is the **Sculpture Museum** housing works by a variety of Greek sculptors such as Ioannis Boulgaros and Vitalis. The **Byzantine Museum** has many old icons; and another museum contains items used in the church service.

Parallel with Evangelistra Street, on the other side of pine shaded public park, is a main street with the fine **archaeological museum** This contains finds from

189

the Sanctuary of Poseidon and Amphitrite, including a sundial and a sea monster in various pieces. There are also huge Archaic storage vases with fine decorations.

Although blessed with numerous eating and drinking establishments, Tinos town never has enough chairs for visitors in the summer, and the ships from Tinos to Athens often lack seats, although surplus passengers are let on all the same. Two landing areas operate, often simultaneously, and it is always best to ask the ticket agent which pier to queue up at in the tourist pens. There is a **yacht supply station** in the port.

From Ag. Fokas it's a short walk to **Kionia,** the site of the recently excavated **sanctuary of Poseidon and Amphitrite,** discovered by the Belgian archaeologist Demoulin in 1902. The name Kionia derives from the many columns which were found there. What remains of the famous sanctuary are the temple, treasuries, entrances, the little temple, baths, the fountain of Poseidon and inns for pilgrims. In many ways the ancient cult of the sea god and his wife Amphitrite resembled the current cult of the icon—which is especially noted for saving ships from storms. The beaches east of town, at **Ag. Ioannes Porto** and **Xera,** tend to be less crowded than Ag. Fokas and Kionia.

At **Vryokastro,** a few minutes beyond Ag. Fokas, are the walls and other remains of an ancient settlement, and in the region one may also see a Hellenistic tower. **Xera** and **Porto** are remote swimming coves.

North of Tinos is the **Kehrovouni Convent** (regular bus from Tinos pier), built in the 12th century and one of the largest in Greece. It is here that Sister Pelagia had her dream of the Virgin, who twice appeared, telling her where to find the icon—supposedly painted by St Luke. You can still visit her old cell and see her embalmed head within. She was canonised in 1971. **Arnados** to the west is a charming little village, as is **Thio Choria.** From here a rough track leads down to a usually deserted beach.

In the winter Tinos turns green, a colour that lingers until May. From then on the island has a rather desolate, barren appearance, striped with sun-parched terraces, in many places totally void of trees. Against this background the dovecots and their white residents add a charming touch. Some of the best are only a few kilometres above Tinos town; other exceptional ones may be seen around Smardaki. In the heart of the cluster of small villages above Tinos is the famous Venetian fortress, **Xombourgo,** on a 564-metre (1850-ft) hill. Although ruined, the view of many surrounding islands makes the climb worth while. The hill was first inhabited around 1000 BC, and a few walls remain of this ancient settlement. Later inhabitants used the ruins to construct their own buildings, especially the Venetian Gizi, who built Santa Elena. Besides the medieval houses, there is a fountain and three churches in the Venetian walls. The easiest approach is from **Xinara,** seat of the Catholic arch-diocese. From here, too, you can walk to the site of one of the ancient towns called Tinos, found in the 8th century BC. A large building and Geometric period temple were discovered here. At **Loutra,** one of the prettier villages, the Catholics founded a monastery of Jesuits (17th century) and a school is still run by the Ursulines. A long valley runs down from Komi to the sea at **Kolympidra**, which has a fine sandy beach where many people camp.

A paved road follows the mountainous ridge overlooking the south-west coast of Tinos. From **Kardiani** you can walk down a difficult path to a remote beach. From **Isternia**, a pleasant village with plane trees, you can drive down to the far more popular Ormos, or **Ag. Nikitas beach,** with rooms and tavernas. This part of Tinos is famous for its green marble, and the island has a long tradition in working the stone. Several well-known Greek artists came from or worked in **Panormos** known locally as **Pyrgos.** Just by the bus stop is a small **museum** and the **residence of sculptor Giannolis Halepas;** the old grammar school, built in the first flush of Greek independence, is now a School of Fine Arts. A shop near the main square exhibits and sells students' works—Byzantine eagles are still popular motifs. Below Pyrgos the public bus continues down to the beach at **Panormos bay,** with tavernas and rooms. **Marlas,** further north, is in the centre of the old marble quarries. From the tip of Tinos it's only a nautical mile to the island of Andros.

PANEYERIA

15 August and 25 March at the Panayia Evangelistra, the two largest in Greece; 15 June, Ag. Triada at Kardiani; 26 October, Ag. Dimitriou in Tinos town; 21 December, Issodia of Mary at Tripotamos; 20 October, Ag. Artemiou at Falatados; 29 August, Ag. Ioannes at Komi (Catholic); 19 January, Megalomatas at Ktikades

WHERE TO STAY

Because Tinos has long been receiving visitors—pilgrims to the shrine—it has some fine, old-fashioned hotels, rarely found on the other islands. One of these is the **Hotel Tinion** on the left end of the harbour as you sail in (tel. 0283 22 261) rated class B and perhaps the *grande dame,* of Tinos' hostelries, a double here is around 7000 dr. From the same period is the nearby **Thaleia,** on Panatiou Street (tel. 0283 22 811), though it's decidedly scruffy; for its faded grandeur you'll pay 2500 dr. for a double.

For something more modern, the **Tinos Beach** is close to the capital on Ag. Fokas Beach, at Kionia (tel. 0283 22 626/8); by far the largest of the island's accommodation, it also has bungalows. Prices are 12 000 dr. There are also quite a few rooms to rent in the town of Tinos, though little elsewhere; as mentioned above, it will be tough getting anything at all during the great feast days, though on 15 August sleeping outside isn't a terrible price to pay if you want to witness the greatest pilgrimage in Greece.

EATING OUT

You can find inexpensive food throughout the town, though the restaurants near the ferry docks tend to be hurried and rather mediocre. For a better meal,

Michalis Taverna on Gavou Street serves good mousaka and lamb dishes for 400–700 dr. If you're not too picky about quality, a memorable meal can be had in a little taverna off Evangelistra Street, currently called **O Patsos** ("the Madman") run by Greek–American Sotiris Fisas, who is almost as much an institution as the holy icon. His establishment is adorned with murals of plump mermaids and photos of the ships Mr Fisas served on in the navy, all of which, he will tell you, were sunk.

TOURIST POLICE
5 Plateia L. Sohon, tel. (0283) 222 55.

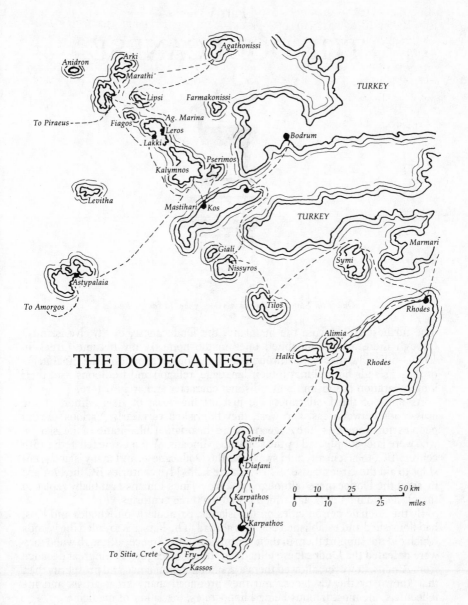

Anidron

Arki

Marathi

Agathonissi

Lipsi

Farmakonissi

TURKEY

To Piraeus

Fiagos

Ag. Marina

Leros

Lakki

Bodrum

Pserimos

Kalymnos

Levitha

Mastihari Kos

TURKEY

Giali

Marmari

Nissyros

Symi

Astypalaia

Tilos

Rhodes

To Amorgos

Alimia

Halki

THE DODECANESE

Rhodes

Saria

Diafani

Karpathos

0   10   25   50 km

0   10   25   miles

Karpathos

To Sitia, Crete   Fry

Kassos

Part V

THE DODECANESE

One of the Statues in Bronze overlooking the Harbour at Rhodes

The furthest group from the mainland, the Dodecanese, or "twelve islands" (though there are 16 inhabited ones in the nomos) only became Greek in 1947—officially, that is, for throughout numerous occupations, the inhabitants of these islands have clung to their language, religion and traditions. But their long separation has given them a distinct character and architecture.

As most of the Dodecanese lie just off the coast of Asia Minor, at the crossroads between east and west, they flourished very early. Various ancient peoples now known as "the Aegeans" were the original inhabitants of the islands, who were later subjugated by the seafaring Minoans. When Crete fell in the 15th century BC, the Acheans held sway over the Dodecanese, and many islands sent ships to aid the Greek cause at Troy. In the 12th-11th centuries BC the Dorians invaded the Dodecanese (although on some islands Ionians eventually replaced them), heralding a dark age which lasted for three centuries.

By the Archaic period cities on the islands, particularly on Rhodes and Kos, had flourished and established colonies abroad. The Persians invaded the islands which did not support them in their ventures against Greece, although when they were defeated the Dodecanese joined the Athenian league. Their great distance from Athens, however, allowed them a greater independence and prosperity than that known by the Cyclades, and they produced many great artists and intellectuals, the most famous being Hippocrates, the father of medicine.

After the death of Alexander the Great, Ptolemy of Egypt controlled most of the Dodecanese. One of the greatest sieges in antiquity took place when one of Ptolemy's rival generals, Antigonos, sent his son Dimitrios to take Rhodes from Ptolemy: the island was the victor. In 164 BC powerful Rhodes made an alliance with Rome, enabling her to exert a great imperialist influence of her own over many of the Greek islands.

St Paul visited some of the Dodecanese and began their early conversion to the Christian faith. St John the Theologian was exiled from Asia Minor to Patmos, where he converted the inhabitants, and wrote the *Apocalypse*. The islands were later incorporated into the Byzantine Empire. At the end of the 11th century the Crusaders began to pass through the Greek islands, and especially through the Dodecanese, marking the beginning of the end of Byzantium. Although their ostensible purpose was to rid the Holy Land of infidels, they were not averse to plunder and to carving out their own little principalities in the captured lands. One of the greatest ironies in history was in 1204 when they sacked Constantinople itself, a Christian capital as great as Rome.

Jerusalem fell to the Ottoman Empire in 1291, and the Knights of St John, a wealthy order made up of men who were the cream of European nobility, and who had organised a hospital for pilgrims in Jerusalem, retreated to Cyprus. Eighteen years later they set up their headquarters on Rhodes, buying it and the rest of the Dodecanese from Admiral Vinioli, the head Genoese pirate there at the time. In 1309 they built a hospital and fortified Rhodes and the other islands against the numerous would-be invaders and adventurers of the day. The Knights themselves played pirates quite often in swift vessels made on Symi. As could be expected, the Sultan of the Ottoman Empire did not view these ventures in a favourable light, especially since the Knights let Christian pirates through their territory unmolested, but stopped ships carrying Muslim pilgrims.

In 1522 Sultan Suleiman the Magnificent attacked Rhodes (the third major Muslim offensive on the Knights) and all the islanders of the Dodecanese who were able, rallied to its defence. Only the information of a traitor caused the defeat of the Knights after a long siege. Suleiman permitted them and their followers to depart in safety with their possessions to Malta. Turkish occupation lasted until 1912, when the Italians took "temporary possession" of the Dodecanese, an occupation made "permanent" after the Greek débâcle in 1922, by the second Treaty of Lausanne. The fascisti poured money into the islands, sponsoring massive public works programmes, reforestation, archaeological excavations and historical reconstructions. While Turkish rule had been depressing and sometimes brutal, fascist Italian rule, in its attempts to outlaw the Greek religion and language, was just as awful. After the Second World War, the islands were united with Greece, the last territory gained by the government, and the islands were granted many duty-free concessions and they began to exploit their rich tourist potential.

Of the islands, Rhodes and Kos have succeeded (too well, some might say) in their efforts; the charter flights and busloads of package tourists are relentless, the climate, beaches, and natural beauty of these islands make them popular all year round. Another island much frequented in the summer is Patmos, with its magnificent monastery of St John. The other Dodecanese are less well known but none the less charming. A certain village on Karpathos maintains the dress and customs of 300 years ago; tiny Kastellorizo, tucked under the bulge of Turkey, is haunted with war-ruined mansions; Kalymnos is the sponge capital of Greece; the volcano on Nissyros still smokes; rocky Kassos has a glorious but tragic history; lovely neo-Classical mansions decorate Symi; Astypalaia, Halki and Tilos are small and serene; and Leros, the island of Artemis, often serenades the visitor with the strains of the santouri, or hammer dulcimer.

Nearly everyday there is large ferry from Piraeus to Patmos, Leros, Kalymnos, Kos and Rhodes—a 20- to 24-hour journey all told. Smaller excursion boats and the noble *Panormitis* link the smaller islands; two hydrofoil companies also ply the most popular routes, some running daily, others a few times a week. There are flights to Rhodes, Kos and Leros direct from Athens; inter-Dodecanese flights also connect Karpathos, Kassos and Kastellorizo. Kos and Rhodes have connections with Turkey, the Rhodes–Marmaris ferries running all year round.

Lastly, there is an agency based in Romford, Essex, called "Twelve Islands" which specialises in arranging flights and good accommodation (some out of the ordinary that you would never find on your own) in the Dodecanese, they go out of their way to accommodate children, which is unusual.

ASTYPALAIA

CONNECTIONS
Four times a week with Rhodes, Amorgos and Piraeus; less frequently with Kos and Kalymnos.

Located halfway between Amorgos and Kos and thus the westernmost island of the Dodecanese, Astypalaia has much of the character of a Cyclade, particularly in the architecture of the houses. Although it is also rocky like a Cyclade, there is a rich valley, Livadia, half an hour's walk from the port, on which the island's agriculture is centred. The greatly indented coastline offers many sheltered bays renowned for their fishing—in antiquity the island was called Ichthyoessa for all its fish. Astypalaia's relative inaccessibility make it a good place to go if you want to beat the summer crowds, although there are times when you may find yourself wishing the locals had more than a couple of streets to exercise their scooters on in the evening. The womens' traditional costumes are famous for their elaborate detail and beauty.

HISTORY
The name Astypalaia means "old city" in Greek, but mythology claims that the name is derived from a sister of Europa, the mother of King Minos. It is thought by some that inhabitants from this island settled the ancient capital of Kos, which

was also called Astypalaia. In Classical times the island was most famous for a tragically short-tempered boxer named Kleomedes, who, in competing in the Olympics, killed his opponent and was thus disqualified. He returned to Astypalaia, seething with rage, and took his disappointment out on the local school building, knocking it down and killing all the children within.

From 1207 to 1522, the Quirini family of Venice occupied the island, styling themselves the Counts of Astypalaia, and building a castle in Chora. During the Italian occupation of the Dodecanese another fortification called Kastellano was built in the east of the island, south of Vathi.

WHAT TO SEE

The capital of the island, **Astypalaia** (or Skala), also serves as its main port, picturesquely piled beneath the glowering Venetian castle and ruined windmills down to a sandy stretch of beach. Up the narrow streets, lined with pretty white houses (many fitted with Turkish-style balconies) is **Chora,** the Venetian capital; on the gate of the **fortress** one can still see the Quirini coat-of-arms. Within its walls are the ruins of the houses on tiny streets, and two churches, **St George** and the **Madonna of the Castle,** one of the most beautiful in the Dodecanese, with its white-tiled dome, which inside is decorated with intricate lace-like designs. The fortress is being slowly restored, and is great fun to explore.

Livadia with Astypalaia's best beach, is a little to the west, in the greenest part of the island.

A little further to the south is Astypalaia's unofficial nudist beach. The island's highest point, 610 metres (2000 ft) is just behind Livadia. From Astypalaia town one can walk to the monastery, **Ag. Libies,** or go by taxi to the more remote villages of **Analypsis** and **Vathi,** which is near the Italian **Kastellana.** At Vathi are the caves of **Drakou** and **Negri,** both stalactites and stalagmites. It is possible to visit the caves on foot or by boat, but take a flash-light with you.

PANEYERIA

21 May, Ag. Konstantinos; 15 August, Panayia.

WHERE TO STAY

Astypalaia is blessed with three class D hotels and one class E, plus a number of rooms in private houses, all in Skala. Prices for the D class hotels are all about the same—1700 dr. for a single, 2200 dr. for a double. Of the three, the **Paradissos** (tel. 0242 61 224) may not be paradise, but it's clean and well run. The E class **Gallia** (tel. 0242 61 245) isn't much cheaper. You can also find rooms at Livadia where many people camp out as well. There are also rooms in remote Analypsis by the taverna there, and in Vathi. There's an organised campsite at Deftero Marmari beach (tel. 0242 61 338).

EATING OUT

Most of the island's eateries are clustered around the wharf and serve local fare at inexpensive prices. Food seems to taste better, however, in the tavernas at Livadia, though the menu is the same.

TOURIST POLICE
See regular police, Chora, tel. (0242 61 207).

HALKI

CONNECTIONS
Three times a week with Rhodes, Karpathos, Kassos and Sitia (Crete); once a week with Santorini and Piraeus; caique (daily in high season, twice a week at other times) from Kamiros Skala, Rhodes. (If you take the 1.30 pm bus from Rhodes town, rest assured that the captain will wait for you.) On most Sundays there's a small boat to Tilos.

Little Halki, with its small port adorned with half derelict neo-Classical mansions, reminds many people of a miniature Symi. Despite its proximity to Rhodes, it is a wonderfully quiet place, with only a few hundred inhabitants and no cars; many of those visitors it does get come back year after year, although except for the one town, Halki is basically a big arid rock. Its name (also spelled Chalki, among other variations) comes from the Greek word for copper which was mined here long ago.

The main claim to fame of **Skala,** the one town, is that its church, Ag. Nikolaos, has the tallest campanile in the Dodecanese. Other than that, it's an infectiously charming hamlet, full of rabbits, which seem nearly as relaxed as its residents.

From Skala a 15-minute walk along the "Boulevard Tarpon Springs" (just wide enough for a single delivery van) will take you to the small sandy beach. Those who are determined to "see" something should continue walking along the boulevard for another hour up to **Chorio,** the old and now abandoned capital of Halki. Here the Knights of St John built a castle on the earlier akropolis and used much of its building materials. The church within has a few Byzantine frescoes; the view from here is excellent.

One can hire a caique to several quiet swimming coves—Areta, Kania, Yali and Trachia are among the best. The most scenic excursion, however, is to the isle of **Alimia,** which has many trees and a deep harbour where Italian submarines hid during the war. Now it is a beautifully tranquil place to fish, swim and picnic.

However, big changes are planned for Halki thanks to UNESCO which has allocated several million dollars to promote the local fishing economy and tourism. Abandoned houses are currently being converted to guesthouses, and a centre is being built for the study of the rare Mediterranean monk seal, whose population is declining.

PANEYERIA
2 August, Ag. Ioannis; 15 August, Panayia.

WHERE TO STAY
Although the UNESCO development will soon change things, currently accommodation on Halki is limited to a few private homes with rooms (about 1800 dr. for a double) and the small but very lovely **Captain's House,** a turn-of-the-century mansion with three lovely rooms resently remodelled by a returned Greek navy admiral and his British wife. One of Halki's largest trees shades the terrace and the belvedere offers a fine view over the sea and town. It's located near the church. Rooms are 4000 dr. for a double, but you'll be lucky to get one in season.

EATING OUT
One can be exact: here there are four restaurants along the waterfront in Skala. Avoid the one with the brand new kitchen, the others are good; the one furthest from the centre of town the least expensive. There's also a very decent taverna on the beach, run by a man who commutes to Halki in the summer from New Jersey. A meal here costs about 700 dr.

KALYMNOS

CONNECTIONS
Daily to Piraeus, Rhodes, Kos, Leros and Patmos; less frequently to the other Dodecanese; twice a week to Karpathos, Paros and Samos; once a week to Amotgos and Syros; daily boats to Pserimos, Kos and Astypalaia; daily caique from Myrties to Xirokambos, on Leros; special boat to connect passengers with Kos airport, arriving on that island at Mastihari.

Kalymnos is a dry, rocky island with several fertile valleys. However, even the most fleeting visitor will notice that this island is preoccupied with sponges. Kalymnos is the last place in Greece still to have an active fleet of sponge divers.

Kalymnos today: In the past the sponge fleet left home for seven months of the year to work off the coast of North Africa. Today it makes only one four-month trip a year, diving (owing to political considerations) in Greek and Italian waters. The fleet leaves a week after Easter this being designated Sponge Week on Kalymnos. This is the occasion for a big celebration of food, free drinks, local costumes and dances. In the Sponge Dance, the local school master mimes the part of the sponge fishermen while his pupils play the sponges. The last night of Sponge Week is tenderly known as To Dipnos tis Agapis, or the Feast of the Lovers. It ends with the pealing of church bells, calling the divers to their boats for another dangerous four months at sea. Oldtimers remember when, not so

0   2   5 km
0   1   2   3   miles

KALYMNOS

Emporios

Skalia

KALAVROS

Arginonta

Kastelli

TELENDOS

Stimena

Massouri

Telendos

Kyra Psilas Monastery

Myrties

*Profitis Ilias
(701m/2300ft)*

Platis Yialos

Dasos

Platanos

Linaria

Vathi

KYRIAKI

Panormos

Pigadia

Chorio

Ag. Nikolaos

Argos

Kalymnos (Pothia)

Thermapiges

Vothini

*Kephalos
Cave*

To Leros

To Kos

NERA

To Piraeus

long ago, it was common to see sponge divers crippled, paralysed, or made deaf by their hazardous occupation. When the industry went into decline on Kalymnos, many sponge divers left to pursue their livelihood off the shores of Florida, which partly accounts for the large numbers of Greek–American visitors in the summer.

Sponge fishing is definitely an art. In ancient times the divers strapped heavy stones to their chests to take them down to the sea bed, speared the sponges with tridents, and were then raised to the surface by a lifeline when they gave the signal. Today the divers wear oxygen tanks and attack the sponges with axes, going down to a depth of 90 metres (300 ft). When fresh from the sea the sponges are smelly and black, and have to be stamped on and soaked until they are clean. Later some are treated to achieve the familiar yellow colour which we see in the shops.

HISTORY

Neolithic remains have been found at Vothini, along with a cave shrine to Zeus, dating habitation in Kalymnos back to prehistoric times. After the destruction of Crete, Dorians from Argos settled the island, naming their capital after their mother city. Homer mentions ships from Kalymnos at Troy, and archaeologists have uncovered Homeric tombs on the island. An ally of Persia, the Queen of Halikarnassos, conquered the island at the beginning of the 5th century BC, but after Persia's defeat Kalymnos joined the Athenian league.

In the 11th century AD the Turks launched a sudden attack on the island and killed almost everyone. The few surivivors fled to fortified positions at Kastelli and Kastro, the latter growing to become the capital of the island in a position which was virtually impregnable. The Genoese Vinioli family occupied Kalymnos, but later sold it to the Knights of St John, who strengthened the fortress of Kastro. In 1522 they abandoned it to succour Rhodes and the Turks quickly took their place. During the Italian occupation, Kalymnos rioted when the fascists tried to close the Greek schools, and the islanders painted everything in sight blue and white—the Greek national colours—as a sign of solidarity with the motherland.

WHAT TO SEE

Pothia, the port, the capital, and second largest city in the Dodecanese, encompasses the harbour and much of the island's largest valley. While at first it may seem a bit dull it soon works its charm on visitors. There are many lovely old mansions along the back streets of Pothia, walled orchards, and from the town's upper levels some fine views. Local sculptors Michail Kokkinos and his daughter Irene have adorned Pothia with statues; next to "Poseidon" and the Olympic Hotel the city operates a very helpful tourist information office from April to October. Near the waterfront towers a monument to Liberty with the history of sponge diving in relief. The tourist police are to be found in a pink Italian-constructed confection on the sea, the island's most fanciful architecture. On the far side of it is the sponge diving school. There is a museum in an old mansion containing a typical miscellany of local antiquities and items from grandma's attic, including a barrel organ. The town has one of Greece's rarer institutions—an orphanage, and until recently it was here that many of Orthodox priests came to choose their brides. There is a small beach near the yacht club, and beyond that a radioactive spring at **Thermapiges,** reputed to cure rheumatism, arthritis and digestive and kidney disorders. Above the town at night shines a huge illuminated cement cross.

From Pothia you can take a caique to **Nera** islet, south of Kalymnos, with a monastery and a small taverna, or to **Kephalos Cave,** a half-hour trip and walk of a couple of kilometres. Accidently discovered in 1961, the cave was found to have been a sanctuary of Zeus; it is full of multicoloured stalactites and stalagmites.

Another cave never thoroughly explored, is the **Cave of the Nymphs** or the **Cave of the Seven Virgins,** for the seven maidens who hid themselves there during a pirate raid and were never seen again. A few traces of ancient nymph worship may still be seen—bring a torch. The cave's entrance is at Flakas, by the hospital. This neighbourhood, just behind Pothia, is called **Myli** for the three monumental though derelict windmills that loom up at the side of the road. On the left, up on a hill, a ruined **Castle of the Knights** may be seen. It is also called Chryssocheria (Golden handed) for the church of the Virgin later built within its walls, on the site of an ancient temple of Dioscuri. A treasure was once supposedly discovered there, and the area has been thoroughly combed on the off-chance of more.

Myli blended imperceptibly into **Chorio,** the old capital of Kalymnos, a pretty white town that grew up around **Pera Kastro,** the striking though very dilapidated castle that rises over the village and served as a place of refuge during the perilous Middle Ages. The village within the walls was inhabited from the 11th to the 18th centuries, and on a cloudy day is most un-Greek in its gloomy greyness. Although the town is in ruins, the nine chapels within are kept freshly whitewashed by the faithful in Chorio. In Pigadia, just beyond Chorio, is the ruined church **Christ of Jerusalem,** built by the Byzantine Emperor Arkadios in gratitude for his shelter at Kalymnos during a terrible storm. The church was constructed out of stone from a temple of Apollo on the site.

A road branching off at Chorio brings one to **Argos,** named by the Dorian settlers who came from Argos on the mainland of Greece. Although there are some ruins there, scholars think that the Doric city was not at precisely the same location as the present village. North of Chorio the road passes Kalymnos' best beaches: **Kantouni, Panormos** (known locally as **Elies** because it sits in the olive groves), **Myrties** and **Massouri** (bus every half hour from Pothia), although as beaches go they're only just adequate. Here, though, is the buzzing centre of Kalymnos' tourist industry, and they do all have some shade. From Myrties frequent caiques make the short trip to the islet of **Telendos.**

In the 6th century AD Telendos broke off from Kalymnos in an earthquake.

Facing the strait is the monastery of **Ag. Konstantinou** and a fort, **Kastro,** both dating back to the Middle Ages. Another monastery, **Ag. Vassilos,** is in better condition than the derelict Ag. Konstantinou. One may also see the ruins of **Roman houses** on the islet and there are two small beaches. Fishermen live there for the most part, and are privileged with magnificent sunsets. On the mountain of Telendos one can see the form of the sleeping or **marble princess.** A similar marble prince faces her on the Kalymnos side of the strait.

North of these beaches is **Kastelli,** to which the survivors of the terrible Turkish massacre fled. Kastelli overlooks the sea in a wild region of rocky cave mouths full of fangs. The church **Panayia** is below. **Arginonta** gives its name to the entire northern peninsula, which is perfect for strenuous, isolated walks in the hills. Non-walkers must take taxis, as public transport does not reach so far **Emporios,** the northernmost village, is within walking distance of some exceptional countryside, and **cyclopean walls** and a tower are very close by. The tower may well have been a Neolithic temple; a sacrificial altar was found in the vicinity. There are quiet beaches at Arginonta and Emporios (bus twice a day from Pothia).

The narrow valley of Vathi ("the deep") consists of three charming, green villages, superbly situated at the mouth of a deep fjord. Groves of mandarins and lemons provide the valley's main income, and houses and white-walled roads fill in the gaps between the trees. In the middle village, Platanos there are more Cyclopean walls. North of Vathi you can walk to the Monastery of **Kyra Psilas,** the Tall Lady. Near Vathi, but accessible only by sea, is the **Cave of Daskaleios,** another ancient cult centre with stalactites and stalagmites.

PANEYERIA
15 August, Panayia; 14 September, Stavros on Nera islet; 27 July, Ag. Panteleimonos at Brosta; a week after Easter, the Iprogros (sponge week), and when the divers return, although each boat is likely to come in at a different time and celebrations are not as general as at the Iprogros.

WHERE TO STAY
In Pothia, where most people stay, the **Thermae Hotel** (tel. 0243 29 425) is a pleasant class C hotel right on the waterfront, located over a restaurant. Doubles with a bath are 2800 dr. Less expensive, with a certain dilapidated charm is the nearby **Alma** at 8 Patr. Maximou (tel. 0243 28 969), where doubles are 1800–2500 dr. There are also private rooms, though it may take some tramping about to find them; you can get a list at the tourist office, next to the fancy **Olympic Hotel,** which has fairly reasonable rates—3000 dr. for a single and 4000 dr. for a double, with bath (tel. 0243 28 801). Most of the other accommodation is at Massouri, Panormos and Myrties. In Massouri the **Massouri Beach Hotel** has comfortable doubles for about 4000 dr. (tel. 0243 47 555). In Myrties the **Hotel Myrties,** class D (tel. 0243 28 912) has good clean doubles for 2000 dr. a night.

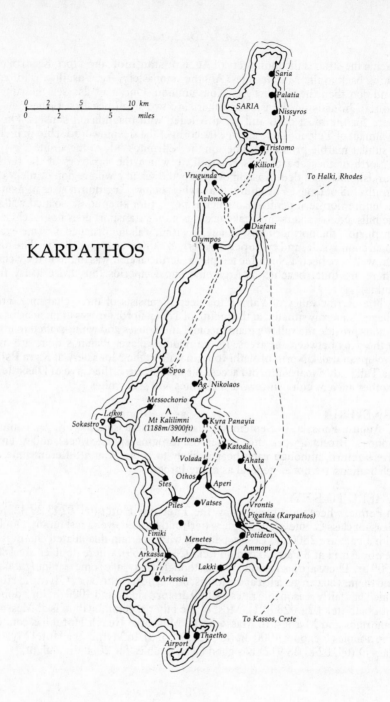

KARPATHOS

Saria
Palatia
SARIA
Nissyros
Tristomo
Kilion
Vrugunda
To Halki, Rhodes
Avlona
Diafani
Olympos

0   2   5   10 km
0   2   5   miles

Spoa
Ag. Nikolaos
Messochorio
Lefkos   ^
Sokastro Mt Kalilimni   **Kyra Panayia**
              (1188m/3900ft)
          Mertonas   **Katodio**
          Volada   **Ahata**
          Othos   **Aperi**
      Stes
      Piles *Vatses*
                        Vrontis
                        Pigathia (Karpathos)
      Finiki *Menetes* **Potideon**
      Arkassa   **Ammopi**
              Lakki
      Arkessia

To Kassos, Crete

Airport *Thaetho*

EATING OUT

In Pothia most of the restaurants are on the far end of the quay, on the other side of the tourist police and municipal palace. You can get reasonably priced seafood at **Uncle Petros.** If you want to dine and watch the crowds go by, try the taverna **Thermae,** belonging to the hotel, right in the middle of the waterfront, with efficient service and reasonable prices. Also in the heart of things is the **Stelios Restaurant,** the international spot, where an average meal is 700–1000 dr. Hidden away in a back street behind the harbour (you'll have to ask directions) is the friendly, family run **Xefteries taverna** where fresh fish and roast lamb dinners won't send you running to the bank. The exotic looking **Tropicana** comes as bit of a surprise, also in the quiet back streets of the town, and a drink in its South Pacific atmosphere, as you check out the menu, is a pleasant way of passing time. For sponge ambience, dine at the **N.O.K.**; again the food is so-so but the decor is intriguing. There are tavernas by all the beaches.

TOURIST INFORMATION

NTOG, next to Olympic Hotel, tel. (0243) 29 310
Tourist police, see regular police on the waterfront, tel. (0243) 29 310.

KARPATHOS

CONNECTIONS

By air, daily, with Rhodes, several times a week with Sitia, Crete, and at weekends with Kassos. By ship: three times a week from Piraeus and on to the other Dodecanese and Crete, four times a week with Rhodes and Kassos, once a week with the Cyclades. All ships call at both Diafani and Pigathia (Karpathos). Small boats daily in the summer connect the two ports, and at weekends there's a caique from Pigathia to Kassos.

Long and thin, ruggedly mountainous in the north and fertile in the south, Karpathos has two distinct personalities; some people even believe that the northerners and the southerners originally belonged to different races; and grew up isolated from one another. The road connecting the two was only finished in 1979. For students of folklore, and anthropologists, the isolation of the north has made it a fascinating place to study. In Olympos, the chief village, women still wear their traditional costumes, and bake their bread in outdoor ovens; many of the men, even the younger ones, continue to play the traditional instruments, the three-stringed lyra, the goatskin bagpipe tsabouna, and the laouto. So far the increasing number of visitors each year has not spoiled this unique village, but a new addition to the island's airport, making it capable of receiving much larger planes than the little "sky vans" that land there now, is scheduled to be finished by 1989 at the latest, and may change things. Although it is doubtful that Karpathos will find a permanent place on the package tourist's map (Karpathos economically doesn't need tourism; land is very expensive and it is difficult for big operators to buy any land), it is only the small size of the planes and the difficulty and length of the sea voyage which has, until now, kept the island from being crowded.

HISTORY

One of the many ancient names of Karpathos was Porfiris, or "Red", for a red dye once manufactured on the island and used for the clothes of kings. Other ancient names described the number of cities on Karpathos, from Tripolis to Tetrapolis, Hetapolis and Oktopolis. The present name is thought to derive from the days of the pirates, when the Vrontis Gulf hid pirate ships which would rush out to attack and plunder any passing vessel. Disgruntled captains dubbed the island Arpaktos, or "robbery island", and the name was eventually corrupted to Karpathos.

Four ancient cities are known to have existed on the island. One, Nissyros, is on the islet of Saria to the north and is believed to have been founded by people from the island of Nissyros. Iron and silver were mined during these ancient days at Assimovorni. The delicious scarus is abundant in Karpathian waters, and the Roman Emperor Luculus sent special ships to the island to catch them for his dinner. Any signs of prosperity, however, had long ended when pirates made the island their centre and one of its villages, Arkessia, a slave market. Things were so rough that the Turks, it seems, didn't really want Karpathos. They only sent a cadi, or judge, to the island a few times a year and he never stayed longer than necessary, having to rely on the Greeks to protect him from the pirates. Today the Vrontis Gulf and Arkessia Bay are said to be full of sunken pirate treasure.

WHAT TO SEE

The capital of Karpathos, known as Pigathia though now more frequently known as **Karpathos,** was in ancient times called Poseidonion, the town of the sea god. This ancient town was abandoned in the Byzantine era though there are a few remains on the old akropolis overlooking Vrontis Bay, where many Mycenaen tombs have been excavated. The modern town is just that—modern, with many new buildings, and it's no accident that the National Bank branch has such an air of prosperity: Karpathos has the distinction of receiving more money from its emigrants abroad than any other island in Greece.

The most distinctive building in town is the Italian-built town hall, near the playground, which contains an early Christian baptismal font. From here it is a short walk to the long stretch of sand around Vrontis Bay. The beach is well shaded, with a pleasant taverna, and on the beach, within an enclosure, are the ruins of a 5th-century basilica, **Ag. Fotini,** recently discovered by accident. Several of the columns have been raised in their places. Across the bay you can see the monastery of Ag. Nikolaos, now deserted, a cave there; Kamara, has sweet water.

Buses to other points on the island run fairly infrequently. There are none at all to Olympos; other villages are only served once a day, some only once or twice a week. One of the few roads that is paved runs south from Karpathos to **Ammopi,** a sandy beach and small resort area, though there is little shade. Indeed, the whole southern section of the island is rather sparsely covered, the few trees bent over by the wind. The road continues south to the airport. This was the site of the ancient kingdom of Thaetho, although little now remains. More can be seen of ancient Arkessia to the north: a Mycenaean akropolis with Cyclopean walls on a rocky headland. The surrounding cliffs are riddled with caves that have offered shelter to shepherds for centuries. By the sea are the ruins of an early Byzantine church, **Ag. Sophia.** If you brush aside the dirt and plants you will see brightly coloured mosaics. The best parts of these are now in the museum at Rhodes. The ruined basilica around the chapel, Ag. Anastasia, dates from the 5th century. The coast below is jagged and wild, but there is a small beach. **Finiki,** a small harbour with a good, inexpensive restaurant, is a stopping point for the sponge divers of Kalymnos, and a caique port to Kassos. Although the sea on this western side of Karpathos, facing Crete, is usually calm, it can be very rough between Karpathos and Rhodes.

On the slopes of Karpathos' tallest mountain, Kalilimni, second highest point in the Dodecanese, is a pretty village, whose name in Roman letters becomes **Piles.** From here a rough road continues up the west coast to **Lefkos,** with a white sandy beach, pine trees and numerous archaeological sites, including a large stone that strikingly resembles a Celtic menhir. A short walk away are the ruins of a small medieval fort; there was another on the offshore islet of **Sokastro.** There is a small hotel and a few rooms to rent in Lefkos, which many consider the most beautiful spot on Karpathos.

Othos, inland, has more greenery than most villages on the island, and here a traditional house has been opened as a small ethnographic museum. Neighbouring **Volada** is the site of a ruined castle built by the Cornaro family of Venice; there is a good restaurant here, Klimataria.

Aperi, overlooking Vrontis Bay, was the capital of Karpathos for many years, and the village still has a cathedral and the island's school. Nearly everyone here has lived in Baltimore or Jersey City. One kafeneíon still proudly displays a picture of Roosevelt; another, the Eleftheria Café run by a PASOK leprechaun, is full of curios and rubber items from the 1960s. In the new cathedral you can pay your respects to Karpathos' most venerated icon of the Virgin, credited with several miracles, among them that of saving the life of a young boy who was pushed off a cliff. He went on to become a rich American lawyer and contributed the funds for many of Aperi's new buildings. A track leads down to **Ahata,** a quiet pebbly beach, but it is very steep.

Other quiet beaches along the east coast are Apella, Kyra, Panayia and Ag. Nikolaos, accessible by land, though much easier to approach by caique from Karpathos. The scenery around Apella is particularly dramatic. **Messochorio** in the mountains is a pretty village hidden from the sea. From here or Spoa you can begin the rugged six-hour trek along the mule path to Olympos, or take the slightly less difficult road by taxi, a $2\frac{1}{2}$-hour (and rather expensive) proposition. Unfortunately, a massive forest fire in 1983 has left most of the island between Spoa and Diafani denuded and melancholy.

The easiest and least expensive way to reach Olympos from Karpathos is by caique to **Diafani,** the village's port, from where a minibus makes the connection to Olympos (or you can walk in about 2 hours). Diafani has a beach with flat rocks and is within walking distance of several others.

Olympos, Karpathos' prettiest village, is draped over a stark mountain ridge, a long line of ruined windmills running like vertebrae down the village's spine. To the west there are magnificent views of mountains plunging headlong into the sea, especially at sunset. Decorative painted balconies, many sporting Byzantine eagles, adorn the houses which in many places are literally stacked one on another. The village church has smoke-darkened frescoes, perhaps going back to the 18th century.

The origins of Olympos are shrouded in mystery. Some evidence suggests that the original inhabitants of northern Karpathos came from Phrygia in Asia Minor; certainly the village was isolated for so long that linguists were amazed to find people here using words last seen in Homer. Some matrilinear customs have survived, a family's property going to the eldest daughter, the "kanakara"; if you're lucky enough to be in Olympos during a paneyeri, you can recognise the kanakaras by the weight of gold coins they wear on chains, coins their grandfathers earned while working abroad. The women wear their lovely costumes every day, including fine goatskin boots (it is said that snakes hate the smell of goat). The boots, which last for years, are handmade in the village and are perhaps the one souvenir you can buy at Olympos.

The best time to visit Olympos is during the weekends, when the women bake bread and vegetable pies in their outdoor ovens, and when the two kafeneíons are filled with Karpathos' Celtic sounding music. In the kafeneíon across from the church the owner displays a certificate from the Governor of Alabama, thanking him for his service in the state militia! Another thing to do is watch the miller grind the wheat in the last working windmill. Otherwise, there is little to do but stroll the quiet streets and absorb what you can of a vanishing way of life.

From Olympos one can drive most of the way to **Avlona,** a village inhabited only during the harvest season by farmers from Olympos, who work the surrounding valley. It is interesting to visit because you can see many old tools still in use. From Avlona it is a rough walk down to **Vrugunda** (Vrykus), the ancient Phrygian kingdom—a stair, a breakwater, burial chambers and walls. In a cavern in Vrugunda a chapel of Ag. Ioannis hosts one of the island's largest paneyeria, a two-day event that is celebrated in the traditional style of sleeping out, roasting meat over an open fire and dancing to the island's music.

On Sundays you can take a boat from Diafani to the islet of **Saria,** which dots the "i" of Karpathos. Here was the ancient kingdom of Nissyros, of which little remains, although it is believed the inhabitants came from the island of the same name. A chapel now stands on the site of the old basilica. More interesting are Ta

Palatia ("the palaces"), actually a post-Byzantine pirate base, the houses built in the dolmus style, with barrel-vaulted roofs. It is a good walk up from the landing place, so wear sturdy shoes.

PANEYERIA
25 March, Evanglismos at Pigathia; 1 July, Ag. Marinas, near Menetes; 15 August, at Olympos and Menetes; 27–29 August, Ag. Ioannis at Vrugunda; 23 August, Panayias near Mertonas; 6 September, Larnitisa; 8 September, tis Panayias at Messochorio.

WHERE TO STAY
If you've the money the most charming place to stay in the capital is the **Pension Romantica** (tel. 0245 22 460/1). Located in a grove of citrus trees, and a short walk from the beach, it has 32 rooms and serves a delicious breakfast—a lovely place to get away from it all. Rates are 3500 dr. for a double, with bath. Even closer to the beach is the **Hotel Porfyris** (tel. 0245 22 294), where a clean, pleasant double is about the same price. Even if you have to go on the pension plan there, the food in the hotel restaurant is very good. On the cheap side there are quite a few small pensions (the **Artemis,** run by a schoolteacher is very clean and on a quiet cul-de-sac), but if you're a woman, beware of staying at George's pension. He may have the least expensive rooms on the island but will assuredly drive you nuts.

In northern Karpathos, there are several hotels in Diafani (the **Mayflower,** with its 6 rooms where the ferry boat lands is clean and has a paperback exchange; 2200 dr. for a double), but it's more fun to stay up in Olympos, at one of the two small pensions, **Artemis Pension** or **Pension Olympos,** which charge 800–1000 dr. a person.

EATING OUT
Food in Karpathos is relatively inexpensive, and one of the best places for it is **George's** (not to be confused with the George in **Where to stay**), located by the sea just below the bank. The murals inside are surreal but the seafood is good and the retsina very delicate, almost perfumed. Dinners here are around 700 dr., 1000 dr. for fish. There's also a good taverna on the beach (from the main road, follow the little signs), and you can eat good fish, believe it or not, up at the **Artemis** in Olympos, since the owner is a fisherman. The **Mayflower** restaurant in Diafani is also good and serves fish at 800 dr. or so.

TOURIST POLICE
See regular police on the waterfront, Pigadia, tel. (0245) 22 218.

KASSOS

CONNECTIONS
By air: almost every day with Rhodes, weekends with Sitia and Karpathos; by sea: twice a week with Piraeus, four times a week with Rhodes and Karpathos, three times a week with Halki and Crete; weekend caique from Finiki, Karpathos.

The southernmost Dodecanese island and one of the most remote Greek islands, Kassos is a barren rock with steep coasts and sea grottoes, with an odd beach or two wedged in between. The port, Emborio, is small, and if the sea is rough, as it often is, landing can be difficult.

HISTORY
Homer mentions Kassos in the *Iliad*, for the island sent ships to Troy to aid the Acheans. An ancient city was built where the present village of Poli is today, and at Hellenokamera cave there are Pelasgian walls (Mycenaean). During the Turkish occupation, Kassos retained a good deal of its autonomy, especially with regard to its ships, which it quickly put at the disposal of the Greek cause when the War of Independence was declared, in 1821. For the first three years of the war the Greeks generally came out ahead in the struggle, but the Sultan, angered by these set-backs, prepared powerful counter-attacks through Ibrahim Pasha, son of the Ottoman Empire's governor of Egypt. In June 1824 Ibrahim left Egypt with a massive fleet to crush the Greek rebellion. His first stop was Kassos, which he decimated, slaying the men and taking the women and children as slaves. The few who managed to escape went to an islet off the north-western coast of Crete, Grambousa, where they were forced to turn to piracy for survival flying the Greek flag proudly in Turkish waters. But Kapodistria and the Great Powers put a stop to their activities, and their refuge, Grambousa, returned to Turkish rule. Thousands of Kassiotes later emigrated to Egypt to work on the Suez Canal.

WHAT TO SEE
Fry is the little capital of the island, where the islanders' main occupation, fishing, is much in evidence. Every year on 7 June a ceremony is held there in memory of the massacre of 1824, and many people from Karpathos also attend, coming on the special boats which sail that day.

There are hardly any trees on Kassos because, it is claimed, Ibrahim Pasha burnt them all down, but many lighthouses stick out above the rocky terrain. A road and the island's one bus link Fry with Kassos' four other small villages. There is a lovely cave with stalactites called Hellenokamara near the beach at **Ammoua. Poli** is built on the island's ancient akropolis, and you can still see a few of the walls at Kastro. Beyond the villages a path leads across the island to **Khelathros Harbour,** with the best beach on the island. Another nice beach is on **Armathia,** the only inhabited islet off Kassos; there are frequent excursions from the port.

PANEYERIA
14 August, at Ag. Marina; 23 April, Ag. Georgios; 7 July, at Fry; late July, Ag. Spyridon.

WHERE TO STAY
The place to stay is the **Hotel Anagennissis** (tel. 0245 41 323), comfortable and run by an engaging former American. Prices range from 2800 dr. for the rooms facing the sea with bath, less for those in the back. There are also several pensions and rooms, and another small hotel, the class C **Hotel Anessis** (tel. 0245 41 201), where the doubles tend to be a little less. All of the above are in Fry.

EATING OUT
There are a handful of tavernas in Fry, a good one near the clock tower, where a typical meal costs 600 dr. There are also a couple of tavernas in Ag. Marina and Emborio.

KASTELLORIZO (MEGISTI)

CONNECTIONS
By air: 3 times a week from Rhodes; boat twice a week from Rhodes.

The furthest east of all Greek territories, Kastellorizo is one of the strangest islands in Greece. It is six hours by ship from Rhodes and in spitting distance of Turkey (where many of the inhabitants go to do their shopping). It is also the smallest island of the Dodecanese, 3 km by 6 (2 miles by 4), yet the mother hen of its own small clutch of islets; hence its official name, Megisti, or "the largest". One nautical mile away lies the Turkish town of Kaş ("eyebrow"); the Turks look upon the island as its "eye"; the Italians called it the "Red Castle" or Kastello-rizo. Dry, depopulated, more than half ruined by numerous vicissitudes, its streets are patrolled by turkeys, and its inhabitants noticeably affected by the isolation. The new airport may change some of that, but at present it remains a quiet if quirky backwater surrounded by a crystal sea brimming with marine life. And while there aren't any beaches, the local people will never fail to tell you that there are plenty of rocks.

HISTORY
According to tradition, Kastellorizo's first settler was King Meges of Echinada. who gave his name to the island. He must have come early indeed, as signs prove

that Kastellorizo was inhabited from Neolithic times. Mycenaean graves have also been discovered, and Homer mentions the island's ships at Troy. When the Dorians came they began to fortify their new home, building two forts on the island, the Kastro by the present town and one above on the mountain, called Palaeokastro—the akropolis of the ancient capital. Apollo and the Diskouri, the patron gods of sailors, were worshipped, and the island had a great fleet of ships based in its large sheltered harbour, which traded with ancient Lycia in Asia Minor, bringing its wood to ports in Africa and the Middle East. From 350 to 300 BC the island was ruled by Rhodes, and in Roman times the pirates of Cassius used it as their hideout. The island was converted to Christianity from the time of St Paul, who preached on the coast of Asia Minor at Myra.

During the Byzantine period Kastellorizo's fortifications were repaired, and this work was continued by the Knights of St John in the 13th century. They gave the island its present name, for the red rock of the castle which they used as a prison for knights who misbehaved on Rhodes. The Sultan of Egypt captured the island in 1440, but ten years later the King of Naples, Alfonso I of Aragon, took it back. Although Kastellorizo belonged to the Ottoman Empire by 1523, the Venetians later occupied it twice during their struggles against the Turks, in 1570 and in 1659. In the War of Independence the islanders, the first in the Dodecanese to join the cause, seized their two fortresses from the Turks but were forced by the Great Powers to give them back in 1833. In 1913 Kastellorizo revolted again only to be subjugated by the French. During the First World War the island was bombarded from the Turkish coast. In 1927 an earthquake caused extensive damage but the Italians, then in charge, did nothing to repair the island, as it had failed to co-operate with their programme of de-Hellenisation. There was another revolt in 1933, but it was crushed by soldiers from Rhodes. By now the island was in sharp decline—in 1941 only 1500 inhabitants remained of an initial 15 000, living mostly from the sea and the lands they owned on the coast of Asia Minor.

This, however, does not end the tale of misfortunes suffered by this tiny but brave island. During the Second World War the Allies, fearing a conflict, sent everyone to the Middle East. Although this was done for their safety, the islanders were not allowed to take many of their more precious belongings with them, and the occupying troops pillaged the houses. To hide their crime, they burnt the town, destroying more than 1500 homes. As if this was not enough, the ship carrying the refugees home after the war sank, and many people were drowned. Those who survived came home to discover that they had lost literally everything, and that there was nothing to do but emigrate.

WHAT TO SEE
There is only one town on the island, also called **Kastellorizo,** full of ruined houses and mansions, some burnt, others crumbling from earthquakes or bombardments. One can see how wealthy some of the inhabitants once were from the remaining interiors, with elegant coffered ceilings and lovely carved balustrades.

Some are being restored, others are inhabited by cats and chickens. Small tavernas line the waterfront, so close to the sea that it is relatively easy to dispose of an unpopular dinner companion in the drink. A hotel occupies one lip of the harbour, and on the other is the **fort** (kastro), last repaired by the eighth Grand Master of the Knights of St John, Juan Fernando Heredia, whose red coat-of-arms is another possible explanation for the name of the island. A ladder takes one to the top, which affords a fine view of the surrounding seascape and of Turkey. Recently an inscription in Doric Greek was discovered at the fort, proving the existence of an ancient castle on the same site. A tomb nearby yielded a golden crown, and in the mosque is a small **museum** (open 5 pm–7.30 pm) containing photographs of the days of past prosperity, a few frescoes, folk costumes and items found in the harbour.

Above the fort there is a **weaving school** where two girls may spend two months making just one large rug.

Another path leads up to a **Lycian tomb**, cut into the rock, with Doric columns. The whole south-west coast of Turkey has similar tombs, but this is the only one to be found in modern Greece. The cathedral of Ag. Konstantinos and Helena contains granite pillars from a temple of Apollo in Anatolia. From town a steep path with steps leads up to four white churches and **Palaeokastro,** an ancient Greek fortress. On the gate there is a Doric inscription from the 3rd century BC referring to Megiste; walls, a tower and cisterns also remain.

There are no beaches on the island, but the sea is clean, and there are a multitude of tiny islets to swim out to. An excursion which should not be missed is to the **Blue Cave**, or Parastas, an hour by caique from the town. It is best to go in the morning when some light filters in, for the entrance is very low, one must duck to enter. The blue effects of the water inside have led to comparisons with the Blue Grotto of Capri. There are many stalactites and a seal which lives inside; if you bring a light there's a chance you may see him.

The fishing around Kastellorizo is excellent, and serves as the main occupation for the island's 200 souls. Almost everyone, however, is ready to leave, and the only reason they stay is to keep the island Greek. The Turks deny it, but many Greeks will tell you that if the population of the island drops below 200, it will revert to Turkey. Whatever the case, the Greek government pays people to stay there (at the time of writing, 9000 drachmas a month), it has built a de-salination plant, and has bent over backwards to bring Greek television, radio and now an airport to the island. If relations with Turkey improve, the island may even become an official port of entry.

PANEYERIA
20 July, Profitis Ilias; 21 May, Ag. Konstantinos; 24 April, Ag. Georgios.

WHERE TO STAY
The island's most comfortable digs is the class C **Hotel Megisti,** located on one lip of the excellent natural harbour. A double here is about 4000 dr. (tel. 0241

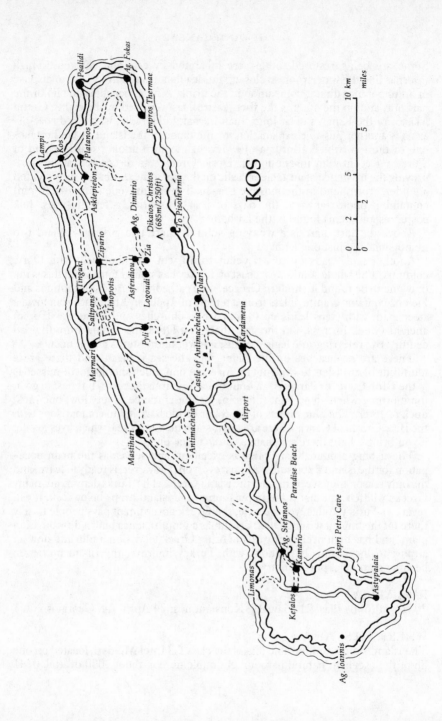

KOS

29072); for something less expensive, just take up one of the offers you'll receive as you get off the boat. As like as not the room you get will be as quirky as its owner.

EATING OUT
Nearly everything's by the harbour; the fish is inexpensive and fresh (and the only thing that doesn't have to be shipped in). Expect to pay between 600–1000 dr. for a full dinner. At least once a week in the summer, a tour agency in Kaş brings over a boatload of visitors for "Greek Night" which considerably enlivens the evening.

TOURIST POLICE
See regular police in the harbour by the post office.

KOS

CONNECTIONS
By air: direct from London and several other European cities, three times a day with Athens, once a day with Rhodes, three times a week with Leros. By hydrofoil: daily with Rhodes, Patmos and Symi. Three times a week with Leros. Once a week with Samos. Also connections with Kalymnos, Halki, Nissyros, Karpathos and Kastellorizo. In season, daily boat to Bodrum, Turkey. Ferry every day to Piraeus, Rhodes, Kalymnos, Leros and Patmos; small boats daily in season to Patmos, Nissyros, Pserimos, Kalymnos and Astypalaia. Three times a week the *Panormitis* links Kos with the smaller Dodecanese.

Dolphin-shaped Kos with its natural beauty, wealth of antiquities, beaches and comfortable climate is Rhodes' major Dodecanese rival in the tourist industry. The two islands have many similarities, and it used to be a cliché that if Rhodes was too crowded for your taste, try Kos. That may no longer be true; Kos is one-fifth the size of Rhodes and it's visited by at least a fifth as many people. But here they tend to hire bicycles instead of taking tour buses, and the percentage of Greeks to foreigners seems much higher.

HISTORY
Evidence found in Aspri Petra cave dates Kos' earliest inhabitants to 3500 BC. A Minoan colony flourished on the site of the modern city of Kos, which later gave way to the Mycenaeans who traded extensively throughout the Mediterranean. After their decline Kos' history is obscure although there are references to two of the island's early names, Meropis, after its mythical king, and Nymphaeon, for its numerous nymphs. Astypalaia was the ancient capital, although in 366 BC the inhabitants founded the city of Kos, on the same site as the present-day capital. Poised between the West and East (the ancient city of Halicarnassus, present-day Bodrum in Turkey, is very near), Kos flourished with the trade of precious

215

goods—and ideas. Halicarnassus was the birthplace of the father of history, Herodotus, and in the 5th century Kos produced the father of medicine, Hippocrates. His school on the island, where he taught pupils a theory of medicine based on waters, observations, and special diets, was renowned throughout the ancient world. Doctors today still take the Hippocratic oath when entering practice. When Hippocrates died an, Asklepieion (a temple to Asklepios, the god of healing) was founded, and people from all over the Mediterranean world came to be healed in its hospital, up into Roman times. The Romans also prized the island for its silk industry, the only one in the Mediterranean, producing a fine, transluscent cloth.

Kos also claims the school of Bucolic poetry and its principle exponent Theocritus. The Hellenistic ruler, Ptolemy II Philadelphos, was born here, and many of the Ptolemies were sent to Kos for their education.

Kos' wealth and position excited the envy of others, and from the 6th century it was invaded by Persians, Romans and Saracens. The gods themselves, it seems, were jealous, and earthquakes in AD 142, 469, 554 and 1933 levelled most of the island's buildings. In 1315 the Knights of St John took control of Kos, and, beginning in 1391, built fortifications using material from the ancient city. Later Grand Masters who continued the work had no qualms about using the works of art from the Asklepieion to furnish the stone for their walls. In 1457 and 1477 the Turks besieged the Knights without success, but they gained the fortress after the fall of Rhodes.

WHAT TO SEE

Kos, the capital and main port, lies in the north, in the region of the dolphin's eye. Its garden setting, the multitude of flowers and stately palm trees, make up for its lack of architectural interest, for most of the buildings were constructed on anti-seismic principles following the 1933 earthquake. The disaster had one good side-effect, however, for it opened up new archaeological excavations, carried out throughout the city by the Italians. Current opening times of the sites and the museum are listed in the **Tourist Information Office,** facing the harbour on the Akti Kountouriotou, where you'll also find many tourist cafés and restaurants. One block up in Plateia Eleftherias, there are more cafés near the **Museum** (open 9 am–3 pm, Sunday 9.30 am–2.30 pm, closed Tuesdays, entrance 200 dr.). The prize exhibit there is the statue of Hippocrates from the 4th century BC, and there are many Hellenistic and Roman vases, statues and mosaics from the Casa Romana and the Asklepieion.

Dominated by the 18th-century **Defterdar Mosque** (still used by Kos' 50 or so Muslim families, but not open to the public), Plateia Eleftheria also has the city's fruit market and the **Porta tou Forou,** the gate to Kos' ancient **Agora,** Within the walls the Knights once had their city, after the earthquake, excavations revealed the Roman Agora, the harbour quarter of the city, a temple of Aphrodite, and a 5th-century Christian basilica.

On the northern end of the Agora, the Plateia Platanou is almost entirely filled by the so-called **plane tree of Hippocrates,** its huge boughs now supported by an intricate metal scaffolding instead of the marble columns that once kept the venerable old tree from disaster. Signs in eight languages warn people not to touch for fear of insecticides. Yet it still seems quite healthy, and though experts are certain that the tree isn't old enough for Hippocrates to have taught under (though it may well be the oldest plane tree in Europe) it is true that the great healer claimed that the shade of a plane tree was the most salubrious. Indeed, the Turks found it delightful, and built a fountain under it, and near it the lovely **Mosque of the Loggia** (1786). On 1 September the citizens of Kos come to pluck a leaf from the tree to include in their harvest wreaths as a symbol of abundance.

A stone bridge off the square takes you over the fosse to the entrance of the **Castle of the Knights** (open 9 am–3 pm, Sunday 9.30 am–2.30 pm, closed Tuesdays, entrance 200 dr.). Begun in the mid-14th century, it served along with their castle across the strait in Bodrum as the outer defence of their main base in Rhodes. It was built in two stages (both times making ample use of stone from the ancient city), much of the second stage defence was built by Grand Master d'Aubusson after an earthquake in 1495, and the tower overlooking the harbour bears his name and coat-of-arms. There are many such inscriptions and reliefs throughout the castle, a number of which have found their way into the Antiquarium, neat stacks and rows of defunct marble. The splendid weeds and stillness within the castle attracted the German film director Werner Herzog, who set most of his *Signs of Life* within its walls; however, the elaborate cockroach traps and hypnotised chickens that played such a large role in the film are no longer in evidence.

From the Plateia Eleftheria take Vas. Pavlou which leads to Kos' other main archaeological sites in the area known as the Seraglio, where Minoan and Mycenaean houses were found, as well as later structures. Across from the Olympic Airways office stands a ramped Hellenistic **Altar of Dionysios,** and across Grigoriou St is the **Casa Romana** (open 9 am–3 pm, Sunday 9.30 am–2.30 pm, closed Tuesdays, entrance 200 dr.), excavated and reconstructed by the Italians in the 1930s. The house and neighbouring baths fell in the earthquake of AD 554; the house has well-preserved mosaics and offers a fair idea of the spacious elegance that rich Romans could afford. To the west along Grigoriou St is the **Roman Odeon,** or concert hall, with its rows of marble seats. Opposite are the **western excavations,** again begun by the Italians in the 1930s. On one side are the great Hellenistic walls around the akropolis, now marked by a minaret; on the other side runs a finely paved street, the main artery of Roman Kos, lined with houses (many, like the house of Europa, containing fine mosaics), a gymnasium and baths that are quite well-preserved and were used for a basilica by 5th-century Christians. In the baptistry you can see a well-preserved font. Alongside the baths and basilica runs the colonnade of the covered running track,

Roman Baths, Kos

or xystos, used in the winter months. The **stadium** was at the northern end of the xystos, down Tsaldari St. Only a few of the seats have yet been excavated, but on the far side near the church is a well-preserved aphesis, or starting gate.

Many places in Kos hire out bicycles, the ideal transport to the **Asklepieion** (open daily 8 am–7 pm, Sunday 9 am–6 pm, entrance 250 dr.) a few kilometres inland. Discovered by the German Herzog in 1902, following the description in Strabo, it has been partially restored by the Italians. This was one of the most sacred shrines to the healing god Asklepios, worshipped by the Asklepiada, a secret order of priests who found that baths in a beautiful setting did much to remedy the ills of body and soul. Snakes were the symbol of the cult, as they were believed to search out healing herbs. Built after the death of Hippocrates, himself a member of the Asklepiada the Asklepieion, as it is seen today is essentially Hellenistic with some Asiatic influences here and there. Several times the sanctuary was decimated by earthquakes and rebuilt, only to be dismantled by the Knights, who found it a very convenient source of stone blocks. Nowadays, the Greeks have big plans to build a "City of Hippocrates" near the present Hippocrates Foundation, where they would hold every five years an international medical olympiad. It is amusing to speculate on what that might encompass.

On the lowest level are Roman baths, built in the 3rd century AD; on the next of the great terraces is the entrance and another large bath, and near the stair are the remains of a temple dedicated by the Kos-born physician G. Stertinius Xenophon, who went on to become the Emperor Claudius' personal doctor, and who murdered his patient by sticking a poisoned feather down his throat. Shortly after that he retired to Kos. On this level there is also a spring, where water has flowed for over 2000 years. On the third terrace is the altar of Asklepios, and Ionic temples of Apollo and Asklepios (a few of the columns have been reconstructed by the Italians); on the fourth level was a Doric temple of Asklepios from the 2nd century BC, the grandest and most sacred of all. The view from this top level is superb. On the way back to the capital, **Platani,** Kos' main Turkish settlement, has some good tavernas and cafés.

Buses to other points on Kos leave the city from the terminal behind the Olympic Airways office, but the services are infrequent, and you'll inevitably find yourself at the wrong end of a hundred metre line-up, waiting for a taxi. The official campsite is at Psalidi about 3 km (2 miles) from town. There is a beach here and further along the coastal road at **Ag. Fokas,** and a spa at Empros Thermae. On the north coast there are beaches at Lampi and Tingaki, the latter especially fine, and near the island's salt pans.

Striking inland, two ruined basilicas (Ag. Pavlos and Ag. Ioannis) lie on the outskirts of **Zipario**; from here the road heads up to **Asfendiou,** a pleasant mountain village, though many of its houses have been abandoned as families moved down into town, **Zia** has become the official "traditional village" of the package tours. From Zia, in an hour, you may climb **Mt Oromedon,** or even Kos' highest peak, Dikaios Christos. This is the region of Pryioton described by Theocritus, and Mt Dikaios produced much of the marble used by Kos' sculptors. From Pyli it is a rough walk up to **Palaiopili,** a ruined Byzantine settlement surrounded by concentric walls camouflaged in the rocks. Within the walls is the church of Ypapandi, supposedly built in the 11th century by the Blessed Christodoulos before he went to Patmos. It, and Ag. Nikolaos nearby, have 14th-century frescoes some in excellent condition. In Pyli itself is the Charmyleion, a hero shrine converted into the church of Stavros.

A sandy beach stretches between the villages of **Tolari,** and **Kardamena,** the latter a fishing village where ceramics are made, now a major resort.

A quieter place to stay (though rapidly being developed) is **Mastihari** on the other side of the island. Frequent boats leave Mastihari for Kalymnos and Pserimos (see below), and it is the port for the ungainly village of **Antimacheia,** near the airport and the **Castle of Antimacheia,** built as a place of incarceration in the mid-14th century. Within its great triangular walls is a ruined settlement, two churches, cisterns and, over the gateway, the arms of d'Aubusson.

Out towards the dull region of the dolphin's tail, near the beach at Kamario, stand the extensive ruins of the twin basilicas of **Ag. Stefanos** (5th century, with mosaics, Ionian columns and remains of an atrium and baptistries) and out at sea, the scenic rock of Ag. Nikolaos. A superb beach near here, **Paradise** at Kamari, for once deserves its name. Great swimming for children, but you'll have to fight your way through the forest of umbrellas to get to the water.

Kefalos to the west is high up on the headland of the dolphin's tail. When the hotels are full on the rest of the island you can usually find a room in one of the houses in this village. South of Kefalos are ruins of yet another castle used by the Knights, one that inspired many travellers' tales in the Middle Ages, all involving a dragon. Mandeville claims the serpent was none other than Hippocrates' daughter, enchanted by Artemis and awaiting a knight brave enough to kiss her to transform her back into a maiden. Neolithic remains were found in the **Aspri Petra cave** near Kefalos, which is also near the site of the ancient capital of Kos, **Astypalaia,** the birthplace of Hippocrates where some ruins remain. On a hill above the town is a fort used by the Knights. Isthmioton, another ancient city on the peninsula, was very important in the past and sent its own delegation to Delos. The **monastery Ag. Ioannis** is 65 km (4 miles) west of Kefalos, the scenery once lovely, now wasted by fire, but still impressive. Nearby **Ag. Theologos** beach provides some of the island's most secluded swimming.

PANEYERIA
23 April, Ag. Georgios, with horse races at Pylio; 8 September, Panayias at Kardamena; 29 July, Ag. Apostoli at Antimacheia; 29 August, Ag. Ioannis at Kefalos; 25 March, Evangalismos at Asfendiou; 21 November, Isodia tis Panayias at Zia; 6 December, Ag. Nikolaos at Kos. In August the **Hippocrates Cultural Festival** attracts people from all over Greece, and includes art exhibitions, concerts of classical and modern music, and screenings of Greek and foreign films.

WHERE TO STAY
In Kos in the old days those in need of a cure would stay in the Asklepieion and sacrifice a chicken to the god. If you want to do the same, there's the new **Hippocrates Palace Hotel** (tel. 0242 24 401) with its Olympic Health Centre, this a medical spa supervised by the famous Dr Christian Barnard. However, it will cost you more than a chicken—rates are 12 000 dr. for a double, with half board in season. The nearby A class **Oceanis** is in the same price range (tel. 0242 24 641). Well located on the harbour is the new **Astron Hotel** (tel. 0242 23 704), a pretty class B with a rooftop garden, sporting a charming view of the sea and city. Rates here are 6500 dr. upwards for a double.

In the lower price brackets, the **Helena Hotel,** at 5 Megalou Alexandrou St (tel. 0242 22 740) is very pleasant, with its pretty balconies and prices at 3000 dr. for a double. For something less expensive, get the list of rooms and pensions at the tourist office, and in the summer have plenty of telephone change handy; these places fill up fast.

If you don't mind the overwhelming package tourism atmosphere, Kardamena has scores of rooms in its pensions and hotels. Dominant here is the **Norida Beach hotel** complex (tel. 0242 91 231) where doubles begin at 8000 dr. Smaller and less expensive is the **Stelios** (tel. 0242 91 293) on the main square and the sea, with doubles at 3800 dr., though do book well in advance. Even more than in Kos, accommodation fills up quickly in Kardamena, though if you come early in the day you can probably find a room in a private house. Other accommodation is to be found in Mastihari, Kefalos (always the last place to fill up) and Tingaki, which is more pricey than the other places, though the **Pension Meni** (tel. 0242 29 217) has doubles at around the 3000 dr. mark. Inquire at the NTOG office in Kos about renting a house in Asfendiou; currently they are being refurbished as part of the organisation's Traditional Settlements scheme. At the opposite extreme there's a huge **Club Méditerranée** complex near Ag. Stephanos. The campsite at Psalidi (tel. 0242 23 275) charges 250 dr. per person, 500 dr. per tent.

EATING OUT

Because it tries to please all, the typical restaurant food in Kos is notoriously bland and dull. As on Rhodes, you'd do well to avoid all places that advertise their dishes with illuminated photos on the façade—the tell-tale sign of mediocrity. In town the most traditional food is in the newer quarter of town, on Psarron Street at the **Hellas** and **Agellos** tavernas where prices are moderate—600 to 800 dr. for a meal, complete with *mezedes*. On the waterfront at Vass. Giorgiou the **Miramare** is largely unchanged by tourism and serves good Greek dishes at reasonable prices. The nearby **Bristol** offers, among other goodies, Chinese food. The sparkling **Le Chevalier** has a French menu with French prices to match. The **Kastro,** near the ancient Agora, belongs in the same league, but the setting is lovely. More down to earth is the ouzeri **Nikos O Vrahos** in Plateia Konitsis, one block up from the Agora, where a selection of delicious dishes will provide a wholesome, inexpensive meal.

Outside Kos town most of the beaches have tavernas, one of the better ones located above Paradise Beach, serving traditional Greek dishes for 700 dr. with Turkey as a backdrop. If you're from Montreal, introduce yourself to the owner, who commutes there with his entire family every year.

In Mastihari the long established **Kalia Kardia** (700–900 dr.) is the best of several; in Kardamena you'll find plenty of beefsteak or chicken with frites.

TOURIST INFORMATION
NTOG, waterfront, tel. (0242) 28 724.
Tourist police, with regular police, by the castle, tel. (0242) 22 222.

PSERIMOS

Located between Kos and Kalymnos, Pserimos has a beautiful sandy beach, making it a popular destination for day trippers from the larger islands though it's a quiet paradise if you choose to stay longer. Fewer than a hundred people live on Pserimos, although its paneyeri on 15 August attracts many times that number of visitors from Kos and Kalymnos. Regular boats run between Kos town, Mastihari and Kalymnos.

WHERE TO STAY
The seaside **Pension Tripolitis** (900 dr. a person) is pleasant, if it's full, you can sleep out on one of the island's more distant beaches, a kilometre from the village.

EATING OUT
Besides the Tripolitis there are three tavernas on the main beach that fill up with daytrippers at lunchtime, but regain their serenity in the evening.

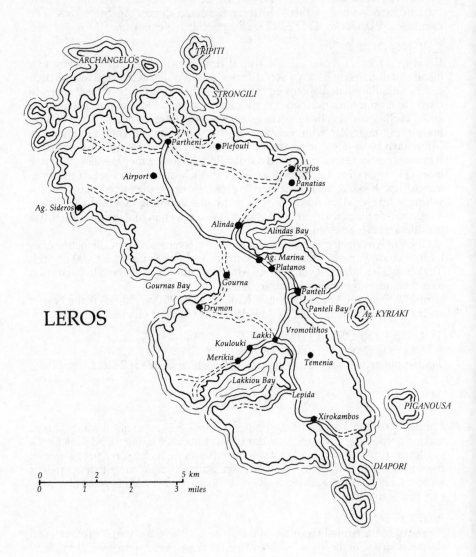

ARCHANGELOS

TRIPITI

STRONGILI

Partheni · Plefouti

Airport ·

Kryfos
Panatias

Ag. Sideros ·

Alinda · Alindas Bay

Ag. Marina
Platanos

Gournas Bay   Gourna

Panteli
Panteli Bay   Ag. KYRIAKI

LEROS   Drymon

Lakki   Vromotithos
Koulouki
Merikia   Temenia

PIGANOUSA

Lakkiou Bay
Lepida

Xirokambos

DIAPORI

0   2   5 km
0   1   2   3   miles

LEROS

CONNECTIONS

By air, daily from Athens and three times a week from Kos. Ferry every day from Rhodes, Kos, Kalymnos and Patmos. Hydrofoils four times a week from Ag. Marina to Patmos and Kos, once a week to Pythagorio (Samos); six times a week excursion boat from Ag. Marina to Lipsi. Daily boat from Myrties (Kalymnos) to Xirokambos. Once a week connections with the other Dodecanese on the *Panormitis*.

With one of the most serrated coastlines of all the islands, Leros defies easy description. Unlike many of the other Dodecanese, most of the visitors are Greek, and many of those who come to Leros tend to combine their holiday with a visit to a relative in one of the island's three mental hospitals, built during the Italian occupation. Indeed, here more than on the other islands you are aware of the Italians, some older residents can't even speak Greek. Although there are several beaches, none of them is anything special, and in the hotels you need all your mosquito defences. However, the people are friendly, and you can walk almost everywhere; there are enough incongruities to make a visit interesting, if not occasionally bizarre.

HISTORY

When the hero Meleagros died, his sisters mourned him so passionately that Artemis turned them into guinea fowl and put them in her temple at Leros, the wooded island dedicated to her. This worship of the goddess of the chase and the guinea fowl might be traced back to Ionian colonists from Miletus. Homer includes Leros in his catalogue of ships; along with Kalymnos, it is one of his Kalydian isles. Leros sided with Sparta in the Peloponnesian War, despite its Ionian ancestry. Under the Byzantines, it was part of the theme of Samos, but in 1316 it was sold to the Knights of St John and governed by the Duke of Naxos as part of the monastic state of Patmos. The town and harbour of Lakki were badly battered by the combined allied air forces in 1943 during a prolonged bombardment; photographs taken by German paratroopers at the time are on display in the Kastis Travel Agency. During the later Cyprus dispute the Greek government dismantled the military installations to show that it had no warlike intentions against Turkey. When the junta took power in 1967, Communist dissidents were exiled on Leros and kept under the strictest surveillance.

WHAT TO SEE

Platanos, in the centre of Leros, is the capital of the island. It is crowned by the **Kastro,** a Byzantine fortress renovated by the Knights of St John and the Venetians, and used even today as a military observation post. Although it seems steep and inaccessible, a fairly easy footpath leads up from the town which is picturesquely piled below. Once at the top you have a splendid view of "four seas": the bays of Panteli, Alindas, Gournas and Lakkiou. Two old churches

Aghia Marina Harbour, Leros

have been repaired by the Greek Archaeology Service, **Moni Megalochiro** and **Kyras Kastrou**. The latter has the following legend: during the Turkish occupation a miraculous icon of the Virgin with a candle set sail from Constantinople and landed at Leros. The inhabitants, led by the bishops, met it and carried it in great procession to the cathedral. The next day, however, the icon was nowhere to be found, but before dismay had spread too far the Turkish captain of the Kastro found it with its candle in the powder stores, a strange incident considering that the door was firmly bolted and locked. The icon was returned to the cathedral, but the next night the very same thing happened. And the next night, and the next. Finally the Turkish captain grew weary of the affair and gave the powder storeroom to the Christians, who turned it into the church Kyras Kastro. Here the wilful icon has decided to remain ever since. During the Second World War the Germans and the Italians used Kastro as an observatory.

In Platanos there is a small museum in the main square, housing local finds, which is usually open in the morning. It is a short walk from Platanos to the beach at **Panteli** in one direction and **Ag. Marina**, Leros' main resort—such as it is—in the other direction. North of Ag. Marina **Alinda,** the old commercial port of Leros, also has a long beach. Near here are the ruins of an Early Christian basilica along with a few vestiges of the ancient city, as well as a British war cemetery from the battle of 1943. Other beaches nearby are at **Gournas,** near the monastery Ag. Sideros which was built on a small islet linked to the main island by a long causeway.

Frequent buses run between Platanos and the island's main port, **Lakki**. If Fellini had been a Greek, he would use this town as a set. The streets are perfectly paved and wide enough to accommodate several lanes of traffic, though usually they're perfectly empty, stately fascisti art deco buildings, genteelly dilapidated, stand forlornly among the empty lots. Night life here centres around the grandiose cinema (inside, it's open air and specialises in cannibal and air crash films). Near the waterfront there's a monument to the many who perished when the Greek ship, the *Queen Olga*, was attacked by German planes and sank in Lakki's harbour during the war. A path leading up from the jetty goes to the nearest beach at **Koulouki,** popular for unofficial camping. At Lepida, across the harbour, the Moni Panayia is built on the ruins of an old lighthouse, and further south, overlooking Xirokambos, is the fort Paliokastro, built near an older fortification dating back to the 3rd century BC. The church inside has mosaics and Xirokambos itself has a pleasant pebble beach with several tavernas and a campsite.

Partheni on the northern shore had an ancient temple to Artemis, near the present church of Ag. Matrona. This was the centre of guinea fowl worship on Leros, and today is the centre of military activity on the island; it was the base used by the colonels to detain political dissidents. There is a better beach with a taverna nearby at **Plefouti.**

PANEYERIA

Carnival at which the children don monks' robes and visit the homes of the newly married, reciting verses made up by their elders; 16–17 July, Ag. Marinas at Ag. Marina; 6 August, Sotiros at Platanos; 15 August, Panayias at the Kastro; 20 August, foreign tourist day at Alinda; 20 October, Ag. Kyras at Partheni; 26 September, Ag. Ioannis Theologos at Lakki. Often at the paneyeria you can hear the Greek hammered dulcimer, the santouri.

Starting on 26 September, three days of memorial services are held for those who lost their lives on the *Queen Olga*; Greek naval vessels always attend this annual commemoration.

WHERE TO STAY

In these days of the cloned concrete beach hotel, you can still stay at the elephantine **Leros Palace Hotel** (tel. 0247 22 940) in the heart of Lakki, where the corridors seem endless, the ceilings high enough to accommodate a trapeze, and you get free audio from the cinema next door. It's the perfect place to stay in Lakki, and the price (if nothing else) is right: 1600–2200 dr. a night for a double, breakfast extra. The nearby **Miramare** has rooms in the same price bracket (tel. 0247 22 053). Other, arguably more comfortable, lodgings may be had at Alinda, in Ag. Marina Bay such as the **Hotel Maleas Beach,** class C (tel. 0247 23 306) and the **Pension Chryssoula,** brand new and boasting the best view in town (tel. 0247 22 460). Rates for the first are 3800 dr. a double, for the Chryssoula 2500 dr. a double. In Panteli there are a number of pensions, including **To Rodon** (tel. 0247 22 075) with doubles for 2500 dr. There's a campsite at Xirokambos (tel. 0247 22 236).

EATING OUT

In Lakki the fare is generally limited to fast food and pizza, a notable exception being **O Sotos** taverna (behind the Leros Palace Hotel), which enjoys an excellent reputation, especially for its fish dishes. Avoid the first taverna on leaving the ferry—the food is dreadful and served stone cold. In Xirokambos **Nick and Anna's Taverna** is friendly and inexpensive with fresh fish for about 800 dr. Ag. Marina has most of the island's tavernas. If you're walking down from Platanos, there's a little taverna directly on your right owned by a charming Italian couple, though the food they serve is mostly Greek (and good). A meal here runs around 800 dr. In Platanos you can dine lightly but well on souvlaki at the café near the top of the main square.

TOURIST INFORMATION

Information booth on quay.
Tourist police, see regular police, tel. (0247) 22 222.

LIPSI (LIPSO)

CONNECTIONS

Once a week with the other Dodecanese by the *Panormitis*; frequent excursion boats from Leros, Patmos and Samos.

Lipsi is a little gem of an island midway between Leros and Patmos, its lovely beaches of late a magnet for day excursions from its larger neighbours. However it is still as quiet a place as one can find with good food and good swimming, near the fine harbour and beach. Other beaches nestling along Lipsi's jagged coastline are at Katsadia and Lendori; the best, **Plati Yialo,** is a half-hour walk to the south (it is also accessible by taxi). Another pleasant stroll leads to a green cultivated valley beyond the town, where a good wine is produced. One tradition connects the island with Calypso, and there certainly is a similarity, in the name if nothing else.

WHERE TO STAY

There's only one hotel on Lipsi, the **Kalypso** (tel. 0247 41 242), where a double costs around 2000 dr. Plenty of other rooms in the village besides. Otherwise you can sleep out at Katsadia or Lendori beach.

EATING OUT

The tavernas on the waterfront are good and not very expensive; a fish dinner here will set you back about 800 dr. Some of the cafés serve breakfast.

NISSYROS

CONNECTIONS

Ferry three times a week from Piraeus. In summer, nearly every day excursion boat from Kos and Kardamena; also less frequently connections with Rhodes,

Symi and Tilos. Once a week connections to other Dodecanese and Crete. Hydrofoil once a week from Rhodes and Kos.

In the great war between the gods and the giants, one of the casualties was the fiery Titan Polybates, who so incurred Poseidon's wrath that the sea god yanked off a chunk of Kos and hurled it on top of Polybates as he attempted to swim away. This became the island of Nissyros, and the miserable Polybates, pinned underneath, eternally sighs and fumes unable to escape.

Geologically Nissyros was indeed once part of Kos, and Polybates is the Dodecanese' only volcano, and even in its dormant state it dominates the character of Nissyros. Its fertile slopes are green with olives, figs, citrus groves and almond trees, and its inhabitants have traditionally worked the pumice fields, both on Nissyros and its little sister islet **Yiali** The coasts of both islands are a jumble of black volcanic boulders and black sandy beaches, though Yiali also has a fine golden, sandy beach.

WHAT TO SEE
Nissyros, despite the advent of day trippers, has retained its quiet charm. Even the new houses constructed in jewel like **Mandraki,** the capital and port, conform to the old style: tall and narrow with small wooden balconies. Of late it has become fashionable to paint them in deep, almost gaudy colours. One of the houses near the church has been opened as a small Historical and Ethnographical Museum, with household implements and costumes and a tiny library of books about the island.

Fortunately most of the streets of Mandraki are too narrow for traffic, but the town has been kind enough to signpost the way to its major attraction: the stair up to the monastery of **Panayia Spiliani** (1825), in a cave within the walls of the old Venetian **Kastro,** Inside is a much venerated icon of the Virgin, loaded down with a bushel of gold and silver offerings, and a finely-carved iconostasis. The Kastro itself isn't much, but the height offers a spectacular view at sunset. Higher up, at **Paliokastro,** are impressive Cyclopean walls.

Just east of Mandraki is the thermal spa of **Loutra,** where the hot volcanic springs are famed for curing arthritis and rheumatism; further to the east is Nissyros' best beach, **Palli,** where there's a new hotel under construction, as well as several excellent tavernas.

The excursion not to be missed on Nissyros, however is to **Polybates,** the volcano. Buses for the crater leave the port, coinciding with the arrival of the tourist boats, or there is the regular village bus from Mandraki up to Emborios and Nikia, two villages perched up on the top of the crater's rim, from where you can walk down. The winding road takes you across most of the island until it begins to twist its way down into an other-worldly landscape of pale greys and yellows, the smell of sulphur so pungent that you can almost see the stink lines radiating out of the great crater. After passing several geothermal pools, the bus stops near the great fuming heart of Polybates. A zigzag path descends to the floor of the crater, when you can feel the great heat and turmoil of the volcano

227

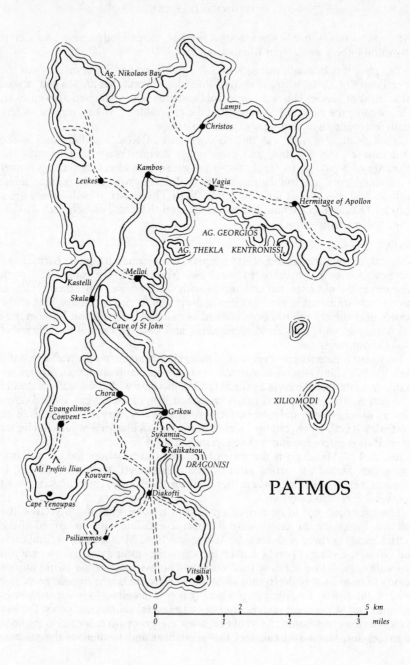

Ag. Nikolaos Bay

Lampi

Christos

Kambos

Levkes

Vagia

Hermitage of Apollon

AG. GEORGIOS

AG. THEKLA KENTRONISSI

Melloi

Kastelli

Skala

Cave of St John

XILIOMODI

Chora

Evangelimos
Convent

Grikou

Sykamia

Kalikatsou

DRAGONISI

Mt Profitis Ilias

Kouvari

Cape Yenoupas

Diakofti

PATMOS

Psiliammos

Vitsilia

| 0 | | 2 | | 5 km |
| 0 | 1 | | 2 | 3 miles |

underfoot (wear stout shoes—not sneakers!).
Small fumaroles still emit steam and stench, and weird and eerie as it is no one stays too long. Even hotter is the natural sauna below **Emborios,** in a cave heated by hot springs. The village with its ruined Byzantine fort and ancient walls offers good views of the crater 300 metres (1000 ft) below, as does pretty **Nikia.**

PANEYERIA
29 June, Ag. Apostoli at Palli; 27 July, Ag. Panteleimonos at Nikia; August 15, Panayias at Mandraki.

WHERE TO STAY
The most comfortable place to stay in Mandraki is the **Hotel Romantzo** near the ferry dock; it has a large shady terrace and a good restaurant and costs 2800 dr. for a double (tel. 0242 31 340). Alternatively the small **Tria Adelfia** (tel. 0242 31 344) has doubles for about the same price. There are also a number of rooms to rent in the village, and the adequate **Pension Sunset** with doubles for 1800 dr.

EATING OUT
All of the tavernas in Nissyros are exceptionally friendly and reasonably priced. Not far from the public lavatories is the **Taverna Tsardka** where you can eat some of the best mousaka in Greece with a bottle of wine for 600 dr. Another relaxed place is the **Taverna Nissyros,** in the centre of Mandraki, where prices are about the same.

TOURIST INFORMATION
Tourist police, see regular police on the quay, tel. (0242) 31 201.
Tourist office, tel. (0242) 31 459.

PATMOS

CONNECTIONS
Hydrofoils in the summer to Kos, Rhodes, Leros and Pythagorio, Samos; daily boat to Lipsi (see below); every day to Piraeus, Kalymnos, Leros, Kos and Rhodes; frequent excursions to Pythagorio and Ikaria; once a week to Paros and Mykonos, also to Arki, Agathonisi, Nissyros, Tilos, Symi, Chios, Lesbos and Limnos.

Of all the Greek islands, Patmos is the most sacred to the Christians, both Orthodox and Western alike, for here St John the Divine received his Revelation, and here, in the 11th century, was founded a monastery more wealthy and influential than any in Greece except for Mt Athos. Many find even today a spirituality in Patmos that the other islands lack, a quiet solemnity, a sacred (though hardly Apocalyptic) aura that seems especially strong in the evening, after the cruise ships have sailed away. If swimming *au naturel* and dancing the night away is what you look forward to, you won't want to stay long on Patmos. It is a quiet place, especially up at Chora, and people tend to retire early to bed.

HISTORY

Patmos was inhabited from the 14th century BC, with the capital near present-day Skala, its akropolis and fortifications at Kastelli. It was a subject to Asia Minor and not very important. In AD 95, however, the island's destiny was forever altered when St John the Divine (also known as the Theologian) was exiled here from Ephesus during the Emperor Domitian's persecution of Christians, and while living here in a cave he had the visions that resulted in the Book of Revelation. Most believe he stayed only a year before returning to Ephesus. Patmos was abandoned from the 7th to the 11th centuries, its barren, volcanic rock not worth the risk posed by pirates, until 1088, when the Blessed Christodulos, a saintly hermit, founded a monastery on the site of an ancient temple of Artemis and an old basilica. The land and funds for building came from the Byzantine Emperor Alexis Comnenus. There's an apocryphal tale which relates that when Alexis' fortunes were down, Christodulos had predicted his ascent to the throne, whereupon Alexis promised that should his words come true he would grant him any wish in his power. When events in 1088 did indeed occur as the hermit had foretold, Alexis kept his promise. The entire island of Patmos was given to the monastery, which managed to retain absolute control of it for centuries against a thousand afflictions ranging from poverty to pirate raids. Under the Duke of Naxos, Patmos was left a relatively independent monastic state. In the 13th century the village of Chora was built in the shadow of the monastery, so that when in danger the population could take refuge behind its powerful walls. Patmos flourished particularly during the 16th to 19th centuries, and its school of theology and liberal arts, founded in 1713, cast a healthy glow over the long, dark domination of the Turks. The monastery's control of the inhabitants lessened as the latter grew rich from trade at sea. By 1720 the monks and laymen had divided the land between them, and Patmos began to establish colonies abroad. With the advent of the steamship the island declined like other island shipping centres.

WHAT TO SEE

All visitors to Patmos land at **Skala,** the port and main tourist centre which has many hotels and rooms to rent. There's a fair-sized beach in the town, and a statue of Protergatis Xanthos Emmanuel, recalling an uprising he led against the Turks in 1821. Skala itself didn't even exist until that year, so fearsome were the pirate raids even at the beginning of the last century. Near the beach, marked by a red buoy, is a reminder of another Patmian menace, the evil magician Yenoupas, who at the urging of priests from the temple of Apollo challenged St John to a duel of miracles. Yenoupas' miracle was to dive into the sea and bring back effigies of the dead; John's was to ask God to petrify the submerged magician,

230

which ended the game rather quickly. Behind Skala you can visit what was once one of the world's largest De-salination plants, work now performed by a reservoir. The water tastes better, but there still isn't enough to meet the island's needs in the summer. You can also walk up to the site of the ancient city, **Kastelli,** in about 20 minutes, a walk rewarded more with stunning views than any archaeological excavations, as the site remains unexplored.

From Skala the island's bus leaves several times a day for **Chora** and other destinations (timetable posted near the Italianate port authority building). From Skala you can see the whitewashed town clustered around the mighty walls of the castle-like monastery, and if you have the time it isn't too strenuous to walk up from Skala, taking in the ever-widening panorama spread out below. Even if there were no monastery, the ascent would be worth while for the view and to see the lovely, almost Cycladic town, with its numerous mansions dating from the heyday of Patmos' once great merchant fleet. A whole day can be spent just visiting its many churches, though many people head straight for the **Monastery of St John the Theologian** (open 8 am–12 noon and 2 pm–6 pm; Thursdays and Fridays 8 am–12 noon; no shorts and women must wear skirts). There is a good guide by S. A. Papadopoulos sold in the monastery that describes its history and the many beautiful frescoes and works of art given to it over the centuries. Inside its massive walls (restored after heavy damage in the earthquake of 1956) are the remains of its founder, the Blessed Christodulos, along with an icon of St John given to the monastery by Alexis. Beautiful frescoes cover almost all paintable surfaces in the church area. In the Treasury Museum are the Codex Prophyrius, St Mark's gospel written in the 6th century; the deed from Emperor Alexis giving the island to the monastery, signed and sealed, remains of the temple of Artemis on which the monastery was founded (supposedly built by

Monastery of St John the Theologian, Patmos

Orestes, in gratitude for being rid of the Furies) and many beautiful icons and ship pendants made of diamonds and emeralds donated by Catherine the Great. The library contains thousands of ancient codices, manuscripts and rare books, but may only be visited with permission from the abbot.

Of the 40 or so churches in Chora, the **Convent of Zoodochos Pigi** (1607) has fine frescoes and icons and can be visited mornings and late afternoons. The others, **Ag. Dimitrios** (11th century) being the oldest, are very likely to be locked, and anyone wanting to visit will need to look for the caretaker, which isn't always easy, as Chora is one of those very old, silent places where the streets always seem to be deserted.

On Maundy Thursday (by the Orthodox calendar) Chora is packed with locals visitors and TV crews for the Niptiras ceremony, when the abbot of the monastery re-enacts Christ's washing of his disciples' feet, a ceremony once performed by the emperors of Byzantium. It takes place either in Plateia Ag. Levias or Plateia Loza, depending on the weather.

It's a 15-minute walk down from Chora to the **Monastery of the Apocalypse** (same opening hours as the Monastery of St John), where a flower-bedecked stairway leads down to the cave where St John lived and dreamed. The cave itself has been converted to a church and one is shown the rock where the good saint, rested his head and hand (though one can't help thinking he must have been a contortionist to manage it), and the massive overhanging roof, split in three sections by the voice of God.

Caiques from Skala run almost every day to the island's best sandy beach, **Psiliammos** and to **Lampi** of the beautiful pebbles. Accessible on foot but much less attractive beaches are at **Melloi** and **Grikou**. There are other beaches in the region, often deserted, such as the one at Sapsila. In the fertile **Sykamia** an old Roman bath claims to have been used by St John to baptise the inhabitants he converted. **Stavros,** a tiny village to the south, has the **Kalikatsou rock,** where carved rooms in rather unlikely places and other signs lead some to suggest that it was the 11th-century hermitage mentioned by Christodulos. Across the island from here, a grotto on **Cape Yenoupas** was the home of the evil magician of the same name, and even today it is said to be hot and smelly inside.

Heading north, **Kambos** lies in the centre of Patmos' main agricultural valley and has a popular sandy beach. Further along are more wild and windswept shores at Levkes. Even more remote is the 19th-century **Hermitage of Apollon,** which is near a small mineral spring (ask for directions in Kambos).

PANEYERIA
Besides the Maundy Thursday Niptiras ceremony, the monastery holds important services for St John on 8 May and 26 September; more popular (feasting and dancing) paneyeria take place 5 August (Sotiris) at Kambos and 15 August, Panayias, also at Kambos; 14 September, Stavros; 27 July, Ag. Panteleimonos, on the islet of Xiliomodi.

WHERE TO STAY

On the edge of Skala there's the **Hotel Byzance,** recently opened but designed in the traditional style featuring a roof garden with lovely views over the port and a small restaurant. A double here costs 3800 dr. (tel. 0247 31 052). On the whole, however, the private rooms in Skala are very comfortable and better value than the hotels, and you're sure to be offered one as soon as you get off the boat. There are also rooms (rather hard to find) up in Chora, the excellent camp ground at Melloi, and hotels at Grikou—the **Panorama** has furnished apartments near the sea, tel. 0247 31 209. Prices here are 6500 dr., studio apartments 4500 dr.; the **Flisvos Hotel** is less expensive (tel. 0247 31 380), with doubles 2500 dr. a night. You can also find rooms in Kambos.

EATING OUT

There are two good restaurants in Chora: **Vangelis,** in Plateia Ag. Levias (follow the little signs) with solid Greek fare at average prices (500 dr.). At the more elegant **Patmian House,** in one of the town's old mansions, the food is very good but more expensive (open only for dinner).

In Skala you'll get better food at better prices the further you go from the waterfront establishments, which cater to the cruise ships. One place worth looking for is near the edge of town—head straight back from the central square—it's owned by a jovial family from Kalymnos who serve grills and other Greek food for around 800 dr. a person, including wine.

TOURIST POLICE

See regular police, tel. (0247) 31 303, in the harbour.

Agathonissi is a remote island off Patmos, connected only once a week with the outside world, like the even smaller **Arki.** (The *Panormitis'* route is: Rhodes, Kos, Kalymnos, Leros, Agathonissi, Arki, Lipsi, Patmos and Samos) These are poor islets, inhabited only by a few fishing families. On Agathonissi are two villages, Megalo Chorio and Mikro Chorio, and a few ancient remains have been found there. Occasional caiques run from Patmos to Arki, usually on Sundays. There are two cafés, a bit of beach, but no electricity. Occasionally caiques from Arki or Patmos run to the even smaller **Marathi,** which has a better, sandy beach and a taverna.

RHODES (RODOS)

CONNECTIONS

By air: In summer at least five daily flights from Athens; daily with Herakleon (Crete), Kos, Mykonos, Paros, and Karpathos; six times a week with Kassos; five

RHODES

Scale:
0 — 5 — 10 — 20 km
0 — 5 — 10 miles

To Symi, Kos
To Piraeus, Karpathos, Halki
To Kastellorizo

Rhodes
Ialysos
Ixia
Trianda
Therme
Paradissi
Tris
Kallithea
Kato Kalamonos
Kremasti
Asgourou
Koskinou
Airport
Pastida
Tholos
Damatria
Soroni
Maritsa
Kallithies
Kallithea Bay
Fanes
Kalamonas
Ladiko
Kalavarda
Epano
Dimilia
Psinthos
Faliraki
Salachos
Kalamonas
Petaloudes
Kamiros
Mt Profitis Ilias
Afandou
Skala
(790m/2600ft)
Eleousa
Archipolis
Afandou Bay
Kamiros
Apollona
Mandriko
Nani
Plantania
Epta Pigi
Kolymbia
To Halki
Kritinia
Archangelos
Embona
Malona
Massari
Mt Ataviros
(1215m/3986ft)
Faraclos
Ag. Isidoros
Laerma
Haraki
Chimarasi
Kalathos
Siana
Vliha Bay
Fourni
Monolithos
Istrios
Pilona
Profilia
Lardos
Lindos
Asklipio
Pefki
Apolakkia
Arnitha
Vati
Chiotari
Gennadi
Messanagros
Lahania
Ag. Pavlos
Kattavia
Plimiri
Prassonisi Cape

SYMI

NIMOS
To Rhodes
Emborio
Nos
Yialos
Chora
Pedi
Taxiarchis
Michael
Panormitis
SESKLI
STROGGILOS

times a week with Thessaloniki and Sitia (Crete); three times a week with Mytilini and Santorini; twice a week with Kastellorizo.

By sea: year round, daily ship to Marmaris, Turkey and twice a week to Limassol (Cyprus) and Haifa (Israel). Daily ferry boat to Piraeus (16–24 hours), Kos, Kalymnos, Leros, Patmos and Symi; four times a week to Karpathos and Kassos; three times a week with Halki, Tilos, Nissyros, Sitia and Ag. Nikolaos (Crete), Samos and Astypalaia; twice a week to Amorgos, Santorini, Anafi and Kastellorizo; several times a week a caique runs from Kamiros Skala to Halki.

By hydrofoil: daily with Kos, Patmos and Symi, three times a week with Leros, once a week with Samos, also connections with Kalymnos, Halki, Nissyros, Karpathos and Kastellorizo.

Rhodes is the largest of the Dodecanese, with the group's highest mountain (Mt Ataviros, 1215 metres/3986 ft). It is ringed by sandy beaches, bedecked with flowers and draped with fertile farmlands and vineyards (some unfortunately destroyed in a sweeping fire in 1987), blessed with some 300 days of sun a year and adorned with monuments evoking a long, colourful history, and so it's little wonder that Rhodes has become the queen of tourism in Greece. It is a year-round resort for cold northerners, a major destination for the package tour and it's not quite fair to judge it in comparison with Greece's other islands. Rhodes is rather a Euro-playground, a modern tourist Babylon, where people feel compelled to emblazon "No Problem!" and "Relax" on their bosoms. If large crowds of tourists bother you, head for the south of the island or try smoking a smelly cigar and pretend you only speak Albanian. Or Greek.

HISTORY

Inhabited since the Stone Age, Rhodes was later invaded by the Minoans who built shrines to the moon at Philerimos, Lindos and Kamiros. The Acheans took the island in the 15th century BC, and Homer mentions that the Rhodians sent nine ships to Troy, led by Tlepolemos, son of Heracles, who met an unhappy end before the walls of Troy. The island had several names in antiquity, among them Telchinia for its first mythical inhabitants, the Telchines, and Ophioussa, for its numerous vipers, even today some villagers wear high goatskin boots when working out in the fields.

The three cities mentioned by Homer—Lindos, Ialysos and Kamiros—long dominated the island's affairs, and the position of Rhodes on the main trade route between the Middle East and the West led to an early importance both in trade and naval power. Around 1000 BC the three cities became part of the Doric Hexapolis (in response to similar Ionion confederacy), the other cities being Kos, Cnidos and Halicarnassus, a confederacy united politically, religiously and economically. For four centuries they knew great prosperity and colonised from Naples to the Costa Brava in Spain.

Rhodes sided with the Persians in both of their major campaigns against Greece, but upon their defeat joined the Delian confederacy. In 480 BC, in order to prevent rivalries among themselves and to increase their wealth and strength,

235

the three ancient cities united and founded one central city, Rhodes, on the northern tip of the island. Hippodamos of Miletus, the geometrician and city planner, designed the new town with straight streets, as he had with Piraeus. It was considered one of the most beautiful cities of ancient times, surrounded by walls encompassing a much greater area than that delineated by the existing medieval walls. Famous schools of Philosophy, Philology and Oratory were founded, and the port had facilities far in advance of its time. Although Lindos, Kamiros and Ialysos still existed, they lost all their importance and most of their populations to the mighty new city.

During the Peloponnesian War, Rhodes sided with whichever power was in the ascendancy at any given time, and later supported Alexander the Great. He in turn lent his support to Rhodes in order to increase the island's commercial importance in contrast to that of Athens. The Rhodians surpassed that city, taking in most of the Mediterranean trade and building up a great navy that ruled the waves. Rhodian colonies were founded all over the known world. Under Alexander and after his death a thriving trade began with Egypt, and although the island was independent, it allied itself with Ptolemy in the Hellenistic struggles between the generals of Alexander. The other great powers at the time left the Rhodian fleet with the task of controlling piracy and creating trade and navigation laws; these were later adopted by the Romans and indeed by commercial traders today.

Then another general of Alexander, Antigonas, in his campaign to unite the old empire, ordered the Rhodians to fight with him against his rivals, mainly Ptolemy of Egypt. Loath to lose their lucrative Egyptian trade, the Rhodians refused and so Antigonas sent his son Dimitrios Poliorketes (The Besieger) into the attack with the army of Syria and the Phoenician fleet. The ensuing year-long siege by one of the greatest generals of all time against the greatest city of the day has gone down in history, not only as a contest of great strength and endurance, but for the battle of wits between the two sides. Over and over again Dimitrios would invent some new ingenious siege machine, such as the ten-storey Helepolis siege tower only to have it ingeniously foiled by the defenders (who dug a hidden, shallow ditch in the path of the great Helepolis, thus tumbling it to the ground). After a year both sides grew weary of the affair and made a truce, Rhodes agreeing to assist Dimitrios' father Antigonas except in battles against Ptolemy. They also sent important hostages with Dimitrios to guarantee their promises.

So Dimitrios departed, leaving the Rhodians all of his vast siege machinery. This they either sold or melted down, in order to construct a great statue of their patron god Helios of the sun. The famous sculptor from Lindos, Chares, was put in charge of the project, which took 12 years to complete and cost 20 000 pounds of silver. Accounts say it was anywhere from 30 to 40 metres (90 to 120 ft) tall (at her crown the Statue of Liberty stands 34 metres/111 ft). Although the popular conception of the Colossus has it astride the entrance of Rhodes harbour, it is technically impossible—most scholars believe it stood near the present Castle of

236

the Knights. Considered one of the Seven Ancient Wonders of the World, it lasted only from 290 to 225 BC, when an earthquake brought it crashing to the ground. There it lay for almost ten centuries, until AD 653 when the Saracens who had captured Rhodes sold it as scrap metal to a merchant from Edessa. According to legend, it took 900 camels to transport it to the ships.

In 164 BC, when they had repaired their city and walls after the siege of Dimitrios (the city at that time was even larger than it is today), the Rhodians made a treaty with Rome. Alexandria was then the only rival of Rhodes in wealth, and tiny Delos its only rival in Mediterranean trade. A famous school of rhetoric on Rhodes attracted Romans such as Cicero, Cassius, Julius Caesar and Mark Anthony. However, entanglement in Roman politics and the oscillations of power within the Roman Empire often brought evils to Rhodes along with privileges. When Rhodes supported the successors of Julius Caesar, Cassius cruelly sacked the island, destroyed or captured its fleet, and sent many of its treasures to Rome. This began the decline of Rhodes, which lost control of the many islands she administered, along with much of the trade she once had. This trade had fallen off almost completely by the time of the end of the empire and Pax Romana. In the first century St Paul preached on the island and converted many of the inhabitants to Christianity.

Byzantium brought many invaders and adventurers to Rhodes, including the Arabs, the Genoese, the Venetians and the Crusaders. In 1191 King Richard the Lionheart and Philip Augustus of France came to Rhodes in search of mercenaries. After the fall of Jerusalem in 1291, the Knights Hospitallers of St John took refuge on Cyprus, but by 1306 they had become interested in the wealthier and better positioned Rhodes. They asked the Emperor Andronicus Palaeologus to cede them the island in return for their loyalty, but the rulers of Byzantium knew better than to trust the Franks after they had sacked Constantinople in 1204. The Knights, under Grand Master Foulques de Villaret, then took the matter into their own hands. Although they purchased the Dodecanese from the ruling Genoese pirates, it was a prize they had to fight for spending three years besieging the inhabitants.

By 1309, with the help of the Pope, the Knights had Rhodes and began to build their hospital and inns, eight in all, one for each of the "tongues", or different nationalities which comprised the Order (England, France, Germany, Italy, Castile, Aragon, Auvergne and Provence). Each tongue had a bailiff, and they in turn elected the Grand Master of the Knights, who lived in a special palace. There were never more than 600 men in the Order, originally devoted to the care of pilgrims who came to the Holy Land. As occasion dictated they became more and more warlike, and although they built a hospital on Rhodes, defence and raiding were their primary concerns. They were also extraordinarily wealthy, especially after the other great Order of the Middle Ages, the Knights Templars was dissolved in 1312. The popes gave much of their wealth and property to the Knights of St John.

The Knights erected a new wall around the town, replacing the outdated

Byzantine fortifications. Italian engineers, the best of their time, designed the new works throughout the 14th, 15th and 16th centuries, some of the most splendid defences of the day. The knights were besieged without success by the Sultan of Egypt in 1444, and by Mohammed II the Conqueror in 1480, but in 1522 Sultan Suleiman the Magnificent conquered the island. The siege lasted for six months, and Suleiman was on the point of giving up when a traitor told him that the Knights could not hold out. So he redoubled his efforts and the Knights were forced to surrender. They were permitted to leave in safety for Malta, with their Christian retainers and possessions, and thus became the Knights of Malta. In 1831 they ended up in Rome.

Turkish rule brought 400 years of darkness to Rhodes. When the inhabitants revolted during the War of Independence, the Turks reacted by slaughtering a quarter of the population. The Italian rulers in 1912 brought material prosperity but spiritual tyranny. They claimed that the island was their inheritance from the Knights of St John, although of course only an eighth of the knights had been Italian. Mussolini even had the Palace of the Grand Masters reconstructed (it and many other of the medieval buildings of the old town were destroyed in the Great Gunpowder Explosion of 1856, when lightning struck an old Turkish powder magazine). During the Second World War Rhodes remained in the hands of a German garrison until May 1945. Before then a large part of the Jewish population on the island, almost 2000, had died in Nazi prison camps. Rhodes, with the rest of the Dodecanese, officially joined Greece in 1945, whereupon the government declared it a free port, boosting its already great tourist potential.

MYTHOLOGY

Long ago, when Father Zeus handed out lands to all the gods and goddesses, he forgot to leave a portion for Helios, the god of the sun. Dismayed, Zeus asked Helios what he could do to make up for his omission. The sun god replied that he knew of an island just emerging off the coast of Asia Minor which would suit him admirably. Zeus gave it to him willingly and Helios named this new home of his "Rhodes" after his nymph wife, the daughter of Poseidon and a Telchine. The nine Telchines, with their flippers and dog heads, were the first inhabitants of the island, and are accredited with founding the three ancient cities of Kamiros, Ialysos and Lindos. The three grandsons of Rhodes and Helios with these names are other possible founders, as is Tlepolemos, who led the nine ships of Rhodes to Troy.

Kamiros even had a fourth mythological founder, Althaemenes, son of the Cretan King Catreus, himself the son of Minos. An oracle predicted that Catreus would be slain by one of his offspring. To prevent the prediction from coming true, Althaemenes went to Rhodes, where he founded Kamiros and built an altar of Zeus, surrounding it with magic metal bulls that would bellow if the island were invaded.

Oracles, however, are not made for nothing, and in later life we find Catreus going to Rhodes to visit his son, whom he had missed dearly for so many years. He arrived at night, and what with the darkness and the bellowing of the metal bulls, Althaemenes could neither see nor hear and was thus unable to identify his father and the Cretans. Naturally thinking that they were invaders, he slew them. When he realised his error in the morning he begged Mother Earth to swallow him up, which she did.

WHAT TO SEE

Rhodes town on the northern tip of the island is still the capital, and few island ports present such an opulent face to the visitor arriving by sea. Rising out of a lush garden are the massive walls of the old town and the Castle of the Knights; here and there graceful minarets add an Eastern touch, as does the seaside city market with its arched colonnade, bright with strings of lights at night. Monumental Italian public buildings loom to one side, on the other three windmills turn lazily. If your vessel is small, you enter the smallest of the city's three harbours, **Mandraki,** passing by the guardian bronze deer, male and female, high on their columns. Here is the site of the old fort of **Ag. Nikolaos,** with its small church. On larger ferry and cruise ships you enter the **commercial harbour,** nearer the Old Town walls.

The **walls,** 4 km (2½ miles) long, are very well preserved, considered a masterpiece of late medieval defences (they are only accessible with guided tours along their perimeter on Mondays and Saturdays at 2.45 pm for 300 dr.). Constructed on the foundation of the old Byzantine walls, mainly under the direction of four Grand Masters, d'Aubusson, d'Amboise, del Carretto and Villiers de l'Isle Adam, on average they are 12 metres (40 ft) thick. The walls are curved to better deflect missiles, and the landward sides were surrounded by a large moat 30 metres (100 ft) wide. Each section of the Knights was assigned a

The Harbour at Rhodes

239

certain area of the wall to defend (Catalan and Aragon together). Bastions and towers strengthened the defence of the wall, and many gates connected the Old Town with the village outside, the most magnificent of these being the **Gate of Emery d'Amboise** near the Palace of the Grand Masters, built in 1512. The Turks later blocked up the two harbour gates; they also made a law that all Greeks had to be outside the inner walls by sundown or forfeit their heads.

Inside the inner wall, or **Collachium,** which the Knights could defend if the outer wall were taken, are the different Inns and the **Palace of the Grand Masters** (open 8 am–7 pm, Sunday 8 am–6pm, closed Tuesday, entrance 300 dr.), also called Castello, for indeed it is more of a castle than a palace. The actual construction of the palace, on the site of a sanctuary of Helios, was completed in the 14th century and it survived intact under the Turks (who used it as a prison) until the Great Gunpowder Explosion of 1856 left it in ruins. Mussolini ordered its reconstruction as it stands today, and the Italians filled it with lovely mosaics and Hellenistic sculptures brought from Kos. They added an elevator and modern plumbing, intending to make it Il Duce's summer villa. However, the war ended before he could ever use it. In the garden below the palace a Sound and Light show is held most evenings (in English on Monday and Tuesday at 8.15 pm, Wednesday, Friday and Saturday at 9.15 pm, Thursday 10.15 pm).

The quiet, medieval Ippoton St (the street of the Knights) leads down from the palace. Of all the streets in the Old Town, this most evokes the past—not a single souvenir shop mars its length. Many of the Inns are in this area, including the French Inn, the Italian Inn, and the House of Villaragout on the street itself. The Inn of Provence and one of the Spanish Inns are on an alley by the French Inn. At the end of the street, if you turn toward Argyrokastro Square you will find the fine Auvergne Inn, today a cultural centre, and a 14th-century building constructed by Grand Master Roger de Pins and perhaps the original hospital of the Knights. The English Inn is nearby, built in 1483, but hard hit by an earthquake in 1851. Rebuilt by the British, it was bombed and renovated again in 1947. This was a praiseworthy effort, especially since the English left the Order of St John when the Pope excommunicated Henry VIII. The British consul of Rhodes (17, 25 Martiou St, tel. (0241) 27 306, open 8.30 am–1.30 pm) has the key to it.

The Hospital of the Knights, restored by the Italians, is in Plateia Symis and now houses the **Archaeology Museum** (open daily except Tuesday 8 am–7 pm, Sunday 8 am–6 pm, entrance 300 dr.), its star attraction the lovely Aphrodite of Rhodes, who provided the title for Lawrence Durrell's excellent book on the island, *Reflections on a Marine Venus.*

Also in Plateia Symis are the ruins of a **temple of Aphrodite,** dating from the 3rd century BC and discovered by the Italians in 1922. Another temple of the same epoch was dedicated to **Dionysos** and can be found near a corner in the wall behind the Ionian and Popular Bank. Also here is the **Museum of Decorative Arts** (open weekdays 8 am–1pm, Sunday 9 am–1 pm, closed Tuesdays, entrance 200 dr.), with folk arts and handicrafts from all over the Dodecanese, including costumes, embroideries and an interior of a traditional room. Nearby is the **Byzantine Museum,** housed in a 13th century church. The **fountain** on Argyrokastro Square is a reconstruction, found in the Byzantine fort at Arnitha. The tourist shops (amusingly for the isle of eternal sun, many sell only umbrellas and fur coats) get more dense as you approach the main shopping street of the Old Town, Sokratous St, its principle landmark the slender minaret of the lovely **Mosque of Suleiman,** across from the clock tower. Built in 1523 by Suleiman the Magnificent after he conquered Rhodes, the mosque is now closed.

The mosque marks the start of an area known as the **Turkish Quarter,** a fascinating zigzag of narrow streets. Turkish balconies of latticed wood project overhead beside crumbling stone arches and houses built directly over the street. On the square off Archelaos Street are the **Turkish baths,** built in 1765 (open daily except Sunday 5 pm–7 pm). Although heavily bombed, they have been restored to full working order by the city. The **Turkish library** is near the Mosque of Suleiman, containing some rare Persian and Arabian manuscripts. Another mosque, **Ibrahim Pasha,** is off Sophokles St. It was built in 1531, and the minaret was restored by the Italians.

Kastellania Palace, on Hippocrates Square, was built by d'Amboise in 1507 and served as a tribunal. It is near the **Evriaki,** or Jewish quarter of town. The **Plateia Evrion Martyron** (the Square of Hebrew Martyrs) recalls the Jewish inhabitants of Rhodes sent off to die in the concentration camps. A fountain with three seahorses is in the centre. At the end of Sokratous St the ruins of the **Virgin of Victory** church still stand, built by the Knights in thanksgiving for their defeat of the Turks in 1480.

NEW TOWN

Outside the walls, next to the taxi stand and the Sound and Light Show, is the Tourist Information Office of the City of Rhodes, open 8 am–8 pm, the National Tourist Office is up the hill at the corner of A. Papagou and Makariou Sts (open 8 am–2 pm), complete with a light-up map for the lost tourist. At either you can pick up a copy of the English paper, appropriately named "The Rhodes Tourist". Buses for points east on the island depart from Papagou St, for the west they leave from the **market,** with its seafront row of sweetshops which also sell inexpensive food. Excursion boats to Lindos, Symi and other destinations, as well as the diving school boat, dock near here.

To the north is an ensemble of fascisti-style public buildings—post office, theatre, city hall—all ungainly piles. On the shore, though, are the fine **Governor's Palace** and the church **Evangelismos,** both built by the Italians, the latter modelled on the Knights' church of St John in the Old Town, destroyed in an earthquake. Many Turkish notables are buried next to the **Mosque of Murad Reis,** named for the head pirate-admiral of the Egyptian Sultan, killed on the island in 1522 and buried in the circular turban. The mosque has a lovely, though crumbling, minaret. Next to it looms the once grand but now forlorn Hotel des Roses, awaiting resurrection of some kind, and a long stretch of beach that is invariably crowded. At the northernmost tip of the island is the **Aquarium** (open

241

daily 9 am–9 pm, entrance 150 dr.), the only one in all the Balkans, with tanks of Mediterranean fish and sea turtles, and a wonderful horror show collection of stuffed creatures, their twisted grimaces the result not of any prolonged agony but amateur taxidermy. Another beach stretches from the aquarium down the west coast, but it's often deserted—the west coast of Rhodes is frequently battered by strong winds.

Many places in town hire out bicycles, scooters and cars, but any reasonably active visitor can walk to **Mt Smith,** named after Admiral Sydney Smith who kept watch on Napoleon's Egyptian escapades from here. On the way there (north Epirous St) are the ruins of an **Asklepieion,** or temple to the god of healing, and the **Cave of the Nymphs,** Mt Smith was the ancient akropolis of the Rhodians. On the top, the Italians have partly reconstructed a **temple of Pythian Apollo** (later associated with the sun god Helios). It belongs to the Doric order and dates from the 2nd century BC. A few columns also remain of temples of Zeus and Athena, and one can distinguish the outline of a 3rd-century BC **stadium,** The **ancient theatre** has been reconstructed, and hosts Classical dramas in July (see the Tourist Office for programme details).

Other Rhodian efforts to amuse visitors include the **Casino** at the Grand Hotel on Akti Miaoulis where the guests may win or lose their fortunes at roulette and baccarat **Folk dances** by the Nelly Dimoglou company are performed nightly, except Saturday, in the Old City Theatre from June until October (for information tel. (0241) 20 157 or 27 524). At lovely Rodini Park, peacocks strut where Aeschines built his School of Rhetoric in 330 BC, in July through August merry drinkers join them at the **Wine Festival**. It is open from 7 pm to 1 am, and buses bring revellers to and from Mandraki harbour. As well as Rhodian and other Greek wines, there is music, dance and food, although one must pay for the food.

EAST COAST

Just south-east of Rhodes, **Kallithea** is an old thermal spa in a magnificent kitsch Italianate, Moorish building, no longer used, although there are plans for its restoration. Kallithea has small sandy coves for swimming; **Faliraki** further south is a major resort near a long sandy beach.

One can play golf at **Afandou** one of the three golf courses in Greece. It has 18 holes and there are also tennis courts. There are fine beaches in the bay below, and at **Ladiko** Anthony Quinn has his own personal stretch of sand. At **Kolymbia** village down the coast many large farms are supplied with water from the tiny village of **Epta Pigi,** the Seven Springs.

Archangelos, continuing down the main highway is the largest village on Rhodes. From there one may visit the two churches Archangelos Gabriel and Archangelos Michael (the village church), considered two of the prettiest on the island; another, Ag. Theodoroi, has old frescoes. The villagers have a reputation for their musicianship and their bootmaking; local cobblers can make footwear to order. The ruined castle on the hill belonged to the Knights.

One of the strongest forts of the Knights is below Malona at **Faraclos**. It was occupied originally by pirates, whom the Knights chased out, repairing the walls and using it as a prison. Even after the rest of the island was conquered, the Castle of Faraclos held out against the Turks, only falling after a long determined siege. There is also a cave there and a lovely enclosed beach at the fishing hamlet of Haraki.

Beautifully situated **Lindos** is the second most important town on Rhodes, both historically and for today's tourists. Of the three ancient cities it was the largest and most important, inhabited from 2000 BC; the first temple on its magnificent akropolis dated back to 1510 BC. Of its many colonies, the city which has become Naples, Italy is the most famous. Part of its early importance lies in its natural harbour, the only one on Rhodes, and in its early ruler Cleobulos, one of the Seven Sages of Greece, who lived during the 6th century BC: his maxim "Nothing to Excess" was engraved on the oracle at Delphi. He created a reservoir which supplies water to Lindos to this day. Lindos today is a charming place, a National Historical Landmark, where no new building is allowed. The narrow pebbled streets are lined with elegant 15th, 16th- and 17th-century "Captain's mansions", built during the Turkish occupation when merchants from Lindos managed most of the island's trade. Almost all of these have been restored, many by foreigners. Below the village are two fine beaches and towering high above within the walls of a Knights' castle, is the **Akropolis,** one of the most stunningly sited in all of Greece.

You can either rent a donkey or walk up the narrow, serpentine streets to the **akropolis** (open daily 8 am–5.30 pm, Sunday 8 am–4.30 pm, entrance 400 dr.), lined with a solid display of blouses, tablecloths and other items put out for sale by the good women of Lindos, who sit by their wares, needlepoint in hand, as if weaving the fates of the thousands of tourists who pass them every day. The akropolis is reached by a high stairway built by the Knights of St John. Note the trireme carved in the rock before climbing, a statue of Agesander, priest of Poseidon, once stood there, sculpted by Pythocretes, better known for his Victory of Samothrace. At the top of the steps one passes through two medieval vaulted rooms. To the right is a 13th-century **Church of St John** in poor repair, and straight ahead is the raised Dorian arcade of Lindian Athenas, the patron goddess of the city. From here the "stairway to Heaven" leads up to the **Propylaea** and the **temple** itself, of which only seven columns are standing, were built in the 4th century BC and reconstructed by the Italians. The pride of the temple was the golden inscription it once contained of Pindar's Seventh Ode.

The view from the akropolis encompasses a wide area, most striking towards the small, circular deep blue harbour where St Paul landed in AD 58. The small chapel dedicated to him has a huge paneyeri on 28 June. In the larger bay the once great Lindian navy of 500 ships berthed.

Many of the houses in the village have collections of the famous Lindian ware, painted plates occasionally dating back to Byzantium. The inhabitants learned the art from the East and produced some true masterpieces in the folk tradition, a few of which can be seen at the **Papakonstandis** mansion, now the Lindos museum. Lindos also has a reputation for embroideries dating back to the time of Alexander the Great. A sperveri, the fine bridal dress that all Lindian girls once wore, can be seen at **Kashines house** In the **Panayia church** in the centre of town are many excellent Byzantine works of art. The Church itself was founded in 1779. There is a beach, Palestra, many restaurants, and a huge plane tree in the square which makes waiting for the bus a pleasant experience. At a distance, by the harbour, is the **tomb of Cleobulos,** now converted to the church Ag. Milianos.

Lardos, west of Lindos, is a pretty little village. The beach below it has sand dunes: indeed the whole south-east coast of Rhodes is a series of sandy beaches, many of them deserted, though good fish tavernas and rooms to rent may be found at **Pefki,** just south of Lindos and at **Chiotari, Gennadi** and **Plimiri.** At the southernmost tip, **Prassonisi Cape,** the landscape takes on an other-worldly aspect in its desolation. Skiadi Monastery is the only place in the area to spend the night.

UP THE WEST COAST

Apolakia, like the whole of this section of coast, is very subject to wind. It is a charming village and produces the best water melons on Rhodes. Further up the coast, **Monolithos** is the most important village of the region, surrounded as its name implies by huge monoliths. On a rocky cliff 200 metres (650 ft) high is a castle built by the Grand Master d'Aubusson. A fairly difficult footpath winds its way to the top. In the walls is the frescoed chapel of Ag. Panteleimon (15th century), and at sunset there are magnificent views over Halki. Below, the shady bay of **Fourni** has a beach, and caves with signs of ancient occupation, and not far away is the monastery Ag. Anastasia.

One of the most traditional villages left on Rhodes is **Embona** in the mountains, where the dances of the women are exceptional. Old people wear their traditional dress every day. Increasingly though, the village is visited by tour buses from Rhodes **Mt Ataviros,** the Dodecanese' highest peak (1215 metres/3986 ft) is a two-hour climb from Embona. Here Althaemenes is said to have built the temple of Zeus Atavros, though little remains of it now. But there are views of the whole island from the summit, and on a clear day they say you can see Crete from the peak; perhaps poor Althaemenes used to come up here when he longed, like all Cretans, for his mother island. Althaemenes supposedly founded the village below Embona, **Kritinia,** which he named in honour of Crete.

Kamiros, one of the three ancient Dorian cities of Rhodes, was abandoned in the dark ages, covered with the dust of centuries and forgotten until 1859, when two archaeologists, Biliotti and Salzmann, began excavating where some villagers had uncovered a few graves. The city which was eventually brought to light is well preserved, the **cemetery,** in particular, rendered many beautiful items and in archaeological terms was one of the richest ever discovered in Greece. An excellent water and drainage system, supplied by a large reservoir, served the many houses which have been excavated. Also to be seen are the baths, the agora with its rostrum for public speeches, the Great Stoa with its Doric columns near the akropolis, and a temple, possibly of Apollo Kamiros (open daily 8 am–7 pm, Sunday 8 am–6pm, entrance 200 dr.).

Kamiros Skala, a modern fishing village about 16 km (10 miles) south of Kamiros, may have been the city's port; today it serves as the port for the caique from Halki.

On a high hill over the village of **Salakos** are the ruins of another medieval fort; the village below is praised for its shade and fresh water, some of which comes from the Spring of the Nymphs. This region, well wooded, with views of the sea, is one of the prettiest in Rhodes, and a tranquil place to walk. Further up the road leads to Mt Profitis Ilias (790 metres/2600 ft). The trees here belong to the Prophet Elijah, who according to legend slays anyone who cuts them down.

Another enchanting spot, if you manage to get there before the tour buses, is the **Valley of the Butterflies,** or Betaloudes. Intersected by a tiny stream, the valley is long and shady, full of fairy-tale trees and wooden bridges. From June to September a sooty orange species of butterfly (*Callimorpha quadripuctaria*) flocks here, attracted by the sweet resin of the storax tree, which is used to make frankincense. The butterflies rise in a cloud when you clap your hands (open daily 9 am–6 pm, entrance 100 dr.). A little way up the road is a monastery, **Panayia Kalopetra,** claimed to have been built by the hero who began the Greek revolution in 1821, Alexander Ypsilantis. Below Kalamonas is the very popular beach Paradissi and the airport.

Kremasti, a village of few tourists, is best known for its wonder-working icon, Panayias Kremasti, for which one of the biggest paneyeri in the Dodecanese takes place between 15 and 23 August, climaxing on the 23rd. Villagers bring out their native costumes and are said to dance a wonderful sousta. On **Mt Phileri-mos** nearby stood the akropolis of the ancient city of **Ialysos,** called Orychoime. Ialysos, the least important of the three ancient cities, is situated near Trianda village, but its akropolis presents the greatest interest. On the site of an older Phoenician temple are the remains of a **temple of Athena** from the 3rd century BC, and a 4th-century **Doric fountain,** discovered by the Italians. A basilica built in the first millennium has been restored with frescoes. The **cemetery** yielded finds from Mycenaean to Hellenistic times. At the Byzantine fortress at Orychoime, Our Lady of Philerimos, the Genoese fought John Cantacuzene in 1248, there are a few Byzantine churches nearby.

Nearby **Trianda,** a resort area, was settled by Minoans in 1600 BC, and may have been damaged in the explosions and subsequent tidal wave from Santorini. Near here at Avra beach there is **Greece Miniature,** a scaled down model of Greece and its islands for the bored tourist to meander around. Some people at **Asgouru** practise the Muslim faith, and the mosque and minaret there were once part of a church of St John. There are many oak trees in the area around Rodini Park.

Caiques leave Mandraki in the mornings for the following beaches: **Lardos,**

Tsambika, Faliraki, Kallithea, Ladiko, Kolymbia and **Lindos**. Most are on the east coast.

PANEYERIA
In August, dance festivals at Kallithies, Maritsa and Embona; 29–30 July, Ag. Soula at Soroni, an occasion for donkey races; 28 June at Lindos; 14 June, Profitis Ammos at Philerimos; 26 July, Ag. Panteleimonos at Siana; 7 September, at Monastery Tsabikas, when barren women go to pray for fertility; 14–22 August at Kremasti; 26 August, Ag. Fanourious in the Old Town; 5 September, Ag. Trias near Rhodes; 13 September, Stavros at Apollona and Kallithies; 26 September, Ag. Ioannis Theologos at Artamiti; 18 October, Ag. Lukos at Afandou; 7 November at Archangelos; carnival at Apokries; Scandinavian mid-summer festivities in Rhodes town.

WHERE TO STAY
Rhodes has a plethora of accommodation in every class and price range. Many places are booked solid by package tours 12 months of the year, but there are so many rooms available on the island that you're bound to find something, though it may be inconvenient.

In Rhodes town, at the top of the list, is the **Grand Hotel Astir Palace** on Akti Miaouli (tel. 0241 26 284), a deluxe hotel with the island's casino, a nightclub, tennis courts and what's reputed to be the largest swimming pool in the country. Singles here begin at 12 000 dr., doubles 16 000 dr. In the same category is the **Miramare** (tel. 0241 24 251/4), which is directly on the beach in Ixia and offers bungalows as well as hotel rooms. Rates here are 10 000 dr. a single, 14 000 dr. a double and 18 000 dr. for a bungalow. Also in Ixia the **Rodos Bay** (tel. 0241 23 661/5) has bungalows by its private beach as well as a pool. The rooftop restaurant has one of Rhodes' finest views. Prices here begin at 8500 dr. for a double, 12 500 dr. for a bungalow.

There are scores of class B, C and D hotels in and around Rhodes town, especially in the new quarter. One of the best value here is the **Ambassadeur,** a class C hotel at 53 Othonos & Amalias (tel. 0241 24 679) where a double is 5000 dr. a night.

Most of the inexpensive (and honestly most interesting) places to stay are in the old town. Look around Omirou Street, where the cleanest and friendliest spot is **Steves Pension** at no. 60 (tel. 0241 24 357) where a double is around 2500 dr. Another, very informal, pension is the **Apollon** at no. 28, with laundry facilities and hot showers and doubles for 2000 dr., 600 dr. for the courtyard space. Very clean and with roof space available if it's full. **Dionysos Pension** at 75 Platanos is located just off the main drag, again for around 2300 dr. a double. A little more expensive, near the Square of the Jewish Martyrs (look for signs) **Nikos Pension** (tel. 0241 23 423), with some baths attached; the rooms are very comfortable and quiet.

In Lindos, where it's illegal to build hotels, nearly every other house has been converted into a holiday villa, and if you want to stay at one you'll have to book through a holiday company before you arrive. Nearby is the new **Lindos Bay Hotel** (tel. 0244 42 212) on the beach and within walking distance of town. A double here begins at 7000 dr.

Other, less expensive (on the whole) beach hotels run down the west coast of the island solidly to Paradisos. In the south half of the island the pickings are sparse—little rooms over tavernas and the like. To get away from the sun and fun crowds, there are two Swiss chalets that lost their way and ended up in the eastern Mediterranean, near the top of Mt Profitis Ilias to be specific, in the midst of a pine forest. These are the **Elafos** (the stag) and the **Elafina** (doe), both class A, quiet and comfortable and not as silly as they sound. The telephone is 0246 21 221 for both; rates are around 6000 dr. for a double. There's a campsite at Lardos, 2 km from Lindos (tel. 0244 44 203).

EATING OUT
The cheapest food to eat in Rhodes is in the market, where you can get several varieties of souvlaki and grilled meats in the numerous little tavernas. In the old town there are several places that specialise in fish, much frequented by the locals, especially **Coralli** near the corner of Sokratous and Ippodamou Streets. Good Greek food may be had in the little square off Sofocleous Street, at the **Taverna Trata,** where the owner grills the orders right out in front; dinners here average 1000 dr. **Spilia** at 24 Eshilou is also good and known for its impromptu entertainment, but you never know on which night. **D'Angleterre,** on Diakou St is, oddly enough, neither French nor English, but a rather ritzy Danish restaurant with all the authentic Nordic grub to keep any viking happy, with the price of a full meal at least 2000 dr. Cheaper, on Akti Miaouli, is another Danish restaurant, **The Danish House,** where it's almost the real thing and good value at about 1500 dr. for dinner with healthy belts of schnapps and Danish beer.

In Lindos prices are very lofty and the service the rudest in all Greece. Nearly everyone who has dined there has a story to tell. In Kamiros Skala there are several tavernas—actually you'll find one anywhere there's a hint of a beach.

TOURIST INFORMATION
NTOG, Papagon and Makariou St, tel. (0241) 23 255.
City of Rhodes Tourist Information Centre, Sound and Light Sq, tel. (0241) 35 945.
Tourist Police, Papagon and Makariou St, tel. (0241) 27 423.
British Consulate 17, 25th Martiou, tel. (0241) 27 306.

SYMI

CONNECTIONS
At least one tourist boat a day from Rhodes; hydrofoils from Rhodes and Kos; two ferries a week with the other Dodecanese and Piraeus; in season hydrofoils

from Rhodes and Kos. Infrequent connections with Sitia and Ag. Nikolaos, Crete.

Few other islands have the crisp brightness of Symi, with its theatre of half-restored, half-derelict neo-Classical mansions, stacked one on top of the other like a Cubist lemon meringue. There are few trees to block the sun, for Symi is a dry island, unable to support many visitors. Most who do come arrive and depart on the excursion boat from Rhodes, and when they're gone, Symi regains much of its serenity. The island is especially popular among the English, many of whom rent houses here. Although Symi can get hot in the middle of summer, its climate is quite pleasant for the rest of the year.

HISTORY
According to legend, Symi was a princess of Ialysos on Rhodes, who was stolen away by Glaukos, the builder of the *Argo*, and ended up on the little island that bears her name. If such was the case, their descendants inherited Glaukos' shipbuilding skills, a craft they have excelled in throughout their history (and one largely responsible for the current lack of trees).

Pelasgian walls in Chorio attest to the prehistoric settlement of Symi, the first inhabitants probably coming from Karia. In the *Iliad* Homer tells how the island mustered three ships for the Acheans at Troy, led by King Nireus. After Achilles Nireus was the most beautiful of all the Greeks, but that didn't prevent the Trojans from killing him. In historic times Symi joined the Dorian Hexopolis initiating the island's domination by Rhodes, which lasted throughout antiquity. The Romans fortified the akropolis at Chorio, which became a Byzantine fort, later renovated by the first Grand Master of the Knights of Rhodes, Foulques de Villaret. From the Kastro the Knights could signal to Rhodes, and they favoured the swift Symiote skiffs for their raiding activities.

During this time the island began to know a certain measure of prosperity primarily through shipbuilding and trade. When Suleiman the Magnificent came to the Dodecanese in 1522, the Symiotes avoided a battle by offering him beautiful sponges, which became their yearly tribute to the Sultan in return for a relative degree of independence. Like the Knights, the Turks made use of the swift Symiote ships, this time for relaying messages. In order to keep Symi thriving, the Sultan declared it a free port and gave the inhabitants the rights to dive freely for sponges in Turkish waters.

Little Symi thus became the third most important island of the Dodecanese, a position it held from the 17th to the 19th centuries. Rich mansions were constructed befitting the islanders' new prosperity. Many of them also bought land in Asia Minor. Schools thrived. Even after certain privileges were withdrawn because of its participation in the 1821 revolution, the island continued to flourish. The Italian occupation and the steamship, however, spelt the end of Symi's glory. The Italians closed up the lands of Asia Minor and thus the island's lumber source for shipbuilding, and the steamship killed the demand for wooden sailing vessels altogether. At the end of the Second World War the treaty giving the Dodecanese to Greece was signed on Symi on 1 March 1948.

WHAT TO SEE

Symi's capital is divided into two quarters: Yialos in the harbour region and Chorio, the older settlement on the hill. In **Yialos** are centred most of the tourist facilities and what is left of the island's shipyards. In honour of its shipbuilding history, a copy of the stone-carved trireme of the Lindos akropolis has been erected by the harbour. Near it is the restaurant and pension **Les Katerinettes,** where a plaque commemorates the signing of the 1948 treaty in the building. At the end of the harbour, in an ungainly concrete clock tower, is the local Tourist Office, only open in summer. Beyond the clock tower, the statue of the fishing boy, and the Nireus hotel is the small **Charani** bay where many ships wait to be finished or repaired. Here especially one can see the result of the bombing during the Second World War, which damaged so many of Symi's lovely old houses. There are no beaches near Yialos, but **Nos,** at the end of Charani, is where the local people swim. There are plans to build a marine museum in the vicinity.

Most of the houses in Yialos date from the 19th century. Older architecture may be seen at **Chorio,** connected to the neo-Classical port by a dirt road or the stairway from Plateia tis Skala. Mansions, mostly neo-Classical, line the way. By the derelict windmills is a **stone monument** erected by the Spartans for their victory over the Athenians off the coast of Symi, a battle mentioned by Thucydides. Houses in Chorio are similar to Cycladic houses, small and asymmetrical, although the residents have often incorporated neo-Classical elements to ornament their doorways and windows. Many houses have very lovely interiors with carved woodwork.

Among the most interesting buildings at Chorio are the **19th-century pharmacy;** the fortress-mansion **Chatziagapitos;** and the churches with their pebble mosaics of evil mermaids sinking hapless ships. The island's **museum** is also up at Chorio, containing objects dating from Hellenistic times to the present. At the **Kastro,** the Byzantine and medieval walls were built from ancient material, including the temple of Athena referred to in an ancient inscription. The coat-of-arms belongs to D'Aubusson and the most interesting church of the village is by the walls, called **Megali Panayia,** with frescoes and post-Byzantine icons.

From Chorio it is a half-hour walk to **Pedhi,** the only fertile area on Symi. On a small bay, it has a beach and is the best place on the island to camp out.

A new road from Chorio links the town with the island's other main attraction, the **monastery of Taxiarchis, Michael Panormitis** (in the summer there are also caiques, and the tourist boat from Rhodes often stops there). The monastery, at the extreme south of the island is dedicated to Symi's patron saint, who was also adopted by Greek sailors. The monastery dates from the 18th century (at least). The **iconostasis** in the church is a remarkable work of carved wood, and there are many 18th-century frescoes and gold and silver ship votives. In the

249

sacristy are more rich gifts from faithful sailors, and little bottles which drifted to shore with money for the monastery. Panormitis also has one of the best beaches on the island, and there are restaurants and cafés and rooms to rent, more reminiscent of a tourist pavilion than a religious sanctuary Sesklia, an islet near Panormitis, belongs to the monastery. Its ancient name was Teutlousa, and Thucydides writes that it was here that the defeated Athenians took refuge after their sea battle with the Spartans during the Peloponnesian War. A few Pelasgian walls remain, and there are also a few ruins on the nearby islet Stroggilos.

The other sites of Symi are also religious in nature. Of the 77 churches, the most interesting is Michael Roukoumiotis, an hour's walk from Yialos. Built in the 18th century, it is a rather strange combination of Gothic and folk architecture. Its paneyeri is held beneath the old umbrella-shaped cypress tree. Ag. Emilianos is on an islet in the bay of the same name, connected to the shore by a causeway with a pebbly beach nearby Ag. Noulias (18th century) is a half-hour walk from Chorio, and nearby Ag. Marina had a famous school before the revolution broke out.

PANEYERIA
5 May, Ag. Athanasios; 21 May, Ag. Konstantinos; 4 June, Analypsis; 24 June, Ag. Ioannis; 17 July, Ag. Marinas; 6 August, Nymborio and Panormitis; 15 August, Panayias; 8 November, Taxiarchis at the monastery.

WHERE TO STAY
Except for the rooms at the Monastery, all the island's accommodation is in town. The two prettiest places to stay are both in old sea captains' mansions, each lovingly restored with fine wood interiors. These are the Aliki (tel. 0241 71 665) and the Dorian (tel. 0241 71 181); rooms here are 5500–7500 dr. Symi Tours by the harbour (tel. 0241 71 307) has a large listing of houses for rent in town. On the less expensive side there are rooms to let here and there, usually on the condition that you stay three nights (to economise on sheet washing—water is scarce). The Pension Les Katerinettes near the boat landing is very pleasant (tel. 0241 71 676); another option in town is the Pension Agli (tel. 0241 71 392) in Plateia tis Skalas, where rates are around 2500 dr. for a double.

EATING OUT
Les Katerinettes restaurant has good food, if a bit expensive (1500 dr. for a full meal). For a meal with a view, try George's near the top of Chorio, where dinner is around 800–1000 dr.

TOURIST INFORMATION
Clock Tower, Gialos, tel. (0241) 71 215.

TILOS

CONNECTIONS
Twice a week Dodecanese steamer to the other islands and Piraeus; in the summer occasional tourist boat and hydrofoil from Rhodes, Symi and Kos; twice a week from Halki. Infrequent connections with Crete.

One of the least visited islands in Greece, Tilos still tries to do its best for visitors; one village, Livadia, has even gone so far as to build communal bungalows from public funds. It is a wonderful place to do nothing; a dreaminess surrounds all practical activities and the visitor who neglects to wind his watch is in danger of losing all track of time. While parts of Tilos are arable and there's water (though it's turned off in the evening), much of it is desolate, though pockets of sandy beach may be found along the island's indented shoreline. The only really remarkable thing about Tilos is that mastadon bones were discovered in one of its caves. The other remarkable thing is that it has managed to stay just about the same over the years.

WHAT TO SEE
The islanders live in two settlements: the port **Livadia,** with a rocky beach; 8 km (5 miles) up the road, the capital **Megalo Chorio.** This is on the site of ancient Tilos, and near the castle you can see Pelasgian walls built by the earliest known residents (if you discount the mastadons) dating from 1000 BC. The castle, or Kastro was built by the Venetians, incorporating a Classical gateway and stone from the ancient akropolis. There is a pleasant beach and taverna near Megalo Chorio at **Nausica,** and paths lead down to other small beaches. In Megalo Chorio a one-room museum awaits a brilliant discovery. Further north is the deserted village of Mikro Chorio and the cave where the mastadon bones were discovered. The best beaches are at **Erestos** and **Plaka.**

Besides no water in the evenings, be warned that transport between Livadia and Megalo Chorio may be hard to find (except when a ship comes in) and there is little fresh food available except around midsummer; even the bread is shipped in from Rhodes. But the people are very kind and help as much they can.

PANEYERIA
25–27 July, Ag. Panteleimonos; 28 June, Ag. Pavlos; 17 January, Ag. Antonio at Megalo Chorio.

WHERE TO STAY
In Livadia you'll find Tilos' one hotel, the **Hotel Livadia,** a slightly down at heel class E establishment with doubles at 2000 dr. a night (tel. 0241 52 202). When

it's full you can start looking for rooms in the village (but not before). There are also rooms up in Megalo Chorio and at Erestos; the fancy apartments in Livadia are always booked by a holiday company. You can also camp out on any beach without protests.

EATING OUT
There are little tavernas in Livadia and the **Blue Sky** near the ferry boat landing, the most likely place to change money on the island (though don't count on it). The food is nothing special here or anywhere else on Tilos, but it's inexpensive and pure Greek. There are also a couple of tavernas in Megalo Chorio and at Erestos.

TOURIST POLICE
See regular police in Megalo Chorio, tel. (0241) 53 222.

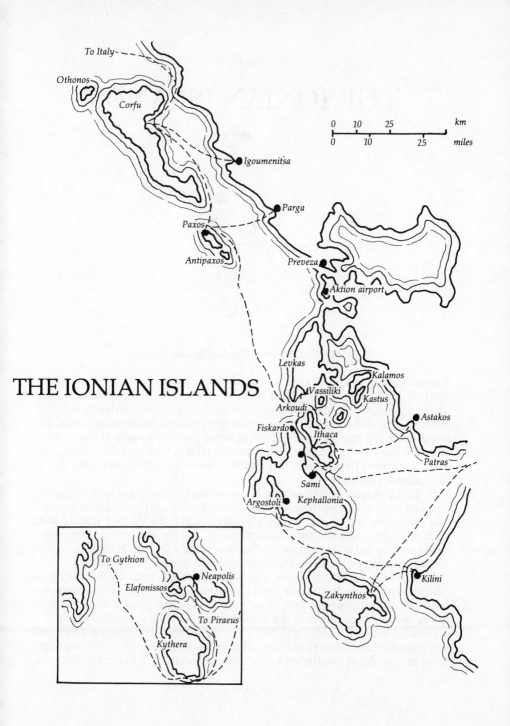

Part VI

THE IONIAN ISLANDS

To Italy

Othonos

Corfu

Igoumenitsa

0   10   25   km
0   10   25   miles

Parga

Paxos

Antipaxos

Preveza

Aktion airport

Levkas

Kalamos

Vassiliki

Kastus

Arkoudi

Astakos

Fiskardo

Ithaca

Patras

Sami

Argostoli

Kephallonia

Kilini

Zakynthos

To Gythion

Neapolis

Elafonissos

To Piraeus

Kythera

THE IONIAN ISLANDS

The "Heyl Aphrodite", Staatliches Museum, Berlin

The seven main islands scattered randomly in the Ionian Sea, from Corfu in the north to Kythera at the southern tip of the Peloponnese, have been lumped together politically since the Byzantine era and thus more or less share a common history, although individually the seven are quite distinct, both geologically and in character. Until recently connections between the islands were scanty at best. Now—at least in the summer—you can with relative ease visit six of them, and there's a ferry to Italy (usually to Brindisi, Otranto or Bari) from Corfu, Paxos, Kephallonia and Ithaca.

In the off season getting around becomes more difficult not only in making connections but because from late October to March there is frequent heavy rain. The rains give the Ionian islands a lushness which the Aegean islands lack; springtime, especially in Corfu, is breathtaking, and the autumn wild flowers are nearly as beautiful as those in spring. Summers tend to be hot, lacking the natural air-conditioning provided on the other islands by the meltemi wind.

Corfu, with numerous direct flights from abroad, remains the queen of tourism, with its lovely Venetian town and natural beauty. The other islands are relatively unspoilt, earthquakes, most notably the great disaster of 1953, have ruined most of their old Venetian buildings, but not their quiet charm.

Situated between Greece and Italy, the Ionian islands for many years were out of the mainstream of Greek politics, although from the beginning of their history to the present day the inhabitants have remained undeniably Hellenes. Not to be confused with Ionia in Asia Minor, the name Ionian here is derived rather from Io of mythology, one of the victims of Zeus' love whom Hera, his wife, unjustly punished. About to be caught in the company of Io, Zeus changed the girl into a white cow, but Hera was not fooled. She asked Zeus to give her the cow as a present, and kept it under careful surveillance. With the help of Hermes, Io escaped, only to be followed by a terrible stinging gad fly which chased her all over the world. One of the first places through which she fled was the eastern part of the Adriatic Sea, which has since been named the Ionian Sea in honour of the tormented girl.

Very little remains of the ancient past on the islands, although they were probably settled in the Stone Age by people from Illyria (present-day Albania) and then by the Eretrians. Homer was the first to mention them, and were he the last they would still be immortal as the homeland of crafty Odysseus. From the 8th century BC, mercantile Corinth colonised the islands and they were of no small importance in trade and relations between Greece and the colonies to the west, particularly Sicily. One of them, Corfu, became so strong that when Corinth's policies went counter to her will, she challenged and defeated at sea the mother city, allying herself with Athens (Corinth was an ally of Sparta). This event triggered off the disastrous Peloponnesian War, as it forced the Spartans either to submit to this expansion of the Athenian Empire and control of western trade, or to attack. They attacked.

The Romans incorporated the Ionian islands into their province Achaia, a classification still current today in Greek administration. After the fall of the Roman Empire, Goths from Italy over-ran the islands, and it is because of their wholesale decimations that so few monuments of antiquity remain today. The Byzantine Empire realised the strategic importance of the islands as a bridge between east and west and fortified them. During the Second Crusade, however, the Normans took the islands by surprise and established garrisons on them, which they used as bases to plunder the rest of Greece. With a great deal of difficulty the Byzantines succeeded in forcing them out of Corfu at least, although the Normans were almost immediately replaced by the Venetians, who claimed the islands in the land grab after the Sack of Constantinople in 1204. The southern islands became part of the County Palatine of Kephallonia when the claims of the Sicilian Norman pirates, Vetrano and Count Orsini, were eliminated by the crucifixion of the former. Corfu, however, was occupied for 150 years by the Angevins, a rule so bitter that the inhabitants surrendered their island to the "protection" of Venice.

Venetian rule was hardly a bed of roses, even though it was Christian (the Orthodox and the Catholics never stopped considering each other heretics). The average Greek in fact preferred the Turks, who allowed the people a measure of self-government and demanded fewer taxes. Some of the Ionian islands actually did come under Turkish rule. The Ottomans were expelled in 1499, although they returned as the Venetian Republic weakened. Despite all their faults, the Venetians were at least more tolerant of artists than the Turks, as Muslims forbade all representations of the human figure, and in the 17th century the Ionian islands provided a refuge for painters, especially from Crete. The Ionian school of art, as it is known, is noted for its fusion of Byzantine and Renaissance styles.

In 1796, after Napoleon had conquered the Venetian Republic, he considered the Ionian islands of the utmost importance to his schemes and took them with the Treaty of Campo Formio. In 1799 a combined Russo–Turkish fleet took the islands from him, forming the independent Septinsular Republic under their protection (and safeguarding the islands against any danger of attack from the notorious tyrant of Epirus, Ali Pasha, who coveted them).

Although the Septinsular Republic did not last long (it was nullified by the Treaty of Tilsit in 1807 which returned the islands to Napoleon), it was the first time in almost four centuries that any Greeks were allowed independent rule, and it helped to inspire the later revolution in 1821; the British taking of the Ionian islands in 1815 was considered another sign of encouragement.

Although the British re-formed the Ionian State, they retained the right of military protection and appointed an English High Commissioner who took precedence over the Ionian parliament. Sir Thomas Maitland, the first High Commissioner, has gone down in history as probably the most disliked British representative ever to govern; he assumed dictatorial powers, and deeply offended the Greeks by giving the city of Parga, an important port on the mainland, to the tyrant Ali Pasha, obeying an obscure clause in the 1815 treaty that no one expected him to comply with. All the Pargians then emigrated to Corfu, rather than submit to Ali Pasha. Other High Commissioners were little better (at least from the Greek point of view) and the Ionian State never stopped demanding or conspiring for union with Greece. The British (since they now had Cyprus) agreed to cede the islands in 1864—but only after blowing up all the fortresses on Corfu. During the Second World War Italy took the islands, but Mussolini's dream of creating another Ionian State under Italian protection was shattered in 1943 when the Germans occupied the islands. Many of the Italian troops joined the Greeks in their resistance, and many were killed by their former allies in the Axis, marking one of the turning points in the fall of Italian fascism.

A couple of notes: the cheapest and easiest way to reach the islands from Athens is by bus. All of these depart from the suburban station at 100 Kifissou St, reached by city bus from Omonia Square. Phone numbers for bus times are (in Athens) 512 94 43 for Corfu; 512 35 83 for Lefkas; 512 94 98 for Kephallonia and Ithaca; and 512 94 32 for Zakynthos. Secondly, there's a long-established company that specialises in renting villas on Paxos, Ithaca, Kephallonia, Zakynthos and Kythera called Greek Islands Club; you can get their brochure by writing to Villa Centre Holidays, 66 High St, Walton-on-Thames, Surrey, KT12 1BU, tel. (0932) 220477.

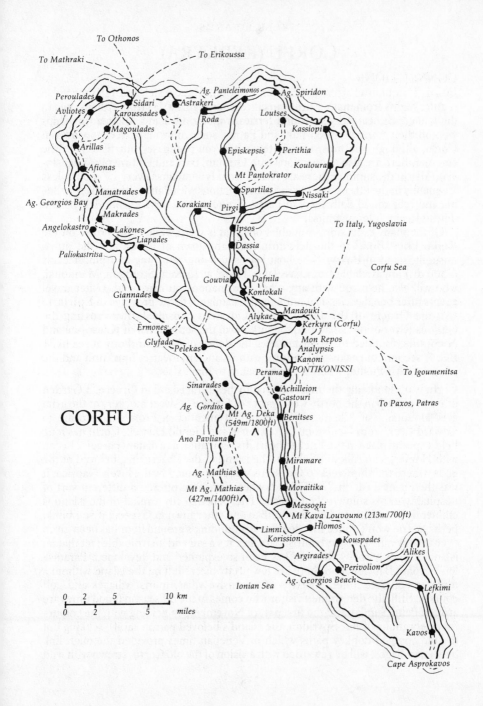

To Othonos

To Erikoussa

To Mathraki

Peroulades
Avliotes
Sidari   Astrakeri
Ag. Panteleimonos   Ag. Spiridon
Karoussades   Roda   Loutses
Magoulades   Kassiopi
Arillas   Episkepsis   Perithia
Afionas   Mt Pantokrator   Kouloura
Manatrades   Spartilas
Ag. Georgios Bay   Korakiani   Pirgi   Nissaki
Makrades   Ipsos
Angelokastro   Lakones   To Italy, Yugoslavia
Liapades   Dassia
Paliokastritsa   Corfu Sea
Gouvia   Dafnila
Giannades   Kontokali
Ermones   Mandouki
Alykae   Kerkyra (Corfu)
Glyfada   Mon Repos
Pelekas   Analypsis
Kanoni
Perama   PONTIKONISSI   To Igoumenitsa
Sinarades
Ag. Gordios   Achilleion
Gastouri   To Paxos, Patras
CORFU   Mt Ag. Deka   Benitses
(549m/1800ft)
Ano Pavliana
Miramare
Ag. Mathias
Mt Ag. Mathias   Moraitika
(427m/1400ft)   Messoghi
Mt Kava Louvouno (213m/700ft)
Limni   Hlomos
Korission   Kouspades
Argirades   Alikes
Perivolion
Ionian Sea   Ag. Georgios Beach
Lefkimi
0   2   5   10 km
0   2   5   miles   Kavos

Cape Asprokavos

CORFU (KERKYRA)

CONNECTIONS

By air: Frequent charter flights from London, Manchester and Glasgow; also regular flights from many European cities; four flights a day from Athens, two in the winter. By sea: All year round ferries from Brindisi and Ancona (the ships stop on their route between Italy and Patras, some allowing a free stop-over in Corfu, although you must specify this when you purchase your ticket). In the summer there are also connections with Otranto, Bari and Dubrovnik (Yugoslavia). Also in the summer there are ferries from Igoumenitsa every $1^{1}/_{2}$ hours, less frequently in the off season. In season connections with Patras, Ithaca, Kephallonia and year round daily ferry to Paxos. Frequent bus service from Athens and Thessaloniki to Igoumenitsa.

Of the many excursions available, one that is worthwhile is the cruise on the **Rena 'Love Boat'** to the delightful mainland town of **Parga** and the quiet, unspoilt island of **Paxos.** The boat leaves at 8 am, returning at 7 pm. Tickets (3500 dr.) are available from Vassilakis Travel at 13 Xen. Stratigou, Mandouki, who will also help you with any other information you may need. Other travel agents offer one day classical tours to the mainland; to the province of **Epiris,** to visit the **Oracle of the Dead,** which Odysseus consulted after crossing the perilous River of the Dead into the unknown, the settlements of **Kassopea** and **Nicopolis,** founded by Augustus after the defeat of Mark Anthony at sea in 31 BC. A second tour takes in **Dodoni,** with its ancient theatre, **Ioannina** and the **island of Ali Pasha,** where a tiny museum to him exists.

Corfu is undoubtedly the most luxuriantly beautiful island in Greece, a Garden of Eden cast up in the north-west corner of Greece, a sweet mockery of the grim grey mountains of Albania, so close and so unenticing. From Shakespeare to Edward Lear, from Gladstone to Lawrence and Gerald Durrell, Corfu has long held a special place in the English heart. Its reputation as a distant paradise began with Homer, who called it Scheria, the island of the Phaeacians, beloved of the gods, where the shipwrecked Odysseus was entertained by the lovely Nausica; it was the magical isle in *The Tempest*, where Prospero offered a different sort of hospitality to his shipwrecked guests. The Venetian city-capital of the island is eminently beautiful, and elegant, unlike any other town in Greece; if you blink, perhaps, you won't notice that nearly every building's ground floor has been given over to souvenir shops and tourist bars. For it's a sad and unavoidable fact that no island, except perhaps Rhodes, has been so exploited and developed. Paradise has become Babylon, and there are few pretty places left on the island without a monster concrete hotel, enclaves of expensive villas, tourist villages and golf courses. Still, the determined visitor who comes in the off season (good times are around Palm Sunday and the first part of November, coinciding with the colourful celebrations of Ag. Spyridon, the island's beloved patron saint), seeking out the old cobbled donkey paths which in Venetian times provided the main link between villages, will be rewarded with a vision of the old Corfu, strewn with wild flowers, scented with the blossoms of lemons and kumquats, silvery with forests of ancient olives. Just don't go out without your wet-weather clothes.

HISTORY
The ancient name of Corfu was Corcyra, after a mistress of the sea god Poseidon. She bore him a son on the island, called Phaeax, who became head of the Phaeacian race; their king's daughter Nausica found the travel-worn Odysseus washed up on the shore of Corcyra. In 734 BC the Corinthians colonised the island, settling the ancient city at Paliapolis. Modern Analypsis was the site of the citadel-akropolis.

Thriving on trade, Corcyra became the richest of the Ionian islands, but internally it was cursed with violent political rivalries between the democrats and the oligarchs. Although the Corcyrian fleet defeated the ships of mother Corinth when the island rebelled in 664 BC—Greece's first recorded sea battle—strife among the inhabitants had weakened Corcyra so much that by the beginning of the 4th century BC it was captured by Syracuse, and then in turn by King Pyrrhus of Epirus and in 229 BC by the Illyrians. Whatever the island's political misfortunes, it was well known in antiquity for its fertility and beauty; under the Romans Nero paid it a special visit in AD 67 and danced at the temple of Zeus in modern Kassiopi.

The remnants of the population that survived the ravages of the Goths founded a new town where they would be better protected on the two hills of Cape Sidaro in the modern town ("Corypho" in Greek means two peaks, thus the name "Corfu"). In the 8th century, walls, castles and moats fortified the town, but they fell to the surprise attack of the Normans in 1081. The Normans, especially under Robert Guiscard and his son, proved a great menace to the Byzantine Empire, and in 1148 the Emperor Emmanuel Comenus sent a special force and fleet to dislodge them. When the siege of the Byzantines made no progress, Emmanuel came himself to lead the attack the following year. By causing subversion among the Normans themselves, he succeeded in winning back the island.

In 1204, when Venice came to make her claim on Corfu, the inhabitants resisted strongly, and although the Venetians succeeded in taking the island's forts, the islanders aligned themselves with the Despotat of Epirus, an Orthodox state. Fifty years later, however the King of Naples, Charles I of Anjou, took Corfu and the rest of Achaia when his son married the princess of Villehardouin. Angevin rule, which lasted 120 years, was intolerant and hateful, forcing the Corfiots to turn to Venice in 1386, to give their island to the "protection" of the Republic.

In 1537 a serious threat, not only to Corfu but to all of Europe, landed at Igoumenitsa in the form of Sultan Suleiman the Magnificent. Suleiman, the greatest of the Turkish rulers, was determined to take Corfu and from there base his attack on Italy and Western Europe. This was in spite of a peace treaty between Turkey and Venice, which did little more than allow Suleiman to plan his attack in the utmost secrecy. When the Corfiots discovered, only a few days in advance, what was in store for them, the people tore down their houses to repair the fortress and in order to leave nothing behind for the Turks. The terrible pirate-admiral Barbarossa was the first to land on the island and he began a siege of the city, during which he suffered massive losses. Thousands of Corfiots who had been pitilessly abandoned outside the fortress suffered too, caught between the Venetians and the Turks, and they fell prey to the worst of Barbarossa's fits of rage at his setbacks. Those who were not slaughtered were taken to the slave markets of Constantinople when Suleiman, discouraged by his losses and bad weather, ordered the withdrawal of the siege.

Only 21 years later Venice, under pressure from the Corfiots, increased the fortifications of Corfu. The canal between the present town and the fortress was dug at this time. Many houses in the town were left unprotected, however, and when the Turks reappeared in 1571 under Ouloudj Ali, these and the rest of the homes, trees and vineyards on Corfu were destroyed. This time the Turks took no prisoners, contenting themselves with massacring the population. The devastation was underlined two years later by another pirate admiral, Sinan Pasha: of the entire Corfiot population, only a tenth survived on the island after the three Turkish rampages.

In 1576 Venice finally began to build the necessary walls for the safety of the Corfiots, together with the Fortezza Nuova, designed by the great expert Sammicheli, and a vast number of other fortifications that no longer exist but were considered superb in their day. The Turks came again in 1716, attacking the new fortifications for one terrible month, only to be dispersed by a tempest, and, as legend claims, by Ag. Spyridon, the patron saint of Corfu.

After the fall of Venice, the French occupied Corfu but quickly lost it again in a fierce battle against the Russo–Turkish fleet. When Napoleon finally got back what he considered his own, he himself designed the new fortifications of the town. They were so strong that the British, when allotted the Ionian islands, did not care to attack them, even though the French commander Donzelot refused to give them up. The French government finally had to send word to Donzelot to come home, and in 1814 Corfu came under British protection, according to the wish of Count John Capodistria. Capodistria, soon to be the first president of Greece, was a son of Corfu and at that time was working for the Tsar of Russia.

But while Capodistria had asked for "military protection", the British, centred on Corfu, took upon themselves all the affairs of the Ionian State. One of the first things they did was to demolish part of the Venetian fortifications in order to build new, more powerful ones in their place, calling upon the Ionian government to pay more than a million gold sovereigns to cover the cost of these marvellous new structures. But in 1864, when Britain had decided to pull out, their condition for letting the Ionian islanders unite with Greece was the destruction of the fortresses of Corfu—those same fortresses the British themselves had just built, and the more historic Venetian buildings. A wave of protest from all corners of the Greek world failed against British determination, and in 1864 the fortifica-

260

tions were blown up, leaving the few ruined relics one can still see today. In 1923 Mussolini bombarded and occupied Corfu after the assassination on Greek territory of an Italian delegate to the Greek–Albanian border council. An even worse bombardment occurred in the Second World War, when the Germans blasted the city for ten days to force its Italian garrison to surrender; a year later, in turn, the British and Americans bombed the Germans. In the end a quarter of the city was destroyed, including 14 of the loveliest churches.

WHAT TO SEE

Corfu town, or Kerkyra, the largest town in the Ionian islands, was first laid out by the Venetians in the 14th century, when the medieval town, crowded onto the peninsula of Cape Sidaro (where the old fortress now stands) needed to expand. The first quarter to be built was Campiello, which has narrow three- or four-storey houses on narrow streets. When the new walls were built in the 16th century, the city expanded at a more leisurely pace the Venetians with the old Italian flair for city planning, laying out an exquisite series of central streets and small squares. The British knocked down a number of the old Venetian walls to permit further expansion, and then contributed a number of elegant Georgian public buildings; the city thus has a unique combination of styles.

Besides Campiello, the old city is divided into a number of small quarters. The newer part of the town (19th century/residential) to the south is called Garitsa. If you arrive by ship from Italy, you enter the city through its back door at **Mandouki** or New Port, on the west side of the New Fortress. Mandouki isn't one of the more attractive parts of town, but it's a good place to look for cheap rooms and food. The ferries from the mainland and islands call on the east side of the New Port, at the **Old Port.** The central city bus depot is in Plateia Theotoki–San Rocco Square; buses to the villages leave from Solomou St by the New Fortress.

The **New Fortress,** or Neo Frourio, where many people get their first look at the town, was built by the Venetians following the third attack on the island. Its walls originally encompassed a much greater area in order to protect the town, but these were destroyed by the British. It bore the main brunt of the Turks' siege of 1716. Nowadays it serves as a Greek naval base, and although you can't get inside you can stroll around the walls adorned with the lions of St Mark. One street near the fortress is named for the crafty and heroic Marshal Schulenburg, a soldier of fortune from Saxony, who outwitted the Turkish High Admiral in the Great Siege—the last major attempt of the Ottoman Empire to expand in the west. Near the bus station stands the 1749 **Catholic Church of Tenedos,** so named for its icon from the island of Tenedos, brought to Corfu by the Venetians.

From the Old Port you can reach the centre of town through the 16th-century **Spilia Gate,** incorporated into a later structure, or take the narrow steps next to the Hotel Nea Yorki into the medieval **Campiello Quarter;** the **Jewish Quarter,** equally old and picturesque, lies at the south end of the fortress walls.

Although the synagogue remains in the heart of the quarter, few of its members survived the Nazi concentration camps to return after the war.

A series of long, parallel streets—the main residential district of the Venetians—all lead to the town's centre, the great green space called the Spinada or **Esplanade,** one of the largest public squares in Europe. Originally the area was left open for defensive purposes; under the French it began to take its present form as a garden and promenade. The French arcades of the Liston on the west edge are full of cafés, the flower beds are immaculately kept, and at night the monuments and trees are floodlit for dramatic effect.

At the far northern end of the Esplanade is the Georgian **Palace of St Michael and St George** with its two great gates. Designed by Sir George Whitmore, the palace was built as the residence of Sir Thomas Maitland, first High Commissioner of the Ionian islands. In 1864 it served as the residence of the King of Greece, then fell into disuse until it was renovated in 1953 to house the **Museum of Far Eastern Art** (open daily 8.45 am–3 pm; closed Tuesdays), the only one of its kind in Greece. The impressive collection, a gift to Corfu from two diplomats, Gregory Manos and Micholos Chadjivasiliou, contains 10 000 works from all the countries of the Far East dating back to 1000 BC. The palace also contains the public library, the tourist and traffic police, and the NTOG office. Notable features of the building are the symbols of the seven Ionian islands that adorn the façade.

Just in front of the palace is another oddity left over from British rule—the **cricket ground,** where little boys play football until their older white-clad brothers chase them off the field. In the summer, matches are held, pitting the two local teams against visitors from Britain and Malta.

Numerous monuments embellish the Esplanade. Towards the centre is the **memorial to Sir Thomas Maitland,** another work of Sir George Whitmore, designed in the form of an Ionian rotunda. Near here is the British-built bandstand, where the local bands (you can often hear them practising in the evening on the upper floors of the old quarters) perform in the summer. There is a heroic marble **statue of Marshal Schulenburg,** and most charmingly, a seated statue of Corfu's favourite Englishman, Frederick North, Earl of Guilford (better known as Lord North) (1769–1828), who with Capodistria founded the first university in Greece. The **Guilford Memorial** portrays him in ancient robes, a touch which he, a man who loved Greece would probably have appreciated. A statue of his friend, Count Capodistria, first president of Greece, stands towards the southern end of the Esplanade.

The **Old Fortress,** on Cape Sidaro, is separated from the Esplanade by the moat, or contra fosse, dug over a 100-year period by the Venetians. The original site of modern Corfu was on the two little hills of the cape; scholars have identified the site with the Heraion akropolis mentioned by Thucydides. Of the mighty walls—the work of centuries—most were blown up by the British; others have fallen into decay. Part of the fortress is still used by the Greek army, but you can wander through the interesting Venetian tunnels and battlements. The drawbridge can still be seen, as well as **St George's,** the church of the British garrison, the Venetian well, and cannons dating back to 1684. Best of all, however, is the view of the city from the hills. In the summer a **Sound and Light Show** (in English on weekdays, French on Sundays, Italian on Mondays, from 1st to 31st August) features the history of the fortress. There are also evening performances of **folk dancing** from 1st June to 30th September (combined ticket 350 dr.).

The church of the patron saint **Ag. Spyridon** is in the old town, not far from the Ionian and Popular Bank of Greece. The church is easy to find, as its bell tower protrudes above the town like the mast of a ship, with its flags and Christmas lights. Ag. Spyridon was the Bishop of Cyprus in the 4th century; when Constantinople fell, his bones were brought in a sack of straw to Corfu. The church was built in 1596 to house the precious relics, now contained in a silver Renaissance reliquary near the iconostasis and brought out with great pomp on the paneyeri of the saint. According to the Corfiots, the good saint has brought them safely through many trials, frightening both cholera and the Turks away from his beloved worshippers. He even gave the Catholics a good scare when they considered placing an altar in his church; the night before its dedication, he blew up a powder magazine in the Old Fortress with a stroke of lightning, to show his displeasure. The Orthodox Palm Sunday, Easter Saturday, 11 August and the first Sunday in November are dedicated to huge celebrations for Ag. Spyridon.

In the Ionian Bank there's a **Museum of Paper Money**, with Greek banknotes dating back to 1820. Across the square from the bank, the 1689 **Church of the Holy Virgin Faneromeni** contains some fine icons of the Ionian School.

The square gives on to the main street **Nikiforou Theotoki,** one of the prettiest in the town; from there head up E. Voulgareos St to the elegant square with Corfu's **Town Hall,** a lovely Venetian confection begun in 1691; a building that later did duty as the municipal opera house. The **Catholic Cathedral of St James** on the square was seriously damaged by the German bombing in 1943; only the bell tower survived intact. The rest has been reconstructed. The **British Consulate** is nearby on another lovely street, Guilford St.

There are several buildings of note in the Campiello Quarter to the north, between the Old Port and the Esplanade especially the 1577 **Orthodox Cathedral,** dedicated to Ag. Theodora Empress of Byzantium and one of the main forces responsible for the restoration of icon worship in the Orthodox Church following the Iconoclasm. Her remains were brought to Corfu along with those of Ag. Spyridon. The cathedral façade dates from the 18th century and the interior is richly adorned with 16th- to 18th-century works of art. A short walk from the Cathedral brings you to the **Byzantine Museum of Corfu,** up the steps from Arseniou St, with fine exhibits of Byzantine icons (entrance fee 200 dr.). On a narrow stairway nearby, off Philharmoniki St, is a **church of Ag. Nikolaos,** which has the odd distinction of once serving as the parish church for the King of Serbia. After the defeat of the Serbian army by the Austro–Hungarians in 1916,

263

the King, his government, and some 150 000 Serbians took refuge on Corfu, making the town their capital. A third of them died shortly thereafter from a plague and are buried on Vido island. It was on Corfu that the king proclaimed the new state of Yugoslavia in 1917. You can take the little ferry out to **Vido island** from the Old Port; the islet was heavily fortified especially after the Turks built a gun battery on it to attack the Old Fortress in 1537. The walls were demolished by the British, and today the island is a quiet refuge with footpaths and a little beach, and a memorial to the Serbians.

Garitsa Bay to the south of the Old Fortress is believed to have been the harbour of King Alcinoos of the Phaeacians. The star attraction in the district of Garitsa is the **Archaeology Museum** (open 8.45 am–3 pm, except Tuesdays; entrance fee 100 dr., free on Sundays), with an excellent collection of finds from the island and nearby mainland, including the famous wall-sized Gorgon Pediment discovered near the 5th-century BC temple of Artemis Kanoni. Other items are from the nearby **Menecrates tomb,** found in the 19th century in an excellent state of preservation. It dates from the 7th century BC and can be seen at the junction of Marassli and Kiprou St, by the police station. South of Garitsa is the suburb of **Anemomilos** ("windmills"), where you can swim at the beach of Mon Repos for a small fee. Mon Repos palace above was built by Sir Frederick, the second High Commissioner of the Ionian State, for his Corfiot wife. The Greek royal family later adopted it as a summer villa and the Duke of Edinburgh was born there. The 11th-century church of **Ag. Iassonos and Sosipater** (two martyrs instructed by St Paul) can also be visited at Anemomilos. The martyrs' tombs and rare icons are inside; the church is one of the island's best examples of Byzantine architecture.

It is a short stroll to **Analypsis,** just south of Mon Repos. Near the Venetian church, along the wall of Mon Repos, a path leads down to the **spring of Kardaki,** which flows from the mouth of a lion; the Venetians used it to supply their ships. The cold water is good, but an inscription above warns: "Every stranger who wets his lips here to his home will not return." Below the spring are the ruins of a 6th-century BC temple. It is one of the most tranquil spots in Corfu.

Kanoni, at the southern tip of the little peninsula, is named for the old cannon once situated on the bluff, where two cafés now overlook the pretty bay, the harbour of ancient Corcyra. Two islets protected it: that of the picturesque convent **Panayia Vlancharina,** now connected to the shore by a causeway, and **Pontikonissi,** the Isle of the Mouse, with a 13th-century chapel, **Ag. Pnevmatos.** Pontikonissi was the Phoenician ship that brought Odysseus home to Ithaca, but which, on its way home, the angry Poseidon smote "with his open palm, and made the ship a rock, fast rooted in the bed of the deep sea", according to the *Odyssey.* Bus no. 2 from Corfu town passes all the above suburbs of gardens and trees, its route ending at Kanoni.

An official **port of entry,** Corfu harbour offers yachts over-wintering facilities, berthing and supplies.

264

The roads on the east coast of Corfu are quite good and developers have followed them nearly every inch of the way. To the immediate north begins a long series of beach, hotel and restaurant complexes, along with most of the camp sites including **Kontokali, Gouvia, Dassia, Ipsos** and **Pirgi. Kouloura** further north is only a kilometre or so from the rugged Albanian coast. The brothers Durrell have left their mark on this part of Corfu, having lived in a seaside villa here in the 1930s. Both have written about the island: Lawrence Durrell in *Prospero's Cell* and his brother Gerald, the naturalist, in *My Family and Other Animals*. At Kouloura the 16th century **Kouartanou Gennata** is part Venetian mansion and part fortified tower, and there are two other 17th-century mansions, **Vassila** and **Prosalenti**. Behind Kouloura looms **Mt Pantokrator,** at 900 metres (3000 ft) the highest point on the island. You can climb it fairly easily from Strinilas or Perithia, two inland villages (to reach the latter, take the bus to **Loutses** and walk past the ruins of Venetian forts).

Kassiopi lies at the northern end of the good paved road. This once important town was founded by Pyrrhus of Epirus in the Hellenistic Age, and it flourished in particular under the Romans who built great walls around it. A famous shrine of Zeus Cassius attracted the Emperor Nero in AD 67, and Cicero also visited the town. Robert Guiscard with his Normans took the Byzantine fortress and then conquered the rest of the island from here. Indeed, as all pirates and adventurers from the north passed by Kassiopi to reach Corfu town, the history of the town is crowded with bloody battles, especially against the Venetians. When the latter finally took the fortress they destroyed it to avenge themselves on the local people. Without their defences the Kassiopians suffered unduly at the hands of the Turks and the town lost all of its former status. One can still see the ruined fortress above the village, now full of wild flowers and sheep. Although still a fishing village, Kassiopi has discovered the profits to be made from the tourist trade and has become one of Corfu's busiest resorts, with a more refined atmosphere than Benitses. Most of the visitors are housed in smart apartments, as there are no hotels. There is good swimming in the sandy coves near the town.

If you take the road from **Spartilas** to **Perithia,** a village nestling in the hills, you'll have a rough but memorable ride through some of the island's most beautiful countryside. **Ag. Panteleimonos,** another inland village, has the huge ruined tower mansion **Polylas,** complete with prisons used during the Venetian occupation. All along the north coast from **Roda** (where egg and chips seems to be everyone's special of the day) to **Sidari** are fine sandy beaches, considered among the best on Corfu; Sidari, though almost entirely given over to tourism, is one of the loveliest spots on the island, with its lush greenery (nearby a river flows into the sea) and picturesque sandstone cliffs, eroded by the wind to form strange caves. There are less crowded beaches near Sidari at **Peroulades, Arillas, Ag. Georgios** and **San Stefano,** a rather characterless bay with villas and served by two hotels. This area in the north-west corner of Corfu, is all covered with forests though the roads are poor and Ag. Georgios bay in particular is hardly developed, although well worth the trip for its beautiful beach. Between Sidari and Roda, **Karoussades,** with the 16th-century mansion of the famous Theotoki family, is a pretty agricultural centre; there is good swimming at sandy **Astrakeri** beach.

North-west of Corfu are three islets, **Othonos** (the largest), **Erikoussa** and **Mathraki,** the westernmost territory of Greece. Nowadays the easiest way to visit the islands is on an organised excursion from Sidari or Corfu, or in the summer from San Stefano. On Othonos a well-preserved medieval fort, **Kastri,** can be seen on a pine-covered hill. Olives and grapes are produced locally, and fresh fish is always available. Many places on the islets are still without electricity, and the population consists mainly of women as their husbands fish, or work in America.

Paliokastritsa, with its beautiful sandy coves, olive groves, mountains and forests, has become the major resort area in west Corfu. On a hill above the town the famous **Paliokastritsa monastery** was built in 1228 on the site of an old Venetian fortress. Inside, a one-room museum contains some very old icons; from outside there is a pleasant view of the sapphire sea below. Along with Kassiopi, Paliokastritsa is considered to be a possible home of the princess Nausica, where the shipwrecked Odysseus found shelter. Today the Barracuda Club for skin divers has its headquarters here. Other fine views may be had from the village of **Lakones** and its famous Bella Vista. Lakones is the hub of the loveliest walks on Corfu, especially to the formidable **Angelokastro** (you can also walk from Paliokastritsa). Built in the 13th century by the Byzantine despot of Epirus, Michael Angelos, it is mostly ruined, but makes an impressive sight perched on the wild red rocks over a 300-metre (1000-ft) precipice. Angelo-kastro played a major role during the various raids on the island, sheltering the surrounding villagers (as well as the Venetian governor, who lived there). However-er, the defending Corfiots were rarely content to stay behind the walls of Angelokastro, often attacking their attackers instead.

East of Paliokastritsa stretches the fertile **Ropa plain,** where most of the island's agriculture takes place. To the south are good beaches and big resorts at **Ermones** and **Glyfada,** the latter dominated by the Grand Glyfada Hotel and its many water sport activities **Pelekas,** up on a mountain ridge, was Kaiser Wilhelm's favourite spot to watch the sunset; bus loads of people come out every evening in the summer to do the same, from a tower known as the **Kaiser's Throne.** During the day, the beach at Pelekas is Corfu's unofficial naturist beach. After sunset the village reverberates to the sound of disco music and is alive with young fun-seekers.

Ag. Gordios has a 2½-km (1½-mile) beach that so far has hardly been developed. A Byzantine castle at **Gardiki,** south of Ag. Gordios, was also constructed by the despot of Epirus, Michael Angelos II, answering a great need during troubled times. Lagoudia, two islets off the south-west coast, are the home of a tribe of donkeys; some of their ancestors were eaten by a boatload of Frenchmen who were wrecked there for three days.

Fine beaches, deserted for the most part, line the south-west coast to **Ag. Georgios. Lefkimi,** in the centre of a large fertile plain, is the second most important village of the island but not very interesting for the tourist; nearby **Kavos,** however, has an important monastery, **Prokopios** and an excellent beach as does **Asprocavos,** both famous for their white sand. Heading north **Moraitika, Miramare** and **Benitses** are tourist villages. Its British pubs and rowdy crowds have turned Benitses into Corfu's Torremolinos, to the point where many of the resort's former enthusiasts have moved out of earshot. Corfu's casino is in the **Achilleion** by Gastouri, perhaps the best kitsch palace in all of Greece. It was built in 1890 by the Empress Elisabeth of Austria, and dedicated to that lady's passion for the hero of Homer's *Iliad.* Inside there are many bizarre paintings of Achilleus, and in the park a statue of the wounded Achilleus. When Elisabeth was assassinated by an Italian anarchist, Kaiser Wilhelm made the Achilleion his summer residence from 1908 to 1914. The small museum (open 8 am–7 pm, Sundays 9 am–7 pm) contains, among its curious collection of imperial mementoes, the Kaiser's riding saddle, from which he dictated some of his plans for the First World War. **Perama,** believed to be the site of King Alcinoos' wonderful garden, offers more luxury than any other place on this luxurious island, and many people rent villas there.

PANEYERIA
10 July, Ag. Prokopios at Kavos; 14 August, The Procession of Lights at Mandouki; first Friday after Easter, Paliokastritsa; 5–8 July, at Lefkimi; 15 August, Panayias at Kassiopi; 21 May, Union with Greece; procession of Ag. Spyridos in Corfu town on Palm Sunday, Easter, 11 August and first Sunday in November.

WHERE TO STAY
For old-style elegance no, hotel on Corfu can compete with the **Cavalieri Corfu,** located on the Esplanade at 4 Kapodistriou (tel. 0661 39 041) in a renovated French mansion. Comfortable, air conditioned and rated class A, doubles start at 8000 dr. and shoot way, way up in season. Less expensive and a little further along the Esplanade is a class C hotel, the **Arcadion** at 44 Kapodistriou (tel. 0661 37 671). Rates are 5000 dr. for a double, and 3000 dr. for a single.

In the old port there's the **Astron Hotel** in a charming neo-Classical structure at 15 Donzelotou (tel. 0661 39 505); although in season its class B rates are 6000–7500 dr. for a double, 3000–4000 dr. for a single, they fall considerably in the off season. Next to it, in another old building, is the gallant class D **Hotel Nea Yorki** (tel. 0661 39 922), where a double is 3000 dr. a night. If you'd prefer something newer, there's always the **Europa** at the New Port (Mandoukion, tel. 0661 39 304) which has, along with modern, clean rooms, a self-service laundrette. Rates here are 3500 dr. for a double. For something less dear, go to the National Tourist office in the palace (tel. 0661 39 730 or 30 265) and pick up their list of rooms to let in town. Most of these are in the old quarters and cost 700 dr. upwards for a bed in season.

The Monastery on Corfu

For rooms and information on accommodation outside Corfu town, contact the Tourist Police near the waterfront on 43 Arseniou St, or at the palace. There's a cache of luxurious high rise palaces in Kanoni, like the **Corfu Hilton,** a hotel and bungalow complex (tel. 0661 36 540) and one of the few hotels in Greece with a bowling alley. A double here will set you back a cool 19 500 dr. Much lower on the price scale, but in an equally commanding position is the **Royal,** a C class hotel that could be luxury class, with its three swimming pools on descending levels, roof garden and its fine view over Mouse Island. Its doubles go for up to 6000 dr. in summer, but these rates drop dramatically in the off season (tel. 0661 37 512). North of Corfu town, at Komeno Bay, the luxury class **Astir Palace** charges 18 500 dr. for its doubles with half board (tel. 0661 91 481). For something different, but in the same price range, there's the **Castello** in Dassia, north of the town (tel. 0661 30 184) in an idyllic country mansion, with frequent bus service to the beach. A double here is around 18 000 dr., a single 14 000 dr. There are plenty of hotels in the moderate price range, however, such as the **Pirros** (tel. 0661 91 206) at Kontokali, the **Galaxias** at Gouvia (tel. 0661 91 566), the **Doria** at Dassia (tel. 0661 93 582) at around 3000–4500 dr. for a double, but its best to book a little time ahead. Some very presentable D class hotels, where you'll pay about 2800 dr. for a double are **Kostas** (tel. 0661 93 205) at Ipsos, or the **Louvre** at Gouvia (tel. 0661 91 506), but don't expect any original masterpieces here. On the opposite end of the scale, Corfu's **Youth hostel** is in the same vicinity (take bus no. 7 from San Rocco Square, tel. 0661 91 202). An IYHF card is required, and rates are 400 dr. a person. In lovely Paliokastritsa everything is overpriced, but if you're lucky (or book early) you may get one of the 8 rooms right on the beach at the **Pavillion Xenia** (tel. 0663 41 208), with a good restaurant below. Prices start at around 5500 dr. for a double, the view and location priceless. Alternatively there's the **Hermes** (tel. 0661 41 211), with less charm, but its prices compensate—about 2800 for a double. A double at the **Grand Hotel Glyfada** runs to 11 5000 dr. in season (tel. 0661 94 201). There's a campground a mile and a half inland from Paliokastritsa (tel. 0663 41 204); others are at Messoghi, Kontokali (the nearest to Corfu town), Ipsos, Karoussades (these two the best on the island), Pirgi and Dafnila. Nearly every village has rooms to let, some, like Kassiopi, Pelekas and Kavos, with long listings. Lastly, for dramatic modern architecture on the beach, stay at the **Ag. Gordios** on Ag. Gordios (tel. 0663 36 723) where a double in the honeycomb is 6000 dr. Villas can be rented all over the island from 4000 dr. upwards. Details from any travel agency.

EATING OUT

The food is usually good on Corfu, and even in the town you can still find low priced Greek dishes at such places as **Gisdakis** near San Rocco Square, where you can eat a full meal for 600 dr. Just as good is **Dionysos**, off N. Theotoki. **Averof**, at Alipiou and Prossalendou Street, is a long established favourite of locals and visitors alike, where prices are just a bit higher. For more atmosphere and higher prices, there's the **Acteon** on the Esplanade—places around here tend to be very, very expensive. One of the most popular and reliable tavernas is **Koromios** in Garitsa, south of the fortress, where it's difficult to run up a bill of more than 700 dr. Mandouki, where the ferry boats from Italy dock, boasts some excellent little eating establishments. In Xen. Stratigou St, **Babis** is everything a Greek taverna should be—noisy, friendly, inexpensive and efficient with super food at 600 dr. a meal. Further up the road is the smarter **Orestes,** with a little garden opposite. If you order their seafood specialities, you'll pay 1500 dr. There are several other fish restaurants in the same area. A little way out of town to the south at Kynopiastes is the **Gloupos,** where you can eat and watch the folk dancing for 1500 dr., and a little further on the **Tripa** ("the Hole") provides a folklore floorshow with dinner at 1200 dr. If you want to splash out, there's plenty of scope. In town the **Bella Napoli** serves international cuisine, particularly Italian dishes, naturally. Dinner for two can be 5000 dr. At Analypsis, the **Top of the Hill Bistro** offers non-Greek surprises such as Lobster Thermidor and convincing curries. **Rex's restaurant,** just off Volgaros St. has interesting Greek specialities in the medium price range. A favourite with many is the **Asterix Wine Bar,** serving immaculately prepared crêpes, and the magic potion is, of course, its wines. **Pizza Pete,** in Arseniou St, overlooking the old port, prides himself on the best in town—a pizza meal will run to 1000 dr. Out on the road to Kontokali (take a taxi) the **Mandarin Chinese Restaurant** has an excellent reputation for top class food and swift service, and its splendid view does justice to the Peking Duck. For a full blow-out, reckon on 2500 dr. For an organised evenings entertainment, **Danilia's Village** is a reconstruction of a typical, old Corfiot settlement, with museum, shopping arcade, folklore museum, and displays of traditional Ionian dancing. It's one of Corfu's bigger attractions and a

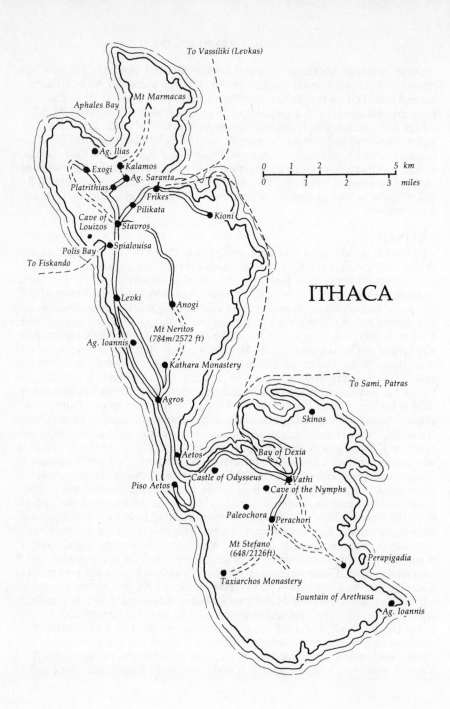

To Vassiliki (Levkas)

Aphales Bay

Mt Marmacas

Ag. Ilias

Exogi · Kalamos
Platrithias · Ag. Saranta
Frikes
Pilikata
Cave of · Stavros · Kioni
Louizos
Polis Bay · Spialouisa
To Fiskando

Levki
Anogi

Mt Neritos
(784m/2572 ft)
Ag. Ioannis

Kathara Monastery

ITHACA

5 km

miles

Agros

To Sami, Patras

Skinos

Aetos
Bay of Dexia

Castle of Odysseus
Vathi
Piso Aetos
Cave of the Nymphs

Paleochora
Perachori

Mt Stefano
(648/2126ft)
Perapigadia

Taxiarchos Monastery

Fountain of Arethusa
Ag. Ioannis

colourful night out, although the food doesn't match the quality of the floor show. Tickets (4000 dr. for the evening) available from most travel agents or hotel reception.

TOURIST INFORMATION
NTOG, Governors House (Palace of St Michael and St George), tel. (0661) 39 730.
Tourist police, next door to above, tel. (0661) 30 265, and at 31 Arseniou St.

CONSULATES
Great Britain: Leof. Alexandras, tel. (0661) 30 055
West Germany: Leof. Alexandras, tel. (0661) 31 755
France: Polyla St, tel. (0661) 26 312

ITHACA (ITHAKI)

CONNECTIONS
In summer, daily with Patras and Sami, Kephallonia, with connections to Lefkas, Corfu and Italy, daily with Ag. Efthimia and Astakos. Frequent connections in summer between Stavros and Fiskardo, and between Frikes and Vassiliki, in Lefkas.

"Every traveller is a citizen of Ithaca", reads a sign in the port. Ithaca is one of those places that has become a compelling and universal symbol although many who have heard of it have no idea where it is, and those who do visit it usually have a hard time reconciling the island's reality with their idea of Odysseus' beloved kingdom. And yet re-read your Homer before you come, and you'll find that nearly all of his descriptions of Ithaca fit this small mountainous island—it is indeed "narrow" and "rocky" and "unfit for riding horses". Some ancient and modern scholars, most famously the archaeologist Dörpfeld, have theorised that Homer's Ithaca was elsewhere—Lefkas and Kephallonia are popular contenders. Don't believe them. Thiaki as the locals call their home, the symbol of all homes, is the real thing, and "even if you find it poor," as Cavafy says, "Ithaca does not deceive. Without Ithaca your journey would have no beauty".

Ithaca has a jagged, indented coast (as Homer says), but no exceptional beaches and its roads are in such a condition that most islanders prefer to travel to distant villages by caique. Its excellent harbour makes it a big favourite with sailors and best of all, it has changed little over the years. The atmosphere is relaxed and low-key, quiet and pleasant.

HISTORY
Inhabited from 2000 BC, Ithaca, home of the intrepid Odysseus, has become the eternal symbol of the journey's end. The island and the four cities of Kephallonia

were probably the extent of Odysseus' Mycenaean kingdom, when ancient Ithaca knew its greatest prosperity. In the last 200 years scholars and archaeologists have come to the island looking for signs of Odysseus. Schliemann came, after his great discovery of Troy, and since he always found what he was looking for, he unearthed a large structure which he called "Odysseus' Palace", and though it dates from a time far later (700 BC), the name has stuck. Other finds indicate that at least the ancients considered Ithaca Homer's Ithaca. Inscriptions indicate that Odysseus was worshipped as a divine hero, coins were found with Odysseus' picture, and pottery decorated with the cock, the symbol of Odysseus, has been found on the island. Homer describes the palace of Odysseus as above "three seas" and a hillock in Stavros matches the description, furthermore it is the site of two ancient fortifications which might have been used for signals and beacons to the palace. There's the Fountain of Arethousa, where Odysseus met his faithful swineherd Eumaeus, and the cave where he hid the treasure given him by the Phaeacians.

After the Mycenaeans, Ithaca lost most of its importance and even its name; for a period it was known merely as "Little Kephallonia". By the time of the Venetians, invaders and pirates had so despoiled the island that it was all but abandoned, and the Venetians offered generous incentives to those who would settle and farm. Once again Ithaca prospered, but unlike the other Ionian islands, it never had an aristocracy. Ironically, union with Greece in 1864 initiated the great migration from the island, many Ithakians going to Romania, Australia and South Africa. Like their countryman Odysseus the islanders are well known as great sailors, and even those who call Ithaca home spend much of the year away at sea.

WHAT TO SEE

Vathi, built around the end of a long sheltered bay, is the capital of the island, although little larger than a village itself. Its beautiful harbour, with a wooded islet **Lazaretto** and its church as centrepiece with mountains on all sides, attracts many yachts. Although devastated by the 1953 earthquake, Vathi was reconstructed in the same style and is considered a "traditional settlement" of Greece. One building that survived is the mansion of the Drakolis family, who brought the first steamship to Greece, which they named the *Ithaka*. **The Archaeology Museum** is behind the Mentor Hotel, housing a collection of vases, offerings and other objects, many dating from Homeric times. In the **Church of the Taxiarchos** an icon of Christ is believed to be from the brush of El Greco. An annual conference on Homer, the International Odessa Congress, has taken place in Vathi since 1981.

West of Vathi it's a half-hour walk to the **Cave of the Nymphs** or Marmarospilia (signposted) where Odysseus hid the gifts of King Alcinoos. The cave is especially interesting for the hole in the roof—"the entrance of the gods"—through which passed the smoke of the sacrifices burnt within. The cave has a few stalactites—bring a torch. Below is the **Bay of Dexia,** where the Phaeacians

272

put the sleeping Odysseus on shore. South of Vathi above the little beach and islet of **Perapigadia,** flows the **Fountain of Arethusa.** According to the myth, Arethusa wept so much when her son Coryx was killed that she turned into a spring and it was here that Odysseus, disguised as a beggar, first met the faithful Eumaeus. The water flows from the rock Coryx—also mentioned by Homer—and is good to drink, though it has a reputation for increasing the appetite.

The only other real village in the south of Ithaca is **Perachori,** also within walking distance of Vathi. Perachori lies in the island's most fertile region and dates from the Venetian settlement, though the first houses were built in **Paleochora,** where you can see the ruins of the fortified houses and churches, one without its roof still adorned with fading Byzantine frescoes. In Perachori the villagers will show you which path to take. Another road from the village goes up to the **Monastery of the Taxiarchos,** founded in the 17th century near the top of Mt Stefano. Although not all that much remains to be seen, the views from the monastery and the road are good. In August Perachori hosts a celebrated wine festival.

Ithaca has an hourglass figure, with a waist only 500 metres wide. This narrow mountain stretch is called **Aetos,** and there is a beach in the bay below and at **Piso Aetos** in the west. Overlooking the bays is the so-called **Castle of Odysseus,** actually the citadel of the 8th century BC town of Alalcomenes. Impressive Cyclopean walls and the foundations of a temple remain. Although Schliemann and others believed this was the site of Odysseus' city, more recent evidence (1930) favours a site near Stavros.

Just north of Aetos is the so-called **Field of Laertes** or Agros, from where a road ascends the slopes of Mt Neritos (formerly Mt Korifi—Ithaca is slowly reclaiming its Homeric names) to the **Monastery of Kathara,** founded in 1696. From the monastery you can see the Gulf of Patras, and even though the monastery is now abandoned, the Church of the Panayia is kept open in the summer for visitors to see the frescoes and icon attributed to St Luke. From Kathara the road continues to **Anogi,** passing many large and unusually-shaped boulders. The village retains some Venetian ruins, including a campanile and the **Church of the Panayia** with very old frescoes.

The second and better road from Argos follows the west coast. At Ag. Ioannis, just opposite Kephallonia, is a lovely, seldom-used beach, with many trees. **Levki,** the small village to the north, was an important base and port for the resistance movement during the war, and when it was destroyed by the 1953 earthquake, Britain officially adopted it and helped to rebuild it. Further north is **Stavros,** the most important village in the north, overlooking the lovely **Polis Bay** ("city bay"), its name referring to the Byzantine city of Ierosalem, which sank into it during an earthquake in the 10th century. A bust of Odysseus in the centre of Stavros looks out over the bay, which has one of Ithaca's more popular beaches. The **Cave of Louizos** on the bay was an ancient cult sanctuary, where archaeologists found a number of items dating back to the Mycenaean age; one of the gods worshipped here was Odysseus. By common scholarly consent his palace was located at **Pilikata,** just north of Stavros. Although the ruins you see on the site are of a Venetian fort, excavators have found evidence underneath of buildings and roads dating back to the Neolithic era. Some of the finds from Pilikata and the Cave of Louizos are in the small but interesting **Stavros Archaeological Museum** in Pilikata. The site also fits the Homeric description almost perfectly, in sight of "three seas" (the bays of Frikes, Polis and Aphales) and "three mountains" (Neritos, Marmacas and Exogi). Before going up to Pilikata, ask in Stavros for the key.

North of Stavros, **Frikes** is a tiny fishing village and port for Fiskardo in Kephallonia and Vassiliki in Lefkas, as well as for daily caiques to Vathi. There's a new hotel here and rooms and tavernas, as there are too in nearby **Kioni** one of Ithaca's prettiest villages, which has better beaches. Kioni means "column", and an ancient one still stands on the altar in the village church. In **Platrithias,** the centre of a group of small settlements north of Stavros, there's a small ethnographic museum, at Kolieri. This fertile area is one of the most pleasant on the island to stroll through; it was here that Odysseus was ploughing his field when the Acheans came to take him away to Troy.

PANEYERIA
15 August, Platrithias; 24 June, Ag. Ioannis, at Kioni; mid-August to mid-September, theatre and cultural festival at Vathi; 5–6 August, Sotiros at Stavros; 8 September, Kathara Monastery; 1 May, Taxiarchos and August wine festival, Perachori.

WHERE TO STAY
Ithaca as a whole has very little accommodation, and most of what there is is in Vathi. Most modern and most expensive is the **Hotel Mentor,** class B, on Georgiou Drakouli Street, tel. 0674 32 433. A bit out of the centre, on the far side of the bay, a double here is 6500 dr. a night. A bit less dear and more convenient is the **Odysseus,** also in the B category (tel. 0674 32 381), where doubles run around 4500 dr., singles 3000 dr. Although C class, the **Nostos Hotel,** at Frikes, has high rates—4200 dr. a double, 2700 dr. a single (tel. 0674 31 644). The **Pension Aktaeon** is small and affordable at 2500. for a double (tel. 0674 32 387). Less expensive, but get there early in the summer to find a room, is the **Pension Enoikiazomena** behind the town hall, on a narrow alley off Odysseus Street. The rooms are old but charming in a grandmotherly way; in the entrance there's a robot made out of cigarette boxes. Try to get a room looking out over the bay; doubles are 2000 dr. There are also a few rooms to rent, here and in Perachori, Kioni and around Stavros.

EATING OUT
Across the street from the Pension Enoikiazomena there's a tiny place simply called **Taverna,** where pots of genuine Greek home cooking simmer on the stove and the prices are embarrassingly low (300–500 dr). Others are near the main

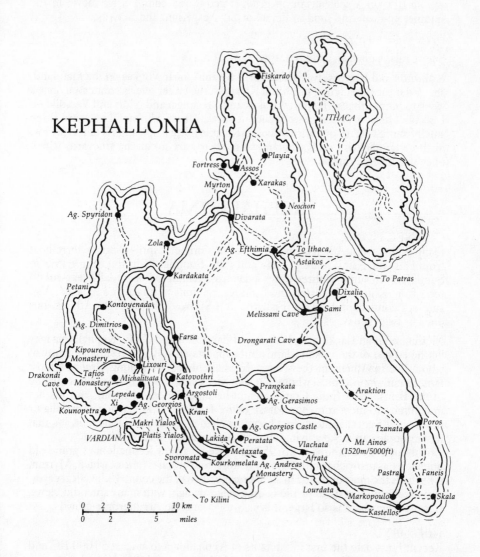

KEPHALLONIA

ITHACA

Fiskardo

Playia

Fortress
Assos
Myrton
Xarakas

Ag. Spyridon
Neochori

Zola
Divarata

Ag. Efthimia
To Ithaca,
Astakos

Kardakata
To Patras

Petani
Dixalia

Kontoyenada
Melissani Cave
Sami

Ag. Dimitrios
Farsa

Drongarati Cave

Kipoureon
Monastery
Lixouri

Drakondi
Cave
Tafios
Monastery
Michalitsata
Katovothri

Prangkata
Araktion

Lepeda
Argostoli
Ag. Gerasimos

Xi
Ag. Georgios

Kounopetra
Krani

Makri Yialos
Ag. Georgios Castle
Tzanata
Poros

VARDIANA
Platis Yialos
Lakida
Peratata
Vlachata
∧ Mt Ainos
(1520m/5000ft)

Svoronata
Metaxata
Afrata

Kourkomelata
Ag. Andreas
Monastery
Pastra
Faneis

Lourdata
Markopoulo
Skala

To Kilini
Kastellos

0   2   5   10 km
0   2   5   miles

square (the ones specialising in grills is good) and charge a bit more; in the summer you can find food in Perachori, Frikes, Kioni and Stavros.

TOURIST POLICE
See regular police at Vathi, tel. (0674) 32 205.

Kalamos and **Kastus,** two islands off Meganisi, near Mitikas on the mainland, are under the jurisdiction of Ithaca. Kalamos, the larger one, is connected once a week to Sami, Ithaca, the port Astakos and Meganisi, and Nidri and Vassiliki on Lefkas. There is also a more frequent service from Mitikas. There are three small fishing villages on its rocky coast: Kalamos, Episkopi, and Kefali. Only two or three families live on Kastus, now unable to care for all the vineyards which once produced a fine wine.

KEPHALLONIA

CONNECTIONS
Daily flights from Athens, several a day in summer; April–October ferry boat from Patras to Sami, Ithaka, Corfu and Italy. Summer hydrofoil from Patras to Sami; ferry in summer three times a day from Killini to Poros; daily year-round ferry from Kilini to Argostoli and from Ag. Ephimia to Ithaka and Astakos. Also summer connection between Fiskardo and Stavros, Ithaka. From Athens, bus once or twice a day.

Mountainous and lacking the lushness of Zakynthos and Corfu, Kephallonia may be the largest of the Ionian islands but supports only 30 000 residents, many of whom live in Athens in the winter. Kephalloniotes are among Greece's most famous emigrants (one of whom, Constantine Yerakis, went on to make a fortune in the British East India Company and became Regent of Siam), and it's not uncommon to meet someone whose entire family lives in Canada, Australia or the United States: if the tourist boom has had a positive social benefit, it's that more people can make a living on their beautiful but untamed island.

Although the earthquake in 1953 destroyed many of Kephallonia's grand old houses it has many charms to woo its visitors: fine beaches (one of which, Myrton, is perhaps the most dramatic in all of Greece), two of the country's loveliest caves, and great pine forests to picnic in and walk through, with many splendid views. Because the island is so large, it is easy to escape the summertime crowds.

HISTORY
Recent finds date the first inhabitants of Kephallonia to at least 50 000 BC and perhaps earlier; Fiskardo man, as the archaeologists have dubbed him, has proved to have many similarities with his peers in western Sicily and Epirus. The island is also exceptionally rich in its Mycenaean finds. Although the name of the island does not occur in Homer, it is believed that the "glittering Samos" of the

Odyssey refers to Kephallonia's mountains, and that the island may well have been part of the kingdom of Odysseus, and certainly the home of many of the ill-mannered Suitors.

Historically the first mention we have of the island is that it was ruled by four city-states: Sami, the most powerful, Pali, Krani and Pronnoi. Hesiod refers to a renamed sanctuary of Zeus which stood on the top of Mt Ainos. Little else, however, is known of the "Kephallonian Tetrapolis" until the Roman invasion, when the besieged Sami held out heroically for four months before the inevitable defeat, and the equally inevitable sale of its citizens into slavery.

In 1082, the Norman baron Robert Guiscard besieged the island unsuccessfully and died of fever in the village that has taken his name—Fiskardo. If the Kephalloniotes breathed a sigh of relief then, it was too soon; for the next 800 years the island, like its sisters, was to become the plaything of the Normans, of Venice, the Vatican, and a motley assortment of dukes and counts in need of a tax income. Most famous of its occupiers was the pirate Count Matteo Orsini, who lived at the end of the 12th century. In 1483 the Turks captured the island, but lost it again when Venice and Spain under the Gran Capitan de Cordova besieged and captured the fort of Ag. Georgios and slaughtered the Turkish garrison.

After this the fortress was repaired and the town nearby became the Venetian capital. A huge earthquake caused heavy damage to Ag. Georgios, and by the 18th century it was abandoned, Argostoli becoming the island's new capital. In 1823 Lord Byron came to Kephallonia as an agent of the Greek Committee in London, where he was as ever a great inspiration to those fighting for the independence of Greece. At the village of Metaxata he wrote *Don Juan* before going on to Messolongi on the mainland, where he died. During the British occupation of the Ionian islands, the Kephalloniotes demanded Greek union there more stridently than anyone else, and many of the nationalist leaders were imprisoned there. Ioannis Metaxas, prime minister-dictator of Greece from 1936 to 1941, came from Kephallonia; and it was he who said the historic "No" to Mussolini's ultimatum at the beginning of the Second World War. In 1943, the Italian occupiers of the island joined forces with the EAM (Greek National Liberation Front) and for seven days fought the invading Germans. Three thousand of the Italians who were forced to surrender died in the subsequent mass executions ordered, it is said, by Hitler himself.

WHAT TO SEE

When Kephallonia was so badly damaged by the earthquake in 1953—only Fiskardo, in the extreme north, survived unscathed—the wealthy emigrants of the island donated large sums of money for the reconstruction of its villages. A fair portion of their money has gone to rebuilding the island's capital **Argostoli,** situated on a thumb of the great bay in the south. Part of this is so shallow that the British, during their rule, built the **Drapanos Bridge** over it, with its many low arches and commemorative obelisk, considerably shortening the trip to the other side of the bay. The port of Argostoli is especially safe and used for winter berthing of yachts and larger ships.

Argostoli has more public buildings than most island capitals; most of them are grouped around the large, central **Plateia Vallanou.** Here there's a **National Tourist Office** open from April to October. Pre-earthquake Argostoli was famous for its bell towers, some of which have been rebuilt—be sure to note the German Expressionist-style tower of the Catholic church near the square. Two museums are nearby: the **Archaeology Museum** contains a room of Mycenaean finds—bronze swords and gold jewellery, coins from the four ancient cities of Kephallonia, and a bronze bust of a man from the early 3rd century BC that's startlingly modern. The **Koryalenios Historical and Folklore Museum** in the basement of the library on Ilia Zervou St contains the Venetian records of the island, icons, a traditional bedroom and other ethnographic items.

There are a number of hotels in Argostoli and two sandy beaches south of the town, the organised **Platis Yialos** and the free **Makri Yialos.** A pleasant walk along **Lassi,** the little peninsula north of Argostoli, leads to one of Kephallonia's peculiar geological features—**Katavothri** or the "Swallow holes", where the sea is sucked into two large tunnels under the ground. No one knew where the water came out until 1963, when Austrian geologists poured a vast quantity of dye into the water. Fifteen days later it appeared in the lake of the Melissani cave and at Karavomylos, near Sami, on the other side of the island. The sea mills that harnessed the rushing water, which were destroyed by the earthquake, have since been reconstructed. On the other side of the peninsula is the lovely **lighthouse of Ag. Theodoros,** reconstructed in its rotunda of columns. On the other side of Argostoli, above the lagoon formed by the Drapanos Bridge, you can see the massive 7th-century BC walls on the akropolis of ancient **Krani.**

Bus services to the rest of the island have been improved and next to the KTEL station on the waterfront there is a local tourist office to help you plan excursions. Many taxi drivers specialise in trips around the island, and caiques go to the more popular beaches. There is a car ferry across the Gulf of Argostoli six times a day from Argostoli to Lixouri.

Lixouri is Kephallonia's second city, all new houses on wide streets and in itself not terribly interesting. In the central square near the waterfront stands a statue of poet Andreas Laskaratos, a local man of letters of the 19th century, remembered in particular for his dislike of the church. He was a poor man with a large family to support, and he kept heckling the priests so much that they finally excommunicated him—this is aforismos, in Greek, meaning that the body will not decompose after death. Laskaratos, in response, hurried home, collected his children's shoes and returned to the priest with the request that he should please aforismos the footwear, too, as he had no money to buy new shoes! On the east side of Lixouri, the **Iakvatos Mansion,** now a library and icon museum, is one of the few buildings in the south to have survived the earthquake.

South of Lixouri, the territory of ancient Pali, there are a number of beaches—

Michalitsata and **Lepeda,** both sandy, and **Ag. Georgios** further south, a long stretch of golden sand, most easily reached by caique. Just south of it the famous **Kounopetra** once created the optical illusion of opening and closing; the earthquake, however, fouled up the magic, and likewise destroyed the houses on the pretty, deserted **Vardiana islet** off the coast. This large peninsula of Kephallonia is rocky and full of caves. The most interesting one, **Drakondi Spilio,** can be reached from the monastery of **Ag. Paraskevi Tafion.** Another monastery, **Kipoureon** perched on the west cliffs, has spectacular views and overnight rooms. South of Manzavinata there's another fine beach, **Xi,** a long crescent of reddish sand. Inland the main road passes through the village of **Soulari,** where **Ag. Marina** has a lovely gilded iconostasis and icons.

North of Lixouri there are more beaches: **Ag. Spyridon** near town, safe for children; **Petani,** pretty and quiet and rarely crowded. Even more remote—accessible by a minor road—is another beach called **Ag. Spyridon,** a stretch of sand tucked into the northernmost tip of the Pali peninsula.

South-east of Argostoli, the **Livatho district** has most of Kephallonia's villages, situated in a fertile region of valleys and rolling hills. At one village, **Metaxata,** Byron wrote most of his great satirical poem *Don Juan.* Nearby **Kourkomelata** was rebuilt by the wealthy Kephalloniote shipowner Vergotis; everything is bright, new and pastel-coloured, reminiscent of a suburb of California. From **Peratata** you can visit the historic church of **Ag. Andreas,** its prize possession a sole of the saint's foot. The earthquake shook loose the whitewash that had covered the interior, revealing frescoes that date back to 1700 and have now been restored. Above the church looms the **Castle of Ag. Georgios,** and the ruined town that until 1757 was the capital of Kephallonia. Most of the impressive ruins you see date from the early 16th century, when the citadel was rebuilt by Nikolaos Tsimaras. Held by the Byzantines, Franks, Turks and, after the fierce siege of 1500, the Venetians, it retains most of its walls, a ruined Catholic church, some forgotten coats-of-arms, and a bridge built by the French during their occupation. The castle commands a wonderful view of the surrounding plains and mountains.

To the east lies the green **plain of Omalos** and the **monastery of Ag. Gerasimos,** containing the body of the patron saint of the island. If 50% of Corfiots are named Spiros after St Spyridon, then 50% of the Kephalloniotes are named Gerasimos after their saint, who is known for curing mental disturbances, especially if one keeps an all-night vigil at his church on the night of 27 October, his feast day. The monastery architecturally is most notable for its grotesque and ungainly bell tower. From the Argostoli–Sami road a branch leads off to Megalos Soros, the highest point of majestic **Mt Ainos,** at 1500 metres (5 ft) the highest point in the Ionian islands. Before the Venetian shipbuilders came to the island the mountain was blanketed with the unique Kephallonian black pine—*Abies cefalonica*—so dense that the Venetians called Ainos the "Black Mountain". In 1962 what has survived of the forest was declared a national park, and it's still impressive to stroll among the tall trees seemingly on top of the world; on a clear day the Peloponnese, Zakynthos, Ithaca, Lefkas, the Gulf of Patras and even Corfu are spread out below as if on a great blue platter.

Along the south coast there are good sandy beaches at **Afrata, Trapezaki** and **Lourdata** (the longest and most crowded). Kephallonia's most popular resorts are in the south-east corner, and its most famous religious event also takes place here, in the village of **Markopoulo**. On 15 August, small harmless snakes "inoffensive to the Virgin Mary", with little crosses on their heads, suddenly appear in the village streets. Formerly they slithered to the church, went inside and mysteriously disappeared near the Virgin's icon. Nowadays the villagers collect them in glass jars and bring them to the church, where they are released after the service and immediately disappear. Although the sceptical believe that the church is simply along the route of the little snakes' natural migratory trail, the faithful point out that the snakes fail to appear when the island is in distress—as during the German occupation and in the year of the earthquake.

Kastellos is a pretty place with springs, greenery and a beach, and becomes more popular every year, as too does **Skala,** boasting another long beach. Near Skala a Roman villa was excavated, and it is worth a visit for its 3rd-century mosaic floors, portraying Envy being devoured by wild beasts and two men making sacrifices to the gods. To the north of Skala a 7th-century BC temple of Apollo has also been discovered, though most of its stones were used to construct the nearby chapel of Ag. Georgios.

The road between Skala and **Poros** has been improved but is still narrow and difficult, but worth the trouble for the scenery and the pretty "Poros Gap". Because of its direct connection with Kilini, Poros is rapidly developing as the island's major resort area.

Sami is the port for ships to Patras and Italy, and is a growing resort in its own right, with beaches and two campsites, although the town itself is not very interesting. On the two hills behind the port are the **walls of ancient Sami,** where the citizens put up a heroic resistance to the Romans in 187 BC. Sami is also the best base for visiting the region's numerous caves, two of which have been developed to receive visitors **Drogarati cave,** near the hamlet of Haliotata, is a fairyland of orange and yellow stalactites and stalagmites; one of its great chambers has such fine acoustics that in the summer concerts are occasionally held there. The other cave, **Melissani** ("purple cave") is a half-hour's walk from Sami. It's a breathtaking sight, with its lake and steep sides and can be explored in one of the small boats provided. About 120 metres (400 ft) long and 30 metres (100 ft) high, the cave is a vast play of blue and violet colours, caught by the sun which sneaks through a hole in the roof. The salt water inside supposedly came from under the island, all the way from Argostoli's "swallow holes". Both caves are open from 8 am to 7 pm in the summer, but close after October. There are other, undeveloped caves in the vicinity of Sami, many with lakes and precipitous drops, best of which is **Anglaki cave,** near Poulata.

Ag. Efthimia, the port for Ithaca and Astakos, also has a harbour for yachts and a hotel. On the northernmost tip of Kephallonia, tiny **Fiskardo** derives its name from a mispronunciation of Guiscard, the Norman prince who died there and was buried in a cairn (by the hotel). Only at Fiskardo were some of the old Venetian houses saved from the earthquake, and they give the visitor an idea of what the rest of the island looked like before 1953.

South-west of Fiskardo, on the way back to Argostoli, is the magnificent castle of **Assos,** far below the mountain road on a small peninsula. Built by the ancient Greeks, it was restored by the Venetians who sent a proveditor to govern it. Two harbours are formed by the peninsula, and on one of them is the little fishing village of Assos, once sleeping and charming, now unfortunately "discovered". Just to the south of it lies the superb beach of **Myrton,** embraced by cliffs, spectacularly snow white against an incredibly blue sea.

PANEYERIA
15 August and 21 October, Ag. Gerasimos; 15 August, Panayias at Markopoulo; 23 April, Ag. Georgios; 21 May, Ag. Konstantinos near Argostoli; carnival celebrations on the last Sunday and Monday before Lent; Easter festival in Lixouri; 21 May, Festival of the Radicals (celebrating union with Greece) in Argostoli; 23 June, Ag. Ioannis, at Argostoli; first Saturday after 15 August, Robola Festival of wine in Fragata.

WHERE TO STAY
Hotels in Argostoli are surprisingly expensive; for example, the class C **Cefalonia Star** at 50 Metaxa St (tel. 0671 23 180) will set you back 4200 dr. for a double. Alternatively there's the **Xenia** at about the same price, but in high season you must take half board, and the rates go up accordingly (tel. 0671 22 233). Nicer priced is the nameless pension nearby, over the bar just opposite the ferry boat docks, with the wonderful, almost life-sized painting of Canadian suburbia. The owners are sweethearts and their clean if small doubles are only 1900 dr. a night. On the beach Platis Yialos there's the **White Rocks,** an A class hotel-bungalow complex with air conditioning and other assorted comforts (tel. 0671 28332/4 with doubles up to 11 000 dr.

In Sami there are more rooms to rent and two decent, clean hotels, the **Hotel Ionian** near the ferry (tel. 0674 22 035), where doubles are 3000 dr. upwards and the **Hotel Kyma** (tel. 0674 22 064), where singles are 1800 dr., doubles 3000 dr. There's also a campsite (tel. 0674 22 480) near Sami with washing facilities and showers for a measly 300 dr. a person.

Other accommodation may be found in Lixouri, Poros, Lassi, Skala, Ag. Afimia and Fiskardo. In Assos, there's the A class **Mediterranee** (tel. 0671 28 760) with all mod cons and airconditioned doubles start at 5000 dr. in the off season, but its high summer rates will have you reaching for the faithful credit card, with doubles hovering around 12 000 dr. On a more realistic level the C class **Irilena** has singles for 2600 dr., doubles 4000 dr. Alternatively, there's the old **Pension Myrto** with all of six rooms, doubles at 2000 dr. In Fiskardo, four

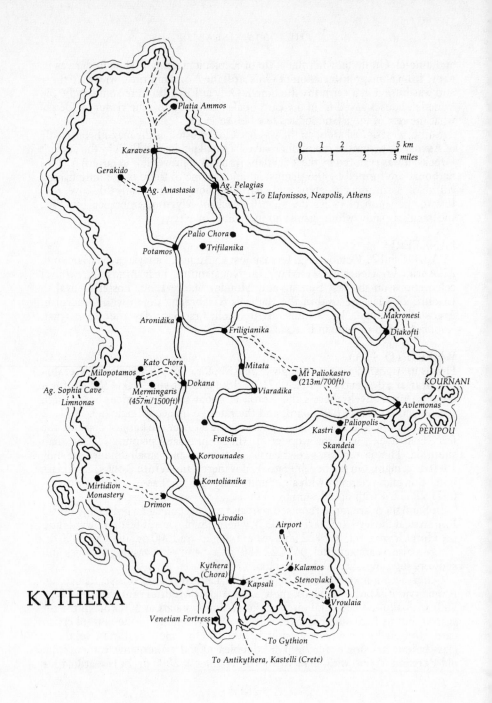

Platia Ammos

Karaves

Gerakido

Ag. Anastasia

Ag. Pelagias

- - To Elafonissos, Neapolis, Athens

Palio Chora

Potamos

Trifilanika

Makronesi

Aronidika

Friligianika

Diakofti

Kato Chora

Mitata

Mt Paliokastro
(213m/700ft)

KOURNANI

Milopotamos

Dokana

Ag. Sophia Cave
Limnonas

Mermingaris
(457m/1500ft)

Viaradika

Avlemonas

Fratsia

Kastri

Paliopolis

PERIPOU

Skandeia

Korvounades

Kontolianika

Mirtidion
Monastery

Drimon

Livadio

Airport

Kythera
(Chora)

Kalamos

Kapsali

Stenovlaki

Vroulaia

KYTHERA

Venetian Fortress

- - To Gythion

To Antikythera, Kastelli (Crete)

0   1   2   5 km
0   1   2   3 miles

typical houses have been renovated by the NTOG; for reservations, write Paradosiakos Ikismos Fiskardou, Kephallonia (tel. 0674 51 398).

EATING OUT
Ask where to eat in Argostoli and you'll always, it seems, be referred to the taverna next to the Rex cinema, where the eating is Greek and cheap (500 dr). **Kalafate,** on the waterfront, is also good and reasonable, and on the main square there's a classy Italian pizzeria for homesick Italians, called **La Gioconda** (400–600 dr. for a pizza). In Lixour, **Anthony's** by the ferry, is good and around 600 dr. for a meal. The best eating, on the whole, is at Fiskardo, where the restaurants are used to loads of yachtsmen dropping in. Two highly recommended places are **Nikolaos** on the alley, with Greek food, grills and pizzas and the **Erodotoes Tavern,** less expensive (600–800 dr) and more traditionally Greek.

TOURIST INFORMATION
NTOG, Argostoli (0671) 22 847.
Tourist police, see regular police, Argostoli (0671) 22 200.

KYTHERA

CONNECTIONS
At least one flight a day from Athens. Hydrofoils from Gythion, Neapolis and Monemvassia daily in summer; also hydrofoil once a week from Piraeus and Nauplion. Regular ferry boat from Monemvassia, Neapolis, Kastelli and Piraeus twice a week.

The opening of the Corinth canal doomed any commercial importance Kythera once had by virtue of its position between the two seas. Today, unless one takes the small plane from Athens, the island is rather difficult to reach. It is totally unconnected with its sister Ionian islands far to the north-west, so much so that politically it now belongs to Attica and is administered from Piraeus. In this century the population has decreased by more than half; as 100 000 people of Kytheran origin now live in Australia, the island is jokingly called a Kangaroo colony, while some call Australia "Big Kythera". All the emigrants who can, come back to Kythera in the summer, constituting its main tourist rush. With only a few hotels and houses with rooms to let, the island is one of the quietest in Greece, and the foreigners who do visit are usually of the hardy Hellenophile type anxious to escape their own countrymen, or the wealthy who have scattered their villas all over Kythera. The island is not without its charms, though it hardly matches the luxuriance of Antoine Watteau's lovely painting, "Journey to Cythère".

HISTORY
When Zeus castrated his father, Cronus, then ruler of the world, he cast the bloody member into the sea. This gave birth to Aphrodite, the goddess of love,

who rose out of the sea foam at Kythera. Later she went across to Cyprus, and was thus referred to as either the Cypriot or the Kytherian. An ancient sanctuary was dedicated to Aphrodite on Kythera, the most sacred of all such sanctuaries in Greece.

Aphrodite was known as Astarte by the first settlers of Kythera, the Phoenicians, who came to the island for a shellfish, the murex, from which they extracted a purple dye to colour royal garments, and from which the island derived its other early name, Porphyrousa. The Minoans from Crete used Kythera as a trading station, for it is centrally situated between Crete and the mainland, and between the Aegean and Ionian Seas. This cross-road location, while encouraging commercial activity, also encouraged raids, and Kythera was invaded no less than 80 times in known history. Particularly frightful were the visits of the Saracen Arabs from Crete: in the 10th century they caused the island to be deserted, as the people sought refuge on the mainland, returning only when Nikephoros Phokas won Crete back for Byzantium.

The rulers of Kythera during the age of Byzantium were the Eudhaemonoyannis family from Monemvassia. The Venetians occupied the island in 1204, but with the help of Emperor Michael Palaeologos, Kythera was regained for the Eudhaemonoyannis, and it served as a refuge for Byzantine nobles when the Turks took the Peloponnese, most of them living at Paliochora. However, in 1537, Barbarossa stopped at Kythera on his way home from the unsuccessful siege of Corfu and destroyed the town. The Venetians occupied the island again in the 15th century and they called it "Cerigo", the name by which it is known in the old history books. The Turks took the island early in the 18th century. In 1864 it was ceded to Greece by the British with the rest of the Ionian islands.

WHAT TO SEE
Kythera, or **Chora**,the capital of Kythera, is a pretty blue and white village, 275 metres (900 ft) above the port of Kapsali, impressively surrounded by the **Kastro**, finished by the Venetians in 1503. The location was supposedly selected by pigeons, who took the tools of the builders from a less protected site and carried them to a hill above the village of Kapsali. There are ten old **Venetian mansions** in Chora still retaining their coats-of-arms, and a small **museum**, generally open in the mornings, which contains artefacts dating back to Minoan times. A few of the inhabitants have rooms to let, and there's a class B hotel. Below, a 20-minute walk down, **Kapsali** has a large house with rooms to let owned by Emmanuel Comnenus (probably a descendant of the Byzantine nobles who fled to Kythera from Mystra), two restaurants and two beaches, along with a yacht supply station.

Buses leave Kythera about once a day for the major villages of the island. Alternatively there are taxis which charge a set fee for different excursions. **Kalamos**, just east of Chora, is within walking distance. One of the churches of the village, Ag. Nikitis, has a pretty bell tower, and there is a taverna by the square. A dirt road leads across some wild landscapes to Vroulaia, a pebble beach and taverna, where many people pitch their tents. **Skandeia** at Paliopolis was the port of the ancient town of Kythera, mentioned by Thucydides, and ruins of the settlement may be seen at the site called **Kastri**. The ancient town itself was above Paliopolis on the **Paliokastro** mountain, and here worshippers came to the ancient temple of Urania Aphrodite to pay their respects to the goddess. The Christians, however, destroyed the renowned sanctuary to build the church of Ag. Anargyroi. Remains of the akropolis walls can still be seen at Paliokastro.

From Paliopolis the coastal road leads to **Avlemonas,** where the Minoans had a trading settlement dating from 2000 BC until the rise of the Mycenaeans. By the sea is a small octagonal fortress built by the Venetians, who left a coat-of-arms and a few rusting cannon inside. There is also a small beach.

Back in the heart of the island, just north of Kapsali at **Livadio,** with its golden wheatfields run wild from a lack of labour, is a pretty bridge of 13 arches. From Livadio via Drimon a paved road leads to the most important religious establishment of Kythera, the **Monastery of the Panayia Mirtidion**. A golden icon of the Virgin and child, faces blackened with age, attracts a huge number of pilgrims to the monastery on 15 August. Situated on the rugged west coast among cypress trees, Mirtidion is ornamented with many flowers, peacocks, and a tall carved bell tower. Two small islets off the coast are apparently pirate ships which the Virgin turned to stone. At the monastery are many lodgings set up to house pilgrims on feast days.

North of the monastery, also accessible from Livadio, **Milopotamos** is the closest thing to Watteau's vision of Kythera. It is the island's loveliest village, crisscrossed with tiny canals of clear water, (so much water, in fact, that the toilet in the valley is in a constant state of flush). This valley, in the middle of town, is called Neraida, or Nymph, and a good restaurant there has music and dancing at night. An old watermill lies along the path to the waterfall, very lovely amid the ancient trees, flowers and banana plants. On quiet days one can even hear the nightingales singing.

Kato Chora lies just below Milopotamos in the walls of a Venetian fortress built in 1560. Above the gate of the deserted town a bas-relief of the lion of St Mark accompanies a Latin inscription. Inside, many of the old stone houses are open for exploration. By the sea below is the cave **Ag. Sophia,** at the end of a rugged, descending road. In the past the cave was used as a church of Ag. Sophia, and inside there are frescoes and mosaics, besides stalactites and stalagmites and small lakes. It is quite a large cave and incredibly is said to go all the way to Ag. Pelagias—where indeed a sign points down a rocky hill to a site called Ag. Sophia.

Palio Chora, also known as Ag. Dimitriou on the north-east coast of Kythera, south of Ag. Pelagias, was built by the Byzantine noble Eudhaemonoyannis in the Monemvassian style. High on the rocks it was hidden from the sea—Barbarossa found it only by capturing the inhabitants and forcing them to tell him where it was. Beside the ruins of the fort is a terrible abyss down which the mothers threw their children before leaping themselves, to avoid the Turks. Most of the island's ghost stories and legends are centred on this tragic place.

Potamos, despite its name, has no river. It is the largest village in the north part of the island, all blue and white like Chora. It has a bank and the Olympic Airways office, and the largest building at the edge of town is the island's retirement home. At **Gerakido** to the north-west one can see yet another tower, this time built by the Turks in the early 18th century. **Platia Ammos** is a fine beach just east of Karaves, and south of it another beach may be found at **Ag. Pelagias,** the northern port of the island, and its most pleasant resort.

From Ag. Pelagias one can see the islet **Elafonissos,** connected by ship three times a week, or more frequently in the summer by caiques. The village, also called Elafonissos, is mostly inhabited by fishermen and sailors. A new village, **Kata Nisso,** is under construction with a hotel, for little Elafonissos has two gorgeous sandy beaches a kilometre or so long, as yet hardly discovered by tourists.

Another islet, **Antikythera,** lies to the south of Kapsali. Ships call there twice a week in between Kythera and Crete. Fewer than 150 people live there in two settlements, Potamos and Sochoria, and it is very rocky with few trees. By Potamos are the ruins of ancient **Aigilia** with a wall dating back to Classical times.

PANEYERIA
15 August, Panayias Mirtidion; 29–30 May, Ag. Trias at Mitata.

WHERE TO STAY
When it comes to finding a place to stay on Kythera you may be hard pressed. In Kythera town there's the small B class pension **Keti,** with doubles going for around 4000 dr. (tel. 0733 31 318). Up in Ag. Pelagias the ten-roomed **Kytheria** pension has doubles for 3500 dr. (tel. 0733 33 321), and in Manitochori, **Ta Kythera** (again, another small pension) has clean, pleasant double rooms averaging 4000 dr. For families and longer stays there are furnished apartments in Kapsali (tel. 0733 31 265) and at Pitsinades, with rates ranging from 4000 dr. to 8500 dr. per day. Other than that there are a few rooms to be had at Ag. Pelagias, Potamos, Kythera town and Milopotamos.

EATING OUT
Kapsali has the most in the way of restaurants, including the American style **Kapsi Kamales,** where you can dine for around 1000 dr. There are a number of typical, simple tavernas offering straightforward Greek food at Greek prices up in Chora; there's also the restaurant in Milopotamos and in Ag. Pelagias there's a limited selection of tavernas and, for the economically minded, an excellent self-service restaurant.

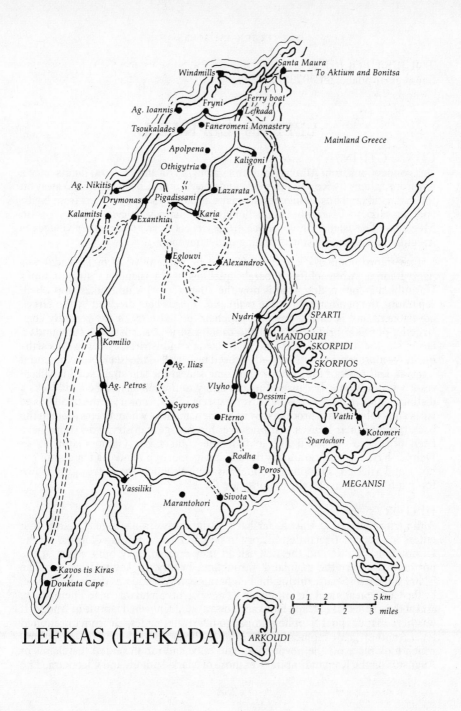

Santa Maura
To Aktium and Bonitsa
Windmills
Ferry boat
Fryni
Lefkada
Ag. Ioannis
Faneromeni Monastery
Tsoukalades
Mainland Greece
Apolpena
Kaligoni
Othigytria
Ag. Nikitis
Lazarata
Drymonas
Pigadissani
Kalamitsi
Exanthia
Karia
Eglouvi
Alexandros
Nydri
SPARTI
MANDOURI
Komilio
SKORPIDI
SKORPIOS
Ag. Ilias
Ag. Petros
Vlyho
Dessimi
Syvros
Vathi
Fterno
Kotomeri
Spartochori
Rodha
MEGANISI
Poros
Vassiliki
Marantohori
Sivota
Kavos tis Kiras
Doukata Cape
0   1   2   5 km
0   1   2   3 miles

LEFKAS (LEFKADA)

ARKOUDI

TOURIST POLICE
See regular police, tel. (0733) 31 206.

LEFKAS (LEFKADA)

CONNECTIONS

Bus connections from Athens (four times a day), Arta and Preveza; flights once a day from Athens (twice a day at week-ends) to Aktium, 26 km (16 miles) away on the mainland, and bus connection from the airport; in summer, boats from Nydri and Vassiliki to Fiskardo (Kephallonia) and Stavros (Ithaca). Daily boat to Meganisi. The island's bus service from Lefkas town to the other villages is irregular and generally stops running mid-afternoon.

Lefkas (more popularly known in Greece by its genitive form Lefkada) was named for its white cliffs. It barely qualifies as an island; in ancient times Corinthian colonists dug what is now the 20-m (66-ft) wide Lefkas ship canal, separating the peninsula from the mainland. This is kept dredged by the Greek government and is easily crossed by a chain-pulled ferry or the recently constructed pontoon bridge; beyond the canal a series of causeways surrounds a large, shallow lagoon (salt is one of Lefkada's industries). A series of earthquakes—most recently in 1948—destroyed nearly all of the island's architectural interest, and most of the visitors who come stay at the still small seaside village resorts in the south. Because of its proximity to the mainland, Lefkada lacks a distinct island character. It is, however, especially well known for the hand-made laces and embroideries produced by its women, many of whom keep a loom in the back room of their houses. To preserve this cottage industry, workshops have been organised—if you'd like to visit one contact Eva Giannoulatou at 23 Delpferth St. Lefkas is gradually developing its tourist potential-a fair amount of hotel and villa construction is underway and although there are quite a few foreign holiday-makers, the majority are Greek.

HISTORY

Although inhabited at least as far back as the Early Bronze Age, Lefkada first enters the scene of recorded history in 640 BC, when it was colonised by the Corinthians. To defend the new island they created, they built a fort at the northern tip, near the mainland, throughout history the key to Lefkada. The island sided with Sparta during the Peloponnesian War and was devastated twice, by the Corcyraeans and the Athenians. The ancient capital was near Themodern, and at the white cliff of Cape Doukata stood a once renowned temple of Apollo. It was here that the poet Sappho plunged to her death, in despair from unrequited love. Another great moment in the island's history was the Battle of Aktium, which took place off the north coast, and once and for all settled the claims of Augustus on the Roman Empire over those of Mark Anthony and Cleopatra. The

Byzantines lost the island to the Franks in the 13th century, and they built the original fortress of Santa Maura, a name later adopted for the whole of the island. When Constantinople fell in 1453, the mother of the last Emperor Constantinos XI, Helene Palaeologus, founded a monastery in the walls of Santa Maura, which the Turks when they took Lefkas in 1479, turned into a mosque. They also took many of the inhabitants of the island to the Turkish slave markets.

In 1500 the combined Spanish and Venetian forces under de Cordova captured Lefkas and Santa Maura in the name of Christianity, but the very next year Venice made a treaty with Turkey and returned the island. Francesco Morosini, however, after losing his own fortress at Herakleon, Crete, was determined to win Lefkas back for Venice in 1684, and he did with the help of a great number of Greeks from the Ionian islands. With the fall of the Serenissima Republic of Venice, the French and then the Russians took Lefkas, the latter establishing it as part of the Septinsular Republic and adding fortifications. They also widened the canal. In 1807 the tyrant Ali Pasha of Epirus moved to take Lefkas, but was held back by forces under the Secretary of State, Count John Capodistria, who is said to have sworn to the cause of an Independent Greece with rebellious refugees on the island, including Kolokotronis.

WHAT TO SEE

As you approach **Lefkas,** the capital of the island, you pass the **Fortress of Santa Maura,** part of it in the sea near Arkanania on the mainland; most of what remains dates from the Venetian and Turkish reconstructions. It survived the periodic earthquakes better than the town, which is nearly all new and is remarkable for the fragile state of the upper storeys of its buildings—an antiseismic measure. Another unusual feature of the town are the bell towers near the 18th-century Venetian churches, which resemble oil drills. Solidly built of stone, the churches have survived the tremors. Examples of the Ionian school of painting can be seen in Ag. Minas and Ag. Dimitrios.

There are three small museums in Lefkas town: the **Archaeology Museum,** housing mostly the finds made by Dörpfeld in Nydri; the **Icon Museum,** with works mostly of the Ionian school, housed in the municipal library; and the **Lefkada Sound Museum,** at 29 Kalkani St, founded by a local collector and the only museum of its kind in Greece, with old gramophones sent over by relatives from the United States, records of Cantades and popular Greek songs of the 1920s, and one of the first discs recorded by a Greek company, "Orpheon" of Constantinople, founded in 1914. There are also a number of antiques from Lefkada (open daily, free).

Just above Lefkas is the 17th-century **Faneromeni Monastery,** rebuilt in the 19th century after a fire. It is a charming and serene place, with wonderful views of the town and lagoon below. There are pebbly beaches along the causeway, near the derelict windmills. The central bus station is at the far end of town and buses to the coastal villages are frequent.

The rest of the island still retains much of its rural charm, and it's not unusual

289

A Country Taverna, Lefkas

to encounter women still dressed in their traditional costumes. A short distance from town on a hill near the east shore, are the ruins of ancient **Leukas,** the Corinthian city, although there's little to see except the walls and traces of a theatre. Further south is **Nydri** one of Lefkada's small resort towns, looking out over the lovely wooded islets of **Mandouri, Sparti, Skorpidi** and **Skorpios,** the last famous for belonging to the Onassis family. From the sea you can spy Aristotle's tomb and excursion boats now have permission to land on the beaches if no-one is in residence. On the plain behind Nydri, Wilhelm Dörpfeld, who assisted Schliemann in the excavation of Troy, found a number of Bronze Age tombs that he believed proved his theory that Lefkas was the Ithaca of Homer. He died in 1940 and is buried near the house in which he lived, on the peninsula facing the town.

Sit at a café in Nydri at twilight—there's one so near the shore you may sit with your feet in the sea—and watch Mandouri float above the horizon on a magic carpet of mist to the croaking of the frogs. The mansion on Mandouri belongs to the family of the poet Aristelis Valaoritis who, like Angellos Sikelianos, came from Lefkas. Both poets were inspired by the combination of mainland and island cultures there.

Vlyho, the next village south, is a quiet, shady charmer and in walking distance of sandy Dessimi beach. From **Syvros,** one of the larger villages in the interior, you can climb to the cave **Karouha,** the largest on the island. **Rodha** and **Sivota** (with a taverna, and hotels under construction) are popular swimming places with the local people. **Vassiliki** is a shady, charming village with beaches. From here one may take a caique (or go by road from Komilio) to see the 60-metre (200-ft) white cliffs of **Cape Doukata,** the original Lover's Leap, where Sappho, rejected by Phaon, hurled herself into the sea below. There is in fact some evidence that the leap was not always a fatal cure for unrequited love; priests serving at the temple of Apollo Lefkada (of which only the scantiest ruins remain) made the jump safely (*katapontismos*) as part of their cult. Later, Romans rejected by their sweethearts made the dives (taking the precaution of strapping on feathers or even live birds and employing rescue parties to pull them out of the sea below). The cliffs are a famous landmark for sailors; Byron's Childe Harold "saw the evening star above Leucadia's far-projecting rock of woe" as he sailed past. Today, a lighthouse marks the historic spot.

The west coast of Lefkas is rocky and rugged as far as **Ag. Nikitis,** which has a sandy beach and night club. Just south of here a new road allows access to **Kathisma,** a good place to swim with a snack bar on the beach. **Ag. Petros** is the prettiest village on this side of the island. In the interior several villages have notable churches with frescoes, like the Red Church (Kokkino Eklisia) in **Alexandros,** and the 15th century church at **Othigytria,** its design incorporating Byzantine and Western influences.

PANEYERIA
Carnival festivities, with a parade; in August, the Arts and Letters Festival and large International Folklore Festival, in Lefkas town; 11–13 August, Ag. Spyridon, at Karia, when the people bring out their old costumes; 30 May, Faneromeni Monastery; 11 November, Ag. Minas in Lefkas; 26 July, Ag. Paraskevi near Ag. Petros.

WHERE TO STAY
Most of the island's accommodation is in the main town, on the waterfront overlooking the canal. The **Xenia** (tel. 0645 24 762) has double rooms with half board (compulsory in high season) for 6400 dr., bed and breakfast (low season) for 4100 dr. More comfortable in the same price range is the **Hotel Lefkas** (tel. 0645 23 916). Next door, the **Niricos Hotel,** also a class B, has doubles at 4000 dr., singles 2800 dr. (tel. 0645 24 132). Less expensive and on the main drag is the small and pleasant **Byzantium Hotel** (tel. 0645 22 629) where doubles at 1900 dr. and singles 1200 dr. (showers extra) are very good value. Rooms in private homes on the island start at 1500 dr. In Nydri, Vlyho and especially in Vassiliki you can usually find a room without too much difficulty from 1700 dr. upwards. At Nikiana, between Lefkas town and Nydri, the new **Galini Hotel** provides comfort at a price—its roomy doubles go for up to 10 000 dr. in the summer (tel. 0645 92 431). In Ag. Nikitis smart rooms with private bath and overlooking the sea are around 3500 dr. There are campsites at Dessimi Beach near Vlyho (tel. 0645 95 225), at Poros Beach further south (tel. 0645 95 298 & 0645 95 475) and at Vassiliki (tel. 0645 31 308).

EATING OUT
Restaurants are numerous and reasonably priced on Lefkas and portions seem to be larger than elsewhere in Greece. In Lefkas town **Pyrofani** taverna has a good

EXOLITHARO LAKKAS

Ipparandi

Lakka

Kastanitha Cave

Ag. Charalambos

Palietatika

Longos

Koutsi

Romanatika

Zenembissatika

Vassilatika

Kalodikatika

Manessatika

Apergatika

Arvanitakeika

To Corfu

PANAYIA

Magazia

Boikatika

Platanos

Ag. Ioannis

Kastro

Ag. Nikolaos

Ortholithos Cave

Xlonatika

Gaios

Vlachoplatika

Makratika

Fanariotika

Zenembissatika

Oxias

MONGONISSI

Ag. Spiridou

KATSIONISSI

PAXOS

0   1   2   5 km
0   1   2   3 miles

Antipaxi

Ag. Emilianos

Agrapoia

ANTIPAXOS

DASKALIA

variety of Greek dishes and seafood. For a change, **La Vela** (behind the Xenia) produces some tasty Italian novelties for about 1500 dr. for a full meal. Eat at least once at **Kavos** on the beach at Nydri for the view and consistently good food for 600 dr. In Vassiliki the best value is the grill, where you can eat well for 1000 dr. on average.

Meganisi lies off the south-east coast of Lefkas. Every day except Monday a caique goes there from Lefkas and Nydri and twice a week the larger ships call at **Vathi,** its port and largest settlement. It is a rocky islet but not without beauty. The only time when many people go there is for the paneyeri of Ag. Konstantinos on 21 May at the hamlet of Kotomeri. **Arkoudi,** another islet south of Lefkas, is inhabited by a few fishermen and shepherds.

TOURIST POLICE
See regular police, Lefkas town, tel. (0645) 95 207 and in Vassiliki, tel. (0645) 31 218.

PAXOS

CONNECTIONS
Daily boats from Corfu in the summer, two or three times a week in summer to Parga; also connections with Patras, Kephallonia, Ithaca and Italy in summer. Connections are far less frequent in the off season. In the summer you may well be asked to have a room reservation before boarding a ferry to the island which is small, wooded, and fearful of campers and their fires.

Tiniest and yet one of the most charming islands in the Ionian Sea, Paxos and its little sister Antipaxos have long served as a kind of outlet from the mass package tourism and overdevelopment of Corfu. Paxos (or Paxoi) is so small and so flat you can easily walk its 8-km (5-mile) length in a day, its one road twisting through the immaculate groves of olives that brought the islanders most of their income before tourism. Paxos' olive oil is still considered among the best produced in Greece and has won many international prizes. Besides the beauty of the silvery trees (there are some 300 000—each family owns at least 500) and the tidy stone walls, the little island has some of the friendliest people you'll find anywhere in Greece.

HISTORY
Paxo was happily little affected by history. What mention it has received is derived from its seven sea caves—Homer mentions one, Ipparandi, describing it as having rooms of gold. In another cave the Greek resistance hero Papanikolaos hid and waylaid passing Italian ships in the Second World War, a trick unfortunately copied by the German U-boats which came later.

Plutarch recounts an incident of great moment that took place off the shore of

Paxos, at the beginning of the 1st century AD. Thamus, the pilot of a ship sailing near the island, heard a voice call his name and say, "When the ship comes opposite Palodes, you must announce the death of the Great God Pan" When Thamus did so at the designated spot, great cries of lamentation arose. So the old gods were replaced with a new, marking the end—and the beginning—of a Great World Age.

WHAT TO SEE

Gaios, the pretty little capital of the island, is named after a disciple of St Paul who brought Christianity to Paxos and is buried there. Most of the island's people live here, and it's where you'll find a small sandy beach and all of Paxos' facilities, including a tiny **aquarium** on the harbour-front. The streets of Gaios are fortunately too narrow for cars, although human traffic jams occur during the day in the summer, when day trippers from Corfu and cruise ships sail into the little port; in the evening, however, the island regains its composure.

On a rocky islet facing the harbour is the well-preserved **Kastro Ag. Nikolaos,** built by the Venetians in 1423, and an old windmill, and beyond it, the islet of **Panayia,** which on 15 August is crowded with pilgrims. In the evening they come back to Gaios and dance all night in the village square. **Mongonissi,** another islet, is connected by caique—belonging to the family which owns a pretty little restaurant there—which brings customers over for dinner in the evening. Caiques may also be rented for a tour of the island, to see its seven sea caves of brilliant blue. Most are located among the sheer cliffs on the western side of Paxos, one of the more impressive being **Kastanitha,** 185 metres (600 ft) high. Another distinctive cave, **Ortholithos,** has a sentinel-like monolith at its entrance. It is possible to penetrate about 5 metres (18 ft) inside by caique. Homer's **Ipparandi** does not have the golden rooms he mentions, although it often shelters seals. **Grammatiko** is the largest cave of them all. When sailing around the island, you can also see the **Mousmouli Cliffs** and their natural bridge **Tripitos**.

The road from Gaios across Paxos was donated by Aristotle Onassis, who found the island charming. At its northern end is **Lakka,** a tiny port where the ferries from Corfu usually call (connected by minibus with Gaios). Lakka has a small beach, and the Byzantine church in the village has particularly musical Russian bells. If you ask, someone in the village will give you the key so that you can climb up in the belfry and ring them. The **Grammatikou mansion** near Lakka dates from the 19th century and is fortified with a tower. In **Boikatika** village the church Ag. Charalambos contains an old icon of the Virgin and in nearby **Magazia** are two churches of interest, Ag. Spyridon and Ag. Apostoli; the latter's churchyard affording an impressive view of the Eremitis cliffs. At **Apergatika** the Papamarkou mansion dates from the 17th century.

PANEYERIA

Easter Monday procession from Gaios to Velliantitika; 15 August, Panayias; 11 August, Ag. Spyridon; 10 February, Ag. Charalambos.

ZAKYNTHOS

Kianoun Cave (Blue Grotto)
Korithi
Askos
Sklavou Skinari
Cave
Volimes
Ano Volimes
Ag. Gerasimou Cave
Xinthia Cave Orthonies
Anafonitria Alikes Alikanes
Katastari Kipseli Planos
Pigadakia Yeraki Tsilivi
Maries Kallithea Tragaki
Megali Cave Skoulikado Ag. Kalipado
Ag. Ioannis Yiri Dimitrios Gaytani Bohali
Exo Chora Ag. Marina Vanato Zakynthos
Louha Ag. Kirikos Sarakinado To Kilini
Kampi Ag. Pandes
Ag. Leon Fiolitis Lagadakia Argassi
Vouyiato Mt Xirokastello
Macherado Airport Skopos
Ag. Nikolaos Lagopoda Ano
Mouzaki Kalamaki Vassilikos
Pantokrator Romiri
Lithakia Lagana Vassiliki
Agalas PELOUZA
Pitch MARATHONISSI
Keri

0   1   2   5 km
0   1   2   3 miles

WHERE TO STAY
The only official accommodation is at the class B **Paxos Beach Bungalows** (tel. 0662 31 211) in Gaios (as is everything else). The chalet bungalows are pleasant, comfortable and near the beach, and go for 7000 dr., but are solidly booked in season. For families the **Tranaka** has furnished apartments for 12 000 dr. a day (enquire at travel agent on quay). Everyone else stays in private rooms, which are invariably pleasant, tidy and double, and average 1800 dr. In Lakka there's the **Pension Lefkothea** (tel. 0662 31 807) with doubles for 2000 dr.

EATING OUT
Take the caique to Mongonissi for the excellent restaurant there (800–1100 dr.) and to while the day away on the beach. There are a handful of tavernas in Gaios (the **Taka Taka** serves solid Greek fare and fish, the former inexpensive, the latter about 1200 dr. for a meal). There are also some tavernas in Lakka and Longos.

TOURIST POLICE
See regular police in Gaios, tel. (0662) 31 222.

South of Paxos lies tiny **Antipaxos,** with only a few permanent residents. From June until September four or five caiques leave Gaios daily for its port **Agrapoia,** and out of season one may rent a boat to make the 40-minute trip. Although both Paxos and Antipaxos were created with a resounding blow of Poseidon's trident (the sea god thought that the gap between Corfu and Lefkas was a bit too large), the two islands are very different in nature. Rather than olive oil, Antipaxos produces good white and red wines, and rather than being rocky, its coasts are enhanced by fine sandy beaches **Voutoumia** and **Vrika** are praised for being "softer than silk". There is no accommodation on the islet—if you are lucky you may find a room in a house, but those planning to stay should bring a sleeping bag. This could well be the uncontaminated paradise you've been seeking.

ZAKYNTHOS (ZANTE)

CONNECTIONS
Daily flights from Athens. Three times a week to Kephallonia. Several charters from major European cities. Daily year-round hydrofoil from Patras; ferry three or four times a day from Kilini. Bus two or three times a day from Athens. Ferry on Sundays to Kephallonia.

Of all their Ionian possessions the Venetians loved Zakynthos the most for its charm and natural beauty "Zante, fiore di Levante"—the flower of the East—they called it, and built a city even more splendid than Corfu on its great semi-circular bay. Unfortunately, the earthquake of 1953 turned it into rubble. Nevertheless, the disaster did nothing to diminish the soft, luxuriant charm of the landscape and its fertile green hills and mountainsides: the valleys with their vineyards, olive groves and orchards, the brilliant garland of flowers and beautiful beaches (the flowers are best in spring and autumn, a time when few foreigners visit the island). The Italians made a lasting impression—many islanders are descendants of Venetian settlers and belong to the Catholic Church. They sing the Italianate Cantades, the lyrical songs for which the island is famous.

HISTORY

According to tradition, the island was named for its first settler, a son of Dardanus from Arcadia. Homer mentions the island in both of his works; in the Trojan War the Zantiots fought under the command of Odysseus, although their island later became an independent, coin-minting state which set up colonies throughout the Mediterranean. One called Zakanthi was founded in Spain and later demolished by Hannibal. General Levinus took the island for Rome in 214 BC, and when the inhabitants rose up against their conqueror he burnt all the buildings on Zakynthos.

Uniting with the Aeolians, the Zantiots forced the Romans to leave, although in 150 BC Flavius finally brought the troublesome island under control. Pliny refers to Mons Nobilis on Zakynthos (now Mt Skopos), identifying its cavern as the entrance to the underworld.

In AD 844 the Saracens captured the island from their base in Crete, but the Byzantine forces were strong enough to expel them. The Norman–Sicilian pirate Margaritone took Zakynthos in 1182, and three years later Byzantium lost the island to the County Palatine of Kephallonia, first governed by Margaritone. One of his successors ceded the island to the Venetians in 1209. They kept the island for almost 350 years, although the Turks captured and pillaged it between 1479 and 1484. The aristocratic social system of the Venetians and wealthy Zantiots caused so much resentment among the commoners that they rose up in "the Rebellion of the Popolari" and took control of the island for four years. When the Turkish forces occupied Crete in the 17th century, many Cretan artists took refuge on the Venetian Zakynthos, initiating a great artistic movement on the island. It was the centre of the famous Ionian school of painting, which produced such artists as Doxaras, Koutouzis and Kantorinis. The song cult of the Cantades flourished and in the 18th century two national poets Andreas Kalvos and Dionysos Solomos, were born on the island and did some of their writing here; Solomos is known as the poet of the Greek War of Independence and wrote the lyrics to the Greek National Anthem.

The Zantiots responded actively to the ideas of the French Revolution, forming their own Jacobin Club and destroying the hated rank of nobility. The Russians in 1798 forced the French garrison and the inhabitants to surrender, after a siege of months, and when the Septinsular Republic established aristocrats of its own, Zakynthos rebelled again in 1801. During the War of Independence many rebels on the mainland found asylum on the island.

WHAT TO SEE

The capital of the island, also called **Zakynthos,** was rebuilt after the earthquake, the inhabitants gamely trying to incorporate some of the lost city's charm into the dull lines of modern Greek architecture. But it is the natural surround-ings of the town that one most remembers—the fine curve of the harbour, the ancient akropolis rising above, crowned with a castle, and to the right the unusual form of **Mt Skopos** ("lookout"), the Mons Nobilis of Pliny. A path leads to the top from the edge of the town; in the old days someone would daily make the two-hour ascent to scan the horizon for pirate ships.

The city itself is long and narrow, and can easily be explored by horse-drawn cab or the odd, double-pedal canopied vehicles for hire in the square. The most conspicuous architectural features of the buildings are the arcades, all full of shops selling the local speciality, mandolato (white nougat with nuts) **Plateia Solomou** is the centre of the town, home of the Tourist Police, the restored 15th century church of **Ag. Nikolaos** and the **Neo-Byzantine Museum** (open 8.45 am–5 pm, closed Tuedays) with works of the Ionian school and icons and other works of art salvaged from the fallen churches. Another museum, two blocks up at Ag. Markou Square, is the **Solomos Museum,** near the mausoleums of Dionysos Solomos and Andreas Kalvos, and contains mementoes of the poets and other famous sons of Zakynthos, as well as photographs of pre-earthquake Zakynthos. Little 17th century **Kyra ton Angelous,** another reconstructed chapel, is near the Xenia Hotel. At the south end of town a huge church was constructed to house the relics of the island's patron saint, **Ag. Dionysos**; it is filled with gold and silver ex-votos and fine frescoes.

Looming over the town is the well preserved **Venetian Kastro,** an hour's walk from Plateia Solomou. It's an easier walk than Mt Skopas, one rewarded with views not only of Zakynthos, but of the Peloponnese and the Bay of Navarino, where the most famous battle of modern Greece was fought.

Because of a recent oil spill the town beach isn't all that good—better to take a bus to **Vassiliki** at the far end of the eastern peninsula (rooms and camping available) and the charming, pine-shaded sandy strand at **Porto Roma**, but bear in mind that because of the infrequent bus service you may well have to fork out 1000 dr. to get back to town by taxi. Out in the bay the little islet **Pelouza** to the south was colonised in 1473 BC by King Zakynthos; today many come there to fish. **Kalamaki** and **Argassi** are two villages with sandy beaches on either side of Mt Skopos, at the beginning of currant country. **Lagana** is Zakynthos' most developed resort, packed on summer weekends with families from the Peloponnese. The sand is good and fine, and there are some curious rock formations by the sea. Behind Lagana extends the **plain of Zakynthos,** a lovely region to cycle through with its old country estates.

Further south is **Keri,** with another sandy beach below; a kilometre or so away the **Pissa tou Keriou** are natural pitch wells, used, as in ancient times, to caulk boats. These were well known in antiquity, referred to by both Herodotos and Pliny. There are tavernas by the beach and fine views from the village of Keri. Like **Exo Chora** in the west, the village is a hunting centre. Zakynthos abounds in rabbits and fowl (the hunting season is from 25 August to 15 March). Northwards, in a cluster of farming villages, **Macherado** stands out with its lovely church of **Ag. Mavra,** housing a beautiful old icon of the saint. The church bells are noted for their musical quality. In nearby Lagopoda there is also the pretty **Eleftherias monastery. Ag. Nikolaos** is a very pretty village, on a hill at the edge of the region. **Katastari,** to the north-west of Zakynthos town, is the island's second largest town, and marks the north edge of the plain. Below is the beach (with pensions and tavernas) at **Alikes,** a wonderful long stretch of sand which continues west around the bay of **Alikan.** From Katastari you can drive or take a taxi up to **Anafonitria** and its monastery, a survivor of the earthquake, with frescoes and the cell of Ag. Dionysos, along with a medieval tower.

Unlike the low rolling hills and plain of the east, the west coast of Zakynthos is mountainous, the steep cliffs plunging into the sea. It is also a region with caves **Ag. Gerasimou, Xinthia** (track from Anafonitria) with sulphur springs—evidence of the island's volcanic origins—and **Sklavou** are the most interesting, excluding of course Kianoun Cave, also known as the **Blue Cave.** Kianoun can be visited by caique, either from Zakynthos town or Alikes. The cave glows with every imaginable shade of blue.

Volimes to the south-west of Korithi is one of the largest villages of the island; to go swimming there wear swim shoes, so hot are the rocks and sand. **Ano Volimes** just above it is a pretty little mountain village.

A small islet some 50 km (30 miles) south of Zakynthos, called **Strophades,** has a Byzantine monastery which served as a fortress for many years, until the Saracens finally overcame the defence of the monks and plundered it. Today only the building remains, and a lighthouse. The island is a popular resting station for migratory doves. If you're looking for an out-of-the-way, romantic destination you won't find a better one.

PANEYERIA
The Carnival in Zakynthos lasts for two weeks prior to Lent, and is known for its masked singers and dancing among the general festivities. For the paneyeri of Ag. Dimitriou on 24 August and 17 December Zakynthos town is strewn with myrtle and there are fireworks at the church. During Holy Week the inhabitants also give themselves over to an infectious merriment. Slightly more modest is Zoodochos Pigi in the town on 10 November. In July the Zakynthia takes place with cultural activities; at the end of August and beginning of September, the International Meeting of Medieval and Popular Theatre, with performances.

WHERE TO STAY
There are hotels in town and around the island in about equal proportion, though on the whole it's more pleasant to stay outside the centre. In Zakynthos town, you can choose between the **Strada Marina** at 14 K. Lombardou St (tel. 0695 22 761). Nicely located on the quay, it is, however, a shade overpriced at 5000 dr. a double. More reasonable are the **Rezentsa Hotel** at 36 Alex Roma St (tel. 0695 22 375), clean and pleasant with singles for 1800 dr., doubles for 2500 dr., and the **Hotel Alfa** on Tertseti St (tel. 0695 22 416) for the same price. The tourist police off the Plateia Solomou have a list of rooms to let.

Outside the town, most of the accommodation is at Laganas, which has almost 20 class C hotels and scores of rooms to rent and the people to fill them up. Unless you like that sort of thing, head to more serene haunts such as Planos, where a double in the C class **Cosmopolite** will set you back 3000 dr. (tel. 0695 28 752), Tsilivi, Porto Roma or Keri, which is serene and has the cheapest rooms on the island. In Tragaki the A class **Caravel** (sister to the one in Athens) will lighten your wallet to the tune of 12 000 dr. for a double with all the trimmings (tel. 0695 25 261). There are campsites at Tsilivi (tel. 0695 24 754) and at Laganas (tel. 0695 22 292), and the popular **Turtle Bay Club** is on its own little bay. The owners will meet you at the ferry.

EATING OUT

In Zakynthos town, you can eat well at **P. Evangelos** on Alex Roma St for 1000 dr.; the food is freshly prepared and good. There are several expensive places on Ag. Marko square and more moderate ones around the city hall. A good place to try the local wine is **Cava Korgianiti** at 52 Calvou St. For a meal with a view, there's **Alla** up on Filikon 38, located in one of the few houses to have survived the earthquake (800–1200 dr. for dinner).

TOURIST POLICE

In the harbour, tel. (0695) 22 550.

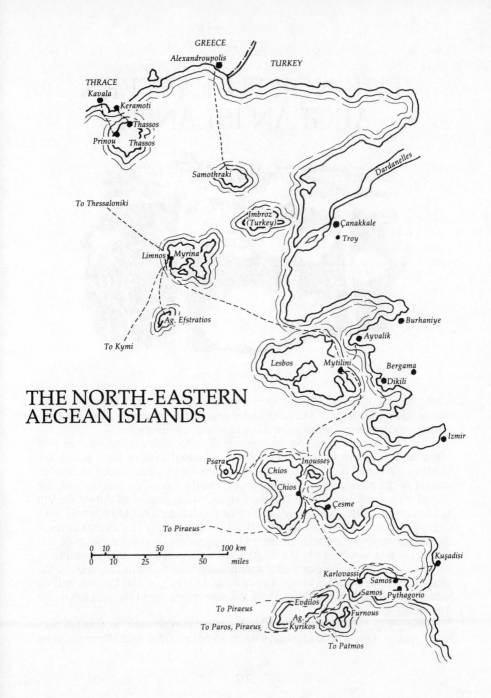

GREECE

Alexandroupolis

TURKEY

THRACE

Kavala

Keramoti

Thassos

Prinou　*Thassos*

Samothraki

Dardanelles

To Thessaloniki

Imbroz (Turkey)

● *Çanakkale*

● *Troy*

Limnos　*Myrina*

Ag. Efstratios

To Kymi

● *Burhaniye*

● *Ayvalik*

Lesbos　*Mytilini*

● *Bergama*

● *Dikili*

THE NORTH-EASTERN
AEGEAN ISLANDS

● *Izmir*

Psara

Inousses

Chios

Chios

● *Çesme*

To Piraeus

0	10		50		100 km
0	10	25		50	miles

● *Kuşadisi*

Karlovassi

Samos

Samos　*Pythagorio*

Evdilos

Furnous

To Piraeus

Ag. Kyrikos

To Paros, Piraeus

To Patmos

Part VII

THE NORTH-EASTERN AEGEAN ISLANDS

Christos Rachon, Ikaria

The grouping of these seven major islands (Chios, Ikaria, Lesbos, Limnos, Samos, Samothrace and Thassos) under one title is done nowadays for convenience rather than for any cultural or historical consideration.

What they have in common, however, is their location off the coast of Asia Minor and Northern Greece. The Ionians colonised most of them during the Dorian invasion of the 12th century BC, when the invaders forced the earlier settlers of the mainland to seek new homes in the east. The Ionians took the coastal regions of Asia Minor and the islands, which flourished during the 7th and 6th centuries BC, producing some of the greatest geniuses of ancient Greece such as Pythagoras, Sappho and probably Homer himself. The ancient cities of the islands were very important in early Greece, not only in commercial trade and the production of wine and olive oil (the soil is ill-suited for other agriculture), but in the religious sphere as well. Samothrace is famous for its sanctuary of the gods of the underworld, Limnos was dedicated to the god Hephaestus, and on Samos the temple of the goddess Hera was considered one of the wonders of the Ancient World.

These prosperous independent islands slipped into obscurity as they fell prey to the greater powers around them, who attacked first from Asia Minor and then

302

Agiasmata

Kabia

Giossona

Ag. Gala

Nagos

Melanios

Marmaros

Kardamila

Parparia

Pirama

Volissos

Pitios

Skala
Volissos

Katavasis

Sidirounta

Anevatos

Vrontados

Karyes

Neo Moni

Chios

Kambos

Lithion

Karfas

Vessa

Tholopotami

Kallimassia

Pass Limani

Kataraktis

Mesta

Armolia

Olymbai

Fana

Kalamoti

Pirgi

Kommi

Emborio

CHIOS

| 0 | 2 | 5 | | 10 km |

| 0 | 2 | | 5 | miles |

from the West, and then from Asia Minor again in the form of the Ottoman Empire. They were annexed to Greece only in 1912, following the Balkan Wars.

The North-Eastern Aegean islands were the last to be discovered by the summer invasions of visitors, partly due to their great distance from Athens— Ikaria, the closest island to Athens, is a 10-hour journey by ship. Almost all the islands, however, now have airports to shorten the trip, although anyone planning to fly there during the summer should reserve a seat as much as two months in advance (Olympic Airways). Connections between the islands are regular if not exceptionally frequent.

CHIOS

CONNECTIONS
By air: three flights a day from Athens, twice weekly with Samos, Lesbos and Mykonos. By ship: daily with Piraeus and Lesbos. Daily in summer to Cesme, Turkey, out of season less frequently. Four times a week to Psara; twice a week with Limnos and Kavala; twice a week with Samos; once a week with Patmos, Kos, Rhodes and Thessaloniki; several times a week to Rafina from the second port, Mesta. Daily excursion in summer to Inousses.

Chios is a wealthy island, not only because of the numerous shipowning dynasties it has produced, but also for its mastic trees, or lentisks, which thrive in Chios as they do nowhere else in the world. In August the sweet sap drips down the shrub-like trunks of the trees, glistening like liquid diamonds in the sun, and by September it is ripe for the mastic manufacturer. Mastic gum, sweets and a liqueur are the major products of Chios.

The geography of the island surprises one with its variety. While some parts are so barren that one can go for a long way without seeing a touch of green, other places are thickly forested, and still others are fertile agricultural plains yielding citrus fruits, olives, almonds and wine. A large mountain range cuts across the island, giving rise to its Homeric epithet of "craggy"; the highest peak, Mt Profitis Ilias, rises to a height of 1297 m (4255 ft). Byzantine and medieval monuments abound, and the International Society of Homeric studies is based on Chios, where a conference is held every summer.

HISTORY
Inhabited from approximately 3000 BC, Chios was later colonised by the Pelasgians who left walls near Exo Didyma and Kourounia and a temple of Zeus on top of Mt Pelion. The Acheans followed the Pelasgians, and they in turn were usurped by the Ionians. A strong tradition asserts that Homer was born on the island in the 9th or 8th century BC, though this claim is disputed chiefly by Smyrna but also by a number of other places across the Mediterranean. At that time Chios was an independent kingdom with colonies abroad (notably Voroniki

in Egypt). By the 7th century BC Chios reached the climax of its importance, famed for its sculpture workshop and system of government. Solon himself studied it and adapted parts of it in his Athenian reforms. Around 490, a Chiote named Glaucus invented the art of soldering metals; less nobly, the island was the first state in Greece to engage in slave trading. As a member of the famous Ionian confederacy, Chios joined Athens in the Battle of Lade (494 BC) in an unsuccessful attempt to overthrow the Persian yoke. Fifteen years later, however, after the battle of Plateia, Chios regained its independence, and held on to it even after Athens moved the treasury of Delos to the Akropolis, subjugating other former island allies as tribute-paying dependencies.

Later, Chios allied itself with Rome and fought the enemy of the Empire, Mithradates of Pontus (8 BC), only to be defeated and destroyed, although it was liberated two years later when Mithradates in his turn was destroyed by General Sulla. A few hundred years later Chios made the mistake of siding with Galerius against his brother-in-law Constantinos the Great. The latter then conquered the island and carried off to Constantinople many precious sculptures of antiquity, including, it is thought, the bronze horses which ended up in front of St Mark's in Venice after the sack of Constantinople in 1204. In 1261 the Emperor Michael Paleologos gave Chios to the Genoese for their assistance in reconquering Byzantium. Under the Genoese, and the Giustiniani, Chios once again prospered thanks to "Maona", a company chartered in 1344 to govern and defend the island. The Genoese lost Chios to the Turks in 1566.

The Turks were fond of the island, especially for its mastic, which they chewed to sweeten their breath, and granted Chios many benefits, including a degree of independence. Despite this, Chios rebelled with the rest of Greece in 1822, and the Sultan, furious at this subversion of a favoured island, ordered the rebellion to be mercilessly quelled. This led to one of the worst massacres in history. In a few days 30 000 Greeks were murdered, and 45 000 others were taken into slavery. All who could fled to other islands, such as Syros. The massacre deeply moved the rest of Europe; Delacroix painted his masterpiece of the tragedy and Victor Hugo wrote about it. On 6 June of the same year, the Greek Admiral Kanaris took revenge on Kara Ali, who had carried out the slaughter by blowing up his flagship, killing Kara Ali and 2000 soldiers. In 1840 Chios attained a certain amount of autonomy under a Christian governor, and it was incorporated into the Greek state in 1912.

MYTHOLOGY
Merope, daughter of King Oenopion, was pledged in marriage to Orion, the handsomest man in the world and a great hunter. Oenopion had little enthusiasm for marrying his daughter to anyone, for he loved her very much himself. However, he promised her to Orion on the condition that he rid Chios of its ferocious beasts, a task the young man easily performed. But rather than give Orion his reward, Oenopion kept putting him off, and finally Orion took the matter into his own hands and violated the girl. For this the king poked out his

eyes. Orion then set out blindly, but the goddess of dawn, Eos, fell in love with him and persuaded Helios the sun god to restore his sight. Before he could avenge himself on Oenopion, however, Orion was killed. His foolhardy boast that he could rid the world of all harmful creatures made Mother Earth send a giant scorpion after him. Orion fled the scorpion, but his friend Artemis, the goddess of the hunt, killed him by mistake. In mourning, she placed his image among the stars.

WHAT TO SEE

The town and main port of Chios, also called Chios or Chora, still belongs very much to its people and not to the tourists, although whether this will be so after the extending of the airport's runway (due in 1989) to accommodate international charters, remains to be seen. The town is mostly new and reflects the island's considerable wealth in its spanking new apartment blocks and high-rise (at least by island standards) offices. There is also an old town dating from the Turkish occupation, which lies within the walls of the **fortress,** a Byzantine structure repaired by the Genoese under Giustiniani (Chios has recently been twinned with Genoa). The ancient Macedonian castle had stood on the same site before Mithradates destroyed it in 86 BC. During the period of Turkish rule the Greeks settled outside the walls, and the gate was closed every day at sundown. Inside is a ruined **mosque** and in the Turkish cemetery is the **tomb of Kara Ali,** who ordered the massacre of Chios. In a tiny **prison** by the gate Bishop Plato Fragiadis and 75 leading Chiotes were incarcerated as hostages in incredibly crowded, inhumane conditions before they were all hanged by the Turks in 1822.

The **main square,** Plateia Vounaki, with its café and sweetshops, is a few minutes' walk away. On one side stands a statue of Bishop Plato Fragiadis, and in the municipal gardens behind the square is a statue of "Incendiary" Kanaris. Also in Plateia Vounaki is an old mosque—note the *Tugra,* the swirling "thumb-print of the Sultan" that denotes royal possession. Tugras, though common in Istanbul, are rarely seen elsewhere, even in Turkey, and this one is a mark of the favour that Chios enjoyed from the Sultan. Today the mosque houses the **Post-Byzantine Museum** (at writing closed for repairs). Near Plateia Vounaki is the **Korais Library**, the fourth largest in Greece with 95 000 volumes, including the private collection of Philip Argentis, and in the same building is the **Folklore Museum** of the Argentis Society, containing locally made costumes and handicrafts.

The new **archaeology museum,** on Michalon St in the new part of town, contains many lovely finds from the island, some marked with ancient Chios' symbol, the sphinx; there's also a letter from the Chiotes to Alexander the Great. Near the sea here there are modern swimming facilities. **Karfas,** the nearest beach to the capital, and gradually being developed, has sand as fine as flour. On the quay are shops selling sticky mastic products; here too is Michalakis Travel, where you can hire a bicycle. Buses depart from the station at the corner of

Mylonadi and Vlattarias Sts near the Plateia Vounaki (timetable posted in the window).

A trip to **Neo Moni** is perhaps the most beautiful excursion on Chios. Perched high above the town among the pine-wooded mountains, Neo Moni was "new" in 1042, when Emperor Constantinos Monomarchos VIII had it built to replace an older structure erected by three monks who found a miraculous icon of the Virgin in a burning bush. Constantinos built them a new monastery in gratitude for a prophesy, given by the Virgin through a monk, that he would return from exile and gain the throne of Byzantium. This new, powerful monastery ruled most of the island. Later the Empresses Zoe and Theadora donated the mosaics inside. These are still some of the most beautiful examples of Christian art, although they were badly damaged in the earthquake of 1881, which brought down the dome, since restored. As well as the mosaics there are other interesting items on display in the church, including a large clock which keeps Byzantine time (the sun rises and sets at 12 every day). One can also visit the chapel which houses the bones of the victims of Kara Ali, and there is an ancient refectory, a huge underground vaulted cistern, an old olive press and ruins of a settlement that once surrounded the monastery. Women should wear a skirt to visit Neo Moni. It is open in the mornings until noon and in the afternoons from 5 pm to 8 pm. Just south of Nea Moni the forest land suffered considerable damage by fire in the summer of 1987.

A rough road leads to the monastery **Ag. Pateras,** built in honour of the three monks who founded Neo Moni. The present Ag. Pateras dates from 1890, and only men are allowed inside. Further up the road is the striking, deserted medieval village of **Anavatos,** the scene of some of the worst Turkish atrocities. Above Anevatos is a medieval castle. If you plan to walk there, take provisions and wear good shoes—it's a good 8-km (5-mile) walk. By **Karyes** on the way back to Chios town is a church to **Ag. Markos,** built in 1835. Karyes is a pretty mountain village known for its healing waters.

Near **Vrontados** just north of Chios town was the church of **Ag. Isidoros,** built on the site where the first church of Chios was founded in the 3rd century. A later church, erected by Emperor Constantinos the Great, fell in an earthquake and was replaced by three successive structures, the last ruined by the Turks in 1822. Saint Isidoros was buried on Chios, but his relics were transferred to Venice in the 12th century, where a chapel at St Mark's was constructed to house them. In 1967 Pope Paul ordered the return of one of Isidoros' bones to Chios, and it was placed in the town's cathedral. Seventh-century mosaics discovered at the ruined church can now be seen in the museum.

The beach at **Vrontados** is pebbly, and above it are three windmills. On the far side of the harbour is the **Petra Omirous** (Homer's Stone), known locally as **Daskalopetra** (teacher's stone), a rather uncomfortable natural rock throne where the poet is said to have sung and taught, though archaeologists believe it was actually part of an ancient altar. A strange legend relates that Christopher

Columbus stopped at Vrontados before going on to America! At Vrontados the International Society of Homeric Studies has its base. The **Monastery of Panayia Myrtidiotissa** nearby, built in the 19th century has the robes of Gregory V, the Patriarch of Constantinople.

Kardamila, the largest village of northern Chios, is actually two villages: the picturesque upper town and the seaside Marmaros, blessed with many philanthropic gifts from wealthy Chiote shipowners. By **Nagos beach** to the north are the ruins of a **temple of Poseidon,** and nearby **Giossona** was named for Jason of the Golden Fleece, though the legend fails to make the island one of the Argonauts' ports of call. A medieval village in the mountains, to which taxis have a monopoly on transport, is **Pitios,** which has claims to be the birthplace of Homer; one can still see his "house" and olive grove. A 12th-century Aegean tower dominates the village: one can find food at the café. The landscape from Pitios towards Chios town is lunar in its burnt emptiness, but just above the village is a lovely pine forest, filled with fire warnings.

Further to the west the **Monimoudon Monastery** near Katavasis dates back to the 13th century. Byzantine nobles were exiled in the medieval fortress at Volissos, known as the Castle of Belisarius. The local saint Ag. Markella came from Volissos, considered to be another possible birthplace of Homer, or at least the village where the great poet took his baths, and the home of the Homeridai, who claimed descent from him. The beach below the town, **Limnia,** has a restaurant and a few rooms to let. Another medieval tower rises above the middle of little **Pirama,** where the lovely church of Ag. Ioannis contains some very old icons. **Parparia** to the north is a medieval hamlet of shepherds, and at **Melanios** many Chiotes were slain before they could flee to Psara in 1822. On the north-west shore stands the church **Ag. Gala,** by a cave which drips milk ("gala" in Greek means milk). Legend claims that it is the milk of the Virgin, and the church was built during Byzantine times.

South of Chios town towards **Vavili** the church **Panayia Krina** was built in 1287, with old frescoes of the Cretan school inside. At **Sklavia** are many 14th-century Genoese villas and gardens, and a few towers remain. The name Sklavia was derived from the Greeks forced to work as slaves for the Genoese nobility. This whole region of the island, south of Chios town and including **Thymiana** and **Kampos,** is very beautiful with its orchards surrounded by tall medieval walls, the gates often inscribed with some forgotten coat-of-arms. Many of the large medieval houses have a water wheel, which with the meadows, wooden bridges and ancient trees, creates a scene of rural peace unique on the Greek islands. Among the Genoese country mansions that of the **Argenti** in Kambos has been restored to the old style, including the oxen-turned "Hesiod's water wheel". Mastodon bones have been discovered at Thymiana. The best way to explore Kambos is on a bike.

South of Karfas on the coast is the **Ag. Minas monastery,** built in 1590. In 1822 it was the site of one of the worst massacres on Chios, when women and children from the surrounding villages took refuge there, thinking to escape from the maddened Turks. A small, hopeless battle took place before Ag. Minas was over-run and all 3000 of the Greeks were slain, their bodies thrown down the well. Recently their bones have been recovered and set in an ossuary by the church (closed in the afternoons until 6 pm).

Further south, **Kontari,** the beach of Kambos, may have been the site of Levkonion, although a more likely candidate is the old mastic exporting port of **Emborio** further south. Archaeologists have discovered signs of a settlement dating from 3000 BC. East of the port a 7th-century BC **temple of Athena** was found on the ancient akropolis, surrounded by ancient walls. Levkonion, mentioned by Thucydides, was an ancient city and rival of Troy. A wealth of amphorae found under water here hint at the extent of Chios' wine trade. The beach at Emborio is black and pebbly and hauntingly beautiful. Some way from the shore are the ruins of a 6th-century **Christian basilica** with mosaics.

The southernmost region of Chios is mastic land, and the villages here were almost all built during the Middle Ages. **Pirgi** in the centre is the largest, dating from the 13th century. It was defended by a Byzantine-style fort, whose walls consisted of the thick outer walls of the houses. Pirgi is fascinating to explore in its excellently preserved medieval state, with tiny arched streets and houses decorated with sgraffito, geometric black and white designs scratched into the surface of the walls. While seen here and there elsewhere in Greece, Pirgi is unique in that nearly every house has its sgraffito, giving a charming, fairytale effect. In the main square of the village they are particularly lavish. The 12th-century **Ag. Apostoli** is decorated with frescoes from the 16th century. The inhabitants of the village preserve many of their traditional customs and dress. Near the bus stop is the central mastic co-operative for the region.

Two other medieval villages, **Olympi** and **Mesta,** are on the road from Pirgi. Near the former once stood the Great Temple of Faneo Apollo, which has an oracle that Alexander the Great is said to have consulted. Only the fountain by the temple remains today, other items excavated from the site are now in the Chios museum. Mesta, with its stone houses and narrow, arched streets, is another medieval charmer, where you can almost hear the silence. Two churches in Mesta are worth visiting: the medieval **Ag. Paraskevi** and the 18th-century **Taxiarchis.** North of Pirgi ancient walls and wild rock formations, along with a 12th-century **Panayia Sicelia,** can be seen at **Tholopotami. Armolia** is the site of the castle **Oreas tis Kastro,** a Byzantine fort which was the abode of a beautiful but fatal seductress. Armolia is known for its potteries **Nenita** and **Kalamoti** are other mastic-growing medieval villages east of Pirgi. To the south, **Fana,** has a fine, wild beach.

PANEYERIA
8 August, Ag. Emilianos at Kallimasia; 12 August, Ag. Fotini at Kallimasia; 15 August, Panayia at Pirgi, Nenita, Kambos and Ag. Georgios; 22 July, Ag. Markella at Volissos and Karies; 26 July, Ag. Paraskevi at Kastello and Kalamoti; 27 July, Ag. Pandeleimon at Kalamoti.

WHERE TO STAY

In Chios town you can stay where the shipowners hobnob, in the large **Chandris Chios** on the sea at Prokymaea (tel. 0271 25 761), class B and wielding a bizarre 1960-ish lobby with cellophane chandeliers. A double here ranges from 8000 dr. to 15 000 dr., singles 7000 dr. to 11 000 dr. Next to it is the more convivial **Hotel Kyma** (tel. 0271 25 551). The main body of the hotel was built by a local shipowner in the style of the Villa Roma, a fine painted ceiling adorning the lobby. There's a new addition, but try to stay in the older part, for the sea view and atmosphere. Most rooms have bathrooms *en suite*, and breakfast is available. Doubles are around 6000 dr., a single 4500 dr. Less expensive is the **Filoxenia**, near the waterfront, towards the centre of town, where a double with bath is around 3000 dr. (tel. 0271 22 813).

In Kambos there's a nine room B class pension, the **Perivoli**, quiet and serene and 4500 dr. for a double (tel. 0271 31 513), though it's best to get directions from the tourist policeman before setting out. In medieval Mesta the NTOG has refurbished some of the old houses as *guesthouses*, each furnished with local handicrafts and giving on to a courtyard. Each house can accommodate up to five people—a bargain at 2300 dr. a night. For reservations, contact Paradosiakos Ikismos, Mesta (tel. 0271 76 319), or the regional office in Lesbos (tel. 0251 27 908). In Mesta, Armolia, Pirgi and Olympi the **townswomen's agrotourist co-operative** rent rooms for around 2000 dr. a night. There are also rooms in private houses to be found at Kardamila and Karfas. A campsite is scheduled to open at Pantoukios (between Chios town and Kardamila) in 1988.

EATING OUT

For fish, go to one of the restaurants in Karfas that have made it their speciality. There are also several inexpensive restaurants in town. Open to all is the **Chios Marine Club**, a modern concrete affair behind the Chandris Hotel, with an alternative to Greek cuisine, at a price. A few metres beyond is **Tassos** taverna, with reliable Greek food at normal prices. On the port, where the ferries dock, is a *psistaria* (grill) with a wide variety of freshly grilled meats, a full dinner costing no more than 1000 dr. Next door is an *ouzeri* serving very good fresh *mezedes*. Nearly all the seaside villages have at least one taverna, but they're nothing special.

TOURIST POLICE

The Tourist Police tel. (0271) 23 211, are to be found at the far end of the quay, next to the regular police and the customs house, from where you can take the boat to Turkey.

Three times a day caiques leave Chios for **Inousses** which consists of nine islets in all. On the largest is a School of Navigation, along with other buildings donated by the great shipowners who were born here. Near the village is a medieval fort; there are a few small beaches for swimming, and two D class hotels, the

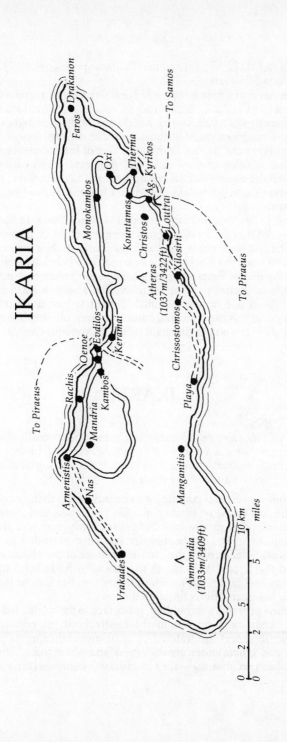

IKARIA

- Drakanon
- Faros
- Therma
- Oxi
- Monokambos
- Ag. Kyrikos
- Kountamas
- Christos
- Loutra
- Xilosirti
- Atheras (1037m/3422ft)
- Chrissostomos
- Playa
- Evdilos
- Keramai
- Oenoe
- Rachis
- Kambos
- Mandria
- Armenistis
- Nas
- Manganitis
- Ammondia (1033m/3409ft)
- Vrakades

To Samos

To Piraeus

To Piraeus

To Piraeus

miles
0   5   10 km
0   2   5

Prassonissia (tel. 0272 51 313) and the **Thalassoporos** (tel. 0272 51 475) with doubles at around 2500 dr.

Psara to the west of Chios is connected only a few times a week with the larger island. Archaeologists have discovered there signs of the 13th century BC Achean settlement near Paliokastro, which was built by refugees who fled to Psara from the misgovernment of the Turks, for the tiny rocky islet had been generally ignored by the Sultan. During the War of Independence the Psariotes contributed many ships to the cause, and they even invented a weapon, the bourleta, which the captains of the revolution used to destroy the Turkish fleet. So irksome were the rebel attacks from Psara that the Sultan finally demanded vengeance on the islet.

On 20 June 1824, he sent 25 000 troops to destroy Psara. In the subsequent slaughter only 3000 of the 30 000 men, women and children managed to escape to Eretria. The rest were either slain with the Turks in their own explosions, or were massacred when the Turks finally swarmed into Paliokastro after the heroic battle. Thus the islet of Psara was annihilated as the Sultan had ordered. Today 500 people live on Psara, a very quiet place with an inn, a small taverna and a small beach. As in Mesta, the National Tourist Organisation offers unusual accommodation, in this case in an old church cloister, offering bed and breakfast (tel. 0272 61 293, or contact the main office in Mytilini, Lesbos, tel. 0251 27 908).

IKARIA

CONNECTIONS
Ferry five or six times a week to Piraeus and Samos, occasionally also to Paros: in summer, once or twice a week with Patmos, Chios and Lesbos. Tourist excursions to Furnous several times a week. Note that some ships call at the island's northern port, Evidlos and not the main port, Ag. Kyrikos.

More accustomed to Greeks coming for its curative baths than to foreign tourists, Ikaria over the past few years has begun to do a little here and there (but not too much) to accommodate its new breed of guests. Each year there are a few more rooms and houses to let; the breakwater has been extended to ensure safer landings at its gale-ridden port (the Ikarian sea is one of the wildest corners of the Aegean), and the large "Welcome to the Island of Radiation" sign that once greeted visitors and gave many an adventurous traveller second thoughts about disembarking has been discreetly painted over.

Most of Ikaria presents a forbidding, rocky face to the world, and much of it is inaccessible except on foot; but in the centre both the popular north and less-visited south shores are watered by clear mountain springs that keep the villages cool and green under groves of oak and plane trees. The island also enjoys natural air conditioning—after its radioactive springs Ikaria is best known for its wind. The god of wind himself is said to abide atop the long mountainous spine that neatly divides the island in two. If it's calm on one side, it's sure to be blustery on the other, and you may leave with the impression that it was the wind that did in Ikaros and not the sun.

Ikaria itself still has many rough edges as well; some of the roads are appalling, public buses often only make cameo appearances, and the accommodation, restaurants and bars are very simple and unpretentious. But such is its charm. Few islands have so stubbornly clung to their traditional identity, or indeed their very soul. It is an island that means to keep its secrets—perhaps sumbolised by the statue of a sphinx recently erected on the road between Ag. Kyrikos and Xilosirtis.

HISTORY
In mythology, Ikaros, when fleeing Crete with his father Daedalus, flew too near to the sun with the lovely wings his father had made him. When the wax that held the feathers together melted, the boy plummeted to his death off the south coast of an island thereafter known as Ikaria. More prosaically, its name was probably derived from the Latin word for fish. The most common name of Ikaria in ancient times was Oenoe, or wine island. So much wine was produced on ancient Ikaria that some considered it to be the birthplace of Dionysos, the god of wine. An inscription found on the akropolis describes Oenoe as being second only to Athens in sending the yearly contributions to Apollo on Delos. During the age of Byzantium it is thought that the island was a place of exile, for the ruins of a palace have been found in Kambos. There was another large settlement at Therma.

During the Turkish occupation the inhabitants imprisoned their Turkish rulers and for five months Ikaria was an independent state with its own flag and stamps. At the end of 1912 the island joined Greece. Later Greek governments sent political dissidents to Ikaria, who succeeded in making the population one of the most left-wing in Greece.

WHAT TO SEE
Ag. Kyrikos, the capital and largest port on the island, is in fact rather small, with trees outnumbering the buildings. The statue at the end of the breakwater honours Ikaros, who doesn't seem very airworthy even here. The little pier on the other side of the town has a constant bezina taxi service to Therma, only ten minutes away (there is also a road), where most of the island's hotels and restaurants are located. Buses from the square leave once a day for the villages. The string of kafeneions along the waterfront see most of the social life, and the restaurant with the portside terrace often has live music in the summer. Shops in "Agios" sell Ikaria's locally made sweets and thyme honey.

People come from far and wide to **Therma,** where the radioactive baths cure chronic rheumatism, arthritis, gout and spondylitis; one is even reputed to make women fertile. The baths are considered among the most radioactive in Europe; one was so strong that it had to be closed. Further up the coast (accessible only by boat) **Faros** has a well preserved, round Hellenistic tower from the 3rd century BC. This is near the ancient city of **Drakanon,** of which only a few 5th-century BC remains can be seen on the akropolis. Another ancient city of Ikaria was at **Katafyion,** where the akropolis that remains is Archaic. The name Katafyion means "shelter" and refers to an underground passageway beneath the church. One day, it is said, the Turks came to Katafyion with evil intentions, but as it was Sunday all the villagers were at church. The Turks decided to wait outside and capture the people as they came out. They waited and waited, then impatiently broke their way into the church. It was empty! The priest had opened the secret trap door in the floor, and everyone escaped from the Turks in safety.

The second most popular spring on Ikaria is also on the south side of the island, called **Therma Lefkados,** or Loutra. Situated in the pine trees by the Anyfantis Hotel, some of its water is so hot that the local people on picnics use it to boil their eggs. Athanatos Nero (the fountain of youth) runs between the pretty little **Evangilistria** and **Xilosirti** where local people can show you exactly where Ikaros fell. Like most of the villages of the island, Xilosirti is spread out among the trees, particularly apricot trees: Ikarian apricots are said to be the best in Greece. On the way up to the mountain village of **Chrissostomo** is Hartia, a lovely place to visit. All but deserted, it has many springs, and plane trees. After centuries of isolation, **Manganitis,** the westernmost village on the south shore was, in 1987, finally reached by a new road and tunnel bored through impassable rock. Built on a steep hillside, its lonely position belies the fact that it is one of the liveliest spots on Ikaria, with parties lasting until dawn.

The north side of the island, with its vast pine forests, vineyards, sandy beaches and excellent roads and guesthouses, attracts far more tourists. The most popular destinations are Evdilos, Armenistis and Gialiskari, the latter boasting Ikaria's unofficial nudist beach. **Evdilos,** the largest village, also serves as a steamer stop once a week on the route to Piraeus and Samos. In nearby **Kambos** are the ruins of the **Palatia,** or Palace, dating from the Byzantine settlement of Doliche, or ancient Oenoe, the capital of Ikaria in antiquity. **Ag. Irene** church in Kambos is Byzantine, and the local museum houses finds mostly dating from that era. Above Kambos are the ruins of the **Kastro of Koskinou,** near the village of the same name. It was built in the 10th century.

Rachis, by a monastery of the same name is called the Little Switzerland of Ikaria, with tall pines growing down the mountainside to a sandy shore. Many people come here to camp, and there are rooms and tavernas which are usually full in the summer. Further west **Armenistis** is a large, attractive village with the island's best beach and most rooms to let; it's also the point of departure for **Pappas** village and ancient **Nas.** In Nas a marvellous statue of Artemis was discovered about a hundred years ago, the eyes of which are said to have followed the viewer from three different angles. The local priest, however, decided that it was the work of the heathen if not the devil himself and ordered it to be thrown in the lime kiln! Thus perished the Artemis of Ikaria, never to hold its sacred spot in the Louvre. At Nas one can still make out the ruins of the ancient harbour.

Rocky but well watered Ikaria abounds in fruit trees of all kinds. Raki and a delicious honey are made from the koumaro bush. A special canned sweet is also produced in the Ikarian sweet factory. In the summer paneyeria occupy the attention of the whole island, when many of the numerous Ikariotes who live abroad come home just to celebrate. These feasts are run in the old style: one orders a prothesi, which consists of a kilo of goat meat, a bottle of wine, a huge bowl of soup and a loaf of bread—enough to feed four. At one of the larger paneyeria at Christos (above Ag. Kyrikos) 2200 pounds of meat are consumed each year. But the biggest festival of all is on 17 July, in honour of the defeat of the Turks by the Ikariotes in 1912. Feasts, speeches, music and folk dancing in costume are part of the day's agenda.

PANEYERIA
Other paneyeria are on 26 July, Ag. Paraskevi in Xilosirti; 27 July, at Ag. Panteleimonos; 6 August at Christos; 8 September, at Playa and Manganitis; 17 September, Ag. Sophia at Mesokambos; 15 August at Akamatra and Chrissostomos.

WHERE TO STAY
In the capital there are quite a few small pensions and rooms, and in Loutra, a mile west of Ag. Kyrikos, there are some hotels proper, such as the C class **Adam's** (tel. 0275 22 418) with doubles in the region of 3000–3500 dr., and in the same price range is the slightly larger **Marina** pension (tel. 0275 22 188). Nearly everything else is in Therma, these catering primarily for the arthritic; nicest here is the class C **Apollon** (tel. 0275 21 477) which includes one of the baths if you'd like to take a dip. Rates here are 3500 dr. for a double. On the more popular north side of Ikaria you'll have to rely primarily on rooms, many of them in Evdilos, where there's also the **Evdoxia** pension, with pricey doubles at around 5500 dr. (tel. 0275 31 502). There's a lot more rooms in Armenistis. The current rate on the island for a double room in a private home is 1600–2000 dr., and no one cares (at least no one official) if you sleep on the beach.

EATING OUT
The best restaurants are in Therma, where, as the locals will tell you, you can even get pizza. In Ag. Kyrikos there's a little taverna tucked in an alley a couple of blocks from the waterfront where a meal is around 700 dr.; there's also the large restaurant by the sea which sometimes has entertainment in the summer. In all the villages, even Manganitis, you can at least get a meal of souvlaki and salad on summer evenings; after September, forget it.

TOURIST POLICE
See regular police, tel. (0275) 22 222.

Connected by caique from Ag. Kyrikos, Ikaria and Samos, **Furnous** (locally known as Furni) is a very quiet, very pleasant little island just about midway

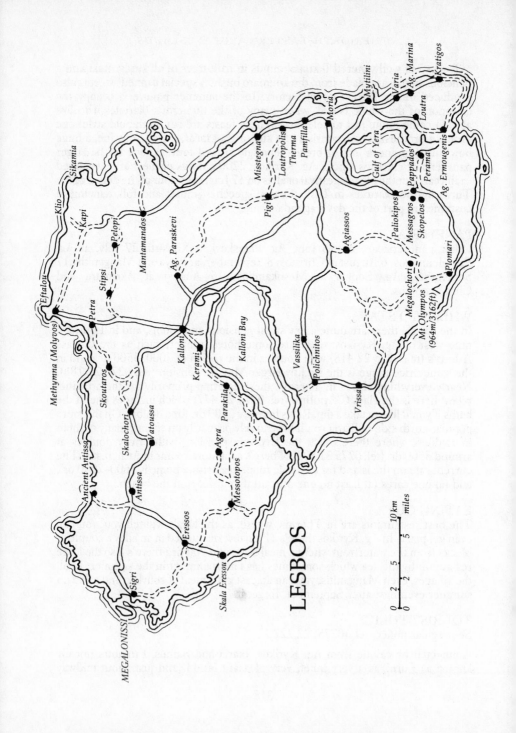

LESBOS

Mytilini
Varia
Ag. Marina
Kratigos
Loutra
Moria
Ag. Ermougenis
Pamfilla
Therma
Loutropolis
Misstegma
Perama
Pappados
Gulf of Yera
Paliokipos
Messagros
Skopelos
Megalochori
Plomari
Mt Olympos
(964m/3162ft)
Agiassos
Pigi
Ag. Paraskevi
Mantamandos
Pelopi
Stipsi
Kapi
Klio
Sikamia
Eftalou
Methymna (Molyvos)
Petra
Skoutaros
Skalochori
Vatoussa
Kalloni
Kerami
Parakila
Agra
Messotopos
Antissa
Ancient Antissa
Eressos
Sigri
Skala Eressou
MEGALONISSI
Kalloni Bay
Vassilika
Polichnitos
Vrissa

0   2   5   10 km
0   2   5   miles

between its two larger sisters, Samos and Ikaria. Actually consisting of two islets, the larger Furnous is blessed with a huge circular harbour that hid a group of Algerian pirates for many a year, from where they would ambush passing ships. Today the harbour is better known for its fish, especially the much loved barbounia and lobster, which, though plentiful, isn't cheap; the surprising number of fishing boats in the harbour supply much of the fish sold in Athens.

Chora, the "capital" and largest village, is a pleasant little town with many trees, belying the barren rockpile which Furni resembles from its outer coasts. There is a sandy beach, but unfortunately it's in the harbour, and not as clean as one might wish. Several caiques, however, run trips to the crystal-clear outer beaches, mostly of the pebble variety. Rooms and taverns may be found in Chora, which is connected by the one road to the island's other village, Chrissomilia. Thymena is the village on Furni's smaller islet.

PANEYERIA
23 April, Ag. Georgios; 6 December, Ag. Nikolaos.

LESBOS (MYTILINI)

CONNECTIONS
By air: numerous charters from various European cities. Five daily flights from Athens, daily with Thessaloniki, four times a week with Limnos, three times a week with Rhodes, twice a week with Chios and Samos (with connecting flights from these islands to Mykonos). By sea: daily ferry boat from Piraeus and Chios; approximately twice a week with Limnos, Ag. Efstratios, Samos, Ikaria, Kavala and Thessaloniki; once a week with Patmos, Kos and Rhodes. In the summer, daily boat to Ayvalik (near ancient Assos) in Turkey.

Officially named Lesbos, but more often called Mytilini after its principal city, the island is the third largest in Greece, famed for its olive oil. Its undulating hills are said to support 11 million olive trees, which glisten silver in the sunlight, while the higher peaks are swathed in deep pine forests. The island has long been a cradle of poetry and art; Sappho ran a marriage school here for young ladies, to whom she dedicated many of her love poems; Alcaeus and Terpander, "father of Greek music", were born here, as too were Arion, inventor of the dithyramb, Longus, author of *Daphnis and Chloe*, and Theophilos (1873-1934), a poor villager who earned his ouzo by painting some of the finest primitive art modern Greece has produced. Even more recently, the last Greek to win a Nobel Prize, poet Odysseus Elytis, came from Lesbos. On the other hand, it was also the birthplace of the Barbarossa brothers, Greeks turned pirates for the Sultan, and the worst terrors the Aegean has ever known.

For the most part Lesbos is an island of quiet villages, and the tourists tend to stay in just a few areas. Its size makes transport difficult unless you have a car or scooter. Although much of the island is quite lovely, it has little that stands out in particular—an attractive artist's colony, a bit of a petrified forest, a handful of charming villages, a few rather ordinary beaches. Like Evia, it is still very much a place where the people go about their everyday business unconcerned with the great wave of international tourism that has swept over the other islands.

HISTORY
Like many of the islands that hug the coast of Asia Minor, Lesbos both enjoyed the benefits and suffered the penalties of its situation between East and West as early as the Trojan War. Homer describes the island as an ally of Troy, suffering raids by both Odysseus and Achilles. In the 10th century BC Aeolians from Thessaly colonised the island and the coast of Asia Minor. On the whole the Aeolians lacked the intellectual spark of the Ionians, but by the 6th century BC they had managed to make Lesbos one of the cultural centres of ancient Greece, especially under the rule of Pittachos, one of the Seven Sages of ancient Greece. He went far in healing the rivalry between Lesbos' two principle cities, Mytilini and Methymna, and promoted trade with Egypt.

Methymna, having lost the fight for island dominance, got back at Mytilini when that city decided to leave the Delian league and join Sparta in the Peloponnesian War, in 428 BC. Methymna appealed to Athens, which decided to decimate the rebellious city. According to Thucydides, an order was sent for a great massacre. However, soon after the ship with the order sailed, the Athenians reconsidered, and sent a second ship countermanding the massacre. The second ship arrived in the nick of time, and the citizens were spared.

In the 4th century BC, Lesbos changed hands frequently, its most memorable ruler being Hermeias, who ruled both the island and the Troad on the mainland. Hermeias was a eunuch and a student of Plato's Academy, and he attempted to rule his principality on the precepts of the *Republic* and the ideal city state; Aristotle helped him found a branch of the Academy in ancient Assos and married Hermeias' niece. Later the island was occupied by Mithradates of Pontos, who was in turn ousted by the Romans in a battle believed to be Julius Caesar's first.

Like Chios, Lesbos was given by the Byzantine Emperor Michael Palaeologus to the Genoese for their help in restoring the Byzantine Empire (1261). In 1462 Mohammed the Conqueror captured the island, despite the heroic resistance led by Lady Oretta d'Oria. Lesbos remained in Turkish hands until 1912.

MYTHOLOGY
Even in myth Lesbos is connected with music and poetry. The mythical-historical musician Arion was a son of the island, accredited with the invention of the dithyramb. His talents brought him great wealth. After a musical contest in Italy, where he had won all the prizes, the crew of the ship bringing him back to Lesbos decided to throw him overboard and keep his treasures for themselves. Arion was allowed to sing for the last time, after which he dived into the sea. His

318

song, however, had charmed the dolphins, and they saved his life, carrying him safely to shore. The ship's crew were later executed for their treachery. Another myth deals with the great poet Orpheus, who was torn to pieces by furious followers of Dionysos and thrown into a river of Thrace. His beautiful head floated to Lesbos, where the inhabitants carried it to a cave. There Orpheus' head sang and prophesied so well that no one went to Delphi any more to hear Apollo. This angered the god, who came to Lesbos to tell Orpheus' head to be quiet.

WHAT TO SEE

The capital of Lesbos, **Mytilini** (which is how most Greeks refer to the whole island), is a large town of magnificent old mansions, impressive public buildings, and beautiful gardens. Its two harbours are divided by what was once an islet, but today is a peninsula, with a **Byzantine-Genoese castle** on top. This was the ancient akropolis of Mytilini, where a temple of Apollo (600 BC) stood. In the area where a canal once flowed between Mytilini and the islet, the remains of an ancient trireme were found, stranded in the accumulation of sand and sediment which filled in the "Euripos of the Mytilineans". The present **kastro** was founded in the 6th century, and in 1373 the Genoese repaired it with any available material from various epochs. One can still see ancient pillars crammed in between the stones. Inside are numerous buildings left by the various occupants of the fortress, and a well-preserved Roman cistern and Turkish medrese.

In the **north harbour,** the least picturesque side of town, are many small antique shops selling some very unexpected items. By the pine forest above the town to the north-west, one may find the **ancient Theatre,** built in the Hellenistic period. It was one of the largest of ancient Greece and Pompey admired it so much that he used its plans to build a theatre in Rome (55 BC). Just north of the north harbour is a wooded hill where campers pitch their tents, and there is a small beach by the shore, **Tsamakia.**

Heading towards the south harbour, the **Tourist Police** are to the immediate right of the point where passengers disembark at the pier. Behind here, on 8 November St, is where the **Archaeology Museum** is soon to be rehoused, and although highlights of the museum's collection include reliefs found in a Roman house, depicting scenes from the comedies of Menander, as well as mosaics and prehistoric finds from Thermai, these cannot be seen in their entirety until 1989.

Dominating the town the cathedral **Ag. Athanasios** (16th–17th century) should be visited for its carved wooden iconostasis. Near **Ag. Therapon** are Turkish fountains, and in front of the church is the **Byzantine Museum,** containing an array of icons; by **Ag. Kyriaki** are some of the walls of ancient Mytilini. Between the new **Municipal Theatre** (1968) and the post office behind it, the placards advertise films that often include some real classics, a cut above the "shoot 'em ups" offered on other islands.

It's not hard to escape from the city; there are numerous places where you can hire cars, scooters or bicycles to explore the rest of the island. Buses depart from

319

two separate stations: distant villages are served from the far end of the harbour, nearer ones from the centre. Buses from the latter station can take you just south of Mytilini to **Varia,** the home town of Theophilos. His house is now a museum—the best on the island, containing some 80 examples of his work, pictures that evoke the island's charm far better than any photograph. Near here is the **Museum of Modern Art,** with works by the Mytilini artist Eleftheriades (possibly better known by his adopted French name Theriade), and minor works by Picasso, Gogol and Chigal. Buses also leave here for the beaches near Mytilini—Neapolis, Achivala and Kalimari. **Neapolis** is just south of Varia and has the ruins of a 5th-century basilica. This whole peninsula is one of the prettiest areas of Lesbos. There are two long beaches, one at **Kratigos** and another at **Ag. Ermougenis,** where there is a taverna. From Skala Loutron a ferry crosses the Gulf of Yera for Perama.

Therma to the north is the health spa of Lesbos; just south of it lies **Pirgi Therma** with the 12th-century Panayia Troullouti. A settlement existed at Therma from before 3000 BC until Mycenaean times, and its five successive levels of civilisation were excavated by Winifred Lamb between 1923 and 1933. Ancient Therma had connections with Troy, and during the Trojan War the Acheans burnt it to the ground; the dates match the traditional dates of the Trojan War (1250 BC). A large Turkish tower stands near the baths, and there are rooms and restaurants and a beach nearby. **Mantamandos** further north is a large village with a restaurant, Mayeriou, and the interesting 18th-century church Taxiarchos Michael, with a famous black icon of St Michael. The story behind it is that at the monastery pirates killed all the monks except one, who collected the blood soaked earth and moulded it into the icon. Mantamandos is one of the villages on the island that has preserved the custom of sacrificing a bull and feasting at Easter time—a folk custom directly descended from antiquity. From Klio to the north a track leads down to a good beach and to pretty **Sikamia,** one of the more remote corners of Lesbos, locally renowned for its mild winters.

Methymna, locally called Molyvos, its Venetian name, is the most popular and prettiest town on Lesbos; Mytilini's arch rival for a long time, it has now dropped to third in terms of population. It was the birthplace of Arion, and the site of the tomb of the Achean hero Palamedes, who was buried by Achilleus and Ajax. Achilleus besieged the ancient fortress of Methymna, but with little success until the daughter of the King of Methymna fell in love with him and opened the city gates to him. Despite her kindness to him, Achilleus had her slain for betraying her father. From Roman times onwards Methymna was frequently attacked. In 1373, when Lesbos belonged to the Genoese, Francesco Gattilusio repaired the old Byzantine fortress on top of the hill, but it fell to Mohammed the Conqueror in 1462.

Modern Molyvos is a symphony of red-tiled roofs, flowers and windows stacked above the lovely harbour and long beach, reaching up to the striking **Genoese Castle** perched on top, with views of Turkey. Besides the town beach, there are others nearby at Petra and **Eftalou,** the latter with hot springs. Both

320

have tavernas and are less crowded than Molyvos. In the summer Molyvos sponsors a theatre festival presented by several different companies.

Charming **Petra**, besides its beach, is noted for its church high up on a precipice, Panayias, dating from the 18th century. **Kalloni,** a large village further south, is by the ancient city of Arisbe; its akropolis was located where the medieval **Kastro of Kalloni** is today. Arisbe flourished until a few of the local young men abducted some girls from Methymna, whereupon the stronger city responded by destroying Arisbe and enslaving all its people. Also near Kalloni one may visit the **Ag. Ignatius Limonos Monastery,** built in the 16th century and containing fine examples of local art. There are three tavernas by **Skala Kalloni beach** and Kalloni Bay, where sardines are caught. At **Ag. Paraskevi** to the east, bulls are sacrificed and eaten in the springtime as in Mantamandos, here in conjunction with horse races.

South-central Lesbos, west of the city of Mytilini, is dominated by **Mt Olympos** (964 metres/3162 ft). Nineteen mountains in the Mediterranean called Olympos have been counted, almost always they were peaks sacred to the local sky god, who, in this most syncretic corner of the world, became associated with Zeus, and thus his mountain home became known as Zeus' home, or Olympos. At the foot of this mountain lies the lovely village of **Agiassos**. Despite its discovery by tourists it remains one of the most interesting settlements of the island. As well as its picturesque houses, there is a medieval castle, the Kastelli, nearby, and the **church of the Panayia,** founded in the 12th century by the Archbishop of Mytilini, Valerios Konstantinos, to house an old icon of Mary saved from the iconoclasts. The present church building was constructed in 1812 after a fire destroyed the older structure, and it has one of the most beautiful 19th-century interiors of all Greek churches. On 15 August the village is thronged with pilgrims. From the **Kipos Panayias** taverna (up the steps from the bus stop) one has a splendid view of the village and its orchards of fruit trees that produce very good black plums. The region with its chestnut and pine groves, is one of Lesbos' prettiest, and the road west to Polichnitos is especially lovely.

Polichnitos has a thermal spa and a beach with tavernas. On the south coast **Vrissa** was the home town of Briseis, but only a wall remains of the ancient Trojan town which was destroyed in 1180 BC. The modern village was built by the survivors. A Genoese tower stands west of Vrissa. **Plomari** to the east has an ouzo distillery producing Greece's best aperitif, and at the small port of **Ekranto** there is a restaurant. By **Pappados** is the ruined Paliokastro, of uncertain date, and at **Perama** there is a good sandy beach and ferry across the Gulf of Yera to **Loutro**. South of Loutro is another good sandy beach, **Ag. Ermogenis**.

The north-west quarter of Lesbos is volcanic, and the home of wild horses— some believe they may be the last link with the horse-breeding culture of the Troad in the Late Bronze Age, often referred to by Homer in the *Iliad*. The largest village here, **Eressos,** minted coins depicting Sappho and is thought to have been her birthplace. Ancient Eressos was north of the present village, near the castle **Xokastro,** and some ruins remain. Nearer the sea, by the **Skala**

Eressou, a Byzantine fortress rises on Vigla hill. Although it stood up to the Genoese siege in 1333, it later surrendered to Mohammed the Conqueror after the rest of the island had been captured. There is a good (and popular) beach near here. Nearby **Apotheka** is a ruined village still retaining a long wall and tower. The modern village of **Antissa** lies inland north of Eressos. Further north again, on the coast, is the site of the Bronze Age town of the same name. Once an islet, **ancient Antissa** was joined to Lesbos in an earthquake. Orpheus' head supposedly ended up here. The Romans later destroyed the town to punish the inhabitants for their support of the Macedonians. **Hourekastro,** a Genoese fort, faces the sea over the ruins of the ancient town, which produced another of Lesbos' great poet musicians, Terpander, inventor of choric poetry. Near Antissa is the **Ag. Ioannis Theologos Ipsilos Monastery,** high on a promontory. Founded in the 9th century and rebuilt in the 12th, there are many old ceremonial items inside. At **Sigri** and the coastal islet Megalonissi are **petrified trees.** These were buried in volcanic ash for hundreds of thousands of the years, and what you see now is only visible because the ash has been eroded away. Some of the best specimens may be seen in Sigri itself; to see those at the site entails a long walk, and inevitable disappointment. But Sigri does have a charming beach, and a Turkish castle (1757) by the shore still has its canons.

PANEYERIA
26 August, Ag. Ermolaou at Paliokipos; 8 May, Ag. Theologos at Antissa; 26 July, at Ag. Paraskevi; 2nd day of Easter and 15 August, at Agiassos; Ag. Magdalinis at Skopelos; end of September, at Plomari; "Week of Prose and Drama" in May.

WHERE TO STAY
In Mytilini itself the **Sappho Hotel** on the waterfront is a picturesque if somewhat noisy place to stay in the city. Rated class C, a double here is 4500 dr., a single 3000 dr. (tel. 0251 28 415). In the same area is the E class **Megali Vretannia** (Grande Bretagne) with little resemblance to its Athenian namesake—but prices are low–2500 dr. for a double (tel. 0251 28 449). However, on the whole you're better off in one of the many pensions; get the list from the tourist police near the ferry quay. On Neapolis Beach near the city, there's the **Lesvos Beach** (tel. 0251 61 531/2) with furnished apartments for lengthy stays. Rates are 5000–8500 dr. a day.

In Molyvos there are a collection of hotels and pensions, which tend to be expensive and full. If you book in advance, the **Poseidon** (tel. 0253 71 570) is pleasant and intimate, with only six rooms; rates begin at 4000 dr. in high season. Slightly set aside from the town and near the beach is the B class **Delfinia**, with comfortable double rooms at 8000 dr., singles at 5200 dr. (tel. 0253 71 373). By the harbour is the **Sea Horse** pension where doubles (if you can get one) in high season are up to 5000 dr. (tel. 0253 71 320). Rooms in private houses start at around 1700 dr.—ask at the tourist information office.

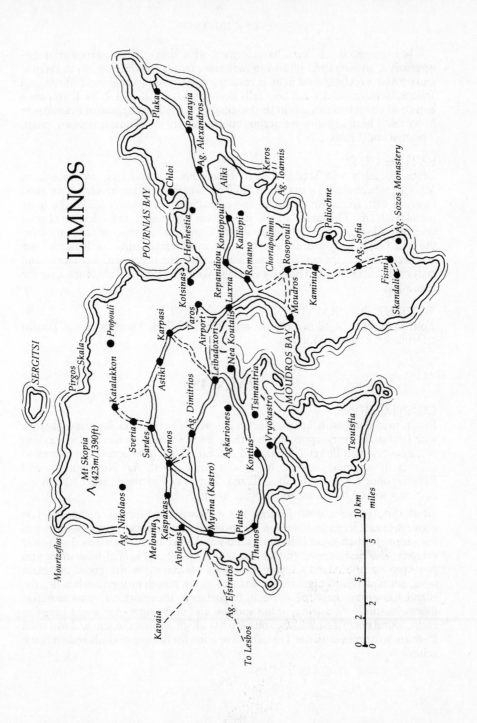

LIMNOS

SERGITSI

Mourtzeflos

Pirgos
Skala

Ag. Nikolaos

Mt Skopia
∧ (423m/1390ft)

Katalakkon

Propouli

Sveria
Sardes

Kornos

Ag. Dimitrios

Astiki

Karpasi

Varos

Airport

Leibadoxori

Repanidiou Kontopouli
Luxna

Nea Koutalis

Romano

Ag. Alexandros

Panayia

Plaka

Chloi

POURNIAS BAY

Hephestia

Kotsinas

Aliki

Keros
Ag. Ioannis

Chortapolimni

Rosopouli

Kalliopi

Moudros

MOUDROS BAY

Tsimantria

Vryokastro

Kontias

Agkariones

Platis

Thanos

Myrina (Kastro)

Kaspakas
Melouna
Avlonas

Ag. Efstratos

Kavaia

To Lesbos

Tsoutsfia

Kaminia

Paliochne

Ag. Sofia

Ag. Sozos Monastery

Fisini

Skandali

10 km
miles

0   2   5

0   2   5

The womenfolk of Petra have formed what they call an **agrotourist co-operative**, pooling their houses to rent more than a hundred rooms to visitors, and provide excellent food at their restaurant. Rooms start at about 2500 dr. and are immaculately clean and tastefully decorated (tel. 0253 41 238). If you are a bona fide artist, you can stay at the lodgings of the Athens School of Fine Arts in Molyvos. There are also numerous rooms to rent in Plomari, Eressos, Sigri, Thermai and Vrissa.

EATING OUT
Lesbos is fairly well supplied with restaurants and tavernas; try **Asteria** in Mytilini, where a meal costs about 1000 dr. Nearly all of the beaches have good tavernas with fresh fish, at prices more reasonable than on some of the more popular islands. The main "street" in Molyvos has an attractive selection of good tavernas, all serving freshly prepared oven dishes and a variety of offerings from the grill. Get in early to claim a table on the small terraces that overlook the town and beach. Also in the centre of town is an English run bistro, with a colourful and tasty choice of salads, and Sunday specials, like Roast Beef and trimmings, for the homesick.

TOURIST INFORMATION
Tourist police, Mytilini harbour, tel. (0251) 22 776. There is also a Tourist information office in Molyvos.

LIMNOS

CONNECTIONS
By air: twice daily with Athens, once a day with Thessaloniki, four times a week with Lesbos. By ferry: approximately three times a week with Kavala and Lesbos; twice a week with Piraeus, Chios and Ag. Eftstratios (also occasional excursion caiques in summer); once a week with Kimi (Evia), Ag. Konstantinos and Rhodes; once a week with Chios, Ikaria, Samos and whatever other islands are currently served by the meandering, poky old *Kyklades*.

Of all the Aegean islands, Limnos lies the lowest and flattest, rising only just above the sea. Green and lovely in the spring, it turns a crackling yellow-brown in the summer, when water is in short supply and is occasionally switched off in the evening. Besides farming (notice the odd scarecrows), animal husbandry and bee-keeping (the island's thyme honey was favoured by the gods) the main occupation of Limnos is military; situated at the mouth of the Dardenelles the island has always been of strategic importance. Its volcanic origins manifest themselves today in astringent hot springs, and in the once-renowned Limnian earth, found near Repanidi, the soil here has a high sulphur content and was used from ancient times until the Turkish occupation for healing wounds and stomach aches.

HISTORY

Limnos has an exceptionally interesting if murky past and mythological tradition. Homer claims that the island's first inhabitants were from Thrace, while Herodotos makes them Tyrrhenian, inscriptions from before the 6th century BC on the island show similarities to the Etruscans, as do some of the ancient burials. These points—as well as Etruscans' own traditions—have convinced many scholars that the Etruscans originally immigrated to Italy from Asia Minor. Whoever they were, the Limniotes before the 6th century BC were not Greek.

Pre-dating them, however, was a Neolithic civilisation, Paleochoe, dating back to 4000 BC, considered the most advanced in the Aegean. Some believe that these ancient people of Limnos were the first to colonise Troy; certainly there were close cultural contacts between the two in the Mycenaean era. Hephestia was the Classical capital, and for a time the island attracted adherents of the Cabiri cult until the religion was centred on Samothrace. Limnos was taken by the Venetians in the 13th century, and then retaken by Kario for Byzantium. In 1475 Mohammed the Conqueror sent Turkish troops to Limnos. They would have captured the island were it not for the leadership of the Limniote heroine Maroula, who seized her dying father's weapons and shouted the battle cry. In 1478, however, Mohammed himself came and took the island and the Turks held it until 1912. In the First World War Moudros Bay became famous as a naval base of the Allies in the Gallipoli campaign.

MYTHOLOGY

Limnos was the island of the iron and fire god Hephaistos, for it was there that he landed when a furious Zeus hurled him from Mt Olympos for daring to defend his rebellious mother Hera. The fall left Hephaistos crippled forever, despite all the care lavished on him by the islanders. The ancient capital of Limnos was named for the god, who was so beloved that when his wife, the goddess of love Aphrodite, betrayed him with Ares while he paid the island a visit, the women of Limnos stopped worshipping her, and even tossed her cult statue into the sea. In fury, Aphrodite retaliated by making their breath and underarms stink (though Robert Graves says this may have been because they worked with woad, a putrid substance used in the manufacture of tattoo ink). This led the good men of Limnos to prefer the company of captive Thracian women to that of their own wives. This led to further incidents: the women of Limnos doctored their husbands' wine to make them sleep, and then slit their throats, throwing their bodies into the sea. Henceforth the smelly women of Limnos lived as Amazons, warlike and independent. When Jason and the Argonauts appeared on the horizon, the women would have attacked had not one of them realised that a shipload of Greek heroes was just what they needed to continue the Limniote race. So the Argonauts, rather than facing battle at Limnos, met only the kindest courtesy. A son born to Jason, Euneus, went on to become King of Limnos during the Trojan War, supplying the Acheans with wine.

The Acheans' best archer, Philoctetes, spent the ten years of the Trojan War

325

on Limnos, suffering from a wounded foot. Philoctetes was the son of Hercules, who inherited his father's famous bow when Hercules was dying in the torment caused by Nessus' shirt, for Philoctetes was the only one who would light his father's pyre. In a fit of pique, caused by Zeus making Heracles an immortal, Hera sent a poisoned snake after Philoctetes when he and the Acheans landed on Limnos on their way to Troy. Throughout the war the poor man lingered in pain on the island where his companions left him, living in a cave, with only his bow. After the death of Achilleus, an oracle declared that Acheans could only capture Troy with the aid of Philoctetes' bow. Odysseus and Neoptolemos' son of Achilleus, went to take it from him by trickery (recounted in Sophocles' play *Philoctetes*) in the end, according to most accounts, Philoctetes himself took his bow to Troy, where he slew Paris.

In Classical times the expression "Limnian deeds" connoted some especially atrocious act. The phrase was first used by Herodotus in his account of an event in the Persian War, when some Limnians brought home some Athenian women they had captured. When their children began putting on airs, the Limniotes supposedly slaughtered them and their mothers.

WHAT TO SEE

Myrina on the west coast serves as the island's port and capital and is the only town of any size. It is sometimes known as Kastro, after the romantic **Turkish fortification** built over the promontory that divides the shore here in two; although there isn't much inside, the walk up to the castle is worth while for the view of the island. Its foundations are Classical, and inscriptions suggest that a temple of Artemis once stood on the site. The ten rooms of the **museum,** in the mansion of the Turkish pasha north of the centre, display a well-arranged collection chronicling the history of Limnos. Upstairs are prehistoric remains, mostly from Paleochoe, divided into four different periods by colours, the oldest the "Black" period, is from 4000 BC. Downstairs are more recent discoveries from Hephestia, Chloi and Myrina.

From the cape beyond the pretty beach of **Akti Myrina,** it is said that the women of Limnos hurled their hapless husbands into the sea. This north side of Myrina has most of the town's night life (such as it is), along the Promenade and the long sandy Greek beach (the Turkish beach is on the south side of town).

The long main shopping street runs down to the southern commercial harbour (Limnos is an official port of entry), passing the banks, the post office, OTE, etc. Some of the old houses are built in the Turkish or Thracian style, and although Myrina isn't an exceptionally pretty town, its gardens and old houses give it a touch of charm. From the north harbour there are caiques to the **Morasiti sea cave**.

Unfortunately buses for other parts of the island are few and infrequent, and there are many villages that have only one service a day, so there's no way to get back the same day. However, there are many taxis and moped and car hire firms in Myrina. South of Myrina are a number of quiet beaches, at **Platis** and

Thanos, and here and there all the way to **Kontias,** many with shade and good places to camp. South of Kontias at **Vryokastro** are the ruins of a Mycenaean fort.

Other beaches, the locally popular **Tsimantria** and **Nea Koutalis** both with restaurants, are on Limnos' great natural harbour, **Moudros Bay.** From here in the First World War the Allies' Mediterranean Expeditionary Force launched its attack on the Dardenelles in April 1915, during which time Winston Churchill, Lord of the Admiralty, visited the island; in 1918, after the defeat at Gallipoli, the armistice with the Turks was signed here on board a ship. East of Moudros town (even today dependent on the large military presence) is a British Commonwealth war cemetery. Limnos' airport (civil and military), is at the north end of the bay, where the island is only a few kilometres wide.

On Pournias Bay to the north, **Kotsinas** was the medieval capital of Limnos. A statue of the heroine Maroula stands here and a spring with good water flows down a long stairway by the church **Zoodochos Pigi.** Ancient walls remain, and there is a good beach and view of the island from the top of the village. Ancient **Hephestia,** further east along the coast, derives its name from the god who made a rather ungraceful landing there when tossed from Mt Olympos. Part of the theatre remains, together with houses and an agora. There is also a medieval fortress at the nearby village **Kokkino.** Another ancient site, excavated by the Italian School of Archaeology (which has done almost all the work on Limnos) is **Chloi,** the site of one of the most ancient sanctuaries of the Underworld deities, the Cabiri (associated with the earth gods of fertility). In the Archaic period women came here to pray for fertility. The Italians found a 6th–7th century BC temple of initiation, dedicated to Thracian Aphrodite; in fact there are two buildings, the old and the more recent. The **cave of Philoktetis** is also at Chloi.

Plaka lies on the tip of the north-eastern Cape Hermaeon, where some say a beacon fire was lit by order of Agamemnon to signal the end of the Trojan War, a signal relayed over the islands back to Mycenae. About 30 metres (90 ft) off shore here are the ruins of **Chryse,** a very ancient city submerged by an earthquake. A temple of Apollo was discovered in a reef. On a calm day you can see some of the marble blocks of Chryse from a boat.

There are two lakes on the east side of Limnos, **Aliki,** which has salt water, and **Chortapolimni,** which is dry in the summer and filled by river torrents in the spring. On the east coast lies Limnos' major archaeological site, **Paliochne** (partly signposted from Kaminia). Here the Italian School discovered four different layers of settlements, one on top of the other. The oldest Neolithic town pre-dates the Egyptian dynasties, the Minoan kingdoms of Crete, and even the earliest level of Troy. Walls and houses remain of the next oldest city (2000 BC) which was probably destroyed by an earthquake; here the Italians found the oldest baths in the Aegean; the third city dates back to the Copper Age, while the last settlement on the site dates from the Bronze Age and was contemporary with the Mycenaeans—the Limnos of Homer—dating from 1500 to 100 BC. Unfortunately there's little to see other than the walls of the second city and the

327

foundations of houses. The now abandoned **Ag. Sozos Monastery** to the south looks over the sea from a high cliff. This whole south-eastern peninsula is planted with vineyards.

North of Myrina **Mt Skopia** is the highest point on Limnos, and can be climbed from Ag. Nikolaos where the road ends. **Pirgos** on the coast has a small fort. Mikro Kastelli, and ancient tombs have been found in the region. Nearby **Skala** has some pretty sea caves that one may see by boat from Myrina or perhaps Kotsinas. **Astiki** to the south is one of the larger villages of the island.

PANEYERIA
23 April, Ag. Georgios at Kalliopi—horse races are run by the locals, who bet goats on the outcome; 26 October, Ag. Dimitrios at Ag. Dimitrios; 15 August, at Kaminia and Tsimantria; 6 August, Sotiris at Vlaka; 7 September, Ag. Sozos; 21 May, Ag. Konstantinos at Romano.

WHERE TO STAY
The locals call it "Little Switzerland", but otherwise the posh deluxe bungalow complex on the beach in Myrina is known as the **Akti Myrina** (tel. 0254 22 681). Owned by Swiss interests, it has its own nightclub, four restaurants, private stretch of beach, swimming pool, tennis courts and its own caique. Wooden chalets house 125 rooms; a bungalow starts at 25 000 dr. At the Akti Myrina international tourism begins and ends on Limnos, otherwise there's the class C **Lemnos** on Plateia 28 Octovriou (tel. 0254 22 153) where a double costs around 3800 dr., or the more reasonable **Aktaeon** at 2 Arvanitaki (tel. 0254 22 258) where you can get a double for less than 3000 dr. There are also a limited number of rooms to let in the town, which tend to be overpriced. If you want to camp out, try Plati beach, a little over a mile from Myrina.

EATING OUT
There's a small selection of tavernas and grills along the waterfront, including a couple of fish tavernas in the fishing harbour; the taverna where the boat docks is undoubtedly the best deal in town, a full dinner costing around 700 dr. Along the northern waterfront, or Promenade, is a stretch of pizzerias and cafés. Outside the capital it's harder to find food at places other than the beach tavernas at Plati and Thanos.

TOURIST POLICE
Tel. (0254) 22 200.

The little triangle of **Ag. Efstratios** (twice weekly ferry from Kavala and Limnos, in summer once a week from Kimi, at least two caiques a week from Limnos) lies 37 km (23 miles) south of Limnos, similarly flat and volcanic, and part of the same nomos. Rich in minerals (including petroleum), the islet has been inhabited from Mycenaean times, and on the north coast one can see the walls and ruins of the ancient settlement, which lasted into the age of Byzantium. In 1967 an earthquake struck Ag. Efstratios, and ruined its port and major village, now standing

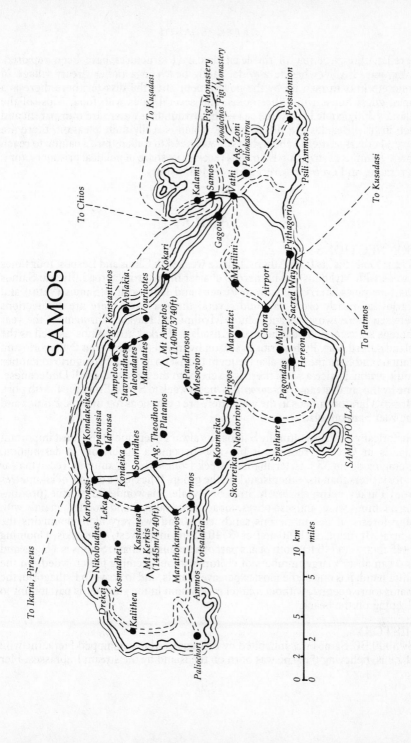

SAMOS

To Chios

To Kusadasi

Pigi Monastery
Zoodochos Pigi Monastery
Ag. Zoni
Paliokastrou
Possidonion

Kalami
Samos
Vathi
Psili Ammos

To Kusadasi

Gagou
Mytilini
Chora
Airport
Sacred Way
Pythagorio

Kokari
Avlakia
Vourliotes
∧ Mt Ampelos
(1140m/3740ft)

To Patmos

Ag. Konstantinos
Stavrinidhes
Ampelos
Valeondates
Manolates
Pandhroson
Mesogion

Mavratzei
Myli
Hereon
Pagondas

Kondakeika
Ipaiousia
Idrousa
Souridhes
Ag. Theodhori
Platanos
Koumeika
Neohorion
Spathare

Kondeika

Skoureika

SAMIOPOULA

Karlovassi
Leka

Ormos

Nikoloudhes
Kastanea
∧ Mt Kerkis
(1445m/4740ft)
Marathokampos
Ammos – Votsalakia

To Ikaria, Piraeus

Drekei
Kosmadhei
Kalithea
Paliochori

10 km
miles

0   5   5   2
0   5   2

derelict, though a few of the least damaged structures have been repaired. Everyone else lives beside a wide, sandy beach in a rather dreary village of concrete huts thrown up by the government after the disaster; here there is a small guest house with nine rooms, and several cafés with food. Most of the island's 300 people live off the sea—the surrounding waters are transparent and rich in fish. Besides the village beach, which is really quite pleasant, there are several others scattered about, but you will need to walk or hire a caique to reach them. In times of strife Ag. Efstratios receives its share of political prisoners, for it is remote, and even today receives very few visitors.

SAMOS

CONNECTIONS

By air: Daily flights from Athens, twice a week with Chios and Lesbos, four times a week with Mykonos and numerous charter flights from abroad. By sea: Samos has four ports. Ferry boats from Piraeus and Ikaria call at Samos (Vathi) and Karlovassi nearly every day, and several times a week there are connections between these two ports and Chios, Mytilini and Kavala. Throughout the year there is an excursion boat between Kusadasi, Turkey and Samos, as well as the island's third port, Pythagorio. In season hydrofoils run between Pythagorio and Patmos and Kos; there are also frequent tourist boats from Pythagorio to Patmos and Furnous; twice a week there is a service to the large and small Dodecanese, one by the small steamer *Panormitis*. Once a week to Syros. From the fourth port, Ormos Marathokampos in the west, there are excursions to Furnous, Patmos and the islet Samiopoula.

Historically and agriculturally Samos has always been one of the most important islands in Greece; recently it has also become a major tourist destination, averaging some 35 charter flights a week from spring to autumn, receiving far more visitors than the other islands in the group. It lies just a couple of kilometres from Turkey, across the lovely Strait of Mycale. It is wonderfully fertile (producing a famous wine, and also olives, tobacco and raisins) and wooded, mainly with pine forests; it has numerous sandy coves and two very high mountains the central Mt Ampelos (1140 metres/3740 ft) and in the west, Mt Kerkis, a looming 1445 metres (4740 ft), both peaks part of a mainland chain. Samos is a big island and can absorb large numbers of visitors without seeming too crowded; on the other hand, it is one of the most expensive islands, and to arrive in Pythagorio, the major tourist centre, without a hotel reservation in the summer is paramount to sleeping on the beach.

HISTORY

By 3000 BC Samos was inhabited by Pelasgians who worshipped Hera, the wife of Zeus, believing that she was born on the island by the stream Imbrassos. Her first temple was built by the mythical king Angaios, who was a member of the crew of the *Argos* on its quest for the Golden Fleece. In the 11th century BC the Ionians invaded Samos, and by the Archaic period the island was enjoying a great prosperity, and producing an excellent wine. In 670 BC Samos became a democratic state and its citizens grew wealthy from commercial activities. The swift battleship *Samaina* was designed there; in 650 BC a Samian captain named Kolaios became the first man to sail through the Straits of Gibraltar. The great philosopher Pythagoras was born on Samos in the 6th century BC. Not only did he invent the right-angle theorem for which all schoolchildren know his name, but he was the first to note the mathematics of music and the planets and the beauty of proportions, an idea that brought perfection to Classical architecture and sculpture. Aristarchus, a later Samian mathematician, was the first in history to put the sun in the centre of the universe. In the late 6th century Samos was ruled by the famous tyrant Polycrates, probably the most powerful man in Greece at the time. Samos then became a grand imperialistic power, taking even Delos. Under Polycrates the grand temple of Hera was built, and the engineering miracle, the Efplinion tunnel, was dug through a mountain to bring water to the then capital of the island, modern Pythagorio.

Throughout ancient times Samos' politics were ruled by a feud the island had with its chief rival in the region, Miletus; whatever Miletus did, Samos tended to do the opposite, siding in turn with the Persians, the Spartans and the Athenians in the great disputes of the age. During their second invasion of Greece, the Persians occupied Samos and kept their fleet at the island. In the battle of Plataea (479 BC) the Greek fleet attacked them at Mycale the strait between Samos and Turkey, soundly defeating them (helped by the defection of the Samians in the Persian navy to the Greek side). After the battle of Mycale, the Persians no longer posed a threat to Greece from the sea. Samos allied itself with Athens following the battle, and under that city's influence became a democracy, and even sheltered Athenian democrats during the Revolution of the Four Hundred (411 BC), but during the Peloponnesian War, Lysander commander of the Spartans, took the island.

In 129 BC Rome incorporated Samos as part of her Asia Province, and Augustus often visited the island in the winter, granting it many privileges, despite the fact that his enemies Antony and Cleopatra had lived there for a short time.

After the sack of Constantinople Samos was captured by the Venetians and Genoese. In 1453, when the Turks came to take their place, the inhabitants took refuge on Chios, leaving their island deserted for 80 years. Gradually the population returned, and many Turks also settled on the fertile island, although life became uncomfortable for them in 1821 when the Samians joined the revolution. The second battle of Mycale was fought against the Turks in 1824, and again the enemy from Asia Minor was defeated at sea, this time when Kanaris blew up a Turkish frigate. Although the Great Powers excluded Samos from joining Greece in 1830, it was granted semi-independence under the

331

"prince of Samos", a Christian governor appointed by the Sultan. In 1912, the Samian National Assembly took advantage of Turkey's defeats in the Balkan Wars to declare unity with Greece, under the leadership of Sophoulis, later Prime Minister of the country. The union was ratified at the end of the war.

WHAT TO SEE
Samos, the capital and main port of the island, dates from the 19th century, when it was called Stephanoupolis; more recently it was known as Vathi, although this name now applies only to the "deep end" of the city's magnificent harbour. By island standards, Samos is a smart town with many new buildings, all harmonised by their bright red-tiled roofs. In 1987 a fierce fire destroyed much of the land around Vathi.

The **public garden,** with its dishevelled flower beds and a small zoo, is near the centre of town; behind it is the new building of the **Archaeology Museum** (open 8.45 am–2.30 pm, 9 am–2 pm on Sundays, closed Tuesdays, entrance 200 dr.) which has a fine collection of griffin heads (the ancient symbol of Samos), grave reliefs, and pottery, mainly from the sanctuary of Hera. Another museum, the **Byzantine Religious Museum,** is in the Bishop's office at 28th Oktroviou St. Open Tuesday and Thursday mornings, it contains items used in the church liturgy. There are several cafés in Plateia Pythagorio, which is guarded by a stone lion and shaded by palms. The bus station is further down the waterfront, city KTEL buses run frequent services to Pythagorio, Kokkari and Karlovassi. The nearest (but often crowded) beach to Vathi is Gagou, to the west.

East of Vathi, with the best views over Asia Minor and the beautiful strait at Mycale, is the monastery **Zoodochas Pigi,** begun in 1756. Its church has many intricate wooden carvings. The whole coast here is very attractive, and there are good sandy beaches at **Possidonion** and **Psili Ammos.**

Pythagorio on the south-east coast is the most popular village on Samos and the island's ancient capital, renamed in 1955 (when it was Tigani) to honour Samos' most famous son. Many relics remain of the golden age of the tyrant Polycrates, the most impressive being the **Efplinion tunnel** a couple of kilometres north of the town. Efplinos, the chief engineer of Polycrates, had it dug by slaves who worked on the project for years; some started on one side of **Mt Kas;** some on the other, and they met each other exactly in the middle. The tunnel is more than 900 metres (1000 yards) long, and used to bring water to Pythagorio from the springs of Mt Ampelos. Recently the tunnel (open mornings) has been electrically lit, so it no longer seems as old and mysterious; visitors are allowed in the first 300 metres. The middle of the tunnel has collapsed.

The **long walls** that surrounded ancient Pythagorio are also very impressive, although they were partly destroyed by Lysander when the Spartans took Samos. They were 6500 metres (7100 yards) long, running all the way to Cape Fonias, and protected with towers and gates. The modern village of Pythagorio was built on the **ancient harbour mole,** another masterpiece of Efplinos; some of its foundations may still be seen. Little remains of the **ancient theatre** (en route to

332

the tunnel), but above Pythagorio is **Spiliani,** the cave where the prophetess Sybilla Feto spoke of a one and true god. The cave has a lake inside, and a church **Panayia Spiliani,** built in 1836. Lycurgos Logothetis, a hero of the 1821 Revolution, built a **fort** by the town and there is also an **archaeological museum** in the Community Hall (open daily 9 am–2 pm) housing finds from the area. In 1985 excavations of the city itself, underneath modern Pythagorio, were begun in several areas, and you never know when you'll trip over a trench in a vacant lot. The nearest beaches to town are at Fonias and Iratis Bay.

To the west of Pythagorio, the **Sacred Way** (nowadays the airport road) once took the faithful the 8 km (5 miles) to the **Hereon,** or the Temple of Hera, the second largest temple ever built in Greece and considered by some as one of the Seven Wonders of the Ancient World, though just like another ancient wonder, the Temple of Artemis just over the strait at Ephesus, only a single column of its original 133 stands today. The site was sacred as early as the Bronze Age; the Great Temple was begun under Polycrates and stood 108 metres by 52 metres (354 ft by 171 ft). Twice a year a grand celebration took place there, in honour of Hera's birth by the Imbassos stream nearby and her marriage to Zeus. In mythology Zeus had to use cunning to seduce an uninterested Hera (perhaps because he was her brother), and they spent a 300-year-long wedding night on Samos. Other curiosities at the site include the **altar, a Mycenean wall,** other small temples and buildings, and a **tribute** sent by Cicero. The damage to the great temple and other antiquities is attributed to various invaders and Christian piety. The site is open 9.30 am–4 pm every day. **Sarakini castle** nearby was built by a naval officer of the same name in 1560. Hereon town today is a pleasant backwater with a small number of hotels and tavernas on its short stretch of beach.

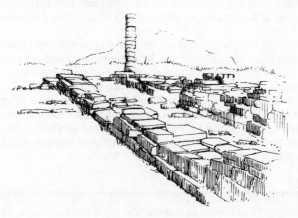

The Temple of Hera, Samos

Chora, just north of Hereon, was the capital of Samos from 1560 to 1855, and today is a charming, quiet village, except when the nearby airport is being used. To the north **Mavratzei** has the **Timios Stavros Monastery,** built in 1592, and a good deal of ceramics and pottery is made in the village itself. In **Mytilini** to the north animal fossils dating back 15 million years have been placed in the **Paleontology Museum** in City Hall, on the main street (open weekdays 7.30 am–3 pm). Interestingly enough, Samos had a reputation for fierce monsters in mythology. The museum's prize exhibit, among the bones of ancient hippopotami and rhinoceroses, is a 13-million-year-old fossilised horse brain. Another pretty village in the region is mountainous **Pirgos,** by the lovely **Koutsi,** which, with its trees, clear waters and mountains, is a popular destination for a lazy afternoon.

Votsalakia rates as the best beach among the Samians, and it and nearby **Psili Ammos** have restaurants and pensions **Marathokampos** village, a little to the north, builds boats, and the **Ormos Marathokampos** is another pretty beach in the area, connected by bus from Karlovassi to the north. All three of these beaches are still relatively quiet; Ormos Marathokampos serves as the region's port. On the slopes of Mt Kerkis north of Marathokampos, **Kastanea** has many beautiful chestnut trees, as its name implies.

Karlovassi, Samos' second city and port, was to be a centre of the tanning industry, an idea that failed but left its port area rather dreary. The city itself, though, is pleasant, and neatly divided into old, middle and new Karlovassi. There are many old houses, some veritable mansions, and an interesting bridge. Near the town there are two monasteries: **Panayia tou Potamou** (Our Lady of the River) dating from the 10th century, and **Profitis Ilias,** founded in 1703. Fewer tourists come to Karlovassi than to Vathi or Pythagorio, although the town does have swimming places nearby (a city bus goes to **Potami,** where there is sand and shade), tavernas, restaurants and a night club. Not all the ships calling at Samos also stop at Karlovassi, so always check if you intend to leave from that port.

Buses run along the north coast of the island between Vathi and Karlovassi, passing the pretty seaside village of **Ag. Konstantinos.** Further east a road leads up the slopes of Mt Ampelos to Manolates, one of the beauty spots of Samos. Here you can eat under the plane trees, and listen to the songs of nightingales. There is good swimming at the pebbly beaches of **Avlakia** and **Kokari,** the latter now a busy resort. In between them you can walk from Vourliotes to the island's oldest monastery, **Our Lady of Vrontiani,** founded in 1560. There are many other villages, small, quiet and verdant, throughout Samos, which has been known since antiquity as "The Island of the Blest".

PANEYERIA

27 July, Ag. Panteleimonos at Kokari (one of the most popular); 6 August, Celebration of the Revolution, all Samos; 29 August, Ag. Ioannis at Pythagorio; 21 November, Panayia Spiliani by Pythagorio; 26 July, Ag. Paraskevi at Vathi; 8

September at Vrontiani Monastery; 20 July, Profitis Ilias celebrated in many villages throughout the island.

WHERE TO STAY

Samos is very difficult for travellers who just drop in; nearly every available room seems to be booked from June to September. In Samos town there are two lovely pensions: the **Athina** at 34 Efplinou St and the **Ionia Pension** at 5 Kalomiri, run by the friendly Evagelia Zavitsanou (tel. 0273 28 782). Both offer doubles for around 2000 dr. If they're full, get the tourist police (next to the **Hotel Xenia)** to help out. Both the Xenia (class B, tel. 0273 27 463) and the **Samos** hotels (class C, tel. 0273 28 377) are modern and clean and face the huge natural harbour. Rates for the Xenia are 6200 dr. in summer and the Samos has doubles with bath at 3800 dr. The helpful NTOG office in Samos town will help you find a room if you're in difficulty.

Pythagorio is packed with small up-scale pensions that are also inevitably full, as well as a typical selection of class C hotels, all costing more than they should. One of the better bargains, if you can get one of its eight rooms, is the D class **Alexandra** at 11 Metamorfosseos (tel. 0273 61 429) with doubles at just under 2000 dr. Many people these days avoid both Samos and Pythagorio and stay in Kokkari, conveniently linked by frequent buses to Samos town. Prices are more reasonable here; for comfort, stay at the **Kokkari Beach Hotel** (tel. 0273 92 263), located, as it's name suggests, right on the shore; doubles here are between 4500 dr. and 6500 dr. a night. Less expensive, and also near the sea, is the **Pension Galina** (tel. 0273 92 331) with doubles around 3800 dr.

To the west there are rooms and pensions on the bucolic slopes of Mt Ampelos, at Platanos and above Ag. Konstantinos, where you'll find the idyllic and inexpensive **Pension Paradisos.** In Karlovassi there's the class B **Merhope Hotel** (tel. 0273 32 650), a favourite of many for its old world service. Rates are 3200 dr. upwards for a double. There's a **Youth hostel** as well in Karlovassi (tel. 0273 32 872) with beds for 400 dr. Peace and quiet can be found at the **Hotel Kerkis Bay** (tel. 0273 37 202) in Ormos Marathokampos, where doubles start at 6000 dr. in season. In Hereon there are a group of small C and D class hotels with prices ranging from 2200 dr. to about 4000 dr., a typical one being the **Faros** (tel. 0273 61 193) with doubles at 2700 dr.

EATING OUT

Samos grows much of its own food and produces its own wine, so eating is usually quite good. The **Samos Wine Festival** takes place every year in August and dancing groups from Athens perform dances from various parts of Greece. In Samos town there's a good taverna near the main square that serves excellent fish dishes for around 1500 dr. The waterfront has a collection of good tavernas which are all reliable (but expensive if you order fish). Less pricey are the numerous snack bars. The waterfront in Pythagorio is one solid café-taverna, and it's worth your while to check their menus before sitting down—not all are

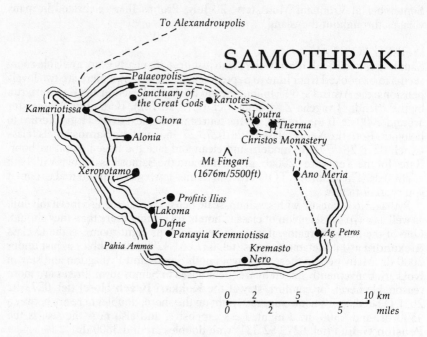

To Alexandroupolis

SAMOTHRAKI

Palaeopolis
Kamariotissa
Sanctuary of
the Great Gods • Kariotes
Loutra
Chora
Therma
Alonia
Christos Monastery

Mt Fingari
(1676m/5500ft)
Xeropotamo
Ano Meria

Profitis Ilias
Lakoma
Dafne
Panayia Kremniotissa
Ag. Petros
Pahia Ammos
Kremasto
Nero

```
0      2      5          10 km
0      2      5          miles
```

expensive. Right on the waterfront in Kokkari, **Stathis** taverna serves very tasty, fresh Greek food for 650 dr. Lobster is more reasonably priced here, too. By the port of Karlovassi there are three restaurants, including a decent pizzeria. In Hereon the sea laps up to the few tavernas situated there, and the food is straightforward and inexpensive.

TOURIST INFORMATION
NTOG, Samos town, tel. (0273) 28 530.
Tourist Police, Samos town, tel. (0273) 27 333.
NTOG, Pythagorio, tel. (0273) 61 022.
Tourist Police, Pythagorio, tel. (0273) 61 100.
NTOG, Kokkari, tel. (0273) 92 333.
Police in Karlovassi, tel. (0273) 31 444.

SAMOTHRAKI (SAMOTHRACE)

CONNECTIONS
By sea: Daily ferry from Alexandroupolis, in summer twice a day; twice a week from Kavala. By air: flights three times a day from Athens to Alexandroupolis.

In the far right-hand corner of Greece, Samothraki is one of the least accessible islands for the average tourist; its rocky shores are uncluttered by day trippers or people just passing through—in a way, they would seem frivolous. For this is a sombre, dramatically stern, rugged island, rising to a peak in the lofty Mountain of the Moon (Mt Fingari), where the sea god Poseidon sat and watched the tides of the Trojan War. Often whipped by the wind and lacking a natural harbour with only a small strip of arable land between the mountain and the sea, it nevertheless was one of the best known and most visited islands of antiquity, for here was the cult centre of the great gods of the Underworld, from all over the Mediterranean people came to be initiated into its mysteries.

HISTORY

Once densely populated and forested, Samothraki owes its importance to its position near the entrance to the Dardenelles. Settled in the Neolithic period, an Iron Age population from Thrace built the first temple on the island (the rock altar beneath the Arsinoeion). In the 8th century BC Aeolians from Mytilini colonised Samothraki and mingled apparently peaceably with the earlier settlers, worshipping Athena and the Great Gods of the Thracians, whose language survived at least in religious rituals, until the 1st century. The mythographers state that Dardanos, the founder of Troy, was a Samothrakian, another Classical tradition has it that Samothraki was itself colonised by the Samians, though the geographer Strabo suggests that the Samians were just boasting because of the island's name. (Strabo also claimed that Samothraki resembled a woman's breast!) By the 5th century BC, Samothraki had reached the height of its importance, itself colonising present-day Alexandroupolis, sending a ship to the battle of Salamis and joining the Delian alliance. Although, like the other islands, her military importance declined with the rise of Athens, Samothraki by this time had become the religious centre of the whole North Aegean drawing a constant stream of pilgrims and adherents to its Sanctuary of the Great Gods.

The Great Gods were chthonic deities (of the earth and Underworld), darker and older and more powerful than the Olympian gods of the state religion, whom even Homer could have fun with. But no one dared to sport with the Great Gods; indeed, no writer dared even reveal what exactly went on at the sanctuary, but it is likely that mysteries included rites of initiation similar to those at the Greek world's major cult centre at Eleusis. A great mother goddess figured in the worship, a Thracian fertility goddess (Axieros Cybele) who was later connected with the Greek Demeter, her other attributes later personified by Aphrodite and Hekate, the Queen of the Night, the goddess of witches. Of secondary importance was her consort, Kadmilos-Hermes, but equal to him were the demonic twins, the powerful Cabiri (later to become associated with the Greek Dioscuri) who protected sailors and are thought to have been Phoenician in origin.

The sanctuary had two levels of initiation, and had surprisingly few restrictions, unlike Eleusis. Anyone male or female, free or slave, could be initiated, and one didn't even have to be initiated to attend the mysteries. There were two levels of initiation, the second thought to have included an unusual moral standard, confession and baptism. Ambassadors from all over the world were invited to the sanctuary's high feasts in the summer, where ceremonies are believed to have taken place at night, by torchlight. Lysander of Sparta, Herodotos Philip II of Macedon and nearly all the Ptolemies were among the well-known initiates, and in mythology even the Argonauts, at Orpheus' suggestion, joined the cult for extra protection before entering the Hellespont.

Hellenistic and Roman rulers continued to patronise the sanctuary. Occasionally they used Samothraki as a naval base, relying on its sacred soil for protection.

In the Roman period, the island began to suffer from invasions and earthquakes. St Paul stopped here, but failed to convert many of the locals, who continued to repair the damaged sanctuary until the 4th century AD. During the age of Byzantium Samothraki was depopulated and forgotten. Pirate raids forced the remaining inhabitants to the hills, where they settled Chora. The Genoese ruler Gattilusi fortified the castle affording them some protection. After the fall of Byzantium to the Turks, Samothracians were sent to resettle Constantinople. Under the Turks life was very quiet, apart from a few uprisings during the War of Independence. Samothraki joined Greece in 1912.

WHAT TO SEE

Kamariotissa, the port of Samothraki, has most of the island's tourist facilities and a rocky beach with changing facilities. Samothraki's three bus routes go from Kamariotissa, and every now and then there are caique excursions to the island's one sandy beach at **Pahia Ammos,** and around the whole of Samothraki—the only way to visit the spectacularly rugged southern coast and the waterfall **Kremasto Nero** ("hanging water").

Buses run frequently from Kamariotissa to **Chora,** the island's capital, high on the slopes of Mt Fingari. Spread out in an amphitheatre below the ruins of a Byzantine castle, Chora is quiet and picturesque, with its Thracian-style homes and red-tiled roofs. Samothraki's only bank is here, as well as several private rooms. From here (or from Therma) you can make the 5–6-hour ascent of **Mt Fingari** (1676 metres/5500 ft), locally known as Mt Saos, and on a clear day enjoy the view as Poseidon did, a stunning panorama of the North Aegean from the Troad in the east to Mt Athos in the west. The paths up are not clearly marked, however and it's best to go with a guide, or at least get clear instructions before setting out. Mt Fingari wears a snow cap for nine months of the year and has long been a landmark for seamen.

Alonia, near Chora, is the island's second largest town, a pretty agricultural village. Other villages—Xeropotamo, Lakoma and **Profitis Ilias** are very small, though the last is pretty and shady and offers views of Turkey. From **Lakoma** a rough track leads to the church Panayia Kremniotissa, from where the energetic can walk to sandy Pahia Ammos.

Buses also run frequently to **Palaeopolis,** where the ancient **Sanctuary of the Great Gods** has been excavated since 1948 by Dr Karl and Phyllis Williams

Lehmann, who have written an excellent guide to the site, on sale in the adjacent museum. (Both the sanctuary and the museum are open daily 9 am–7 pm Sundays 10 am–430 pm)

A visit is best begun in the museum, which has been arranged to help you understand Palaeopolis, as well as displaying artefacts uncovered on the site, or at least those that were missed by previous excavators; the French, of course, took the prize, the famous Winged Victory now prominently displayed in the Louvre, discovered in 1863 by the French consul at Adrianople; the museum displays a plaster copy, a gift from the French.

The sanctuary itself, well labelled and impressive in its ruined grandeur, lies a short distance from the museum. The **Anaktorion** (the House of the Lords) is the first building you reach, dating from the 6th century BC, though the present structure is mainly Roman, here the first-level initiations were held in its inner sanctum. Next to it is the **Arsinoeion,** the largest circular building of the ancient Greeks, 20 metres (66 ft) in diameter. It was dedicated to the Great Gods in 281 BC by Queen Arsinoe, wife and sister of Ptolemy Philadelphos, in thanksgiving for being made fertile. In its walls is an ancient altar, thought to have belonged to the original Thracian cult. The neighbouring rectangular foundation belonged to the **Temenos,** where the celebrations may have taken place; adjacent stand the five re-erected Doric columns of the **Hieron,** where the upper level of initiation was held, a structure restored in the 3rd century AD. Here you can still see the stones where the initiates' confession was heard, as well as the Roman viewing benches. .

The bare outline remains of the theatre on the hill; here also is the **Nike Fountain,** named for the great Hellenistic statue discovered there. The Victory, donated by Dimitrios Polorketes (the Besieger) in 305 BC, once stood as the figurehead of a great marble ship, supposedly it was a gift of thanksgiving for Dimitrios' naval victory over Ptolemy II. Ptolemy II himself donated the monumental gateway to the sanctuary known as the Propylae of **Ptolemaion.** Near here is a small theatre-like area and a Doric building, dedicated by Philip and Alexander, Hellenistic rulers of Macedon. It was at a ceremony in the sanctuary that King Philip II of Macedon first met Olympias of Epiros, later to become the mother of Alexander the Great.

The buildings on the site were extensively dismantled to construct the medieval Genoese castle—the **Ruinenviereck** near the Nike Fountain—and the two watchtowers along the road. The road continues west through shady plane groves and along rocky shores, past many good campsites towards Samothraki's little hot spring spa, **Loutra,** and its budding resort, **Therma,** with a typical island beach.

PANEYERIA
6 August, at Sotirou in Chora; 26 July, Ag. Paraskevi, near Palaeopolis; 20 July, Profitis Ilias at Kormbeti; 15 August, Panayias at Loutra; 8 January, Ag. Athanassios at Alonia.

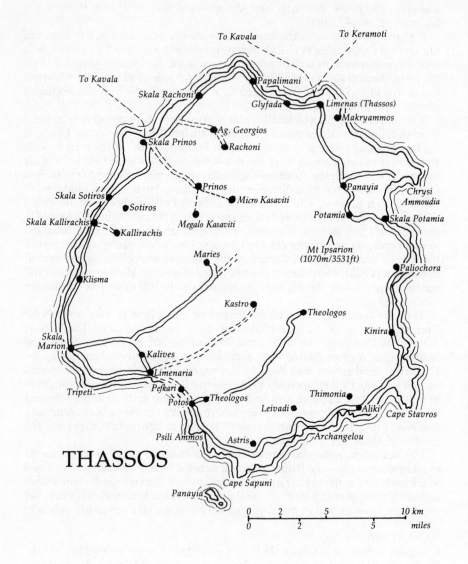

To Kavala

To Keramoti

Papalimani

Skala Rachoni

Glyfada

Limenas (Thassos)

To Kavala

Makryammos

Ag. Georgios

Skala Prinos

Rachoni

Panayia

Chrysi
Ammoudia

Prinos

Micro Kasaviti

Skala Sotiros

Potamia

Skala Potamia

Sotiros

Skala Kallirachis

Megalo Kasaviti

Kallirachis

Mt Ipsarion
(1070m/3531ft)

Maries

Paliochora

Klisma

Kastro

Theologos

Kinira

Skala
Marion

Kalives

Limenaria

Tripeti

Pefkari

Thimonia

Potos

Theologos

Aliki

Leivadi

Cape Stavros

Psili Ammos

Astris

Archangelou

THASSOS

Cape Sapuni

Panayia

| 0 | | 2 | | 5 | | 10 km |
| 0 | | 2 | | 5 | | miles |

WHERE TO STAY

In the port of Kamariotissa there's the brand new class C **Niki Beach Hotel** (tel. 0551 41 561), with 38 rooms by the sea. Rates are 4500 dr. for a double in season. For archaeology lovers, the little **Xenia Hotel** (tel. 0551 41 230), is in the grove by the Sanctuary of the Great Gods. A double here will set you back about 4000 dr. but in season you may have to take half board. Up in Chora there's a small pension and rooms to rent (expect to pay around 1800 dr. a night). There are also rooms in Therma and Profitis Ilias. When you step off the ferry in Kamariotissa there's a small booth where the Room Renters Association has a list of all available rooms. There is a campsite at Loutra.

EATING OUT

In the summer you can do fairly well in Samothraki. The waterfront in Kamariotissa is lined with cafés and tavernas, all typical and inexpensive. Particularly good is the **Aigeon Taverna**, which has a wide choice of Greek food, including the local speciality, kid. Small tavernas spill over on the premises of neighbouring shops, so you could well find yourself eating *souvlaki* in a hardware store. There is fresh fish in the town's only fish taverna, and the *ouzeri* in the middle of the waterfront grills delicious giant shrimp over the coals. Chora and Therma have a number of simple tavernas. In the winter everything closes down except for one or two places in the port.

TOURIST POLICE

In Chora, near the Kastro, tel. (0551) 41 203.

THASSOS

CONNECTIONS

Ferry from Kavala to Prinos almost every hour; from Kavala to Thassos' capital (Limenas) three times a day; from Keramoti (a 20-minute bus ride from Kavala) to Thassos eight or nine times a day. There are daily flights from Athens to Kavala, and buses from Athens and Thessaloniki; Kavala airport is also open to international charter flights.

Northernmost of all the islands in Greece, Thassos is also one of the fairest in the land, almost perfectly round and mantled with fragrant, intensely green pinewoods, plane trees, walnuts and chestnuts. Unlike most of the other islands, it is almost never afflicted by the meltemi winds, but enjoys a moist climate, much subject to lingering mists; on summer days the intense scent of the pines by the calm sapphire sea nearly overwhelms one with a sensuous languor. Also unlike many of the other islands, it is well watered; a necklace of sandy beaches divides the forest from the sea, and—perhaps best of all—its relative inaccessibility to foreign visitors has kept it a virgin in spite of the orgy of package tourism that has

341

deflowered so many of the Greek islands. However, with the recent opening of Kavala airport to international charter flights, it is inevitable that an increasing number of visitors will affect the all-Greek character of this beautiful island. At present, though, the hotels are small and geared to families from northern Greece (and Yugoslavia when the exchange rate permits). Many people camp out, either on the organised sites or elsewhere, even though it is, as usual, forbidden. Prices are still reasonable, and despite the new oil rigs north-west of the island, the water is still very clean.

One problem most people have in Thassos (apart from the trouble it takes to get there) is that the island must be shared with the mosquitoes, so come prepared, especially if you intend to sleep out. Thassos is also badly affected by forest fires; 1985 was an exceptionally bad year, and there were days when the fires raged out of control. Be extra careful.

HISTORY

Herodotos informs us that Thassos was first inhabited by the Phoenicians in 1500 BC. This is uncertain, though when the Parians came to set up a colony (at the command of Hercules, they said) in 710 BC, the island was inhabited by a Thracian tribe. The likeable poet of Paros, Archilochus, sent to do battle with them, was out-manoeuvred and ran away into the trees, dropping his shield in his haste, then went on to write about the incident, probably the first self-deprecating poem in history. The Parians who stayed on as colonists had better luck, extracting some 900 talents of gold a year from the rich mines of Thassos and from the lands they annexed on the mainland. The 6th century BC saw the height of the island's prosperity and political independence.

In 490 and 480 BC the island was attacked by the Persians; the first time its walls were razed, so, when the second time Xerxes arrived, the defenceless islanders threw a fabulous feast for the army and sent it on its way to Salamis. When the island later revolted against the Delian league, Athens sent Kimon to teach it a lesson which he did—after a two-year siege. After that Thassos was ruled by Athens or Sparta (whenever it had the upper hand). Philip of Macedon seized its mainland gold mines.

In 197 BC the Romans defeated the Macedonians, and Thassos gladly became part of the Roman Province, sheltering the defeated Roman Republicans after their defeat at the battle of Philippi. Among the various marauders who troubled the island during the age of Byzantium, the Genoese took the most permanent possession of it in the 14th century. The Turks chased them out in 1460 and occupied Thassos themselves. Russia took over from 1770 to 1774. In 1813 the Ottoman Sultan granted the island to Mohammed Ali, Governor of Egypt, who had been brought up in nearby Kavala. Mohammed had asked for the island he knew so well, and the Sultan hoped that by giving it to him he would remain a good subject of the Empire. Thassos continued to be ruled by Egypt until 1902, when the Turks returned briefly before the island's union with Greece during the Balkan Wars, in 1912.

342

WHAT TO SEE

The capital and port of the island is officially Thassos, locally called **Limenas,** or sometimes just Limen (even more confusingly, the island's second town is Limenaria). The flags of the world line the waterfront, so everyone can feel at home. Limenas is built on the site of ancient **Thassos,** which covered a far greater extent than the modern town. Various excavations of the ancient city lie scattered among the new. The ancients used an amazing amount of marble—the island's highest peak, Mt Ipsarion, is one great block of it. (Ecologically minded residents are concerned about the current widespread quarrying, which is marring the island's soft green contours.) Not only are the remains of the city interesting, but the marble in itself is also quite beautiful, especially in the **Roman Agora** in the centre of town, adjacent to the museum. Entered from the harbour through a gate, you can see the foundations of porticoes and stoas, a massive altar, sanctuaries, and the mysterious paved "Passage of Theoria" leading to a temple of Artemis (7th century BC), both of these pre-dating most of the other structures in the Agora. The **museum** (open every day except Tuesday from 8.45 am–3 pm. Sundays 9 am–2.30 pm) has a fine collection, with the famous 6th-century BC Kriophoros—a young man bearing a lamb on his shoulders—a lion's head carved in ivory, fine reliefs, ceramics, coins, a lovely head of Dionysos from the 3rd century, and some exceptional Roman imperial busts. Also near the Agora is part of an ancient street, an exedra, a few tiers of the **Odeon** and the **Sanctuary of Hercules,** with an altar and an Ionic temple.

A path follows the extensive **walls** and gates of the ancient city and akropolis. What remains was reconstructed after the first Persian invasion and the later Athenian siege, and was most recently repaired, at least in part by the Genoese. Near the two harbours you can see the two naval gates, known as the **Chariot Gate** (with Artemis on the relief) **and the Gate of Semel-Thyone** (with Hermes); near them are two sanctuaries, of Poseidon and of Dionysos. From here the walls extend beyond the ancient moles of the commercial harbour to the **Greek Theatre** on the lower slopes of the akropolis. This is used in the summer for performances of Classical comedies and tragedies by the Northern Greek State Theatre as part of its Philippi and Thassos Festival, not so much for its state of preservation, but for the marvellous view it affords of pinewoods and sea.

From the theatre a path continues up to the **akropolis,** spread out across three summits; from here on a clear day you can see Mt Athos and Samothraki. The first hill sports a Genoese fortress, built out of the temple of Apollo that once occupied the site. The Kriophoros was discovered embedded in its walls, and a fine relief of a funerary feast (4th century BC) can still be seen near the guardroom. The next hill has a **temple of Athena** (5th century BC), but the Genoese treated her no better than Apollo, leaving only the foundations of the temple. Just below, a Hellenistic relief of Pan can still be seen at his sanctuary, and from here the path continues to the third and highest summit of the akropolis.

The so-called **Secret Stair,** carved into the rock in the 6th century, descends

343

precipitously from here to the walls and the watchful stone eyes of the **Apotro-paion** (to protect Thassos from the Evil Eye), the well-preserved Gate of Parmenon, and most interesting of all, a short distance further on, the **Gate of Silenus**, the largest. The vigorous bas-relief of the phallic god (6th century BC) has lost its most prominent appendage to some "moral cleansing" of the 20th century, but is still impressive. Continuing back towards the modern town are, respectively, the **Gate of Dionysos and Hercules** with an inscription, and the **Gate of Zeus and Hera** with an Archaic relief.

The town beaches are sandy but are also the most crowded on the island, although a half-hour's walk in either direction will bring one to prettier, emptier and cleaner beaches. There is a healthy night life at Limenas, and the evening volta along the waterfront is well worth seeing. This is a stupendous parade in the summer months, perhaps because most of the tourists who come to Thassos are Greek. There is a yacht supply station at Limenas.

Thassos has one main road which follows the coastline all the way round the island. Buses make the circuit several times a day. Of the many beaches, Kalirahi, Pefkari, Pharos, Panayia, Potamia, Rachoni and Aliki are considered the best; **Makryammos** is lovely but has become a high-class tourist beach with an entrance fee of 120 dr. for use of its facilities; Archangelos and Ag. Ioannis are isolated and forested. Directly south of Limenas, along a picturesque road, lies **Panayia,** the most charming village of Thassos. Its old Macedonian houses, decorated with carved wood, overlook the sea. The **church Panayias** has an underground spring, **Chrysi Ammoudia**, inside. There are many restaurants in town and by the beach.

To the south of Panayia is another large, pretty mountain village, **Potamia,** which also has a beach below, lined with many tavernas. **Kastro** in the centre of the island, was the refuge of the Limenarians in the days of piracy, but was abandoned in the 19th century. High up on a steep precipice (a good track leads up from Kalives), some of its old houses have recently been restored. **Aliki** on the south coast was an ancient settlement, and ruins are strewn about its sandy shore. Another ancient settlement was at **Thimonia** nearby, where part of a Hellenistic tower still stands. Further along, the **Monastery Archangelou,** a convent under the jurisdiction of Mt Athos, may be visited (proper attire, even long sleeves, is required); paradoxically, the sandy beach below, nestling in the cliffs is frequented by naturists. **Astris,** above pretty Cape Sapuni, has several ancient towers, and is one of a number of places in the Mediterranean that claims the Sirens, whose singing almost lured Odysseus to his destruction.

Continuing clockwise around the island, **Psili Ammos** and **Potos** have some of the island's best beaches, the latter especially popular with foreigners. From Potos you can take the road up to **Theologos,** the 19th-century capital of the island and one of its greenest spots, where the water from the mountain springs literally flows through the streets. One of the old houses of the village has been done up as a museum of popular crafts, here also are the ruins of the castle **Kourokastro,** and in the church Ag. Dimitrios are icons 800 years old. **Pefkari** on the coast below is a lovely beach with pine trees along the sand. It can be reached by caique from **Panorama** or Limenaria. **Limenaria,** the second largest town on Thassos, draws a fair crowd of tourists in the summer. In 1903 the German Spiedel Company arrived in Limenaria to mine the ores in the vicinity—its plant can still be seen south of town, while the company's grand offices, locally known as the **Palataki,** "Little Palace", stands alone in a garden on the headland. From Limenaria excursion boats tour the coast of Mt Athos—the closest women can get to the great monastic state. Limenaria has retained more of a village atmosphere than Limenas. It is surrounded by trees, with a huge stretch of shady beach.

The west coast of Thassos is lined with beaches, usually less frequented than the beaches on the east coast. There are small resorts at the three Skalas—**Marion, Kallirachis** and **Sotiros.** The village of Sotiros proper, just inland, is the least changed of the island's villages, and has a pleasant taverna. **Skala Prinos** has the closest connections to Kavala, although there isn't much to the village itself. Inland from here is the village of **Prinos,** beyond which lie the two smaller villages of **Megalo** and **Micro Kasaviti,** worth a visit for their lovely setting and charming old houses, many of which have been bought up and renovated by Germans. **Rachoni** and **Ag. Georgios** are two quiet inland villages. A small islet off the north coast, **Thassopoula,** is pretty and wooded but full of snakes, according to the locals.

PANEYERIA
6 August, Metamorphosis tou Sotirou at Sotiros; end of July–beginning of August, traditional weddings performed at Theologos; first Tuesday after Easter, all over the island; 15 August, Panayia at Panayia; 26 October, Ag. Dimitrios at Theologos; 18 January, Ag. Athanasiou at Kastro; 27 August, at Limenaria with special dances; 6 December, Ag. Nikolaos at Limenas; 28 April at Ag. Georgios. (Thassos festival runs from 10 July to 15 August.)

WHERE TO STAY
Between the middle of September and the middle of May it is illegal to rent a room in a private house on Thassos; in season the tourist police in Limenas have a list of available rooms. The island is well endowed with hotels, however, such as the pleasant class B **Timoleon** (tel. 0593 22 177) in Limenas, where a single is 3700 dr., a double 5200 dr. Rates drop by 15% in the off season. The **Akti Hotel** on the waterfront (tel. 0593 22 326), is less expensive but clean, weighing in at 3700 dr. for a double. One street back from here is the spacious **Amfipolis,** recently converted from a tobacco warehouse, with A class doubles going for 8000 dr., singles at 5500 dr. (tel. 0593 23 101). The poshest place to stay on the island is the very modern **Makryammos Bungalows** on the much lauded soft sandy beach of the same name, near Limenas (tel. 0593 22 101). Bungalows start at 14 000 dr. In Skala Prinos the C class **Europa** has 12 double rooms at 3500 dr. (tel. 0593 71 212).

In Limenaria rooms are very plentiful and relatively cheap, and there's an overpowering class E hotel, the **Papageorgiou** (tel. 0593 51 205), where you can get a room and a bath for 2000 dr. Thassos has two campsites, the least expensive at **Panayia** (tel. 0593 61 472). Two others are to be found at **Prinos** (run by NTOG, tel. 0593 71 270), and at **Pefkari** (tel. 0593 51 190). The **Ioannides Rahoni** campsite, with its excellent facilities, is ideal for families and is beautifully situated on a sandy beach under the pine trees; it's between Prinos and Limenas (tel. 0593 71 377). For something different you can find rooms in the pretty village of Panayia, where there's also the small E class **Hotel Helvetia** (doubles 2000 dr., tel. 0593 61 231), or completely off the beaten track at Kastro, where some of the old homes are available to let. For real isolation, permission can be obtained from the Forestry Commission to stay at the hostel on **Mt. Ipsarion**, for a small fee. Details from the tourist police or tourist information office.

EATING OUT

Every beach, it seems, has at least one taverna, and the towns are very well supplied, with everything from snack bars to chi chi restaurants, all catering to Greek tastes. At the eastern end of the harbour, towards the town beach, the **Platanakia** serves fish at the appropriate price, and just beyond, the **New York Pizza Restaurant** seems to cover all options with traditional Greek food, giant pizza for five (about 1500 dr.), various pasta dishes and occasionally fresh mussels. One street back from the main seafront is the **Asteria** *psistaria* with lots to offer from the spit including, for those not squeamish, revolving goats' heads sporting lascivious grins. A few steps along, and less macabre, is **George's Restaurant** and although the menu outside is extensive, in reality the choice, like the name, is typically Greek. A few steps further will bring you to the **Thessaloniki Taverna**, where you can eat the day's special in its shady garden under the trees. 800 dr. at any of these places will buy you an excellent meal with wine.

As you step off the boat at Prinos, **Kyriakos Taverna**, in front of you, has good fresh food and a wider than average selection. Next door, **Zorba's** is just as popular, and an added treat is the traffic policemen assailing your eardrums with their whistles, as they frantically usher cars on board the waiting ferries.

TOURIST POLICE

Tourist police in Limenas, on the waterfront, tel. (0593) 22 500.
Tourist Information booth on quay in Limenas.
Tourist Police in Limenaria, see regular police, tel. (0593) 51 111.

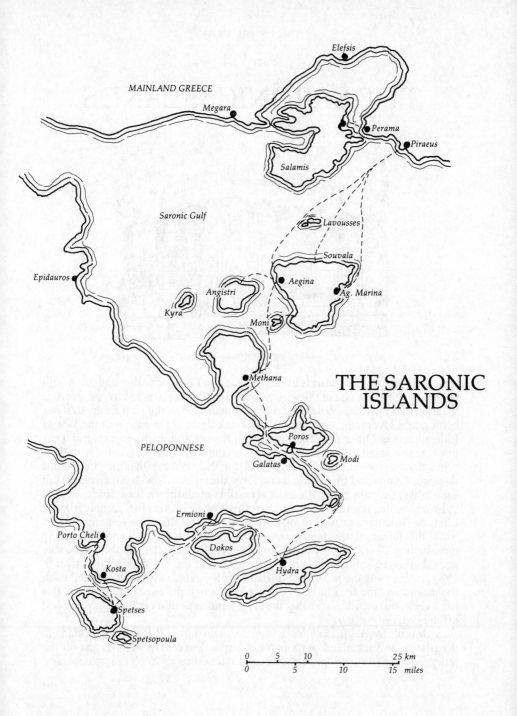

MAINLAND GREECE

Elefsis

Megara

Perama

Piraeus

Salamis

Saronic Gulf

Lavousses

Souvala

Epidauros

Angistri

Aegina

Ag. Marina

Kyra

Moni

Methana

THE SARONIC ISLANDS

Poros

PELOPONNESE

Modi

Galatas

Ermioni

Porto Cheli

Dokos

Kosta

Hydra

Spetses

Spetsopoula

| 0 | 5 | 10 | | 25 km |
| 0 | 5 | 10 | 15 | miles |

Part VIII

THE SARONIC ISLANDS

The Temple of Aphaea, Aegina

The history of the five islands in the Saronic Gulf is inextricably bound up with the sea. Aegina was one of the most powerful maritime states in Greece; Poros is the island of Poseidon; Salamis gave its name to one of the world's greatest sea battles, and Hydra and Spetses led the Greek fleets in the battles of the War of Independence. Other than their links with the sea and their geographical location, the five small islands have little else in common. This, combined with their proximity to Athens, makes them ideal for the visitor with little time at his disposal. Connected by hydrofoil and ferry almost hourly with Athens and with each other, they are by far the most accessible of all the Greek islands.

From the beginning of this century tourists began to visit the Saronic islands. First the Athenians came, buying or renting villas for the three summer months while the father of the family commuted to and fro at weekends. After the introduction 20 years ago of such conveniences as fresh water supplies, electricity and telephones, sun and fun seekers from all over the world began to arrive. In 1985, Aegina was the most visited island in all Greece; Hydra has earned itself the nickname "the St Tropez of Greece", although the once quiet Spetses also has a claim on the title. Note that the only island to permit camping is Moni, just off the coast of Aegina.

Hydrofoils for Aegina *only* leave from the main port of Piraeus; others going to the islands and mainland ports beyond Aegina leave from Zea Marina on the other side of Piraeus. Some are express services directly to Hydra and Spetses;

others call at Aegina, Poros, Hydra and Spetses. Regular passenger ships for all Saronic ports, and car ferries to Aegina and Poros, leave from Piraeus' central harbour.

AEGINA

CONNECTIONS
Every hour by hydrofoil (40 minutes) until late afternoon, or by boat 1½ hours from Piraeus; frequent connections with Methana (the closest port to Epidau-

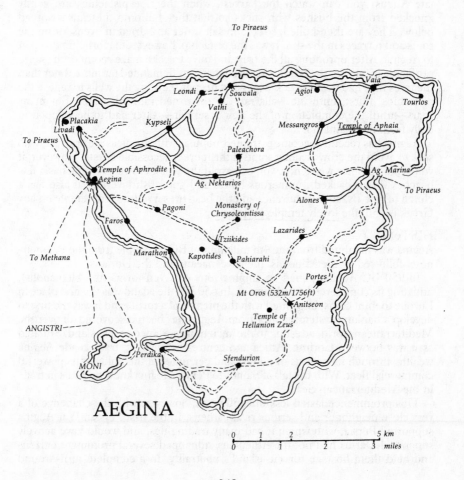

AEGINA

ros). Ferries go either to Aegina town or to Ag. Marina on the east coast; at weekends some call at Souvala. Note that the Flying Dolphin hydrofoil to Aegina departs next to the municipal bus stop to Athens airport; if you have only one day left in Greece and want to see one last island, it's the obvious choice.

Connections between Aegina and Piraeus are so frequent that some residents commute to work in the city, and there are those who jokingly call the island a suburb of Athens. However, unlike Salamis, Aegina has none of the grime of the mainland, and still retains its traditional economy of fishing and agriculture. The pistachio nut is king of the agricultural products; Greeks know them as "Aegina peanuts" and claim that they are the best in the world. If you come to the island in late August you can watch the harvest, when the ripe pistachios are gently knocked from the bushes with sticks so that they fall onto the canvas spread below. They are then hulled, soaked in salt water and dried in ovens, or on the roofs and terraces in the sun. It was the pistachio, however, that brought drought to Aegina. After uprooting all the fruit and olive trees to make room for the more profitable pistachio, the farmers realised that they demanded far more water than the trees they had destroyed. Deeper and deeper they dug the wells to relieve the pistachios' thirst, until the wells ran dry or turned into salt water. For many years—until the completion of the new reservoir—water had to be shipped in daily from the mainland.

Aegina has recently become extremely popular with the pleasure craft set, who seek to avoid the crowds along some of the more inaccessible coasts. However, if you avoid summer weekends, you can avoid the worst crowds. Aegina has a few beaches (often packed), numerous hotels and good fish tavernas; it also has a clutch of fine Byzantine churches and the best-preserved ancient temple on any Greek island, the lovely temple of Aphaia.

HISTORY
Aegina was inhabited from the 4th millennium BC by people from the Peloponnese, followed by the Minoans, the Mycenaeans and the Dorians.

In 950 BC Aegina joined an amphictyony of seven towns (the Heptapolis), initiating its commercial development. In 650 BC the island was the first place in Europe to mint coins, imprinted with the picture of a turtle, and it was the first to develop a banking system; money from Aegina has been discovered all over the Mediterranean world, attesting to the ancient importance of the island. Situated as it was between Corinth, Attica and centres in the east, trade made Aegina wealthy through its exports of pottery and perfumes in the holds of its powerful commercial fleet. With the fall of Samos to Persia, Aegina knew no rivals in trade in the Mediterranean Sea.

This prominence lasted less than 50 years, however, with the challenge of a very close neighbour and serious rival: Athens. In the first Persian War Aegina supported Persia, with which it had many trading ties, and would have actively supported Darius had not the Athenians kidnapped several prominent citizens and held them hostage for the island's neutrality. In a complete turn-around

Aegina sent 30 ships to aid the Greeks at the Battle of Salamis, and won the first choice of spoils for the most heroic conduct. Even so, Perikles could not forgive Aegina for its prosperity and competition with Athens; he called it "a speck that blocked the view of Piraeus". In 458 BC the Athenian fleet defeated the triremes of Aegina, and three years later the city of Aegina was forced to surrender to the siege of the Athenians, who made the inhabitants destroy their fortifications and hand over their fleet.

When the Peloponnesian War broke out, the Athenians deported all the Aeginetans, who were welcomed by the Spartans and were later returned to their homes by Lysander. Saracens, Venetians and Turks took the island many times the last occupation of the Ottomans lasting from 1715 to 1821, when Aegina was one of the first places in Greece to be liberated. Many refugees came to the island from other parts of Greece. In 1828 Aegina became the capital of free Greece under Capodistria, who was elected there. The first modern drachma, bearing a phoenix rising from the ashes, the first newspaper and, less pleasant, the first prison of Greece were created on Aegina although a year later the capital was relocated in Nauplia.

MYTHOLOGY
The name Aegina comes from one of Zeus' many loves, with whom he fathered Aeacus, the first king of the island. Aeacus to honour his mother, renamed what was then Oenone "Aegina". This was too much for the ever jealous and ever unjust Hera. She punished Aeacus for being an illegitimate son of Zeus by plaguing Aegina with poisonous serpents, polluting the water and causing all the people to perish. Aeacus begged his father Zeus for help, wishing for as many inhabitants to repopulate his island as there were ants on a nearby oak, a wish Zeus granted. Thus the new Aeginetans were known as the Myrmidons. Aeacus went on to father three sons—Peleus, Telemon and Phocos. When out of jealousy Telemon and Peleus killed Phocos, their father's favourite, and were forced to flee the island, Telemon went to nearby Salamis, and Peleus to Thessaly. These two brothers, in turn, fathered two of the greatest heroes of the Trojan War, Ajax and Achilles respectively. When Aeacus died, Zeus appointed him one of the three judges of the dead along with Minos, his arch enemy, and Rhadamanthys, his other son from Crete.

WHAT TO SEE
Aegina town has some lingering grandeur from its days as the capital of Greece; today it is simply the capital of the island and its main port. Its large harbour, a distinctive crescent, was financed in 1826 by Samuel Greenly Howle, an American philanthropist and one who loved Greece. Directly on the harbour, and built at the same time, is a chapel dedicated to Ag. Nikolaos, patron of sailors.

In ancient times Aegina also had a "secret port" just north of here, often referred to by ancient writers—secret because only the local people knew the entrance. Overlooking it, on the **Hill of Kolona,** stood the ancient city, dating back to the Early Helladic period. Excavations here revealed a road, a walled settlement and a temple. The name of the hill, however, comes from the one remaining standing column from what is now identified as the early 5th-century **Temple of Apollo** (once thought to belong to Aphrodite, after a description by Pausanias). Unfortunately most of it was used to build the quay. Graves were found in the vicinity; one, found in the 1880s, yielded the British Museum's "Aegina Treasure" of gold ornaments in the Minoan style, dating back to the 16th century BC. A new **Archaeology Museum** has been constructed at Kolona, replacing the old one in town (indeed, Aegina had Greece's first archaeology museum, though most of its collection soon went to Athens). Inside is an interesting collection of finds from the Neolithic era to the Classical period. Also at Kolona you can see a mosaic reconstructed from an ancient synagogue discovered in the town.

Other sights relate to the brief days of glory when Aegina was the capital of Greece. The first government building was the pink **Tower of Markellos,** near the large Ag. Nikolaos church. It is grim and austere, as is the hastily erected **Residence** (now the public library) on Kyverneou St. Capodistria, the first president, slept in his office on the upper floor here, while downstairs the mint churned out the drachmas of the new state. When the rest of his government moved on to the new capital at Nauplia, the once dapper count from Corfu lingered here, estranged from his own government, suspected by nearly all, until his assassination. On the waterfront you can also see many elegant buildings from the past behind the tourist clutter, and the numerous horse-drawn carriages are a nice touch.

An evening stroll around the waterfront is particularly pleasant for the lovely sunsets (probably due to the dirty atmosphere emanating from Athens) which bathe the town in a gentle light far different to the daytime glare. Colourful fishing boats solidly line the waterfront. They no longer fish for the famous katsoulas, once a speciality of Aegina but today almost extinct, nor do the sponge boats operate any more, having been pushed out of business by synthetics. Now the small marida (whitebait) comprises most of the catch, which one can try with Aegina-produced retsina in one of the many tavernas at the port. Aegina has a yacht supply station. There are two beaches near the capital, one by the secret port, the other, more shady beach, to the south of town. Caiques leave the harbour for Moni islet, and a boat to Angistria. Buses serving the rest of the island depart from the square near the quay.

Aegina lends itself to travel by bicycle or scooter, both of which may be easily hired in town. However, it's not far to walk north of Aegina town to **Livadi,** where a plaque now marks the house in which Nikos Kazanzakis wrote his best-known novel, *Zorba the Greek*. Further afield, on the north coast, **Souvala** is the island's spa, with radioactive baths recommended for rheumatism and arthritis, and there is also a beach and hotels. A road south from Souvala leads to ruined **Paleach-ora,** the Byzantine and medieval capital, of the island founded in the 9th century during the raids of the Saracens. Here Ag. Dionysos came from Zakynthos after

352

his brother's death to live at the **Episkopi cathedral**. The town was destroyed twice, first by Barbarossa in 1538 and then by Morosini in his siege of 1654. At Paleachora are the remains of 20 or so 13th-century churches, it is said that there were once 365, but most were torn down to build new houses. Many of those remaining have frescoes inside. Above the crumbling old village is the partly ruined **Venetian castle** of 1654. If you visit Paleachora in the morning, the caretaker is usually there with the keys to the churches (be sure to wear your walking shoes). Some of the paintings inside are quite lovely, such as the **Basilica of Ag. Anargyroi,** the **Chapel of Taxiarchis,** and Ag. Dionysios' **Cathedral of the Episkopi**.

Far more recent is the **convent of Ag. Nektarios,** former bishop of Aegina, who was canonised in 1967, the most recent of Greek Orthodox saints. His remains are in the church, and he is considered the protector of Aegina. On 9 November, a large pilgrimage is made to the convent to commemorate the date of the saint's death in 1920. An hour's walk to the south leads to the 17th century **convent of Chrysoleontissa,** a fortress-style monastery housing an icon of the Virgin responsive to prayers for rain. Inside is a fine carved wooden iconostasis. The nuns at the convent are well known for their hospitality and for the delicious products of their farm. East of Paleachora is the pretty village of **Messangros,** surrounded by the vineyards and pine groves that combine to make Aegina's excellent retsina.

On the pine-covered hill above Messangros is the prize attraction of the island, the beautiful **temple of Aphaia**. Like Apollo and Artemis, Aphaia was a child of Leto. She often went hunting with her sister and followed her cult of virginity. Minos of Crete fell in love with her, but she would have nothing to do with him, he chased her, and she fled him for nine whole months. Unable to bear it any longer, Aphaia threw herself into the sea, but was rescued by kindly fisherfolk. Artemis later made her a goddess, although she was hardly known outside Aegina.

The temple of Aphaia (open 9am-6pm) was built in the Doric order in the early years of the 5th century BC, and today it is the best-preserved temple on the Greek islands. Of the 32 original columns, 25 still stand (some reconstructed). The pediment sculptures, prize examples of Archaic art, depicting scenes of the Trojan War, were purchased by Ludwig of Bavaria in 1812 and can now be seen in the Munich Glyptothek. In the great hall of the temple, where a statue of the goddess once stood, examples of 19th-century graffiti can now be seen. Outside the temple are the ruins of an ancient wall, the altars, a cistern and some of the houses of the priest. There is a café across the road from the temple, offering a splendid view of the east coast of Aegina, including **Ag. Marina,** the seaside resort of the island with a long sandy beach. Ag. Marina is the final destination of the bus from Aegina, which leaves every half-hour.

One of the most popular excursions on Aegina is to cycle to **Perdika** (partridge) in the south. Still relatively untouched by tourism, Perdika is a pretty fishing village and the best place to find fresh fish on the island. One can also swim at its small beach. Inland on **Mt Oros** is the third temple of Aegina, dedicated to Zeus. The walk there from Marathon village takes about two hours. Its reward is a magnificent view from the summit, although little remains of the Mycenaean sanctuary of Zeus, called Hellanion for the ancient name of the mountain.

PANEYERIA

9 November, Ag. Nektarios; 6 December, Ag. Nikolaos at Aegina; 14 September, Stavros in Paleachora; 6–7 September, Ag. Sostis in Perdika; 23 April, Ag. Georgios at Ag. Georgios.

WHERE TO STAY

In Aegina town most of the accommodation is on the oldish side, and there are many relatively inexpensive places to stay (at least for such a popular island). One of the more comfortable places is the **Pension Xenon Pavlou** at 21 P. Aeginitou (tel. 0297 22 795), a block from the waterfront. Rates here start at 2000 dr. for a single, 3000 dr. for a double. Opposite the beach, the **Hotel Brown** at 4 Toti Hatzi (tel. 0297 22 271) has a friendly staff; for peace and quiet, ask for a room in the back. A double here is 3500–4500 dr. For B movie atmosphere, stay at the **Hotel Miranda** beyond the football field on the far end of the beach (tel. 0297 22 266) which doesn't look as though anyone has touched it since 1958. The large garden in front has gone to weeds, and the midget behind the desk in the tiny, gloomy lobby can be decidedly surly. But the price for one of its wistful rooms is right: singles at 1700 dr., doubles 2500 dr. The friendly **Leoussis Agency** near the boat dock can also help you find an inexpensive room as well as a villa. The tourist police are also helpful and open all year.

In Perdika there's the **Moondy Bay Bungalows,** with a well-tended garden, swimming pool and its own jetty (tel. 0297 61 146). Rates are between 7500 dr. and 10 000 dr. for a bungalow; book well in advance. There are also plenty of hotels (too many) on Ag. Marina beach, and you'll pay from 2800 dr. to 4500 dr. for a C class double room here, and not much less for a D or E class. In Souvala the **Xeni** (tel. 0297 52 435), with seven rooms, will give you relative comfort for about 3000 dr. a double, but there are a few cheaper rooms in private houses, and in nearby Vathi. The only camp ground in the Saronic islands is on the islet of Moni.

On Angistri island there's no shortage of accommodation, most of it centred around Skala, and it's all much of a muchness. The **Hotel Anagennissis** is right on the beach here, with doubles at about 2500 dr. (tel. 0297 91 332), and for about the same price there's the **Aktaeon** in the village (tel. 0297 91 222), You'll also find rooms to let in private homes.

EATING OUT

Aegina town is packed with eateries all along the waterfront where you can eat anything from hamburgers and souvlaki to lobster. For reasonably priced fish try

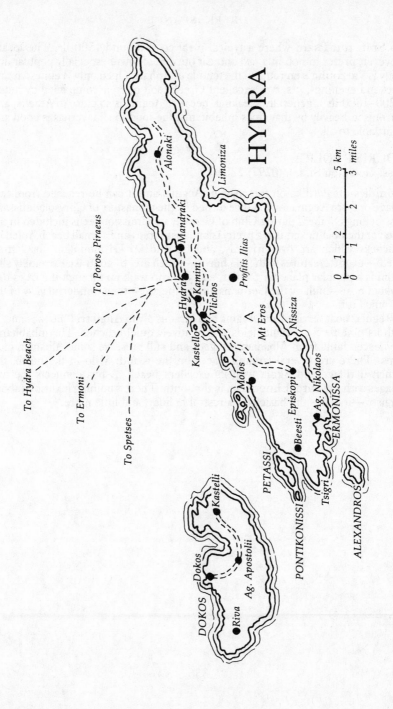

HYDRA

To Poros, Piraeus

To Hydra Beach

To Ermoni

To Spetses

Alonaki

Limoniza

Mandraki

Kamini

Hydra

Vlichos

Kastello

Profitis Ilias

Mt Eros

Nissiza

Molos

Beesti Episkopi

Ag. Nikolaos

PETASSI

Tsigri

ERMONISSA

PONTIKONISSI

ALEXANDROS

DOKOS

Dokos

Kastelli

Ag. Apostolii

Riva

0   1   2   3 miles

0   1   2   3   4   5 km

To Spiti tou Psara where a typical meal costs around 1500 dr. The locals, however, prefer to hop in a taxi and eat outside of town; especially popular and lively is **Vatzoulia's** en route to the temple of Aphaia. Open only Wednesday and weekend evenings, it serves excellent Greek food often accompanied by music (1200–1800 dr.); generally speaking, because Aegina is so close to Athens, and patronised heavily by that city's inhabitants, the food in all tavernas is good and affordable to all.

TOURIST POLICE
Vass. Georgiou St, tel. (0297) 22 391.

Moni lies off Perdika on the coast of Aegina, and it can be reached from that village or from Aegina town. Once owned by the monastery of Chrysoleontissa, it now belongs to the Touring Club of Greece; an admission fee is included in the price of the boat ticket. It is a pretty island, with trees and a small beach, ruled by peacocks which are over-friendly, and by wild kri kri mountain goats from Crete—exotic creatures with long horns—which are, by contrast, extremely shy. Moni is a popular place for picnics, and you can walk up through the trees to a lookout post—built by the Germans during the war—for a wonderful view of the Saronic Gulf.

Regular boat service from Aegina and Piraeus ply to **Angistri** ("hook island"), with its pine forests, fertile fields and relatively quiet beaches. The inhabitants are descendants from Albanian refugees and still preserve some Albanian customs. There are several landing places on the island: **Milo** in the north, the principal village and **Skala** with its excellent beach. A bus connects the two villages with the third, **Limenaria,** in the south. There's nothing luxurious about Angistri—it offers the basics for a restful holiday, and little more.

HYDRA

CONNECTIONS

Passenger ships connect Hydra with the other Saronic islands and ports five or six times a day; twelve hydrofoils a day from Zea Marina (Piraeus), some going "express" to Hydra in about 1½ hours; hydrofoil connections to Porto Heli and Nafplion in the Peloponnese.

Hydra's role in the War of Independence has earned it a major place in the nation's history books and a picture on the 1000-drachma note; its extraordinary harbour, piled high with the tall, sombrely elegant mansions of its legendary sea captains, once served as the backdrop to Greece's largest fleet of sailing ships. Now restored and inhabited by artists and their followers, they serve as the setting for oil paintings and trendy models. Hydra is expensive, and because accommodation is limited, most visitors come only for the day.

HISTORY

In the 6th century BC the tyrant Polycrates of Samos bought dry, rocky Hydra with the tribute he captured in Sifnos. However, no permanent settlers lived on the island until the 15th century, when Greeks and Albanians from Epirus escaped there from the Turks. By the late 18th century, Hydra had become a major refuge for rebels, many fleeing the tyranny of Ali Pasha. Hydra is a rocky, barren island, and through necessity the new arrivals turned to the sea for their livelihood: shipbuilding, a large merchant marine fleet—and piracy. By the 18th century Hydra was very much its own little island state, sending only sailors as an occasional tribute to the Sultan, who prized their prowess in his fleet. By the end of the 18th century the island had a fleet of 150 merchant ships, a population of 25 000, and considerable wealth, the Albanians in particular making their fortunes by daring to run the British blockade in the Napoleonic Wars. When Ibrahim Pasha visited the island, he bestowed on it the title "Little England".

Hydra was one of the major centres of insurgency, and in 1821 it sprang into the revolution with enthusiasm. A merchant and pirate fleet of 150 ships was fitted out for war with funds given by the wealthy merchants and sea captains, most notably the prominent Koundouriotis family. Under such leaders as Miaoulis, commander-in-chief of the Greeks, Tombazis, Voulgaris and Tsamados, the Hydriots terrorised the Turkish fleets, especially with their fire ships. Under the cover of night, a few brave Greeks would row a decrepit vessel full of explosives alongside the Turkish ships, ignite it and swim for their lives. The Turks, should they notice it in time, could only do the same, as they had little defence against a lighted bomb. After the war, sponge fishing became the islanders' major occupation, but then that too declined through lack of demand. In the 1950s life on Hydra was very quiet indeed, until it began to attract artists, beginning with the Greek Hadjikyriakos Ghikas, which turned a new page in the island's history.

357

WHAT TO SEE

Sailing into Hydra's steep-sided port, capital and only town of **Hydra** is a breathtaking experience. The island seems to be a barren rock as you sail along the coast, then suddenly your vessel makes a sharp turn, and there it is: the scene that launched a thousand cruise ships. The grey and white mansions, built in the late 18th century by Venetians and Genoese architects, are unique on the islands and lend Hydra its special character. The island has no cars, but many narrow streets that peter out into stairs, rewarding the wanderer with many charming scenes and views, and surprising tranquillity. Although many of the artists have fled the cosmopolitan onslaught, a branch of the **School of Fine Arts** survives in the fine old residence of the Tombazi family, and there are several galleries amid the boutiques and jewellery shops. Another school, recalling an older tradition, the **Skoli Borakis Naftilias,** Greece's oldest school for merchant marine captains, is in the old Tsamados house. The loveliest mansions—and the largest—belonged to the Koundouriotis family, which produced two important men in Greek history: Georgios, who converted his merchantmen into warships at his own expense, and Pavlos, who went on to serve as president of Greece.

The churches in Hydra also reflect the wealth and influence which the island once enjoyed with their marble campaniles and gold chandeliers. **Panayia tis Theotokou,** next to the port, has a lovely iconostasis and silver chandelier; dating from the 17th century it was once the church of a convent, the cells of which are now used for town offices. There is also a statue of Miaoulis, the famous fighter for the revolution on the high seas. It is said that Nelson once captured Miaoulis on one of his adventures, but Miaoulis in turn captured Nelson with his charm. In his honour the **Miaoulia celebrations** are held in the town on 20 June, complete with mock re-enactments of the Hydriot admiral's battles.

Of course the main thing to do in Hydra is to walk around and soak up local colour. A climb up to **Kalo Pigadi** is an easy and worthwhile excursion just above the town (go by Miaoulis St). There are some old 18th-century mansions on top and two deep wells with fresh water. The one real beach on Hydra is a 20-minute walk away at **Mandraki,** the old shipbuilding docks (arsenal) of the Hydriots and there are some recent fortifications there. One may also swim at **Kamini** (Italian for "whitewash", which was once made there) although the beach is mostly rocks. Kamini is packed with Hydriots and visitors who come to watch the moving Good Friday candlelit procession that culminates here; the "epitaphios", after passing through the streets of the town is brought here to the sea. Another place to swim is the sea cave **Bariami** nearer to town converted into a kind of swimming pool.

Other swimming holes and inland excursions require more walking but that is a guaranteed way to escape the crowds of tourists who stay close to the cafés and shops in the town. At **Kastello** are the ruins of a thick-walled castle down near the shore. Further on, **Vlichos** has a couple of good tavernas. A pine forest and cove for swimming make **Molos** a popular place for outings; according to ancient tradition a nearby cliff was used to dispose of the aged and sick who produced nothing for the island. Wealthy hunters have their lodges at **Episkopi,** in a region of pine forests. Another excursion inland is to the **Profitis Elias monastery** and the nearby convent **Ag. Efpraxia,** an hour on foot above the town. The view from the top is lovely and one may buy textiles woven by the nuns on their ancient looms.

PANEYERIA
15 August Panayias in town 13-14 November Ag. Konstantinos of Hydra the island's patron saint mid-June the Miaoulia 20 July Profitis Elias Good Friday and Easter. 25 July at Ag. Efpraxia.

WHERE TO STAY
It is absolutely impossible to come to Hydra in the summer and expect to find anywhere to stay without a reservation. Now that you've been warned here are some to choose from: **Pension Cavos** (tel. 0298 52 581) is perhaps the most charming with only four rooms in a typical Hydriot house. Rates here are 4500 dr. for a room. Equally pleasant and just a bit larger the **Hydra Hotel** is similarly located in a historic mansion once belonging to a sea captain (tel. 0298 52 597). A double here is 4200 dr. In the centre of town, the fully-air-conditioned **Hotel Greco** charges 6000 dr. for a double (tel. 0298 53 200). Outside the town, at Mandraki there's the **Miramare,** class A, with mandatory pension (tel. 0298 52 300) a double here is 5700 dr. Somewhat larger than the others, the **Hotel Leto** might be able to squeeze you in at short notice (tel. 0298 52 280); doubles are 4000 dr. Least expensive and right in the heart of things the **Hotel Sophia,** class D (tel. 0298 52 313) offers singles for 1700 dr., doubles for about 2500 dr., showers included.

EATING OUT
For the privilege of sitting and eating on the lovely quay of Hydra expect to pay through the nose for anything from a cup of coffee upwards. The one taverna that keeps human prices is near the cathedral called **The Three Brothers**; expect to pay between 600 and 800 dr. for their excellent Greek cooking. Also resonably priced are **The Well,** serving old Greek favourites, and the **Hydra Corner,** which often has live *bouzouki* music to accompany your meal from the grill. Hydra's new French restaurant **La Grenouille** serves classic dishes in a cool garden setting, and is expensive. Out at Kamini, the tranquil taverna run by the Mavromatis family seems worlds away from the cosmopolitan port, and 30 metres behind it, the **Anastasakis** taverna serves some of the best traditional Greek food on Hydra for a moderate price.

TOURIST POLICE
Navarhan N. Botsi, St, tel. (0298) 52 205.
For general information, hydrofoil and boat tickets, accommodation, etc., contact **Pan Travel** on the quay (tel. 0298 53 260).

From Hydra it is an hour's caique trip to the islet of **Dokos,** which produced a kind of marble called marmaropita, grey and red and as hard as steel, used in building. The beach at Dokos is longer than at most ports but there is little accommodation on this islet, almost untouched by tourism. As no regular service goes to Dokos it is best to round up as many people as can fit into a caique, thus making the trip more reasonable.

POROS

CONNECTIONS

Car ferry from Piraeus, Aegina, Methana several times a day; several car ferries daily to Galatas; frequent passenger ships and Flying Dolphin hydrofoils to other places on the Saronic Gulf. Galatas is four hours from Athens by land, and water taxis (benzinas) make the short trip across the strait on demand.

Of the four major islands in the Saronic Gulf, Poros, for some unknown reason, receives the most package tours. At one point it's only 370 metres (400 yards) from the mainland and sailing through the narrow Strait of Poros on a large ferry boat is a unique experience—you feel as if you could touch the balconies of the waterside buildings (or at least see what their inhabitants are watching on television). Curiously, Poros actually consists of two different islands from different geological periods: larger Kalavria is pine-forested and embellished with innumerable quiet sandy coves; little Sferia is a volcanic leftover that popped out of the sea during the eruptions at Methana on the mainland. The two are joined by a sandy belt of land and a bridge.

Although Poros itself has little to offer in the way of excursions, it is close to some of the principal sights in the Peloponnese: the ancient theatre of Epidauros with its festival of ancient Greek drama, ancient Troezen (of Theseus, Phaedra and Hippolytus), and its impressive Devil's Bridge, and nearer to Galatas, the fragrant Lemonodassos ("forest of lemon trees"), some 30 000 in all, visible to the left from Poros.

HISTORY

"Poros" means passage, but in antiquity the entire island was known as Kalavria. It was the headquarters of the Kalavrian league, a 7th-century BC amphictyony, or maritime confederation, that included seven cities: Athens, Aegina, Epidauros, Troezen, Nauplia, Ermioni, Orchomenos and Pasiai. One of the few things known about the Kalavrian league is that it operated under the protection of the sea god Poseidon, to whom Poros was sacred. A famous sanctuary of the god stood in the centre of Kalavria. Not much remains of it today except for the memory of the great Athenian orator, Demosthenes, who roused his city's love for freedom against Alexander the Great. Years after the Macedonians had defeated the Athenians at Chaeronea (338 BC) Demosthenes still had little, if anything, kind to say about the Macedonians and in 322 Antipater went after him. Demosthenes sought sanctuary at the temple of Poseidon; cornered there by Antipater's men he took poison (significantly from the tip of his pen) and died.

One of the bays of Poros is called Russian Bay, recalling some of the confusing events that occurred on Poros in 1828, when emissaries of the Great Powers (British, French and Russian) gathered here for a conference on the new Greek kingdom. The Russians were always close friends with the first president, Capodistrias—too close, thought many independent-minded revolutionaries from Hydra and Poros, who formed their own "constitutional committee". On its orders, Admiral Miaoulis seized the national fleet base at Poros in 1831 and when ordered by the Great Powers to hand it over to the Russians, he blew up the flagship instead.

The name of the island's other bay, Askeli, is derived from the mythological princess Skylla of Poros, whose father, the king, had a magic lock of hair that made him immortal. When Minos of Crete besieged her father's castle, Skylla fell in love with the handsome Cretan king as she watched the battle. To prove her love for him, she cut off her father's magic lock of hair while he slept and brought it to Minos proclaiming her affection. By killing the king, Minos

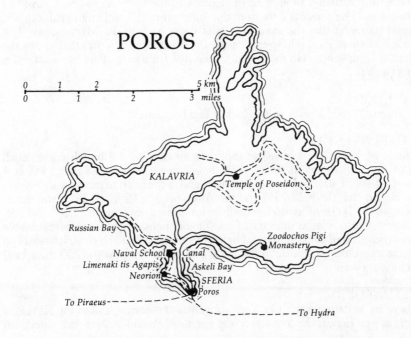

POROS

KALAVRIA

Temple of Poseidon

Russian Bay

Zoodochos Pigi
Monastery

Naval School   Canal
Limenaki tis Agapis   Askeli Bay
Neorion   SFERIA
Poros

To Piraeus

To Hydra

succeeded in taking Poros the next day. But rather than thank and love Skylla for her help, he was revolted by what she had done and left for Crete without her. Desperately, Skylla swam after him, but she was attacked by her father's spirit in the form of an eagle, and drowned in the bay which still bears her name.

WHAT TO SEE

Poros, the capital and port of the island, faces Galata on the mainland, almost like a reflection. Like Hydra, many of its inhabitants trace their history back to Albanian forebears who fled Turkish depredations in their homeland. These days it's given over almost completely to the needs of tourists, except for the **Naval Training School,** a kind of public school housed in the buildings of the first arsenal of the Greek State (which moved its facilities to Salamis in 1877). A water ski school offers lessons in the beautiful port.

A new crop of hotels has sprung up on Kalavria in recent years, some on the often polluted beach of **Neorion,** to the west, and **Askeliou** and **Kokkinos,** which are rather cleaner to the east. Although they are hot stuff for Poros, true beach lovers will probably turn up their noses at all of them. From Kokkinos a bus route continues to the 18th-century **monastery of Zoodochos Pigi** which has a lofty gilt iconostasis with impressive paintings but no longer any monks. A new road in front of the monastery climbs to the plateau of Palatia and the wonderfully situated though scant remains of the once renowned **temple of Poseidon**. The remains date from the 6th century BC, although evidence was found revealing that the sanctuary itself dates back to the Mycenaeans. The ancient city was also up here and Pausanias, who visited it, writes that he saw the tomb of Demosthenes in the precinct. The view from here of the Saronic Gulf is spectacular.

PANEYERIA

15 August; Good Friday at Zoodochos Pigi monastery.

WHERE TO STAY

Hotels on Poros are expensive; the most pleasant of the bunch is the small **Pension Anessis** (tel. 0298 22 111), though one of its spotless rooms will cost you 4000–6000 dr. Slightly less expensive and in the heart of the busy waterfront are **Saron** (tel. 0298 22 279) and the **Aktaeon** (tel. 0298 22 281), and out at Neorion the B class **Pavlou** has doubles for around 4500 dr. (tel. 0298 22 734). There are also a large number of guesthouse-pensions with more reasonable rates (many open summer only). Highly recommended is the establishment run by George Douras (tel. 0298 22 532). The room rates (900–1200 dr. a bed) include showers.

EATING OUT

There are restaurants all over town, as well as at Neorion, and in the Kokkinos area, as well as near the monastery and temple of Poseidon. Near the waterfront

362

try the **Epta Adelfia** with good food at the best prices in Poros (600-800 dr. for a meal). For fish try **Lagoudera,** directly on the waterfront, where a portion of red mullet is 1400 dr. Also on the waterfront is the **Africana**—but don't expect wildebeest or cous-cous—it's a Chinese restaurant with well prepared dishes for about 500 dr. There's food and music at **Zorba's** on Askeli Bay.

TOURIST POLICE
On the waterfront tel. (0298) 22 462.

SALAMIS (SALAMINA)

CONNECTIONS
Ferry frequently from Perama to Paloukia, or from a point south of N. Peramos to Faneromeni (less frequently). Small boats all through the day from Piraeus to Paloukia, Ambelaka, Selinia or Kamatero. Also ferries from Megara to Faneromeni.

Salamis faces Perama and the shipyards of Piraeus, the famous Strait of Salamis, where the great naval victory over the Persians took place, is only 3 km (2 miles) wide and as a result of its proximity to Piraeus, the island has lost much of its identity. Excepting the frescoes in the Faneromeni convent, neither nature's nor man's creations are particularly inspiring. The south-east side of Salamis is the prettiest part of the island, with its pine forests and beaches, although they are only accessible by private car and on foot. The villages of Salamis are connected by an efficient bus system. Moulki, also called Eantion, and Selinia are popular seaside villages among families from Athens and Piraeus.

HISTORY
When Telemon and his brother Peleus slew their brother Phocos (see Aegina), Telemon fled to Salamis, the island of serpents. It acquired this name from the destructive serpent killed by its first king, Cychreus, who, it seems, nurtured one of its offspring which went on to become an attendent of Demeter at Eleusis. It was Cychreus' daughter whom Telemon married in order to become king of the island; however, his son, Great Ajax, a hero of the Trojan War, was born of his second wife, a princess of Athens. When Megara and Athens quarrelled over the possession of Salamis in 620 BC, it is said that Solon visited the tomb of Cychreus to invoke his aid in the dispute, and when the Spartans, who judged the dispute, decided to give the island to Athens, they did so on the strength of the Salamian serpent at Eleusis and Telemon's marriage to an Athenian! During the Battle of Salamis, the Athenians claimed that Cychreus appeared among their ships in the form of a mighty serpent to spur them on to victory.

Solon made Salamis an Athenian colony in order to protect Piraeus. During this time Kamatero was the capital of Salamis, and on Mt Patsi there are remains

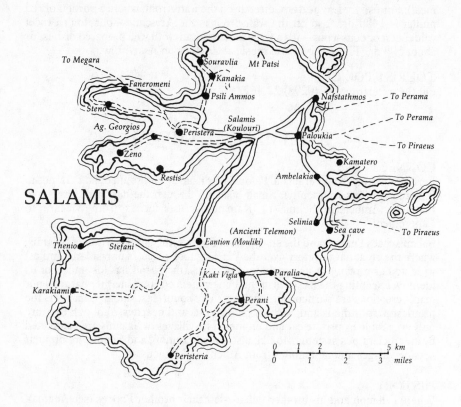

To Megara

Souravlia Mt Patsi

Kanakia

Faneromeni

Psili Ammos

Nafstathmos — To Perama

Steno

— To Perama

Salamis
(Koulouri)

Ag. Georgios

Peristera

Paloukia

— To Piraeus

Zeno

Kamatero

Restis

Ambelakia

SALAMIS

Selinia
(Ancient Telemon)

Sea cave

— To Piraeus

Thenio

Stefani

Eantion (Mouliki)

Karakiami

Kaki Vigla

Paralia

Perani

0   1   2   5 km
0   1   2   3 miles

Peristeria

of towers which were used to communicate with the mainland. The island was
also defended to the west against possible Megarian aggression.

In September of 480 BC a massive Persian fleet under Xerxes, the King of
Kings, moved into Faliron Bay with the intention of conquering Greece once and
for all. Greek commentators numbered the Persian fleet at 1200 (surely an
exaggeration), and the Athenians and their allies at only 378. The Greeks knew
they were coming and made preparations, sending the old men to Salamis and
the women and children of Athens to Troezen. Numerous accounts of the
subsequent battle have been passed down to us, most poetically *The Persians* of
Aeschylus, who participated in the battle.

364

The Greeks won as much by their wits as by the use of their superior, highly manoeuvrable ships. Themistokles, the Athenian commander-in-chief, had a rumour leaked to Xerxes that the Greeks, hearing of a Persian land invasion in the Peloponnese, had split up and were in disarray. Xerxes decided to take advantage of the supposed situation, and in the darkness, ordered his fleet to block up the Strait of Salamis at Megara and in the east. Certain of victory, Xerxes had his silver throne carried to the summit of Mt Egaleo in Perama, where he watched the battle unfold.

But Themistocles had been warned of the Persian plan. At dawn he moved his triremes up against the strongest Persian vessels, which began the attack. At first the Greeks fell back—then quickly spun their swift ships around and drove the bulkier craft of the Persians into the dangerous shallows that the defenders knew so well. Helpless, Xerxes' fleet foundered and his ships in the south fled back to Faliron Bay. The King of Kings watched his incredible defeat in anguish and was eventually forced to create a diversion in order to escape back to Persia with his 300 remaining ships. The army he left behind was defeated later at Plataea, thus ending the Persian threat.

The victory at Salamis gave the Athenians a moral boost which brought about their golden age. It also demonstrated the might of their navy, leading them to form the Delian league and control the fate of so many islands. As for Salamis, it gave birth to the tragedian Euripides and then fell back into obscurity.

WHAT TO SEE

Salamis, the rather uninteresting capital of the island, is nicknamed Koulouri ("croissant") for its shape. There are no hotels although one may find a room to rent. There is a small beach by the town and in its harbour there are Japanese pearl oysters—stowaways on the Japanese freighters that have stopped there.

Above Koulouri is **Mt Profitis Elias,** from which one can see the whole island. From Koulouri a bus leaves every hour for **Faneromeni,** the convent and ferry-boat landing stage. Situated in a large pine forest popular with picknickers and campers, Faneromeni dates from 1661, although the stones of its foundation are from an ancient temple. In the convent's church, Metamorphosis, are huge fascinating frescoes of the Last Judgement, containing more than 3000 figures. These were painted in the 18th century by Georgios of Argos and his pupils and they have been restored to their original state. The best time to find the convent open is in mid-morning or around 5 pm. Across the road, by the sea is a fine open-air taverna and there are many places to swim all along the shore. To the east is the beach **Psili Ammos** (village and taverna) which unfortunately smells of petrol much of the time.

South of Koulouri is the pleasant village of **Mouliki,** also with a beach. One can find accommodation there or sleep out under the pine trees nearby. From Mouliki a bus goes to **Kaki Vigla,** and a rough road from there leads to **Ag. Nikolaos,** a monastery with a 15th-century chapel. Between Ag. Nikolaos and Kaki Vigli one can find excellent, isolated camping sites and many of the beaches

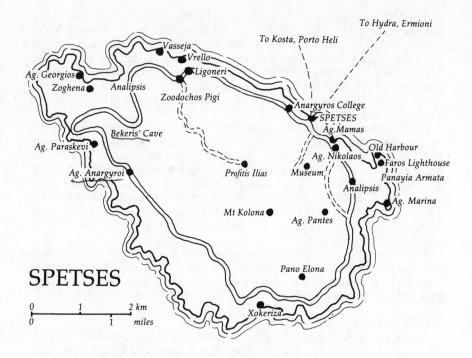

To Hydra, Ermioni

To Kosta, Porto Heli

Vasseja
Vrello
Ligoneri
Ag. Georgios
Zoghena
Analipsis
Zoodochos Pigi
Anargyros College
SPETSES
Ag.Mamas
Bekeris' Cave
Ag. Paraskevi
Old Harbour
Ag. Nikolaos
Faros Lighthouse
Ag. Anargyroi
Profitis Ilias
Museum
Panayia Armata
Analipsis
Ag. Marina
Mt Kolona
Ag. Pantes

SPETSES

0   1   2 km
0   1   miles

Pano Elona

Xokeriza

are sandy. On the east coast of Salamis **Paloukia,** the ferry-boat landing stage has a naval festival at the end of August. The boats are met by buses which leave for the villages.

South of Paloukia **Ambelakia** has become a ships' rubbish dump and is very smelly. Should members of the Ugly Art Movement search for an ideal setting for a colony in Greece, Ambelakia awaits them. **Selinia,** a few kilometres south of Ambelakia, is a collection of summerhouses, though the beach is nothing special.

PANEYERIA
The biggest celebration is the great pilgrimage to the convent of Faneromeni on 4 September: Salamis is also noted for its religious processions during Holy Week; also 5 June at Metamorphosis, and the last Sunday of Carnival at Koulouri.

WHERE TO STAY
Most of the hotels on Salamis are very simple and "ethnic". The best on the island is the **Gabriel Hotel** (tel. 0146 62 275) in Eantion, where a double is around 3500 dr. In Selinia there are several small pensions and hotels, like the **Vorsalakia** at 64 Themistocleous (tel. 0146 53 494), where rooms are 2500 dr.

366

for a double; in the same street and for about the same price is the **Akroyali** (tel. 0146 53 341).

EATING OUT
Because Salamis gets very few foreign tourists, its tavernas are very Greek and the food tasty and inexpensive.

SPETSES

CONNECTIONS
Hydrofoils from Piraeus and the other islands; also connections with Ermioni, Porto Heli and Nauplio (once or twice a day). Other routes continue to Monevassia, Leonidion, Neapolis and Kythera. Three times a day passenger boats call at many of the same ports in the Saronic Gulf; frequent excursion boats to Porto Heli, Kosta and other small beaches and ports on the mainland.

Spetses is a charming, pine-scented island, the furthest in the group from Athens, a factor that for a long time kept it quieter and more relaxed than its more accessible sisters. Sadly, that's no longer the case and it's not unusual to see helicopters flying in, depositing members of the jet set. The hotels, cafés and even the streets are packed, especially with the British who have practically colonised the island. Spetses is not new to tourism—its first hotel was built in 1914, and since the Second World War, families have come for its safe beaches and excellent climate—but there is a new, trendy atmosphere which seems foreign and strange. As it is, unless you're terribly lonely, you may want to avoid Spetses in July and August.

HISTORY
Archaeologists have found evidence at Ag. Marina proving that Spetses (ancient Pityoussa) has been inhabited since 2500 BC. The modern name of the island may come from the Italian word for spice "spezie", given it by the Venetians. Like the other islands in the group, it attracted many refugees from the mainland during the Turkish occupation. Shipbuilding began on the island in the early 17th century; by the 19th century Spetses was renowned for its seamanship and, like Hydra, thanks to the daring of its merchantmen in blockade running, it was wealthy. It joined the revolution early, raising the flag on 2 April 1821, and two days later won the first naval victory of the war, capturing three Ottoman ships near Milos. Many of the island's subsequent victories were won by the famous capitana of Spetses, Lascarina Bouboulina, the indomitable muse of patriotic Greek writers and artists and the 50-drachma note.

WHAT TO SEE
The capital and port of the island is officially Spetses, but it's more often known as **Dapias,** though this properly refers only to the sloping square you see as you

leave the quay. The Dapia, still bristling with cannon, was the centre of the town's fortifications—now the centre of its café society. The pebble mosaics commemorate the revolution that was planned here in 1821. There's also a bust of La Bouboulina, who lived in a house on the Dapia, and behind the bust stands the large yellow mansion of island philanthropist Sotiris Anargyro, founder (in 1927) of a boys' school on the English model, the **Anargyrios and Korgialenios School,** where John Fowles taught and wrote *The Magus* (another book by Fowles, *Islands* is a good read while staying on Spetses, or on any other island for that matter).

Spetses' **Museum** (open mornings) is housed in the late-18th-century mansion of Hadziyiannis Mexis. On the ground floor the furnishings of the original occupants have been preserved, and in the museum proper you can see a box holding Bouboulina's remains, the flag ("Freedom or Death") of the War of Independence, some ancient coins, paintings and costumes. Of the churches in town, the cathedral **Ag. Nikolaos** by the old harbour is the oldest; it once served as a monastery where Napoleon's brother Paul stayed. On its clock tower the Spetsiots raised their flag in 1821 (a bronze cast of it may be seen in the pretty square of pebble mosaics opposite). The **old harbour** also serves as the town beach and yacht marina. A story is told that when the Turks came to occupy the island, the inhabitants created mannikins, with bright red fezes and Turkish-appearing uniforms, and set them up along the shore. Seeing them from a distance, the Turkish commander thought that the island had already been taken and sailed on! The old harbour is a serene place, with large white houses.

Two other fine churches are up at **Kastelli,** the oldest quarter of town, the 17th-century **Koimistis Theotokou,** with frescoes, and **Ag. Triada,** with a marvellous, carved iconostasis.

368

The only cars allowed on Spetses are official vehicles, one taxi and the municipal bus. Horse-drawn fiacres provide the most romantic means of transport and will take you part of the way around the island; benzinas or boat taxis (for hire at the new harbour) can take up to four people to other places along the coast; scooters may be hired, although they hardly seem necessary—you can walk all the way around the island in a day on the partially asphalted road that encircles Spetses. The buses go as far as Ag. Anargyroi (from the town beach) and to Ligoneri (from the Possidonion Hotel).

The entire jagged coastline of Spetses is embellished with beaches whose access often depends on the reliability of your shoes. It's an easy walk, however, to the **Faros** (lighthouse) to visit the church **Panayia Armata,** built after the victory on 8 September 1822. Inside, a large painting by Koutzis commemorates the heroic scene. One may also walk to **Ag. Marina,** a beach and night centre on the island in the summer. Further south along the coast one sees the idyllic islet **Spetsopoula,** circled by a paved road; it is the private island of the wealthy shipowner Niarchos.

Ag. Anargyroi, with its shady beach and good taverna, is the most popular destination on the island. From there it is a short walk to **Bekiris' cave.** This Turkish name is derived from 1770, when Muslims from Albania came to take revenge on the Spetsiots for siding with Russia in the war. They burnt the houses, and the women and children of the island took refuge in the cave. It is said that one mother killed her whimpering baby to prevent discovery, but just as many other stories say that the refugees were eventually discovered and slain. One can enter from the sea or there is a low entrance by land (be sure to duck). The best time of day to go is in the afternoon, when the sun shines inside. One can see the beginning of a tunnel, said to have run to Profitis Ilias monastery until it was blocked up by an earthquake. There are also a few stalactites.

From **Vrello** in the north one can walk up to Profitis Ilias, although it is far more pleasant just to stay in Vrello, which is in that region of Spetses called **Paradise** for its beauty.

PANEYERIA

The most colourful festival of the year takes place on the nearest weekend to 8 September, when the Spetsiots commemorate their victory over the Turks in the Straits of Spetses, in 1822. The Ottomans, coming to attack the island, were held at bay throughout the day by the island's fleet, and in the end withdrew when confronted with a drifting fireboat. The battle is re-enacted in the harbour, with fireworks and folk dancing and other festivities. Also, first Friday after Easter, at Zoodochos Pigi; 26 July, Ag. Paraskevi at Zogheria; 1 July and 1 November, Anargyroi; 23 April, Ag. Georgios.

WHERE TO STAY

The classy place to stay on Septses is the grand old **Possidonion Hotel,** an Edwardian palace and one of the dominant features of the skyline, built by Sotiris

Anargyro in 1914 to revitalise the island economy. For its old time luxury, rates start at 7000 dr. for a double, 5500 dr. for a single (tel. 0298 72 208). Also popular is the class C **Hotel Myrtoon** (tel. 0298 72 555) with a roof garden and bar. A double here goes for around 3800 dr. in season; for both of the above reserve well in advance. There are several pensions on Botassi Street (where you can also find the tourist police). A little way out of town, at Ag. Mamas, there are a few low-key hotels and pensions, such as the D class **Klimis,** with doubles hovering around 2800 dr. As you disembark at the port there are two travel bureaus that seem to control the rooms on the island especially Takis Travel Office. Not a few people get fed up and sleep on the beach.

EATING OUT
The best seafood on Spetses is at **Trehandiri** near Ag. Nikolaos; prices are fairly high (expect to pay at least 1500 dr.) but the food is worth it and you have a fine view over the harbour. For the island's speciality, Psari Spetsiotiko (sea bream in spicey sauce), try the less expensive **Mandelena's** on the waterfront in the new harbour. For something in the 600–800 dr. range try the excellent dishes at **Stelios,** also in the new port.

TOURIST POLICE
Botassi St, tel. (0298) 73 100.

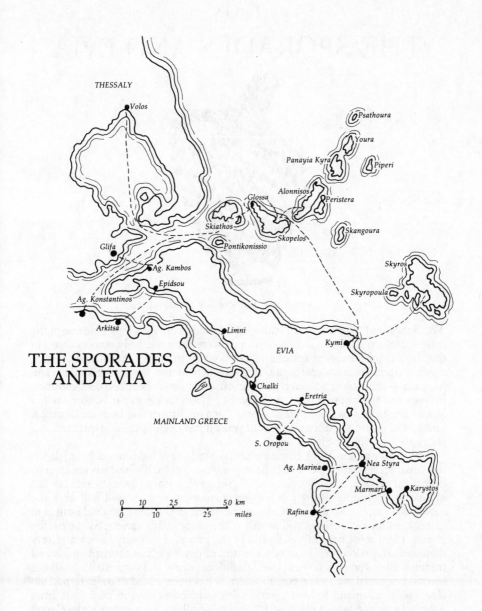

THESSALY

Volos

Psathoura

Youra

Panayia Kyra

Piperi

Glossa

Alonnisos

Peristera

Skiathos

Pontikonissio

Skopelos

Skangoura

Glifa

Ag. Kambos

Epidsou

Skyros

Ag. Konstantinos

Skyropoula

Arkitsa

Limni

Kymi

EVIA

THE SPORADES
AND EVIA

Chalki

Eretria

MAINLAND GREECE

S. Oropou

Ag. Marina

Nea Styra

Marmari

Karystos

Rafina

0   10   25   50 km
0   10   25   miles

Part IX

THE SPORADES AND EVIA

A Minoan Vase with Leaf Motif

The Sporades ("sporadic" or "scattered") islands were for a long time one of the least visited corners of Greece—not only were they relatively inaccessible but they lacked the historical associations evoked by so many other islands. Then, slowly, Greek vacationers began to make two of the islands—Skiathos and Skopelos—their own, attracted by their exquisite sandy beaches, cool summer, breezes and thick pine forests. A vanguard of Germans began to restore the old homes on Alonnisos for summer villas. Then an airport was built on Skiathos, linking the island to Athens; in recent years it has been opened to international charters—and the rest is history.

Perhaps it was inevitable. Some immortal hand or eye has framed these islands to fit nearly everyone's idea of a holiday paradise. Yet each island has retained its individual character, although that of Skiathos, with its lovely beaches, has increasingly become blurred as European tourism cast its dull pall over the island. Skyros, the hardest to get to, remains one of the more original islands in Greece, its tourist facilities still mainly of the home-made variety; Skopelos, the greenest and most naturally endowed of the group, is still very Greek and very dignified; and Alonnisos is an odd mixture of cosmopolitan tourism and island tradition (the women still wear their traditional dress and card wool). Evia, the second largest island in Greece, historically has been a land of quiet farms, too close to the mainland to have a personality of its own (you can take a bus from Athens to its capital Chalkida in 1¼ hours). Still, its long, scarcely developed coastline is beginning to attract both Greek and foreign visitors escaping the crowds elsewhere.

The Sporades were first settled by Thracians in misty prehistoric times. In the 16th century BC the Cretans colonised the islands, introducing the cultivation of olives and grapes. When the Minoan civilisation fell, Mycenaeans from Thessaly, known as the Dolopians (of the same race as the Acheans), settled the Sporades, using them as bases for their enterprises at sea, for they were great sailors. Much of the rich mythology of the islands had its historical roots during this period: Achilles himself was raised on Skyros.

The Chalkidians in the 8th century BC captured the Sporades as stepping stones to further their ambitions in Macedonia. These new invaders continued the sea traditions of the Dolopians, inciting hostility from Athens. In the 5th century, Athens sent General Kimon to crush the rival fleets of the Sporades. The Athenians then colonised the islands, and their culture dominated and was accepted by the inhabitants. Thus, of all the islands of Greece, the Sporades had the closest ties and friendship with the Athenians, who managed to present themselves as liberators rather than conquerors. The government of the islands was run on the model of Athenian democracy, and Athena became a prominent goddess in the local pantheon.

When the Spartans defeated Athens in the Peloponnesian War, the Sporades were part of their spoils, although their reign on the islands was short. A greater threat to Athenian influence came in the person of Philip II of Macedon. His dispute with Athens over the possession of the islands attracted the attention of the entire Greek world, as suspicions began to surface—later proved correct—that the Macedonian king intended to unite all of Greece against Persia. Philip eventually took the islands and Athens itself, although the conquest of Persia was left to his son Alexander.

Even during the Roman occupation (beginning in the 2nd century BC), the Sporades retained their connections with Athens, which still, even after its own fall to General Sulla in 88 BC, nominally held sway over some of the Sporades. Christianity, with a good helping of pagan rites, spread over the islands in the 2nd and 3rd centuries. The Byzantines sent many of their exiles there, who formed the local aristocracy. In 1207 the Venetian Gizi family made their claim on the Sporades. Philip, the most notorious of the dynasty, usurped authority from a senior relative and ruled the area as a pirate king, claiming that no one could stop him. His pride, however, was forced into submission when Likarios, the admiral of Emperor Michael Palaeologos, took him in chains to Constantinople, where he only gained his liberty by handing the islands over to the restored Byzantine Empire. Afterwards possession of the islands changed hands a few more times between Greeks and Franks, until Constantinople fell to Mohammed the Conqueror in 1453. The islanders quickly invited the Venetians to reoccupy their lands, which the Venetians willingly did, although they, too, were forced out when their agreements with the Ottoman Empire crumbled before the violent attacks of the terror of the Aegean, Barbarossa.

373

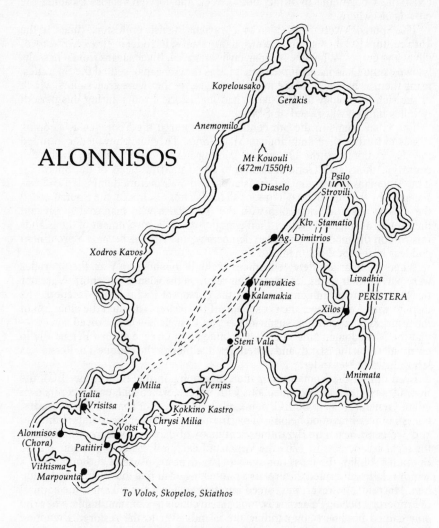

ALONNISOS

Kopelousako

Gerakis

Anemomilo

Mt Kououli
(472m/1550ft)

Diaselo

Psilo
Strovili

Klv. Stamatio

Ag. Dimitrios

Xodros Kavos

Vamvakies
Kalamakia

Livadhia
PERISTERA

Xilos

Steni Vala

Mnimata

Milia

Venjas

Yialia
Vrisitsa

Kokkino Kastro
Chrysi Milia

Alonnisos
(Chora)

Votsi

Patitiri

Vithisma
Marpounta

To Volos, Skopelos, Skiathos

| 0 | 2 | 5 | 10 km |
| 0 | 2 | 5 | miles |

After taking the Sporades, however, the Turks manifested little interest in them, sending only a cadi to assure the payment of taxes; the islands were so subject to raids that a permanent Turkish population never settled there. In the 1821 revolution, Thessalian insurgents found refuge on the islands, which also helped the cause financially. In 1830 the Treaty of London included them in the original kingdom of Greece.

GETTING TO THE SPORADES

If you're departing from Athens, Alkyon Tours, at 98 Academias (tel. (01) 362 2093) has long specialised in travel to the islands, and has all the latest bus and boat timetables. Skyros can only be reached from or via Kymi, in Evia, from where there are weekly sailings (at least) to the other Sporades. The main ferry ports to Skiathos, Skopelos and Alonnisos are Volos in Thessaly and Ag. Konstantinos. Hydrofoils also ply these routes daily in summer from Volos and Ag. Konstantinos to these islands. The only other connection is the occasional boat from Limnos to Skopelos.

You can safely camp on the islands (in Skiathos only at the official camp site) except for Alonnisos. The only luxury facilities are on Skiathos; pensions predominate on Skopelos, while on Skyros most available accommodation is in private rooms.

ALONNISOS

CONNECTIONS

At least once a day with Volos, Skopelos and Skiathos; several times a week with Ag. Konstantinos; with Kymi at least once a week.

Generally the least known of the four main islands, Alonnisos is the queen of its own little archipelago of nine islands. It once produced a large crop of grapefruit, but the trees on the island all perished from disease; a similar fate has recently afflicted many of the grapevines in the area. More significant for the island's current condition was the earthquake of 1965, which devastated the principal town, Chora. The government transferred all the people to a new village by the sea, and Chora, magnificently situated high up above the sea, was abandoned— until some Germans, enchanted by the serenity and the view, began to buy and repair the old homes, agreeing together to do without such conveniences as running water and electricity. There's one stretch of paved road, and others are planned, but for the time being nine-tenths of Alonnisos is accessible only on foot; this is fine walking country, the heights inhabited only by the rare Eleanora's falcon.

HISTORY

The history of Alonnisos is complicated by the fact that the modern Alonnisos is not ancient Halonnesos, but actually bore the name Ikos. The confusion resulted from an early Greek government's over-enthusiasm for restoring the ancient place names. In this case, the mistake was rather fortunate, "Alonnisos" being rather more musical to the ear than Ikos. As for ancient Halonnesos, its location is uncertain, some think it may have been tiny Psathoura, northernmost of the islets that surround Alonnisos, where the extensive ruins of an ancient city lie submerged off shore. Another possibility is Kyra Panayia, a fertile island with two fine harbours.

Inhabited from Neolithic times, Ikos, as it was known then, was part of the Cretan colony of Prince Stapylos, who began the cultivation of the vine which was later to make Ikos famous. In the 14th century BC the Mycenaeans took over the affairs of the island. The most famous of the Ikian settlers was Peleus, the father of Achilleus, who died on the island. In Classical times two cities thrived on Ikos, exporting wine. The Athenians established a naval base there in the 4th century, and later, in Roman times, General Antonius gave Ikos to Athens (42 BC).

During the Middle Ages Ikos, gradually becoming known as Achilliodromia and later Liadromia or simply Dromos (road), was subjected to Skopelos. Barbarossa wreaked havoc on the island in 1538 when it was added to the Ottoman Empire.

As for ancient Halonnesos (wherever it may be), in Classical times it belonged to Athens, although in the 4th century BC the pirate Sostratos governed it de facto. Philip of Macedon took it from him, quoting the famous speech of Demosthenes "Concerning Alonnisos", which initiated the troubles between Athens and Macedonia. Skopelos took the island in 341 BC when Philip offered to return it to Athens; Philip, however, crushed these opportunists and the island lost all its importance, until even its identity faded from human memory.

WHAT TO SEE
The island's port, **Patitiri,** the relief village built by the government after 1965, and the fishing hamlet of **Votsi** have all merged together in recent years. Most of the buildings are new, but perhaps to make up for their dull design many have luxuriant gardens. The limpid waters off Alonnisos provide a good income for local fishermen, and the whole port area is lined with almost identical, shady tavernas. There's a small beach at Patitiri, and another at Votsi, but most people opt for one of the many caique excursions to the island's coves. The one really sandy beach is at Vrisitsa, though there are many others on nearby Peristera. Mopeds can be hired (even cars go as far as Kalamakia these days) if you feel the need to get somewhere quickly.

South of Patitiri are two beaches, **Vithisma** and **Marpounta.** The remains of a round temple of Asklepios, the god of healing, can be seen in the sea at the latter. There was a 5th-century BC settlement (almost certainly ancient Ikos) at the beach **Kokkino Kastro,** but it too sank into the sea; you can make out some of its walls from shore. It's a two-hour walk from Patitiri, or one may go by boat. A shorter walk or even shorter drive should be made to the old capital of the island, **Chora,** situated above Patitiri. Walkers can choose between two delicious routes:

the mule path is hedged with raspberry bushes, while the road is lined with pear and nut trees. The walls of the town were built by the Byzantines and repaired by the Venetians, and ghosts are said to dance around the 17th-century church **Christos**. As well as the summertime Germans, several local families have returned to Chora, and you can see the old women, in their traditional pale blue and white dresses and scarves, their long braids hanging about their shoulders. The sunsets from the walls are quite lovely. The two oldest churches on Alonnisos are in Chora: **Ag. Athanasios** and **Ag. Georgios**. From Chora it's a 20-minute walk down to Vrisitsa beach.

Steni Vala and **Kalamakia**, both on the east coast, have small pensions, beaches and tavernas. They are well sheltered in the embrace of nearby Peristera islet, and offer the best fishing and water sports on the island; frequent boat excursions connect them with Patitiri. The delicious astakos is plentiful off the remote northern coast, by **Kopelousako** beach and the old shepherd's village of Gerakis. At **Ag. Dimitrios** are the ruins of a Byzantine fountain and another ancient settlement in the sea; fossils of prehistoric beasts were found at Megliamos. The beach is also lovely and usually deserted.

PANEYERIA
1 July, Ag. Anargaroi; 26 July, Ag. Paraskevi; 15 August, Panayias; 17 July, Ag. Marina; 40 days after Easter, Analypsos.

Peristera (Dove) islet, following the east coast of Alonnisos, was part of the island until separated by a natural upheaval. Also known as Xiro, the island is endowed with many sandy beaches. There are three tiny shepherds' hamlets, Mnimata, Livadhia and Xilos, the last having the ruins of a castle nearby. Every ten days a caique goes to **Psathoura,** where one of the most powerful lighthouses in Greece guides passing ships. It is another candidate for the island of the Sirens as well as of ancient Halonnesos. The submerged city may be seen in the sea by the lighthouse, as well as a sunken volcano.

Lovely, well wooded **Panayia Kyra** (Pelagos) is two or three hours by caique from Alonnisos. Now uninhabited (except for wild goats) the island once supported two monasteries, the original one founded by monks from Mt Athos in the Byzantine period, and the other on the east coast, at a later date; although they are now empty the island is still owned by Mt Athos. At the one port, Ag. Petros, you can see the remains of a 12th-century Byzantine ship in the waters; when it was discovered its hold was filled with ceramics. Panayia Kyra has some pleasant beaches and a pretty cave (believed to have been the home of the Cyclops).

There is another monastery on **Skangoura**, connected with that on Mt Athos, which offers excellent fishing in its many sea coves and caves. **Pappou** swarms with hares, while on **Youra** (ancient Geronta) a special breed of goat skips about the rocks. A large empty house is said to have belonged to King Konstantine, should he ever desire to come to Youra to visit the goats! A few Classical and Roman remains have been discovered there; the most spectacular is another

377

Cyclops cave with stalactites (bring a light). Another islet, **Piperi,** is a wild life sanctuary, the home of numerous monk seals.

WHERE TO STAY
Most of the island's accommodation is in Patitiri and Votsi, though the spiffier hotels and pensions tend to be booked solid by packagers. To make up for it, there are plenty of rooms to rent in private houses and generally plenty of people to offer them to you when you get off the boat. The **Marpounta Bungalows,** if you can get a room, are the most comfortable lodgings on Alonnisos, near the sea at Votsi; tel. 0424 65 219, rates are fairly high—at least 8500 dr. for a twin bungalow. In Alonnisos town the **Alkyon** (if not fully booked) is a pleasant pension with doubles averaging 6000 dr. (tel. 0424 65 450). Less expensive is the simple pension **Ioulieta** in Patitiri, where doubles are around 3000 dr. For a room, take pot luck or go to Ikos Travel near the wharf, which has a listing of rooms. There are also a few rooms available in Chora (though harder to find). There's also an official campsite, **Ikoros Camping** (tel. 0424 65 258) at Steni Vala.

EATING OUT
If you wanted to splurge and have a feast of Mediterranean lobster (*astakos*), Alonnisos is the place for it; many of the seaside restaurants in Patitiri serve it as well as other marine delectables. For good food and a magnificent view, eat at the **Paraport Taverna** up in Chora, where a meal costs about 1200 dr. There are tavernas at all the most popular beaches.

SKIATHOS

CONNECTIONS
By air: At least four flights a day from Athens, three a week from Thessaloniki, and numerous charters from European cities. By sea: Daily from Volos, Ag. Konstantinos, Skopelos and Alonnisos. Hydrofoils daily in summer from Volos and Ag. Konstantinos with connections to Skopelos and Alonnisos. Daily excursions boat to Skopelos and Alonnisos.

Racy Skiathos is not for the sun-shy teetotaller. It's beach life by day and bar life by night, with few places of historical interest to distract the scholar. Not so long ago a peasant island community, Skiathos has been catapulted faster than most into the frantic world of tourism, with all the pros and cons that this inevitably entails. It is now one of the most popular destinations in Greece, and with good cause. It is a stunningly beautiful island; its magnificent beaches (by most counts there are 62) provide some of the best swimming in Greece, and its lush foliage is a pleasure to the eye. Add to this a host of lively bars and restaurants and you have the ingredients for a potent, heady cocktail.

HISTORY

While the great Persian fleet of King Xerxes was on its way to its eventual defeat at Salamis in 480 BC, it encountered a fierce storm in the waters off Skiathos, which wrecked so many of Xerxes' ships that he put in at Skiathos to make repairs, in the bay that still bears his name. According to tradition, during his stay Xerxes built the world's first lighthouse on the islet of Kyrminx, now a reef called Lepheteris, which is still a menace to sailors sailing between Skiathos and the mainland. Xerxes took such an extraordinary measure in order to slip past the Athenian guardships that patrolled the area. A few vestiges of the lighthouse still exist.

The rest of Skiathos' history follows that of the other Sporades. the Gizis took the island and built the fort on Bourtzi islet by the present-day town, which was settled in 1790 by refugees from Limni on Evia. The Skiathiot navy assisted the Russians in the campaign at Cesme, when they defeated the Turkish fleet. In 1805 the island began to revolt against the Ottomans, and sent its ships to aid the Greek cause so enthusiastically that Skiathos itself was left unprotected and prey to marauders. It was one of the first places to be touched by the Orthodox reformist movement, Kollivades, emanating from Mt Athos (although the name Skiathos means "shadow of Athos" it was derived from a preHellenic source). A

local writer, Alexandros Papadiamantis (1851–1911) immortalised Skiathos by setting the scenes of his novels there, although the books have yet to be translated into English.

WHAT TO SEE

The capital, **Skiathos,** is the island's only town and is a spread of traditional white-washed houses, many of them sporting rich bougainvillaea between the freshly washed sheets hanging out to dry. Like most Greek island towns, a walk through the back streets is worthwhile to absorb the feeling of the place. Don't expect to encounter many donkeys, though. You're more likely to find yourself dodging high speed trial bikes. The town has two harbours, separated by the pretty **Bourtzi** promontory, where a medieval fortress now serves as a primary school. For a sweeping panorama of Skiathos town and the neighbouring island of Skopelos, take the steps at the end of the old harbour past the cafés and souvenir shops which line the bustling waterfront. Late afternoon sees the place really come to life and cocktail hour seems to last forever as you sit and people watch. If this flagrant hedonism pricks the conscience, you can get your shot of culture by locating the house of Skiathos' illustrious poet, **Alexander Papadiamantis,** situated just off the main street, which bears his name.

The boats bobbing up and down in front of the cafés in the old harbour will take you to most beaches and you'll hear the owners calling out their destinations. Some offer round the island trips but be warned that on the north side there is a fairly uninteresting stretch and the water on that side can be rough—many a day tripper comes back green. The excursion to **Meteora** on the mainland to see the monastries in the sky is fascinating but a long haul. If you want to get about the island under your own steam, there are a number of places to rent cars and scooters. Be careful on the roads—traffic is fast moving and if on a bike keep an eye out for gritty curves and the demon taxi drivers.

Buses to other parts of the islands run hourly in season from the new harbour (in summer your feet may not touch the floor throughout the journey, but you could make some new friends). Taxis also operate from here and are in great demand, so don't be shy to share.

The island's main road runs from town along the southern flank of the island ending up at the legendary **Koukounaries,** whose sweeping crescent shaped bay fringed by pine trees is so well known in Greece. The most convenient beach to town is **Megali Ammos,** although it's generally crowded. Moving westward, **Ahladies** beach, dominated by the large Esperides hotel (with tennis court open to the public) is also densely populated for most of the summer season. Beyond that, **Kanapitsa** beach, situated on the **Kalamaki** peninsula, is 5 km from the town, and is a popular cove for swimming and watersports, and there's a restaurant by the water. Nearby **Vromolimnos,** hard to pronounce and even harder to find, is one of the finest places to swim on the island, and when the rest of Skiathos is bulging at the seams, you'll always find room to play frisbee on **Platanias.** Even the seedy snack bar doesn't manage to spoil its charm. Convenient by bus or boat is **Troulos,** its attractive taverna waiting to welcome the round-the-island trippers, so be sure to get there well before or after them as the place becomes full and extremely busy at lunchtime. On the other side of Koukounaries lies **Krassa,** nowadays called **Banana** beach, perhaps because it's where you can peel off everthing. Definitely not for the modest, it's always cheek by cheek in the high season. To get there, head up the hill with the sea on your left when you get off the bus at Koukounaries. Next door is the lovely **Ag. Eleni,** the last beach accessible by road, a somewhat quieter spot with a view across to the Pelion peninsula on the mainland.

On the north coast, **Mandraki,** reached by footpath from the lagoon behind Koukounaries, has lovely sand (and a snack bar). More isolated is sandy **Aselinos** an hour's walk from the 17th-century monastery **Panayia Kounistra,** itself accessible by hired car or bicycle. The icon for which the church is named was found dangling in a tree. The beach at **Kastro** is equally isolated and **Lalaria** is a marvel of silvery pebbles, accessible only by boat, as are the nearby sea grottoes—**Skotini** ("the dark cave"—bring a light), **Galazia,** "the blue", and **Chalkini,** "the copper".

One of the two most interesting walks across Skiathos is to **Kastro,** the medieval settlement and place of refuge during times of danger. The walk takes a little over two hours and the path is well marked from Ag. Konstantinos near Skiathos town. The ruins within the crumbling walls include Byzantine churches and a Turkish hammam; the view from the top is quite lovely. (Boats sometimes make the excursion.) A detour on the path could be made to the monastery **Panayia Kechis,** dating from the 15th century and the oldest on the island. Inside are some fine 17th-century icons. Another walk from town (about an hour) begins just before the turning to the airport road and leads to the only occupied monastery left on the island, **Evangelistria** (8 am–12 noon and 5–7 pm proper attire required). The monastery was founded in 1797 by monks from Mt Athos during the Kollivades movement. On its tall blue and white flagpole, it is said, the Skiathiots raised the Greek flag in 1827—the first to do so (though Spetses, for one, would dispute this). There is a small museum there. There are hourly excursion boats in the summer to **Tsougrias Islet,** facing Skiathos town, and it's well worth the half hour boat ride from the harbour. In the sixties the Beatles wanted to buy it. It's an ideal place to escape the droves of summer visitors, with its fine sand and excellent swimming. The simple snack bar usually provides freshly caught marides (white bait), which you can enjoy at a table under the trees, but you may have to share your food with the resident wasp population. Tsougrias has two other beaches, accessible on foot, where you really can play Robinson Crusoe for the day. If you can't summon the energy to join the queues for bus, boat or taxi, dive off the rocks at the **Bourtzi,** where a drink at the little bar by the water's edge will make you feel part of your own Martini ad.

PANEYERIA
15 August, at Evangelismos; 27 August, Ag. Fanourios; 26 July, Ag. Paraskevi; 27 July, Ag. Panteleimonos.

WHERE TO STAY
Skiathos has accommodation to suit everyone's taste and pocket, but remember that in high season finding a bed can be a trial, especially in the torrid month of August, when it seems the island will sink beneath the weight of its occupants. If you want to escape the madding crowd you'll find peace out at the **Skiathos Palace Hotel,** which enjoys dubious luxury class status, but it does have a superb view of Koukounaries bay. Doubles here are a pricey 18 000 dr. in high season (tel. 0427 22 242). At **Nostos,** 5 km from town, the **Nostos Hotel** commands a majestic position and at night glitters like a real palace; an Olympic size pool is handy for those who can't face the long trek down to the sea, and its rustically decorated interior makes a refreshing change. Don't expect snappy service though. Double rooms are 14 000 dr. (tel. 0427 22 420). Closer to town is the B class **Esperides** at Ahladies beach. As large hotels go it's one of the best and thus popular with the major tour operators; singles go for 10 000 dr. and doubles 14 000 dr. (tel. 0427 22 245). The **Lalaria** hotel on the main road at Megali Ammos is a comfortable walk from town and is a modestly sized, sleepy establishment. Doubles are 7000 dr. (tel. 0427 22 900). In town itself there are many offerings, most notably the **Meltemi,** on the new harbour front, but generally booked solid in summer months. However, have a drink at their pleasant outdoor bar and watch the antics of the flotilla yachties as they moor and unmoor with zealous gung-ho. Rates here are 7000 dr. for a double (tel. 0427 22 493). A few steps beyond is the colourful **San Remo Hotel,** whose terraced rooms give you dress circle seats to observe the harbour traffic and wave at the greenhorn passengers on the incoming charter jets. Doubles are 8000 dr. (tel. 0427 22 078). Follow the harbour front around to find the **Alkyon,** a standard B class hotel with its cooling marble lobby offset by comfortable rooms overlooking the hotel's pleasant gardens. Singles start at 3500 dr., doubles 6000 dr. and is very good value for money (tel. 0427 22 981). Another good bet is the centrally placed **Australia Hotel,** just off Papadiamantis St, behind the post office. It's simple and cheap (3000 dr. for a double, tel. 0427 22 488).

Rooms for rent can be found all over the town, but you'll have to search them out; it's not common practice in Skiathos to meet incoming boats or planes to hawk cheap rooms. Wander up the hilly streets and ask the ladys sitting on their doorsteps. Prices are rising at a brisk pace, so expect to pay up to 2800 dr. for a double. Out at Megali Ammos there are a number of charming pensions on the beach. The rooms are basic but the thriving flora on the terraces lend an exotic atmosphere to the place. If you come unstuck in your quest for a room, stroll into any of the tourist offices on the waterfront.

EATING OUT

Eating out in Skiathos is a hit and miss affair. Some of the most beautifully located tavernas serve mediocre food, as in the cases of the **Bourtzi** and the hard to find but equally spectacular **Tarsanas**. Generally speaking, avoid the tavernas on the steps at the western end of the old harbour, as they tend to be expensive, but look out for the **psistaria** lodged between them where they serve good spit-roasted chicken and *souvlaki* at low prices, and you have the same view as those next door. By common consent the best bargain in town is **Stavros** (in Evangelistrias St, 50 metres from the post office). Dimitrios, one of the owners, is the calmest waiter in Greece. Especially good for oven ready food, steak and chops at 800 dr. for a full meal. **Ilias** taverna (rather more difficult to find, it's two blocks past Stavros on the left) is traditionally everyone's favourite, but going a little up market lately. South African and British island residents, jockeying for position on the local social scale, like to be recognised by the owner. Try the shrimp *youvetsi*, rabbit *stifado* and all sorts of other enticing dishes on display. (Closed lunchtime and all day Sunday.) Prices for a full dinner range from 1500 dr. to 2000 dr. At **Limenaki,** on the waterfront past the new harbour, you can enjoy such luxuries as avocado, shrimps and pepper steak, as near to the real thing as you'll find in Greece without paying through the nose for it. While sampling some of the standard but well prepared dishes at **Dionyssos,** just off the main street, the waiters will treat you to a floor show of Greek dancing—dinner with wine around 1000 dr. The **Akti,** at the far end of the new harbour, has a special licence to stay open most of the night, so join the other insomniacs and low life for an early morning pizza of spaghetti from the oven; it's cheap. At least once head out of town to **Stathis,** another taverna where the ex-pats hang out in force. Some unusual menu items include goulash, chicken livers in cream, a so-so curry and a wide assortment of salads. The staff can be abrupt so stay calm. Dinner here runs to 2000 dr.

Having eaten, you'll be spoilt for choice when it comes to bars as there are many, but they're not cheap. An oasis of tranquillity in the Skiathos summer madhouse is the **Adagio** Bar, opposite Stavros taverna in Evangelistrias St. Pleasant decor and classical music soothe the eye and ear, and Sophia, the multi-lingual owner, will give you a genuinely warm and friendly welcome. A favourite place for an after dinner drink and the only night bar to serve Irish coffee. The **Kentavros,** in Papadiamantis Square off the main street, is always popular for its lively but not deafening music. The **Admiral Benbow Inn** (Polytechniou St) provides a corner of old England and is a charming little bar. On the same street the **Borzoi,** for years the place to go, is still worth a try after midnight if you can afford the drinks. Two popular bars catering for those with a love of loud, loud music and the possibility of a date with a local beau are the **Banana** bar and **Stones,** where you'll need your Norwegian phrase book to get you through the evening. The **Scorpio** disco in the centre of town livens up around 2.30 am, when some of the other bar owners close down and congregate there to dance to the great music. Half the fun is guessing what is really coming

The Harbour and Capital of Skiathos, The Sporades

out of those bottles. On a warm summer evening the picturesque waterfront bars come into their own, the best being **Jimmy's,** the **Porto Fino** and the **Oasis,** where the chic hang out. Your first, and last watering hole may well be the **airport** bar, whose owner spent many years in Switzerland learning and skilfully combining German, French, Italian and English. Probably one of the few people alive who can get all four languages into one sentence.

TOURIST POLICE
See regular police, tel. (0427) 21 111.

SKOPELOS

CONNECTIONS
Ferries daily from Volos, and most days from Ag. Konstantinos; once or three times a week from Kymi. Daily to Skiathos, less frequently to Alonnisos. Once or twice a week to Limnos. Note that the ferries usually call at both Skopelos town and Loutraki, the port of Glossa.

Where Skiathos has given its all to tourism, Skopelos remains far more reserved; indeed a good many of its tourist facilities are actually operated by outsiders who leave as soon as the tourists and their money stop arriving. Yet it is an exceptionally beautiful island, more dramatic than Skiathos, its beaches as lovely (and safe for children), its entire 100 km^2 (40 sq. miles) shaded by pine forests. The two main towns, Skopelos and Glossa, are, along with Skyros town, among the finest in the Sporades. There's an accepted if unofficial campsite, many small pensions and a modest amount of night life. Skopelos has learned to take the summer invasion in its stride, if not perhaps with any great enthusiasm. Traditionally, at least half of the young men on the island spend most of their lives working abroad or at sea; the easy money to be had catering to the needs of tourists simply does not appeal to them.

HISTORY
Known in antiquity as Perparethos, Skopelos formed part of the Cretan colony ruled by Staphylos (some say the son of Theseus and Ariadne). In 1927 a wealthy Minoan tomb was excavated in the bay that has always borne Staphylos' name, so

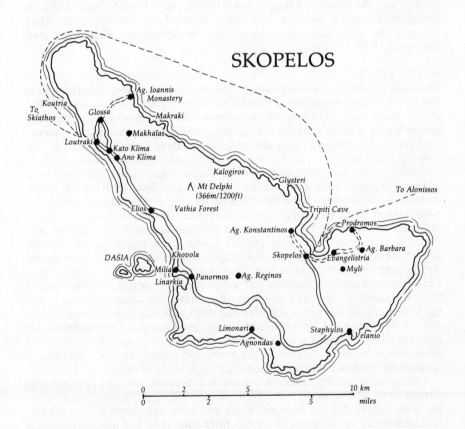

SKOPELOS

there was no doubt in the archaeologists' minds as to whose grave they had uncovered. Tradition–history–mythology recounts that King Pelias, usurper of the Iolkan kingdom in Thessaly, settled Skopelos in the 13th century BC; Pelias later ordered his rival Jason to undertake the quest for the Golden Fleece. Under Athens, Skopelos retained a certain amount of autonomy and minted its own coins. Dionysos and Demeter were the most popular gods on the island. During Roman times it was given its present name, which means "cliff". The first bishop of Skopelos in the 4th century, Reginos, became the island's patron saint. When Philip Gizi played pirate he used Skopelos as his headquarters, his capture meant a decline in local excitement, enabling the inhabitants to return to a peaceful way of life until Barbarossa decimated the community.

The island gradually regained its population, including many refugees from the Turks. Skopeliot sailors fought with the Russians at Cesme, and the Russian admiral gave the islanders a larger church bell in thanks for their help. A British consul on Skopelos, Stephan Dapondes, founded an academy there. After assisting the Thessalian mountaineers in the Revolution, Skopelos joined Greece in 1830.

WHAT TO SEE

Skopelos or Chora, is an exceptionally pleasant town, its collage of old blue slate and new red-tile roofs arranged around the steep amphitheatre overlooking the port, a memorable sight beneath the ruins of the Venetian kastro. The older houses have a definite Venetian touch, such as the Fragomacholas house; newer ones are built in a sturdy Thessalian style, while others seem Macedonian. The newer houses have been harmonised by incorporating older features such as balconies in their structure, and the Greek national instinct for planting a seed wherever it might have half a chance to grow manifests itself in the house gardens. Above the town is the **Venetian castle** of Gizi, which was so strong that Skopelos was left untouched during the War of Independence. Tradition claims that there are 123 churches in the town, of all shapes and sizes. One, **Zoodochos Pigi,** claims an icon by St Luke, another, **Christo,** has an exceptional interior. Within the Kastro (once the site of a temple of Athens) stands the 9th-century **Ag. Athanasios,** with frescoes from the 16th century. At a place called **Ampeliki** the ruins of an Asklepieion lie half-submerged in the sea. At the other end of the town stands the fortified monastery **Episkopi.** The ancient church is believed to mark the site where the island's patron saint Reginus was martyred in 362. In the vicinity of Chora you can also visit the **Fournou Damaskinon,** the giant oven where Skopelos' famous prunes are dried in August. There is a long sandy beach immediately next to the town and a shady row of sweet shops specialising in loukoumades (hot honey pastries) in the evening.

Among the excursions within easy distance of Skopelos town is a caique trip to **Tripiti cave,** whence come many of the island's lobsters. Opposite the town on the hills overlooking the harbour, there are three monasteries. The closest, **Evangelistria,** was founded by monks from Mt Athos, but today serves as a convent. Generally open mornings and late afternoons, it offers one of the best views of Skopelos town, and woven goods for sale. Further afield the monastery **Metamorphosis** was recently abandoned, but still hosts one of the island's biggest paneyeria; over the ridge, looking towards Alonnisos, is, **Prodromos,** again now inhabited by nuns (same hours as Evangelistria). One path connects them all; a road for vehicles ascends to Metamorphosis. On the other side of the bay near the pleasant shingle beach **Ag. Konstantinos** are the ruins of a Hellenistic water tower; if this beach is overcrowded, try **Glysteri,** a 3-km (2-mile) walk to the north.

Buses run regularly from Skopelos to Glossa along the island's one main road. Along the route is **Staphylos beach** where the Minoan tomb was discovered, now the island's main family beach; **Velanio beach,** on the other side of a small headland is an unofficial nudist beach. **Agnondas,** the next stop, serves as a kind of emergency port when the sea is rough and landing at Skopelos town is impossible; a special bus then relays passengers to the capital. Inaccessible from land is nearby sandy **Limonari beach,** one of the island's best and a popular boat destination from Agnondas.

From Agnondas the road cuts through the pine groves to another popular campsite and beach, **Panormos.** Many people, however, prefer nearby **Milia,** which is shady and pebbly (path from the main road). Further along, **Elios** beach has a number of prefabricated concrete homes—emergency shelters thrown up after the 1965 earthquake.

Glossa, high on its hill, is a beautiful village constructed mainly during the Turkish occupation, situated in the woods high above the sea. The houses survived the 1965 earthquake that ruined parts of Skopelos. One of the more peculiar architectural features is the toilet on the balcony of many houses. There's a pebble beach, and a taverna under the plane trees at **Loutraki,** the town's port, 3 km (2 miles) below. Most of the island's almonds grow in the region of Glossa, which also boasts three 4th-century BC towers, at **Mavragani, Helliniko** and **Sendouka.** Near the church **Ag. Nikolaos** in Loutraki are the 7th-century ruins of an earlier basilica. There are also the remains of a fortress at **Selinus.**

South of Glossa are three little villages, **Makhalas, Kato Klima** and **Ano Klima,** where one may find rooms to rent. **Kalogiros** on the north coast is a settlement of country houses, most easily reached by caique. From Glossa you can walk across the island to the church **Ag. Ioannis** on the rugged north coast, perched like an eagle's nest over the sea—the last part of the walk is up a hundred steps carved in the rock. It takes about an hour to get there; ask in Glossa for instructions, and take a canteen of water.

Ag. Barbara, a short walk from Skopelos town, is a fortified monastery containing frescoes from the 15th century. Two islets are accessible by caique from Skopelos: **Tripiti,** with a sea cave and excellent fishing and lobsters, and **Ag. Georgios,** which has a 17th-century monastery and a herd of wild goats.

387

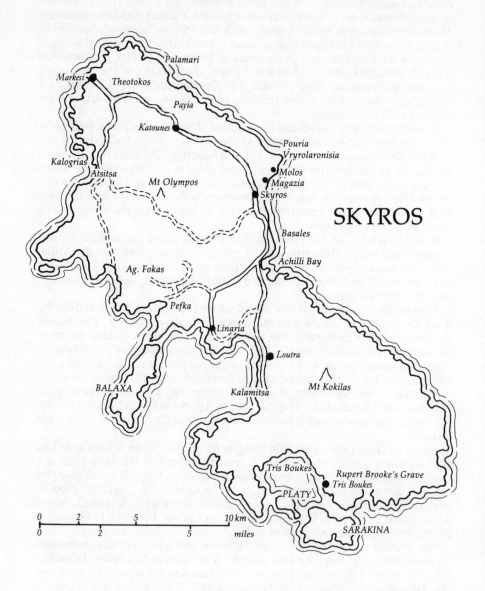

Markesi

Palamari

Theotokos

Payia

Katounes

Pouria

Vryrolaronisia

Kalogrias

Molos

Atsitsa

Magazia

Mt Olympos

Skyros

Basales

SKYROS

Ag. Fokas

Achilli Bay

Pefka

Linaria

Loutra

Mt Kokilas

BALAXA

Kalamitsa

Tris Boukes

Rupert Brooke's Grave

Tris Boukes

PLATY

SARAKINA

0   2   5   10 km

0   2   5

miles

PANEYERIA
25 February, Ag. Reginos; 6 August, Megosotiri on Skopelos Bay; 15 August, Panayias in Skopelos; 9 November, Esothia Theotokos at the edge of the town; 25 November, Christos, also in the town.

WHERE TO STAY
Like Skiathos, Skopelos is expensive; unlike Skiathos, there are no huge slabs of hotels. Skopelos town is for most people the best place to stay; among the choices is the **Xenia Pension** (tel. 0424 22 232), where doubles are 4500 dr., or the **Hotel Adonis** (tel. 0424 22 231), where a double is more expensive at 6000 dr. in high season, and it has a fast food restaurant on the ground level. There are also a fair number of pensions, such as the **Drossia** (tel. 0424 22 490—doubles a reasonable 2800 dr.) and rooms to let. Outside town you can find rooms at Loutraki, the port of Glossa, and the **Pension Valentina** (tel. 0424 33 694), where doubles are about 3000 dr. In Panormos there's the spacious **Panormos Beach Pension,** catering mostly to packagers, with doubles a little pricey at 7000 dr. (tel. 0424 22 711). For about the same price the **Rigas** is the place to stay at Staphylos (tel. 0424 22 618). Near the port at Skopelos an agency specialises in finding rooms in houses (a free service); ask there for possibilities elsewhere on the island.

EATING OUT
On the waterfront of Skopelos town, try **Jimmy's** for local specialities at moderate prices; others nearby specialise in good but pricey fish. There are good tavernas around Panormos and the other beaches, and an inexpensive one at Loutraki. At Skopelos, on the harbour, there's also one of the few places that play jazz on the Greek islands—**Platanos.**

TOURIST POLICE
See regular police, Skopelos town, tel. (0424) 22 235.

SKYROS

CONNECTIONS
Daily flight from Athens. Ferry from Kymi, Evia twice a day (2¹/₄ hours). Hydrofoil twice a week from Volos, Skiathos, Skopelos and Alonissos.

Of all the Sporades, Skyros is the most difficult to reach from Athens—under ideal conditions it takes about seven hours by land and sea. An alternative, if you cannot get a direct flight, would be to fly to Skiathos and connect with a hydrofoil on the appropriate day, at present Thursday and Sunday. For many years connections even from Kymi were so limited that the people of Skyros eventually got together to purchase their own ferry. This inaccessibility, of course, accounts in a large part for the island's charm and the staying power of many of its old traditions. The older men, in particular, still don their baggy blue trousers and flat leather sandals with many straps, and the women often wear their long skirts and yellow scarves. The interiors of Skyriot houses are often adorned with carved wood and painted plates, the latter a local mania dating from the days of the wealthy Byzantine exiles. When these nobles lost their power, which had been so resented by the locals, they sold their dinner ware, creating the Skyriot status symbol which the women have since bought, traded and displayed with great enthusiasm. Thus a Skyriot sailor in a distant land knows exactly what gift to bring his wife or mother: a plate. Some in Skyros are from as far away as China.

The very early inhabitants of the island are said to have worshipped goats, and cattle and vestiges of this cult remain even on modern Skyros. During the carnival, three characters dance down the street led by a man in a goatskin costume and sheep bells called the Old Man, followed by the Frangos (the European) and the Korela (a man dressed up as a woman). These perform the Horos tou Tragoun, or the Goat Dance, an ancient rite that gave us the word "tragedy" ("goat song"). Every day during the carnival the Old Man, the Frangos and the Korela make their way up to the monastery of Ag. Georgios, the patron saint of Skyros. Satires are produced, making fun of almost everything, along with other, more traditional festivities.

HISTORY
Long ago the two distinct parts of Skyros were two separate islands: present-day southern Skyros was wild and rocky, while the north was fertile and pine-forested. A type of small native pony, the Pikermies, ruled the southern part undisturbed except at harvest time, when they were rounded up to assist the farmers in the north. This state of affairs has gone on for countless years, perhaps even back to the day when the Athenian hero Theseus, having met a serious decline in his popularity, sought asylum with the king of Skyros, Lycomedes, who betrayed his sacred obligations as host when he lured Theseus to the pinnacle of the akropolis and gave him a push, hurling him to death on the rocks below. It is said that there his bones lay until the Persian Wars, when the Athenians saw his ghost leading them on to victory. When informed of this, the oracle at Delphi ordered the Athenians to bring Theseus' bones back to Athens—just the excuse they needed to take the island for themselves. In 476 BC Kimon captured it, enslaved the inhabitants and found the bones of Theseus, which he took back to Athens and enshrined in the Theseion.

So many Athenians then came to settle the island that Athens treated it on equal terms and the island paid no tribute. The Dionysia, in honour of the god of wine, was the biggest festival on the island, which also worshipped Achilleus (a bay on the island is still named after the Achean hero). Like Lesbos, it has a Mt Olympos, a name probably given it by the Athenian settlers, adopting the native sky god's cult into their own state religion of Zeus and his Olympians.

Skyros remained part of Athens until 86 BC when General Sulla captured the city. During the Byzantine period, many important people were exiled to Skyros marking the beginnings of a rather tyrannical upper class. Barbarossa took Skyros for the Sultan in 1538, and it is thought there was a small Turkish settlement on the island.

MYTHOLOGY

When a prophecy said that Achilleus, son of the goddess Thetis and Peleus, would either win great glory at Troy and die young, or live at home to a ripe if inglorious old age, his doting mother thought to hide him from the Acheans by disguising him as a girl and hiding him among the women at King Lycomedes' palace in Skyros, a situation he profited from by fathering a son, Neoptolemis. A prophecy, however declared that the Acheans would never win the Trojan War without Achilleus, and so Odysseus went in search of the young hero. The crafty Odysseus suspected Thetis' ploy, and in order to make Achilleus reveal himself, he brought a chest full of treasures when he called on King Lycomedes. These included perfumes, jewellery, finery—and a sword, which the young transvestite in the crowd of women seized joyfully for his own, just as Odysseus had anticipated. Thus Achilleus joined the Acheans. When an arrow in his heel ended his life, Odysseus returned to Skyros to fetch his son Neoptolemis to Troy, and the war was eventually won.

WHAT TO SEE

There are basically only two settlements on Skyros: **Linaria,** a colourful fishing village and port with ticket offices and (connection by bus) the capital **Skyros,** or Chorio, with most of the island's facilities.

Skyros is striking, reminiscent of a Cycladic town, its white houses stacked one on top of the other along the steep, narrow streets; from the distance it sweeps like a full skirt around the massive rock of the ancient akropolis, high over the sea. The ruins of a Venetian **kastro** occupy the site of the Classical fortifications (traces can still be made out here and there) from where Lycomedes pushed Theseus. The Venetian walls were built by the Duke of Naxos—note the lion of St Mark over the gate. Just below here, in the walls, is the monastery of **Ag. Georgios** the Arab, founded in 962 by Nikephoros Phokas, "the Pale Death of the Saracens", after his liberation of Crete. The emperor gave it to his friend, Athanasios, who later incorporated it with the Great Lavra monastery of Mt Athos. Scholars believe the church was built over a temple of Dionysos and though once famed for its miracles, it is now only occasionally occupied by local priests. Below the church is another dedicated to Ag. Athanasios.

There are two museums in town, an **archaeology museum** (closed Tuesdays) with a few odds and ends, and the more interesting **Faltaits Museum of Folklore** (open daily 10 am–1 pm & 6 pm–8 pm, entrance free), both on Brooke Square, where a **Statue of Immortal Poetry,** by sculptor M. Tombros (1931) commemorates the English poet Rupert Brooke, who is buried on Skyros: there's not much to say about it, except that nobody likes it. The Faltaits Museum contains a collection of domestic items and fine embroideries made on the island, including traditional Skyrian costumes made to order; there are also model houses in the traditional style which you can examine if you're not lucky enough to stay in a real one in the town. Carving wooden furniture is still a local occupation, and in early August there's an annual exhibition of local handicrafts. You can buy chairs and tables made in Skyros, but taking them home is about as easy as shipping an elephant to Alaska. (You can, however, check out Olympic Airways' world-wide freight service.)

From the town a path leads down to a long sandy beach **Magazia,** named after the Venetian magazines once kept here and behind it stretches the island's one fertile plain. Next to Magazia is Molos beach, with accommodation and tavernas. If these two beaches seem crowded there are others near at hand, at **Basales, Achilli** and nearby **Papa ta Chomata** ("Priests' Land"), which is popular among nudists. From Ormos Achilli, Achilleus is said to have embarked for Troy.

The bus runs intermittently between Linaria, Skyros town and Molos. The only way to visit the rest of the island is on foot or by hired moped. The northern half of Skyros is more accessible and well wooded, and there are many small sandy beaches just off the dirt tracks which more or less follow the coast. Because of the number of military installations on the island you are forbidden to take photographs in many areas. One track criss-crosses the island to the beach at **Atsitsa,** which has a taverna, as does **Pefkos,** where the island's variegated marble is quarried.

In the south the bus goes as far as **Kalamitsa,** one of the loveliest beaches, also with a taverna and a small pension. Signs of one of ancient Skyros' three rival towns, Chrission, were found near here, an ancient tomb, locally said to be Homer's, and traces of an Early Christian basilica. From Linaria, the port, you can visit the grottoes **Pentekali** and **Gerania Spilies,** and take a caique to the islet **Skyropoula,** that lies between Skyros and the mainland. Skyropoula has two beaches and another cave, **Kavos Spili,** and a herd of the wild ponies that once ruled the rocky southern half of Skyros, but are now rarely seen (though some have been domesticated and on 21 and 22 August they are ridden by children in organised races at Molos).

It's possible to take a taxi or caique (far more pleasant on a calm day) or make the two-hour walk to **Tris Boukes** and the **grave of Rupert Brooke** at the southernmost point of Skyros. On 23 April 1915, Brooke, on his way to the Gallipoli campaign, died of blood poisoning in a hospital ship just off Skyros and was buried at dawn the next morning. His well-tended grave is maintained by the Anglo-Hellenic society. It was only a year before he died that he wrote his famous poem anticipating his death:

> If I should die think only this of me:
> That there's some corner of a foreign field
> That is forever England.

PANEYERIA

Carnival; 23 April, Ag. Georgios; 2 September, Ag. Mamon near Kalikri (Ag. Mamon is the patron of shepherds, and their festival also includes traces of ancient rites); 12 March, in town; 27 July, Ag. Panteleimon, near Pefkos.

WHERE TO STAY

There are three basic places to stay on the island, at the port Linaria, where the A class **King Likomedes** has doubles for 12 000 dr. (tel. 0222 91 949), on Skyros beach (Magazia or Molos) or in Skyros town. On the beach the most comfortable place is the class B **Hotel Xenia** on Magazia beach (tel. 0222 91 209), where doubles are 6000 dr. in season. Less expensive is the small pension run by M. Balotis nearby. In Molos, further down, there are two motels, the **Panagou** (tel. 0222 91 381) and the **Demitris** (tel. 0222 91 763). Both are A class, their doubles between 5000 dr. and 8000 dr., triples from 8000 dr. to 11 000 dr., but these rates drop in the off season. You can get a very pleasant double with bath en suite at **Pension Venetsanos** (tel. 0222 91 386) for 3500 dr. There are, of course, a fair number of rooms for rent in private houses. No one cares if you sleep on the beach, though there is a conveniently placed campsite in Magazia.

In Skyros town there are scores of rooms to let, many of them in charming traditional houses (just mind you don't break the plates). Current rates for a stay of more than two days are about 900 dr. per person per night. The E class **Pension Elena,** for example, has a limited number of rooms for 1950 dr. (tel. 0222 91 738).

A rather different holiday may be had at **The Skyros Centre,** a small hostelry geared to mind and body relaxation. It offers community atmosphere and activities, including workshops and therapeutic recreational programmes involving dance and music. It's annexe, out in Artitsa, concentrate more on physical activities, including windsurfing. Courses are fairly expensive and you have to find your own way to and from the island; if it's what you're after, contact The Skyros Centre, Skyros, for further details.

EATING OUT

Moraiti restaurant, on the main street, is a great spot to eat, with good food and location (dinners are around 800 dr.), but certainly not the only place to watch the bustling pedestrian traffic. In fact any of the tavernas here serve excellent Greek food and on the whole prices are lower than on most islands and the atmosphere livelier; perhaps the good retsina of Skyros has something to do with it. Incidentally, if you've been waiting for the right moment to eat lobster, this could be it, as seafood prices are surprisingly low on Skyros. Down in Magazia the **Green Corner,** by the campsite entrance, will provide a lobster dinner for two for under 5000 dr., and the **campsite taverna** itself can be fun, especially at the weekends when there is often spontaneous dancing to the live Skyrian music. Around the corner, overlooking Magazia beach, is the **Aigeon Taverna,** serving fresh hot Greek food, which seems to taste that much better in such an attractive setting.

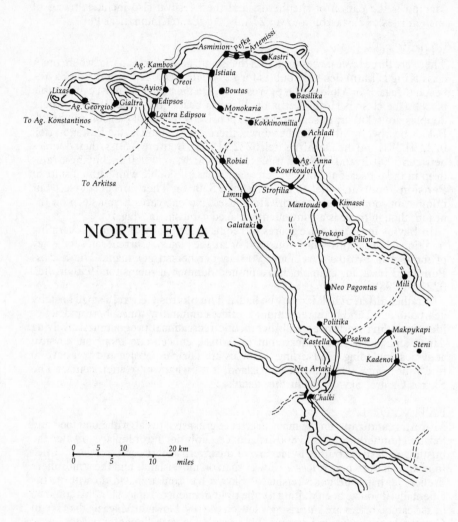

NORTH EVIA

Asminion · Pefka
Artemissi
Ag. Kambos
Oreoi
Istiaia
Kastri
Lixas
Ayios
Boutas
Basilika
Ag. Georgios
Gialtra
Edipsos
Monokaria
To Ag. Konstantinos
Loutra Edipsou
Kokkinomilia
Achladi
Robiai
Ag. Anna
To Arkitsa
Kourkouloi
Limni
Strofilia
Kimassi
Mantoudi
Galataki
Prokopi
Pilion
Neo Pagontas
Mili
Politika
Makpykapi
Kastella
Psakna
Steni
Kadenoi
Nea Artaki
Chalki

0   5   10   20 km
0   5   10   miles

Of the two bouzouki night clubs, the **Ta Trapezakia Mesa** at Basales is the more popular, with a bottle of wine at 1000 dr.

TOURIST INFORMATION
NTOG, near Brooke Square, tel. (0222) 91 616.
Tourist police, see regular police, Skyros town, tel. (0222) 91 274.

EVIA (EUBOEA)

CONNECTIONS
Bus every half-hour, and train every hour from Athens to Chalki (1½ hours), the main bus terminal of the island. The terminal in Athens is Liossion, from where you can also travel direct to Kymi (and Skyros) and many other points in Evia, but for Rafina (also the main port for the island of Andros), buses leave Athens from the Mavromateon terminal. Ferry boats link Evia with the mainland from Rafina to Karystos (three times a day), Rafina to Marmari (three times a day), Rafina to Nea Styra (eight times a day), Arkitsa to Edipsos (twelve times a day), Oropos to Eretria (every hour), and Glifa to Agiokambos (every two hours).

The second largest island in Greece after Crete, Evia is separated from Boeotia on the mainland by the famous Euripos Strait, now crossed by a short bridge. The currents of the Euripos Strait or canal change every six hours or so, a phenomenon that so puzzled the great Aristotle that, according to tradition, it drove him to his death. Despite its great size and proximity to Athens, and despite its often beautiful scenery, Evia has only recently begun to receive tourists, both Greek and foreign, and in quite large numbers; they tend to stick almost exclusively to the established coastal resorts. Evia is one of the country's principal food producers, and was much favoured by the Turkish peasantry, some of whom still remain by special agreement. Although nearly every hill on the island is crowned with some Frankish or Byzantine fortification, there are relatively very few Classical remains, which confirms Evia's relative lack of importance in ancient history. Quiet rural farming has been the Eviot's way of life for centuries, and it remains so today.

HISTORY
Inhabited in prehistoric times by settlers from Thessaly, and later by Dorians, Aeolians and Ionians, Evia is first mentioned by Homer. Seven city-states divided the long island amongst themselves, but the most powerful were the two great rivals, Chalki and Eretria, great commercial ports that set up colonies as far away as Sicily. Between them lay the most fertile land in Evia, the Lelantine Plain which, they constantly quarrelled over. The cities extended their disagreement into international affairs which did neither of them any good: Chalki joined Boeotia in a war against Athens, and when it was conquered by Athens (506 BC),

the land was divided; the Eretrians, of Ionian origin, fought with Athens in the Ionian uprising on the Asia Minor coast, the only city to do so, and in return, when Darius came to punish the Athenians, he sacked Eretria and enslaved its citizens. In the 5th century BC the whole island came under the rule of Athens.

In 338 BC Macedonia took Evia, and the Romans who followed them used the name of an Eviot tribe, the Graeci, to refer to the entire Hellenic people, an error which Europeans have perpetuated. After the Latin conquest of Constantinople, the Franks divided the fertile land into three baronies, under the King of Thessalonika, Boniface de Montferrat. This began the great castle-building period on the island, each lordling the master of his own little fort. Over the next hundred years, Evia came under the sway of Venice, who made it the kingdom of Negroponte "black bridge" (a corruption of Euripos). When the Turks took the island in 1470, they did not even allow a puppet Frankish governor to remain, but occupied the island themselves, settling more permanently than they did elsewhere in the Aegean. In 1830 Evia became part of the original Greek kingdom.

MYTHOLOGY
Evia, split from the nearby mainland with a blow of Poseidon's mighty trident, was the sea god's favourite island. He lived in the Evian Gulf in a fantastic palace with his wife Amphitrite. South of this gulf is the Myrtoan Sea, named for a son of Hermes who was a charioteer of King Oenomaus. Oenomaus had a beautiful daughter and a team of divine horses. Anyone who desired his daughter's hand was required to race the chariot of the king, which was invincible. Myrtilus, the king's charioteer, himself wished to marry the princess, a fact that the hero Pelops, a challenger in Oenomaus' race, took advantage of. If, Pelops suggested, Myrtilus would replace the lynch pins in the axles of the king's chariot with wax (thus enabling Pelops to win the race and the princess), then Pelops would allow Myrtilus to share the girl. The charioteer eagerly agreed, and events unfolded as predicted: Oenomaus' chariot collapsed in the heat of the race, the king was killed and Pelops was given his daughter. He and Myrtilus left with her in the direction of Evia, but Pelops, never intending to keep his bargain with Myrtilus, pushed him into the sea where he drowned. His father Hermes then named the sea in his son's honour.

WHAT TO SEE
Chalki, the bustling industrial rhinocerus-shaped capital of Evia, stands at the narrowest point of the strait that divides the island from the mainland. Its location has long been the main source of its prosperity, for should Chalki wish it could seriously block trade between Athens and the north. Its name derives either from bronze (chalkos), another early source of its wealth, or perhaps from chalki, the sea snail prized in antiquity for making the purple dye of kingly cloaks. The city had so many colonies in the north of Greece that the entire peninsula, Chalkidiki, was named for the city. Among its famous colonies are Messina and Cumae.

By the 7th century Chalki had asserted its position over Eretria as the island's

396

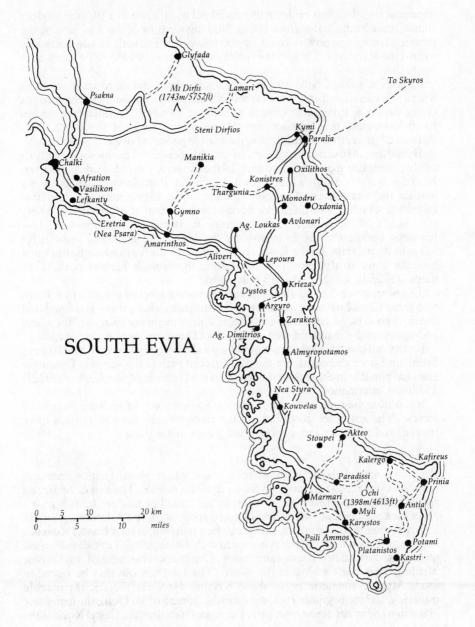

Glyfada

Psakna

Mt Dirfis
(1743m/5752ft)
∧

Lamari

To Skyros

Steni Dirfios

Kymi
Paralia

Chalki

Manikia

Oxilithos

Afration
Vasilikon
Lefkanty

Thargunia

Konistres

Monodru
Oxdonia

Gymno

Ag. Loukas

Avlonari

Eretria
(Nea Psara)

Amarinthos

Aliveri

Lepoura

Krieza

Dystos

Argyro

Zarakes

Ag. Dimitrios

SOUTH EVIA

Almyropotamos

Nea Styra
Kouvelas

Stoupei

Akteo

Kalergo

Kafireus

Paradissi
∧
*Ochi
(1398m/4613ft)*

Prinia

Marmari

Antia

Myli
Karystos

Psili Ammos

Platanistos

Potami
Kastri

0   5   10   20 km

0   5   10   miles

dominant city. The first bridge to the mainland was built in 411 BC (the modern sliding draw bridge dates from 1962). Nothing remains of the ancient city, the former akropolis is now covered by the ruins of a **Turkish castle** (curiously named the Karababa, Turkish for "black father") built in 1686. The climb up is worth the view.

Facing the strait, Chalki puts on an attractive face, and there are many cafés where you can sit and speculate on the still unexplained mystery of the Euripos (some days the current may change as many as 14 times). In the new town, on Leof. Venizelou, the **Archaeology Museum** has some of the finest items discovered in Eretria, including the fine marble pediment of a temple of Apollo. A **Byzantine Museum** is nearby, in an old mosque. The mosque (with its marble fountain) marks the entrance to the **Kastro**, the old Turkish quarter. Near the mosque the city's best-known church, **Ag. Paraskevi**, began its life as a basilica and was converted by the Crusaders in the 13th century into a Gothic cathedral, which has resulted in a curious architectural amalgam inside. Every year, in late July, a market, "the paneyeri of Ag. Paraskevi", enlivens Chalki for ten days, people coming from all over the island and mainland to hunt for bargains on the stalls. In the Kastro you can also see the **Turkish aqueduct** that brought water to the city from Mt Dirfis, the island's highest peak (1745 metres/5725 ft, some 25 km/ 15 miles away).

The nearest beach to Chalki, **Asteria**, has restaurants and every facility. Boats also leave Chalki daily for the islet of **Tonnoiron**, where there is a hotel and beach. A good bus service connects Chalki with all the major villages of the island and towns on the mainland such as Thebes. There is a yacht supply station.

From Chalki you can take a taxi or bus a good way up the slopes of **Mt Dirfis** to **Steni**, and from there walk up the well-marked path to the summit. Overnight stays are possible in Steni or in the refuge of the Hellenic Alpine Club tel. (0221) 25230 for information.

If you have the time and energy, there is no better way of seeing Evia than by bicycle. The roads are good and not too steep (though the east coast is quite rugged) and there are many springs and places to camp out.

SOUTH EVIA

Beginning with the southernmost tip of Evia, where poor Myrtilus drowned, **Karystos** was renowned long ago for its cipollino marble. Today it is the largest village and most popular holiday resort in the area. The modern town is near a Mycenaean settlement—Karystos is located at one of the few defensible points in Evia. For that reason, in 1030, the Byzantines built the famous **Castel Rosso**, a huge fortification that the Turks occupied with 400 families. Turkish rule in the town was particularly harsh, and many Christians who refused to become Muslims were dealt a blow of the sword. The Castel Rosso may be visited in lovely **Myli**, a kilometre or so above Krystos. Here are the ancient **marble quarries,** and the beginning of the path to the summit of **Mt Ochi**, through some of the most dramatic scenery on Evia. Far more intact than the Castel Rossa is the

398

14th century coastal fort called **Bourdzi**. A long sandy beach stretches to one side of Karystos, excellent for a good night's sleep and known as Psili Ammos.

In the region of Karystos is another beach, 13 km (8 miles) away at the **Borou Hotel**. Above the town is a large cave called **Ag. Triada**, which can be explored by torchlight. You can also visit a monastery, Ag. Mavra. The **Katochi cave** by Kastanas seems to have been used as a small hotel in the past. At **Platanistos** there are large plane trees and a stream; visitors can stay overnight in rooms in the houses. At **Cape Kafireus**, the notorious Cavo Doro where tempests are all too common, are a few ruins of a Byzantine fortress, repaired by Admiral Likarios, the right-hand man of the Emperor Michael Paleologus who restored the Byzantine Empire, beginning in Evia at this ruined fort.

Along the west coast are two small port resorts, **Marmari** and Nea Styra, connected by ferry from Rafina. **Nea Styra** is a pleasant, peaceful backwater with a stretch of sandy beach providing excellent swimming. Near Nea Styra are the "homes of the Dragons", which is actually a Venetian fortress. Ancient **Styra** lies above the modern town. Nearby are also the ruins of the Mycenaean **Dryopes**.

Further north, by Evia's largest lake, are the walls of the akropolis of ancient **Dystos**, built during the Classical period and very well preserved. Homes and streets of the ancient lakeside city may be explored. At **Lepoura** a branch of the good road heads north to **Kymi**, with a turn off it to **Oxdonia**, an attractive east coast resort crammed together beneath a castle. The scenery along the Lepoura–Kymi road through the valley of Oxilithos is exceptionally lovely, pastoral and embellished with castles. **Kymi**, the main port for Skyros (with occasional connections to the other Sporades), is a very green village perched high above the sea, surrounded by forests. Many Greeks have built summer villas in the hills, some of quite ambitious design. While there are many restaurants and rooms to rent, Kymi has little night life. Below the pretty village is the port **Paralia Kymi**, with a yacht supply station and an average beach, generally crowded. Not far from Kymi at Cheili are the ruins of a Mycenaean fort, and to the north on a sheer rock, rises the Byzantine castle Apokledi. Above the town is the castle of Ag. Georgios, built during the Turkish occupation, and just below it is the monastery Metamorphosis. At Avlonari, a village south of Kymi, one may visit a small fortress with a Venetian church inside.

Aliveri, back on the road from Karystos to Chalki, is an old red-roofed village inhabited mainly by miners and men working in the nearby power station. There is a beach just below it and restaurants and pensions in town. Near Aliveri are the ruins of three ancient towns: **Amarinthos,** where the tall Venetian tower stands by the bay of Aliveri; **Tamynae,** above Aliveri, and **Porthmos,** near the beach.

Eretria, connected to the main land by ferry from Oropou, is also known as Nea Psara; the modern town was founded by refugees from the island of Psara, who rather unfortunately built their new town over the ruins of the old. Still, Eretria is the most complete ancient site on Evia, as well as the biggest holiday resort after Edipsos. Ancient Eretria reached its prime during its great rivalry with Chalki, when the two cities fought over the Lelantine Plain, they agreed not to use weapons of any sort, solving their dispute through wrestling contests and general fisticuffs. Eretria lost, and suffered an even worse disaster in 490 BC when the Persians decimated the city. The Eretrians rebuilt their city, earning themselves a reputation for their excellent ceramics, and generally stayed allied with Athens until 87 BC, when Mithridates sacked the city. It was never rebuilt.

The **museum** and akropolis lie at the top of Arcaiou Theatrou St. The museum isn't much (the best of the finds went to Chalki) but the excavations near the museum revealed some of the excellent masonry of the walls, a 4th century BC palace (complete with bath tub) and the **theatre**, or at least the parts of it which have survived the building of Nea Psara. Most interesting here is the survival of part of the ancient mechanism that boosted the plots of many a play, the **deus ex machina**. From the **akropolis** you have an excellent view of the fertile Lelantine Plain, subject of so much contention, and, on a clear day, Mt Parnassos on the mainland. In the town itself stand the ruins of a temple of Apollo Daphnephoros, who enjoyed a popular following throughout Evia. Near Eretria is the developed Malakonta beach, with many hotels and restaurants.

NORTH EVIA

Sadly the northern half of Evia, once covered with forests, has recently suffered devastating fires, and much of the landscape is charred and desolate. By good fortune the fires spared some of the best scenery, around Prokopi. Two villages just north of Chalki, **Psakna** and **Politika**, have castles, but the most striking one is in **Prokopi**, at the end of a series of magnificent ravines called the **Kleisoura,** often narrow and full of trees. Prokopi is an enchanting place, with its fortress built on a nearly inaccessible precipice. Sometimes known by its old name Ahmet Aga, the modern town is largely inhabited by Greeks from Urgup, Turkey, who came over in the population exchange after the great fiasco; with them they brought the relics of St John the Russian, who went from being a soldier in the Tsar's army to a slave in Urgup (1730), to a saint of the Russian Orthodox Church (in 1962). **Limni**, on the west coast is a charming sleeping bay with beaches and a slowly growing resort community.

From Limni a main road under construction goes up the coast, while another avoids the challenge of the mountains, taking a diversion across the island and back again to the south-east coast, to the major tourist attraction on Evia, Loutra Edipsos. One passes the village of **Artemissi** along the way, where a naval battle took place between the Greeks and the Persians in 480 BC. Here also the statue of Zeus (or Poseidon), one of the prizes of the National Archaeological Museum in Athens, was discovered. Below Artemissi is a pretty beach, **Pefka** (so called because it sits under the pine trees), with rooms available. This entire north coast of the island is dotted with beaches, popular with people from the city of Chalki.

Istiaia is the largest village en route to Edipsos and is prettily situated in the hills. Founded by Thessalians, they defied Athens so often that Perikles took the town and exiled the inhabitants, repopulating Istiaia with Athenians, who actually formed the nearby settlement of **Oreoi**, which dominated Istiaia for a time. The entire population of Evia rebuilt or renovated the fortress of the town, and there are other medieval fortifications at Oreoi. In the main square stands an expressive bull from the Hellenistic era, found offshore in 1962.

Edipsos owes part of its popularity to its thermal, sulphurous waters, reputed for curing rheumatism, arthritis and gallstones, and a good many other problems, including depression. It has been famed since ancient times, when it was believed the springs were connected to those at Thermopylae. Aristotle referred to Edipsos, and Augustus, Hadrian and General Sulla visited the baths. There are frequent connections with Arkitsa on the mainland, on the major route from Athens to Thessaloniki. Signs of the spa's long history can be seen, and there is a long, lovely beach. A seaside village on the peninsula facing Edipsos, **Lixas,** is connected with Ag. Konstantinos on the mainland. There are tourist facilities in the village, and a beach at **Ag. Georgios.**

PANEYERIA
15 August, at Kymi, Oxilithos, Haito, Satsaroni and Koupeios; 26 July, Ag. Paraskevi, long celebrations at Chalki, Myli and Rukia; 17 July, Ag. Marinas near Karystos; 21 May, Ag. Konstantinos at Vitalakimis; 27 May, St John the Russian at Prokopi.

WHERE TO STAY
Evia's coasts have nearly all the facilities for tourists, most of whom are Greek; major centres are Chalki, Edipsos, Karystos, Limni, Kymi and Eretria (the last especially popular among foreign visitors). In Chalki, you can stay at the class A **Lucy,** directly facing the Euripos strait on 10 L. Voudouri (tel. 0221 23 831), where doubles begin at 5000 dr. The nearby **Iris Hotel** at 3 Plateia Gefyras (tel. 0221 22 246) charges considerably less: around 2500 dr. for a double. Most people, however, don't care to linger in busy workaday, Chalki. In **Eretria** (near Psara) just south of Chalki there are many new hotels (mainly filled with package tourists) and old favourites like the **Delfis** (tel. 0221 62 380), where the rates are 4500 dr. for a double. Slightly cheaper is the **Xenia** (tel. 0221 61 202). In Nea Styra further south you'll find no bargains (typical is the **Aktaeon** on the beach, tel. 0224 41 261) with rates at 3500 dr. a double. The **Venus Beach Hotel** has twin bungalows for around the 4000 dr. mark (tel. 0224 41 226). Karystos, way at the southern tip of the island, has more to offer, from the seaside **Apollon Resort Hotel** on Psili Ammos beach (tel. 0224 22 045), with cosy doubles at 6500 dr. to the **Hironia Hotel** in town by the sea (tel. 0224 22 238), where you can get a single room for around 2500 dr., a double for up to 4500 dr.

In Kymi, the most pleasant place to stay is the **Hotel Krinion** (tel. 0222 22 287) in the Plateia G. Papanikolaou, where a pleasant room with a balcony is only 1300 dr. for a single, 2300 dr. for a double. Down in Paralia Kymi there are a few rooms to be had, and two hotels under the same management—the **Beis,** an anonymous C class with doubles around 3000 dr. and next door the scruffy **Aegeon,** doubles at around 2000 dr. (tel. 0222 22 604 for both). In Limni the

Hotel Avra (tel. 0227 31 220), has very nice doubles for 3800 dr., and the **Ilion** is cheaper with doubles up to 2500 dr. (tel. 0227 31 768). In Edipsos there is no shortage of hotel accommodation. The **Aegli Hotel**, 18 Paraliakis (tel. 0226 22 215) is perhaps the best for grand old spa atmosphere. Rates are about 5000 dr. upwards for a single, 6500–9000 dr. a double. For something more modern and air conditioned, **Gregolimano-Roi Soleil** (tel. 0226 33 281) is secluded and exclusive and 8000 dr. for a double, 12 000 dr. for a bungalow.

In the resort Istiaia most of the accommodation is apartments or rooms; the **Hermes** (tel. 0226 52 245) charges around 2800 dr. for a double, and cheaper is the **Neon** (tel. 0226 52 226) with doubles 2000–2500 dr. Further along in Orei, a pretty little town, although the beach isn't spectacular, the **Corali Hotel** is reasonable with simple rooms at 2500 dr. for a double (tel. 0226 71 217) and the pension **Kentrikon** (tel. 0226 71 525) is small and cheap. There is also a number of rooms in private homes. Pefki, a cool, busy beach town popular with Greek holidaymakers, has a small number of pleasant hotels, among them the **Galini**, with doubles around 4000 dr.

Unfortunately there's no central clearing house for rooms on Evia; you just have to go to each village and take pot luck. Most are on the coasts. Villages in the interior have little or no facilities.

Evia is a very popular place for camping, both with tents and trailers, and although there is an official campsite on Malakonta beach, near Eretria, most of the camping is freelance (but, again, check what other people are doing first).

EATING OUT

On the whole Evia is not expensive, except for Eretria, where prices have been jacked up to accommodate foreign currencies. The best places to eat seafood are Limni, where the **Avra** taverna seems to have the monopoly and Karystos, along the waterfront, where the fish somehow tastes better. In the latter, **Melissa** on T. Kotsika Street has a wonderful reputation, a fish dinner will cost around 1500 dr. here. In Paralia Kymi there's an excellent taverna, **To Aigeo**, on the waterfront; you may have to wait a while to be served in high summer, but the food is good and cheap, with a meal costing 800 dr. or so. Istiaia has a number of restaurants lining the waterfront, and in Orei there's a superb *souvlaki* place and an even better *ouzeri*, which serves delicious seafood *mezedes*, on the harbour front. Pefki has a small selection of decent tavernas, and on Sundays there's a smell of lobster wafting through the air.

TOURIST POLICE
2 Eleftheriou Venizelou, Chalki, tel. (0221) 24 662.
3 Okeanidou St, Edipsos, tel. (0226) 22 465.

LANGUAGE

Although modern Greek, or *Romaíka* is a minor language spoken by few non-Greeks, it has the special distinction of having caused riots and the fall of a government (in 1901). In Greece today there are basically two languages, the purist or *katharevóusa* and the popular or *demotikí*. Both are developments of ancient Greek, but although the purist is consciously Classical, the popular is as close to its ancient origins as French is to Latin. While many purist words are common in the speech of the people, the popular dominates, especially in the countryside.

Until the turn of the century all literature appeared in the purist language. What shook Athens with riots in 1901 was the appearance of the *Iliad* and the *New Testament* in the demotic. When the fury had died down a bit, more and more writers were found to be turning their pens to the demotic. Cavafy, the first great modern Greek poet, wrote in both the popular and purist. In its "moral cleansing" of Greece the Papadopoulos government tried to revive the purist, but with little success.

Knowing the language of any country makes the stay twice as enjoyable; in Greece, especially, people spend much of the day talking. But modern Greek isn't a particularly easy language to pick by ear, and it is often spoken at great velocity (if you speak slowly someone is sure to interrupt). If you buy a modern Greek grammar, check to see if it has the demotic and not just the purist. Even if you have no desire to learn Greek, it is helpful to know at least the alphabet—so that you can find your way around—and a few basic words and phrases.

THE GREEK ALPHABET

Α	α	álfa	(short a as in father)
Β	β	víta	(v sound)
Γ	γ	gámma	(slightly gutteral g or y sound)
Δ	δ	thélta	(hard th as in though)
Ε	ε	épsilon	(short e as in bet)
Ζ	ζ	zíta	(z sound)
Η	η	íta	(long e as in bee)
Θ	θ	thíta	(soft th as in thin)
Ι	ι	yóta	(long e as in be; sometimes like y)
Κ	κ	káppa	(k sound)
Λ	λ	lámtha	(l sound)
Μ	μ	mi	(m sound)
Ν	ν	ni	(n sound)
Ξ	ξ	ksi	(x as in ox)
Ο	ο	omicron	(o as in open)
Π	π	pi	(p sound)
Ρ	ρ	ro	(r sound)

Σ	σ (ς)	sigma	(s sound)
Τ	τ	taf	(t sound)
Υ	υ	ipsilon	(long e as in bee)
Φ	φ	fi	(f sound)
Χ	χ	chi	(German ch as in doch)
Ψ	ψ	psi	(ps as in stops)
Ω	ω	omega	(o as in open)

Note: i is as i in machine.

DIPHTHONGS AND CONSONANT COMBINATIONS

αι	(short e as in bet)
ει, οι, υι	(i as in machine)
ου	(oo as in too)
αυ	(av or af sound)
ευ	(ev or ef sound)
ηυ	(iv or if sound)
γγ	(ng as in angry)
γκ	(hard g; ng within word)
ντ	(d; nd within word)
μπ	(b; mp within word)

VOCABULARY

Yes	ne or ah me (This is accompanied by a short nod or tilt of the head)	Ναί
no	óchi, óxi (This is accompanied by a backwards jerk of the head, with a click of the tongue, smack of the lips or raise of the eyebrows)	Ὄχι
yes	málista (This is the formal yes)	Μάλιστα
I don't know	then xéro (An even greater throwing back of the head, or a display of empty hands)	Δὲν ξέρω
I don't understand (Greek)	then katalavéno (helliniká)	Δὲν καταλαβαίνω (Ἑλληνικά)
Does someone speak	Iné kanés poo na milá	Εἶναι κανείς ποὺ νὰ μιλᾶ

404

English?	angliká?	ἀγγλικά;
go away	fíyete	Φύγετε
help	voíthia	βοήθεια
my friend	o fílos moo (m)	ὁ φίλος μου
	ee fíli moo (f)	ἡ φήλη μου
please	parakaló	Παρακαλῶ
thank you (very much)	evcharistó (párapolí)	Εὐχαριστῶ (πάραπολύ)
you're welcome	parakaló	Παρακαλῶ
it doesn't matter	then pirázi	Δὲν πειράζει
all right	en táxi	Ἐν τάξει
excuse me	signómi	Συγγνώμη
pardon?	oríste?	Ὁρίστε;
be careful!	proséchte	Προσέξατε!
nothing	típote	Τίποτε
what is your name?	pos sas léne?	Πῶς σᾶς λένε;
how are you?	ti kánete?	Τί κάνετε;
hello	yásou	Γειάσου
goodbye	yásou, andío, hérete	Γειάσου, Ἀντίο, χαίρετε
good morning	kaliméra	Καλημέρα
good evening	kalispéra	Καλησπέρα
good night	kaliníkta	Καληνύκτα
what is that?	ti íne aftó?	Τί εἶναι αὐτό;
what?	ti?	τί;
who?	piós? (m), piá? (f)	ποιός; ποιά;
where?	poo	ποῦ;
when?	póte?	πότε;
why?	yiatí?	γιατί;
how?	pos?	πῶς;
I (am)	egó (íme)	ἐγὼ (εἶμαι)
you (are) (sing)	isí (íse)	ἐσὺ (εἶσαι)
he, she, it (is)	aftós, aftí, aftó (íne)	αὐτὸς, αὐτὴ, αὐτὸ (εἶναι)
we (are)	imés (ímaste)	ἐμεῖς (ἔμαστε)
you (are) (pl)	isís (íste)	ἐσεῖς (εἶστε)
they (are)	aftí (m), aftés (f), aftá (n) (íne)	αὐτοὶ, αὐτὲσ, αὐτά (εἶναι)
I have	écho	ἔχω
You have (sing)	échis	ἔχεις
he, she, it has	échi	ἔχει

we have	échomen	ἔχομεν
you have (*pl*)	échete	ἔχετε
they have	échoon	ἔχουν

I am lost	échasa to thrómo	''Εχασα τό δρόμο
I am hungry	pinó	Πεινῶ
I am thirsty	thipsó	Διψῶ
I am tired	íme kourasménos	Εἶμαι κουρασμένος
I am sleepy	nistázo	Νυστάζω
I am ill	íme árostos	Εἶμαι ἄρρωστος
I am poor	íme ftochós	Εἶμαι πτωχός
I love you	sagapóh	Σ'ἀγαπῶ

good	kalá	καλά
bad	kakó	κακό
so-so	étsi kétsi	ἔτσι κ'ἔτσι
slow	sigá sigá	σιγά σιγά
fast	grígora	γρήγορα
big	megálo	μεγάλο
small	mikró	μικρὸ
hot	zésti	ζέστη
cold	crío	κρύω

SHOPS, SERVICES, SIGHTSEEING

I would like	tha íthela	Θὰ ἤθελα
where is?	poo íne?	Ποῦ εἶναι;
how much is it?	póso káni?	Πόσο κάνει;

bakery	artopoíon	᾿Αρτοποιεῖον
bank	trápeza	Τράπεζα
beach	paralía	παραλία
bed	kreváti	κρεββάτι
bookshop	vivliopolío	Βιβλιοπολεῖο
book	vivlío	βιβλίο
butcher	kreopolíon	Κρεοπωλεῖον
church	eklisía	᾿Εκκλησία
cinema	kinimatográfos	Κινηματογράφος
food (see also page 410)	fayitó	φαγητὸ
hospital	nosokomío	Νοσοκομεῖο
hotel	xenodochío	Ξενοδοχεῖο
hot water	neró zestó	νερό ζεστό
house	spíti	σπίτι
kiosk	períptero	Περίπτερο
money	leftá	λεφτά

museum	mooséo	Μουσείο
music	musikí	μουσική
newspaper (foreign)	efimerítha (xéni)	ἐφημερίδα (ξένη)
pharmacy	farmakío	Φαρμακείο
police station	astinomía	Αστυνομία
policeman	astifílaka	ἀστυφύλακα
post office	tachithromío	Ταχυδρομείο
restaurant	estiatório	Ἑστιατόριο
ruins	archéa	ἄρχαῖα
sea	thálassa	Θάλασσα
shoe store	papootsís	Παπουτσῆς
shower	doush	ντούς
student	fititís	φοιτητής
telephone office	OTE	OTE
theatre	théatro	Θέατρο
toilet	tooaléta	τουαλέττα
tourist policeman	astifílaka toristikí	ἀστυφύλακα τουριστηκή
a walk	vólta	βόλτα

TIME

what time is it?	ti óra íne?	Τὶ ὥρα εἶναι;
month	mína	μήνα
week	evthomáda	ἑβδομάδα
day	méra	μέρα
morning	proí	πρωί
afternoon	apóyevma	ἀπόγευμα
evening	vráthi	βράδυ
yesterday	chthés	χθές
today	símera	σήμερα
tomorrow	ávrio	αὔριο
now	tóra	τώρα
later	metá	μετά
it is early	íne norís	Εἶναι νωρίς
it is late	íne argá	Εἶναι ἀργά

TRAVEL DIRECTIONS

I want to go to …	thélo na páo sto (m), sti (f) …	Θέλω νὰ πάω στὸ, στή …
how can I get to …?	póso boró na páo sto (m), sti (f) …?	Πόσο μπορῶ νὰ πάω στὸ, στή …;
can you give me a ride to …?	boréte na me páte sto (m), sti (f) …?	Μπορείτε νὰ μὲ πάτε στὸ, στή …;
where is …?	poo íne …?	Ποῦ εἶναι …;

407

how far is it?	póso makriá íne?	Πόσο μακριὰ εἶναι;
when will the ... come?	póte tha érthi to (n), ee (f), o (m) ...?	Πότε θά ἐρθει τὸ, ἡ, ὁ ...;
when will the ... leave?	póte tha févi to (n), ee (f), o (m) ...?	Πότε θά φύγει τὸ, ἡ, ὁ ...;
from where do I catch ...?	apó poo pérno ...?	'Απὸ ποῦ παίρνω ...;
how long does the trip take?	póso keró tha pári to taxíthi?	Πόσο καιρὸ θὰ πάρη τό ταξίδι;
please show me	parakaló thíkstemoo	Παρακαλῶ δεῖξτέμου
how much is it?	póso káni?	Πόσο κάνει;
the (nearest) town	o horió (o pió kondá)	τὸ χωριὸ (τὸ πιό κοντά)
good trip	kaló taxíthi	Καλὸ ταξίδι
here	ethó	ἐδῶ
there	ekí	ἐκεῖ
close	kondá	κοντά
far	makriá	μακριά
full	yemáto	γεμάτο
left	aristerá	ἀριστερά
right	thexiá	δεξιά
forward	embrós	ἐμπρός
back	píso	πίσω
north	vória	Βόρεια
south	nótia	Νότια
east	anatoliká	'Ανατολικά
west	thitiká	Δυτικά
corner	gonía	γωνία
square	platía	πλατεῖα

DRIVING

where can I rent ...?	poo boró na enikiáso ...?	Ποῦ μπορῶ νά ἐνοικιάσω ...;
a car	énan aftokínito	ἕνα αὐτοκίνητο
a motorbike	éna mechanáki	ἕνα μηχανάκι
a bicycle	éna pothílaton	ἕνα ποδήλατον
where may I buy petrol?	poo boró nagorázso venzíni?	Ποῦ μπορῶ ν'ἀγοράζω βενζίνη;
where is a garage?	poo íne éna garáz?	Ποῦ εἶναι ἕνα γκαράζ;
a mechanic	éna mikanikó	ἕνα μηχανικό
a map	éna chárti	ἕνα χάρτη
where is the road	poo íne o thrómos	Ποῦ εἶναι ὁ δρόμος

408

to . . . ?	yiá . . . ?	γιά . . . ;
where does this road lead?	poo pái aftós o thrómos?	Ποῦ πάει αὐτὸσ ὁ δρόμος;
is the road good?	íne kalós o thrómos?	Εἶναι καλός ὁ δρόμος;

exit	éxothos	ΕΞΟΔΟΣ
entrance	ísothos	ΕΙΣΟΔΟΣ
danger	kínthinos	ΚΙΝΔΥΝΟΣ
slow	argá	ΑΡΓΑ
no parking	apagorévete ee státhmevsis	ΑΠΑΓΟΡΕΥΕΤΑΙ Η ΣΤΑΘΜΕΥΣΙΣ
keep out	apagorévete ee ísothos	ΑΠΑΓΟΡΕΥΕΤΑΙ Η ΕΙΣΟΔΟΣ

NUMBERS

one	énas (*m*), mía (*f*), éna (*n*)	῎Ενας, μία, ἔνα
two	théo	Δύο
three	tris (*m, f*), tría (*n*)	Τρεῖς, τρία
four	téseres (*m, f*), téssera (*n*)	Τέσσερεις, τέσσερα
five	pénde	Πέντε
six	éxi	῎Εξι
seven	eptá	῾Επτά
eight	októ	᾿Οκτώ
nine	ennéa	᾿Εννέα
ten	théka	Δέκα
eleven	ántheka	῎Ενδεκα
twelve	thótheka	Δώδεκα
thirteen	theka tría	Δεκατρία
fourteen	theka téssera	Δεκατέσσερα
twenty	íkosi	Εἴκοσι
twenty-one	ikosi énas/mía/éna	Εἴκοσι ένας/μία/ένα
thirty	triánda	Τριάντα
forty	saránda	Σαράντα
fifty	penínda	Πενήντα
sixty	exínda	᾿Εξήντα
seventy	evthomínda	῾Εβδομήντα
eighty	ogthónda	᾿Ογδόντα
ninety	enenínda	᾿Ενενήντα
one hundred	ekató	῾Εκατό
one thousand	chília	Χίλια

MONTHS/DAYS

January	Ianooários	Ἰανουάριος
February	Fevrooários	Φεβρουάριος
March	Mártios	Μάρτιος
April	Aprílios	Ἀπρίλιος
May	Máios	Μάϊος
June	Ioónios	Ἰούνιος
July	Ioólios	Ἰούλιος
August	Avgoostos	Αὔγουστος
September	Septémvrios	Σεπτέμβριος
October	Októvrios	Ὀκτώβριος
November	Noémvrios	Νοέμβριος
December	Thekémvrios	Δεκέμβριος
Sunday	Kiriakí	Κυριακή
Monday	Theftéra	Δευτέρα
Tuesday	Tríti	Τρίτη
Wednesday	Tetárti	Τετάρτη
Thursday	Pémpti	Πέμπτη
Friday	Paraskeví	Παρασκευή
Saturday	Sávato	Σάββατο

TRANSPORT

the airport	to arothrómio	τὸ ἀεροδρόμιο
the aeroplane	to aropláno	τὸ ἀεροπλάνο
the bus station	ee stási ton leoforíon	ἡ στάση τῶν λεωφορείων
the bus	o leoforío	τὸ λεωφορεῖο
the railway station	o stathmós too tréno	ὁ σταθμὸς τοῦ τραίνου
the train	to tréno	τὸ τραῖνο
the port	to limáni	τὸ λιμάνι
the port authority	to limenarchíon	τὸ λιμεναρχεῖον
the ship	to plíon or to karávi	τὸ πλοῖον/τὸ καράβι
the steamship	to vapóri	τὸ βαπόρι
the car	to aftokínito	τὸ αὐτοκίνητον
a ticket	éna isitírio	ἕνα εἰσιτήριο

OPEKTIKA	**Orektiká**	**Hors d'oeuvre**
Τσατσίκι	tsatsíki	yoghurt and cucumbers
Ἐληὲς	eliés	olives
Ντολμάδες	dolmáthes	stuffed vine leaves
Διάφορα ὀρεκτικά	thiáfora orektiká	diverse hors d'oeuvre

410

ΣΟΥΠΕΣ	Soupes	Soups
Αὐγολεμονο	ávgolemono	egg and lemon soup
Σοῦπα ἀπό χόρτα	soúpa apó chórta	vegetable soup
Ψαρόσουπα	psarósoupa	fish soup
Μαγειρίτσα	magirítsa	giblets in egg and lemon soup

ΖΥΜΑΡΙΚΑ	Zimárika	Pasta and Rice
Πιλάφι σάλτσα	piláfi sáltsa	pilaf
Σπαγέττο	spagéto	spaghetti
Μακαρόνια	makarónia	macaroni

ΛΑΔΕΡΑ	Lathéra	Vegetables
Πατάτες	patátes	potatoes
Ντομάτες γεμιστές	tomátes yemistés	stuffed tomatoes
Μελιτζάνες γεμιστές	melitzánes yemistés	stuffed aubergines/ eggplants
Πιπερίες γεμιστές	piperíes yemistés	stuffed peppers
Φασόλια	vasólia	beans
Φακή	fakí	lentils
Χόρτα	chórta	greens

ΨΑΡΙΑ	Psária	Fish
᾽Αστακὸς	astakós	lobster
Καλαμαράκια	kalamarákia	little squid
Ὀκταπόδι	oktapóthi	octopus
Μπαρμπούνια	barboúnia	red mullet
Γαρίδες	garíthes	prawns (shrimps)
Μαρίδες	maríthes	whitebait
Συναγρίδα	sinagrítha	sea bream
Μπακαλιάρος (σκορδαλιά)	bakaliáros (skorthaliá)	fried cod (with garlic and vinegar sauce)
Στρείδια	stríthia	oysters
Λιθρίνια	lithrínia	bass

ΑΥΓΑ	Avgá	Eggs
᾽Ομελέτα Ζαμπὸν	omeléta zambón	ham omelette
᾽Ομελέτα μὲ τυρί	omeléta me tirí	cheese omelette
Αὐγά τηγαιτά (μπρουγὲ)	avgá tigetá (brouyé)	fried (scrambled) eggs

ΕΝΤΡΑΔΕΣ	Entráthes	Entrées
Κοτόπουλο	kotópulo	chicken
Μπιφτέκι	biftéki	beefsteak

411

Κουνέλι	kounéli	rabbit
Παστίτσιο	pastítsio	meat and macaroni
Μουσακά	mousaká	meat and aubergine/ eggplant with white sauce
Σκώτι	skóti	liver
Μοσχάρι	moskári	veal
Αρνάκι	arnáki	lamb
Μπριζόλας χοιρινὲς	brizólas chirinés	pork chops
Σουτςουκάκια	tsoutsoukákia	meat balls in tomato sauce
Λουκάνικο	lukániko	sausage

ΣΧΑΡΑΣ	**Skáras**	**Grills**
Σουβλάκια	souvlákia	meat on a skewer
Κοτολέτες	kotolétes	veal chops
Κότα ψητή	kóta psití	roast chicken
Κεφτέδες	keftéthes	meat balls

ΣΑΛΑΤΕΣ	**Salátes**	**Salads**
Ντομάτες	tomátes	tomatoes
Ἀγγουράκι	angouráki	cucumbers
Ρωσσικὴ	rossikí	Russian salad
Χοριατικιά	choriatikiá	village salad with cheese
Κολοκυθάκια	kolokithákia	courgettes/zucchini

ΤΥΡΙΑ	**Tiriá**	**Cheeses**
Τυρόπιττα	tirópitta	cheese pie
Φέτα	féta	goat cheese
Κασέρι	kaséri	hard buttery cheese
Ροκφὸρ	rokfór	blue cheese
Γραβιέρα	graviéra	like Gruyère

ΓΛΥΚΑ	**Glyká**	**Sweets**
Παγωτό	pagotó	ice cream
Κουραμπιέδες	kourabiéthes	white Greek biscuits
Λουκομάδες	loukomáthes	hot honey fritters
Χαλβά	halvá	sesame seed sweet
Μπακλαβά	baklavá	honey pastry
Γαλακτομπούρεκκον	galaktoboúrekkon	custard pastry
Γιαοῦρτι	yiaoúrti	yoghurt
Ρυζόγαλο	rizógalo	rice pudding
Καταϊφι	kataífi	shredded wheat with nuts and honey

Μπουγάτσα	bougátsa	custard tart
Ἀμιγδαλωτά	amigthalotá	almond cookies

ΦΡΟΥΤΑ	**Frúta**	**Fruit**
Ἀχλάδι	akláthi	pear
Πορτοκάλι	portokáli	orange
Μῆλο	mílo	apple
Ροδάκινο	rothákino	peach
Πεπόνι	pepóni	melon
Καρπούζι	karpoúzi	watermelon
Δαμάσκηνο	thamáskino	plum
Σύκα	síka	fig
Σταφύλια	stafília	grapes
Μπανάνα	banána	banana
Βερύκοκο	veríkoko	apricot

		Miscellaneous
Νερό (βραστό)	neró (vrastó)	water (boiled)
Ψωμί	psomí	bread
Βούτυρο	voútiro	butter
Μέλι	méli	honey
Μαρμελάδα	marmelátha	jam
Ἁλάτι	aláti	salt
Πιπέρι	pipéri	pepper
Ζάχαρη	zákari	sugar
Λάδι	láthi	oil
Ξύδι	xíthi	vinegar
Μουστάρδα	mustárda	mustard
Λεμόνι	lemóni	lemon
Γάλα	gála	milk
Τσάϊ	chái	tea
Σοκολάτα	sokoláta	chocolate
Λογαριασμὸ	logariasmó	the bill/check
Στὴν ἡγειά σας!	stíniyásas	to your health!

FURTHER READING

Clogg, Richard and Yannopoulos, George, *Greece Under Military Rule* (London 1972)

Dakin, Douglas, *The Unification of Greece 1770–1923* (London 1972)

Heurtley, W. A., Darby, H. C., Crawley, C. W. and Woodhouse, C. M., *A Short History of Greece from Early Times to 1964* (Cambridge and New York 1966)

Kousoulas, George D., *Revolution and Defeat: The Story of the Greek Communist Party* (Oxford 1965)

Legg, Keith R., *Politics in Modern Greece* (Stanford, Calif., 1969)

Mavrogordato, J., *Modern Greece 1800–1921* (London 1931)

O'Ballance, Edgar, *The Greek Civil War 1944–1949* (London and New York 1966)

Pallis, A. A., *Greece's Anatolian Adventure and After* (London 1937)

Papandreou, Andreas, *Democracy at Gunpoint* (New York 1970, London 1971)

Stephens, Robert, *Cyprus: A Place of Arms* (London and New York 1966)

Sweet-Escott, Bickham, *Greece: A Political and Economic Survey 1939–53* (London and New York 1954)

Ware, Timothy, *The Orthodox Church* (Baltimore, Ma. 1963, London 1964)

Woodhouse, C. M., *The Greek War of Independence* (London 1952, New York 1967)

Woodhouse, C. M., *Modern Greece: A Short History* (London 1977)

In London a likely place to find these books is at the Hellenic Book Service, 122 Charing Cross Road, London WC2, tel. (01) 836 7071. In Athens the best bookstore for English books on Greek subjects can be found on 4 Nikis St, Syntagma Square, and is called Eseftheroudakis.

INDEX

Islands are indexed both individually and within each group of islands. Alternative spellings or names are shown in brackets.

417

URBAN LANGUAGE SERIES

ROGER W. SHUY, GENERAL EDITOR

TEACHING BLACK CHILDREN TO READ

EDITED BY

JOAN C. BARATZ & ROGER W. SHUY

CENTER FOR APPLIED LINGUISTICS : 1969

INTRODUCTION TO THE SERIES

The Urban Language Series is intended to make available the
results of recent sociolinguistic research concerned with the
position and role of language in a large metropolitan area.
The series includes descriptions of certain aspects of urban
language, particularly English, as well as theoretical considerations relevant to such descriptions. The series also includes studies dealing with fieldwork techniques, matters of
pedagogy and relationships of urban language study to other
disciplines. Where appropriate and feasible, accompanying
tape recordings will be made available. Specifically excluded
from consideration are aspects of English as a second language
or second language learning in general.

It is hoped that the Urban Language Series will prove useful to several different kinds of readers. For the linguist,
the series will provide data for the study of language performance and for the development of linguistic theory. Historically, linguists have formulated theory from individual
rather than group performance. They have had to generalize
about what constitutes "standard" or "non-standard" from intuitive judgments or from very limited data. This series is
designed to make available large portions of language data as
well as analyses in order to broaden the knowledge from which
linguistic generalizations may come.

For the sociologist the series will provide access to
the nature of social stratification by means of language. It

is the contention of some scholars that a person's use of
language is one of the most important cues to his social
status, age, race or sex.

For the educator, the series will offer among other
things a description of the very things which are most
crucial to the classroom—the linguistic correlates which
separate the accepted from the unaccepted.

Although the value of focussed attention on the special
problems of urban language has been recognized for some time,
relatively few substantial studies have been published. To
a certain degree, this series represents a pioneering venture
on the part of the Center for Applied Linguistics.

Roger W. Shuy
Director, Sociolinguistics Program
Center for Applied Linguistics

TEACHING BLACK CHILDREN TO READ

PREFACE

Reports from city after city with substantial numbers of
economically deprived black children have indicated that
reading achievement for this group is well below the national
norms. In general, the reading failure of these children has
been viewed as one requiring remediation, i.e. a <u>deficit model</u>
has been employed which implies that there is something wrong
with the child that has prevented him from learning to read.
This something is most often presumed to have a neuro-
physiological base (e.g. dyslexia) or to be related to environmental factors that are presumed to be detrimental to
the acquisition of reading skills (e.g. no books in the home).

   The present volume is also concerned with the failure of
black children in our public schools. It is, however, not
concerned with remediation; rather, its focus is on literacy.
The primary concern of the papers in this collection is that
of language and the relationship of language to reading. Not
remediation but how to teach reading is the issue here.

   Although each author suggests different ways of handling
certain aspects of the child's speech in teaching reading,
all the papers in this volume recognize and deal with the
role of the child's own language behavior in the process of
learning to read.

   These papers were written over approximately a four-year
time span. They were developed in most cases independently,
although some drew on the insights of the earlier papers.

ix

Several of the articles were written specifically for this volume while others are reprinted from various journals.

McDavid states in his paper the fundamental proposition that "a reading program in any language, at any stage in a student's career, is likely to be effective in proportion to its use of the language habits that the student has acquired in speaking." His focus is on phoneme-grapheme relationships, particularly as they conflict across regional dialects.

Goodman also takes as basic to any reading program the premise that "literacy is built on the base of the child's existing language." He focuses on dialect differences that can impede learning to read, and suggests possible solutions which might avoid these barriers.

Labov discusses the difficulties in teaching black children to read arising from the "ignorance of standard English rules on the part of speakers of non-standard English" and from the "ignorance of non-standard English rules on the part of teachers and text writers." His discussion of sources of reading problems for non-standard speakers deals mainly with differences in phonology between standard and Negro non-standard English.

Baratz takes as a basic premise that the reading problem in the United States in regard to the black population is no different from literacy problems of emergent nations around the world. She feels that the child's different syntactic structures must be incorporated into the teaching procedures. A difference model, rather than a deficit model, is proposed for teaching black children to read.

Shuy also focuses on differences in the child's language system as a basis for suggested developments of beginning reading materials. He provides a possible linguistic rationale for consideration in the construction of such materials.

Fasold's paper deals with some of the problems of orthographic presentation of dialect materials to children. A systematic framework for the use of standard orthography in dialect texts is presented.

The Wolfram and Fasold paper is an attempt to illustrate some practical applications of the theoretical considerations of several of the preceding articles.

In the final paper, Stewart, who for some time now has been a staunch advocate of dialect-based texts, also focuses sharply on the child's different language system. He discusses the nature of the child's reading problem with particular emphasis on language interference as a prime source for the child's failure in school. While he calls for the use of dialect materials, Stewart elaborates on some of the difficulties inherent in constructing and programming such materials.

During the four-year time span of these papers there have been changes in the rhetoric concerning the American Negro. In McDavid's paper (1964), and even more so in Goodman's paper (1965), although some of the dialect speakers that are being described are clearly Negroes, no reference to race is made--the black man was still "the invisible man". Finally, however, the overt identification is made: Labov (1966-67) addresses himself to describing reading problems of Negro children, while in 1968, Baratz, Fasold, Shuy, and Wolfram use such terms as black, Negro inner-city, ghetto dwellers, and Afro-American synonymously.

J.C.B.
R.W.S.

Washington, D.C.
January 1969

CONTENTS

DIALECTOLOGY AND THE TEACHING OF READING

by Raven I. McDavid, Jr.

Dialect associations of phonemes and graphemes may vary strikingly from one part of the culture to another. English patterns of phonemic-graphemic correspondences involve several layers of cultural convention, and some of the practices of some subcultural subdialects may be sharply at variance with the normal practices of a speaker. These complexities of association make it difficult for someone not only to spell a word he normally confines to the spoken informal style, but to pronounce a word which he is accustomed to meeting only in print. And if words of the last group are frequently mispronounced in oral reading, there is a reasonable supposition that they will be as frequently misapprehended in silent reading. This supposition, like many others, needs to be tested, but pending disproof, I shall continue to assert it.

More important than this, and amusing examples that may be drawn from anyone's recollections,[1] is the basic problem: to what extent do dialect differences in American English complicate the task of teaching in American schools the reading of matter written or printed in English? I shall here use reading in its widest sense, to include not only simple

. . . .

Reprinted by permission from The Reading Teacher 18:3.206-13 (December 1964).

literacy but the skill—the art, in fact—of understanding
materials of increasing complication, whether scientific or
aesthetic in their essential bent.

Here we have to ask ourselves a few questions, some of
which, like desperate Pilates, we cannot expect to have adequately answered in this life: (1) What is the process of
learning to read, in linguistic and sociolinguistic terms?
(2) What is dialectology? (3) What is the general dialectal
situation in American English? (4) How does this situation
affect the problem of the classroom teacher, as a teacher of
reading? (5) How much do we know about various kinds of dialect differences in American English? How much more can we
hope to know? (6) How do these differences, as we know them,
affect the problem of the classroom teacher of reading in the
American dialectal situation?

What is the process of learning to read, in linguistic
and sociolinguistic terms? On this question I gladly yield to
the greater expertise of the professionals. There are many
forces converging to a point when a teacher guides a student
into the ability to understand the graphic representation of
the language the student can already manipulate orally and understand aurally. But even here a few propositions can be restated:

A reading program, in any language, at any stage in a
student's career, is likely to be effective in proportion to
its use of the language habits that the student has acquired
in speaking.

All children by the age of six use extremely complicated
syntactic patterns; furthermore, children's vocabularies are
frequently underestimated, rarely overestimated.

Our culture demands a high degree of reading skill of
anyone who hopes to participate adequately in its benefits;
but conversely, more than any other culture ever known, it
provides frequent opportunities for children to develop at

an early age associations between the language and its graphic
representation. It is an ironic fact that the culturally
most deprived groups actually make the greatest use of the
entertainment medium that provides the greatest opportunities
for developing these associations—television.

All instructional programs which are concerned with
developing skills might learn from the intensive language
programs of World War II and develop drill materials based
on functional situations and substitutions in patterns.
Admittedly limited in my knowledge of the subculture of professional teaching of reading, I find none of the so-called
basal readers that has yet done this.

What is dialectology? Dialectology is the study of
language differences within a speech community, with a dialect
simply defined as a variety of a language, generally mutually
intelligible with other varieties of that language, but set
off from them by a unique complex of features of pronunciation, grammar, and vocabulary. Dialect, thus used, is not
a derogatory term but a descriptive one; it is equally applicable to the Gullah of Edisto Island (locally /'edisto
'ɔilənt/) and to the quaint and curious subspecies of cultivated Eastern New England speech employed by the Senators
from Massachusetts. These differences are often apprehended
intuitively or informally, but they can always be classified
objectively provided comparable data have been elicited.
The methods of eliciting such data and the techniques of
classification have been described on many occasions: the
handbooks of the linguistic atlases of Italy and of New England present rather detailed accounts of methods and procedures.

What is the general dialectal situation in American
English? Dialects in American English are less sharply set
off from each other than those in British English or in any

of the better known languages of Western Europe. With few
exceptions, an American from one region can understand one
from another region without difficulty. The more recently a
part of the country has been settled, the less sharp are the
dialect differences; in the Rocky Mountain and Pacific Coast
states there are no differences as great as those between
Boston, New York, and Albany.

Second, there is no single regional variety of speech
that has established itself as prestigious, and therefore to
be imitated more than all others. In Italy the educated
speech of Florence has been preferred since the fourteenth
century; in France, the Francian of Paris; in England, the
upper-class speech of London, now half embalmed in the guise
of Received Pronunciation (RP). But in the United States
the educated speech of Boston, New York, Atlanta, Chicago,
San Francisco or Seattle stands on a par with that of Richmond or Charleston or St. Louis or any other cultural center.
The time is largely past when a teacher attempts to impose
on his students a dialect from another region.

Third, there is extreme mobility, both regional and
social, epitomized by the fact that the great-grandson of an
Irish common laborer was our last president, and was succeeded
by the son of a southern marginal farmer. The son of an Italian immigrant has been secretary of Health, Education and
Welfare, and the rolls of Congress are studded with those
whose ancestors were the humblest of people, who rose by
their own merits. And the records of internal migration are
at least as complex, as any linguistic geographer can tell
us. The movements of Daniel Boone from Virginia to North
Carolina to Kentucky and finally to Missouri typify the
search of Americans for new frontiers, physical or economic.
The migrations of children of servicemen or Methodist ministers have always been proverbial; today the children of

corporation executives and junior executives are also likely
to change schools every few years. And teachers themselves,
from all over the nation, are drawn westward by California
gold, or to the large metropolitan areas by higher salaries
and pensions and better working conditions. The typical kindergarten or first grade classroom today is likely to show a
wide range of regional or social dialects, or both.

How does the dialectal situation affect the teacher of
reading? This dialectal situation means that the teacher
must accept a multi-valued conception of standard English,
with a consequent variety of phonemic-graphemic associations.
He must also be ready to face the problem of introducing to
reading materials in the standard language children for whom
standard English is an alien idiom and the dominant culture
an unknown culture.

How much do we know about various kinds of dialect differences? Fortunately, we have at our disposal a large body
of evidence on regional and social differences within American English. Such broad-gauge studies as the Linguistic Atlas
project are largely unpublished as yet, but several significant derivative books and monographs and a spate of articles
have appeared. Other more specialized studies, such as
C.K. Thomas's investigations of the low-back vowels before
/-r-/, have given valuable information on particular problems.
Several specific communities have been investigated, with
emphasis on social differences in dialect; especially notable
is the study of New York's Lower East Side by William Labov,
and that of Metropolitan Chicago by Lee Pederson. Viewed in
terms of linguistic phenomena, we have the following kinds
of information:

1. A delineation of most of the significant dialect
areas east of the Mississippi, and of those in several states
farther westward.

2. As far as segmental phonemes are concerned, rather detailed information on differences in the phonemic systems of these dialects, on the incidence of the phonemes in particular words, and on the phonetic qualities of the phonemes.

3. Rather good sampling of variations in verb forms; less adequate sampling of other matters of inflection and of most matters of syntax.

4. Rather detailed information on representative selections of the folk vocabulary of older America, particularly of the folk vocabulary of rural areas; less adequate information about regional and social differences in the lexicon of more recent aspects of culture, especially of the characteristic vocabulary of urban areas. Enough information, in any case, to permit tentative generalizations about the regional differences in culture, somewhat more accurate than the impressionistic feelings we all have. Certainly enough to realize the complexity of urban culture, where chitterlings and bagels may be sold in the same store, and the daughter of two white Anglo-Saxon Protestants (wasps, familiarly) may come home from kindergarten talking of dreidels.

5. Very little about regional or social variation in the suprasegmentals: stress, intonation, transitions, and terminals. Almost all the evidence on such variations is to be found in nontechnical observations, such as Mencken's summary of the intonation patterns of English in the Pennsylvania German areas. Exceptions to this generality are a few pages in Pike's Intonation of American English (1942) and such incidental comments that in such words as nonsense Sledd and I, like many Middle Westerners, have the sequence /ˊ + ˆ/, but the phonetic qualities of our stress phonemes are such that to Middle Westerners like Joos we seem to be saying /ˊ | ˊ/. The whole range of regional and social variation in these complex phenomena needs detailed investigation.

The same observation can be made about the dialectology of paralanguage and kinesics; again, as with the dialectology of the suprasegmentals, there has been no systematic research, but a number of shrewd intuitive guesses. For these fields, as with the suprasegmentals, we can all concede that the phenomena have only recently been considered systematically structured as a part of human communication, so that the techniques of dialectal investigation would take some time to develop. However, our objective appreciation of the delay in no way mitigates the urgency of the investigation, nor lessens our appreciation of such pioneering work as has been conducted by Basil Bernstein at the University of London or by Rufus Baehr at the University of Chicago, limited as their conclusions may be.

6. Again, there is little systematic evidence available about regional and social differences in children's speech, or differences in the speech of equivalent social groups in the same region but residing in cities, suburbs, small towns, and rural communities. This in no way detracts from the value of Miss Strickland's magnificent study, or of the Loban study at California, or of the work just beginning on the Chicago South Side. It simply recognizes the need to learn far more than we have yet learned.

How do these differences affect the teacher of reading? The implications of this current state of our knowledge of American dialects for the practical work of teaching reading will demand the cooperation of several kinds of scholars and the devotion of skilled teachers. What follows represents the thinking of one person who feels that it is important to put the resources of dialectology, regional and social, at the service of society, and who is willing both to offer his mite and to listen to suggestions as to how that mite can be most profitably invested. Some observations follow.

Whatever the disadvantages of our current system of
writing down English, we are not likely to find a better one
generally adopted. We must assume that students in our
schools are going to have to use the conventional English
alphabet when they read. While we should not discourage the
experimental use of such devices as the Pitman Augmented
Alphabet, we must remember that they are strictly interim
devices, and their use must allow for a systematic phasing
out, and the mastering of the conventional system. Furthermore, any such interim device must be tested in terms of its
adequacy in representing the units of the sound system that
contrast in the various standard dialects of American English.

The regional differences in children's speech are probably diminishing, though undoubtedly there are differences in
experience that might be considered in any program. On the
other side of the coin, however, television now brings a wide
assortment of vicarious experiences to most children in most
areas; one might think in terms of a reading program that
would enable the children to investigate more widely on their
own the worlds of Robin Hood, the cowboys, the spacemen—or
the wide range of materials offered by Garfield Goose—when
the television is being repaired or repossessed.

Social differences present a more complicated problem.
Under the older demographic pattern, most phonological and
lexical details were shared throughout a community, and the
social differences were largely matters of grammar—differences
in particular morphological or syntactic features (e.g., seed
vs. saw, all to once vs. all at once). It was assumed that
newer immigrant groups would have peculiarities of speech,
but that assimilation to the normal patterns of their communities would gradually take place; and by and large this
expectation has been fulfilled, as one may observe from
listening to any presidential news conference. However, in

recent years the prevailing pattern in American cities has
been altered to something once restricted to the rural areas
of the Southeast, and what had been the ideal of a human-
istically oriented plantation culture modeling itself on its
interpretations of the classical societies is now fulfilled
as the nightmare of a technologically determined urban and
suburban civilization, where a high degree of literacy is
essential for any true participation in the benefits of
society. The mudsill of happy slaves on which Southern apolo-
gists erected their myth of an Aristotelian-ordered society
has now become a frustrated and properly resentful, low
skilled and often unemployable proletariat, potentially
threatening the stability of urban society. Set off by skin
color, by ignorance of the values of the dominant culture,
and by a dialectal cleavage which contrasts the pronunciation,
grammar, and vocabulary of southeastern folk-speech and North
Central common and cultivated speech, they find integrated
schools, fair employment, and open occupancy a cruel mockery,
as working-class whites, themselves anthropologically unsophisticated, join the sauve qui peut in search of a suburban haven.

The usual teacher, compulsively in pursuit of middle-
class norms, has no conception of the environment of deprivation, exploitation, frustration, and violence in which the
lower-class urban Negroes live. The normal curiosity of
children about the world is inhibited by properly fearful
parents; absence of mothers means the lack of anyone for the
children to talk to; books are nonexistent; and in a caco-
phonous world the television—potentially a powerful instrument for acculturation—becomes just another source of background noise.

The educational advancement of this new urban group—
which means basically the improvement of their ability to

read—constitutes the greatest challenge to American education. It is likely that teaching some form of standard English as a second language will be necessary; and it might be
easier to start this second language in the kindergartens or
earlier, and use this as the vehicle of reading, and hence
of introduction to the values of the dominant culture.

Paralanguage and kinesics are largely cued into reading
materials by lexical devices, e.g., such verbs as sauntered,
gesticulated, simpered, and whined. Some of this comes into
oral reading in the early grades; relating to it is important
for silent reading in the advanced grades and in college, to
say nothing of later life. Whether these cues can be grasped
informally—as is the usual procedure today—or should be
formally indicated is something that needs exploration.
Where regional and social differences occur, some accounting
may be necessary, but we need to discover those differences
first.

Suprasegmentals, like segmentals, are not adequately
represented by the conventional writing system, but have been
conventionalized over some four centuries by generations of
editors and printers. Where regional and social differences
occur—especially in the same classroom—so that the same
gross phonetics may signal different meanings or different
gross phonetics signal the same meaning, one may hope that
the future teachers will be sophisticated enough to recognize
what is going on and to explain the differences to the student
(and one is unrealistic if he thinks that children in the
early grades cannot detect such differences and wonder about
them). In most cases, it is unlikely that there will be
serious differences in the positions of the terminals (Trager
and Smith's single-bar, double-bar, double-cross), and there
seems to be no reason for failing to order line-breaks in
elementary reading materials according to the positions of

the terminals. (This, I am told by some experienced teachers
of reading, is frowned upon, as interfering with the development of a wide eye-span; but what profiteth a man to span
whole lines at a glance and miss the structural cues to meaning? It would seem that there is really no basic conflict,
but only a question of ordering materials.)

The problems of general differences in the regional and
social vocabularies have been approached in the analysis of
the potential regional and social differences in children's
speech. But there will always be a problem of relating
visual signal and speech signal in words that are associated
primarily with either the spoken or the written side of the
language. A legendary episode in my childhood concerns a
time in 1914 when I brought in the evening paper and remarked
from the headline "/jépən/ (Japan) enters the war" (less
heinous in my community perhaps than elsewhere, since a local
tobacconist was named Gapen /gépən/). And I still recall my
first attempts to render negotiations and cooperate (respectively /nígətèsənz/ and /kúpərèt/, or a rather good second-
grader's /vέləkəsi/ and /mǽŋgi/ for velocity and mangy. Conversely, familiar childhood words like fice or rinktums or
larrows (to pull a few out of my own recollection) may lack
an established orthographic form altogether. Because a dialect is associated with some kind of subculture, there may
be differences in the most feasible words to introduce in a
given set of reading materials.

In the early grades, it would seem that the grammatical
problems, generally social rather than regional, can be
handled as matters of selection, careful allocation to context, and pattern drill. The forms saw and seen are both a
part of the language experience of every American child; the
problem is to make sure that he regularly selects the forms
I saw and I have seen. This of course may be related to the

problem of teaching the standard usage as a second language,
and of associating all reading materials with this usage.
Problems like associating the /-s, -z, -əz/ allomorphs with
the third singular present indicative, where the home dialect
has /φ/, must certainly be handled in this fashion.

Perhaps the most important—and certainly the most
clearly systematized—impact of dialectology on the teaching
of reading will come in the area of phonemic-graphemic associations in the segmentals. (Several scholars, notably
Charles F. Hockett of Cornell, are investigating the relative
frequency of certain kinds of phonemic-graphic associations.)

There are two problems to be considered: (1) structural
differences, presence or absence of such contrasts as do/dew,
cot/caught, morning/mourning, have/halve; (2) differences in
the incidence of phonemes, as found in the variant pronunciations of coop, on, fog. These must be related to the necessity of introducing at the earliest possible moment such forms
as a, the, and the like, the desirability of proceeding from
grosser to finer graphic distinctions, and the distribution
of the learning load so that too many sound-symbol associations
are not thrust upon the student at once. (Leonard Bloomfield,
C.C. Fries, and other linguists have recognized the importance
of getting into the program, as early as possible, the high-
frequency function words.) And somehow, not too late, the
student must be conditioned to the morphographic side of the
English orthographical system, so that he can associate history
and historical and so on.

A complex dialectal problem develops when there is another
language in use at home, whether Acadian French, Milwaukee
German, Yiddish, or Puerto Rican Spanish. This is often further complicated when the students or the parents first encounter English as a nonstandard type. However, these are
best treated here as differences in degree and not in kind.

A student of dialectology is not, <u>per se</u>, an authority on all problems of reading, or necessarily on any of them. His role is, rather, that of a consultant, to collaborate with the others involved in this most important problem in American education—to be a devil's advocate if necessary— by attempting to anticipate some of the problems teachers and students may have in using materials in a different cultural situation from that for which they were originally designed.

NOTES

1. Humorous anecdotes can be documented from such sources as, for example, Mayor Collins of Boston who, on meeting the aristocratic Senator Hoare at a social gathering, asked, "And how is Mrs. W.?"

DIALECT BARRIERS TO READING COMPREHENSION

by Kenneth S. Goodman

The task of learning to read is not an easy one. But it's a lot easier to learn to read one's mother tongue than to learn to read a foreign language, one which the learner does not speak. Actually each of us speaks a particular dialect of a language. Each dialect is distinguished from all other dialects by certain features as: some of its sounds, some of its grammar, some of its vocabulary. The dialect which the child learns in the intimacy of his own home is his mother tongue. All physically normal children learn to speak a dialect. Whatever happens to his language during his life, however fluent and multilingual he may become, this native dialect is his most deeply and permanently rooted means of communication.

Since it is true that learning to read a foreign language is a more difficult task than learning to read a native language, it must follow that it is harder for a child to learn to read a dialect which is not his own than to learn to read his own dialect.

This leads to an important hypothesis: <u>The more divergence there is between the dialect of the learner and the</u>

. . . .

First read as a paper at the meeting of the International Reading Association in Detroit, Michigan, May 6, 1965, this article is here reprinted by permission from <u>Elementary English</u> 42:8.853-60 (December 1965).

dialect of learning, the more difficult will be the task of learning to read.

This is a general hypothesis. It applies to all learners. If the language of the reading materials or the language of the teacher differs to any degree from the native speech of the learners some reading difficulty will result. To some extent also there is divergence between the immature speech of the young learner and adult language norms in the speech community. Children have mastered most but not all of the sounds and syntax of adult speech. A further divergence reflects the fact that older members of any language community are less influenced by language change than are the youth. Thus the teacher may cling to language which is obsolescent in form or meaning. Books particularly lag behind language change since they freeze language at the date of composition. Though this paper is mainly concerned with gross dialect differences it must be remembered, then, that the reading problems discussed apply to some extent to all learners because minor dialect differences are features of even homogeneous speech communities.

The Divergent Speaker

For purposes of discussion we'll call the child who speaks a dialect different from that which the school, text, or teacher treats as standard, the divergent speaker. Divergence, of course, is relative and there is by no means agreement on what standard American English is. Divergent is a good term however, because it is neutral as a value term and it is important, perhaps critical, in considering the problems of the divergent speaker to avoid labeling his language as bad, sloppy, or sub-standard. We need to keep clear that, though some dialects may carry more social prestige than others, they are not necessarily more effective in communication. Gleason has said, "It is a safe generalization to

say that all languages are approximately equally adequate
for the needs of the culture of which they are a part."
Dialects represent subcultures. Therefore it can similarly
be said that all dialects are equally adequate for the needs
of the subculture of which they are a part.

Every child brings to school, when he comes, five or six
years of language and of experience. His language is closely
intertwined with the culture of his community; it embodies
the cultural values and structures the way in which he may
perceive his world and communicate his reactions to others.

His language is so well learned and so deeply embossed
on his subconscious that little conscious effort is involved
for him in its use. It is as much a part of him as his skin.
Ironically, well-meaning adults, including teachers who would
never intentionally reject a child or any important characteristic of a child, such as the clothes he wears or the color
of his skin, will immediately and emphatically reject his
language. This hurts him far more than other kinds of rejection because it endangers the means which he depends on
for communication and self-expression.

Things that other people say sound right or funny to a
child depending on whether they fit within the language norms
of his dialect. He has become exceedingly proficient in de-
tecting slight, subtle differences in speech sounds which are
significant in his dialect and he's learned to ignore other
differences in speech sounds that are not significant. He
uses rhythm and pitch patterns of his language with great
subtlety. He enjoys puns on language which employ very slight
variations in relative pitch and stress. By the time divergent speakers are in the middle grades they have learned to
get pleasure from the fact that an in-group pun based on their
common divergent dialect is unfunny to an outsider like their
teacher who doesn't share the dialect.

All children develop vocabulary which falls generally
within the vocabulary pool of their speech community. Through
repeated experience common for their culture they have begun
to develop complex concepts and express them in their mother
tongue.

In every respect the process of language development of
the divergent speaker is exactly the same as that of the
standard speaker. His language when he enters school is just
as systematic, just as grammatical within the norms of his
dialect, just as much a part of him as any other child's is.
Most important, it is a vital link with those important to
him and to the world of men.

There are some differences between the problems of the
divergent speaker in an isolated rural community where a
single dialect is the common speech and has been for several
generations and the problems of the divergent speaker in the
center of one of our great cities. This latter child may
live in a virtual ghetto, but his friends and neighbors represent a variety of language backgrounds. Transplanted regional
dialects become social class dialects. As the city-dweller
grows older he comes into increasing contact with the general
culture and its language. In the home community the idiolects, the personal languages of individuals, will cluster
closely around a dialect prototype. But the dialects of urban
divergent speakers are much more varied and shade off from
distinct divergent dialects to standard speech. Variables
such as family origin, recency of migration, degree of isolation from influences outside the subculture, attitudes
toward self, personal and parental goals are some of the factors which may determine idiolect.

Divergent Languages or Dialects

Language diversity among divergent speakers complicates
the task of understanding the literacy problems which they

have. The basic problems will be the same but the specific
form and degree will vary among individuals.

Teachers need to give careful consideration to the separate characteristics of several kinds of language divergence.
They need to first differentiate immature language from dialect-based divergence. Language which is immature is always
in transition toward adult norms. Teachers need not worry
too much about immaturity in language since desired change
is virtually inevitable. On the other hand, whatever the
teacher does to speed this change is in the direction the
child is moving. He can confirm the teacher's advice in the
speech of his parents. But if the teacher "corrects" the
dialect-based divergent language, this is at cross purposes
with the direction of growth of the child. All his past and
present language experience contradicts what the teacher tells
him. School becomes a place where people talk funny and
teachers tell you things about your language that aren't true.

Another point that needs to be clarified is the difference between standard regional speech and some imaginary
national standard which is correct everywhere and always.
No dialect of American English ever has achieved this status;
instead we have a series of standard regional dialects, the
speech of the cultured people in each area.

It's obvious that a teacher in Atlanta, Georgia, is
foolish to try to get her children to speak like cultured
people in Detroit or Chicago, just as it's foolish for any
teacher to impose universal standard pronunciations which
are not even present in the teacher's own speech. I'm referring to such hypocrisies as insisting that u before e
must always say its own name and therefore Tuesday is
/tyuzdey/. Cultured speech, socially preferred, is not the
same in Boston, New York, Philadelphia, Miami, Baltimore,
Atlanta, or Chicago. The problem, if any, comes when the

Bostonian moves to Chicago, the New Yorker to Los Angeles,
the Atlantan to Detroit. Americans are ethnocentric in regard to most cultural traits but they are doubly so with
regard to language. Anybody who doesn't speak the way I do
is wrong. A green onion is not a scallion. I live in Detróit
not Détroit. I can carry my books to work but not my friends.
Fear ends with an r and Cuba does not. Such ethnocentrisms
are unfortunate among the general public. They may be tragic
among educators. Too often we send children off to speech
correction classes not because their speech needs correction
but because it isn't like ours. Pity the poor child who finds
himself transplanted to a new and strange environment and then
must handle the additional complication of learning to talk
all over again. And, of course, if the child is a migrant
from the rural South to the urban North, his speech marks him
not only as different but socially inferior. He is told not
just that he is wrong but sloppy, careless, vulgar, crude.
His best defense is to be silent.

    In his classroom the divergent speaker finds several
kinds of language being used. First is the language or bundle
of idiolects within dialects which he and his classmates bring
with them as individuals. Represented in their language or
dialect is the language or dialect of their parents and their
speech community. Next there is the language of the teacher
which will exist in at least two forms. There will be the
teacher's informal, unguarded idiolect and his version of correct standard speech; the way he says things off guard; the
way he strives to speak as a cultivated person. Another version of the standard language will be the literary form or
forms the child encounters in books. To this we must add the
artificial language of the basal reader. Artificial language
is not used by anyone in any communicative situation. Some
primerese is artificial to the point of being non-language,
not even a divergent one.

The Consensus of Language and the Uniformity of Print

Two things are in the divergent child's favor. First, all speakers have a range of comprehension which extends beyond the limits of their own dialect. All of us can understand speech which differs from our own, particularly if we are in frequent contact with such speech. As they grow older, urban children are in increasing contact with a number of dialects other than their own. Secondly, the English orthography has one great virtue in its uniformity across dialects. No matter how words are pronounced, printers across the country usually spell them the same. Though we get some mavericks like guilty and judgment, we spell pumpkin the same whether we say pəŋkin or pəmpkən and something the same whether we say səmpthin or səmpm. This standardization of print for a multidialectal speech suggests that part of the problem of learning to read for divergent speakers could be eliminated if teachers let children read in their own dialects and if teachers got rid of the misconception that spelling determines pronunciation. One child asked his teacher how to spell /ræt/. "R-a-t," she said. "No, ma'am," he responded, "I don't mean rat mouse, I mean right now."

Points of Divergence Among Dialects

Now if we examine the areas in which dialects differ we can perhaps shed some light on the barriers divergent readers face. Let us start with sound.

SOUND DIVERGENCE

Intonation

Dialects differ in intonation. Perhaps what makes an unfamiliar dialect most difficult to understand is its unexpected pitch, stress, and rhythm. Teachers often complain when they first begin to work with divergent speakers that they can't understand a word. But after a short time they seem to tune in on the right frequency. They catch on to the

melody of the dialect. Since intonation is essential in
understanding oral language, it is logical to assume that it
must be supplied mentally by readers as they read in order
for comprehension to take place. How much comprehension is
interfered with if the teacher insists on intonation patterns
in oral reading which are unnatural to the divergent reader
can only be conjectured at this time. But there is no doubt
that this is a source of difficulty to some extent.

Phonemes

Phonemes are the significant units of speech sounds
which are the symbols of oral language. All American dialects
share more or less a common pool of phonemes. But not all
dialects use all these phonemes in all the wame ways. They
pattern differently in different dialects. Since phonemes
are really bundles of related sounds rather than single
sounds, it is likely that the range of sounds that compose a
particular phoneme will vary among dialects. Vowel phonemes
are particularly likely to vary. Even within dialects there
are some variations. Good examples are words ending in -og,
such as /dog/, /fog/, /frog/, /log/; or are they /dɔg/, /fɔg/,
/frɔg/, /lɔg/? In my own idiolect I find I say /frɔg/, /fɔg/,
/dɔg/, /lɔg/, but I also say /cag/, /bag/, /smag/.

Obviously, phonics programs which attempt to teach a
relationship between letters and sounds cannot be universally
applicable to all dialects. The basic premise of phonics
instruction is that by teaching a child to associate the
sounds which he hears in oral language with the letters in
written language he will be able to sound out words. But a
divergent speaker can't hear the sounds of standard speech
in his nonstandard dialect because he does not have them or
because they occur in different places in his dialect than
other dialects. The instruction may be not only inappropriate but confusing. When he reads the lesson he may then

be forced to sound out words which are not words in his dialect. To illustrate: Take a child who normally says /də/
rather than /ðə/ and /nəfin/ rather than /nəθin/. Teaching
him that the digraph <th> represents the first sound in the
and the medial consonant in nothing makes him pronounce words
not in his dialect and throws a barrier across his progress
in associating sound and print.

New Reading Materials and Sound Divergence Among Dialects

Recent attempts at producing beginning reading materials
which have regular one-to-one correspondence between letters
and phonemes will not solve this problem and may actually
compound it since there will be a tendency for teachers to
assume that the matched correspondence of sound and letter
is to be uniform throughout the reading materials. For
example, they might assume frog and log to have the same
vowel sound and so teach the sounds to be the same when a
student might well use /a/ as in father in one and /ɔ/ as in
caught in the other. The matched phonemic-graphemic books
assume that there is a uniform spoken set of sounds that can
by ingenuity and counting of data be inscribed with a uniform
written alphabet. This is not true, when the spoken language
is viewed as a national-international phenomenon or when it
is viewed as a local phenomenon in a heterogeneous cultural
country as one of our urban centers.

Transcription of the sound language in ITA faces the
same problems. It has a wider alphabet and can therefore
transcribe more literary and sensible English than the limited
lexicon of the American linguistic readers. The British ITA
materials, however, cannot be read literally except with the
"received pronunciation" of the BBC. When as an American I
read about "levers" in an ITA book I must say /liyvərz/.
The principle that spelling is the same across dialects is
sacrificed and ITA spelling requires pronunciation narrowed

to one special class dialect. Teachers using these materials
need to make some adjustments for the dialects used by themselves and their students. There may be, no doubt is, a
spoken language in common but it is not so uniform as is the
common spelling system.

Another place where sound divergence among dialects affects the handling of reading materials is the traditional
sets of homophones. Homophones, words that sound alike, will
vary from dialect to dialect. Been and bin are homophones in
my speech. In another dialect been would sound the same as
bean and in still another Ben and been would be sounded alike.
Bidialectal students may bring up new sets of homophones.
One teacher asked her class to use so in a sentence. "I don't
mean sew a dress", she said. "I mean the other so." "I got
a so on my leg", responded one of her pupils.

GRAMMAR DIVERGENCE

The Suffix

Inflectional changes in words involve using suffixes or
internal changes in words to change case or tense. In certain dialects of American English speakers say He see me
rather than He sees me. They are not leaving off an s.
There isn't any in their dialect. Similarly, plurals may
not use an s form. I got three brother, is common in Appalachian speech. One teacher reported to me that her pupils
could differentiate between crayon and crayons as written
words and respond to the difference by selecting plural and
singular illustrations, but they read the words the same,
one crayon, two /kræyən/. The problem is not an inability
to see or say the s. It doesn't seem to belong in the pronunciation of crayons. The inflectional ending s to indicate
plural is not in the grammar of this dialect.

Most Americans will add /əz/ to form plurals of words

ending in /s/ /z/ /š/ /ǰ/ /č/ as in <u>busses</u>, <u>mazes</u>, <u>washes</u>, <u>colleges</u>, <u>churches</u>, but in the Blue Ridge Mountains this ending also goes with words ending in /sp/, /st/, /sk/ as in /waspəz/ /pohstəz/ /tæskəz/ (H.A. Gleason, <u>An Introduction to Descriptive Linguistics</u>, New York: Holt, Rinehart and Winston, p. 62). This kind of difference will be reflected in the child's reading. The differences are systematic within the child's dialect. In terms of the school and teacher they may be divergent, or as we say, incorrect, but in terms of the reader and his speech community they are convergent, that is, correct.

No only suffixes vary, but also verb forms and verb auxiliaries. When a child says, "I here, teacher", as the teacher calls the roll, he is not being incomplete. No linking verb is needed in this type of utterance in his dialect. There is a difference in the syntax of his dialect and other American English dialects. Fortunately such differences are minor in American English. One area of difference seems to be the use of verb forms and verb markers. <u>We was going</u>, <u>They done it</u>, <u>We come home</u>, all are examples of this phenomenon.

Vocabulary Divergence

An area of dialect divergence that people are most aware of is vocabulary. Most people are aware that <u>gym shoes</u> in Detroit are <u>sneakers</u> in New York, that in Chicago you may <u>throw</u> but in Little Rock you <u>chunk</u>, that a Minnesota <u>lake</u> would be a <u>pond</u> in New Hampshire. Perhaps there is less awareness of words which have similar but not identical meanings in different dialects. All words have a range of meaning rather than a single meaning. This range may shift from place to place. The meaning of <u>carry</u> may be basically the same in two dialects but some uses will be correct in one dialect but not in the other.

Vocabulary differences among dialects may cause reading difficulty and must be compensated for by the teacher who uses texts printed for a national market.

I've dealt primarily here with the barriers to learning how to read that result when the readers have divergent languages. There are of course other important problems which grow out of the differences in experience, values, and general subculture of the divergent learners. Readers can't comprehend materials which are based on experience and concepts outside their background and beyond their present development.

The Reading Program for Divergent Speakers

Let's address ourselves to a final question. What is currently happening as the divergent speaker learns to read? I've found that divergent speakers have a surprising tendency to read in book dialect. In their oral reading they tend to use phonemes that are not the ones they use in oral language. Their reading often sounds even more wooden and unnatural than most beginners. There is some tendency to read their own dialect as they gain proficiency, but in general it appears that teachers are more successful in teaching preferred pronunciations than reading. What is lacking is the vital link between written and oral language that will make it possible for children to bring their power over the oral language to bear on comprehending written language.

There seem to be three basic alternatives that schools may take in literacy programs for divergent speakers. First is to write materials for them that are based on their own dialect, or rewrite standard materials in their dialect. A second alternative is to teach the children to speak the standard dialect before teaching them to read in the standard dialect. The third alternative is to let the children read the standard materials in their own dialect, that is, to accept the language of the learners and make it their

medium of learning. The first alternative seems to be impractical on several counts. Primarily the opposition of the
parents and the leaders in the speech community must be reck-
oned with. They would reject the use of special materials
which are based on a non-prestigious dialect. They usually
share the view of the general culture that their speech is
not the speech of cultivation and literature. They want
their children to move into the general culture though they
are not sure how this can be brought about.

The second alternative is impractical on pedagogical
grounds in that the time required to teach children who are
not academically oriented to another dialect of the language,
which they feel no need to learn, would postpone the teaching
of reading too long. Many would never be ready to learn to
read if readiness depended on losing their speech divergence
in the classroom. The problem is not simply one of teaching
children a new dialect. Children, the divergent among them,
certainly have facility in language learning. The problem
involves the extinction of their existing dialect, one which
receives continuous reinforcement in basic communications outside of the classroom. Labov's research in New York indicates
that divergent speakers do not seem to make a conscious effort to use language forms which they recognize as socially
preferred until adolescence. Younger children may hear differences but lack the insight to realize which forms are
socially preferred. Of course, teenagers may deliberately
avoid preferred forms, too, as they reject adult ways and
adult values.

In essence the child who is made to accept another dialect for learning must accept the view that his own language
is inferior. In a very real sense, since this is the language
of his parents, his family, his community, he must reject his
own culture and himself, as he is, in order to become something

else. This is perhaps too much to ask of any child. Even
those who succeed may carry permanent scars. The school may
force many to make the choice between self-respect and school
acceptance. And all this must be accomplished on the faith
of the learner that by changing his language he will do himself some good. As one teenager remarked to me, "Ya man, alls
I gotta do is walk right and talk right and they gonna make
me president of the United States."

The only practical alternative I feel is the third one.
It depends on acceptance by the school and particularly by
the teacher of the language which the learner brings to
school. Here are some key aspects of this approach:

1. Literacy is built on the base of the child's existing
    language.
2. This base must be a solid one. Children must be helped
    to develop a pride in their language and confidence in
    their ability to use their language to communicate their
    ideas and express themselves.
3. In reading instruction, the focus must be on learning to
    read. No attempt to change the child's language must be
    permitted to enter into this process or interfere with it.
4. No special materials need to be constructed but children
    must be permitted, actually encouraged, to read the way
    they speak. Experience stories must basically be in their
    language.
5. Any skill instruction must be based on a careful analysis
    of their language.
6. Reading materials and reading instruction should draw as
    much as possible on experiences and settings appropriate
    to the children. While special dialect-based materials
    are impractical, we may nonetheless need to abandon our
    notion of universally usable reading texts and use a

variety of materials selected for suitability for the
particular group of learners.

7. The teacher will speak in his own natural manner and pre-
    sent by example the general language community, but the
    teacher must learn to understand and accept the children's
    language. He must study it carefully and become aware of
    the key elements of divergence that are likely to cause
    difficulty. Langston Hughes has suggested an apt motto
    for the teacher of divergent speakers: "My motto as I
    live and learn, is dig, and be dug in return."

My own conviction is that even after literacy has been
achieved future language change cannot come about through the
extinction of the native dialect and the substitution of
another. I believe that language growth must be a growth outward from the native dialect, an expansion which eventually
will encompass the socially preferred forms but retain its
roots. The child can expand his language as he expands his
outlook, not rejecting his own sub-culture but coming to see
it in its broader setting. Eventually he can achieve the
flexibility of language which makes it possible for him to
communicate easily in many diverse settings and on many levels.

I'd like to close with a plea. You don't have to accept
what I've said. I don't ask that you believe or that you
agree with my point of view. My plea is that you listen to
the language of the divergent. Listen carefully and objectively. Push your preconceptions and your own ethnocentrisms
aside and listen. I think that you'll find beauty and form
and a solid base for understanding and communication. And as
you dig you'll find that you are indeed dug in return.

SOME SOURCES OF READING PROBLEMS FOR NEGRO SPEAKERS OF NONSTANDARD ENGLISH

by William Labov

It seems natural to look at any educational problem in terms of the particular type of ignorance which is to be overcome. In this discussion, we will be concerned with two opposing and complementary types:

> ignorance of standard English rules on the part of speakers of nonstandard English

> ignorance of nonstandard English rules on the part of teachers and text writers

In other words, the fundamental situation that we face is one of reciprocal ignorance, where teacher and student are ignorant of each other's system, and therefore of the rules needed to translate from one system to another.

The consequences of this situation may be outlined in the following way. When the teacher attempts to overcome the first kind of ignorance by precept and example in the classroom, she discovers that the student shows a strong and

. . . .

Reprinted by permission from A. Frazier (ed.), New Directions in Elementary English (Champaign, Ill., National Council of Teachers of English, 1967), pp. 140-67. This paper was first given at a meeting of the NCTE in the spring of 1966, and summarizes some preliminary findings of research on nonstandard English in urban ghetto areas for the U.S. Office of Education. The view of the problem and the preliminary data given here are in general supported by the findings of the complete study. Several additions and corrections are indicated in the text in square brackets; references to later publications which report the complete results of this research have been added to the footnotes.

inexplicable resistance to learning the few simple rules that
he needs to know. He is told over and over again, from the
early grades to the twelfth, that -ed is required for the
past participle ending, but he continues to write:

I have live here twelve years.

and he continues to mix up past and present tense forms in
his reading. In our present series of interviews with Harlem
youngsters from ten to sixteen years old, we ask them to correct to classroom English such sentences as the following:[1]

He pick me.
He don't know nobody.
He never play no more, man.
The man from U.N.C.L.E. hate the guys from Thrush.

Words such as man and guys are frequently corrected, and
ain't receives a certain amount of attention. But the double
negative is seldom noticed, and the absence of the grammatical
signals -s and -ed is rarely detected by children in the fifth,
sixth, or seventh grades. There can be little doubt that their
ignorance of these few fundamental points of English inflection
is connected with the fact that most of them have difficulty
in reading sentences at the second grade level.

There are many reasons for the persistence of this ignorance. Here I will be concerned with the role played by
the second type of ignorance: the fact that the child's teacher has no systematic knowledge of the nonstandard forms which
oppose and contradict standard English. Some teachers are
reluctant to believe that there are systematic principles in
nonstandard English which differ from those of standard English. They look upon every deviation from schoolroom English
as inherently evil, and they attribute these mistakes to
laziness, sloppiness, or the child's natural disposition to
be wrong. For these teachers, there is no substantial difference in the teaching of reading and the teaching of geography. The child is simply ignorant of geography; he does

not have a well-formed system of nonstandard geography to be
analyzed and corrected. From this point of view, teaching
English is a question of imposing rules upon chaotic and
shapeless speech, filling a vacuum by supplying rules where
no rules existed before.

Other teachers are sincerely interested in understanding
the language of the children, but their knowledge is fragmen-
tary and ineffective. They feel that the great difficulties
in teaching Negro and Puerto Rican children to read are due
in part to the systematic contradictions between the rules
of language used by the child and the rules used by the
teacher. The contribution which I hope to make here is to
supply a systematic basis for the study of nonstandard English of Negro and Puerto Rican children, and some factual
information, so that educators and text writers can design
their teaching efforts with these other systems in mind.

Priority of Problems

Within the school curriculum, there seems to be an order
of priority of educational problems that we face in large
urban centers. Many skills have to be acquired before we
can say that a person has learned standard English.[2] The
following list is a scale of priority that I would suggest
as helpful in concentrating our attention on the most important problems:

a. Ability to understand spoken English (of the teacher).
b. Ability to read and comprehend.
c. Ability to communicate (to the teacher) in spoken
    English.
d. Ability to communicate in writing.
e. Ability to write in standard English grammar.
f. Ability to spell correctly.
g. Ability to use standard English grammar in speaking.
h. Ability to speak with a prestige pattern of pro-
    nunciation (and avoid stigmatized forms).

I would revise this list if it appeared that the teacher could
not understand literally the speech or writing of the child;

weaknesses in c or d could conceivably interfere with the
solution to b. But considering all possibilities, this list
would be my best estimate, as a relative outsider to the
field of elementary education; it is of course subject to
correction by educators.

In dealing with children from English-speaking homes,
we usually assume a. In the extreme cases where the child
cannot understand the literal meaning of the teacher, we
have to revise our approach to teach this ability first.
For the most part, however, we take the first academic
task of the child to be b, developing the ability to read
and comprehend. Certainly reading is first and most urgent
in terms of its effect on the rest of learning, and it is
most seriously compromised in the schools of the ghetto
areas in large Northern cities. The problem of reading is
so striking today that it offers a serious intellectual
challenge as well as a pressing social problem. One must
understand why so many children are not learning to read,
or give up any claim to understand the educational process
as a whole.

Structural vs. Functional Conflicts

We have dealt so far with a series of abilities. Obviously the desire to learn is in some way prior to the act
of learning. Our own current research for the Office of
Education is concerned with two aspects of the problem:[3]

> (a) Structural conflicts of standard and nonstandard
> English: interference with learning ability stem-
> ming from a mismatch of linguistic structures.

> (b) Functional conflicts of standard and nonstandard
> English: interference with the desire to learn
> standard English stemming from a mismatch in the
> functions which standard and nonstandard English
> perform in a given culture.

In the discussion that follows, we will be concerned only
with the first type of conflict.

We should also consider whose speech, and whose learning problems, must be analyzed. Here again there is an order of priority, based on the numbers of people involved, the extent of neglect, and the degree of structural differences involved. In these terms, the educational problems of the Negro children in large cities must be considered most pressing; secondly, those of Puerto Rican and Mexican children from Spanish-speaking homes; and third, the problems of white youth from Appalachian backgrounds and other underprivileged areas.

Is there a Negro speech pattern? This question has provoked a great deal of discussion in the last few years, much more than it deserves. At many meetings on educational problems of ghetto areas, time which could have been spent in constructive discussion has been devoted to arguing the question as to whether Negro dialect exists. The debates have not been conducted with any large body of factual information in view, but rather in terms of what the speakers wish to be so, or what they fear might follow in the political arena.

For those who have not participated in such debates, it may be difficult to imagine how great are the pressures against the recognition, description, or even mention of Negro speech patterns.[4] For various reasons, many teachers, principals, and civil rights leaders wish to deny that the existence of patterns of Negro speech is a linguistic and social reality in the United States today. The most careful statement of the situation as it actually exists might read as follows: Many features of pronunciation, grammar, and lexicon are closely associated with Negro speakers—so closely as to identify the great majority of Negro people in the Northern cities by their speech alone.

The match between this speech pattern and membership in the Negro ethnic group is of course far from complete. Many Negro speakers have none—or almost none—of these features.

Many Northern whites, living in close proximity to Negroes, have these features in their own speech. But this overlap does not prevent the features from being identified with Negro speech by most listeners: we are dealing with a stereotype which provides correct identification in the great majority of cases, and therefore with a firm base in social reality. Such stereotypes are the social basis of language perception; this is merely one of many cases where listeners generalize from the variable data to categorical perception in absolute terms. Someone who uses a stigmatized form 20 to 30 percent of the time will be heard as using this form all of the time.[5] It may be socially useful to correct these stereotypes in a certain number of individual cases, so that people learn to limit their generalizations to the precise degree that their experience warrants: but the overall tendency is based upon very regular principles of human behavior, and people will continue to identify as Negro speech the pattern which they hear from the great majority of the Negro people that they meet.

In the South, the overlap is much greater. There is good reason to think that the positive features of the Negro speech pattern all have their origin in dialects spoken by both Negroes and whites in some parts of the South. Historically speaking, the Negro speech pattern that we are dealing with in Northern cities is a regional speech pattern. We might stop speaking of Negro speech, and begin using the term "Southern regional speech", if that would make the political and social situation more manageable. But if we do so, we must not deceive ourselves and come to believe that this is an accurate description of the current situation. The following points cannot be overlooked in any such discussion:

1. For most Northern whites, the only familiar example

of Southern speech is that of the Negro people they hear,
and these Southern features function as markers of Negro
ethnic membership, not Southern origin.

2. Many characteristic features of Southern speech have
been generalized along strictly ethnic lines in Northern
cities. For example, the absence of a distinction between
/i/ and /e/ before nasals [pin equal to pen] has become a
marker of the Negro group in New York City, so that most
young Negro children of Northern and Southern background
alike show this feature while no white children are affected.

3. In this merger of Northern and Southern patterns in
the Northern Negro communities, a great many Southern features
are being eliminated. Thus in New York and other Northern
cities, we find the young Negro people do not distinguish
four and for, which and witch; while monophthongization of
high and wide is common, the extreme fronting of the initial
vowel to the position of cat or near it, is less and less
frequent; the back upglide of ball and hawk, so characteristic of many Southern areas, is rarely heard; grammatical
features such as the perfective auxiliary done in he done
told me, or the double modal of might could, are becoming
increasingly rare. As a result, a speaker fresh from the
South is plainly marked in the Northern Negro communities,
and his speech is ridiculed. Negro speech is thus not to be
identified with Southern regional speech. [Moreover, there
are a small but significant number of features of Negro
speech which are not shared by whites in the South, such as
the deletion of the reduced and contracted 's representing
forms of is to yield such sentences as He crazy.]

4. The white Southern speech which is heard in many
Northern cities—Chicago, Detroit, Cleveland—is the Southern
Mountain pattern of Appalachia, and this pattern does not
have many of the phonological and grammatical features of
Negro speech to be discussed below in this paper.

5. Many of the individual features of Negro speech can
be found in Northern white speech, as we will see, and even
more so in the speech of educated white Southerners. But the
frequency of these features, such as consonant cluster simplification, and their distribution in relation to grammatical
boundaries, is radically different in Negro speech, and we
are forced in many cases to infer the existence of different
underlying grammatical forms and rules.

We can sum up this discussion of the Southern regional
pattern by saying that we are witnessing the transformation
of a regional speech pattern into a class and ethnic pattern
in the Northern cities. This is not a new phenomenon; it
has occurred many times in the history of English. According to H. Kökeritz and H.C. Wyld, such a process was taking
place in Shakespeare's London, where regional dialects from
the east and southeast opposed more conservative dialects
within the city as middle class and lower class speech against
aristocratic speech.[6] We see the same process operating today
in the suburbs of New York City; where the Connecticut and
New Jersey patterns meet the New York City pattern, in the
overlapping areas, the New York City pattern becomes associated with lower socioeconomic groups.[7]

The existence of a Negro speech pattern must not be confused of course with the myth of a biologically, racially,
exclusively Negro speech. The idea that dialect differences
are due to some form of laziness or carelessness must be rejected with equal firmness. Anyone who continues to endorse
such myths can be refuted easily by such subjective reaction
tests as the Family Background test which we are using in our
current research in Harlem. Sizable extracts from the speech
of fourteen individuals are played in sequence for listeners
who are asked to identify the family backgrounds of each.[8]
So far, we find no one who can even come close to a correct

identification of Negro and white speakers. This result does
not contradict the statement that there exists a socially
based Negro speech pattern: it supports everything that I have
said above on this point. The voices heard on the test are
the exceptional cases: Negroes raised without any Negro
friends in solidly white areas; whites raised in areas dominated by Negro cultural values; white Southerners in Gullah-
speaking territory; Negroes from small Northern communities
untouched by recent migrations; college educated Negroes who
reject the Northern ghetto and the South alike. The speech
of these individuals does not identify them as Negro or white
because they do not use the speech patterns which are characteristically Negro or white for Northern listeners. The
identifications made by these listeners, often in violation
of actual ethnic membership categories, show that they respond to Negro speech patterns as a social reality.

Relevant Patterns of Negro Speech

One approach to the study of nonstandard Negro speech
is to attempt a complete description of this form of language
without direct reference to standard English. This approach
can be quite revealing, and can save us from many pitfalls
in the easy identification of forms that are only apparently
similar. But as an overall plan, it is not realistic. We
are far from achieving a complete description of standard
English, to begin with; the differences between nonstandard
Negro speech and standard English are slight compared to
their similarities; and finally, some of these differences
are far more relevant to reading problems than others. Let
us therefore consider some of the most relevant patterns of
Negro speech from the point of view of reading problems.

Some Negro-white differences are plainly marked and
easy for any observer to note. In the following examples,
the Negro forms are patterns which frequently occur in our

recordings of individual and group sessions with boys from
10 to 17 years old—ranging from careful speech in face-to-
face interaction with adults to the most excited and spontaneous activity within the primary (closed network) group:[9]

Negro	White
It don't all be her fault.	It isn't always her fault.
Hit him upside the head.	Hit him in the head.
The rock say "Shhh!"	The rock went "Shhh!"
I'm a shoot you.	I'm g'na shoot you.
I wanna be a police.	I wanna be a policeman.

Ah 'on' know. [a o no] (marked 2 4 3 above a o no)   I d'know. [aɪdnoᵁ] (marked 2 3 1 above dno)

Now consider the following examples, in which Negro-white
differences are less plainly marked and very difficult for
most people to hear:

Negro	White
He [pæsɨm] yesterday.	He [pæsd̥ɨm] yesterday.
Give him [ðeᴛ] book.	Give him [ðɛ⊥] book.
This [jɔːɤ] place?	This [jɔːᵊ] place?
[ðæs] Nick boy.	[ðæᵗs] Nick's boy.
He say, [kæːᵊl] is.	He says, [kærəl] is.
My name is [bu].	My name is [bu?].

This second series represents a set of slight phonetic differences, sometimes prominent, but more often unnoticed by
the casual listener. These differences are much more significant than the first set in terms of learning and reading standard English. In truth, the differences are so significant that
they will be the focus of attention in the balance of this
paper. The slight phonetic signals observed here indicate
systematic differences that can lead to reading problems and
problems of being understood.

Corresponding to the phonetic transcriptions on the left,
we can and do infer such grammatical constructions and lexical forms as:

He pass him yesterday.
Give him they book.
This you-all place?

> That's Nick boy.
> He say, Ca'ol is.
> My name is Boo.

Each of these sentences is representative of a large class
of phonological and grammatical differences which mark non-
standard Negro speech as against standard English. The most
important are those in which large scale phonological differences coincide with important grammatical differences.
The result of this coincidence is the existence of a large
number of homonyms in the speech of Negro children which are
different from the set of homonyms in the speech system used
by the teacher. If the teacher knows about this different
set of homonyms, no serious problems in the teaching of reading need occur; but if the teacher does not know, there are
bound to be difficulties.

The simplest way to organize this information seems to
be under the headings of the important rules of the sound
system which are affected. By using lists of homonyms as
examples, it will be possible to avoid a great deal of phonetic notation, and to stay with the essential linguistic
facts. In many cases, the actual phonetic form is irrele-
vant: it is the presence or absence of a distinction which
is relevant. Thus, for example, it makes no differences
whether a child says [pɪn] or [pɪən] or [peːən] or [pɛn] for
the word pen; what counts is whether or not this word is
distinct from pin. The linguistic fact of interest is the
existence of contrast, not the particular phonetic forms that
are heard from one moment to another. A child might seem to
distinguish [pɪn] and [pɛn] in Northern style in one pair of
sentences, but if the basic phonemic contrast is not present,
the same child might reverse the forms in the next sentence,
and say [pɪn] for ink pen and [pɛn] for safety pin. A linguistic orientation will not supply teachers with a battery

of phonetic symbols, but rather encourage them to observe
what words can or cannot be distinguished by the children
they are teaching.

Some Phonological Variables and Their Grammatical Consequences

        1. r-lessness. There are three major dialect areas in
the Eastern United States where the r of spelling is not pronounced as a consonant before other consonants or at the ends
of words: Eastern New England, New York City, and the South
(Upper and Lower). Thus speakers from Boston, New York,
Richmond, Charleston, or Atlanta will show only a lengthened
vowel in car, guard, for, etc., and usually an obscure center-
ing glide [schwa] in place of r in fear, feared, care, cared,
moor, moored, bore, bored, etc. This is what we mean by
r-less pronunciation. Most of these areas have been strongly
influenced in recent years by the r-pronouncing pattern which
is predominant in broadcasting, so that educated speakers,
especially young people, will show a mixed pattern in their
careful speech.[10] When the original r-less pattern is preserved, we can obtain such homonyms as the following:[11]

            guard = god   par   = pa
            nor   = gnaw   fort = fought
            sore = saw   court = caught

and we find that yeah can rhyme with fair, idea with fear.

        Negro speakers show an even higher degree of r-lessness
than New Yorkers or Bostonians. The r of spelling becomes a
schwa or disappears before vowels as well as before consonants
or pauses. Thus in the speech of most white New Yorkers, r
is pronounced when a vowel follows in four o'clock; even
though the r is found at the end of a word, if the next word
begins with a vowel, it is pronounced as a consonantal [r].
For most Negro speakers, r is still not pronounced in this
position, and so never heard at the end of the word four.
The white speaker is helped in his reading or spelling by

the existence of the alternation: [fɔːfiːt, fɔrəklak], but
the Negro speaker has no such clue to the underlying (spelling) form of the word four. Furthermore, the same Negro
speaker will often not pronounce intervocalic r in the middle
of a word, as indicated in the dialect spelling inte'ested,
Ca'ol. He has no clue, in his own speech, to the correct
spelling form of such words, and may have another set of
homonyms besides those listed above:

        Carol   = Cal
        Paris   = pass
        terrace = test

   2. l-lessness. The consonant l is a liquid very similar
to r in its phonetic nature. The chief difference is that
with l the center of the tongue is up, and the sides are down,
while with r the sides are up but the center does not touch
the roof of the mouth. The pattern of l-dropping is very
similar to that of r, except that it has never affected entire dialect areas in the same sweeping style.[12] When l
disappears, it is often replaced by a back unrounded glide,
sometimes symbolized [ɤ], instead of the center glide that
replaces r; in many cases, l disappears entirely, especially
after the back rounded vowels. The loss of l is much more
marked among the Negro speakers we have interviewed than
among whites in Northern cities, and we therefore have much
greater tendencies towards such homonyms as:

        toll = toe   all   = awe
        help = hep   Saul = saw
        tool = too   fault = fought

   3. Simplification of consonant clusters. One of the
most complex variables appearing in Negro speech is the general tendency towards the simplification of consonant clusters
at the ends of words. A great many clusters are involved,
primarily those which end in /t/ or /d/, /s/ or /z/.[13] We are

actually dealing with two distinct tendencies: (1) a general
tendency to reduce clusters of consonants at the ends of
words to single consonants, and (2) a more general process
of reducing the amount of information provided after stressed
vowels, so that individual final consonants are affected as
well. The first process is the most regular and requires the
most intensive study in order to understand the conditioning
factors involved.

The chief /t,d/ clusters that are affected are (roughly
in order of frequency) /-st, -ft, -nt, -nd, -ld, -zd, -md/.
Here they are given in phonemic notation; in conventional
spelling we have words such as past, passed, lift, laughed,
bent, bend, fined, hold, poled, old, called, raised, aimed.
In all these cases, if the cluster is simplified, it is the
last element that is dropped. Thus we have homonyms such as:

                past = pass   mend = men
                rift = riff   wind = wine
                meant = men   hold = hole

If we combine the effect of -ld simplification, loss of -l,
and monophthongization of /ay/ and /aw/, we obtain

                [šiwa:ɣ]   She wow! = She wild!

and this equivalence has in fact been found in our data. It
is important to bear in mind that the combined effect of several rules will add to the total number of homonyms, and even
more, to the unexpected character of the final result:

                told = told = toe

The first impression that we draw, from casual listening,
is that Negro speakers show much more consonant cluster simplification than white speakers. But this conclusion is far from
obvious when we examine the data carefully. Table 1 shows the
total simplification of consonant clusters for two speakers:
BF is a Negro working class man, 45 years old, raised in New
York City; AO is a white working class man, of Austrian-German

background, 56 years old, also raised in New York City but with little contact with Negroes.

Table 1

Overall Simplification of /t,d/ Consonant Clusters
For One Negro and One White New York City Speaker

	BF (Negro)		AO (White)	
	Number Simplified	Total Clusters	Number Simplified	Total Clusters
/-st/	29	37	18	23
/-ft/	7	9	0	2
/-nt/	8	16	14	29
/-nd/	8	14	8	14
/-ld/	8	15	2	4
/-zd/	5	8	3	4
/-md/	2	3	0	1
other	4	4	1	4
Total	71	106	46	81

The overall percentage of simplification for BF is 67 percent, not very much more than AO, 57 percent. Furthermore, the individual clusters show remarkably similar patterns; for the larger cells, the percentages are almost identical. It is true that the social distribution of this feature is wider for Negroes than for whites, but the sharpest differences are not in this particular phonetic process. As we shall see below, it is in the nature of the grammatical conditioning that restricts the deletion of the final consonant.

The other set of clusters which are simplified are those ending in /-s/ or /-z/, words like axe /æks/, six /siks/, box /baks/, parts /parts/, aims /eymz/, rolls /rowlz/, leads /liydz/, besides /bisaydz/, John's /džanz/, that's /ðæts/, it's /its/, its /its/. The situation here is more complex than with the /t,d/ clusters, since in some cases the first element of the cluster is lost, and in other cases the second element.[14] Furthermore, the comparison of the same two speakers as shown above shows a radical difference (see Table 2).

Table 2

Overall Simplification of /s,z/ Consonant Clusters
For One Negro and One White New York City Speaker

BF (Negro)			AO (White)		
1st Cons. Dropped	2nd Cons. Dropped	Total Clusters	1st Cons. Dropped	2nd Cons. Dropped	Total Clusters
31	18	98	6	4	69

This overall view of the situation is only a preliminary to a much more detailed study, but it does serve to show that the simplification of the /s,z/ clusters is much more characteristic of Negro speakers than of white speakers. The comparison of these two speakers is typical of the several hundred Negro and white subjects that we have studied so far in our current research.

In one sense, there are a great many homonyms produced by this form of consonant cluster simplification, as we shall see when we consider grammatical consequences. But many of these can also be considered to be grammatical differences rather than changes in the shapes of words. The /t,d/ simplification gives us a great many irreducible homonyms, where a child has no clue to the standard spelling differences from his own speech pattern. Though this is less common in the case of /s,z/ clusters, we have

six = sick   Max = Mack

box = bock   mix = Mick

as possible homonyms in the speech of many Negro children.

4. <u>Weakening of final consonants</u>. It was noted above that the simplification of final consonant clusters was part of a more general tendency to produce less information after stressed vowels, so that final consonants, unstressed final

vowels, and weak syllables show fewer distinctions and more reduced phonetic forms than initial consonants and stressed vowels. This is a perfectly natural process in terms of the amount of information required for effective communication, since the number of possible words which must be distinguished declines sharply after we select the first consonant and vowel. German and Russian, for example, do not distinguish voiced and voiceless consonants at the ends of words. However, when this tendency is carried to extremes (and a nonstandard dialect differs radically from the standard language in this respect), it may produce serious problems in learning to read and spell.

   This weakening of final consonants is by no means as regular as the other phonological variables described above. Some individuals appear to have generalized the process to the point where most of their syllables are of the CV type, and those we have interviewed in this category seem to have the most serious reading problems of all. In general, final /t/ and /d/ are the most affected by the process. Final /d/ may be devoiced to a [t]-like form, or disappear entirely. Final /t/ is often realized as glottal stop, as in many English dialects, but more often disappears entirely. Less often, final /g/ and /k/ follow the same route as /d/ and /t/: /g/ is devoiced or disappears, and /k/ is replaced by glottal stop or disappears. Final /m/ and /n/ usually remain in the form of various degrees of nasalization of the preceding vowel. Rarely, sibilants /s/ and /z/ are weakened after vowels to the point where no consonant is heard at all. As a result of these processes, one may have such homonyms as:

Boot = Boo[15]	seat = seed = see
road = row	poor = poke = pope[16]
feed = feet	bit = bid = big

   It is evident that the loss of final /l/ and /r/,

discussed above, is another aspect of this general weakening
of final consonants, though of a much more regular nature
than the cases considered in this section.

    5. <u>Other phonological variables</u>. In addition to the
types of homonymy singled out in the preceding discussion,
there are a great many others which may be mentioned. They
are of less importance for reading problems in general, since
they have little impact upon inflectional rules, but they do
affect the shapes of words in the speech of Negro children.
There is no distinction between /i/ and /e/ before nasals in
the great majority of cases. In the parallel case before
/r/, and sometimes /l/, we frequently find no distinction
between the vowels /ih/ and /eh/. The corresponding pair of
back vowels before /r/ are seldom distinguished: that is,
/uh/ and /oh/ fall together. The diphthongs /ay/ and /aw/
are often monophthongized, so that they are not distinguished
from /ah/. The diphthong /oy/ is often a monophthong, especially before /l/, and cannot be distinguished from /ɔh/.

    Among other consonant variables, we find the final
fricative /θ/ is frequently merged with /f/, and similarly
final /ð/ with /v/. Less frequently, /θ/ and /ð/ become /f/
and /v/ in intervocalic position. Initial consonant clusters
which involve /r/ show considerable variation: /str/ is often
heard as /skr/; /šr/ as [sw, sr, sɸ]. In a more complex
series of shifts, /r/ is frequently lost as the final element
of an initial cluster.

    As a result of these various phonological processes, we
find that the following series of homonyms are characteristic
of the speech of many Negro children:

pin	= pen	beer	= bear	poor	= pour
tin	= ten	cheer	= chair	sure	= shore
since	= cents	steer	= stair	moor	= more
		peel	= pail		

        find = found = fond   boil = ball
        time   = Tom   oil = all
               pound = pond

    Ruth = roof   stream = scream
    death = deaf   strap = scrap

Changes in the Shapes of Words

The series of potential homonyms given in the preceding
sections indicate that Negro children may have difficulty in
recognizing many words in their standard spellings. They may
look up words under the wrong spellings in dictionaries, and
be unable to distinguish words which are plainly different
for the teacher. If the teacher is aware of these sources
of confusion, she may be able to anticipate a great many of
the children's difficulties. But if neither the teacher nor
the children are aware of the great differences in their sets
of homonyms, it is obvious that confusion will occur in every
reading assignment.

However, the existence of homonyms on the level of a
phonetic output does not prove that the speakers have the
same sets of mergers on the more abstract level which corresponds to the spelling system. For instance, many New Yorkers
merge sore and saw in casual speech, but in reading style,
they have no difficulty in pronouncing the /r/ where it belongs. Since the /r/ in sore reappears before a following
vowel, it is evident that an abstract //r//[17] occurs in their
lexical system: //sɔr//. Thus the standard spelling system
finds support in the learned patterns of careful speech, and
in the alternations which exist within any given style of
speech.

The phonetic processes discussed above are often considered to be "low level" rules—that is, they do not affect
the underlying or abstract representations of words. One

piece of evidence for this view is that the deletable final
/r, l, s, z, t, d/ tend to be retained when a vowel follows
at the beginning of the next word. This effect of a following vowel would seem to be a phonetic factor, restricting
the operation of a phonetic rule; in any case, it is plain
that the final consonant must "be there" in some abstract
sense, if it appears in this prevocalic position. If this
were not the case, we would find a variety of odd final consonants appearing, with no fixed relation to the standard
form.[18]

For all of the major variables that we have considered,
there is a definite and pronounced effect of a following
vowel in realizing the standard form. Fig. 1 shows the effect of a following vowel on final /-st/ in the speech of
four Negro and three white subjects. In every case, we find
that the percent of simplification of the cluster falls when
a vowel follows.

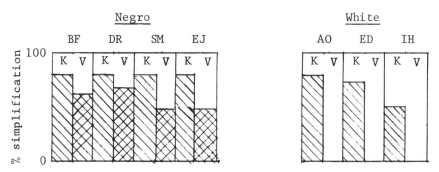

Fig. 1.   Effect of a Following Vowel on /-st/ Final Clusters
          for Four Negro and Three White Speakers

The same argument, however, can be used to argue that
the Negro speakers have underlying forms considerably different from those of white speakers. The white speakers showed
almost as much overall simplification of the clusters before
a following consonant, but none at all before a following

vowel: in other words, their abstract forms were effectively
equivalent to the spelling forms. The Negro speakers showed
only a limited reduction in the degree of simplification when
a vowel followed.

We can explore this situation more carefully when we
consider grammatical conditioning. But we can point to one
situation which suggests the existence of nonstandard underlying forms. In the most casual and spontaneous speech of
the young Negro people whose language we have been examining,
the plural //-s// inflection is seldom deleted. It follows
the same phonetic rules as in standard English: (1) after
sibilants /s, z, š, ž/, the regular plural is [əz]; (2) after
other voiceless consonants, [s]; and (3) elsewhere, [z]. The
regular form of the plural after a word like test, desk, is
[s], as in [desks]. If the rules were so ordered that we
began with the abstract form //desk//, added the //-s//, and
then deleted the /k/ in the consonant cluster simplification
process, we would find the final phonetic form [dɛs:]. We
do in fact sometimes find this form, in a context which implies the plural. But more often, we find [dɛsəz, gosəz,
tosəz] as the plurals of desk, ghost and toast.

[A form such as [dɛsəz] is consistent with an order of
the rules which begins with //des//, or reduces //desk//
immediately to /des/. Then the plural //-s// is added, and
the phonetic rules give us [dɛsəz]. It should be emphasized
that those speakers who use this form do so consistently,
frequently, and in the most careful speech; it is not a slip
of the tongue. On the contrary, clusters such as -sps, -sts,
-sks are almost impossible for many Negro children to articulate. Even with direct modeling, they find it extremely
difficult to repeat the standard forms of wasps, lists,
desks, etc.[18a] It is quite common for children to produce
under pressure such forms as [lɪstsəsəsəs], a recursive

process, as a result of their efforts to produce the -sts cluster.

Forms such as singular [dɛs], plural [dɛsəz] give no support for an underlying spelling form desk. It is true that they are not inconsistent with a spelling desk, for an automatic rule simplifies -sks in 100 percent of the cases, changing -sk+s to -s+s. But there is no way for the Negro child to differentiate mess, messes from des', desses, on the basis of his own native speech forms. Therefore he can only memorize from school lessons which words have final consonants after -s. In the case of verbs such as test, and their derived nouns, there is no problem, for the form testing preserves the final -t; but most words in this class have no derived forms or inflectional forms in which a vowel follows the stem. When the next word begins with a vowel, the effect is often not strong enough to bring out the underlying final consonant in the speech of adults, and the listener does not hear the full form as regularly as he does in testing. There are, of course, dialects which resolve this problem in other ways by changing the rules for epenthetic vowels, yielding deskes, testes and waspes, but this is more characteristic of white Appalachian speech than Southern Negro speech.]

Grammatical Correlates of the Phonological Variables

As we examine the various final consonants affected by the phonological processes, we find that these are the same consonants which represent the principal English inflections. The shifts in the sound system therefore often coincide with grammatical differences between nonstandard and standard English, and it is usually difficult to decide whether we are dealing with a grammatical or a phonological rule. In any case, we can add a great number of homonyms to the lists given above when we consider the consequences of deleting final /r/, /l/, /s/, /z/, /t/, and /d/.

1. <u>The possessive</u>. In many cases, the absence of the
possessive //-s// can be interpreted as a reduction of consonant clusters, although this is not the most likely interpretation. The //-s// is absent just as frequently after
vowels as after consonants for many speakers. Nevertheless,
we can say that the overall simplification pattern is favored
by the absence of the //-s// inflection. In the case of
//-r//, we find more direct phonological influence: two possessive pronouns which end in /r/ have become identical to
the personal pronoun:

      [ðeɪ] book   not   [ðɛ:ə] book

In rapid speech, one can not distinguish <u>you</u> from <u>your</u> from
<u>you-all</u>. This seems to be a shift in grammatical forms, but
the relation to the phonological variables is plain when we
consider that <u>my</u>, <u>his</u>, <u>her</u>, and <u>our</u> remain as possessive pronouns. No one says <u>I book</u>, <u>he book</u>, <u>she book</u> or <u>we book</u>,
for there is no phonological process which would bring the
possessives into near-identity with the personal pronouns.[19]

2. <u>The future</u>. The loss of final /l/ has a serious
effect on the realization of future forms:

     you'll = you   he'll = he
     they'll = they   she'll = she

In many cases, therefore, the colloquial future is identical
with the colloquial present. The form <u>will</u> is still used in
its emphatic or full form, and the <u>going to</u> is frequent, so
there is no question about the grammatical category of the
future.[20] One form of the future with very slight phonetic
substance is preserved, the first person <u>I'm a shoot you</u>:
there is no general process for the deletion of this <u>m</u>.

3. <u>The copula</u>. The verb forms of <u>be</u> are frequently
not realized in sentences such as <u>you tired</u> or <u>he in the way</u>.
If we examine the paradigm, we find that it is seriously
affected by phonological processes:

$$I'm \quad \neq I \qquad we're \quad = we$$
$$you're \simeq you \qquad you're \simeq you$$
$$he's \quad ? \ he \qquad they're = they$$

The loss of final /z/ after vowels is not so frequent as to
explain the frequency of the absence of -s in he's, and it
is reasonable to conclude that grammatical rules have been
generalized throughout the paradigm—still not affecting I'm
in the same way as the others, as we would expect, since
phonological rules are not operating to reduce /m/.

4. The past. Again, there is no doubt that phonological
processes are active in reducing the frequency of occurrence
of the /t,d/ inflection.

$$pass = past = passed \qquad pick \ = picked$$
$$miss = mist = missed \qquad loan \ = loaned$$
$$fine = find = fined \qquad raise = raised$$

At the same time, there is no question about the existence of
a past tense category. The irregular past tense forms, which
are very frequent in ordinary conversation, are plainly
marked as past no matter what final simplification takes place.

I told him [atoɨm]   he kept mine [hikɛpmaᴵn]

The problem which confronts us concerns the form of the regular suffix //-ed//. Is there such an abstract form in the
structure of the nonstandard English spoken by Negro children? The answer will make a considerable difference both
to teaching strategy and our understanding of the reading
problems which children face. To approach this problem, we
have used a variety of methods which it may be helpful to
examine in detail.

The Problem of the -ed Suffix

The first approach to this problem is through a study of
the quantitative distribution of the forms as spoken by Negro
and white subjects in a variety of stylistic contexts. We
contrast the simplification of consonant clusters in two

situations: where the /t/ or /d/ represents a part of the
root form itself [D$_{MM}$] and where the /t/ or /d/ represents
the grammatical suffix of the past tense [D$_P$]. Fig. 2 shows
the results for the speakers BF and AO who were first considered in Tables 1 and 2.

The Negro speaker BF shows almost the same degree of
consonant cluster simplification when the /t,d/ represents
a past tense as when it is a part of the original root. On
the other hand, the white speaker AO simplifies very few
past tense clusters. We can interpret these results in two
ways: (a) BF has a generalized simplification rule without
grammatical conditioning, while AO's simplification rule is
strongly restricted by grammatical boundaries, or (b) BF's
underlying grammar is different. If we were to rewrite his
grammar to show -ed morphemes only where phonetic forms
actually appear, his consonant cluster rule would look much
the same as AO's. Without attempting to decide this issue
now, let us examine a Negro speaker in several styles, and
see if the -ed is affected by the shift.

Fig. 3 shows the percent of /t,d/ clusters simplified
by DR, a Negro woman raised in North Carolina. On the left,
we see the simplification of both D$_{MM}$ and D$_P$ in intimate
family style, discussing a recent trip to North Carolina
with a close relative. The pattern is similar to that of
BF, with no differentiation of D$_{MM}$ and D$_P$. But on the right
we find a sharp differentiation of the two kinds of clusters:
this is the careful style used by DR in a face-to-face interview with a white stranger. Fig. 3 shows us that the grammatical constraint which DR uses in careful speech is quite
similar to the pattern used by the white speaker AO.

Stylistic context is obviously important in obtaining
good information on the underlying grammatical system of
Negro speakers. We may therefore profit from considering

WILLIAM LABOV

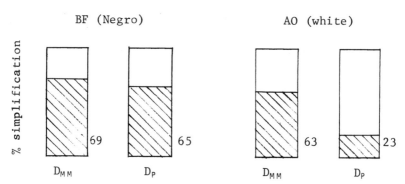

Fig. 2. Effect of Grammatical Status on /t,d/ of Final
Clusters for One Negro and One White Speaker

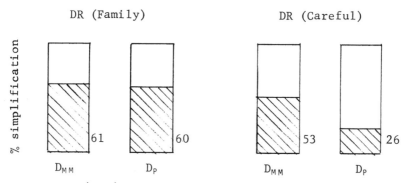

D_{MM}: /t,d/ final in monomorphemic (root) clusters
D_P : /t,d/ final as past tense -ed morpheme

Fig. 3. Effect of Stylistic Level and Grammatical Status
on /t,d/ of Final Clusters for One Negro Speaker

data where this factor is controlled. Fig. 4 shows the overall consonant cluster simplification patterns for two groups
of Negro boys: the Thunderbirds, 10 to 12 years old, and the
Cobras, 14 to 16. These are two peer groups which form
closed networks. Most of the boys are poor readers, and
they represent the groups which respond least to middle-class
educational norms. In the interviews which provided this
data, the groups were recorded in circumstances where they
used the most excited and spontaneous speech, interacting
with each other, and with only moderate influence from

Thunderbirds (five boys, age 10-12)

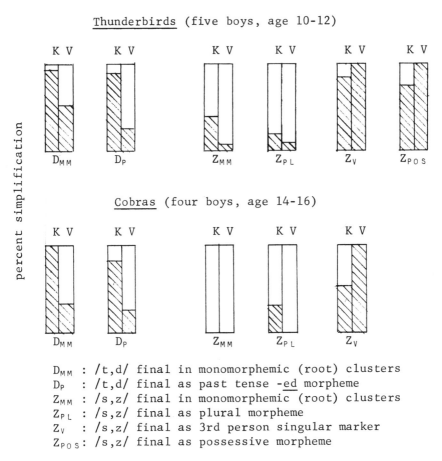

D_MM : /t,d/ final in monomorphemic (root) clusters
D_P : /t,d/ final as past tense -ed morpheme
Z_MM : /s,z/ final in monomorphemic (root) clusters
Z_PL : /s,z/ final as plural morpheme
Z_V : /s,z/ final as 3rd person singular marker
Z_POS: /s,z/ final as possessive morpheme

Fig. 4. Simplification of /t,d/ and /s,z/ Final Clusters for
     Two Groups of Negro Boys From South Central Harlem

outsiders. Each boy was recorded on a separate track, from
a microphone placed only a few inches away from his mouth.
(Recordings made with a single group microphone are of little
value for this type of group interaction since only a small
part of the data is recovered.)

     The Thunderbirds show a very high percentage of simpli-
fication of clusters before consonants: 61 out of 63 for
nongrammatical clusters, and 21 out of 23 for grammatical
clusters. But before following vowels, only 7 out of 14

nongrammatical clusters were simplified, and even fewer—3 out of 13—for grammatical clusters.

We can conclude from these figures that there is a solid basis for the recognition of an -ed suffix: grammatical status does make a difference when the unfavorable phonological environment is set aside. Secondly, we can see that there is a good basis for approximating the lexical forms of standard English: 50 percent of the root clusters conformed to the standard forms in a favorable environment. From another point of view, however, one might say that in half the cases, the boys gave no evidence that they would recognize such spellings as test or hand as corresponding to their [tɛs] and [hæn].

The Cobras, some four years older, are very similar in their /t,d/ pattern. The phonological conditioning has become even more regular—that is, the effect of the following vowel is more extreme. All of the root clusters are simplified before consonants, but only a small percentage before vowels. The effect of grammatical status is no stronger, however. We may conclude that the process of growing up has brought better knowledge of the underlying lexical forms of standard English, but the status of the -ed morpheme is still about the same.

Perception testing. A second approach to the problem of the -ed suffix is through perception testing. It is possible that the speakers are not able to hear the difference between [pɪk] and [pɪkt], [mɛs] and [mɛst]. If the phonological reduction rule was regular enough, this might be the case. We explore this possibility by a perception test of the following form. The subject listens to a series of three words: [mɛs, mɛst, mɛs], and is asked to say which one is different. The test is repeated six times, with various random combinations of the two possibilities. Then a second series is

given with /-st/ before a vowel: [mɛsʌp, mɛstʌp, mɛsʌp], etc.
A person who can hear the distinctions will give a correct
response in six out of six, or five out of six trials.

The Thunderbirds had no difficulty with the perception
test. Three of the boys had perfect scores, and only one
showed definite confusion—in fact, the one boy who came
closest to standard English norms on the other tests described below. It is true that many Negro youngsters have
great difficulty in perceiving phonemic contrasts which are
not made in their own dialect; but in this particular case,
perception of the /-t ~ -st/ distinction has less relevance
to the grammatical status of -ed than any of the other means
of investigation.

Classroom correction tests. A third means of approaching
the grammatical status of -ed is through the classroom correction tests mentioned earlier in the discussion. The subjects are asked to change certain sentences to correct schoolroom English, starting with easy examples like I met three
mens. Several sentences are relevant to the -ed problem:

> He pick me.
> I've pass my test.
> Last week I kick Donald in the mouth, so the
>   teacher throwed me out the class.

As a whole, results on the classroom correction tests show
that the Thunderbirds and the Cobras have little ability to
detect the absence of -ed as a grammatical element to be corrected. They focus upon ain't, or man in He never play no
more, man, but not upon the -ed. Among the Thunderbirds,
only one of the five boys had this ability to supply -ed,
and the Cobras showed no greater perception of the status of
this element.[21]

The -ed reading test. The most effective way of determining the grammatical significance of -ed for the groups we
have been working with is through a series of sentences in

the reading texts used in our interviews. The relevant sentences are as follows:

    (a)   Last month I read five books.
    (b)   Tom read all the time.
    (c)   Now I read and write better than Alfred does.
    (d)   When I passed by, I read the posters.
    (e)   When I liked a story, I read every word.
    (f)   I looked for trouble when I read the news.

These sentences depend upon the unique homograph read to indicate whether the reader is interpreting the -ed suffix as a
past tense signal. The first three sentences show whether
the reader can use the time indicators last month, now, and
the absence of -s to distinguish correctly between [ri:d]
and [rɛd]. In sentences (d), (e), and (f) the reader first
encounters the -ed suffix, which he may or may not pronounce.
If he interprets this visual signal as a sign of the past
tense, he will pronounce read as [rɛd]; if not, he is apt to
say [ri:d]. The distance between the -ed suffix and the
word read is kept as short as possible in sentence (d), so
that here at least there is no problem of understanding -ed
and then forgetting it.

    The overall results of this test show that -ed is inter-
preted correctly less than half the time by the Thunderbirds—
less often than the -ed suffix is pronounced. The Cobras
show no material improvement in this respect. For each group,
only one boy was able to approximate the standard English
performance in this test.

    We can conclude that the original inferences drawn from
Fig. 4, based on linguistic performance in spontaneous speech,
are supported by various other approaches to the -ed problem.
The degree of uncertainty registered in the D_p column for
consonant clusters, even before vowels, indicates that the
-ed cannot function as an effective marker of the past tense
for many children. Though the Cobras are four years older

than the Thunderbirds, they show little change in their use
of -ed. It is also true that some children—a minority in
this case—can recognize -ed as a past tense marker, and use
it effectively in reading, even though they usually do not
pronounce it.

Grammatical Status of the //-s// Suffixes

The same quantitative method which was effective in
interpreting the status of -ed can be used to analyze the
various -s suffixes used by Negro children. Fig. 4 provides
information on consonant cluster simplification as it affects
four different categories of -s:[22]

Z_{MM} monomorphemic -s in root clusters: axe, box
Z_{PL} the plural -s
Z_V the 3rd person singular marker of the verb
Z_{POS} the possessive -'s

For each category, we can compare the extent of simplification before consonants and before vowels.

In the case of root clusters, the Thunderbirds show
only a moderate tendency to drop the final element before
consonants, and a very small tendency before vowels. In
other words, the standard forms are intact. For the Cobras,
this -s is always present.

The plural is rarely lost, and shows the usual effect
of the following vowel. We can conclude that the plural inflection is the same for the Thunderbirds, the Cobras, and
standard English.

In the case of the third person singular marker and the
possessive, an extraordinary reversal is found. For the
Thunderbirds, the situation can be summarized as follows:

Z_V	-K	-V
simplified	17	12
not simplified	4	0

Not only is the extent of simplification higher in Z_V than
for Z_{PL}, but the direction of influence of a following vowel

is reversed. No clusters at all appeared in the most favorable environment for the phonological rule. We can infer
that this is no longer effectively described as consonant
cluster simplification, but rather as a grammatical fact.
The third person singular marker //-s// does not exist in
the particular grammar being used here. The same argument
holds for the possessive //-s// marker, though as noted
above, we cannot extend this argument to infer a loss of the
possessive in general.

A striking fact about this situation is that the older
group has gained in several respects as far as approximation
to standard English forms is concerned, but their development
has not affected the grammatical status of the third person
singular marker.

Consequences for the Teaching of Reading

Let us consider the problem of teaching a youngster to
read who has the general phonological and grammatical characteristics just described. The most immediate way of ana-
lyzing his difficulties is through the interpretation of his
oral reading. As we have seen, there are many phonological
rules which affect his pronunciation, but not necessarily
his understanding of the grammatical signals or his grasp of
the underlying lexical forms. The two questions are distinct:
the relations between grammar and pronunciation are complex,
and require careful interpretation.

If a student is given a certain sentence to read, say
He passed by both of them, he may say [hi pæs ba^I bof ə dɛm].
The teacher may wish to correct this bad reading, perhaps by
saying, "No, it isn't [hi pæs ba^I bof ə dɛm], it's [hi pæst
ba^I boθ əv ðɛm]." One difficulty is that these two utterances
may sound the same to many children—both the reader and those
listening—and they may be utterly confused by the correction.
Others may be able to hear the difference, but have no idea

of the significance of the extra [t] and the interdental
forms of th-. The most embarrassing fact is that the boy
who first read the sentence may have performed his reading
task correctly, and understood the -ed suffix just as it
was intended. In that case, the teacher's correction is
completely beside the point.

We have two distinct cases to consider. In one case,
the deviation in reading may be only a difference in pronunciation on the part of a child who has a different set of
homonyms from the teacher. Here, correction might be quite
unnecessary. In the second case, we may be dealing with a
boy who has no concept of -ed as a past tense marker, who
considers the -ed a meaningless set of silent letters. Obviously the correct teaching strategy would involve distin-
guishing these two cases, and treating them quite differently.

How such a strategy might be put into practice is a
problem that educators may be able to solve by using information provided by linguists. As a linguist, I can suggest
several basic principles derived from our work which may be
helpful in further curriculum research and application.

1. In the analysis and correction of oral reading,
teachers must begin to make the basic distinction between
differences in pronunciation and mistakes in reading. Information on the dialect patterns of Negro children should be
helpful toward this end.

2. In the early stages of teaching reading and spelling, it may be necessary to spend much more time on the
grammatical function of certain inflections, which may have
no function in the dialect of some of the children. In the
same way, it may be necessary to treat the final elements of
certain clusters with the special attention given to silent
letters such as b in lámb.

3. A certain amount of attention given to perception
training in the first few years of school may be extremely
helpful in teaching children to hear and make standard English distinctions. But perception training need not be complete in order to teach children to read. On the contrary,
most of the differences between standard and nonstandard
English described here can be taken as differences in the
sets of homonyms which must be accepted in reading patterns.
On the face of it, there is no reason why a person cannot
learn to read standard English texts quite well in a non-
standard pronunciation. Eventually, the school may wish to
teach the child an alternative system of pronunciation. But
the key to the situation in the early grades is for the
teacher to know the system of homonyms of nonstandard English,
and to know the grammatical differences that separate her own
speech from that of the child. The teacher must be prepared
to accept the system of homonyms for the moment, if this will
advance the basic process of learning to read, but not the
grammatical differences. Thus the task of teaching the child
to read -ed is clearly that of getting him to recognize the
graphic symbols as a marker of the past tense, quite distinct
from the task of getting him to say [pæst] for passed.

If the teacher has no understanding of the child's grammar and set of homonyms, she may be arguing with him at cross
purposes. Over and over again, the teacher may insist that
cold and coal are different, without realizing that the child
perceives this as only a difference in meaning, not in sound.
She will not be able to understand why he makes so many odd
mistakes in reading, and he will experience only a vague confusion, somehow connected with the ends of words. Eventually,
he may stop trying to analyze the shapes of letters that follow the vowel, and guess wildly at each word after he deci-
phers the first few letters. Or he may lose confidence in

the alphabetic principle as a whole, and try to recognize each word as a whole. This loss of confidence seems to occur frequently in the third and fourth grades, and it is characteristic of many children who are effectively nonreaders.

The sources of reading problems discussed in this paper are only a few of the causes of poor reading in the ghetto schools. But they are quite specific and easily isolated. The information provided here may have immediate application in the overall program of improving the teaching of reading to children in these urban areas.

NOTES

1. The research described here is a part of Cooperative Research Project No. 3091, U.S. Office of Education: "A Preliminary Study of the Structure of English Used by Negro and Puerto Rican Speakers in New York City." For much of the field work and analysis, I am indebted to Paul Cohen, Clarence Robins, John Lewis, Jr., and Joshua Waletzky of the project staff. The Final Report on Cooperative Research Project 3091 is available through ERIC, ED 010 688.

2. See "Stages in the Acquisition of Standard English," in Roger Shuy (ed.), Social Dialects and Language Learning (Champaign, Illinois: National Council of Teachers of English, 1965), pp. 77-103.

3. The continuing research discussed here is part of Cooperative Research Project No. 3288, U.S. Office of Education, "A Study of the Non-Standard English of Negro and Puerto Rican Speakers in New York City." The Final Report on Cooperative Research Project 3288 will be available through ERIC at the end of 1968.

4. These observations are based upon experience with many teachers of English, Negro and white, at summer reading institutes, conferences on social dialects, principals' conferences, and other meetings where the speech of Negro people in urban ghettos has been discussed.

5. Many examples of this stereotyping process are discussed

in William Labov, The Social Stratification of English
in New York City (Washington, D.C.: Center for Applied
Linguistics, 1966).

6. H. Kökeritz, Shakespeare's Pronunciation (New Haven: Yale
    University Press, 1953); and H.C. Wyld, A History of
    Modern Colloquial English (Oxford: Basil Blackwell, 1920).

7. Such a phenomenon can be observed in suburban Bergen
    County, along the boundary of the New York City dialect
    area. In Closter, N.J., for example, the socioeconomic
    differentiation of speakers by r-pronunciation seems to
    be much more extreme than in the city itself: middle-
    class children may pronounce final and preconsonantal
    /r/ consistently, while working-class children will be
    completely r-less, and this difference is maintained over
    a wide range of stylistic contexts.

8. The forms for the Family Background test give the listen-
    er a limited choice of ethnic backgrounds: Irish, Afro-
    American, Spanish, Jewish, German, and Other White.
    Within each category, one can specify "S" Southern, "N"
    Northern, or "W" Western.

9. These data are derived from series of interviews with
    individuals and groups in South Central Harlem and ex-
    ploratory interviews in other Northern cities: Boston,
    Philadelphia, Cleveland, Detroit, and Chicago.

10. In New York City, the correlation of /r/ and stylistic
    context follows a very regular pattern, as discussed in
    The Social Stratification of English in New York City,
    and other references cited above. Negro speakers are
    especially sensitive to the prestige status of /r/. The
    systematic shift indicates the importance of controlling
    the stylistic factor, as well as socioeconomic factors,
    in gathering data on speech patterns.

11. In many cases, pairs such as guard-god, nor-gnaw, are
    differentiated by vowel quality. For most Negro speakers
    in Northern cities, they are identical. Pairs such as
    sore-saw or court-caught, which oppose M.E. closed o
    before r to long open o, are differentiated more often
    by vowel quality, especially among older people. In any
    case, the lists of homonyms given here and elsewhere are
    given as examples of possible homonyms illustrative of
    large classes of words that are frequently identical.

    It should be noted that words with mid-central vowels

before r do not follow the r-less patterns discussed
here; r appears much more frequently in such words as
work, shirt, bird, even when it is not used after other
vowels.

12. One English dialect which shows systematic l-lessness is
    Cockney, as described in E. Sivertsen, Cockney Phonology
    (Oslo, 1960).

13. When the /t/ or /d/ represents a grammatical inflection,
    these consonants are usually automatic alternants of the
    same abstract form //ed//. Phonetic rules delete the
    vowel (except after stems ending in /t/ or /d/, and we
    then have /t/ following voiceless consonants such as
    /p, s, š, k/ and /d/ in all other cases. In the same
    way /s/ and /z/ are coupled as voiceless and voiced
    alternants of the same //s// inflection. But in clusters
    that are a part of the root, we do not have such auto-
    matic alternation.

14. The loss of the first element—that is, assimilation to
    the following /s/—is most common in forms where the /s/
    represents the verb is or the pronoun us as in it's,
    that's and let's. In none of these cases is there a
    problem of homonymy, even in the case of let's where
    there is no likelihood of confusion with less. This type
    of simplification will therefore not be considered in any
    further detail. It should be noted that "simplification"
    in regard to the loss of final /s/ is merely a device for
    presenting the data: as we will see, there are several
    cases where we are forced to conclude that the /s/ is not
    there to begin with.

15. This homonym was troublesome to us for some time. One
    member of the Thunderbirds is known as "Boo." We did not
    notice the occasional glottal stop which ended this word
    as a functional unit for some time; eventually we began
    to suspect that the underlying form was "Boot." This was
    finally confirmed when he appeared in sneakers labeled
    BOOT.

16. The word poor is frequently pronounced with a mid-vowel
    [po] even by those who do not have a complete merger of
    such pairs as sure-shore, moor-more. One of our Gullah-
    influenced South Carolina informants on Saint Helena
    Island is named Samuel Pope or Polk, but we cannot de-
    termine which from his pronunciation.

17. The // // notation encloses morphophonemic forms—that

is, forms of words which are the most abstract representation underlying the variants that occur in particular environments as determined by some regular process.
English spelling is, on the whole, morphophonemic rather
than phonemic: the stem academ-, for example, is spelled
the same way even though it is pronounced very differently in academy, academic, academe and academician.

[The situation in regard to r is not quite this regular in white working-class speech. "Intrusive r" does
appear at the end of saw in I saw a parade, and consonantal [r] is sometimes not pronounced in sore arm. But
the general pattern indicated above prevails and provides
enough support for the spelling forms.]

18.   This is precisely what does happen when final consonants
are lost in words that have no spelling forms, no correlates in careful speech, and no regular morphophonemic
alternation. Terms used in preadolescent culture will
occur with a profusion of such variants (which may be
continued in the adolescent years). For example, in
Chicago the term for the base used in team versions of
Hide-and-Seek is the goose. This is derived from the
more general term gu:l with loss of final /l/—a dialect
form of goal. (Cf. the alternation Gould and Gold in
proper names.) A similar phenomenon occurs in New York
City, where the same item is known as the dent—related
to older den. It is worth noting that both of these
cases are characteristic of language change among the
Negro speakers we are discussing, and illustrate the un-
checked consequences of the homonymy we are considering.
A more extreme case may be cited: in one group of teenage Negro boys, the position known elsewhere as War Lord
(the member who arranges the details for gang fights)
has shifted to a term with the underlying form //war
dorf//, or possibly //waldorf// or //ward f//.

18[a].   [For an account of these repetition tests, see Cooperative
Research Report 3288.]

19.   In the Creole-based English of Trinidad, however, we do
find regularly the forms he book, she book, etc. The
grammatical differences between Trinidadian English and
standard English are therefore much greater than those
between nonstandard American Negro English and standard
English. In the same way, we find the past tense irregular forms preserved in the dialects we are studying, but
only the unmarked stem he give, he tell in Trinidad.
See D. Solomon, "The System of Predication in the Speech
of Trinidad," Columbia University Master's Essay, 1966.

20. Given this situation, it is evident that more colloquial
     reading texts with contracted forms he'll and you'll
     will not be easy for Negro children to read. The tra-
     ditional uncontracted he will and you will may seem
     slightly artificial to some, but will not involve the
     problems of homonymy discussed here.

21. In the classroom correction test, the same problem arises
     which affects any test given in the schoolroom: how hard
     is the subject trying to give the right answer? It is
     likely that the boy's general orientation toward the
     schoolroom would tend to reduce the amount of effort they
     put into this particular test; but we can base our con-
     clusions on the type of grammatical feature which is
     noticed and corrected, rather than the total number cor-
     rected.

22. Two other types of //-s// can be isolated: the adverbial
     /s/ of besides, sometimes, etc., and the various con-
     tracted forms mentioned above: that's, it's and let's.
     The first is not frequent enough to provide good data
     for the small groups discussed here, and the second type
     shows a loss of the first element of the cluster with no
     grammatical effect.

ORTHOGRAPHY IN READING MATERIALS FOR

BLACK ENGLISH SPEAKING CHILDREN

by Ralph W. Fasold

Reading is the process of relating written symbols to units
of spoken language. There are only two basic ways in which
writing systems represent speech. In a writing system based
on morphological reference, each meaningful unit of spoken
language is represented by a separate symbol regardless of
how it is pronounced. This system is essentially the nature
of Chinese orthography, and accounts for the fact that written
Chinese is intelligible to speakers of different Chinese languages. Since there is no reference to pronunciation in the
writing system, the same symbols can be used to represent
different languages so long as those languages have roughly
the same lexical items and roughly the same syntax, even
when the lexical items are pronounced very differently in the
various languages.

The other system identifies meaningful units less directly. In this kind of writing system, the symbols refer to
the phonological aspects of the units. Two variations of
writing systems with phonological reference have developed.
One of these is the alphabet, in which each symbol refers to
a sound segment; the other is the syllabary, in which each
symbol refers to a whole syllable. The writing system used
in English is an alphabet, and each letter ideally stands for
one segment in English phonology.

However, the sound segments recognized by modern linguistics exist on various levels of abstraction. This fact

leads to the question: At what level of abstraction could the
English writing system best represent the segments of English
phonology? Once this is determined, it seems reasonable to
ask to what extent the English spelling system actually does
represent these segments. A given spelling is <u>correct</u> with
respect to this representation if it accurately reflects the
segments at that level. A spelling is <u>conventional</u> if it is
the usual spelling for this word. For example, if the segments of the word 'fat' at the appropriate level of abstraction are [fæt] and <u>f</u> is the symbol which represents [f], <u>a</u>
is the symbol for [æ], and <u>t</u> is the symbol for [t], then
<u>fat</u> is the correct spelling, and, since <u>fat</u> is the usual
spelling for the word, it is also conventional. If the segments of the word 'cat' at this same level of abstraction are
[kæt] and the symbol for [k] is <u>k</u>, and the symbols for [æ]
and [t] are <u>a</u> and <u>t</u> respectively, then <u>kat</u> is the correct
spelling for 'cat'. But since the accepted spelling is <u>cat</u>,
the spelling is not conventional. If the appropriate segments of the word 'rough' are [rʌf], then the spelling <u>rough</u>,
while it is conventional, is not correct. Finally, if someone were to spell 'mat' as <u>mta</u>, the spelling would be neither
correct nor conventional. When the relationship between
phonology and the writing system has been established, the
next step is to analyze the ways in which conventional spellings are incorrect and to devise methods for teaching the
child to handle these failures in the writing system.

One conceivable answer to the question of level of abstraction is that the alphabet should represent phonetic segments. In this view, the reader would have a mark on paper
for every acoustic feature perceivable to the human ear.
There are overwhelming objections to this view. First, because there are so many perceivable acoustic differences in
speech sounds, the alphabet would need to contain a tremendous

number of symbols. Second, the English alphabet is clearly
not designed to handle this task, since it contains only 26
symbols. Third, the acoustic features of the pronunciation
of any given word vary from one utterance of the word to
another. In addition, it is obvious that not all acoustic
features need to be marked, since only some of them are used
to keep lexical items separate from each other. Only those
which serve to separate lexical items need to be indicated
in the orthography.

The most popular answer to these objections is that the
writing system should represent segments at the phonemic
level. By phonemic analysis, the tremendous variety of
speech sounds is reduced to a relatively few segments which
are distinctive. As a result, the phonemic spelling principle has been proposed. According to this principle, the
ideal writing system would have only one symbol for one phoneme. The success of an existing orthography would be determined by its degree of deviation from this ideal. This suggests a certain strategy for the teaching of reading, i.e.
that words whose conventional spellings conform to the phonemic principle be taught first and other words be introduced later, as anomalies. A phonemic writing system has
many advantages over a phonetic one. The number of necessary
symbols is reduced to a manageable number and the degree of
deviation from conventional spelling is greatly reduced. In
a phonetic writing system, there is no justification for
using the same symbol for the [p] in 'spit' and the [pʰ] in
'pit', since there is noticeably greater aspiration on the
[pʰ] in 'pit'. But by phonemic analysis, both sounds are
assigned to the same phoneme and can justifiably be written
with the same symbol. On the other hand, the spelling of a
word such as mussel cannot be justified, since the phonemes
of this word are something like /mʌsɨl/. The spelling mussel

fails to conform to the phonemic principle in several ways.
The first vowel should not be spelled with a u since this
symbol is needed for the vowel of words like 'put' (phonemically /put/) and for part of the complex vowel nucleus
of words like 'spoon' (phonemically /spuwn/). The double s
is inappropriate because two symbols are used for only one
phoneme. The spelling e for the phoneme /ɨ/ is not correct
since the e of 'bet' is not the same as the e of 'mussel',
and the symbol e is generally used for the former.

While the phonemic principle results in a great reduction in the number of necessary symbols as compared with
phonetic writing, and while its application considerably
reduces the number of inappropriate spellings in the conventional orthography, it still leaves a number of spelling
anomalies in the conventional system. More serious, the
justification of the phoneme as a linguistic entity has been
called into serious question.[1] If the phoneme is not a real
entity, it can hardly be the basis for the most appropriate
writing system.

An alternative to the phonemic spelling principle has
recently been suggested. In this view, alphabetic symbols
represent phonological segments on a more abstract level.
In generative phonology, there are at least two alternatives
for what this level would be. The alphabetic symbols could
be said to represent segments of the lexical representation.
If this were the case, many conventional spellings would
fail to conform to the principle because the symbols are too
specific in reference. For the word 'street', to take an
extreme example, the first letter in the spelling street is
inappropriate to correspond to the first segment in the lexical representation, since the lexical representation need
only indicate that there is a segment preceding t. The normal constraints on the structure of English morphemes precludes

any segment but)s(in this position.* Similarly, the letter
r represents the only segment possible in its position. A
more appropriate spelling to represent the lexical form of
'street' would be ∅t∅eet, with the zeroes merely indicating
that a segment is present.[2] The other possibility within the
framework of generative phonology is that the alphabetic
symbols represent segments which are fully specified in ac-
cordance with the redundancy conditions on the structure of
English morphemes, but not for any features determined by the
phonological rules proper. Richard Stanley has proposed that
phonological theory include a process by which lexical entries
with partially specified segments are replaced by a representation with all segments fully specified in this way.[3] This
is the level which seems most realistic and at the same time
closest to what the conventional English spelling actually
does represent.[4]

The arguments which show that there is an abstract but
linguistically justifiable level of phonology to which conventional spelling corresponds most neatly are involved ones.[5]
As we have shown above, this spelling fails to meet the requirements of the phonemic spelling principle in several ways.
But as Chomsky and Halle show, this is exactly the correct
spelling to represent the word 'mussel' before the phonological rules proper apply. For a number of reasons, the phonology of English must contain a rule which in one of its
applications reduces the vocalic nucleus)u(in abstract
representations to phonetic [ʌ]. With few exceptions, phonetic [ʊ] and [ʌ] are in complementary distribution in
American English, [ʊ] occurring following nonnasal labial
segments and preceding either double or final)l(or a

---

* In the discussion that follows, alphabetic symbols that
  represent phonological segments on the abstract level are
  given between reversed parentheses, e.g.)s(,)u(, etc.

voiceless alveolopalatal consonant--)š(or)č(--and [ʌ] appearing elsewhere.[6] If the underlying representations of words
containing phonetic [ʌ] are assumed to contain underlying
)u(, rules of great generality in English phonology will
automatically convert this)u(to [ʌ] in the proper environments.[7]

The word 'mussel' must also contain double)s(and
undergo a rule which deletes the first of two identical consonants. English phonology contains a rule which voices
)s(intervocalically. Pairs like 'resent' and 'consent',
and 'resist' and 'consist', illustrate this rule. In 'resent'
and 'resist', the orthographic s is intervocalic and is pronounced [z]. In 'consent' and 'consist', the operation of
this voicing rule is blocked by the presence of)n(, and the
s is pronounced as a voiceless [s]. Similarly, 'dissemble'
(phonetically [dɪsɛmbl̩]) contains a voiceless fricative while
'resemble' (phonetically [riyzɛmbl̩]) has the voiced counterpart. The presence of [s] in 'dissemble' can be explained if
we assume that the underlying form of the word has double
)s(. If this is the case, neither)s(is intervocalic and
the)s(-voicing rule does not apply. At the same time, this
assumption neatly fits the analysis of 'dissemble' into the
prefix 'dis' and the stem 'semble'. But since 'dissemble' is
not pronounced with a geminate [s], there must be a rule which
simplifies geminate consonant clusters. If we extend this
analysis to 'mussel', we can preserve the generality of the
voicing of intervocalic [s] and still account for the pronunciation [mʌsl̩].[8]

Finally, English reduction rules will reduce)el(to
[l̩].

These facts about English phonology lead to the conclusion that the abstract representation of the word 'mussel'
is, in fact,)mussel(. The rules we have discussed derive

the pronunciation [mʌsḷ] from this representation in the
following way:

Underlying representation:	mussel
u → ʌ rule:	mʌssel
Voicing of intervocalic s:	(does not apply)
Geminate cluster simplification rule:	mʌsel
Reduction rule:	mʌsḷ

While the spelling mussel is inadequate either phonetically
or phonemically, it is precisely correct for the representation of the sort of underlying form suggested by Stanley.
Chomsky and Halle point out that many other conventional
spellings are similarly appropriate.[9]

The view of the reading educator about the nature of
the relationship between speech and writing will have implications for the methodology used in teaching reading. Reading involves two tasks: (1) to determine the identity of
words, and (2) to understand the grammatical relationships
between them. The first task is successfully achieved when
the reader associates a part of the printed matter with a
word in his language.[10] Because reading also involves the
second task, i.e. the understanding of the grammatical relationships among words, it may seem that dealing with the
identification of words is not enough. In his book Linguistics and the Teaching of Reading, Carl Lefevre draws attention to the whole sentence before treating word identification.
Since intonation plays an important role in determining syntactic structure in spoken language, Lefevre suggests that
beginning readers should be taught to look for clues to intonation on the printed page. Lefevre believes that readers
will be able to determine the syntactic structure of a written
sentence by imagining what its intonation would be if it were
spoken.[11] However it seems more reasonable to suppose that
reading proceeds in exactly the reverse order. A reader can
determine the proper intonation of a written sentence only

from the syntactic structure. Punctuation is probably best
considered a device for marking off various kinds of phrases
and sentences rather than for indicating intonation directly.
Once the nature of the construction of a sentence is known
to the reader, he can supply the correct intonation because
of his knowledge of the language he is reading. Thus, intonation seems to be of marginal importance to the reading
process. If a reader can identify written words and can
interpret punctuation marks, he has all the information he
needs in order to understand sentences. For this reason,
word identification is the sine qua non of successful reading.

It will be our assumption that words are most efficiently
identified if the printed symbols are interpreted as referring
to phonological segments rather than as direct representations
of lexical items, as is true in Chinese.[12] Furthermore, we
assume that the English spelling system refers approximately
to the phonology of units at the level of lexical representation in the sense of generative phonology, plus the full
specification of redundant features according to the constraints on the form of English morphemes.

Given these assumptions, we are ready to address ourselves to the specific problems of how children learn to
read. We are arguing that spellings like mussel are correct
even though they do not represent the surface pronunciation
of the word very well. One of the crucial arguments that
this spelling is correct involves the comparison of words
like 'consist' with 'resist', and 'resemble' with 'dissemble',
to establish the)s(-voicing and geminate consonant simplification rules. If we suppose that a child learning his first
language uses evidence of this sort in some way in the process of language learning, presumably he will not acquire
the language competence described by these rules until he

learns items like 'resist' and 'consist', 'resemble' and
'dissemble', and realizes that they related. Our argument
that _mussel_ is the correct way to spell 'mussel' assumes that
the reader has acquired the)s(-voicing and geminate consonant simplification rules, among others. If he has not yet
acquired them, the conventional spelling of 'mussel' will be
anomalous.

There are a great many words in English for which the
conventional spellings can be shown correct in spite of the
fact that they do not directly reflect the actual pronunciations of the words. But nearly all of the arguments in
these cases depend on alternations among Latinate lexical
items. In order to show that _a_ is the correct letter to
represent superficially different vowels in 'sane' and
'sanity', and also that the _e_ in _sane_ represents a vowel that
is actually present in the underlying form of 'sane', it must
be assumed that the reader knows both of these words and many
others like them and also knows that they are related. Children are likely to lack some of these crucial lexical items
in their vocabularies, and, as a result, many spellings that
are correct for educated adults would be anomalous to them.
If ghetto children have fewer of these Latinate words in their
vocabularies, this aspect of the problem of orthography would
be more acute for them than for other children. In any event,
the presence or absence of these crucial items for any given
child is an empirical question which would need to be answered
before the type of reading techniques we will suggest could be
put in effect.[13]

Further problems in teaching reading to some black children arise because of the fact that they come to school speaking the Negro dialect -- Black English. The middle-class
child brings to school essentially the same dialect that he
will be taught to read, i.e. standard English. The Black

English speaking child is asked to learn simultaneously the skill of reading and of speaking a new dialect which is different from his own in many important ways. To complicate the problem, his teacher often does not realize this, and what is worse, will condemn as "bad" those aspects of his dialect which differ from the standard dialect.[14] Chomsky and Halle indicate that they expect underlying forms to differ very little from dialect to dialect:

There has, in other words, been little change in lexical representation since Middle English, and, consequently, we would expect (though we have not verified this in any detail) that lexical representation would differ very little from dialect to dialect in Modern English. If this assumption proves to be correct, it will follow that conventional orthography is probably fairly close to optimal for all Modern English dialects, as well as for the attested dialects of the past several hundred years.[15]

What is implicit in the above statement, however, is that all Modern English dialects are direct descendants of the Middle English dialects mentioned. In the case of Black English, a quite different history has been suggested. William A. Stewart has argued that modern Black English (he uses the term Negro non-standard dialect) can be traced to a variety of English creole which was used by slaves early in the history of European settlement of this continent.[16] Many of the features of this creole language originate in the African languages of the slaves. The early creole gradually became more like Standard American English, but many of the features of present-day Black English, in this view, are traceable to this creole and not to early British dialects. If some of these creole features have survived in modern Black English phonology, and furthermore, if they involve the underlying structure of lexical representations, it may well be that Chomsky and Halle's statement does not apply to this dialect of English. Most of the examples of

differences between Black English and Standard English which
Stewart gives are grammatical, but in one article he cites a
difference in phonemic contrast:[17]

Note that in this dialect there are no apico-dental fricatives,
standard English /ð/ and /θ/ showing up as /d/ and /t/ in
initial positions, and usually as /v/ and /f/ elsewhere.

Actually, this description is factually not quite right. The
Black English pronunciation of words which begin with [θ] in
Standard English has the affricate [tθ], if not the fricative
[θ] itself. As a result, the words 'thought' and 'taught'
are not homonyms in Black English and there is a phonemic
difference between /t/ and /tθ ~ θ/ in the dialect. However,
it could be argued that the dental fricative or affricate
phonemes are restricted to word-initial position in Black
English, as /h/ is in Standard English. That is, the apico-
dental consonants appear in word-initial position, but nowhere else. In every other position where a word appears in
Standard English with /θ/, for example, Black English has /f/.
Because of this, there is no problem of a phonemic contrast
in Standard English which is missing in Black English, but
there is a phonemic difference none the less. The problem
is that the phonemic composition of some words is different
in the two dialects. For example, the word 'tooth' is phonemically /tuwθ/ in the standard dialect and /tuwf/ in Black
English. According to the phonemic spelling principle, the
spelling tooth is anomalous for the Black English speaker,
but not for the Standard English speaker.

But since we have seen that there is evidence that the
phonemic spelling principle is not appropriate as a guide for
teaching reading, this is not enough. We must ask what the
form of words like 'tooth' is in their underlying representations. At this level, we see that there is indeed a contrast
between the [f] which matches Standard English [θ], and the

[f] which matches Standard English [f]. In certain situations, words with word-final [f] in Black English are pronounced with a [t]. Consider the two sentences:

> Get off my bike!
> Come back with my bike!

One possible Black English pronunciation of these sentences is:

> [gɪt ɔf ma bayk]
> [kəm bæk wɪf ma bayk]

In rapid speech, the [f] in 'with' can be pronounced as [t], but not the [f] in 'off':

> *[gɪt ɔt ma bayk]
> [kəm bæk wɪt ma bayk]

It is necessary, then, before the phonological rules apply, to designate which kind of [f] is which. Given the system of English phonology, it can be shown fairly convincingly that the appropriate segment to represent the underlying final consonant of 'with' is)θ(, even if it is never so pronounced. To the extent that th is the proper spelling for this segment, the final th spelling is correct for Black English as well as for Standard English.

There may be words ending in th and pronounced with final [f] in Black English which never fall into the environment in which [t] can appear. For these, there is no motivation to specify underlying)θ(. Since the pronunciation is always [f], one would specify the underlying representation for these words as containing)f(. The result is that while the th spelling is correct for some words which end in th in conventional spellings, f seems to be the correct spelling for others.

A similar situation exists for words with medial th spellings. A word like 'nothing' can be pronounced either [nʌfn̩] or [nʌtn̩], whereas a word like 'stiffen' can be pronounced only [stɪfn̩]. Other words spelled with medial th (e.g. 'ether') never fall into the environment in which [t] can be pronounced, so the correct spelling of these words, by our principle, would be with f. Again, some th spellings are correct (e.g. th is correct in 'nothing') and others are not (e.g. the correct spelling of 'ether' would be efer).

But in deciding that some conventional th spellings are incorrect, we are overlooking an important part of the evidence. By far the majority of the people who use the [f] pronunciation of conventionally spelled th do so only part of the time. The rest of the time, [θ] is used. It could be argued that the [θ] pronunciation is a borrowing from Standard English and has nothing to do with Black English phonology. If this were the case, one would expect hypercorrection to extend the [θ] pronunciation to other words with [f], so that one would observe not only both [wɪf] and [wɪθ] for 'with', but [ɔf] and [ɔθ] for 'off'. But this does not happen, since pronunciations like [ɔθ] are never heard. Clearly, Black English speakers know which words are which. The problem is how to account for this knowledge in a linguistic description of the dialect. There are at least three possible solutions. One of these would be to allow the lexical entries of the words which are sometimes pronounced with [θ] to be marked as loanwords from Standard English which, as a result, do not follow the constraints of Black English phonology. The implication is that there are two words 'with'. One is given the underlying representation)wif(, and is marked as a native word. The other is represented as)wiθ(, and is marked as a loanword exempt from the ordinary Black English constraints on the distribution of [θ].

Another solution is to assume that a speaker who uses both [f] and [θ] pronunciations is really a bilingual. Any sentence containing a [θ] pronunciation in medial or final position is not a Black English sentence at all; rather, the speaker has switched to his other language, Standard English.

However, there are innumerable cases in which a word spelled with a final or medial th is pronounced with a [θ], but this is the only feature in the entire sentence which must be considered Standard. To refer to this sort of situation as an example of bilingual code-switching would make the concept of code-switching meaningless.

The third solution is probably the best one. Since we have already seen that there is intradialectal motivation for recognizing underlying)θ(in some words which actually are pronounced with [f], we could merely extend the device to words which never are pronounced with [t] but sometimes are pronounced with [θ].

There is even more evidence that the alternation between [θ] and [f] is an integral part of the structure of Black English. Wolfram has shown that there are markedly more instances of the [θ] pronunciation if the segment is in medial position than if it is in final position.[18] This is the natural situation for the application of what Labov calls the variable rule.[19] Labov observed that the frequency of application of a phonological rule is often systematically determined by the environment. He has formulated a modification of phonological rule form in generative phonology so that the relative frequency of application according to environment can be formally indicated. It seems clear that such a rule for the variation between [f] and [θ] is part of Black English phonology. This being the case, word-medial and word-final)θ(is to be marked in the underlying representation and undergoes this variable rule. Underlying word-medial and word-final)f(does not. These arguments lead us to the conclusion that the th spelling is correct for Black English for virtually all words which are spelled conventionally in this way.[20]

Another example of the relationship of phonological rule to conventional orthography is the case of the final stop

devoicing in Black English. Words ending in final voiced
stops in the standard dialect end in the corresponding voiceless stop in Black English. However, the preceding vowel
nucleus of such words is long in duration, like the vowel
nuclei of words ending in voiced consonants in Standard English. Thus the word 'bit' in Black English is pronounced
[bɪt] while 'bid' is pronounced [bɪːt]. At first it seems
that we have a contrastive difference in vowel length in
Black English, but a consonantal contrast in Standard English. However, we find that the lengthening rule for vowels
before voiced segments operates in Black English before
laterals ([bɪːl] 'bill', but [bɪt] 'bit') and before stops
in non-final position ([bɪːgə] 'bigger' but [bɪkə] 'bicker').
This would suggest that the proper phonemic analysis would
be to allow both /d/ and /t/ to have the allophone [t] in
word-final position, with vowel lengthening before the [t]
of /d/ but not before the [t] of /t/. Such an analysis runs
afoul of the classical problem of phonemic overlapping.[21]
Another possible solution would be to posit phonemic vowel
length, but this would not allow the expression of the
generality about the lengthening of vowels before non-final
voiced consonants. This solution, of course, would render
the conventional spelling bid of 'bid' incorrect by the phonemic spelling principle. If phonemic analysis is abandoned,
there is no problem. The underlying form of these words
clearly has the voiced stop, and there are two ordered rules
in the phonology of Black English such that the first leng-
thens vowels before voiced segments and the second devoices
a word-final stop consonant. The first rule is shared with
Standard English, but the second is peculiar to Black English. Again, the result is that the conventional spelling
is correct for Black English.

A third example of the relationship of phonological

rules to conventional orthography is found in connection with the Black English pronunciation of words which end in a cluster of [s] plus a voiceless stop in Standard English.[22] In Black English, there is no trace of the stop member of such clusters. Thus, 'desk' is pronounced [dɛs], 'risk' is pronounced [rɪs] and 'test' is pronounced [tɛs]. The question which needs to be answered is whether or not the final stop is present in the underlying representation. The answer will automatically solve the concomitant problem concerning whether the spellings desk, risk and test are correct for Black English.

Examination of the plurals of these words indicates that the stop member of the clusters is not present in the underlying representations. The plurals of these forms are typically pronounced [dɛsɪz], [rɪsɪz], and [tɛsɪz], respectively. As is well known, there are three forms of the English plural, depending on the preceding segment. If this segment is voiced, the plural form is [z], as in 'dogs' [dɔgz]. If it is voiceless, the plural is [s], as in 'cats' [kæts]. If the final segment is a sibilant, the plural is [ɪz], as in 'horses' [hɔrsɪz]. The use of [ɪz] as the plural marker for words like 'desk', 'risk' and 'test' indicates that there is no final stop consonant present in their underlying representations in Black English. If it were otherwise, the expected plurals would be [dɛss], [rɪss] and [tɛss], respectively.[23] These plurals would arise by application of the following operations:

        Underlying representation: desk + z
        Voicing assimilation: desk + s
        Final cluster simplification: des + s
        Boundary deletion: dess

However, if the underlying representation does not contain a final stop consonant, the derivation is as follows:

        Underlying representation: des + z
        Vowel epenthesis: des + ɪz
        Boundary deletion: desɪz

But another set of facts complicates the picture. If a suffix beginning with a vowel is added to these forms, the final stop consonant is articulated by the majority of Black English speakers. Thus we get the pronunciations [tɛstɪn] and [rɪskiy] for 'testing' and 'risky'. The conclusion suggested by these forms would seem to be that the underlying representation must contain the final stop consonant, which seems to contradict the conclusion suggested by the plural forms. But both the plural forms and the vowel-suffix forms can be explained if the underlying representations include the final consonant and the rules are properly ordered. Something like the following three rules are needed:

1. Consonant-cluster simplification:

   $sC_{st} \Rightarrow s$ in env. _____ (+X)#, where X does not begin with a vowel

2. Epenthesis:

   $Z + Z \Rightarrow Z + ɪZ$ in env. _____ #

3. Boundary deletion:

   boundary $\Rightarrow \emptyset$

Rule 1 states that of two consonants at the end of a word (# symbolizes word boundary) such that the second is a stop (symbolized by C_{st}) and the first is)s(, the stop is deleted, unless followed by a suffix which begins with a vowel. The epenthesis rule (Rule 2) states that the vowel [ɪ] is inserted before a suffix which consists only of a sibilant (symbolized by Z) if the stem ends in a sibilant. Rule 3 deletes boundaries and is an ad hoc summary of what is a general process in the grammars of natural languages. Given these rules, the derivation of 'test', 'tests', and 'testing' in Black English is as follows:

Rule	test	tests	testing
underlying form	#test#	#test+z#	#test+ɪn#
1	#tes#	#tes+z#	(not applicable)
2	(not applicable)	#tes+ɪz#	(not applicable)
3	[tɛs]	[tɛsɪz]	[tɛstɪn]

The crucial factor in the application of the above rules is the ordering of Rules 1 and 2. A vowel-initial suffix must be present when the consonant-cluster deletion rule takes effect in 'testing', but not in the derivation of 'tests'. This result is achieved by allowing epenthesis to apply after cluster deletion. However, all the facts are accounted for only if the underlying form is recognized as including the stop member of the cluster. Again we see that the conventional spelling is the correct one for Black English.[24]

But there are a number of Black English speakers for whom the above rules are not appropriate. Some speakers pronounce the above three forms as [tɛs], [tɛsɨz] and [tɛsn̩], respectively. For these speakers, there is no reason to set up underlying forms which contain a final stop. That is, the underlying form for 'test' is)tes(. As a result, the correct spelling would be tes, and the conventional spelling test is anomalous.[24]

The problem for the educator then is to identify which speakers fail to have the standard underlying form for these words. It is very easy to determine this by means of a short diagnostic test.

With a few marginal exceptions, there is no reason to develop a special orthography just for Black English speakers. Because of the possible lack of certain crucial lexical items in the vocabularies of children in general, it may prove advisable to use some sort of modified orthography in teaching all young children to read. But in the main, conventional English orthography is as adequate for Black English speakers as it is for Standard English speakers.[25]

We suggest that reading be taught to Black English speakers in three stages. At the first stage, reading passages would be contolled so as to include only words whose abstract

and surface representations and conventional spellings are
largely the same. This would mean that most of the words
would be monosyllabic words without radically different
morphemic alternants. At this stage, the reader learns the
principles of sound-symbol association. At the next stage,
correct and conventional spellings which do not match the
phonetics of the words as pronounced would be introduced.
These words should be chosen so as to be only words for which
the children are likely to know the relevant morphemic alternants. They would be introduced without apology for their
failure to conform to surface pronunciation. Theoretically,
this stage should be completely unobtrusive to the pupil,
but this remains to be seen. The final stage would involve
the introduction of words whose conventional spellings are
not correct, but only after the basic reading and spelling
principles have been firmly established.

    Although our view of spelling correctness and the nature
of the reading process in its beginning stages leads us to
the conclusion that there should be no special difficulties
for Black English speakers in reading caused by the way words
are spelled, this definitely does not mean that there is no
problem and that there is no necessity for teachers to make
special adjustments in teaching reading to Black English
speakers. The adjustments must come in teacher-training and
teacher behavior in the classroom. Teachers must be brought
to the realization of two important facts. First, the teaching of reading and the teaching of spoken Standard English
are two completely different jobs. Second, the correct way
to pronounce certain spellings in Black English is not the
same as the correct way to pronounce them in Standard English. A good example is the word 'test', which we have just
discussed. Even for those Black speakers for whom the correct spelling is test, the correct pronunciation is [tɛs].

A child who reads <u>test</u> is [tɛs] should be praised for his
complete mastery of the reading process, not condemned for
"leaving out the <u>t</u>". The practice of condemning Black English speaking children when they correctly read words in
their dialect can do considerable harm.

     An illustration of the effect of this kind of teaching
from the point of view of a speaker of Standard English
might be instructive. The word 'basically' is spelled <u>basi-</u>
<u>cally</u> but pronounced [beysɨkliy]. There is a phonological
rule in English to delete the underlying)æl(in this environment. Therefore the Standard English speaking child
who knows how to read, reads the spelling <u>basically</u> correctly
as [beysɨkliy]. Since his teacher speaks the same dialect
as he does, he is not likely to be contradicted in this pronunciation. But suppose he were to be told that he has made
a mistake in reading this word because he left out the letters
<u>al</u> and that he should have read [beysɨkæliy]. In addition,
he is made to feel foolish because he has failed to react to
two letters which are clearly present on the printed page.
Yet, he knows full well that [beysɨkæliy] is not the correct
pronunciation, because it does not conform to his knowledge
of English, nor do people around him pronounce the word in
this way. As a result, he doubts an important principle of
reading, which he is beginning to learn, namely, that words
can be identified by spelling which reflects their underlying representation and should be pronounced according to
the ordinary rules of English phonology.

     If the child were consistently corrected in this way,
he might learn a different principle of reading. This new
principle would be that words are indeed identified by their
spellings which reflect underlying forms, but that oral
reading is unlike speaking in that one suspends certain rules
in English phonology so as to make surface pronunciation of

words more closely approximate their underlying forms. The
introduction of this complication would be pointless, but if
the child were to be consistently corrected in this way, he
could still learn to read.

The problem for the Black English speaking child is that
the corrections he receives are <u>not</u> consistent. When he reads
<u>basically</u> as [beysɨkliy], his reading is acceptable, reinforc-
ing the correct principle of reading. But when he is told
that [tɛst] rather than [tɛs] is the correct way to read
<u>test</u>, the above spurious principle of oral reading is rein-
forced. Not being a speaker of Standard English, he has no
way of knowing why some words are to be read according to one
principle and others according to another. As a result, the
child is likely to conclude that there is actually no principle at all. Since there is no way to determine the relationship between written symbols and their pronunciation,
wild guessing is the only way to seek the teacher's approval.
Since wild guessing so rarely produces the desired approval,
complete despair may well be the next step.

This difficulty can be overcome by training teachers in
Black English pronunciations so that they will consistently
accept words that are correctly read according to the rules
of Black English phonology. This means that [wɪf] is a correct reading for <u>with</u>, [bɪːt] is the right way to read <u>bid</u>
and that <u>test</u> is properly read as [tɛs].[26]

An accurate understanding of orthography is obviously
not the whole answer to the problem of teaching reading to
inner-city Negro children. The problems of education in the
inner-city are too intricately involved with issues of social
injustice and deprivation to yield to a single solution.
Nevertheless, an understanding of the relationship of spelling
to speaking is crucial in our attempts to improve reading
instruction for inner-city children.

NOTES

1. For examples of these arguments, see Noam A. Chomsky,
    Current Issues in Linguistic Theory, (The Hague: Mouton,
    1964), and Noam Chomsky and Morris Halle, "Some Contro-
    versial Questions in Phonological Theory", Journal of
    Linguistics 1 (1965) p. 97-138.

2. Even this is not quite right, since the first t repre-
    sents a segment which need only be partially specified.

3. Richard Stanley, "Redundancy Rules in Phonology", Language
    43 (1967) p. 393-436. Stanley's proposal is adopted by
    Chomsky and Halle as an "interim solution"; see Noam
    Chomsky and Morris Halle, The Sound Pattern of English
    (New York: Harper and Row, 1968), p. 385-389. Objection
    to the phonemic spelling principle is not limited to
    generative phonologists, however. See, for example,
    Martin Joos, Review of Axel Wijk, Regularized English in
    Language 36 (1960) p. 250-262, and Henry Lee Smith, Jr.,
    "The Concept of the Morphophone", Language 43 (1967)
    p. 318-322.

4. This suggestion will have to be refined somewhat. One
    such refinement seems to be that the application of cer-
    tain low-level optional phonological rules will have to
    be reflected in the orthography. Thus we find contraction
    indicated in the spelling He's (here), I've (got it) and
    doesn't. In places where Black English has such optional
    rules which are missing in Standard English, this may mean
    that the apostrophe should be used in Black English where
    it is not used in Standard English. Certain manifestations
    of the '-ed' suffix may be deleted by an optional low-level
    rule in Black English. This may mean that the Black Eng-
    lish sentence [yɛstɨdey hiy kʌs ælbɪt awt] should be writ-
    ten Yesterday, he cuss' Albert out.

5. These arguments appear in Chomsky and Halle, op. cit.,
    passim, but see especially p. 3-55.

6. Words like 'put' and 'cushion' are true exceptions to this
    generalization. That is, each such lexical entry must be
    marked as exempt from the rules which govern the comple-
    mentary distribution.

7. See Chomsky and Halle, op. cit., p. 203-205, for the
    details of this argument.

8. <u>Ibid.</u>, p. 46-47.

9. <u>Ibid.</u>, p. 49.

10. Those who teach reading by the "whole word" method expect
    the reader to associate the printed word with the spoken
    word by the general configuration of the written word
    rather than by relating letters to phonological segments.
    The implicit assumption of this method is that English is
    written like Chinese and that the writing system has
    morphological and not phonological reference. As a matter
    of fact, English is <u>not</u> written in this way, but that in
    itself is no reason to assume that people cannot success-
    fully learn to read as if it were.

11. Carl Lefevre, <u>Linguistics and the Teaching of Reading</u>
    (New York: McGraw-Hill, 1964) p. 73.

12. We assume that reading with this interpretation will be
    easier for the straightforward reason that English writing
    clearly <u>does</u> refer to the phonological structure of words.

13. As Chomsky and Halle point out, <u>op. cit.</u>, p. 50.

14. I had the experience of working in a ghetto tutoring pro-
    gram in which a well-meaning teacher often greeted the
    utterance of a distinctively Black English sentence by
    the children with the remark, "Now say it in English".
    The remark was invariably met with bewildered silence.
    The point is that the youngsters did not know the "Eng-
    lish" she was referring to and she assumed they did.

15. <u>Op. cit.</u>, p. 54.

16. William A. Stewart, "Sociolinguistic Factors in the His-
    tory of American Negro Dialects", <u>Florida FL Reporter</u>
    Vol. 5, No. 2 (Spring 1967).

17. William A. Stewart, "Foreign Language Teaching Methods
    in Quasi-Foreign Language Situations", in William A.
    Stewart (ed.) <u>Non-Standard Speech and the Teaching of
    English</u> (Washington, D.C.: Center for Applied Linguistics,
    1964), p. 1-14.

18. Walter A. Wolfram, <u>A Sociolinguistic Description of
    Detroit Negro Speech</u> (Washington, D.C.: Center for Applied
    Linguistics, to appear).

19. William Labov, "Contraction, Deletion and Inherent Vari-
     ability of the English Copula" (New York: mimeographed,
     1968).

20. There may be a small minority of Black English speakers
     who do not have the systematic variation between [θ] and
     [f]. But even these speakers have the variation between
     [f] and [t]. For these speakers, the conventional spell-
     ing th in with is correct, although it may not be for
     tooth.

     We have said nothing about [ð] and [v]. Many of the
     arguments which apply to [f] and [θ] also apply to their
     voiced counterparts, although the situation is a little
     less clear.

21. For discussion of this point, see Wolfram, op. cit.

22. This is a special case of a more general matter involv-
     ing final clusters of continuant plus stop in which the
     voicing of both members is the same.

23. It turns out that these actually are the plural forms of
     these words for many English speakers of both races and
     of all social classes.

24. This argument is essentially that given in William Labov,
     "A Study of the Non-Standard English of Negro and Puerto
     Rican Speakers in New York City, Volume I: Phonological
     and Grammatical Analysis", Final Report, Cooperative
     Research Project No. 3288 (New York: Columbia University
     [1968]), p. 131-133; cf. also Labov's addition to the
     text of his article "Some Sources of Reading Problems
     for Negro Speakers of Nonstandard English" as reprinted
     in this volume, especially pages 49-50.

25. These examples might lead the reader to the conclusion
     that we are deriving Black English forms from their
     Standard English counterparts. However, this is not the
     case. The Black English pronunciations are being derived
     from Black English underlying phonological forms which
     happen to resemble Standard English pronunciations. But
     the evidence for positing the Black English underlying
     forms comes entirely from within the dialect itself.

26. This procedure has been suggested in Kenneth S. Goodman's
     article "Dialect Barriers to Reading Comprehension",
     reprinted in this volume (see pages 14-28).

TEACHING READING IN AN URBAN NEGRO SCHOOL SYSTEM

by Joan C. Baratz

The inner-city Negro child is failing in our schools. His
inability to read is a major challenge to contemporary educators because of its relationship to the child's self-esteem
and his ultimate social effectiveness.

Failure to acquire functionally adequate reading skills
not only contributes to alienation from the school as a social
institution (and therefore encourages dropping out), but it
goes on to insure failure in mainstream job success. There
is certainly a relationship between reading success or failure
on the one hand, and receptivity to or alienation from the
society in which those reading skills are highly valued
(Labov and Robins, 1967). It is almost impossible to under-
estimate the chain of reactions which can be touched off by
early and continued educational failure which so many disadvantaged Negro children experience in even the most well-
intentioned schools. Because the educational system has been
ineffective in coping with teaching inner-city children to
read, it treats reading failure (in terms of grading, ranking,
etc.) as if this failure were due to intellectual deficits of
the child rather than to methodological inadequacies in teaching procedures. Thus the system is unable to teach the child
to read, but very quickly teaches him to regard himself as
intellectually inadequate, and therefore, of low self-worth
and low social value.

Despite the enormous expenditure of energy in remedial

reading programs, children in the ghetto are still not learning to read (National Advisory Council on Education of the
Disadvantaged, 1966). Although the difficulties of teaching
reading to a portion of the population is a unique problem
for the United States, the problem itself is not unique.
The parallels are quite clear between the difficulty we are
experiencing in teaching reading to the disadvantaged Negro
child with those of emergent countries which are attempting
to make a multi-cultured population literate in a single
national tongue.

In his recent report on the Washington, D.C. School
System, Passow (1967) indicated that the central question that
must be answered is: "What are the educationally relevant differences which the District's pupils bring into the classroom
and what kinds of varied educational experiences must be provided by the schools to accommodate these differences?" One
major educationally relevant difference for Washington, D.C.,
as for ghettos across the nation, is that of language. The
Negro ghetto child is speaking a significantly different language from that of his middle-class teachers. Most of his
middle-class teachers have wrongly viewed his language as
pathological, disordered, "lazy speech". This failure to
recognize the interference from the child's different linguistic system, and consequent negative teacher attitudes
towards the child and his language, lead directly to reading
difficulties and subsequent school failure. Understanding
that the inner-city child speaks a language that is well-
ordered, but different in many respects from standard English,
is crucial to understanding how to educate him. Unfortunately,
there is a tendency for the educator to think of the black
child with his non-standard speech as a "verbal cripple" whose
restricted language leads to, or is caused by, cognitive deficits.

If we look briefly at the research and research assumptions concerning the language of Negro children, we can see how this erroneous notion of verbal inadequacy evolved.

When reviewing the literature, one finds three major professions concerned with describing the language and cognitive abilities of black children: educators, psychologists (mainly child development specialists), and linguists. The educators were the first to contribute a statement about the language difficulties of these children -- a statement that amounted to the assertion that these children were virtually verbally destitute, i.e. they couldn't talk, and if they did, it was deviant speech, filled with "errors". The next group to get into the foray -- the psychologists -- reconfirmed initially that the children didn't talk, and then added the sophisticated wrinkle that if they did talk, their speech was such that it was a deterrent to cognitive growth. The last group to come into the picture were the linguists, who, though thoroughly impressed with the sophisticated research of the psychologist, were astonished at the naïveté of his pronouncements concerning language. The linguist began to examine the language of black children and brought us to our current conceptions of the language abilities of these children, namely, that they speak a well-ordered, highly structured, highly developed language system which in many aspects is different from standard English.

We have a fascinating situation here where three professions are assessing the same behavior -- the child's oral language production and comprehension -- but with varying assumptions, so that they see different things. However, it is not merely another example of the parable of the six blind men describing the elephant and asserting that an elephant equaled that portion of the elephant that the blind man happened to be touching -- for in the parable all men were

partially correct, and an elephant could be adequately described in the sum total of their "observations". But when we
look at the assumptions of the educator, the psychologist,
and the linguist, we find that there are actually some premises held by one profession, e.g. the psychologists' view
that a language system could be underdeveloped, that another
profession sees as completely untenable, e.g. linguists, who
consider such a view of language so absurd as to make them
feel that nobody could possibly believe it and therefore to
refute it would be a great waste of time. The educator
worked under the assumption that there is a single correct
way of speaking and that everyone who does not speak in this
"grammar book" fashion is in error. (Indeed, although the
psychologist may not recognize it, he tacitly adheres to this
principle when he defines language development in terms of
"correct" standard English usage.) This assumption is also
untenable to the linguist, who is interested in the structure
and function of an utterance. To him the discussion of a
hierarchial system that says that a double negative, e.g.
they don' have none, is inferior to a single negative, e.g.
they haven't any, is meaningless. The linguist simply wishes
to describe the rules of the system that allow a speaker of
that system to generate a negative utterance -- or any other
complex structure -- that is considered grammatical and is
understood as intended, by the speakers of the system.

The linguist takes it as basic that all humans develop
language -- after all, there is no reason to assume that black
African bush children develop a language and black inner-city
Harlem children do not! Subsumed under this is that the language is a well-ordered system with a predictable sound pattern, grammatical structure and vocabulary (in this sense,
there are no "primitive" languages). The linguist assumes
that any verbal system used by a community that fulfills the

above requirements is a language and that no language is
structurally better than any other language, i.e. French is
not better than German, Yiddish is not better than Gaelic,
Oxford English is not better than standard English, etc.
The second assumption of the linguist is that children learn
language in the context of their environment -- that is to
say, a French child learns French not because his father is
in the home or his mother reads him books, but because that
is the language that he hears continually from whatever source
and that is the language that individuals in his environment
respond to. The third assumption that the linguist works
with is that by the time a child is five he has developed
language -- he has learned the rules of his linguistic environment.

What are those rules and how have they been determined?
By using ghetto informants, linguists such as Stewart (1964,
1965, 1967, 1968), Dillard (1966, 1967), Bailey (1965, 1968),
Labov (1967), Loman (1967) and Shuy, Wolfram and Riley (1968)
have described some of the linguistic parameters of Negro
non-standard English. Differences between standard English
and Negro non-standard occur to varying degrees in regard to
the sound system, grammar and vocabulary.

Although Negro non-standard has many phonemes similar
to those of standard English, the distribution of these phonemes varies from standard English. For example, /i/ and
/e/ may not be distinguished before nasals, so that a "pin"
in Negro non-standard may be either an instrument for writing
a letter or something one uses to fasten a baby's diaper.
Sounds such as 'r' and 'l' are distributed so that 'cat' may
mean that orange vegetable that one puts in salads -- standard
English carrot -- as well as the four-legged fuzzy animal, or
a "big black dude". The reduction of /l/ and /r/ in many
positions may create such homonyms as "toe" meaning a digit

on the foot, or the church bell sound -- standard English
<u>toll</u>. Final clusters are reduced in Negro non-standard so
that "bowl" is used to describe either a vessel for cereal
or a very brave soldier -- standard English <u>bold</u>.

These are but a few of the many instances where Negro
non-standard sound usage differs from standard English. It
is no wonder then, that Cynthia Deutsch (1964) should find
in her assessment of auditory discrimination that disadvantaged black children did not "discriminate" as well as white
children from middle-class linguistic environments. She administered a discrimination task that equated "correct responses" with judgments of equivalences and differences in
standard English sound usage. Many of her stimuli, though
different for the standard English speaker, e.g. <u>pin-pen</u>,
are similar for the Negro non-standard speaker. She attributed the difference in performance of disadvantaged children
to such things as the constant blare of the television in
their homes and there being so much "noise" in their environment that the children tended to "tune out". However,
black children make responses based on the kind of language
they consider appropriate. In the same way that <u>cot</u> (for
sleeping), <u>caught</u> (for ensnared); or <u>marry</u> (to wed), <u>Mary</u>
(the girl), and <u>merry</u> (to be happy) are not distinguished in
the speech of many white people (so that they would say on
an auditory discrimination test that <u>cot</u> and <u>caught</u> were the
same), <u>pin</u> and <u>pen</u> are the same in the language of ghetto
blacks. The responses that the black child makes are on the
basis of the sound usage that he has learned in his social
and geographical milieu, and do not reflect some difficulty
in discriminating.

The syntax of low-income Negro children also differs
from standard English in many ways (unfortunately the psychologist, not knowing the rules of Negro non-standard has

interpreted these differences not as the result of well-
learned rules, but as evidence of "linguistic underdevelop-
ment"). Some examples of the differences are provided below:

1. When you have a numerical quantifier such as 2, 7,
   50, etc., you don't have to add the obligatory morphemes for the plural, e.g. 50 cent; 2 foot.

2. The use of the possessive marker is different. For
   example, the standard English speaker says "John's
   cousin"; the non-standard Negro speaker says John
   cousin. The possessive is marked here by the con-
   tiguous relationship of John and cousin.

3. The third person singular has no obligatory morphological ending in non-standard, so that "she works
   here" is expressed as she work here in Negro non-
   standard.

4. Verb agreement differs, so that one says she have a
   bike, they was going.

5. The use of the copula is not obligatory -- I going;
   he a bad boy.

6. The rules for negation are different. The double
   negative is used: standard English "I don't have
   any" becomes I don' got none in Negro non-standard.

7. The use of "ain't" in expression of the past --
   Negro non-standard present tense is he don't go,
   past tense is he ain't go.

8. The use of "be" to express habitual action -- he
   working right now as contrasted with he be working
   every day.

These are just a few of the rules that the non-standard speaker
employs to produce utterances that are grammatical for other
speakers in his environment.

Baratz and Povich (1967) assessed the language development of a group of five-year-old black Head Start children.

They analyzed speech responses to photographs and to CAT cards, using Lee's (1967) developmental sentence types model. A comparison of their data and Menyuk's (1964) restricted and transformational types of white middle-class children was performed. Results indicated that the Negro Head Start child is not delayed in language acquisition -- the majority of his utterances are on the kernel and transformational levels of Lee's developmental model. His transformational utterances are similar to those appearing above -- he has learned the many complicated structures of Negro non-standard English.

But how did the psychologist manage to come to the erroneous conclusion that the black child has an insufficient or underdeveloped linguistic system? The psychologist's basic problem was that his measures of "language development" were measures based on standard English (Bereiter, 1965; Thomas, 1964; Deutsch, 1964; Klaus and Gray, 1968). From these he concluded that since black children do not speak standard English, they must be deficient in language development.

Despite the misconceptions of the educator and psychologist concerning language and linguistic competence, the linguists for their part have described the differences between Negro non-standard and standard English in some detail. The following is a list of some of the syntactic differences between the two systems:

Variable	Standard English	Negro Non-Standard
Linking verb	He is going.	He __ goin'.
Possessive marker	John's cousin.	John_ cousin.
Plural marker	I have five cents.	I got five cent_.
Subject expression	John_lives in New York.	John he live in New York.
Verb form	I drank the milk.	I drunk the milk.
Past marker	Yesterday he walked home.	Yesterday he walk_ home.

Verb agreement	He runs home.	He run_ home.
	She has a bicycle.	She have a bicycle.
Future form	I will go home.	I'ma go home.
"If" construction	I asked if he did it.	I ask did he do it.
Negation	I don't have any.	I don't got none.
	He didn't go.	He ain't go.
Indefinite article	I want an apple.	I want a apple.
Pronoun form	We have to do it.	Us got to do it.
	His book.	He book.
Preposition	He is over at his friend's house.	He over to his friend house.
	He teaches at Francis Pool.	He teach _ Francis Pool.
Be	Statement: He is here all the time.	Statement: He be here.
Do	Contradiction: No, he isn't.	Contradiction: No, he don't.

But what of these differences? All the linguists studying
Negro non-standard English agree that these differences are
systematized structured rules within the vernacular; they
agree that these differences can interfere with the learning
of standard English, but they do not always agree as to the
precise nature of these different rules. This leads to
varied disagreements as to why a particular feature exists
(i.e. phoneme deletion vs. creolization), but it does not
dispute the fact that the linguistic feature is present.
No one would fail to agree that standard English has a grammatical structure and uniqueness, and many descriptions of
that structure have been written. Yet it is probably true
that no two linguists would agree in all details on how to
write the grammar. This equally explains the current controversy among linguists as to how one writes the grammar of
Negro non-standard English.

This language <u>difference</u>, not deficiency, must be considered in the educational process of the black ghetto child.
In 1953, the UNESCO report regarding the role of language in
education stated that: "It is axiomatic that the best medium
for teaching a child is his mother tongue. Psychologically,
it is the system of meaningful signs that in his mind works
automatically for expression and understanding. Sociologi-
cally, it is a means of identification among the members of
the community to which he belongs. Educationally he learns
more quickly through it than through an unfamiliar medium."

Since 1953, studies implementing the recommendations of
the UNESCO report have clearly illustrated the importance of
considering the vernacular in teaching reading in the national
language (Modiano, 1965). It seems clear that a structural
knowledge of non-standard vernacular and the ways it can
interfere with learning to speak and read standard English
are indispensable to teaching ghetto Negro children. Goodman
(1965) and Bailey (1965), along with Stewart, have all discussed the possibility of interference from the dialect on
acquiring the ability to read. Labov (1967) has also stressed
that the "ignorance of standard English rules on the part of
the speakers of standard English" and the "ignorance of non-
standard English rules on the part of teachers and text
writers" may well be the cause for the reading failures that
occur in the schools. In addition, Wiener and Cromer (1967)
in their article on reading and reading difficulty discussed
the need to determine the relationship between language differences and reading problems, because a failure to be explicit about the relationship between reading and previously
acquired auditory language often leads to ambiguities as to
whether a particular difficulty is a reading problem, language
problem, or both.

But does the black non-standard speaker have to contend

with interference from his own dialect on his performance in
standard English? The following experiment clearly suggests
that he does.

The subjects in this experiment were third and fifth
graders from two schools in the Washington, D.C. area. One
was an inner-city, impact-aid school; all the children in
this school were Negroes. The other was a school in Maryland,
located in an integrated low-middle-income community; all the
children from that school were white.

	Negro	White	Total
Third Grade	15	15	30
Fifth Grade	15	15	30
	30	30	60

A sentence repetition test was constructed that contained
30 sentences, 15 in standard English and 15 in Negro non-
standard. The sentences were presented on tape to each subject, who was asked to repeat the sentence after hearing it
once. Two random orders of the sentences were constructed to
control for an order effect. The sentences were as follows:

1. That girl, she ain' go ta school 'cause she ain'
    got no clothes to wear.

2. John give me two books for me to take back the
    liberry 'cause dey overdue.

3. I's some toys out chere and the chil'run they don'
    wanna play wid dem no more.

4. Does Deborah like to play with the girl that sits
    next to her in school?

5. The teacher give him a note 'bout de school meetin'
    an he 'posed to give it ta his mother to read.

6. John he always be late for school 'cause he don't
    like ta go music class.

7. My aunt who lives in Baltimore used to come to
    visit us on Sunday afternoons.

8. Do Deborah like to play wid da girl that sit next
    to her at school?

9. I asked Tom if he wanted to go to the picture that was playing at the Howard.

10. John gave me two books to take to the library because they were overdue.

11. Can Michael make the boat by hisself or do we gotta he'p him do it?

12. Henry lives near the ball park but can't go to the games because he has no money.

13. Where Mary brovah goin' wif a raggedy umbrella and a old blue raincoat?

14. There are some toys out here that the children don't want to play with any more.

15. If I give you three dollars will you buy me the things that I need to make the wagon?

16. When the teacher asked if he had done his homework, Henry said, "I didn't do it."

17. I aks Tom do he wanna go to the picture that be playin' at the Howard.

18. Henry live beside the ball park but he can't go to the games 'cause he ain' got no money.

19. The teacher gave him a note about the school meeting to give to his mother.

20. She was the girl who didn't go to school because she had no clothes to wear.

21. John is always late to school because he doesn't like to go to music class.

22. Patricia sits in the front row so that she can hear everything the teacher says.

23. If I give you three dollar you gonna buy what I need to make the wagon?

24. When the teachah aks Henry did he do his homework, Henry say I ain't did it.

25. My aunt, she live in Baltimore, and she useda come visit us Sunday afternoon.

26. Gloria's friend is working as a waitress in the Hot Shoppes on Connecticut Avenue.

27. Can Michael build the boat all by himself or should we help him with some of the work?

28. Where is Mary's brother going with a raggedy umbrella
    and an old blue raincoat?

29. Patricia all the time be sittin' in the front row so
    she can hear everything the teacher say.

30. Gloria frien', she a waitress, she be working the Hot
    Shoppes on Connecticut Avenue.

Each subject was asked to repeat exactly what he heard as
best he could. After the subject had responded to all the
stimuli on the tape, he was asked to listen to two stimuli,
one in standard English and the other in non-standard English. After each of these stimuli, the subject was asked to
identify who was speaking from among a group of pictures containing Negro and white men, women, boys and girls, and an
Oriental girl.

The data were analyzed to ascertain what happened to the
following constructions:

Standard Constructions	Non-standard Constructions
Third person singular	Non-addition of third person -s
Presence of copula	Zero copula
Negation	Double negation; and "ain't"
If + subject + verb	Zero "if" + verb + subject
Past markers	Zero past morpheme
Possessive marker	Zero possessive morpheme
Plural	Use of "be"

1. Analysis of variance on repetition of standard constructions.

The data concerning repetition of the seven standard
constructions were subjected to a Winer (1962) multifactor
repeated measures analysis of variance (Table 1). The factors under study were: A, race -- Negro vs. white performance; B, age -- third graders vs. fifth graders; and C,
grammatical feature -- the seven standard constructions
listed above. The analysis of variance indicated that race,
grammatical feature and the interaction of race and grammatical feature were significant beyond the .001 level. The
interaction of age and grammatical feature was significant
at the .05 level.

Table 1

Analysis of Variance of Standard English Sentences

	ss	df	ms	f
Between subjects				
A	128.48	1	128.48	285.51*
B	.09	1	.09	.20
A x B	1.00	1	1.00	2.22
Subjects within groups	25.22	56	.45	
Within subjects				
C	69.98	6	11.66	31.61*
A x C	39.49	6	6.58	21.23*
B x C	4.46	6	.74	2.39**
A x B x C	2.51	6	.41	1.32
C x subjects within groups	103.74	336	.31	
Total	374.97	419		

* Significant beyond .001 level
** Significant at the .05 level

White subjects were significantly better than Negro subjects in repeating standard English sentences. A Scheffé
test (Edwards, 1962) for multiple comparisons of factor C,
grammatical features, indicated that most of the significant
variance could be ascribed to the differential performance
of subjects on the "if" construction. In addition, the plural
feature was significantly more accurate than the third person

singular and the possessive. The significant A x C interaction, race and grammatical feature, was most readily explained by the significant difference between Negro and white
performance on the following grammatical categories: third
person singular, copula, "if" construction, and negation.
The B x C interaction, age and grammatical feature, was
mostly due to the significant difference in performance at
grade three and grade five of the "if" construction and the
plural marker (Table 2).

2.   Analysis of variance on repetition of non-standard
     constructions.

     The data concerning repetition of the seven non-standard
constructions were subjected to a Winer multifactor repeated
measures analysis of variance (Table 3). The factors under
study were the same as those in the previous analysis of
variance: A, race; B, age; and C, grammatical feature. The
analysis of variance indicated that race, grammatical feature, and the interaction of race and grammatical feature
were all significant beyond the .001 level.

     Negro subjects did significantly better than white sub-
jects in repeating Negro non-standard sentences. A Scheffé
test for multiple comparisons of factor C, grammatical features, indicated that most of the significant variance could
be ascribed to the differential performance of subjects on
the "if" construction. The significant A x C interaction,
race and grammatical feature, was most readily explained by
the differential performance of Negro and white subjects on
the "if" and the double negative constructions (Table 4).

3.   Identification of race of the speaker.

     Of the third graders, 73.3% identified the standard
sentence as being spoken by a white man, and 73.3 identified

Table 2

Scheffé Results of Standard English Sentences Analysis

Factor C

Third person	"To be"	"If"	Past Marker	Possessive	Plural	Negation
143.40	155.67	76.65	152.67	140.07	167.96	152.67

Third person is significantly different from the plural and the possessive at the .05 level. The "if" construction is significantly different from all other constructions at the .05 level.

Factor A x C

	Third person	"To be"	"If"	Past Marker	Possessive	Plural	Negation
Negro	51.00	65.88	6.33	69.21	66.30	77.14	54.90
White	92.40	89.79	80.32	89.79	48.44	90.82	85.17

Performance of Negro and white students was significantly different on the third person, "to be", "if", and negation constructions at the .05 level.

Factor B x C

	Third person	"To be"	"If"	Past Marker	Possessive	Plural	Negation
Grade 3	72.46	76.73	39.55	74.60	82.39	86.11	65.63
Grade 5	70.94	78.94	47.10	78.07	72.35	81.85	74.44

Performance of third and fifth graders on the "if" construction was significantly different from their performance on the plural and the possessive

Table 3

Analysis of Variance of Negro Non-Standard Sentences

	ss	df	ms	f
Between subjects				
A	73.20	1	73.20	66.55*
B	.53	1	.53	.48
A x B	.01	1	.01	.009
Subjects within groups	61.63	56	1.10	
Within subjects				
C	44.34	6	7.39	13.19*
A x C	39.49	6	6.58	11.75*
B x C	.82	6	.14	.25
A x B x C	3.42	6	.57	1.02
C x subjects within groups	188.83	336	.56	
Total	412.27	419		

* Significant beyond the .001 level

Table 4

Scheffé Results of Negro Non-Standard English Sentences Analysis

Factor C

	Third person	Be	Zero Copula	"If"	Past Marker	Double Negative	Possessive
	86.79	54.48	106.61	109.30	80.93	109.57	73.06

The use of "Be" was significantly different from performance in regard to the zero copula, the third person singular, the "if" construction and the double negative.

Factor A x C

	Third person	Be	Zero Copula	"If"	Past Marker	Double Negative	Possessive
Negro	52.88	35.27	57.16	87.87	53.39	67.90	42.57
White	33.91	19.21	49.45	21.43	26.54	31.67	30.49

Most of the significance was due to the difference in performance between Negro and white students on the double negative and on the "if" constructions.

the non-standard sentence as being spoken by a Negro. Of the fifth graders, 83.3% judged the standard sentence as being spoken by a white man, while 93.3% judged the non-standard sentence as being spoken by a Negro. Eighty percent of the white children and 76.6% of the Negro children identified standard sentences as being spoken by a white man. Non-standard sentences were judged to be spoken by a Negro 83.3% of the time by both Negro and white children.

In responding to standard English sentences, white speakers did significantly better than black speakers. However, in examining the black child's "errors", it became evident that he didn't fail utterly to complete the sentence; he didn't jumble his response, nor did he use a "word salad". His "error" responses were consistent, e.g. in response to the stimulus: "I asked Tom if he wanted to go to the picture that was playing at the Howard", 97% of the children responded with: "I aks Tom did he wanna go to the picture at the Howard". In response to: "Does Deborah like to play with the girl that sits next to her in school", 60% of the Negro children responded: "Do Deborah like to play wif the girl what sit next to her in school".

This same behavior was evident in the white subjects when asked to repeat Negro non-standard sentences. Black children were superior to white children in repeating these stimuli. Here again the "error" responses followed a definite pattern, e.g. in response to the stimulus: "I aks Tom do he wanna go to the picture that be playin' at the Howard", 78% of the white children said: "I asked Tom if he wanted to go to the picture that was playing at the Howard". Similar "translations" to standard English occurred on the other Negro non-standard constructions.

The fact that the standard and non-standard speakers exhibited similar "translation" behaviors when confronted with sentences that were outside of their primary code indicates quite clearly that the "language deficiency" that has so often been attributed to the low-income Negro child is not a language deficit so much as a difficulty in code switching when the second code (standard English) is not as well learned as the first (non-standard English).

The kinds of "errors" the two groups made (e.g. white subjects adding the third person -s to non-standard stimuli and Negroes deleting the third person -s on standard stimuli) represent an intrusion of one language code (the dominant system) upon the structure of the other code (the newly-acquired system). If, indeed, non-standard were not a structured system with well-ordered rules, one would expect that Negro children would not be able to repeat the non-standard structures any better than did the white children, and one would also expect that non-standard patterns would not emerge systematically when lower-class Negroes responded to standard sentences. Neither of these expectations was upheld. The Negro children were in fact able to repeat non-standard structures better than were the white children, and they did produce systematic non-standard patterns when responding to standard sentences. The converse was true for the whites; they responded significantly better to standard structures and exhibited systematic standard patterns when responding to non-standard stimuli.

The results of this research clearly indicate that (1) there are two dialects involved in the education complex of black children (especially in schools with a white middle-class curriculum orientation); (2) black children are generally not bi-dialectal; and (3) there is evidence of interference from their dialect when black children attempt to use standard English.

Since the disadvantaged Negro child, as the previous study

suggests, like the Indian having to learn Spanish in Mexico,
or the African having to learn French in Guinea, has to contend with the interference from his vernacular in learning
to read, how does his task of learning to read differ from
that of the middle-class "mainstream American" child? When
the middle-class child starts the process of learning to
read, his is primarily a problem of decoding the graphic
representation of a language which he already speaks. The
disadvantaged black child must not only decode the written
words, he must also "translate" them into his own language.
This presents him with an almost insurmountable obstacle,
since the written words frequently do not go together in any
pattern that is familiar or meaningful to him. He is baffled
by this confrontation with (1) a new language with its new
syntax; (2) a necessity to learn the meaning of graphic symbols; and (3) a vague, or not so vague, depending upon the
cultural and linguistic sophistication of the teacher, sense
that there is something terribly wrong with his language.

Although both the middle-class child and the disadvantaged Negro child are at the beginning faced with the task of
relating their speech to a graphic representation that appears
to be arbitrary and without a direct one-to-one correspondence
to their speech (e.g. the "silent e" in love, the "silent k"
in knife, the "k" as represented in cut and kite, and the "s"
as represented in Sue, cement, etc.), the cards are stacked
against the inner-city Negro child because his particular
phoneme patterning is not considered in the curriculum at this
early phase, so that when he reads hep for "help", men' for
"mend", boil for "ball", the teacher presumes that he cannot
read the word. Hep and help, men' and mend, and boil and ball
are homonyms in the inner-city child's vernacular.

Despite the obvious mismatching of the "teachers and text
writers" phoneme system and that of the inner-city child, the

difficulties of the disadvantaged Negro child cannot be
simplified solely to the pronunciation and phoneme differences that exist in the two systems. There is an even more
serious problem facing the inner-city child, namely, his unfamiliarity with the syntax of the classroom texts. Although
the middle-income child also must read texts that are at
times stilted in terms of his own usage, there is no question
that the language of the texts is potentially comparable to
his system. That is to say, although he does not speak in
the style of his reading text, he has the rules within his
grammar to account for the occurrence of the textbook sentences. However, the textbook style is more unfamiliar to
the ghetto child than it is to his middle-class standard-
speaking age mate because much of the reading text is not a
part of his "potential" syntactic system.

Because of the mismatch between the child's system and
that of the standard English textbook, because of the psychological consequences of denying the existence and legitimacy
of the child's linguistic system, and in the light of the
success of vernacular teaching around the world, it appears
imperative that we teach the inner-city Negro child to read
using his own language as the basis for the initial readers.
In other words, first teach the child to read in the vernacular, and then teach him to read in standard English. Such a
reading program would not only require accurate vernacular
texts for the dialect speaker, but also necessitate the cre-
ation of a series of "transition readers" that would move the
child, once he had mastered reading in the vernacular, from
vernacular texts to standard English texts. Of course, success of such a reading program would be dependent upon the
child's ultimate ability to read standard English.

The advantages of such a program would be threefold.
First, success in teaching the ghetto child to read. Second,

the powerful ego-supports of giving credence to the child's
language system and therefore to himself, and giving him the
opportunity to experience success in school. And third, with
the use of transitional readers, the child would have the
opportunity of being taught standard English (which cannot
occur by "linguistic swamping", since his school mates are
all vernacular speakers) so that he could learn where his
language system and that of standard English were similar
and where they were different. Such an opportunity might
well lead to generalized learning and the ability to use
standard English more proficiently in other school work.

The continued failure of programs of reading for ghetto
children that offer more of the same, i.e. more phonics,
more word drills, etc., have indicated the need of a new
orientation towards teaching inner-city children to read.
Any such program must take into account what is unique about
the ghetto child that is impairing his ability to learn within the present system. This paper has suggested that one of
the essential differences to be dealt with in teaching inner-
city Negro children is that of language. The overwhelming
evidence of the role that language interference can play in
reading failure indicates that perhaps one of the most effective ways to deal with the literacy problems of Negro
ghetto youth is to teach them using vernacular texts that
systematically move from the syntactic structures of the
ghetto community to those of the standard English speaking
community.

BIBLIOGRAPHY

Bailey, B. Linguistics and non-standard language patterns.
    NCTE paper, 1965.

-----. Some aspects of the impact of linguistics on language teaching in disadvantaged communities. Elementary English, 1968, 45, 570-579.

Baratz, J. and Povich, E. Grammatical constructions in the language of the Negro preschool child. ASHA paper, 1967.

Bereiter, C. Academic instruction and preschool children. In R. Cobin and M. Crosby (eds.), Language Programs for the disadvantaged, Champaign, Ill.: National Council of Teachers of English, 1965.

Deutsch, C. Auditory discrimination and learning: Social factors. Merrill Palmer Quarterly, 1964, 10, 277-296.

Dillard, J. The Urban Language Study of the Center for Applied Linguistics. Linguistic Reporter, 1966, 8 (5), 1-2.

-----. Negro children's dialect in the inner city. Florida FL Reporter, 1967, 5 (3).

Edwards, A. Experimental design in psychological research. New York: Holt, Rinehart & Winston, 1962.

Goodman, K. Dialect barriers to reading comprehension. Elementary English, 1965, 42, 853-860. [Reprinted in the present volume, pp. 14-28.]

Klaus, R. and Gray, S. The early training project for dis- advantaged children: A report after five years. Society for Child Development, Monograph 33, 1968.

Labov, W. Some sources of reading problems for Negro speakers of nonstandard English. In A. Frazier (ed.), New Directions in Elementary English, Champaign, Ill.: National Council of Teachers of English, 1967. [Reprinted in the present volume with additions and corrections by the author, pp. 29-67.]

----- and Robins, C. A note on the relation of reading fail- ure to peer-group status. Unpublished paper, 1967.

Lee, L. Developmental sentence types: A method for comparing normal and deviant syntactic development. Journal of Speech and Hearing Disorders, 1966, 31, 311-330.

Loman, B. Conversations in a Negro American Dialect. Washington, D.C.: Center for Applied Linguistics, 1967.

Menyuk, P. Syntactic rules used by children from preschool through first grade. Child Development, 1964, 35, 533-546.

Modiano, N. A comparative study of two approaches to the
teaching of reading in the national language. U.S. Office
of Education, Final Report, 1965.

National Advisory Council on the Education of Disadvantaged
Children. March 1966, p. 7.

Passow, A. Toward creating a model urban school system: A
study of the District of Columbia public schools. New
York: Teachers College, Columbia University, 1967.

Shuy, R., Wolfram, W. and Riley, W. Field techniques in an
urban language study. Washington, D.C.: Center for Applied
Linguistics, 1968.

Stewart, W. Foreign language teaching methods in quasi-
foreign language situations. In W. Stewart (ed.),
Non-standard speech and the teaching of English, Washington,
D.C.: Center for Applied Linguistics, 1964.

-----. Urban Negro speech: Sociolinguistic factors affecting
English teaching. In R. Shuy (ed.), Social Dialects and
Language Learning, Champaign, Ill.: National Council of
Teachers of English, 1965.

-----. Sociolinguistic factors in the history of American
Negro dialects. Florida FL Reporter, 1967, 5 (2).

-----. Continuity and change in American Negro dialects.
Florida FL Reporter, 1968, 6 (2).

Thomas, D. Oral language sentence structure and vocabulary
of kindergarten children living in low socio-economic
urban areas. Dissertation Abstracts XXIII (1962), 1014
(Chicago).

Wiener, M. and Cromer, W. Reading and reading difficulty:
A conceptual analysis. Harvard Educational Review, 1967,
37, 620-643.

Winer, B. Statistical principles in experimental design.
New York: McGraw-Hill, 1962.

A LINGUISTIC BACKGROUND FOR DEVELOPING BEGINNING READING MATERIALS FOR BLACK CHILDREN

by Roger W. Shuy

Morton Wiener and Ward Cromer, in their article "Reading and Reading Difficulty: A Conceptual Analysis", describe four different assumptions which are used to explain what is meant by the term "reading difficulty".[1] Each assumption implies a kind of built-in model of remediation. Some researchers, for example, assume that reading difficulty involves a kind of malfunction, usually of the sensory-physiological type. Other investigators feel that reading difficulty involves a deficiency of some sort which must be corrected before adequate reading can take place. Still others attribute reading difficulty to certain things (bad method, anxiety, etc.) which are present but interfering, and which must be removed before good reading can take place. A fourth approach to reading difficulty is one in which the researchers assume that the child would read adequately if the material and method were consistent with his linguistic behavior patterns. Investigators who work under this assumption believe that in order to make the child read, either the material or the behavior patterns must be changed.

. . . .

This article is based on two papers delivered during the spring of 1968. The first was presented at the International Reading Association Pre-Convention Workshop on Psycholinguistics on April 24. The second was read at the Temple University Faculty Workshop in Reading Theory on May 8.

Let us pause to examine the urban Negro child's "reading difficulty" in the light of the Wiener-Cromer taxonomy of research assumptions. We would be hard-pressed to demonstrate that the urban Negro child generally has sensory of physiological defects, or that he lacks some function necessary to the reading process. Nor can we casually observe that the entire population of urban Negro children is made up of individuals who have intrapsychic conflicts. The reading difficulty seems, rather, to stem from a cultural difference characterized, among other things, by a different view of life's problems, a different style of self-presentation, and a different orientation to the printed page. It is almost as though the child "speaks another language", and in the case of the urban Negro child, this is very close to true.

The linguistic system of the ghetto Negro is different in a number of identifiable features from that of Standard English. If this non-standard dialect is interfering with the acquisition of Standard English reading skills, we can take at least two courses. One is to adjust the child to suit the materials. The other is to adjust the materials to suit the child. If the end result is successful it is a matter of indifference which system is used. Those who advocate that we teach the child Standard English before he learns to read assume that since it is a good thing to learn Standard English, he might as well learn it before he learns to read. Most linguists, on the other hand, realize that the complexity of language learning is such that this sort of engineering is too slow-moving to be effective. That is, the social value of learning Standard English is not worth the long delay it would cause in his learning to read. The simple truth is that speaking Standard English, however desirable it may be, is not as important as learning to read.

In any case, the idea of changing the child to suit the

materials seems educationally naïve when one stops to give it careful consideration. The usual practice among educators has been to suit the materials to the child. But even assuming that it were desirable to first teach children Standard English, we have no research to show that children have any great conscious awareness of the fine distinctions of the social dimension of language. Of course they are quite able to use grammatical, phonological and lexical forms in keeping with their own value systems, but these value systems are those of the unsophisticated child, who just may value the speech of a juvenile delinquent, a dope peddler or an athlete who lisps more than the speech of a teacher, an announcer or a judge. Furthermore, pre-adolescent children are relatively unable to articulate what they are doing when they adopt someone's linguistic norms.[2] This is not surprising, since it is also difficult for adults, even language arts teachers, to identify these things. In her doctoral dissertation, Anne E. Hughes asked a random group of urban teachers of disadvantaged pre-school children to identify the language problems of their students.[3] The teachers were first asked to talk about the characteristic linguistic problems. Then they were asked to listen to a tape recording of some of these children and identify the linguistic problems on that tape. The results showed a very low correlation of response to reality.

Eighty percent of the teachers observed that their students have a limited vocabulary. One teacher offered the following reason for this "handicap":

...the children came with a very meager vocabulary...I think it's because of the background of the home and the lack of books at home, the lack of communication with the family, especially, if there are only one or two children in the family. Perhaps if there are more children in the family communication might be a bit better. They might have a few more words in their vocabulary.

Another teacher observed:

"In the inner-city, the child's vocabulary is very limited. His experiences are very limited."

These comments are typical. Neither teacher gave any indication that the home environment might produce a different vocabulary. Both felt, on the contrary, that a lack of school vocabulary was equivalent to a lack of overall vocabulary. This reflects a widely-held but erroneous concept, in which the disadvantaged child is sometimes called non-verbal. Nothing in the current research on Washington, D.C., or Detroit Negroes supports this idea. The notion that children in disadvantaged homes are the products of language deprivation seems to mean only that the investigators proved to be such a cultural barrier to the interviewee that informants were too frightened and awed to talk freely, or that the investigators simply asked the wrong questions.

If the teachers' comments about vocabulary were unsophisticated, their descriptions of their childrens' pronunciation and grammar were even worse. Thirteen percent of the teachers observed that some students can not talk at all when they come to school; many felt that these children could not hear certain sounds, apparently on the assumption that because a child does not relate his sound system to printed symbols, he cannot hear these sounds. One-third of the teachers characterized their childrens' greatest grammatical failure as their inability to speak in sentences or complete thoughts.

This research showed clearly that one of the most important aspects of language development among disadvantaged children centers on imprecise descriptions of the problem, large-scale ignorance of how to make an adequate description, and the interference of pedagogical folklore which passes as knowledge about a conspicuously neglected and underprivileged group of human beings.

The position of a Negro child in an urban ghetto is,
then, that he has a functioning language system which does
not necessarily match the language system of the school.
Recent research on this problem, using sentence repetition
experiments, clearly indicates that middle-class white children have as much difficulty repeating syntactical constructions commonly used by Washington, D.C., Negro children as
the Negro children have in repeating the white middle-class
syntactical forms.[4] The implications of this research point
to a cultural mismatch between student and teaching materials.

The first major task for linguists is to describe and
analyze this language system of the urban ghetto. In many
ways it is similar to that of Standard English but in several
very important ways it is quite different. It differs basically in two ways: (1) the presence of some feature not found
in Standard English, or the absence of some feature found in
Standard English; and (2) a frequency distribution of a feature which is significantly different from that of Standard
English.

A quite romantic picture of the differences between Standard English and Black English would be to say that their
grammars and phonological systems are entirely different.
Current research in New York, Detroit and Washington, D.C.,
has shown that this would be a gross overstatement. If it
were true, there would be little mutual understanding between
speakers of the different dialects. There are, however, significant contrasts that are particularly evident when the verb
systems of lower-class and working-class Negroes are compared
with those of middle-class Negroes and with whites of all
classes. The copula and auxiliary have been the most fruitful
areas of study so far, particularly with regard to a feature
which is present in one social group while absent in another.[5]
There are many examples of frequency distribution differences

between racial and/or social groups.[6] The most notable of these
include recent studies of multiple negation, pronominal apposition, r-deletion, l-deletion, consonant-cluster reduction,
devoicing of word-final stop consonants, among others.

The significance of this sort of research for beginning
reading instruction is of two kinds, depending on whether the
feature is phonological or grammatical.

Phonological features

A careful description of the phonology of Black English
speakers will be of more use to teachers than to writers of
classroom materials. The arbitrariness of the symbolization
process makes it rather unnecessary to recast primers into
graphemic series which delete the r in car (cah), the l in
help (hep), which substitute voiceless stops for voiced ones
in words like red (ret), and which show consonant-cluster
reductions in words like just (jus) and send (sen). Urban
disadvantaged Negroes should not find it difficult to discover that /jəs/ is realized in print as just. Their grapheme rule would be ⟨st⟩ → /s/ in final position. This is
certainly no more unreasonable than other double grapheme
relations as single sounds, such as ⟨th⟩ → /θ/ in thin or
⟨mb⟩ → /m/ in thumb. That is, the decoding process of reading is already imbued with such rules. One might also ask,
however, how different the problem is for urban poor Negroes
than for, say, middle-class whites. There is considerable
evidence to show that in some oral styles, middle-class whites
also reduce these consonant clusters, although not always as
frequently as do Negroes.

In addition to cases in which the reduction of consonant
clusters occurs similarly for urban poor Negroes and Standard
English speakers, there are cases in which the non-standard
Negro cluster reductions are different, depending on the surrounding sounds, from Standard English. For example, in

Standard English if a word ends in /st/ and the following
word begins with /s/, the /st/ cluster is frequently reduced
to /s/, as in /wesayd/ (west side). However, in non-standard
the cluster may be reduced whether or not the following word
begins with /s/, as in /wesindiyz/ (West Indies).

Also for other phonological features linguists can make
good cases for the systematic nature of the disadvantaged
Negro's decoding process. In Detroit, for example, whereas
a middle-class white or Negro might decode ⟨time⟩ as /taym/,
the ghetto Negro might realize it as a front vowel, with a
different glide segment, /tæhm/. If the glide vowel is
entirely absent, as it often is, the main vowel is usually
lengthened, thus producing /tæ:m/. The rules[7] for these
various realizations may be formulated as follows:

Standard	Non-Standard
Rule S 1 ⟨t⟩ → /t/	Rule NS 1 ⟨t⟩ → /t/
S 2 ⟨i...e⟩ → /ay/	NS 2 ⟨i...e⟩ → /æ:/ ∼ /æh/

Thus rules S 1 and NS 1 are identical. Rules S 2 and NS 2
have different correspondent features but the same number of
correspondences. That is, ⟨i⟩ followed by a non-contiguous
⟨e⟩ marker yields a glide /ay/ in Standard English of the
North, whereas here it yields either a different glide,
/æh/, or /æ/ plus a vowel duration /:/ which may be said to
replace or compensate for the loss of the glide vowel.

All of this is meant to indicate that there is nothing
irregular about the phoneme-grapheme relationship of speakers of non-standard. The correspondences are quite similar
in quantity but different in certain shapes. In terms of
entire linguistic structures these differences are actually
very slight. They gain in importance only as social groups
assign values to them.

It is of utmost importance, however, that teachers be
made aware of these systematic decoding processes. A child

who decodes ⟨time⟩ as /tæ:m/ is not deficient in his ability
to pronounce the glide vowel most frequently heard in Standard English. Nor is he misreading the word. Ironically,
he is doing what any good reader ought to be doing -- taking
printed symbols and translating them into his own meaningful
oral symbols. It might be said, in fact, that learning to
read has little or nothing to do with a child's ability to
handle Standard English phonology. But it is tremendously
important for the teacher to understand the child's phonological system in order to distinguish between reading difficulties and systematic features of the child's dialect. It
is also important for the teacher to understand the child's
phonological system in order to organize teaching materials
into consistent groupings. For example, I once observed a
teacher in a ghetto school tell beginning readers that the
vowels of fog, dog, hog, and log were all the same. She then
had the students repeat the words after her, thus: /fag/,
/dɔg/, /hag/, /lɔg/. The students heard the difference.
This teacher never did. Learning the -og matrix is meaningful pedagogy if there is consistency in the production of
that matrix, /ɔ/ or /a/. Either pattern is useful to the
beginning reader who is being taught on the basis of pattern.

Grammatical Features

       If phonological considerations appear to be of no great
consequence to the development of such materials, one might
legitimately ask what importance to attach to grammatical
considerations. In order to do this, we might do well to
suggest some principles upon which such considerations can
be based. Such principles can be expected to be broadly
relevant for judging the effectiveness of such materials but
they should also serve as judgment categories in reading
generally, whether it be for non-standard readers, Standard
readers, speed readers, literature readers, or readers of any

other sort. Three such principles suggest themselves:

1. The grammatical choices should not provide extraneous
   data. In the case of beginning reading materials for
   non-standard speakers, the text should help the child
   by avoiding grammatical forms which are not realized by
   him in his spoken language (third singular verb inflections, for example).

2. The grammatical choices should provide adequate data.
   In the case of beginning reading materials for non-
   standard speakers, grammatical forms which occur in non-
   standard but not in Standard should be inserted where
   they appear natural (the be in "All the time he be
   happy", and the to in "Make him to do it", for example).

3. The grammatical choices should provide sequentially
   relevant data. In the case of beginning reading materials for non-standard speakers, syntactic constructions
   such as adverbial phrases should be reduced to their
   derivative nominalized forms where it is natural to do
   so in the dialect (the as a janitor in the sentence,
   "Samuel's brother is working as a janitor", for example,
   reduced to "Samuel brother, he a janitor".).

A basic difficulty at this point is that the reading
theorists have not adequately defined just exactly what
reading is and, consequently, what reading problems really
are. This puts the linguist at a disadvantage. But even if
we can't define reading, we can at least talk about some of
its characteristics and perhaps discover how the interference
of one grammatical system on another may contribute some
problems therein.

If we are willing to say that some of the characteristics
of reading include the reader's decoding certain graphic symbols for meaning with the aid of some unexplained help from
his knowledge of semantic, phonological, and grammatical

probabilities, and non-linguistic context, then we can pre-
cede along the following lines. It seems likely that these
characteristics of the reading process may operate (here
considerably oversimplified) according to the chart as shown
in Fig. 1.

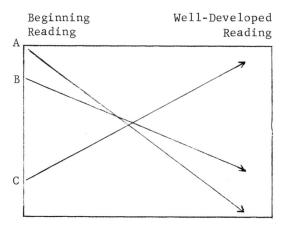

      Beginning   Well-Developed
      Reading   Reading

A - Visual Discrimination
B - Sound-Symbol Relationship
C - Underlying Language Structure

Fig. 1.   Schematic Chart of the Child's Dependence
on Some Characteristics of the Reading
Process

If this schematization in any way reflects reality, it
is obvious that the characteristics necessary for the beginning reader may be called upon in progressively different
degrees as this child moves toward more mature reading abilities. That is, he must call on visual discrimination (A)
and sound-symbol relationship (B) quite heavily at the beginning stages, and he must learn to rely on them less and less
if he wants to read faster and better. His underlying language structure (C), however, though called upon throughout
the reading process, is used increasingly as (A) and (B)
diminish.

The importance of underlying language structure in the

reading process cannot be overestimated and very little has been said about it in the literature of reading. By underlying language structure is meant that ability which even beginning readers have which enables them to avoid misreading via any manner other than by the phonological and grammatical rules of their native language. Thus they do not render cat as cta (an impossible phonological realization in English) although they quite possibly could realize it as cet or cep or any other sequence of sounds allowable in English. Such ability also prevents grammatical misreadings of sentences like The man chased the cat as The man the chase cated or Man the the chased cat. If the reader is going to err, he will err within the framework of possible variants in phonology and grammar -- although not necessarily within the framework of Standard English (e.g. The man done chased the cat). Some linguists maintain that a child has some innate capacity for language learning which accelerates such apparently learned characteristics; or, that underlying language structure characterizes all types of linguistic performance and that, in reading, a person perceives in relationship to such an underlying system. The blind can learn to read despite absent visual discrimination (A) and the deaf can become literate despite an absent sound-symbol relationship (B). The fact that many children learn to read in spite of the inadequacies of reading theory and teaching today may be a silent tribute to the magnificence of the human brain and the marvels of underlying language structure.

Certain kinds of supposed reading errors, then, can be said to result from differing performance realizations of similar underlying language structures. A child who reads He is John's friend as He John friend may be evidencing exactly the same linguistic sense of the writer, with only performance differences.

These realizations, and others like them, give rise to
certain questions:

1. What kind of, and how much, interference is caused by
    the absence of non-standard grammatical features in
    Standard English texts?

2. What kind of, and how much, interference is caused by
    the presence in the text of Standard English grammatical
    features which are not used by non-standard speakers?

3. What kind of, and how much, interference is caused by
    syntactic variations between non-standard and Standard
    English features?

All of the above questions have to do with grammatical
matters in which the underlying structures of Standard English and non-standard are equivalent but in which the surface
realizations vary. It goes without saying that where both
performance and the underlying structure fail to match or,
worse yet, where performance is identical and where the
underlying structures are not equivalent, there are bound to
be reading problems.

It may turn out that there is no more to worry about in
terms of potential cross-dialectal interference for many
grammatical matters than there is to concern us with cross-
dialectal interference in phonological features. In an effort to determine potential reading interference caused by
the conflict between non-standard speech and Standard written
text, let us list some of the outstanding characteristics of
non-standard as they appear in most American Negro ghettos.

Written Expression	Linguistic Feature	Oral Expression
1. John's house	possession	John house
2. John runs	3rd sing. pres.	John run
3. ten cents	plurality	ten cent
4. He jumped	past	He jump
5. She is a cook	copula	She a cook

6. He doesn't have   negation   He ain't got no
   any toys   toys

                                              He don't have
                                              no toys

                                              He don't got
                                              no toys

7. He asked if I   past conditional   He asked did I
   came   question   come

8. Every day when   negative + be   Every day when
   I come he isn't   I come he don't
   here   be here

In the first five items, sound-symbol relationships and
visual discrimination have little if any effect on the non-
standard reader's realization of the written Standard text.
These realization rules may be stated as follows:

Linguistic Feature	Standard	Non-Standard
1. possession	→ -'s	→ ∅
2. 3rd singular verb	→ -s	→ ∅
3. plurality	→ -s	→ ∅
4. past tense	→ -ed	→ ∅
5. copula	→ is	→ ∅

If the non-standard reader has no reason to supply an
oral sound for the Standard written representation of possession, 3rd singular, plurality, past tense and the copula, we
can safely say that the sound-symbol relationship plays little
or no part in his reading ability in these instances. He is
perfectly able to produce non-inflectional word-final sounds
which are identical to those above (e.g. miss, his, buzz,
bet, etc.), discounting the possibility that he has a speech
production problem. As he reads, he must be influenced by
his grammatical system, which, as indeed is the case, contains an unmarked possession, 3rd singular verb, plurality,
past tense and copula. He must become wary of certain morphemes, just as he must become wary of such graphemes as the
l in could and the s in island. Most likely the sound-symbol

relationship (B) has been submerged by reading skills provided by his underlying language structure (C) which, in
turn, leads him to produce language performance consonant
with his dialect even though the visual symbols might argue
otherwise.

Sentences 6 through 8 provide somewhat different kinds
of problems:

6. Negation
   Standard: do + neg + have + any
   Non-Standard: $\begin{bmatrix} \text{have} \\ \text{do} \end{bmatrix}$ + neg + $\begin{Bmatrix} \text{have} \\ \text{got} \end{Bmatrix}$ + no

7. Past conditional question
   Standard: if + S + V (past)
   Non-Standard: do (past) + S + V

8. Negative + be
   Standard: be + neg
   Non-Standard: do + neg + be

In each of the above cases there are sufficiently different sound-symbol relationships between the written Standard and the oral non-standard to suggest that this aspect
of the reading act is called upon scarcely at all in these
instances. Instead, the non-standard speaker who converts
the Standard text into non-standard grammatical patterns
seems to be more influenced by what seems "natural" to him
than by what is found on the printed page.

Research into reading errors produced by speakers of
non-standard is still in its infancy but already several
things have become clear. Children in the intermediate
grades have fewer reading problems of the sort noted in sentences 6 through 8 and produce more "errors" of the sort
found in sentences 1 through 5. This seems to indicate that
the greater the difference between Standard and non-standard
grammatical items, the more likely the intermediate child is

to have developed an ability to read it successfully aloud.
Conversely, the less basic the difference, the less importance it appears to have for the child. This seems to support the notion that sound-symbol relationships are ulti-
mately less basic than grammatical features, since the readers appear to work harder at grosser differences and ignore
smaller ones.

These conclusions, like all conclusions derived from
the study of reading errors, are drawn from the oral reading
experiences of children who develop sufficient reading skills
to read aloud. What is unfortunate about such conclusions,
of course, is that children who can't read well enough to
risk exposing their ignorance cannot be studied in this way
and their performance cannot be measured. It is just possible that one aspect of their reading failure can be attributed to their inability to cope with the grosser differences
of the sort noted in sentences 6 through 8, where currently
available reading pedagogy, with its emphasis on phonics and
word method, only confuses the matter. William A. Stewart
has referred to the grammatical plight of the non-standard
ghetto resident as that of a quasi-foreign language situation,[8] which, if true, would indicate that we have a far
more complicated situation to deal with than normally faces
the reading teacher. The situation is further complicated
by the fact that the many similarities between the Standard
and non-standard grammatical patterns obscure the few but
crucial differences.

If the processes of learning to read and learning to
speak Standard English are entirely separate entities (as
many linguists believe), and if the suggested model of reading acquisition skills noted earlier is accurate, we can
reasonably say that the beginning reader, with his heavy
leaning on sound-symbol clues to reading, ought to be

protected as much as possible from the mismatch between his
social dialect and the written text, in the following ways:

1. Include in the beginning reading materials the grammatical forms which occur in non-standard, even though they
   may be absent in Standard English (cf. sentences 6 through
   8).

2. Exclude from the beginning reading materials the grammatical forms which occur in Standard but do not occur in
   non-standard (cf. sentences 1 through 5).

3. Write beginning reading materials in such a way that the
   syntactic structures of the written text reflect the syntactic structures of the reader's oral language experience
   in a way that is consistent with the task at hand --
   learning to read (cf. sentences 6 and 7).

It is point number 3 which requires explanation at this
time, for we have said very little about syntactic presentation of any magnitude. A major consideration ought to be that
sentences in beginning reading materials be so organized as
to show the clearest possible relationships between constituent elements. For beginning readers, less concern needs to
be shown for problems of monotony than for obscurity or ambiguity. Such obscurity can be seen in the following passage:
"Larry went to the movies. 'At the movies, we had fun',
said Larry". Beginning readers from all social classes are
apt to stumble on the prepositional phrase beginning the second sentence. The experience of our research shows that
children tie it to the first sentence, probably because such
prepositional phrases seldom are found in sentence initial
position in their oral language. Perhaps writers of beginning reading materials should take certain clues from trans-
lators of materials for the new literate or for the only
slightly educated reader. William Wonderly suggest techniques like the following:[9]

1. Avoid complex or derived constructions and stick to
    simple or kernel constructions. Use verbal rather than
    nominal constructions and active rather than passive
    verbs.

    Although it is important for children to eventually
    develop an ability to vary sentence structure by using
    derived constructions (such as nomalizations) and pas-
    sive voice verbs, there is practically no need for such
    variation in beginning reading materials. To illustrate
    his contention that complex derived sentences provide
    excessive embedding for the beginning reader, Wonderly
    uses the sentences; John told George to tell Mary to
    bring her sister, which has at least four base sentences:

    > John told George [something]
    > George told Mary [something]
    > Mary had a sister
    > Mary brought the sister[10]

    Several psycholinguists have suggested that such com-
    plex sentences tend to be stored in the human memory in
    the form of their underived, "kernel" constructions
    (along with their rules for embedding).[11] If this is true,
    then the reading of embedded sentences might be considered
    to be a kind of pre-storage disembedding process. It also
    suggests that beginning readers (of any social class)
    should be provided materials in kernel or near-kernel form,
    even at the price of monotony (a less decisive factor for
    those who have not become over-familiar with the printed
    page).

2. Avoid structural ambiguity. This is, of course, good
    advice for beginning reading materials for any class or
    dialect speaking group. Some of the more humorous say-
    ings of small children stem from unrealized ambiguities
    such as:

Mother: Sally, go see how old Mrs. Jones is today.

Sally: Mrs. Jones, how old are you today?

Such unintentional ambiguities pose unnecessary additional burdens on the beginning reader. The dangers of potential ambiguities for beginning ghetto children are painfully apparent in the following sentences:

Standard	Potential "Reading" by Non-Standard Speaker
1. She arose early today.	She _is_ a rose early today.
2. We jump into the water.	We jump_ed_ into the water.
3. He sat _on_ the bank. [river]	He sat _on_ the bank. [building]
4. Flying planes can be dangerous.	_The_ flying planes... or, Flying _the_ planes...
5. They took the bus to Akron.	They "rode" the bus... or, They "brought" the bus...

Sentences 1 and 2 are ambiguous as a result of the differing grammatical systems between the child's oral language and that of the printed page. Sentence 3 stems from a cultural contrast between reading primer authors and the ghetto child's experience. Sentence 4 is ambiguous because of its underlying (logical) constituent structure and is an example of a type of ambiguity which faces all readers at all levels. Sentence 5 contains an ambiguous lexical form, _took_, which is equally ambiguous for all classes of readers.

The basic problem for beginning readers is similar for Standard and non-standard speakers, but it is by no means identical. As sentences 1 through 3 illustrate, the culture and language of the ghetto must be considered for potential ambiguity for beginning readers who are there.

3. Use redundancy. The nature of underlying language structure, as we are using the term here, insures a certain

amount of redundance. The sentence, LeRoy eats the
carrots contains a number of semi-redundant features.
If school makes any sense to him at all, the beginning
reader's innate knowledge of English keeps him from
reading it LeRoy carrots the eats or LeRoy of house ands.

For beginning readers, this principle means that the
writer should be very careful to load the text with predictable materials and to delay metaphor, simile and
other non-predictable matters until the reader is far
enough along in his learning to be able to tolerate them.
If we are serious about using redundancy which parallels
the ghetto child's oral language practice, we may decide
to include such so-called redundant features as multiple
negatives and pronominal apposition in the beginning
reading materials, e.g.:

He don't have no baseball bat.

My brother John, he struck out.

If redundancy is reinforcing for the language learner
(in this case, the aspiring literate), one must use the
inventory of available redundancies.

If beginning reading materials for ghetto children are
to relate to the oral language of the learners, these considerations must be reflected in the primers. The matter of
the reader's underlying language structure must be given considerable emphasis in these primers, particularly where there
is mismatch between standard and non-standard grammatical
phenomena. There is considerable room for improvement in the
construction of beginning reading material for children of
all social classes and races, but there is drastic need for
adjustment of such materials for the Negro non-standard
speaker, whose grammatical system is sufficiently different
from Standard English to hinder his learning to relate his

oral language to the grammatical forms of the primer.

The problems of producing overcomplex or derived constructions, ambiguous readings and under-redundant material
for Standard English speaking readers has by no means been
solved, but it is even multiplied for non-standard speaking
children, whose derivations, systematic ambiguities and redundancies have only begun to be observed, much less utilized
in reading materials.

NOTES

1. Morton Wiener and Ward Cromer, "Reading and Reading
    Difficulty: A Conceptual Analysis", Harvard Educational
    Review, XXXVII (1967), No. 4, pp. 620-643.

2. Occasionally, however, they can cite lexical matters
    which they think have social consequence.

3. Anne E. Hughes, An Investigation of Certain Socio-
    linguistic Phenomena in the Vocabulary, Pronunciation
    and Grammar of Disadvantaged Pre-School Children, Their
    Parents and Their Teachers in the Detroit Public Schools
    (unpublished Ph.D. Diss., Michigan State University,
    1967). For a summary, see Roger W. Shuy, Walter A.
    Wolfram and William K. Riley, Linguistic Correlates of
    Social Stratification in Detroit Speech, Final Report,
    Cooperative Research Project 6-1347, U.S. Office of
    Education, Part IV, pp. 1-10.

4. Joan Baratz, "Teaching Reading in an Urban Negro School";
    in the present volume, pages 92-116.

5. See Marvin Loflin, On the Structure of the Verb in a
    Dialect of American Negro English, Office of Naval
    Research Group Psychology Branch, Technical Report No. 26
    (Center for Research in Social Behavior, University of
    Missouri), and Ralph W. Fasold, "Tense and the Form Be
    in Black English", in Roger W. Shuy and Ralph W. Fasold
    (eds.), Current Viewpoints Toward Non-Standard "Be"
    (Washington, D.C.: Center for Applied Linguistics, forth-
    coming).

6. See, for example, William Labov, The Social Stratification

of English in New York City (Washington, D.C.: Center for
Applied Linguistics, 1966), and Shuy, Wolfram and Riley,
op. cit.

7. The term "rule" is not used here in the current sense in
   which it is found in theoretical linguistics. That is,
   we are not referring to derivational history. From the
   linguist's viewpoint, a more accurate term might be
   "correspondence".

8. William A. Stewart, "Foreign Language Teaching Methods
   In Quasi-Foreign Language Situations", in Stewart (ed.),
   Non-Standard Speech and the Teaching of English (Washing-
   ton, D.C.: Center for Applied Linguistics, 1964), pp. 1-15.

9. William Wonderly, Bible Translations for Popular Use (New
   York: American Bible Society, 1968).

10. Ibid., pp. 150-151.

11. See, for example, G.A. Miller, "Some Psychological Studies
    of Grammar", American Psychologist, XVII (1962), pp. 748-
    762; and E.B. Coleman, "Learning of Prose Written in Four
    Grammatical Transformations", Journal of Applied Psychol-
    ogy 49 (1965), pp. 332-341.

TOWARD READING MATERIALS FOR SPEAKERS OF

BLACK ENGLISH: THREE LINGUISTICALLY

APPROPRIATE PASSAGES

by Walter A. Wolfram and Ralph W. Fasold

Within the last half century the populations of many urban
areas in the United States have been drastically restructured.
Extensive in-migration by Southern Negroes has resulted in
the growth of many large isolated Negro ghettos. The segregated rural populations of the South have thus become the
isolated Negro communities of our metropolitan areas. Although sociologists, psychologists, and anthropologists have
pointed out the cultural gap that exists between the so-
called ghetto culture and the culture of mainstream middle-
class American society, it has been only recently that the
linguistic consequences of this cultural difference have been
examined. Previously, the speech behavior of many lower
socio-economic class Negroes was simply considered comparable
to that of lower socio-economic white citizens who spoke a
variety of nonstandard English. Even some dialectologists
simply assumed that the speech of the uneducated Negro was no
different from that of the uneducated Southern white. Recent
descriptive and sociolinguistic studies of the variety of
English spoken by urban ghetto dwellers (i.e. Black English[1]),
however, have indicated that there are important systematic
differences between Black English and Standard English.

At this point, one may ask why the speech behavior found
in these isolated Negro communities should differ significantly
from the nonstandard variety of English spoken by the lower
socio-economic class white. In Northern urban areas, one

source of difference can be found in the influence that Southern dialects have on these speech communities. But even in
the rural South, Black English is characteristically different
from the speech of the lower socio-economic class white, and
one must ask why. For an explanation, one need only look at
the distinct history of the Negro in American life, both in
terms of his original immigration and his subsequent segregation. Recently, creole specialists have been particularly
occupied with pointing out the historical derivation of Black
English, tracing its origin to a rather widespread creole
spoken in the Caribbean area. For example, William A. Stewart
notes:

Of those Africans who fell victim of the Atlantic slave trade
and were brought to the New World, many found it necessary to
learn some kind of English. With very few exceptions the
form of English they acquired was a pidginized one, and this
kind of English became so well-established as the principal
medium of communication between Negro slaves in the British
colonies that it was passed on as a creole language to succeeding generations of the New World Negroes, for whom it
was their native tongue.[2]

Present-day Negro dialect, according to Stewart, has resulted
from a process which he labels "de-creolization". That is,
some of the original features characterizing the creole variety of English spoken by the early Negro slaves were lost
through a gradual merging of the creole with the British-
derived dialects with which they came in contact. The lexical inventory of this language variety became, for all practical purposes, identical with English (a process called
"relexification" by Stewart). Due to the persistence of
segregation, however, the process of decreolization was
neither instantaneous nor complete. Thus, the nonstandard
speech of present day Negroes still exhibits structural
traces of a creole predecessor.

     Present research by linguists has focused on Black
English both as a system in itself and as a variety of English

which systematically differs from Standard English. Some of
the differences between Standard English and Black English,
though seemingly small, have important consequences for the
communication of a message. Furthermore, many of the systematic differences between Standard English and Black English
have been overlooked by psychologists, sociologists, and educators, who simply dismiss Black English as an inaccurate and
unworthy approximation of Standard English. To illustrate,
we may briefly cite the Black English use of the form be as
a finite verb, in a sentence such as He be at work. This
characteristic use of be in Black English has been dismissed
as simply an inaccurate attempt by the lower socio-economic
class Negro to approximate the Standard English speech norm.
But such is clearly not the case. A study of the grammatical
and semantic function of this construction employing the descriptive technique of modern linguistic theory reveals that
one function of "finite be" has an "habitual" or "iterative"
meaning for the Black English speaker. There is no equivalent
category in Standard English and such a meaning can only be
conveyed by a circumlocution (e.g. He is at work all the time).
Thus, we see a clear-cut difference between the two grammatical systems. As will be seen in the annotated passages
at the end of this article, there are a number of consequen-
tial systematic differences between Black English and Standard English.

Now let us consider the implications of the above on the
preparation of reading materials in the school system. We
observe clear-cut differences between Black English and Standard English on several different levels (i.e. phonological,
grammatical, semantic) of language organization. The normal
processes which account for dialect differences have been
augmented by a creole substratum. We obviously have a dialect situation which is unique vis-à-vis other dialect

varieties of American English. Some educators have assumed
that one set of reading materials, perhaps "simplified"
(however that may be defined) to avoid structural conflict
between Standard English and Black English, is adequate for
the general school population. Certainly some lower socio-
economic class speakers read extant materials and with some
apparent understanding. We would not argue that the Black
English speaker is going to understand as little Standard
English as a monolingual German speaker reading English, but
we do suggest that there will be an inevitable information
loss. This leads to the question of what type of reading
materials are needed in the inner-city classroom.

Recently, publishers have introduced reading materials
that attempt to relate to the culture of the ghetto. They
have begun to include stories about Negro families in a
ghetto setting, but despite the change in context, the dialogue in these texts is a variety of Standard English which
does not very closely approximate the actual language usage
of black ghetto youth. Somehow, in the cultural adaptation
publishers have largely ignored the linguistic consequences
of cultural differences. Educators are thus faced with an
anomaly which may be greater than the original mismatch of
white middle-class-oriented narratives for black ghetto
youth. One can imagine what the response would be if the
white suburban youth were characterized by Black English
dialogue. Yet, it is precisely this type of anomaly which
is perpetuated by reading material which attempts to establish a cultural context indigenous to the ghetto but retains
the language of white middle-class suburbia. What appears
to be needed, then, is a linguistic adaptation or translation
of reading materials to a language system which more closely
approximates the child's oral language behavior.

Although adaptation or translation of materials is

linguistically justifiable, there remain a number of factors
which must be taken into account. One has to do with orthography. We have opted for standard orthography and conventional spelling. Conceivably this could lead to difficulties
if Black English pronunciations prove different enough from
Standard English, so that there is a serious mismatch between
conventional orthography and the phonology of the dialect.
However, research on Black English phonology has indicated
that conventional orthography is as adequate for Black English as it is for Standard English.[3]

Another factor in the use of the proposed adaptations
is that of applicability. There are many black ghetto residents who have learned Standard English. For these people,
the Black English materials would scarcely be more applicable
than they would be to any other speaker of Standard English.
Because of this, the use of the proposed materials cannot be
indiscriminate, even within ghetto schools. These materials
should be used only with those children who actually use
Black English.

A third factor has to do with the acceptability of the
materials to black people themselves. The degree to which
the adaptations would be acceptable, even to bona fide Black
English speakers, is an unanswered question. Sociolinguistic
research has shown that speakers who use socially stigmatized
speech forms sometimes have the same low opinion of such forms
as do speakers who do not use them. As a result, even though
the Black English materials might be clearer and more natural
to some, they may not be acceptable because of the presence
of these stigmatized forms. One consideration which may tend
to neutralize rejection, however, is the new feeling of racial
pride among black Americans. This pride leads Negroes to seek
those parts of their background, both in Africa and America,
which are distinctive to them. There is an emphasis on black

history, "African bush" hair styles, and neo-African clothing styles. So far this emphasis has not been extended to language. If a realization develops that this dialect, an important part of black culture, is as distinctively Afro-American as anything in the culture, the result may well be a new respect for Black English within the community.

The fourth factor has to do with the acceptability of the materials by educators. One possible objection would be the apparent discrepancy between the use of such materials and widely-advocated plans to teach disadvantaged children spoken Standard English. If a child is given books to read in his socially stigmatized dialect at the same time as he is being taught to replace his Black English with a dialect of Standard English, the two efforts would appear to be at cross-purposes. There are a number of reasons why this difficulty is more apparent than real. First, learning to read another language or dialect and learning to speak it are two different tasks. When the child who speaks Black English is required to learn to read using Standard English materials, he is given two tasks at once: learning to read and learning a new dialect. The Standard English speaking child, by contrast, is only required to learn to read. The success in learning to read is greater when the skill is taught in the mother tongue of the child.[4] In the second place, because of the social dynamics involved, there is some question about the degree to which Standard English can be taught to the ghetto child in the classroom at all. The most successful language learning has, as a component, meaningful interaction between the learner and speakers of the language he is trying to learn. Most Negro children, segregated by race and poverty, will have little opportunity to develop close acquaintanceships with Standard English speakers. There seems to be no reason why we should withhold from

inner-city children materials which may help them learn to
read simply because the use of these materials might interfere with teaching them spoken Standard English, especially
when it may not be possible to teach spoken Standard English
in the classroom in the first place. In any event, it seems
that some of the usual reasons for teaching spoken Standard
English, e.g. to enhance employment opportunities, are not
very relevant to elementary school children at the age at
which reading is taught. Furthermore, there is some evidence
that a young person is well into adolescence before he becomes aware of the social dimensions of language,[5] a fact
which would seem to indicate that formal efforts to teach
Standard English would be most effective if delayed until
junior high school or later--well after reading skills should
have been established.

The best proposals for teaching Standard English to
speakers of nonstandard dialects have as their goal adding a
new dialect to the pupil's linguistic ability, rather than
trying to eradicate his "bad" speech. In programs of this
type, the students are assured that there is nothing wrong
with their speech if it is used in appropriate contexts.
If these assurances are sincere, a good way to demonstrate
this would be to use the dialect in the educational process,
specifically in reading materials.

As an example of how this could be done, we present in
what follows three linguistically appropriate passages.
First, we have taken an original Black English passage, which
is a dramatized enactment of a situation occurring in the
ghetto. In this passage we have simply transcribed and edited
a section from a phonograph record[6] and arranged it as a
quasi-drama. The record contains the reasonably spontaneous
speech of six pre-adolescent Harlem boys. We have made no
grammatical changes in the text so that at places it may

appear that certain forms are importations from Standard English. The second passage is a dialect translation of reading material which was designed for use in inner-city schools.[7] In the third passage we have taken an established piece of literature, the Bible, and translated a passage into idiomatic Black English. In this passage we have not attempted to change the Biblical cultural setting, which is very different from both mainstream middle-class society and the black ghetto. We have approached this translation with the same rigor expected of any serious translation task. That is, we have attempted to be faithful to the form and content of the original manuscript (which, of course, is Greek and not English). Our translation of the Bible passage must therefore be distinguished from attempts to paraphrase the Bible into contemporary cultural parallels of the original message. We have included a Standard English translation of the passage for contrast with the Black English translation. Our annotations indicate those places where there exist clear-cut contrasts between the grammatical systems of Standard English and Black English.[8] Phonological differences are not annotated except where they affect grammatical form. Differences in the semantic content of lexical items have not generally been noted.

DUMB BOY

[Scene I]

Calvin: One day I was walking. Then I met Lennie. Lennie say,[1,2] "Calvin, what happened[3] to your lip?" I said, "Nothing." And then Lenn came over to me and he say,[1,2] "What[4] you mean by nothing?" Like he always say[2] because he's always interested in me and me and him[5] is[6] good friends. So I told him what happened.[3] "This guy named[3] Pierre, he[7] about fifteen..."

Lennie: Yeah?

Calvin: He came over to me...

Lennie: Uh huh.

Calvin: And he hit me in my[8] lip because...

Lennie: Yeah?

Calvin: I...

Lennie: Done[9] what?

Calvin: Had done copied[9] off his paper in school.

[Scene II]

Pierre: Uhh, I told you don't do that no more.[10,11]

Calvin: Come on, please leave me alone, please, please.

Pierre: Next time I catch you copying off somebody in there,
         you know what I'll do? I'll strangle you to death! Don't
         do that no more,[10] hear?

Calvin: I'm sorry.

[Scene III]

Lennie: What's that guy[12] name?

Calvin: Pierre.

Lennie: Where[4] he live at?

Calvin: Around our block.

Lennie: How old is he?

Calvin: Fifteen.

Lennie: How big is he?

Calvin: About the size of the other guy named[3] Pierre around
         our block.

Lennie: Well, tonight it's[13] gonna be a party at 118th Street
         where I live at. You bring him around there, hear?

Calvin: I surely will.

Lennie: O.K.

[Scene IV]

Calvin: So when I walked in there, everything was silent.

Lennie: Is that the guy over there?

Calvin: Yeah.

Lennie: Hey you, what[4] you hit my little brother for?

Pierre: Did he tell you what happened,[3] man?

Lennie: Yeah, he told me what happened.[3]

Pierre: But you...but you should tell your people to teach
          him to go to school, man. I know I didn't have a right
          to hit him. But he was copying off me and the teacher
          said...I forgot to tell the teacher.

Lennie: What[4] you mean you forgot to tell the teacher?
          What[4] you mean tell my parents to make him go to school
          to learn? What[4] you mean by that? What[4] you mean?

Pierre: Just like I said, man, he can't be dumb, man. I
          don't be[14] with him all his life.

Lennie: You basing or you sounding?[15]

Pierre: I ain't doing neither[10] one.

Lennie: That's more like it. But we[7] gonna deal tonight.

Pierre: If you can't face it, .don't waste[16] it. If you
          can't face it, don't waste[16] it.

                      SEE A GIRL*
              [Standard English Version]

          "Look down here," said Suzy.
          "I can see a girl in here.
          That girl looks like me.
          Come here and look, David.
          Can you see that girl?"

_____

*The setting of this story involves a little girl who looks
at her reflection in a puddle. Wiggles is a dog.

"Here I come," said David.
"I want to see the girl."
David said, "I do not see a girl.
A girl is not in here, Suzy.
I see me and my ball."

Suzy said, "Look in here, Mother.
David can not see a girl.
And I can.
Can you see a girl in here?"

"Look down, Suzy," said Mother.
"Look down here, David.
That little girl is my Suzy.
And here is David."

"Mother! Mother!" said Suzy.
"We can see David and me.
We can see Wiggles and a big girl.
That big girl is you."

SEE A GIRL
[Black English Version]

Susan[17] say[1,2] "Hey you-all,[18] look down here.

I can see a girl in here.

The girl, she[19] look[2] like me.

Come here and look, David.

Could[20] you see the girl?"

David, he[19] say[1,2] "Here I come.

Let me see the girl."

David say[1,2] "I don't see no girl.[10]

Ain't no girl[21] in there.

I see me and my ball."

Susan, she[19] say[1,2] "Momma,[22] look in here.

David don't[1] see no girl[10] and I do.

You see a girl in there?"

Momma[22] say[1,2] "Look down there, David.

That little girl[7] Susan.

And there go[23] David."

Susan[17] say[1,2] "Momma![22] Momma![22]

We can see David and me.

We can see Wiggles and a big girl.

You[7] that big girl."

JOHN 3:1-17 [Revised Standard Version]

Now there was a man of the Pharisees, named Nicodemus, a ruler
of the Jews. This man came to Jesus by night and said to him,
"Rabbi, we know that you are a teacher come from God; for no
one can do these signs that you do, unless God is with him."
Jesus answered him, "Truly, truly, I say to you, unless one
is born anew, he cannot see the kingdom of God." Nicodemus
said to him, "How can a man be born when he is old? Can he
enter a second time into his mother's womb and be born?"
Jesus answered, "Truly, truly, I say to you, unless one is
born of water and the Spirit, he cannot enter the kingdom of
God. That which is born of the flesh is flesh, and that which
is born of the Spirit is spirit. Do not marvel that I said
to you, 'You must be born anew.' The wind blows where it
wills, and you hear the sound of it, but you do not know whence
it comes or whither it goes; so it is with every one who is
born of the Spirit." Nicodemus said to him, "How can this be?"
Jesus answered him, "Are you a teacher of Israel, and yet you
do not understand this? Truly, truly, I say to you, we speak
of what we know, and bear witness to what we have seen; but you
do not receive our testimony. If I have told you earthly
things and you do not believe, how can you believe if I tell
you heavenly things? No one has ascended into heaven but he
who descended from heaven, the Son of man. And as Moses
lifted up the serpent in the wilderness, so must the Son of
man be lifted up, that whoever believes in him may have eternal life." For God so loved the world that he gave his only
Son, that whoever believes in him should not perish but have
eternal life. For God sent the Son into the world, not to
condemn the world, but that the world might be saved through
him.

JOHN 3:1-17   [Black English Version]

It[13] was a man named[3] Nicodemus. He was a leader of the Jews. This man, he[19] come[1,2] to Jesus in the night and say,[1,2] "Rabbi, we know you[7] a teacher that come[2] from God, cause can't nobody[24] do the things you be[14] doing 'cept he got God with him."

Jesus, he[19] tell[2] him say,[2,25] "This ain't[10] no jive,[26] if a man ain't born over again, ain't no way[21] he[7] gonna get to know God."

Then Nicodemus, he[19] ask him, "How[4,7] a man gonna be born when he[7] already old? Can't nobody[24] go back inside his mother and get[27] born."

So Jesus tell him, say,[2,25] "This ain't[10] no jive,[26] this[7] the truth. The onliest way a man[7] gonna get to know God,[7] he got to get born regular and he got to get[27] born from the Holy Spirit. The body can only make a body get[27] born, but the Spirit, he[19] make[2] a man so he can know God. Don't be suprised[3] just cause I tell you that you got to get born over again. The wind blow[2] where it want[2] to blow and you can't hardly[10] tell where it's[28] coming from and where it's[28] going to. That's[28] how it go[2] when somebody get[2,27] born over again by the Spirit."

So Nicodemus say[1,2] "How[4] you know that?"

Jesus say, "You call yourself[29] a teacher that teach Israel and you don't know these kind of things? I'm gonna tell you, we[7] talking about something we know about cause we already seen it. We[7] telling it like it is[30] and you-all[18] think we[7] jiving. If I tell you about things you can see and you-all think we[7] jiving[26] and don't believe me, what's[28] gonna happen when I tell about things you can't see? Ain't nobody[21] gone up to Heaven 'cept Jesus, who come[1,2] down from Heaven. Just like Moses done[9] hung up the snake in the wilderness, Jesus got to be hung up. So that the peoples[31] that believe in him, he can give them[19] real life that ain't never[10] gonna end. God really did love everybody in the world. In fact, he loved[3] the people so much that he done[9] gave up the onliest Son he had. Any man that believe[2] in him, he[7] gonna have a life that ain't never[10] gonna end. He ain't never[10] gonna die. God, he[19] didn't send his Son to the world to act like a judge, but he sent him to rescue the peoples[31] in the world."

NOTES

1. "Black English" is appropriate as a label for the dialect of lower socio-economic class Negroes for at least three reasons. First, there is a precedent for designating dialects with color names (Black Bobo, Red Tai, White Russian). In the second place, the current use of the term "black" in throwing off pejorative stereotypes of Negro life matches our efforts to overcome the stereotype that this dialect is simply bad English. Finally, the name "Black English" avoids the negative connotations of terms which include words like "dialect", "substandard" and even "nonstandard".

2. William A. Stewart, "Sociolinguistic Factors in the History of American Negro Dialects", The Florida FL Reporter, Vol. 5, No. 2 (1967) p. 22.

3. Ralph W. Fasold, "Orthography in Reading Materials for Black English Speaking Children" [in the present volume, pp. 68-91].

4. Evelyn Bauer mentions several experiments involving North American Indians in which superior results were obtained when Indian children were taught to read in their own language before attempting to read the national language. (Evelyn Bauer, "Teaching English to North American Indians in BIA Schools", The Linguistic Reporter, Vol. 10, No. 4 (1968) p. 2.)

5. William Labov, The Social Stratification of English in New York City (Washington, D.C.: Center for Applied Linguistics, 1966), p. 421.

6. Street and Gangland Rhythms (Folkways 5589 [1959]).

7. Writers' Committee of the Great Cities School Improve-
    ment Program of the Detroit Public Schools, Gertrude
    Whipple, Chairman, Four Seasons with Suzy (Chicago:
    Follett Publishing Co., 1964), pp. 48-50. Used by per-
    mission. [In preparing reading materials for the ghetto
    we certainly do not recommend working from a Standard
    English text to a Black English version, but in this
    case we have done so in order to point out some contrasts
    between the two versions of the story.]

8. It will be apparent that some of the features discussed
    here are shared both by Black English and other non-
    standard dialects of English.

ANNOTATIONS

[1] Some verbs, like "come" and "say", are not marked for past
     tense in Black English narratives, even when the context
     is past time.

[2] Black English lacks the -s suffix which marks the present
     tense with third person singular subjects in Standard
     English.

[3] When the suffix -ed is realized by a stop following a base
     form which ends in a consonant, the stop is not pronounced
     (thus, the pronunciation /neym/, for Standard English
     /neymd/). This reflects a Black English phonological pat-
     tern in which syllable final consonant clusters in Standard
     English correspond to simple consonants in Black English
     (see note 16). The pattern illustrates how phonological
     constraints in Black English affect the presence of certain
     grammatical categories.

[4] Sentences which would have a pre-posed verbal auxiliary in
     Standard English due to the formation of a content question
     generally have no auxiliary at all in the corresponding
     Black English sentence. For example, the "do" which would
     appear in the Standard English equivalent of questions like
     "what you mean by nothing?" is absent for this reason.

[5] In coordinate noun phrases, the distinction between objec-
     tive and subjective forms of the pronoun is often neutral-
     ized, so that the "objective" form may function as a gram-
     matical subject.

6 Occasionally (and particularly with coordinate constructions), the singular conjugated forms of "be" ("is", "was")
occur with the plural subject in Black English.

7 The present tense form of the copula frequently is not
realized in a number of different syntactic environments
in Black English. Generally, where the contracted form
of the copula may occur in Standard English the stative
condition is indicated simply by word order in Black English.

8 In Standard English, sentences like "kiss her on the cheek"
and "punch Jack in the stomach" involving a verb of physical contact, a personal nominal reference and a body part,
the definite article "the" is used with the body part although it belongs to the same person referred to by the
personal noun or pronoun. In Black English, the possessive
pronoun is used in these constructions instead of the
article.

9 The use of "done" plus the past tense of a verb is a construction indicating completed action. Some speakers
occasionally include a form of "have" as in "had done
copied..."

10 In Black English, negation is typically marked not only in
the main verb phrase, but also in each indefinite deter-
miner or indefinite pronoun in the sentence, as well as in
certain adverbs like "hardly" and "never".

11 An embedded imperative may be retained in its original
quoted form instead of being realized in an infinitive
construction (e.g. "I told you don't do that no more"
instead of "I told you not to do that no more").

12 Black English lacks possessive -s so that possession is
indicated only by the order of items.

13 "It", in Black English, can be used as an "expletive" or
"presentative" in addition to its function as a pronoun
referring to a specific object or participant. In this
usage it is equivalent to Standard English "there".

14 The form "be" can be used in Black English as a verb in
the same constructions in which "is, am, are, was, were"
are used in Standard English, but with a different meaning.
The use of "be" as a main verb denotes iteration or habit-
uation.

[15] The expressions "basing" and "sounding" refer to types of
aggressive verbal behavior. "Basing" is a kind of back-
talk and "sounding" refers to a special type of ritual
insult.

[16] The items "face" and "waste" have rhyming endings in Black
English because the final stop member of a syllable final
consonant cluster is frequently absent.

[17] The use of nicknames like "Jim" for "James" or "Dick" for
"Richard" is rare in ghetto communities. Therefore,
"Susan" is more natural in Black English reading materials
than "Suzy".

[18] Unlike most Standard English dialects, Black English dis-
tinguishes the singular and plural of the second person
pronoun ("you" versus "you-all", pronounced /yɔl/).

[19] A pronoun is often used following the noun subject of a
sentence in Black English. "Pronominal apposition" functions to focus on the "topic" of the sentence and to indicate the re-entry of a participant in a discourse.

[20] In a number of contexts, Black English speakers use "could"
where Standard English has "can".

[21] This construction is a very common stylistic variation of
"it ain't no girl in here" or "it ain't nobody who has
gone up to Heaven" (cf. note 13).

[22] Black children generally call their mothers "Momma".
"Mother" is likely to be taken as an abbreviation for a
taboo term.

[23] The idomatic expression "there go" is equivalent to the
Standard English construction "there is" when it refers
to the existential location of something. Generally, this
construction is limited to the speech of adolescents and
pre-adolescents.

[24] There are two types of emphatic negative sentences in
Black English involving the pre-position of a negativized
auxiliary. Black English, unlike most white nonstandard
dialects, permits both an indefinite subject and the main
verb to carry negative markers. Thus, "...nobody can't
do the things you be doing..." is a grammatical sentence
in the dialect, meaning that nobody can do these things.
To emphasize such a negative statement Black English
speakers may prepose the negativized verbal auxiliary to

the front of the sentence, much as the ordinary English yes-no question formation. Two kinds of stress pattern are associated with this structure. If the stress pattern is "càn't nóbody (do something)", it expresses general emphasis. If the stress pattern is "cán't nobòdy (do something)", it carries the overtone of disbelief.

25 Quotations can be introduced by the form "say" in addition to any other quotative words such as "tell" and "ask".

26 The concept "jive" in the Negro ghetto refers to a particular form of language behavior in which the speaker assumes a guise in order to persuade someone of a particular fact. It is often used to refer to the deception of someone with flattery or false promises.

27 "Get" (or "got") often functions as a passive marker in Black English.

28 When a pronoun ending in /t/ like "it" or "that" precedes the contracted form of "is", the contraction /s/ is pronounced and the /t/ is not (cf. note 7).

29 The expression "you call yourself X" or "you call yourself doing X" implies mild doubt that the hearer really is X or is doing X.

30 The expression "telling it like it is" refers to making an accurate and trustworthy assessment of a situation, without any attempt to exaggerate.

31 -s plural can be suffixed to forms which in Standard English form their plural in some irregular way (suppletive forms, internal change, etc.).

ON THE USE OF NEGRO DIALECT IN THE TEACHING OF READING

by William A. Stewart

By the time he reaches the age of five or six, (i.e. school age, in many societies), every normally developed human being has already mastered the fundamentals of at least one language, and has done so quite accurately without any need for formal instruction from others.[1] Indeed, so intrinsic is the normal child's interest in the language used around him and so apparently spontaneous his acquisition of it, that it is reasonable to suppose a propensity for language to be part of the genetic endowment of the human species -- with only the structural details of each language left to invention, cultural transmission, and historical change.[2] But if it is in man's nature to acquire a language through mere exposure to it at the right time in life, that nature also seems to require (whether for neurological, psychological, or other reasons) that the language behavior encountered be presented in certain ways and take certain overt forms before it can be "picked up" and internalized by the child. For one thing, in the early stages of language acquisition, at least, the language behavior encountered by the child must be socially relevant (by emanating directly from other human beings) and in context (so that the meaning of it can be established). For another (and this may or may not be a further ramification of the social-relevance requirement), the language behavior encountered must be encoded into systematic and perceivable manifestations of human behavior -- usually vocal noises.[3]

Unfortunately, written language does not fulfill any of these requirements. When encountered by a language-acquiring child, written text is not likely to be in the process of emanating from another individual, nor is its meaning likely to be apparent from the immediate situation at the time of encounter. In addition, human beings simply do not seem to be "programmed" to acquire writing systems automatically -- even if these are based on a known or frequently heard spoken language. Consequently, reading and writing skills have to be taught formally in most cases, and subsequent to first-language acquisition. This explains why there are so many people in the world who do not know how to read or write a language, while there is hardly anyone who does not know how to speak a language. In addition, there is the fact that writing is a quite recent phenomenon in contrast to speaking, and therefore still a functionally marginal one in many societies.

This problem exists even when the written language is little more than a graphic rendition of the spoken language of the population, as is more-or-less true for some segments of modern European and American societies. In many parts of the world, however, learning to read (even with substantial amounts of formal instruction) may be rendered infinitely more difficult by a tradition of writing primarily or exclusively in some language other than the one (or ones) which the population normally learns to speak. In the West African countries, for example, practically all writing (and certainly all important writing) is done in English or French, in spite of the fact that scarcely any West African learns English or French as his first language. In those countries, the teaching of reading is nothing less than the teaching of reading of English or French, so that the reading process itself must either follow or run concurrently with the teaching of English

or French as a foreign language.[4] Even in countries in which
the national language is indeed that of the majority of the
population, a situation similar to the West African one may
hold for members of foreign-language-speaking minority groups,
since many of these are expected to function as literates in
the larger society.

For multilingual situations of the West African type,
one of the most promising innovations in the direction of a
viable literacy program is the pedagogical separation of
beginning reading from the encumberment of concurrent foreign
language teaching. This separation is accomplished by the
simple strategy of teaching individuals to read first in
their own native language, and then transferring the reading
skills thus acquired to the task of reading in whatever
foreign language is the ultimate goal of the literacy program. In some cases, it may be necessary for the literacy
specialist to devise an orthography for the native language
of the learners, if this is an unwritten one, while in other
cases an existing orthography may or may not need modification
to facilitate transfer to the ultimate target language. Tra-
ditionally-oriented educators and administrators who do not
understand the rationale for the separation of learning tasks
involved in this approach, and who accordingly see the teaching of initial reading in some normally unwritten or nationally
unimportant language as an utter waste of time, may be surprised to find groups which have been taught literacy by the
native-to-foreign language technique catching up with and even
surpassing groups which have begun reading in conjunction with
the learning of the national (though, for them, foreign) language.[5] But whether innovative or traditional methods are employed, the general multilingualism of areas like Africa,
Asia, and parts of Europe and Latin America makes those involved acutely aware that pedagogical problems related to

literacy can be, and often are, predicated on language-
learning problems.

In the United States, that portion of the national population for which reading in English constitutes reading in a
completely foreign language is relatively small when compared
with the truly multilingual nations just discussed. At present, Spanish-speaking Americans and speakers of American
Indian languages seem to constitute the most well-defined
cases of this. For these groups, such specialized literacy
materials as there are do tend to take the matter of language
differences into account; and even relatively unsophisticated
reading teachers can be expected to realize that retardation
in the reading of English texts by Mexican-American or Navajo
children probably has something to do with the fact that many
of these children do not speak English natively -- even if
the teacher doesn't know exactly what to do about the situation.

Even though aware of a possible relationship between
language differences and serious reading problems in American
school children from foreign-language backgrounds, most reading specialists would not be inclined to consider a similar
cause for reading retardation in children from an English-
speaking background. To be sure, it is recognized that even
these children may experience initial difficulties in relating writing to speech, but this is understood to be little
more than the effect of minimal differences between written
and spoken varieties of the same language -- in this case,
English.[6] At the same time, the apparent overall similarity
between the spoken language which English-speaking children
bring to school and the written language which they encounter
in books is seen to preclude language differences as a primary cause of any failure on the part of such children to
attain normal reading proficiency. When such failure occurs,

there is accordingly a strong tendency to attribute it to
extra-linguistic factors, such as abnormalities or malfunc-
tions either in the child or in his surroundings. These
real or imagined causes of reading retardation include organic (i.e. neurological or physiological) disorders, and
such functional disorders as emotional disturbance in the
child, or his lack of exposure to written language, education,
a stimulating environment, etc. And -- with tragic consequences, as will be seen -- extra-linguistic causes have been
appealed to almost exclusively in recent attempts to explain
why it is that reading retardation is more pronounced among
Negro English-speaking children than among white English-
speaking children in many American schools.

One theory which has been advanced to explain this does
involve an organic principle, though not actually an organic
disorder. It is that racially correlated differences in
reading achievement (as well as achievement in other school
subjects) are simply a manifestation of racial differences
in mean intellectual capacity. This theory is based in large
part on apparent evidence that Negroes tend to score significantly lower than whites on standardized intelligence tests.
The evidence is striking enough to indicate some variable at
work, even though it turns out that few of the relevant
experiments have been well enough designed or controlled to
be entirely reliable, or to show what the different scores
indicate. Furthermore, it has been possible to arrange
experiments which offer some counter-evidence to the theory.[7]
Debate on the issue has been strongly polarized, and often
more socio-political than scientific. On the one hand are
the hereditarians, who maintain that race-related differences
in performance on intelligence tests have a genetic basis.
Aligned against them are the environmentalists, who insist
that these differences, even if real, are but the product of

ecological and experiential factors. Of the two, the hereditarians' argumentation seems especially weak. They claim
that there is a lower intelligence mean for Negroes than for
whites, and either state or imply that this relates directly
to biological differences between the two races. Yet, they
base these claims on studies in which distinctions between
"Negro" and "white" have had more of a social than a biological basis (the real meaning of "Negro" in the United
States). Furthermore, the hereditarians simply have not
given due consideration to nonhereditary variables. As the
environmentalists are quick to point out, the relatively
poorer performance by lower-class Negroes than by middle-
class Negroes shows quite clearly that, whatever the causes
of performance differences may be, they are not racially
distributed to any degree which would indicate a genetic
basis.

From the environmentalist side, a number of reasons have
been suggested why Negroes may seem to do relatively more
poorly than whites on intelligence tests, and in such school
subjects as reading. One possibility sometimes suggested is
that there may be a higher incidence of intellectually debilitating organic disorders among Negroes than among whites. But
the origin of these disorders would not be genetic; rather,
they would be induced in individuals by such features of lower-
class living as poor pre- and postnatal care, substandard
nutrition, physical abuse, etc. Their apparent racial correlation would only be a function of the disproportionately
high percentage of Negroes in the American lower-class population. In a similar vein, a higher rate of debilitating
functional disorders (such as emotional disturbance) is sometimes claimed for Negroes, and this is also attributed to the
rigors of lower-class life.

Although it is perfectly true that both organic and

functional disorders can affect intelligence scores and reading ability (sometimes drastically), the real question is
whether such pathologies are induced regularly enough by the
lower-class condition to account for the regularity with
which the supposed intellectual deficit occurs in the Negro
population. Considering the performance differences between
Negroes and whites, the incidence of pathology in the lower-
class Negro environment would have to be considerable. And
this leads to another pertinent question concerning the
validity of such explanations: Is there any evidence that
the lower-class Negro environment is sufficiently worse than
the lower-class white environment to account satisfactorily
for the intellectual performance differences between lower-
class Negroes and even lower-class whites? In at least some
areas in which lower-class Negroes and lower-class whites
score differently (in Appalachia, for example), their material
condition is remarkably similar. A different explanation --
one which would at least account for a higher incidence of
emotional disturbance among Negroes (if this should prove to
be the case) -- is race prejudice, pure and simple. But then
why do middle-class Negroes score better than lower-class
Negroes, when the former are apparently in more of a position
to feel the brunt of prejudice directly?

     Of the many theories which have been advanced by environ-
mentalists to explain differences in intellectual performance
between Negroes and whites, certainly the most popular have
been those positing as a basic cause some sort of cognitive
or communicative deficit. According to such theories, there
is something about the lower-class (usually Negro) environment,
both social and physical, which inhibits the normal development of abstract thought and well-formed, expressive language
in the growing child. The factors which are believed to in-
hibit cognitive and linguistic development in the lower-class

Negro child are all environmental: excessive noise and disorder, depressing surroundings, the absence of a father,
insufficient verbal interaction with the mother, no contact
with books, limited experiences, etc. That an individual
thus burdened with a "cognitive deficit" and "verbal desti-
tution" would do poorly on any kind of intellectual task
seems almost beyond question, and the impression that this
is so has undoubtedly contributed to the widespread acceptance of environmentalist deficit theories.

Yet, the questions which should really be asked about
these theories are: Do they describe the lower-class Negro
environment accurately? and, Do they demonstrate a causal
relationship between any of the characteristics of such
environments on the one hand and basic cognitive and linguistic development on the other? When furnished, the
answers to these questions may be quite disconcerting to the
deficit theories. For example, there is no real evidence
that lower-class environments are significantly more noisy
or less structured than middle-class ones, nor is it clear
just how noise levels, say, of an inner-city magnitude would
stultify cognitive or linguistic development. And, in view
of the importance of the peer-group as a source of language
models for the growing child, it seems quite risky to assume
that parental involvement is an absolute necessity in even
first-language acquisition. This would especially be true
in lower-class Negro families, where there are usually several
siblings and many, many playmates.

At present, theories that the special educational problems of lower-class Negro children stem from cognitive, cultural, and/or linguistic deficiencies in these children or
their environments seem to be subscribed to whole-heartedly
by most educational psychologists. And, given the prestige
which psychological formulations of learning problems currently

enjoy in educational circles, it is not surprising that deficit theories have been widely accepted by teachers, curriculum
designers, and school administrators as the "scientific" reason
why lower-class Negro children do so poorly in the classroom.
Of course, the acceptance by educators of deficit theories is
facilitated by the fact that, just like their psychological
gurus, few educators are familiar enough with lower-class
Negro life to know how badly such theories represent it, and
by the fact that any conceptual inadequacies in psychological
research designs for measuring lower-class Negro performance
on standardized tests are likely to be effectively obscured
by impressive test specifications (masking the inappropriate-
ness of the tests), by elaborate statistical analyses (masking
the irrelevance of the variables), and by complicated charts
and graphs of the misleading or prevaricating results.[8]

As one would expect, hereditarian explanations of Negro
and white differences in intellectual achievement and school
performance have appealed most strongly to racists, while
environmentalist explanations have found eager acceptance
among egalitarians. Of course, there are many social scientists, social activists, and educators who make it a point
never to discuss such differences, or even acknowledge their
existence. This conspiracy of silence seems to be a manifestation either (depending upon one's point of view) of the
assumption that such differences, while probably debilitating,
are nevertheless innate and unchangeable, and therefore that
nothing would be gained by talking about them, or that the
measurements which show them represent deliberate misrepre-
sentation or some minor procedural mistake in the testing
methodology, so that if one only ignores them they will
eventually waft away by themselves. For those who do believe
in facing up to the data, however, some sort of explanation
of these differences must be sought, if for no reason other

than that American education might come to understand why
what is happening to it is happening. I suspect that the
popularity among egalitarians of the environmentalist deficit
theories as explanations of ethnically-correlated performance
differences derives not only from ethnocentrism, but also
from the conviction that they represent the only honest alternative to hereditarianism short of an egalitarian act of
faith which, far from bringing about an understanding of the
problem, would only serve to obscure its causes all the more.[9]

The fact that debate on the issue of Negro intelligence
has been carried on largely in terms of genetics and ecology
might well come as a surprise to social scientists or educators who are not familiar with American social rhetoric.
For, were a difference in intellectual performance to be
found between two populations in almost any other part of the
world, it would be considered a matter of course to explore
first the possibility that the apparent intellectual dis-
parity might merely reflect cultural differences between the
two groups through a bias in the measurement techniques toward one or the other culture.[10] In the United States, on the
other hand, only the scantiest consideration has been given
to the same possibility -- that being "white" and "Negro"
might involve correlations with more-or-less different American subcultures, and that cultural differences might therefore be responsible for the intellectual performance dis-
parity between the two ethnic groups. Rather, American social
scientists have generally assumed that, once such variables as
social class and regional provenience (particularly rural vs.
urban) are accounted for, Negroes and whites would turn out
to be culturally identical.[11] That this assumption should
remain unchallenged (and, indeed, that it should have been
made in the first place) in the face of such obvious and
omnipresent indications of cultural differences between whites

and Negroes as are evident in musical styles, patterns of
worship, dress, expressive behavior (such as the forms and
uses of laughter), and a host of other cultural domains in
which intra-ethnic variation according to social class and
region never quite obscures the inter-ethnic differences, is
probably due to its compatibility with the American "melting
pot" myth. For it is a basic tenet of that myth that all
foreign immigrant groups are automatically and completely
assimilated to the Anglo-Saxon national culture within one
or two generations, so that cultural differences between
groups of different ethnic or national origin are not to be
expected to last for long. In fact, the Negro is often
singled out by propagators of the myth as a prime example of
just how thorough the assimilation process can be in America --
the implication being that, since American Negroes no longer
exhibit identifiably African behaviors, they must have assimilated completely to the cultural patterns of American whites.

       Although this impression of the cultural relationship of
American Negroes to American whites is inaccurate in many
important ways, it is not difficult to see how it evolved.
For, when Africans and Europeans came together in North America, people tended (as they still do) to regard behavioral
differences as legitimate cultural differences only when they
could be associated with some national or tribal source.
Consequently, observable deviations in the behavior of Negroes
from the norms of whites were considered to be culturally conditioned only so long as the Negroes retained enough identifiably African behaviors to insure their being considered
Africans. However, once the visible trappings of African
tribal cultures were given up by American Negroes (or at
least became subtle enough to escape identification), continued deviations from white behavioral norms were considered
gaffes and gaucheries at best, and more often as evidence of

intellectual immaturity in the Negro and therefore justification for his enslavement. Unfortunately, and in spite of
Emancipation, this blindness to the cultural nature of Negro
and white behavioral differences has persisted down to the
present day, with the white liberal and black revolutionary
alike the simultaneous perpetrators and victims of it that
Massa and Cudjo were on the Old Plantation.[12]

In at least one area -- that of language -- there has
been a growing awareness of the historical and functional
legitimacy of Negro deviations from white behavioral norms.
Long regarded by the public in general and educators in particular as the result of carelessness, laziness, ignorance,
or stupidity, the nonstandard speech patterns of American
Negroes are now coming to be recognized as perfectly normal
dialect forms which are just as much the product of systematic (though formally unspecified) linguistic rules as are
the speech patterns of whites. That the Negro speech of a
given region and social class may differ from the white
speech of even the same region and a comparable social class
is now understood to be the result, not of physiological or
mental differences between Negroes and whites, but rather of
the interrelationship between language history and American
social structure.[13] For, if early written samples of North
American slave speech are at all reliable, it would seem that
the unique characteristics of present-day Negro dialects derive, at least in part, from former pidgin and creole stages.
And this would also explain why the most nonstandard varieties
of Negro dialect are structurally much more deviant from standard English than are the most nonstandard dialects of native
American whites.[14]

Once this is understood, it should become apparent that
language differences, as opposed to language deficits, may
well account for most of the chronic difficulty which so many

lower-class Negro children have with standard English in the
classroom and, later, on the job. For, wherever the structure of standard English differs from that of their own non-
standard dialect, the "interference" of the familiar pattern
in the production of the unfamiliar pattern may occur. This
is, in fact, exactly what happens when a Spanish-speaking
child produces a Spanish-like English utterance. Thus, the
language-learning problems of a Negro-dialect speaker who is
trying to acquire standard English are, in many ways, more
like those of, say, a Spanish speaker who is trying to acquire
English than they are like those of a middle-class, English-
speaking child. For the first two, the task is one of learning structurally different functional equivalents of patterns
which they already know; for the third, the task is merely
one of learning additional and compatible patterns to the
ones already known. In other words, the learning of standard
English by speakers of Negro dialect is more like foreign-
language learning than it is like first-language learning.
For this reason, techniques which have been developed in
foreign-language teaching to deal with structural conflicts
between different language systems are being found to be
much more appropriate for teaching standard English patterns
to Negro-dialect speakers than are the pathology-oriented
methods of traditional speech therapy and remedial English.[15]
And even though the overall structural difference between
Negro dialect of the most nonstandard kind and standard English of the most formal kind is obviously not as great as
between any kind of English and a foreign language like
Spanish, this does not necessarily make it easier for the
Negro-dialect speaker to acquire an acceptably standard
variety of English than for the speaker of Spanish to do so.
On the contrary, the subtlety of the structural differences
between the two forms of English, masked as they are by the

many similarities, may make it almost impossible for the
speaker of Negro dialect to tell which patterns are characteristic of nonstandard dialect, and which ones are not.
Indeed, this may explain why it is that many immigrant populations have been able to make a more rapid and successful
transition from their original foreign language to standard
English than migrant Negroes have from their own nonstandard
dialect to standard English.[16]

Toward the beginning of this paper, it was indicated
that the attainment of such a seemingly rudimentary skill as
literacy in the national language could actually turn out to
be an inordinately difficult task for persons who might not
happen to speak that language -- success in learning to read
being, for them, largely dependent upon success in learning
a new language. Mention was made of the recent development
of special literacy programs for such persons, involving the
teaching of beginning reading in the learner's native language and the subsequent transfer of the basic skills thus
acquired to the reading (and even to the learning) of the
national language. That early in the paper, the possible
implications which the native-to-foreign approach to literacy might have for teaching reading to "disadvantaged" Negroes
could not be explored directly, since, without the inter-
vening discussion, few reading specialists would have been
prepared to see any similarity at all between the reading
problems of linguistic minorities in foreign lands and those
of Negro children in American schools. But once it has become clear that low intellectual performance of whatever kind
on the part of Negro school children could be due, not to
neurological or experiential deficits, but rather to un-
formalized yet real differences between their own cultural
orientation and school expectations, and, more specifically,

once it becomes clear that the chronic difficulties which
such children often have with oral standard English can be
traced to structural differences between nonstandard Negro
dialect (the linguistic aspect of their own culture) and
standard English (the linguistic aspect of the school culture), then the applicability of native-to-foreign literacy
techniques becomes a distinct possibility. After all, might
not learning to read in an unfamiliar dialect have associated
with it some of the problems which have been found to charac-
terize learning to read in an unfamiliar language?

Although no adequate study of the role of dialect differences in the reading proficiency of American Negro children has yet been undertaken, a suggestion of what is likely
to be the case is available from a somewhat comparable European situation. In a Swedish-dialect context, Tore Österberg
found that the teaching of basic reading skills in the non-
standard dialect of the school children in a particular district (Piteå) increased proficiency, not only in beginning
reading in the nonstandard dialect, but also in later reading of the standard language.[17] In fact, one of Österberg's
most dramatic findings was that the experimental group (which
began with nonstandard dialect materials and then changed to
standard Swedish materials) overtook the control group (which
used standard Swedish materials from the very beginning) in
reading proficiency in standard Swedish -- I repeat, standard
Swedish -- even though the additional steps of the bidialectal
approach meant that the students in the experimental group
spent less total time with the standard language.

But even before I became aware of the Österberg study,
with its obvious implications for American education, the
suitability of the bidialectal approach to the reading problems of inner-city Negro children was suggested to me by a
fortuitous experience. In the latter part of 1965, I had

decided to do a Negro-dialect translation of Clement Clarke
Moore's famous Christmas poem "A Visit from St. Nicholas"
(more widely known as "The Night Before Christmas") for
Christmas greetings from the Urban Language Study of the
Center for Applied Linguistics.[18] In order to highlight the
grammatical differences between nonstandard Negro dialect
and standard English, I decided to retain standard-English
word spellings in the nonstandard version wherever possible.
Thus, I wrote it's, the, night, before, and Christmas, even
though a child might be apt to pronounce /is/, /də/, /nay/,
/bifów/, and /kɪsmɪs/. One modification I made in this rule
was that, when the nonstandard pronunciation of a particular
Negro-dialect word was better represented by the spelling of
some standard-English word other than its direct functional
equivalent, that spelling was used. Thus the Negro-dialect
verb /fuw/, though equivalent to fill in standard English,
was spelled full in the poem. In addition, the form and
sequencing of the events in Moore's original version were
recast to make the nonstandard version more in keeping with
Negro discourse style and inner-city cultural reality. Some
idea of what the result of this translation process looked
like can be gotten from the first few lines, which went:

> It's the night before Christmas, and here in our house,
> It ain't nothing moving, not even no mouse.
> There go we-all stockings, hanging high up off the floor,
> So Santa Claus can full them up, if he walk in
>   through our door.

For those who are not entirely familiar with this kind of
dialect, I should probably point out that the Negro-dialect
phrase There go we-all stockings does not mean "There go our
stockings" in standard English. As often used by Negro children, the idioms here go and there go serve to point out
something (not necessarily in motion) to the listener, and
are thus equivalent to standard English here is/are and
there is/are, or to French voici and voilà.

One evening, while I was working at home on the translation of the poem (a draft of which was in my typewriter,
with the original version at the side), two inner-city children dropped by for a visit. While I was busy getting some
refreshments for them from the refrigerator, Lenora (then
about 12 years old) went over to play with the typewriter
and found the draft of the nonstandard version of the poem
in it. Lenora was one of the "problem readers" of the public
schools; she read school texts haltingly, with many mistakes,
and with little ability to grasp the meaning of what she read.
Yet, when she began to read the nonstandard version of the
poem, her voice was steady, her word reading accurate, and
her sentence intonation was natural (for her dialect, of
course). This unexpected success in reading so surprised
Lenora that she began to discuss the experience with her
little brother. They decided that there was something different about the text, but were unable to tell exactly what
it was. To compare, I then had Lenora read the standard English version of the poem, which was sitting beside the typewriter. When she did, all the "problem reader" behaviors
returned.

Now, it must be remembered that both the nonstandard
and standard versions of the poem were written with the same
spellings for similar words, e.g., Christmas in both. Therefore, it was clear that Lenora was reacting primarily to the
difference between a familiar and an unfamiliar type of grammar. For, if she could read standard-English words without
difficulty when they were presented in a nonstandard grammatical framework, then this meant that word-reading or sound-
spelling-meaning correspondences were not the problem that
they seemed to be when she attempted to read standard English.
It struck me that this unplanned "experiment" (later dupli-
cated with other inner-city children) suggested an entirely

different dimension of possible reading problems for inner-
city Negro children than those focused on by such methods as
i.t.a. and phonics. This other dimension is that of structural interference between the grammatical patterns of the
nonstandard dialect which many Negro children speak and the
grammatical patterns of the standard English in which reading materials are invariably written. And, if it has been
considered pedagogically useful to adapt beginning reading
materials to the word pronunciations of middle-class white
children (as has been done in i.t.a. and phonics), then might
it not also be useful to adapt beginning reading materials
to the sentence patterns of lower-class Negro children?

From my own point of view, which is that of a linguist
who has spent most of his life in multilingual, diglossic,
and multidialectal situations, who considers them normal,
and who feels that educational techniques ought to take them
into account, the answer is that beginning reading materials
should indeed be adapted to the patterns of nonstandard Negro
dialect -- and to those of any other nonstandard dialect which
school children in a particular area may speak, for that matter. Yet, I think I can anticipate at least four reasons
which might be given why the "correctness" of reading materials should not be tampered with and, in particular, why
Negro-dialect patterns should not be allowed to appear in
school readers.

One argument which might be advanced against the incor-
poration of nonstandard-dialect patterns into beginning reading materials is that the process ought to be unnecessary;
children from whatever language or dialect background ought
to be instructed in oral standard English as part of their
pre-reading training, and reading materials ought to be written in standard English from the very start. Neat though
this approach may seem, it is simply impossible to carry out

in most rural and inner-city schools. For the fact is that
these schools are full of functionally illiterate, nonstand-
ard-dialect-speaking children of all grades and ages -- many
of whom are simply too far along in the curriculum to be told
to stop trying to read, go back, and take remedial oral English with the kindergarten children and first-graders. Even
if most predominantly Negro schools were to have effective
programs for teaching oral standard English to pre-readers
(and most still do not), the migratory and working patterns
of rural children and the high geographic mobility of inner-
city children would make it difficult for such schools to
insure that the children going into beginning reading would
all have already had instruction in oral standard English.
Consequently, the recognition of nonstandard dialect in reading instruction will probably be necessary for at least some
pupils at all grade levels in such schools. And this is as
it should be. Special oral-language programs for Negro-
dialect speakers and special reading instruction for Negro-
dialect speakers ought, after all, to be complementary
activities, not rival ones.

    Another argument which is very likely to be advanced
against the idea of incorporating Negro-dialect grammatical
patterns into beginning reading materials is that the features of Negro dialect which seem to interfere the most with
the effective oral reading of standard English do not seem to
be grammatical ones; rather, they seem to be phonological
ones (i.e. differences in pronunciation). This is certainly
the impression of many reading specialists, and it agrees
substantially with the view which most speech therapists and
many English teachers have of Negro dialect as more a matter
of deviant "speech" (i.e. pronunciation) than of different
"language" (i.e. grammar). What is more, those who argue
thus can point to a great deal of support for this assumption

from dialectology and linguistics. For it has long been the
view of most dialectologists that American dialects of English differ from each other primarily in details of pronunciation and, to a lesser extent, of vocabulary. In fact,
so fully was this concept of American dialect differences
borrowed from European dialect geography that, when the field
questionnaires for work on an atlas of American dialects were
drawn up, they were designed to elicit phonological and lexical information almost exclusively. (Of course, the results
of the American Dialect Atlas fieldwork reinforced the original
view of dialect differences, since the questionnaires revealed
virtually no grammatical differences!) And, more recently,
some linguists who have studied Negro dialect from a transformational viewpoint have maintained that a few phonological
processes and minor transformations account for most of the
observable structural differences between nonstandard Negro
dialect and standard English. In other words, even apparent
word-form and grammatical differences may, in this view,
represent little more than different phonological and transformational treatments of otherwise similar "underlying"
structures.[19]

It is perhaps inevitable that those who take this view
will see the special reading problems of lower-class Negro
school children primarily as a difficulty in word or sentence
recognition caused by the frequent lack of correspondence
between Negro-dialect pronunciations and standard-English
spellings (which, of course, represent standard-English pronunciations much more closely). That is, the Negro child is
seen as having to cope primarily with such problems as learning that there is a correspondence between the spelling and
meaning of pen and pin in written standard English, even
though the word for the thing one writes with and the word
for the thing one sticks with are both pronounced [pɪn]

(or, alternatively, [pɛn]) in Negro dialect. And the reading
teacher is seen as having to cope primarily with such problems
as deciding, when a Negro child reads aloud /ges/ for guest,
whether he has understood the meaning of the written word and
merely given it its Negro-dialect pronunciation, or whether
he has misread the word as guess.[20]

Now, it is undoubtedly true that sound-spelling-meaning
correspondences between spoken Negro dialect and written
standard English are less regular (or, at least, less obviously regular) than between spoken standard English and
written standard English. Still, they are by no means neat
in even the latter case. For example, speakers of standard
English must learn to deal with the correlation to different
meanings of the written distinction between homophonic son
and sun, just as speakers of Negro dialect (or, indeed, of
southern varieties of standard English) must learn to deal
with what for them are homophonic pen and pin. And, of
course, spellings like of and island are not representative
of the pronunciation either of Negro dialect or standard English. Yet, most speakers of standard English do not seem to
be hindered very much by such sound-spelling-meaning irregu-
larities when they are learning to read -- a fact which would
suggest that absolute parallelism between phonology and
orthography is not really a prerequisite to literacy in English. Indeed, even relatively inexperienced readers seem to
be able to cope with a fair amount of sound-spelling irregu-
larity, provided that they are familiar with the spoken forms
of the words and are able to get sufficient cues for associating the written and spoken forms from the lexical and
syntactic context.

Probably more serious in its consequences for reading
instruction is the way in which differences between Negro
dialect pronunciations and standard English spellings can be

misinterpreted by reading teachers when they attempt to evaluate reading success through viva-voce performance. Unfortunately, there seems to be no simple way of deciding whether, in a particular instance, /ges/ represents a Negro dialect pronunciation of guest, or a misreading of it as guess. It would be more likely to be the former, but the background and training of many reading teachers would incline them to see it as the latter. And, although linguists know that a verb need not be accompanied by an explicit marker of the past tense to have past-tense meaning in Negro dialect (or, sometimes, even in standard English -- cf. hit, which never takes a past-tense marker), most reading teachers would probably assume that, when a Negro child reads a sentence like They guessed who he was to sound more like They guess who he was, this is evidence that he has missed the past-tense meaning of the verb guess. In fact, the Negro child may merely pronounce written guessed as /ges/ for the same reason that he pronounces guest as /ges/ -- because final /st/ clusters turn into /s/ in his dialect. The failure to articulate a final written -ed when reading aloud no more indicates that a Negro child has failed to perceive the past-tense meaning of a written verb having it than reading He hit me yesterday aloud is an indication that the speaker of standard English has failed to perceive the past-tense meaning of hit. Clearly, the requirements for acceptable reading aloud must be distinguished from the requirements for effective reading comprehension.

Even in those cases in which phonological differences between Negro dialect and standard English look like they ought to make phonological identification of the written word more difficult for the Negro-dialect speaker, and thus interfere with reading comprehension, this may not always turn out to be so. For, if the differences are regular enough, which

they often are, then the Negro-dialect speaker may be able to
set up his own sound-spelling correspondences between them --
ones which will be different from those set up by a speaker
of standard English, but which will allow effective word
identification nevertheless. For example, most varieties of
Negro dialect regularly have /f/ and /v/ where standard English has /θ/ and /ð/, respectively. And the standard-English
sounds are regularly represented in the written language by
th (usually standing for the voiceless /θ/, but also for the
voiced /ð/ in certain circumstances). But the fair amount
of regularity between standard English /θ/ and /ð/ and Negro
dialect /f/ and /v/ on the one hand, and standard English
/θ/ and /ð/ and the spelling th on the other allows the
Negro-dialect speaker to set up his own reading rule which
tells him, in effect, "Read /f/ (or, in certain circumstances,
/v/) for th, when not at the beginning of a word." Thus, he
will read /bref/ for breath and, with the additional knowledge
that th before final e usually stands for the voiced counterpart, he should read /briyv/ for breathe. And, since /bref/
and /briyv/ are exactly his functional equivalents of standard
English /breθ/ and /briyð/, the correct word identification
of breath and breathe, in terms of his own spoken vocabulary,
will be made.[21] For the reading of word-initial th, other
reading rules would be set up, since the Negro-dialect reflexes of initial /θ/ and /ð/ in standard English are more
complicated.[22]

    If, as the foregoing observations seem to indicate, the
adverse effects of purely phonological differences between
Negro dialect and standard English on reading comprehension
are but slight, then the case for structural interference in
a Negro-dialect speaker's attempts to read standard English
will have to be made on other linguistic grounds. A substantial number of lexical differences between the two kinds

of English would serve this purpose, but one of the striking
features of the relationship between urban Negro dialect and
standard English is that it involves very little lexical
divergence. Consequently, if there really is significant
dialect interference in the reading process, it can be expected to derive from grammatical differences between Negro
dialect and standard English, and particularly from ones
which are more or less independent of non-significant (for
reading) phonological differences.

There are actually many grammatical differences between
Negro dialect and standard English which, whether caused by
different transformations or by different grammatical processes of a "deeper" type, are nevertheless clearly independent of regular phonological differences between the two
kinds of English.[23] Examples of transformationally-derived
grammatical differences are encountered in the use of question-
type inversion in Negro-dialect verb phrases where standard
English uses <u>if</u> (meaning "whether") with no inversion, e.g.
<u>See can he go</u> for <u>See if he can go</u>, uninverted verb phrases
after certain question words in Negro dialect where standard
English requires inversion, e.g. <u>What it is?</u> for <u>What is it?</u>,
and multiple negation in Negro dialect where standard English
has single negation, e.g. <u>He ain't never bought none</u> for
<u>He hasn't ever bought any</u> or <u>He has never bought any</u>.[24] As
with many of the regular phonological differences between
Negro dialect and standard English, the Negro-dialect speaker
is usually able to establish correspondences between grammatical differences of this type -- provided, of course,
that the context is clear and that such constructions do not
pile up in rapid succession. But even so, misinterpretation
is quite possible when a standard-English construction happens to resemble in form some Negro-dialect construction
other than the one to which it is functionally equivalent.

For example, a seemingly unambiguous standard-English sentence like <u>His eye's open</u> may be misinterpreted by a Negro-dialect speaker as meaning "His eyes are open", simply because it resembles in form the Negro dialect sentence <u>His eyes open</u> (with that meaning) more than it does <u>His eye open</u> (the Negro-dialect equivalent of the original standard-English sentence). And this, incidentally, is yet another example of a case in which <u>viva-voce</u> performance would be of no help to the reading teacher in deciding whether there was a misinterpretation or not, since the pupil's pronunciation of standard English <u>His eye's open</u> and Negro dialect <u>His eyes open</u> would be identical.

Intelligibility problems of a different order -- at once more subtle and more ingrained -- are posed by grammatical differences between Negro dialect and standard English which originate deeper in the respective grammars than do differences of the preceding type. Because they are not likely to involve simple one-to-one correlations, and because they may not even use the same perceptual information about the real world, these deeper grammatical differences are apt to lie beyond the scope of the intuitive methods by which speakers of one dialect normally determine structural equivalences between their own and some other dialect. It is this type of grammatical difference which underlies the dissimilar use of <u>be</u> in Negro dialect and standard English. In Negro dialect, <u>be</u> is used with adjectives and the <u>-in'</u> (= <u>-ing</u>) form of verbs to indicate an extended or repeated state or action, e.g. <u>He be busy</u>, <u>He be workin'</u>. On the other hand, the absence of this <u>be</u> usually indicates that the state or action is immediate or momentary, e.g. <u>He busy</u>, <u>He workin'</u>. The auxiliary or tag for <u>be</u> in Negro dialect is <u>do</u>, e.g. <u>Do he be busy?</u> as a question form of <u>He be busy</u>, while the explicit form use in the non-<u>be</u> construction is usually <u>is</u>, e.g. <u>Is he busy?</u>

as a question form of He busy. This means, of course, that
be and is are entirely different morphemes in Negro dialect.
But in standard English, there is no such grammatical distinction, and be and is are merely inflectional variants of
one and the same verb. Thus, for the two grammatical constructions of Negro dialect, standard English has but one
grammatical equivalent, e.g. He is busy, He is working, in
which the immediacy or duration of the state or action is
left entirely unspecified.

Thus far, this difference between Negro dialect and
standard English in the grammatical recognition or not of a
contrast between extended or repeated states and actions and
immediate or momentary ones may seem to have little significance for reading comprehension, since the Negro-dialect
speaker is obviously not going to encounter his own He busy
and He be busy constructions (which mark the distinction)
in a standard-English text. In form, the closest standard-
English constructions to these will be the He is busy type,
which is functionally equivalent to both of the Negro-dialect
constructions, and the He will be busy type, which represents
a future state or action only. Now, if this were indeed the
extent of the matter, it would certainly be reasonable to
assume that the differences in form between the standard-
English and Negro-dialect constructions would alert the
average Negro-dialect speaker to a possible difference in
meaning between them. But one more bit of information is
necessary to a full understanding of just how much such a
seemingly minor grammatical difference can affect intelligibility. This is that exposure to the standard-English use
of present-tense forms of the copula (i.e. am, is, are) has
made many speakers of nonstandard Negro dialect -- even very
young ones -- aware that their own He busy and He be busy
types of construction are not "proper" in form. Consequently,

they often attempt to "correct" these on their own by adding
one or another of the standard English auxiliaries to their
He busy type of construction, and by changing the be of their
He be busy type of construction into bees (on analogy with
correcting he work to he works) and, when they realize that
even this is nonstandard, into will be.[25] Now, even assuming
that those who do this will always end up with forms like
He is busy (with appropriate person accord of the auxiliary
throughout) for He busy, and He will be busy for He be busy,
it is nevertheless the case that these phonologically and
morphologically "standard" forms are still nonstandard Negro
dialect in their grammar and meaning. This means that Negro-
dialect speakers -- even ones who appear to know "correct"
grammar -- are apt to misread standard-English He is busy
constructions as necessarily implying immediacy (which they
do not), and He will be busy constructions as possibly indicating repetition or long duration (which they do not) as
well as futurity.

Taken altogether, the grammatical differences between
Negro dialect and standard English are probably extensive
enough to cause reading-comprehension problems. Even in
cases where the differences do not actually obscure the
meaning of a sentence or passage, they can be distracting to
a young Negro-dialect speaker who is trying to learn to read,
and who can find but few familiar syntactic patterns to aid
him in word identification. It is true that this child must
eventually be taught to read standard-English sentence patterns, but it is open to question whether he should be made
to cope with the task of deciphering unfamiliar syntactic
structures at the very same time that he is expected to
develop effective word-reading skills. One simple way to
avoid placing a double learning load on the lower-class Negro
child who is learning to read would be to start with sentence

patterns which are familiar to him -- ones from his own dialect -- and then move to unfamiliar ones from standard English once he has mastered the necessary word-reading skills.
In that way, reading ability could actually become an aid to
the learning of standard English.

A third objection which might well be raised to the use of
Negro dialect in beginning reading materials is that it would
reinforce the use by lower-class Negro children of their non-
standard dialect, and thereby serve as a barrier to their
eventual acquisition of standard English. But such a claim
would be predicated on two false assumptions about language
learning and language use. The first false assumption is
that the use of language patterns always constitutes reinforcement of those patterns in the user. Although this is a
popular belief among educators, it is obviously untrue for
native speakers of a language (or a particular variety of a
language) who are using familiar patterns of it. If a
standard-English speaker is asked to repeat (or read) a sentence like Charles and Michael are out playing, he will not
know either the sentence pattern or the individual words any
better when he is through than before he started. The reason
is, of course, that he already knows these aspects of his
language as well as he could possibly learn them. If this is
so, then why is it assumed that, if a Negro-dialect speaker
is allowed to say (or asked to read) a sentence like Charles
an' Michael, dey out playin', he will thereby become more
addicted to Negro dialect? And what sort of magic is a
classroom supposed to have, anyway, that the occasional use
of nonstandard pronunciations or sentence patterns within its
confines is regarded as pregnant with potential effect, while
the almost exclusive use of those same pronunciations and
sentence patterns outside the classroom is regarded as of
little consequence? The second false assumption underlying

this particular argument is that the knowledge and use of one
language or dialect precludes the learning and use of another
language or dialect -- or, put more simply, that people's
capacity for learning and using different linguistic systems
is severely limited. This is a particularly common belief
in America, where very few educators have had any exposure
to multilingualism or bidialectalism. But Europeans would
be likely to be astonished or amused by such an assertion,
since most of them accept it as a matter of course that one
will use a nonstandard dialect in the village home and a
standardized variety of the same language (or even a different language) in the city office. The fact is that, in
America too, there is no linguistic reason why an individual
ought not to be able to produce sentences like <u>Charles an'</u>
<u>Michael, dey out playin'</u> in one situation, and <u>Charles and</u>
<u>Michael are out playing</u> in another. Poor language teaching,
rather than the prior knowledge of another language or dialect, is the principal cause of unsuccessful bilingualism or
bidialectalism.

Instead of being ignored or made the target of an eradi-
cation program, Negro dialect should actually be used as a
basis for teaching oral and written standard English. If
Negro dialect is used to teach initial word-reading skills
to Negro-dialect speakers, then those word-reading skills
can be made the constant in terms of which standard-English
grammatical patterns can be taught through reading and writing. One form which this type of language teaching could
take would be to make the transition from Negro dialect to
standard English in a series of stages, each of which would
concentrate on a limited set of linguistic differences. An
exciting aspect of this approach is that oral language teaching could be combined with the reading program to any degree
felt useful. Take, for example, the Negro-dialect sentence

just cited, and its standard-English counterpart. The former would become the initial stage in such a program, and the latter would be the ultimate goal. In this illustration, I will write the Negro-dialect sentence in standard-English spelling in order to simplify the transition process.

STAGE 1
Charles and Michael, they out playing.

Grammatically, sentences at this stage will be pure non-standard Negro dialect. The vocabulary, also, will be controlled so that no words which are unfamiliar to a Negro-dialect-speaking child will appear. Thus, all linguistic aspects of text will be familiar to the beginning reader, and his full attention can be focused on learning to read the vocabulary. At this stage, no attempt should be made to teach standard-English pronunciations of the words, since the sentence in which they appear is not standard English.

STAGE 2
Charles and Michael, they are out playing.

At this stage, the most important grammatical features of standard English are introduced. In the example, there is one such feature -- the copula. Apart from that, the vocabulary is held constant. Oral-language drills could profitably be used to teach person accord of the copula (am, is, are), and some standard-English pronunciations of the basic vocabulary might be taught.

STAGE 3
Charles and Michael are out playing.

Grammatically, the sentences at this stage are brought into full conformity with standard English by making the remaining grammatical and stylistic adjustments. In the example, the "double subject" of the nonstandard form is eliminated. Oral-language drills could be used to teach this, and additional standard-English pronunciations of the basic vocabulary could be taught.

Although the complete transition from Negro-dialect grammar to standard-English grammar was effected in three stages in the foregoing example, more stages would probably be required in a real program of this type. The actual programming of these stages would have to be carried out by competent linguists, but, once done, the resulting materials ought to be usable in regular remedial-reading classes.

The fourth objection which might be made to the use of written Negro-dialect materials in the school is that it is insulting to Negroes. In part, this view may stem from the mistaken notion that Negro dialect is nothing but "sloppy" speech -- a sort of half-language -- the use of which might be taken as evidence of low intellectual achievement in the Negro.[26] But another possible reason why written materials in Negro dialect might be regarded by many as damaging to the Negro image could be an assumption that such materials are merely a continuation of literary Negro stereotypes of the sort which have appeared over the years in stories, jokes, cartoons, etc., and which have undoubtedly served as entertainment for countless numbers of white racists. That the Negro dialect of many of these stereotypic representations of lower-class Negroes was often more accurate than many middle-class Negroes or liberal whites realize or would care to admit further complicates the matter, since structural similarities between the Negro dialect of literary stereotypes and that of pedagogical materials might be misconstrued as evidence that language of the pedagogical materials has been based on that of literary stereotypes. And, of course,

there will be the inevitable visceral reaction of many up-
wardly-mobile Negroes against any public recognition of
distinctively Negro behaviors -- particularly those which
cannot, like Negro musicality, be easily transvalued into
"soul". Often near-white culturally and linguistically,
Negroes of this type frequently attempt to pass themselves
off on the white power structure as representatives of the
culturally and linguistically non-white Negro school child,
and as natural authorities on his background and learning
problems. At the same time, many of these same Negroes are
inordinately fond of boasting to anyone who will listen
that they never spoke nonstandard dialect, as if the truth
of such a statement were indicative of anything more than
their total unfamiliarity with the very kinds of pedagogical
problems which they claim to know so much about. (Indeed,
when some middle-class Negroes do attempt to demonstrate a
knowledge of Negro dialect, it more often than not turns out
to be a combination of standard-English grammar and peda-
gogically-irrelevant ethnic slang.) Recently, some of these
culturally and linguistically near-white Negroes have even
tried to turn "instant black" through superficial conformity
to the styles and rhetoric of the Black Power movement --
their assumption apparently being that, in the eyes of the
white establishment, a bush and a dashiki are adequate sub-
stitutes for knowledge in qualifying as an authority on Negro
educational needs. And, given the fact that the white-
dominated educational establishment is more committed to the
political goal of placating middle-class Negro social griev-
ances than the professional goal of fulfilling lower-class
Negro educational needs (and is probably even unaware that
there could be a difference), they may be right. The danger
is that Negroes who are embarrassed by or hostile to Negro
dialect may attempt to abort its use in the school curriculum

by any of a number of strategies, such as reiterating the
conventional view that Negro dialect is nothing more than a
mass of unstructured speech errors, or by claiming that Negro
dialect of the type depicted by linguists is either rare or
non-existent among black school children, or, if all else
fails, by the irresponsible yet, to liberal whites, intimi-
dating charge that anyone who works on the theory that
American Negroes and whites have different configurations of
behavior is a racist.

If the more pessimistic of these expectations turns out
to be well-founded, and numbers of articulate Negroes do move
to force school administrators into bypassing or abandoning
programs using Negro dialect, the day will not be saved for
these programs by white linguists. For they, like other white
social scientists, are as easily intimidated by political
pressure from blacks as white school administrators are.
Rather, the day will be saved by other Negroes -- ones who,
often coming from a lower-class background, are aware that
cultural and linguistic differences do exist between American
whites and blacks, who accept the fact, and who want to use
it as a point of departure for increased self-awareness and
inter-ethnic understanding. Even more articulate than their
white-oriented, middle-class counterparts, Negroes with this
new awareness know that such differences are not indications
of intellectual superiority or inferiority, but are rather
exciting indications of unique and equally worthy culture
histories. They recognize that, because of these differences,
Negro and white children will often have unique performance
characteristics and curriculum needs in school, but they see
that American education has traditionally recognized and
adjusted itself only to those of the white children. As a
result, it is with some justification that many of these
Negroes regard the American school system as a singularly

colonialist institution -- one having only slightly more
relevance for lower-class American Negro children than the
British educational system had for native children in Africa
and India. Negroes who are developing this awareness -- and
their numbers are increasing every day -- are simply not
going to sit idly by while white-oriented Negroes attack the
very kind of curriculum which would set this situation right.
For their own good, school administrators, curriculum plan-
ners, textbook publishers, and program funders had better
learn to distinguish between these two types of Negroes, if
only to the extent of realizing that the opinion of a "colored"
friend, associate, or colleague on Negro-dialect materials may
not necessarily be an inside tip on the feelings of Negroes at
large.

Linguists, for their part, ought to be more concerned
about the suitability of a particular set of Negro-dialect
reading materials for a particular population of Negro children than about the popularity of such materials among Negro
adults. The materials will be accepted by the children if
they are authentic -- that is, if the written language of the
materials represents accurately their own spoken language.
For the linguist, this authenticity will only come about
through careful attention to details of grammar, style, and
vocabulary. And the materials will be accepted by Negro
parents and other adults when they see that Negro children
learn to read standard English by means of them, where they
did not by means of traditional reading materials. For the
linguist, the ability of the materials to do this will require meticulous planning of the structural changes which are
to be dealt with in each of the successive stages from "pure"
nonstandard dialect to "pure" standard English. Finally, if
it can be argued, as it has been in this paper, that beginning
reading materials in standard English are not suitable for

children who only speak nonstandard Negro dialect, then it
should be equally apparent that beginning reading materials
in nonstandard Negro dialect will not be suitable for children who only speak standard English. In particular, one
should guard against the danger of assuming that Negro-dialect
materials will be appropriate for all Negro school children.
Earlier, it was pointed out that most middle-class Negroes
do not (and, indeed, many cannot) speak nonstandard Negro
dialect. Although this fact cannot serve as an argument that
Negro dialect is rare or non-existent, it certainly is an
indication that not all Negroes speak Negro dialect. Even
among lower-class Negroes, some individuals (particularly
females) will be found who, either due to a special life
history or because of strong upward mobility, have acquired
and use standard English. And, of course, there will be
individuals who speak something between standard English and
the type of nonstandard dialect I have characterized as "pure"
Negro dialect. This does not make Negro-dialect materials
any the less useful for children who actually speak Negro
dialect; it merely means that any Negro-dialect reading program will have to have an instrument for determining exactly
who does, and who doesn't, speak Negro dialect in the first
place. And if such an instrument could actually measure a
child's initial language on a Negro-dialect-to-standard-
English continuum, then it would also be useful for measuring
that child's progress in standard English as a result of the
staging process of the materials. Although still in an
embryonic state, the bidialectal oral-language proficiency
test designed by Joan C. Baratz and myself is potentially
ideal for this purpose.[27] Even children whose initial language is shown by such a test to be somewhere in between
"pure" Negro dialect and standard English can be worked into
such a program if, as ought to be the case, the language of

its intermediate stages is made to resemble the intermediate dialects in a Negro speech community. Thus, a particular child might be started with, say, Stage Two materials rather than Stage One materials.

Once the decision has been made to develop beginning reading materials using Negro dialect for a particular school population, then a suitable orthography must be selected for the nonstandard sentence patterns. This is an unavoidable problem, since any nonstandard dialect is, by its very nature, unwritten. But it is an important problem, since the effective use of a nonstandard dialect in a bidialectal reading program will depend to a great extent on how easy the orthographic transition between the two linguistic systems can be made. For Negro dialect, four major types of orthography are available to choose from. These are:

1. An autonomous phonemic orthography, in which words are spelled the way they are pronounced (or heard) by a speaker of the dialect. For example, if a Negro-dialect speaker normally pronounces his equivalents of standard English bend and bending /ben/ and /bendin/, then these words will be spelled so as to show these pronunciations, sound-by-sound, e.g. ben and bendin.

2. A systematic phonemic orthography, which attempts to have the spellings represent all the information necessary to determine changes which can occur in the pronunciation of words in different contexts. For example, this type of orthography would spell the Negro-dialect equivalent of standard English bend in a way which would show that a /d/ is pronounced in the word when a vowel follows (as it does with the suffix /-in/), while the same is not true for a word like /mown/, for standard English moan, i.e. /mownin/. This could be accomplished simply by spelling the Negro-dialect form /ben/ as bend, with a "reading

rule" that <u>d</u> after <u>n</u> is pronounced only before a vowel.

3. A literary-dialect orthography, in which the purely dia-
    lectal pronunciations of Negro-dialect words are roughly
    indicated by minor changes in the traditional spellings
    of their standard-English cognates. One important device
    used in literary dialect is the apostrophe, which is sub-
    stituted for certain letters to show that a particular
    sound usually pronounced in a standard-English form is
    not pronounced in its Negro-dialect equivalent (e.g.
    <u>ben'</u> for standard English <u>bend</u>), or to indicate sound
    substitutions (e.g. <u>bendin'</u> with final /n/ for standard
    English <u>bending</u> with final /ŋ/). The examples of Negro
    dialect which were given in the earlier discussion of
    grammatical interference were written in a literary-
    dialect orthography.

4. An unmodified standard-English orthography, with no ef-
    fort made to indicate differences in pronunciation between
    Negro dialect and standard English. For example, the
    spellings <u>bend</u> and <u>bending</u> would be used in writing both
    varieties of English. The Negro dialect in the poem
    "A Visit from St. Nicholas" was written in this way, as
    was that in the three-stage example of transitional read-
    ing materials.

The first two types of orthography are the most scientific,
since they both attempt to indicate the pronunciation of the
dialect accurately, and in its own terms. Each of these systems has its advocates and its detractors, who will be happy
to point out its strengths and weaknesses.[28] An autonomous
phonemic orthography has the advantage of being applicable to
a language or dialect as soon as certain basic facts are known
about its sound system, and long before much is understood
about contextual variations in the structure of words. It is
largely for this reason that most of the orthographies which

have been devised in connection with basic literacy programs
around the world have been autonomous phonemic ones. On the
other hand, a systematic phonemic orthography has the advantage of representing the relationship between variant pronunciations of words much more adequately than is possible
in an autonomous phonemic orthography, and hence tends to
relate more closely to grammatical processes in the language
or dialect. A distinct disadvantage of systematic phonemic
orthographies, however, is that they can only be as well-
formed as the state of knowledge concerning the lexicon and
morphophonemics of the particular language or dialect will
allow. And, since the lexicon of even a "primitive" language
can be quite vast, and the morphophonemics of even a "simple"
dialect quite complex, that knowledge is seldom ever as complete as it ought to be for devising a permanent orthography.
Accordingly, attempts to create such orthographies are likely
to be characterized by a certain degree of instability, engendered by constant additions, corrections, and revisions.

The last two types of orthography are, from a phonological point of view, at least, much less scientific than
the first two. While a literary-dialect orthography does
attempt to indicate Negro-dialect pronunciations, this is
seldom done either consistently or in the dialect's own
terms.[29] And Negro dialect which has been spelled entirely
in the standard-English fashion will offer no clues at all
as to its unique pronunciations. Rather, the effect of these
two types of orthography is to show the relationship of the
one form of English to the other. A literary-dialect orthography, with its altered spellings and ubiquitous apostrophe,
emphasizes the dialect's phonological deviations from standard-English norms, and can create an impression of great
difference -- even without accommodating the actual dialect
syntax.[30] The writing of Negro dialect in an unmodified

standard-English orthography, on the other hand, obscures the
phonological differences between the two and, as a result,
highlights whatever syntactic differences are incorporated
into the writing of the sentences.

In evaluating the relative utility of these four types
of orthography for writing Negro dialect in a reading program
designed to phase into standard English, it is ironic that
the least satisfactory one is that which has proven most effective in basic literacy programs involving only one language or dialect at a time: the autonomous phonemic orthography. What renders this type of orthography unsuitable
for the task at hand is that, precisely because it would
represent the sounds of Negro dialect accurately and in the
dialect's own terms, it would produce Negro-dialect word
spellings which would be too foreign to the spellings of
standard-English cognates to permit an easy transition from
reading and writing the one to reading and writing the other.[31]

Both a systematic phonemic orthography and a literary-
dialect orthography would have essentially the same drawbacks
as an autonomous phonemic orthography, though conceivably to
a lesser degree. But the main argument against both of these
types of orthography is their complexity; the prospective
reader would probably do better to spend his time and effort
mastering the intricacies of the standard-English orthographic
system. And, given what was said earlier about the ability
of the Negro-dialect speaker to set up his own sound-spelling
correspondences between Negro-dialect pronunciations and
standard-English word spellings, the writing of Negro dialect
in an unmodified standard-English orthography ought not to
cause more problems than it avoids.[32]

Apart from the obvious necessity of using the nonstandard
ain't and common contractions like it's, don't, won't, can't,
etc., in writing Negro dialect in a standard-English type of

orthography, I would make one major compromise in the direction of a literary-dialect orthography. That would be to
indicate, by an apostrophe, those cases in Negro dialect in
which a word must take a prefix in order to become like its
standard-English equivalent, e.g. Negro dialect 'bout,
'cause, 'round, and 'posed to for standard English about,
because, around, and supposed to. In the Negro-dialect
materials, word-initial apostrophes would thereby become
graphic indicators of specific lexical points at which later
morphological expansion of the Negro-dialect forms would have
to be carried out in the transition to standard English.[33]
The usefulness of this technique lies in the fact that Negro-
dialect speakers do not always know that a prefix is "missing"
from their version of a particular word. Thus, the Negro-
dialect form 'most (cf. standard English almost), as in
'most always, 'most everybody, is either left that way when
"proper" English is attempted, or it may be "corrected" with
a suffix, -ly, rather than with a prefix. Although this
latter step creates no conflict in meaning for the Negro-
dialect speaker (since his normal equivalent of standard
English mostly is most of..., e.g. Most of it ruined and
They most of them teachers for standard English It has mostly
spoiled and They are mostly teachers), it does produce sequences like mostly always and mostly everybody which are
incongruous and comical when interpreted as standard English.
But even when Negro-dialect speakers do suspect that some
sort of suffix is required to make a particular word into
standard English, they may not be at all sure which standard-
English prefix is required; or they may be sure, but be mistaken. Negro-dialect speakers may know, for example, that
their forms 'cord, 'morial, and 'vorce all require a prefix
in "proper" usage, but then they are likely to overuse re-
(by far the most functional prefix in Negro dialect) to

produce the "corrected" forms record, remorial, and revorce,
with only one matching with standard English record (verb),
memorial, and divorce -- and that a fortuitous one. In effect, this persistent confusion which many Negro-dialect
speakers experience with standard-English pretonic syllables
(often in spite of "hearing" the appropriate forms from
middle-class speakers from time to time) suggests that it
would be of little use to write almost, record, memorial,
divorce, etc., in beginning reading materials for Negro-
dialect speakers, with the hope that they would somehow
"pick up" the right usage from the spellings. It would
seem more effective to write such words as 'most, 'cord,
'morial, 'vorce, etc., in at least the initial stage of
such materials, so that the learner could first become familiar with the reading of their "stems" in terms of his own
pronunciation patterns, and only then to teach the appropriate standard-English prefixes by means of supplementary
spoken drills, preparatory to introducing the standard-
English spellings into the written text.[34]

To close this paper, I have written a very short story,
which I call "Shirley and the Valentine Card", to show what
the written Negro dialect of the initial (i.e. the most non-
standard) stage of a Negro-dialect-to-standard-English reading program might look like, to serve notice on normativists
that standard English has no monopoly on expressiveness, and
to reassure the socio-politically timid that even radically
nonstandard Negro dialect will turn out to be comfortably
unobtrusive if dialectal spellings are used sparingly enough.
I have not gone so far as to structure the text of the story,
as it ought to be in a reading program, by presenting sound-
spelling-meaning correspondences in a systematic way, or by
organizing the distinctive structural features of the dialect
in a way which will facilitate their staging into standard

English. Rather, I present this story simply as a sample of
the language of the story. To that end, I immediately follow
it with a few specific comments on some of its features.

SHIRLEY AND THE VALENTINE CARD

It's a girl name Shirley Jones live in Washington.
'Most everybody on her street like her, 'cause she a nice girl.
And all the children Shirley be with in school like her, too.
Shirley treat all of them just like they was her sisters and
brothers, but most of all she like one boy name Charles.
Shirley, she be knowing Charles 'cause all two of them in the
same grade, and he in her class. But Shirley keep away from
Charles most of the time, 'cause she start to liking him so
much she be scared of him. And that make it seem to Charles
like she don't pay him no mind. So Charles, he don't hardly
say nothing to her neither. Still, that girl got to go
'round telling everybody Charles 'posed to be liking her.
She act like she his girlfriend, too.

But when Valentine Day start to come 'round, Shirley
get to worrying. She worried 'cause she know the rest of
them girls all going get Valentine cards from their boy-
friends. And she know when them girls find out she ain't
get a card from Charles, they going say she been telling a
story 'bout Charles being her boyfriend. So she keep on
thinking 'bout that and worrying all day long, even at school
when she 'posed to be learning something from the teacher and
playing with the other girls. That Shirley, she so worried,
she just don't want to be with nobody. She even walk home
by her own self, when school let out.

When Shirley get home, her mother say it's a letter for
her on the table. Right away Shirley start to wondering who
could it be from, 'cause she know don't nobody 'posed to be
sending her no kind of letter. It do have her name on the

front, though. It say, <u>Shirley Jones</u>. So Shirley, she open
the envelope up. And when she do, she can see it's a Valentine card inside. Now, Shirley take out the card, and she
look at it, and she see it have Charles name wrote on the
bottom.

See, Charles really been liking her all the time, even
though he ain't never tell her nothing 'bout it. So now
everything going be all right for Shirley, 'cause what she
been telling everybody 'bout Charles being her boyfriend
ain't story after all. It done come true!

Comments on the Language of the Story

Although Negro-dialect speakers often narrate their
stories in a past-time setting, I have deliberately put
"Shirley and the Valentine Card" in the somewhat less common
(though still appropriate) simple present throughout. This
is a useful strategy to employ in the writing of initial-
stage reading materials, since it eliminates the need for
introducing nonstandard past-tense verb forms, some of which
would definitely require dialectal spellings, and allows for
the systematic introduction of standard-English past-tense
verb forms at a later time.

The language of the story is essentially a representation, in the kind of standard-English orthography I have
advocated, of a variety of nonstandard dialect which is used
by many lower-class Negro children in the District of Columbia -- the scene of the story.[35] As it stands, this kind of
Negro dialect is almost identical to that of similar children
in such Eastern Seaboard cities as Baltimore, Wilmington,
Philadelphia, and New York. The language of the story is
fairly "pure" Negro dialect, with features from standard
English kept to a somewhat artificial minimum (since, after
all, the idea would be to introduce these systematically in

the course of the reading program of which such a story
would be part). On the other hand, because this story is
arbitrarily directed to the 10-to-15-year-old range, a number
of even more deviant features of the speech of younger children have been omitted, such as possessive pronouns which
(except for the first person singular) are undifferentiated
in form from the corresponding subject pronouns, e.g. he
girlfriend, she boyfriend for his girlfriend, her boyfriend. If materials were being developed for much younger
children, or for regions in which such features occur in a
wider age range (in coastal South Carolina, Georgia, or
Florida, for example), the dialect forms could be modified
accordingly.[36]

The other regional limitations in the linguistic structure of "Shirley and the Valentine Card" are really quite
minor. A marked characteristic of the dialect used is that
verbs in the simple present do not usually take a suffix -s
for any person subject.[37] But in some other varieties of
Negro dialect, particularly those spoken in the South Central
states (Mississippi, Alabama, etc.), the simple present verb
is more often marked with -s for all persons, e.g. I lives in
Jackson. Also, although no examples of possessive noun constructions appear in the story, South Central Negro dialect
often uses a possessive suffix like standard English, e.g.
Shirley's boyfriend, where Eastern Seaboard Negro dialect
simply uses noun apposition, e.g. Shirley boyfriend. Finally, in the Negro dialect of the District of Columbia, as in
most of the Eastern Seaboard, got (or gots) and 'posed to
take do (negative don't) as an auxiliary or tag, e.g. Do you
got a dollar?, Don't they 'posed to go with you?, while in
South Central usage the auxiliary or tag for these verbs is
usually is (negative ain't), e.g. Is you got a dollar?,
Ain't they 'posed to go with you? But the fact that, in

general, the language of "Shirley and the Valentine Card" is
as close as it is to the speech of Negroes of a comparable
age and socio-economic level in so many parts of the United
States shows rather clearly that Negro dialect from South to
North, from East to West, from farm to city, and from store-
front church to playground, is all part of a single sociolinguistic complex, with a single historical origin, and
reveals the emptiness of the claim of some traditionalist
educators that Negro speech varies too much from place to
place for it to be a useful pedagogical tool.[38]

What I have had to say about Negro dialect in the course
of this paper should make it obvious that it is a highly complex yet well-formed and systematic code -- just like any
other language. To speak it well, or to use it effectively
in pedagogical materials, requires a profound knowledge of
its many phonological and grammatical rules, of subtle lexical differences (e.g. that bright means "light-skinned" in
Negro dialect, while it means "clever" in standard English),
and of countless stylistic and idiomatic details (e.g. that
sisters and brothers is the "pure" Negro-dialect form, while
brothers and sisters is an importation from standard English).
This means that attempts to use or to write Negro dialect
should not be made by unqualified persons, black or white,
any more than attempt to use or write, say, French should be.
For one thing, the inner-city slang or "hip talk" of teenagers and young adults should not be confused with Negro dialect in the linguistic sense, no matter how ethnically-
correlated many of the slang terms may be. They are simply
deliberate vocabulary substitutions, and have nothing directly
to do with dialect grammar or phonology. Nor is the "stage
dialect" of Negro bit-players on radio, television, or the
screen necessarily close to real Negro dialect. Often, in

order to insure its being understood by a wide audience, a
stage Negro dialect may be created which is little more than
standard English with a slightly ethnicized or southernized
pronunciation, reinforced by the insertion of such general
nonstandardisms as ain't and the double negative, and perhaps a sprinkling of southern or inner-city Negro lexical
usages like honey child or man.[39] And, although literary
renditions of plantation Negro dialect (such as appears in
Joel Chandler Harris' Uncle Remus, His Songs and His Sayings)
may represent an older form of Negro dialect rather accurately, and thus share many structural characteristics with
present-day Negro dialect, there are still too many inter-
vening variables (nineteenth-century usage vs. twentieth-
century usage, adult speech vs. child speech, rural forms
vs. urban forms, story-telling style vs. colloquial style,
etc.) for that kind of Negro dialect to be directly useful
for the purposes I have been suggesting.[40] If used well by
educators, living Negro dialect can serve as a bridge between
the personal experiences of the Negro child and his acquisition
of mainstream language skills. If used poorly, however, it
will only add to the confusion of pupil and teacher alike.
The language of the Negro child can be made an effective
educational tool, but it must be treated with respect and
understanding.

NOTES

1. Most of the world's languages consist of more than one
   variety, with different varieties (called dialects by
   linguists) having developed in different regions, or
   among different social groups. The dialects of a language can differ from each other in various details of
   pronunciation, grammar, and vocabulary. Every dialect
   is systematic and logical in its own terms, and a grammar and dictionary of it could conceivably be written.

For most languages, however, only one or so of the total
number of existing dialects ever comes to be regarded as
"correct" or "proper" usage (linguists call such a dialect the standard one), with normative grammars and
dictionaries based upon it. Consequently, the structural
characteristics of other dialects which deviate from the
standard one are generally regarded as errors, rather
than as differences; and when they are deviant enough,
such dialects (called nonstandard dialects by linguists)
may be popularly deprecated as "bad" or "improper" speech,
with the implication that they have no structural or
historical justification. Now, the chances of a normal
child who reaches school age having mislearned the language used around him are infinitely smaller than the
chances that he might have learned accurately a non-
standard dialect. Therefore, educators should be much
less prone than they have been to infer that school-
child speech which deviates from the pedagogical norm
necessarily implies poor language learning.

2.   For a discussion of current theory on this aspect of
     human language competence, see Eric H. Lenneberg, The
     Biological Foundations of Language (New York: John Wiley,
     1967).

3.   For obvious reasons, the congenitally deaf do not acquire
     spoken language in this way. However, those having early
     contact with persons who use a manual sign analogue of
     oral language (such as deaf parents or deaf playmates)
     may acquire this sign language in a way and at a rate
     which is strikingly similar to the hearing child's
     acquisition of spoken language. In this sense, even the
     congenitally deaf turn out to be linguistically normal.

4.   In pointing this out, I am not suggesting that the adop-
     tion of a single language, either imported or indigenous,
     as a national language by a multilingual nation is neces-
     sarily an unwise step. There are often many advantages
     in such a policy. At the same time, it means that lit-
     eracy strategies in such a situation cannot be identical
     to those which would be appropriate for a monolingual
     country, or for a multilingual country in which most of
     the languages are written and officially recognized.

5.   See William A. Bull, "The Use of Vernacular Languages in
     Fundamental Education", International Journal of American
     Linguistics, 21:288-294 (1955), reprinted in Dell Hymes,
     ed., Language in Culture and Society (New York: Harper &
     Row, 1964); and Nancy Modiano, "National or Mother Language

in Beginning Reading: A Comparative Study", <u>Research in the Teaching of English</u>, Vol. 2, No. 1 (Spring 1968), pp. 32-43.

6. The i.t.a., phonics, and other "linguistic" methods of teaching beginning reading deal primarily with such minimal written vs. spoken code differences.

7. For a thoughtful critique of the recent literature on this issue, see Ralph Mason Dreger and Kent S. Miller, "Comparative Psychological Studies of Negroes and Whites in the United States: 1959-1965", <u>Psychological Bulletin</u>, Vol. 70, No. 3, Part 2 (September 1968).

8. A classic example of this kind of psychological formulation of deficit theory, with its superficial sophistication and hidden defects, is the much-cited and influential article by Vera P. John, "The Intellectual Development of Slum Children: Some Preliminary Findings", <u>American Journal of Orthopsychiatry</u>, Vol. 33, No. 5 (October 1963). In her study, John measured what she thought to be differences in verbal and classificatory skills in three socio-economic groups of Negro children (lower-lower, upper-lower, and middle-class) through their performance on a series of standardized verbal and non-verbal tests, including the Peabody Picture Vocabulary Test and the Lorge-Thorndike Intelligence Test. Differences in the performance of the three groups led John to conclude that, among other things, "The acquisition of more abstract and integrative language seems to be hampered by the living conditions in the homes of the lower-class children." Quite apart from John's unsubstantiated statement that the problem-source was "the living conditions in the homes", she seems to have failed to grasp the true relationship of her tests to her subjects, and therefore the real meaning of her results. She showed no awareness that the Peabody test contains only standard-English linguistic forms, and that therefore it is a test of verbal ability only when applied to standard-English speaking subjects. And she showed no awareness that the Lorge-Thorndike test is based on middle-class heuristic styles, and that therefore it is a test of non-verbal intelligence only for members of the middle class. Thus, John failed to realize that her results might well indicate little more than differences in language forms and heuristic styles in her three groups (which she quite wrongly characterized as all belonging to "the same subculture"). I mention John's article specifically because it has been responsible for a great deal of

mischief in intervention programs since its publication,
and because its recent reprinting in Gladys Natchez, ed.,
Children with Reading Problems (New York: Basic Books,
1968) is likely to give it the chance to do further mischief in the field of reading. The editor has countered
the effect of John's article somewhat by reprinting with
it the opposing view of Kenneth B. Clark, "The Cult of
Cultural Deprivation: A Complex Social Phenomenon". The
only question is, Will reading specialists perceive the
fundamental philosophical difference between these two
articles, and be able to judge which is closest to fact?

9. Judging from the current educational and social-activist
    rhetoric, it is widely assumed that a gut-level commit-
    ment to the principle of human equality constitutes the
    only special preparation necessary for teaching lower-
    class Negro children. This was the assumption under which
    the Port Royal experiment in freedman education was insti-
    gated in the first years of the Civil War; it was the
    assumption under which Negro education was carried out in
    the segregated school systems after Emancipation; and it
    has been the assumption under which most of the teaching
    of the "disadvantaged" has been carried out since deseg-
    regation. That these attempts at Negro education have
    failed with dismal regularity to match white education in
    quality and effect can certainly be explained, but the
    point is that the failure has occurred despite the long
    and heavy involvement of individuals having a genuine
    commitment to the egalitarian philosophy.

10. Throughout this paper, the term culture is used in the
    modern anthropological sense of a network of customs,
    values, beliefs, and lifeways associated with a particu-
    lar social group or society. Culture may thus include
    such phenomena as material artifacts (e.g. dwellings,
    tools, clothing, ornaments), social institutions (e.g.
    family structure and kinship systems, political organi-
    zations, the church), values and belief systems (e.g.
    religion, codes of morality and etiquette, the world-
    view), and expressive behaviors (e.g. art, music, lan-
    guage, interaction styles). Cultural norms may be
    consciously specified and transmitted (as in the case of
    laws, rituals, and traditions), or their acquisition and
    use may be unconscious (as with particular ways of walk-
    ing, holding one's body, laughing, and expressing em-
    barrassment). The forms of one's language, too, are a
    part of one's culture, even though linguists prefer for
    practical reasons to describe language patterns separately
    from other kinds of cultural phenomena. And, as is true

with language, other basic aspects of one's culture can
be learned quite independently of any formal instruction.
In growing up in his society, a child may "pick up" many
of the cultural patterns used around him quite early --
so early, in fact, that in later life he may not be able
to recall ever having not known them. Indeed, when the
cultural patterns thus acquired are used unconsciously,
as in the way one walks or laughs, there may be no awareness that there is anything socially learned about them.
Rather, the individual concerned is likely to have the
impression that it is simply the "natural" way to walk,
laugh, etc. Again as with language, any national culture may be divided into a number of sub-varieties,
often correlated with geographical location or social
sub-group membership within the nation. And, carrying
the similarity still further, it is also usual that the
norms of only one or so of these sub-cultures may come
to be accepted by the larger society as the "right" way
to behave. But the point is that many kinds of "wrong"
behavior may derive from cultural differences, not cultural deficit. Thus, in spite of its current popularity
among educators and social activists, the idea that the
members of any population are "culturally deprived" is
an anthropological absurdity.

11. Psychologists have, of course, been aware for some time
that cultural differences could affect performance on
standardized intelligence tests. Indeed, it was this
awareness which touched off well-meant but largely unsuccessful attempts to develop useful "culture-fair" or
"culture-free" intelligence tests during the 1940's and
1950's. The social-group classifications which psychologists recognized as having a potentially high
correlation with cultural differences were social class
(i.e. socio-economic status) and ethnicity (which they
usually defined as membership in a social group of
"foreign origin"). See, for example, Kenneth Eels,
et al., Intelligence and Cultural Differences (Chicago:
University of Chicago Press, 1951). The problem was
that psychologists found it difficult to place the
American Negro accurately in this classification. Since
he was obviously not a member of a social group of
"foreign origin" in anything like the sense that Mexican-
Americans, Pennsylvania Germans, or Ashkenazic Jews were,
it seemed logical to consider his intellectual performance
differences to be social-class derived. At the same time,
psychologists were not quite ready to claim that Negroes
performed just like whites of a comparable socio-economic
level (which should have been the case, if the differences

were entirely due to social class), even though they
rejected genetics as a factor in performance differences. The only alternative seemed to be the concept
of cultural "differences" in the Negro as the product
of cultural deficit. That is, "disadvantaged" Negroes
were assumed to differ from whites, not in the kind of
cultures they possessed, but rather in the amount of a
presumably similar culture they possessed. And this
position is still held by most psychologists today.
For example, in the book of readings edited by A. Harry
Passow, et al., Education of the Disadvantaged (New York:
Holt, Rinehart & Winston, 1967), discussions of the
Negro fairly drip with social pathology. One recent
psychological study which has recognized American Negroes
as a distinct ethnic group with cultural characteristics
of its own, irrespective of social class, is that reported in Susan S. Stodolsky and Gerald S. Lesser,
"Learning Patterns in the Disadvantaged", Harvard Educational Review, Vol. 37, No. 4, Fall 1967. Virtually
all of the findings of this study have important implications for American education, but a particularly
relevant one for the teaching of "disadvantaged" Negroes
is that American Negroes of all socio-economic classes
show a relatively high level of verbal ability. (Of the
ethnicities studied by Stodolsky and Lesser, only Jews
showed a higher level in this ability.) The implication
that language skills enjoy an important place in American
Negro social life will come as no surprise to the few
social scientists and educators who know Negro life
firsthand, but it certainly ought to startle the many
who have theorized that the lower-class Negro child
comes from a non-verbal background. On the other hand,
one needn't take too seriously the opposition implied in
Stodolsky and Lesser between "supportive" and "compensatory" education for different ethnic groups, since
there is no reason why an adequate curriculum shouldn't
contain elements of both. Indeed, the type of reading
program which will be outlined in the course of the
present article is at once supportive, in that it focus-
ses on the relatively high verbal ability of Negroes,
and compensatory, in that it develops reading skills
which are not engendered by the ethnic subculture.

12.   For the reader who is interested in pursuing further the
      matter of African acculturation in the New World, an
      important perspective is that found in Melville J.
      Herskovits, The Myth of the Negro Past (New York:
      Harper & Brothers, 1941).

13. See Lorenzo Dow Turner, <u>Africanisms in the Gullah Dia-</u>
     <u>lect</u> (Chicago: University of Chicago Press, 1949), and
     Beryl Loftman Bailey, "Toward a New Perspective in Negro
     English Dialectology", <u>American Speech</u>, Vol. 40, No. 3
     (October 1965).

14. For a pedagogically-oriented survey of the origin and
     development of nonstandard Negro dialects, see William A.
     Stewart, "Sociolinguistic Factors in the History of
     American Negro Dialects" and "Continuity and Change in
     American Negro Dialects", first published in <u>The Florida</u>
     <u>FL Reporter</u>, Vol. 5, No. 2 (Spring 1967) and Vol. 6,
     No. 1 (Spring 1968). Both are being reprinted in
     Harold B. Allen and Gary N. Underwood, eds., <u>Readings in</u>
     <u>American Dialectology</u> (New York: Appleton-Century-Crofts
     [in press]) and, under the cover title "Toward a History
     of American Negro Dialects", in Frederick Williams, ed.,
     <u>Language and Poverty: Perspectives on a Theme</u> (Chicago:
     Markham Publishing Co. [in press]).

15. See William A. Stewart, "Foreign Language Teaching Meth-
     ods in Quasi-Foreign Language Situations" in W.A. Stewart,
     ed., <u>Non-Standard Speech and the Teaching of English</u>
     (Washington, D.C.: Center for Applied Linguistics, 1964);
     William A. Stewart, "Urban Negro Speech: Sociolinguistic
     Factors Affecting English Teaching" in R.W. Shuy, ed.,
     <u>Social Dialects and Language Learning</u> (Champaign, Ill.:
     National Council of Teachers of English, 1965); William A.
     Stewart, "Nonstandard Speech Patterns", <u>Baltimore Bulletin</u>
     <u>of Education</u>, Vol. 43, Nos. 2-4 (1966-1967); J.L. Dillard,
     "The English Teacher and the Language of the Newly Inte-
     grated Student", <u>The Record -- Teachers College</u>, Vol. 69,
     No. 2 (November 1967); Marvin D. Loflin, "A Teaching
     Problem in Nonstandard Negro English", <u>English Journal</u>
     (December 1967).

16. In any language-teaching situation, it is important for
     educators to be acquainted with the extent to which more
     than one linguistic system is involved, as well as the
     extent to which the general population (represented by
     the students) is aware of whatever the case may be. Any
     two coterminously-used linguistic systems can range,
     insofar as the tendency of naïve speakers to equate one
     with the other is concerned, from a completely foreign-
     language relationship (in which the two are impression-
     istically dissimilar in all structural aspects), through
     a diglossic relationship (in which the two are struc-
     turally similar enough in some ways to be considered

varieties of the same language, though different enough
in others to create serious interference problems), to
a relationship of observable yet structurally trivial
dialect variation. In the United States, the relationship of the more nonstandard varieties of Negro dialect
to standard English is in many ways closer to diglossia
than to normal dialect variation of the type which
usually holds for white dialects. For this reason, I
have occasionally lumped such situations together under
the term "quasi-foreign language situations" (see the
first item in note 15 above). For a discussion of the
structural and functional aspects of true diglossia as
it occurs in several parts of the world, see Charles A.
Ferguson, "Diglossia", Word, Vol. 15, No. 2 (August
1959), and William A. Stewart, "The Functional Distribution of Creole and French in Haiti", Thirteenth Annual
Round Table on Languages and Linguistics (= Monograph
Series on Languages and Linguistics, No. 15, Georgetown
University, 1962).

17. See Tore Österberg, Bilingualism and the First School
     Language -- An Educational Problem Illustrated by Results
     from a Swedish Dialect Area (Umeå, Sweden: Västerbottens
     Tryckeri AB, 1961). Although only standard Swedish has
     traditionally been used in Swedish schools, many of the
     children who are educated in those schools come from
     districts in which the vernacular is a nonstandard
     Swedish dialect -- sometimes structurally quite differ-
     ent from the standard language. These children are
     expected to adjust to the language difference on their
     own, although the structural intricacies of standard
     Swedish often make the task almost impossible. The
     similarity of the plight of such children to that of
     Negro-dialect speakers in the United States will be
     apparent to anyone who reads the second chapter of
     Österberg's study.

18. The Urban Language Study, then under the direction of
     J.L. Dillard, was a study of the linguistic structure
     of the nonstandard dialect of Negro school children in
     the District of Columbia. I took the idea for a Negro-
     dialect translation of Moore's poem from the example of
     Emery Nemethy's "Kanaka Christmas" -- a delightful
     Hawaiian Pidgin English version which has been available
     on Christmas cards in my island homeland for many seasons.

19. As far as I have been able to ascertain, the first appli-
     cation of this linguistic view of dialect differences to
     reading theory was made in Peter S. Rosenbaum,

"Prerequisites for Linguistic Studies on the Effects of
Dialect Differences on Learning to Read", Project Literacy
Reports, No. 2 (Ithaca, New York: Cornell University,
1964). To illustrate his thesis that all dialects of
English (including Negro dialect) differ from each other
only in low-level transformations, Rosenbaum gave a few
trivial and contrived examples of equivalent sentences
from unspecified but presumably different dialect sources.
At the same time, he ignored (and was probably unaware of)
grammatical differences between dialects which could not
easily be accounted for by low-level transformations
(such as the he has broke it vs. he done broke it distinction of many rural white dialects). The one time
Rosenbaum did specifically mention Negro dialect, it was
to suggest that the difference between the Negro-dialect
and standard-English use of the overt copula (e.g. is)
was the result of "an extremely low-level transformational
rule which deletes the copula [in Negro dialect] when it
occurs in active non-negative present tense sentences."
In order to make a statement like that, Rosenbaum had to
be totally unaware of such contrasts as He sick vs. He be
sick (the first meaning "He is temporarily ill" and the
second "He is chronically ill") in Negro dialect -- a
distinction which is simply not made in the standard-
English equivalent for both of them: He is sick. Rosenbaum's observation was quite plausible as far as it went,
but it only accounted for a part of the difference between the use of copula in Negro dialect and standard
English. And, although I pointed out the existence of
this grammatical difference between the two kinds of
English in "Social Dialect", Research Planning Conference
on Language Development in Disadvantaged Children (New
York: Yeshiva University, 1966), Labov and Cohen still
seemed to be uncertain about the function of be and the
copula in Negro dialect and standard English in "Systematic Relations of Standard and Non-Standard Rules in
the Grammars of Negro Speakers", Project Literacy Reports,
No. 8 (1967).

20. This view of the reading problems of lower-class Negro
children has been articulated most explicitly by William
Labov in "Some Sources of Reading Problems for Negro
Speakers of Non-Standard English" which originally
appeared in Alexander Frazier, ed., New Directions in
Elementary English (Champaign, Illinois: National Council
of Teachers of English, 1967) [reprinted with additions
and corrections in the present volume, pages 29-67].
So strong is Labov's adherence to the principle of
phonological determinism in accounting for structural

differences between Negro dialect and standard English
that at times the viability of his statements about the
former seems to suffer. For example, after having
theorized that differences in form between Negro-dialect
possessive pronouns and their standard-English equivalents are due to a weakening or disappearance of final
/r/ in Negro dialect (e.g. you book, they book for your
book, their book), Labov makes the claim that "No one
says I book, he book, she book or we book, for there is
no phonological process which would bring the possessives
into near-identity with the personal pronouns." Actually,
possessive pronoun forms such as me, he, she, we (or
we-all), y'all and dem occur frequently in Negro dialect
in the Deep South (as anyone from that region knows),
and most of the same forms occur sporadically in Negro
dialect throughout the rest of the United States (as
many teachers can testify). These forms, which are
strikingly similar to those of the Caribbean Creole
English which Labov asserts (in a footnote to the foregoing quote) that American Negro dialect is so unlike,
demonstrate quite clearly that more than just phonological rules are involved in the difference between the
total set of Negro-dialect and standard-English possessives.

21. Of course, inter-dialectal sound-spelling correspondences
of this type are not going to give rise to successful
word identifications when cognate word forms do not exist
in the two kinds of English. For example, a Negro-dialect
speaker who is able to read bath "correctly" (in terms of
his own phonology) as /bæf/ may puzzle over bathe, which
he ought to read "correctly" as /beyv/ if he can read
breathe as /briyv/. But the problem is likely to be that
the Negro-dialect speaker receives no confirmation of
such a reading from his own vocabulary -- many varieties
of Negro dialect having only verb phrases with /bæf/,
e.g. take a bath, give a bath, as functional equivalents
of the standard English transitive and intransitive verb
bathe.

22. The usual Negro-dialect reflexes of /θ/ and /ð/ have been
discussed in more detail in my "Foreign Language Teaching
Methods in Quasi-Foreign Language Situations" (see note
15 above) and in Ralph Fasold, "Orthography in Reading
Materials for Black English Speaking Children" [in the
present volume, pages 68-91]. At one point, Fasold
questions my description of a Negro dialect without /θ/
and /ð/ phonemes. Since Fasold makes no reference to a
footnote (to the very paragraph that he takes issue with)

in which I point out that many Negro-dialect speakers
do indeed have at least initial /θ/ and /ð/, it can
only be that he thinks I am wrong in maintaining that
any variety of Negro dialect lacks /θ/ and /ð/ phonemes.
If so, then he must be unaware, not only of the usage of
some younger children in the District of Columbia (the
one I chose to describe, since it poses obvious pedagogical problems), but also of that of many adult Negro-
dialect speakers along the South Carolina, Georgia, and
Florida seaboard.

23.   Starting with Rosenbaum (see note 19 above), a number of
      linguists have preoccupied themselves with the problem
      of whether the differences between Negro dialect and
      standard English are all in the "surface structure" (i.e.
      the phonology and, let us say for simplicity's sake, the
      transformations as well) or not -- as if the settling of
      this highly theoretical issue one way or the other would
      have profound implications for language teaching and for
      Negro self-respect. One of their assumptions seems to
      be that, if the differences between two grammars can be
      shown to be limited to the surface structure, then peda-
      gogical concern over these differences would be unfounded.
      But although surface-structure differences are undoubtedly
      easier for one to cope with, this does not necessarily
      mean that the absence of differences from the "deep struc-
      ture" (i.e. the grammatical categories and phrase-structure
      rules) of the grammars of two languages or dialects will in
      itself insure either mutual intelligibility or effortless
      language learning between them. Among other factors, the
      actual number of surface-structure differences between two
      languages or dialects can have an important effect on
      intelligibility and the ease of acquisition. For example,
      although there may be scarcely any deep-structure differ-
      ences between Anglo-Saxon and modern English, the surface-
      structure differences between the two are extensive enough
      to render texts in the former virtually unintelligible to
      speakers of the latter without some very difficult lan-
      guage learning. But, then, it is possible that the lin-
      guistic terminology in which this issue is couched may be
      little more than a scientific veneer covering an essen-
      tially social concern. For, although the linguistic
      alternatives are never evaluated in political terms, pub-
      lic assertions that only surface-structure differences
      exist between Negro dialect and standard English are
      often made (and accepted) with all the conviction and
      prior commitment of public assertions of the Negro's
      rights in American society. Might there perchance be a
      subtle analogy working in the minds of these linguists

(and their audiences) between surface structure and deep
structure on the one hand, and skin color and the "inner
man" on the other? If so, then asserting publicly that
American Negroes have the same linguistic deep structure
as American whites may merely be a way of declaring one's
acceptance of the Negro as an equal. But what if, in
fact, Negro dialect does exhibit certain deep-structure
differences from standard English, and even from white
nonstandard speech? Does this mean that Negroes are
intellectually, socially, and politically unequal to
whites? Does it mean that linguists should ignore such
differences, or attempt to explain them away? The tail-
oring of linguistic statements about dialect differences
to fit current humanistic social rhetoric may indeed
have the desired effect of gratifying middle-class Negro
adults, but I doubt if it will ever contribute much toward solving the school language-learning problems of
lower-class Negro children.

24. As is also the case with many (but not all) of its
     phonological features, Negro dialect shares many (but
     not all) such transformationally-derived grammatical
     differences from standard English with nonstandard white
     dialects -- particularly those spoken in the South.
     In fact, the See can he go construction even extends to
     Southern colloquial standard usage. Correspondences of
     this type are sometimes cited by dialect geographers and
     English-language specialists in an attempt to prove that
     there is no such thing as "Negro dialect" -- that the
     nonstandard speech of American Negroes is structurally
     identical to that of Southern whites. (I call this,
     perhaps uncharitably, the "Ain't nobody here but us white
     folks" theory.) Since I know of no community in even the
     deepest South in which the nonstandard speech of mono-
     dialectal Negroes is identical to that of monodialectal
     whites, and, indeed, since some features of Negro speech
     are conceivably of non-European origin, it may well be
     that such an assertion is but a more primitive version
     of the surface-structure-differences-only ploy mentioned
     earlier (see note 23 above). At any rate, the term
     "Negro dialect" is a sociolinguistic one, like "American
     English", and is meant to indicate the relationship be-
     tween the social identity of a linguistic system's users
     and its structural characteristics. Nonstandard Negro
     dialect is "nonstandard" because it has structural fea-
     tures which deviate from standard usage, and it is "Negro"
     because it has particular configurations of structural
     features which are used exclusively (even though not
     universally) by Negroes. To deny the validity of the

concept merely because Negro speech turns out to share many structural features with white speech is like claiming that American English does not exist because the speech of Americans shares many structural features with that of Englishmen.

25. In most varieties of Negro dialect, be is also used for a future state or action, in which case it never becomes bees, e.g. He be here all the time or He bees here all the time, but only He be here tomorrow. In addition, be in the future sense takes will as an auxiliary or tag, instead of do, e.g. Will he be here tomorrow? as a question form of He be here tomorrow. The Negro-dialect speaker's "correction" of non-future be to will be represents a fusion of the forms of the non-future with the future be -- apparently based on an awareness that the latter can pass muster as standard English, while the former cannot.

26. The view of Negro dialect as faulty or disordered speech has been a common one among speech therapists and, to only a slightly lesser degree, among English teachers. Recently, in an interview reported in Herbert H. Denton's article "Negro Dialect: Should the Schools Fight it?" in The Washington Post (December 22, 1968), Dorothy L. Vaill, the head of the Speech Department of the District of Columbia Public Schools, objected to talking about Negro dialect as a well-formed language, saying "[Negroes] are American people speaking an American language." But, if American Negroes all speak an American language (which they do), then what is wrong with recognizing the existence of these Americans and their distinctive form of American language? Or does Miss Vaill mean that, because Negroes are Americans, they ought to speak an American language (=standard English) -- even if they often don't. Does this speech therapist think that, because Negro dialect is different from standard English, it is un-American? What about Navajo Indians, who are also Americans speaking an American language! And, although this speech therapist is white, the same view can be encountered in Negroes representing a wide spectrum of sociopolitical orientations. For example, the Negro audiologist Charles G. Hurst, Jr., in his Psychological Correlates in Dialectolalia (Howard University, Communication Sciences Research Center, 1965), has characterized Negro dialect as "defective speech...abnormal speech" (p. 1) and as "oral aberrations" involving "phonetic distortions, defective syntax, misarticulations, mispronunciations, limited or poor vocabulary, and faulty

phonology" (p. 2). I even once remember, in a Negro-
nationalist bookstore in Harlem, being assured by a
lady in an African dress that the cause of Negro dialect
was a "lazy tongue".

27.   The test is described briefly in Joan C. Baratz, "Teaching Reading in an Urban Negro School System" [in the
present volume, pages 92-116], and in more detail in her
article, "A Bi-Dialectal Task for Determining Language
Proficiency in Economically Disadvantaged Negro Children",
to appear in Child Development, Vol. 40, No. 3 (September, 1969).

28.   See, for example, Paul M. Postal, Aspects of Phonological
Theory (New York: Harper & Row, 1968).

29.   Although the techniques of literary-dialect orthography
have found their greatest use in the representation of
nonstandard dialects in literature, and thus have tended
to be wanting in linguistic accuracy, there is no reason
why the same techniques could not be used by a linguist
to develop a linguistically sophisticated and pedagogically useful orthography for a nonstandard dialect or
"quasi-foreign" language. In fact, I know of at least
one case where this has already been done. In his
"Writing Haitian Creole: Issues and Proposals for
Orthography" (the Appendix to the unpublished Hudson
Institute document HI-458-D, December 1, 1964), Paul C.
Berry has devised a sociolinguistically sound literary-
dialect orthography for Haitian Creole based on the
orthographic conventions of standard French, the official
and school language of Haiti.

30.   Interestingly enough, some well-known literary creations
of the classic period of Negro-dialect writing (1875-
1925) turn out to be syntactically almost pure standard
English, with most of the differences being in pronunciation (shown by dialect spellings) and vocabulary. This
is especially true of Paul Laurence Dunbar's early dialect poetry -- a fact which is not surprising when one
realizes that he was probably not a native speaker of
the rural, lower-class Negro dialect he was attempting
to represent, and when one stops to think how difficult
it is to write good verse (which Dunbar's was) in even
a familiar dialect.

31.   This, incidentally, proved to be one of the more serious
pitfalls in early literacy programs in Haiti. Rural
peasants were taught to read their native French Creole

in an autonomous phonemic orthography in which, for
example, the words for "there", "that", and "step" were
written la, sa, and pa, because they are pronounced that
way. But the inevitability of an association of Creole
with standard French, so similar in vocabulary, was
overlooked by the literacy specialists. Consequently,
when he attempted to make the transition to literacy in
French, the poor Haitian peasant was left unprepared for
the fact that the same words, with the same meanings and
pronunciations, were written là, ça, and pas respectively.
Berry's Creole orthography, mentioned earlier (see note
29, above), was designed to correct this problem by making
the Creole word spellings resemble more closely those of
their French counterparts.

32. When I first began using standard-English word spellings
for writing Negro dialect texts, I assumed that this was
an entirely new technique. However, a subsequent search
revealed that a number of other writers have hit upon the
same idea independently, and used it for a wide range of
purposes. In the early 1940's, a type of word spelling
very close to standard English was used to set down the
ex-slave narratives which had been collected by the
Federal Writers' Project; see B.A. Botkin, ed., Lay My
Burden Down: A Folk History of Slavery (Chicago: University of Chicago Press, 1945). In the Spring of 1965,
several teacher-parents connected with the Child Development Group of Mississippi (CDGM) wrote spontaneous and
unprogrammed beginning readers in Negro dialect, using
standard-English spellings for the words. Still more
recently, Carl F. Burke, a prison chaplain, has produced
two books of religious texts and verse in an approximation
of Negro dialect grammar (though only slightly nonstandard)
with standard-English word spellings in most places: God Is
For Real, Man (New York: Association Press, 1966) and Treat
Me Cool, Lord (New York: Association Press, 1968). Some
of the passages in Chaplain Burke's books appear to be
based on spoken or written expositions by Negroes, while
others are obviously ex post facto creations by the white
author. Unfortunately, in his attempts to produce his
own Negro-dialect passages, Burke has achieved only mixed
success. For example, he innocently uses punk in the
strictly white sense of "hoodlum" -- apparently unaware
that it means "homosexual" in Negro dialect. Probably
the most ambitious application of the standard-English
word-spelling technique to the representation of Negro
dialect has been that of a young New Yorker who has written an entire novel in an approximation of Harlem teenage
speech. This is Shane Stevens, Go Down Dead (New York:

William Morrow & Co., 1966). Although Stevens' dialect grammar is no always accurate (e.g. dont going get..., for aint going get... -- perhaps a misapplication of the perception that got takes the auxiliary do in that variety of Negro dialect), it is still close enough to be artistically effective.

33. It should be pointed out that not every unit referred to in this discussion as a "prefix" will necessarily be a true prefix in standard-English grammatical or lexical terms (cf. the me- in memorial). From a historical point of view, these units are simply word-initial pretonic syllables which somehow became detached in the process of language transmission. Since re-standardization of the resultant Negro-dialect base forms requires that the appropriate syllables be "prefixed" to them, however, these syllables come to function morphologically like prefixes, and the base forms like stems.

34. The spelling of the prefix ex- makes it the one item which cannot be handled routinely by this technique. The problem is caused by the letter x in the prefix, which represents not only the final /k/ or /g/ of the phonological prefix (that is, the part which may be absent in Negro dialect), but also the /s/ (before consonants) or the /z/ (before vowels) which normally remains a part of the Negro dialect base form, e.g. /spek/ for expect, /zækli/ for exactly. In traditional literary Negro dialect, the remaining /s/ and /z/ of a former ex- were usually indicated by 's and 'z, e.g. 'spec', 'zackly. Yet, this practice is hardly a desirable one for beginning reading texts, since it is not in keeping with the idea of avoiding letter alternations in standard-English spellings. For the present, I feel that the least complicated solution to the problem created by ex- is simply not to make unnecessary use of words with it in the initial stage of the reading materials. At a later stage, such words could be introduced in their full forms, reinforced by oral drills. Fortunately, the one high-frequency Negro-dialect word which it would be difficult to avoid using in even very early texts, i.e. /sep/ for except, can be handled quite easily by the apostrophe technique, i.e. 'cept, since the /s/ of the ex- has coalesced with the initial /s/ (spelled c) in the base form.

35. For a general discussion of Negro speech in the District of Columbia, including the relationship of the nonstandard dialect of Negro children to that of adults, see William A.

Stewart, "Urban Negro Speech: Sociolinguistic Factors
Affecting English Teaching" (cited in note 15 above).

36. In certain extremely nonstandard varieties of Negro dialect in the coastal areas mentioned, pronoun forms may
even be undifferentiated for sex, so that sequences like
He a nice girl (or Him a nice girl) and Here come he
boyfriend (or Here come him boyfriend) are quite normal.

37. The -s in the coastal South Carolina, Georgia, and
Florida variants gots and does for got and auxiliary do
is not a functional suffix, but rather an integral part
of the verb base.

38. In addition to regional variation in a few grammatical
details, there is a certain amount of variation in
Negro-dialect pronunciation. A small part of this
variation may be caused by differences in the basic
phonology (i.e. the inventory of phonemes, their articu-
lation and co-occurrence rules) of regional forms of
Negro dialect, but the greater part of this type of
variation is caused by differences in lexico-phonology
(i.e. the phonemic structure of specific words). For
example, the stressed vowel in the word usually spelled
little may be /i/ in some regions, but /iy/ in others.
Although regional variation in Negro-dialect lexico-
phonology should not be severe enough to require extensive modification of standard-English word spellings in
Negro-dialect reading materials, there may be a few
cases in which dialect pronunciations will be too deviant
for the standard-English spelling, e.g. /čimbli/ for
chimney and /swimp/ for shrimp. Although there will be
a temptation to devise dialect-oriented spellings for
such cases, e.g. chimbley and swimp, the fact that the
standard-English spellings (and pronunciations) would
have to be taught eventually suggests that it might be
better to introduce them to the beginning reader in their
standard-English spelling after the standard-English pronunciation has been taught orally. This procedure would
eliminate a potential source of confusion for the young
reader by avoiding the accumulation in the program of
words with two spellings, one nonstandard and one standard.

39. In the section entitled "An Experimental Investigation of
the Use of Dialect vs. Standard English as a Language of
Instruction" in the recent report on United States Office
of Economic Opportunity Project No. IED 66-1-12, Carolyn
Stern and Evan Keislar describe their attempt to assess
the reaction of lower-class Negro Head Start children in

the Los Angeles area to the use of standard English and
what the experimenters considered to be nonstandard Negro
dialect in a lesson context. The lesson plan consisted
of only one text, written in standard English, with instructions to a "professional Negro actress" to read the
lesson aloud once in standard English and once in Negro
dialect. Tape recordings of these readings were then
played to the subjects, who were grouped à la standard
experimental procedure. The posttests were also treated
in this way. When the results were assessed, the experimenters were surprised to find that their Negro subjects
learned significantly more about the content of the
experimental lesson when it was presented in standard
English than when it was presented in the nonstandard
version. And, although they did see that the match between the nonstandard stimulus in their experiment and
the actual Negro dialect of their subjects was undeter-
mined, they nevertheless concluded that "there seems to
be little support for an increasingly popular notion that
young Negroes would suffer less of a handicap in their
early school years if they were initially taught in a
dialect with which they are familiar. Instead, evidence
has been presented to show that instruction employing
standard English produced superior learning under some
circumstances." On request, Stern was kind enough to
furnish me with the tapes used in that experiment, and
they reveal that the experimenters' concern about the
match between the nonstandard stimulus and the language
of the subjects was more than justified. For, the non-
standard stimulus turned out to be little more than the
kind of Negro stage dialect I have already described --
a kind of language which is grammatically much closer
to standard English than to the nonstandard dialect
which I have heard lower-class Negro children speak in
Los Angeles. Now, this should not be taken as a criti-
cism of the Negro actress; she merely did the job she
was trained, and hired, to do. Indeed, if anyone thinks
that it is even possible to read a standard-English
text aloud as authentic Negro dialect, just let them
try to read "Shirley and the Valentine Card" aloud as
grammatical standard English -- bearing in mind all the
while that, since standard-English speech patterns are
the more formally-defined ones, they ought to be the
easiest to produce in this way. My point is that, when
the experimental subjects responded to this Negro stage
dialect as if it were merely an odd type of standard
English (which it was), their reaction was taken as
clear-cut evidence that they found standard English more
meaningful than their own dialect. And, such is the

aversion of liberal educators to the possibility that
distinctive and viable Negro cultural patterns might
exist, and of traditionalist educators to the possibility that new pedagogical techniques and skills might
be in order, that this conclusion has been enthusiastically received in many quarters as proof positive that
Negro dialect has no place in education, and may not
even exist at all.

40. I understand that, in some experimental classes for
     lower-class Negro children, attempts have been made to
     relate the content of the curriculum to the language of
     these children by giving them the Uncle Remus stories
     to read. As long as this sort of nonsense continues,
     it will be safest to ascribe any reported failure in the
     use of Negro dialect in the classroom to the professional
     incompetence of the would-be experimenters, rather than
     to the linguistic incompetence of the subjects.